MUSIC PUBLISHING
IN THE BRITISH ISLES

A CATALOGUE
OF ALL THE
MUSICK-BOOKES
That have been Printed in *England*, either for Voyce or Instruments.

Musick Bookes in folio.

ALfonso his Ayres.
Alphonso his Lyra Lessons.
Allisons Psalms, of 4 parts, according to the Church Tunes.
Bartlets Ayres.
Coperario's first Booke.
Coperario's second Booke.
Corkins Ayres, first Booke.
Corkins Ayres second Booke.
Cavendish his Ayres.
Campions first and second Books.
Campions third and fourth Books.
Dowlands Introduction.
Dowlands first Booke.
Dowlands second Booke.
Dowlands third Booke.
Dowlands fourth Booke.
Dowlands fift Booke.
R. Dowlands Lute Lessons.
R. Dowlands Ayres.
Daniels Ayres.
Fords Ayres.
Filmers Ayres.
Greaves Ayres.
Humes first Booke.
Humes second Booke.
Jones first Booke.
Jones second Booke.
Jones ultimum vale.
Jones Musicall Dreame.
Jones Muses Garden.
Leightons select Songs of 4 and 5 parts.
Morley's Introduction.
Morley's Ayres.
Morley's Consort.
Maynards Ayres.
Masons Ayres.
Pilkingtons Ayres.
Rosseters Ayres.
Rosseters Consort.
Robinsons Schoole of Musick.
Book of Virginall Lessons by Mr. Bird, Dr. Bull, and Orlando Gibbons.

Musick Books in quarto.

ALlisons 5 parts.
Adsons Courts Masking Ayres, 5 and 6 parts.
Amners set to 3, 4, 5, 6 parts.
Bathes Introduction.
Butlers principles of Musick.
Birds Kirries 3 parts.
Birds Kirries 4 parts.
Birds kirries 5 parts.
Birds 5. parts wherein is Lullaby.
Birds 3, 4, 5, 6 parts, English.
Birds 5 parts Latine, Ne Irascaris. 1 set.
Birds 5, 6 parts Latine, Infælix ego, 2 set.
Birds 1. set of Gradualia. 5, 4, 3 parts.
Birds 2. set of Gradualia. 4, 5, 6, parts.
Birds 2. set English.
Batesons 3, 4, 5, 6 parts, 1. set.
Batesons 3, 4, 5, 6 parts, 2. set.
Bennets Madrigals, 4 parts.
Bevens Canons upon divers plain songs.
Cosins Psalms, 5, 6 parts.
Carltons 5 parts.
Croces 6 parts.
D. Campions Book of Counter-point.
Damons Psalms 4 parts 1. set.
Damons Psalms 4 parts, 2. set.
Easts first set, 3, 4, 5 parts.
Easts second set, 3, 4, 5 parts.
Easts third set, 5, 6 parts.
Easts fourth set, 4, 5, 6 parts.
Easts fifth set, 4, 5, and 6 parts.
Easts sixth set, 5 and 6 parts.
Easts 7. set of fantasies, 2, 3, & 4 parts.
Easts three parts.
Farmers two parts in one.
Farmers Madrigals 4 parts.
Gibbons Madrigals, 5 parts.
Gibbons 3 part fantasies, graven upon Copper.
Holbornes Cittern Booke.
Holbornes Pavin, 5 part.
Hiltons 3 parts Fa la's.
Jones 3, 4, 5, 6, 7, 8 parts.

Musick Books in quarto.

Kirbies 3, 4, 5, 6 parts.
Lichfields 3, 4, 5 parts.
Lessons for the Lute, Orph, & Bando.
Morley's 2 parts English.
Morley's 2 parts Italian.
Morley's Canzonets, 3 parts.
Morley's Madrigals 4 parts.
Morleys 4 parts selected.
Morley's 5 parts selected.
Morley's fa la's English, 5 parts.
Morley's fa la's Italian, 5 parts.
Morley's Ayres 5 parts.
Mundayes 3, 4, 5 parts.
Orlando's d'Lasso's 2 parts, Latine.
Oriana's 5 and 6 parts.
Pilkingtons 3, 4, 5 parts.
Path-way to Musick.
Persons 5 and 6 parts.
Persons Ayres and Dialogues, 4 and 5 parts.
Robinsons Citharen Booke.
Ravenscrofts Book of Catches.
Ravenscrofts Psalms of 4 parts.
Tallis and Birds Latine, 5 and 6 parts.
Taylors Psalms of five parts.
Vauters set of 5 and 6 parts.
Wilbies first set, 3, 4, 5, 6 parts.
Wilbies second set 3, 4, 5, 6 parts.
Warsons 4, 5, 6 parts, collected.
Withornes two parts.
Withornes 4, 5 parts.
Wilkes 3, 4, 5, 6 parts.
Wilkes fa la's, 5, 6 parts.
Wilkes third set, 5, 6 parts.
Wilkes Fantasticks, 3 parts.
Wardsset to 3, 4, 5, 6 parts.
Yongs first set, 4, 5, 6 parts.
Yongs second set, 5, 6 parts.
Youles Canzonets, 3 parts.
Pamelia, a Book of Catches of 3, 4, 5, 6, 7, 8, 9, & 10 parts.
Deutranela Book of Catches and Freemans songs of 2 and 3 parts.

Musick Bookes lately Printed.

MR. *Porters* set of Ayres for 2, 3, 4, and 5 Voyces, with a through Basse after the Italian way.

Mr. *Henry* and Mr. *William Lawes* set of Psalms, to Mr. *Sands* Translation, for 3 Voyces, with a through Basse.

Mr. *Henry Lawes* Musick for 2 Voyces to Mr. *Sands* Translation of the Psalmes, fol. and oct.

Mr *William Childs* set of Psalms for 3 Voyces, after the Italian way, with a through Basse, cut in Copper.

A Booke of select Ayres and Dialogues for 1, 2, and 3 Voyces to sing to the *Theorbo*, or *Basse Violl*, composed by Dr. *Wilson*, Dr. *Colman*, Mr. *Henry*, and Mr. *William Lawes*, and other excellent Masters in Musick.

A Book of Ayres and Dialogues for 1, 2, and 3 Voyces, by Mr. *Henry Lawes*.

A Book of *Catches*, *Rounds*, and *Canons*, collected and published by *John Hilton*.

Musicks Recreation, or choice Lessons for the Lyra Violl to severall new tunings, composed by severall Excellent Masters.

A New Booke of Lessons and Instructions for the *Cithern* and *Gittern*.

A New Book, Entituled, the *Dancing Master*, or plain and easie Rules for the Dancing of Countrey Dances, with the Tunes to each Dance, to be playd on the *Treble Violin*.

Renatus Des Cartes his *Compendium* of Musick in English.

LONDON, Printed, and are to be sold by *John Playford*, at his shop in the Inner Temple neare the Church doore, or at his house in three Leg Alley, in Fetter lane, next doore to the red Lyon.

An early catalogue of Elizabethan music and John Playford's publications. 1653

MUSIC PUBLISHING

IN THE

BRITISH ISLES

from the beginning until the middle of the nineteenth century

A Dictionary of engravers, printers, publishers and music sellers, with a historical introduction

By CHARLES HUMPHRIES
and WILLIAM C. SMITH

Second edition, with Supplement

NEW YORK: BARNES & NOBLE
1970

Published in the United States by
Barnes & Noble, Inc., New York, N.Y.

SBN 389 01369 2

Printed in Great Britain

CONTENTS

	Page
LIST OF ILLUSTRATIONS	v
PREFACE	vii
INTRODUCTION	1
BIBLIOGRAPHY	43
DICTIONARY	49
INDEX OF FIRMS IN PLACES OTHER THAN LONDON	347
LIST OF MUSICAL INSTRUMENT MAKERS AND REPAIRERS	354
SUPPLEMENT	357

LIST OF ILLUSTRATIONS

An Early Catalogue of Elizabethan Music and John
  Playford's Publications. 1653 — *Frontispiece*

Facing page

Book of twenty Songs of four and three parts. 1530 — 24

Fantazies of III. Parts. Orlando Gibbons. *c.* 1606-10 — 25

French Court-Aires. Edward Filmer. 1629 — 56

Select Ayres and Dialogues. John Wilson and
  Others. 1659 — 57

Sonnata's of III. Parts. Henry Purcell. 1683 — 88

Musica Oxoniensis. 1698 — 89

A Collection of New Songs. Vaughan Richardson. 1701 — 120

Pièces de Clavecin. Johann Mattheson. 1714 — *following* 120

Radamisto. G. F. Handel. 1720 — *following* 120

[v]

facing page

The Monthly Apollo.   1724   121

A Pocket Companion.   Richard Neale.   1724   152

The Hymn of Adam and Eve.   J. E. Galliard.   1728   153

The Musical Miscellany.   1729-31   184

Mirth and Harmony.   George Vanbrughe.   1732   185

The Musical Entertainer.   1737-39   216

Sonate a Violina con Viola di Gamba ó Cembalo.
    Francesco Guerini.   *c.* 1740   217

Clio and Euterpe.   1756-62   248

A Collection of New English Songs and a Cantata.
    Edward Miller.   *c.* 1760   249

Sei Sonate ovvero Divertimenti da Camera.   1760.
    Title-page   280

Sei Sonate ovvero Divertimenti da Camera.   1760.
    Sonata I.   281

Three Sonatas for the Harpsichord.   Giuseppe Sarti.
    1769.   Title-page   312

Three Sonatas for the Harpsichord.   Giuseppe Sarti.
    1769.   Sonata I.   313

Catalogue of Subjects or Beginnings of Bland's Divine
    Music.   *c.* 1793   344

Song from " Die Drei Freier ".   *c.* 1806-7   345

PREFACE

F RANK KIDSON'S pioneer work, *British Music Publishers, Printers and Engravers, &c.,* issued in 1900, has long been out of print, and it is to be regretted that the author was unable to undertake a new edition incorporating the results of his later investigations. Although he subsequently published a number of important articles on certain aspects of the subject, and various works have appeared by other writers dealing with specific periods and individual publishers, etc., no comprehensive work covering practically all the known firms up to about 1850 has been issued, and the present volume has been prepared to supply as far as possible that want, in a simple and concise form. It has been inspired by the fine work of Kidson himself and is offered, it is hoped, as a worthy tribute to his memory.

INTRODUCTION

T HE history of the printing, publishing and selling of
music in the British Isles from the fifteenth century to
the present time is given only in outline here, presenting
in chronological order the main facts in the development and
practice of the art and business, together with the names of the
most important contributors, in one way or another, to the
making and marketing of music in these islands. It is a story
of experiment and performance, which produced many examples
of fine and artistic craftsmanship that compare to their advantage with many of the best works produced on the Continent.
The names of scores of small printers, publishers, engravers,
music sellers who worked between the years covered by this
dictionary are hardly known to-day, except to the musical
librarian and specialist, while even of the larger and better
known firms much remains to be said about their methods of
working, the quality and extent of their publications, their
relationships with each other, what they did to stimulate the
British composers by making their music accessible and cheap,
and the part they played in bringing the works of foreign
composers to this country.

Following the invention of letterpress typography on the
Continent, in the middle of the fifteenth century, the early
printers were soon faced with the problem of how to apply the
process to the printing of music; but it was not until the early
days of the sixteenth century that their efforts can be considered
to have achieved real success. In 1473 appeared what is accepted as the earliest book containing musical notation—
Johannes Gerson's *Collectorium super Magnificat*, printed by
Conrad Fyner at Esslingen—but the music consists of five notes
only, stamped or printed, leaving the stave lines to be supplied
in manuscript. About the same time a Gradual was printed,
probably at Augsburg, with the music from movable type, the
notes and staves being separately impressed in black. Before
the end of the century, a number of works, principally liturgical,
containing music were issued on the Continent, the details of
which need not concern us here.

A *   [1]

Various methods were used in these early days, before printing music by type in one printing became the accepted method until the introduction of engraved plates in 1586 or prior to that. As these various processes have all been used in English music printing, it is essential to describe them briefly here. In some of the earliest printed books containing music, a space was left for the lines and notes to be inserted by hand. The printed methods included: (*a*) Printed stave lines with notes in manuscript; (*b*) Stamped or printed notes with lines in manuscript; (*c*) Stamped notes on printed lines; (*d*) Notes and lines from a wood or metal block; (*e*) Notes and lines from type in two printings. The method frequently adopted for liturgical works was to print the stave lines in red and the notes in black, a practice that was followed for many years, particularly in the large service books, round which those engaged in the particular church office could gather, and read from a distance.

It was not until 1495 that the first music printed in England appeared; but it can hardly be considered a very important example. It consists of but eight notes in Higden's *Policronicon*, printed by Wynkyn de Worde at Westminster. In this edition the music was made up from printers' quads and rules. Caxton printed an edition of the same work in 1482; but he left a space for the music to be put in by hand, and in a later edition of Peter Treveris (Southwark, 1527) the music was printed from a wood block. In addition to the above, Steele [1] records only eight works containing music, all liturgical, printed in England before 1530—by Julian Notary and Jean Barbier, Richard Pynson and Wynkyn de Worde; but to these must be added a secular ballad printed by John Rastell probably as early as 1516, and perhaps the music in *A new interlude* which may have been printed by Rastell, c. 1519 or later, or by his successor John Gough, after 1530. Up to this time there was little call for experiment in music printing in this country. Secular music was in no demand, and the notation used for the liturgical works was unsuitable for mensural music. But in the opening years of the sixteenth century a striking advance in musical typography was made by Ottaviano Petrucchi, a native of Fossombrone, who was established in Venice in 1491, where he produced in 1501 his first musical work, *Harmonice Musices Odhecaton A* (a collection of ninety-six secular pieces of three

---

[1] *The Earliest English Music Printing.*

and four parts), which profoundly affected music printing in Britain and elsewhere. Petrucchi printed from a fine distinctive type, in two printings, but so exactly registered as to make the whole pleasing and satisfactory. Not only did he lay the pattern for the printing of mensural music, but from 1504 onwards he adopted separate part-books for the various voices, instead of printing the parts opposite one another on the open pages of the work. This practice of separate part-books was used subsequently for the madrigals and motets, in England and elsewhere, throughout the sixteenth century, although the books of lute songs, etc., were frequently printed with all the parts on one page, or double page, arranged so that the singers and players could sit round the volume. Although the use of part-books may have made performance easier, for the modern collector they have one disadvantage, parts got separated and lost. In consequence, many famous libraries contain numbers of incomplete sets of works, the other parts of which they can hardly hope to obtain. A striking example in English music of much regretted missing parts are those of the 1530 book of twenty songs, referred to later.

The objection to Petrucchi's method was the double printing of the music, which with the text made three printings; and the printers of the time must have felt the need for a one-process method. It is a little uncertain as to who first achieved this successfully. Pierre Haultin (or Hautin) in Paris, about 1525 devised a one impression music type, used by Pierre Attaignant a few years later, while John Rastell and John Gough are variously given the credit for having been the first to discard two impression music printing in England; but their type was rather crude and irregular.

In 1530 this country produced one of the finest printed music works of all time, the well known book of twenty songs usually attributed to Wynkyn de Worde. The British Museum contains the Bassus part (wanting colophon), and the first leaf of the Triplex part (B.M. K. 1. e. 1.), and from these, experts concluded that Wynkyn de Worde was the printer. A few years ago, however, there was discovered in Westminster Abbey Library, the first and last leaves of the Medius part, with a portion of the colophon: "Impryntyd in Londõ at the signe of the black Morẽs," which makes it certain that it was not printed by Wynkyn de Worde, as we know his address at the time.

The work was from fine bold type, with the stave lines from metal blocks. The printer may have got some of his ideas from Petrucchi's work, and his type has also some resemblance to that used by Erhart Oeglin at Augsburg from 1507 onwards.[1]

From 1530 until 1575 only some sixty works containing music appear to have been printed in England—by John Gough, Richard Grafton, Robert Crowley, William Seres, John Kingston and Henry Sutton, John Day, etc.—consisting almost entirely of psalters and other liturgical works, Day's editions of the Sternhold and Hopkins versions of the Psalms being twenty or more of the total number. Not until 1571, when Day issued Thomas Whythorne's *Songes of three, fower and fiue voyces . . . Now newly published,* do we find a secular work, except for a ballad or so, indicating very clearly that secular and popular music, such as there was, had not yet become a matter of interest to printers and publishers, who up to that time, and later, were generally concerned with works other than musical. During this period a number of royal licences to print, particularly psalters, were granted—to William Seres in 1552, and John Day in 1559 and later. Richard Day, following his father, exercised his right to print until 1603, when it passed to others. Thomas Tallis and William Byrd were granted by Queen Elizabeth, in 1575, a patent right for twenty-one years for the printing of music and the importation of music from foreign sources; and the first work issued under the patent was their own *Cantiones, quae ab argumento sacræ vocantur,* printed by Thomas Vautrollier in 1575. One other work not in the stream of religious music should be mentioned—Adrian Le Roy's *A Briefe and easye instrution to learne . . . the Lute,* which was translated from the French, and printed by John Kingston in 1568, who printed another edition in 1574. From 1575 until the beginning of the madrigal period (c. 1586), about fifty works or so appeared, again mainly Sternhold and Hopkins versions of the Psalms by John Day. But from 1586 until the end of the century there were some hundred or more works produced, only forty being psalm books (mostly Sternhold and Hopkins). The remaining sixty or so included madrigals, motets, songs, instruction books; among them Morley's famous *Plaine*

[1] H. M. Nixon, " The Book of XX Songs." (*The British Museum Quarterly.* Vol. XVI, No. 2. April 1951. pp. 33-35.)

and easie Introduction to practicall Musick (1597)—the text-
book for many years to come.

From 1601 to 1620 about one hundred and sixty works
appeared, sixty of them being psalm books (mostly Sternhold
and Hopkins). From 1621-40, when the madrigal period was
over, there were one hundred or more works produced, of which
about three-quarters were psalm books (mostly Sternhold and
Hopkins).

For the purposes of this survey, it is unnecessary to mention
the composers who contributed to this great period of English
music (1575-1640); but it may be of use to place in the order
of their first starting business, the names of the principal
printers, publishers, etc., who played their part in producing
the music, and thus making it accessible to the public. The dates
given are in some cases conjectural, and further details can be
found under the respective entries in the dictionary: Henry
Denham, 1560-89; Thomas Este, 1566-1609; John Wolfe,
1579-1601; John Windet, 1584-1611; Edward Allde, 1584-
1628; Humfrey Lownes the elder, 1587-1629; Peter Short,
1589-1603; William Barley, 1591-1614; William Stansby,
1597-1638; The Stationers' Company, 1604 (first musical work),
etc.; Thomas Snodham, 1609-24.

When Thomas Tallis died in 1585, Byrd became the sole
owner of the patent to print music, and he granted permission
to others to print under his right. When the patent expired,
Thomas Morley was granted in 1598 another patent for twenty-
one years. In consequence, much of the music published during
this period appeared with the names of the owners of the rights
although printed by others. Morley did not exercise his right
to print himself except possibly in one case, if the imprint is to
be accepted on Richard Carlton's *Madrigals to Fiue Voyces*
(1601); but works were printed by his assignes, William Barley,
Thomas Este and Peter Short.

During the period 1530 to 1640 musical typography settled
down into an accepted method of single impression printing
from movable type, the notes having lozenge shaped heads, each
note standing alone, which was generally the practice until the
introduction of the tied note in 1687, although oval shaped notes
were used on the Continent about 1532.[1]

Steele gives some interesting details of the prices of musical

[1] *See* Steele for specimens of printing 1495-1600.

[5]

works during the period covered by his survey, examples of which are the following: Morley's *Arte of Music*, 1597, four shillings; a Lute Book, four shillings; Scotch Psalms, 1575, two shillings unbound, three shillings bound; Psalm Books, "with the notes," eight shillings and more. A Manual cost two shillings in 1526, twenty pence in 1528, two shillings in 1534, and four shillings in 1554. A Processional cost one shilling and eight pence in 1526 and three shillings in 1554; a Gradual eight shillings and four pence in 1547 and fifteen shillings in 1556; a book of prick-song, three shillings and four pence in 1536. Of the prices of the Elizabethan madrigals and motets there is little information until we come to the various Henry Playford catalogues of 1690 and 1697, described later on, which contain a number of priced items of the Elizabethan period that were being sold at two or three shillings each; but these may have been reduced prices owing to the lack of interest in the works at the time, or because Playford was anxious to get rid of his stock.

With the gradual decline in popularity of the madrigal from 1620 to 1640, the reasons for which it is difficult to find—other than the dearth of composers able to follow in the steps of the great Elizabethans—some new movement was necessary if English music was to survive. And strangely enough a rebirth took place in the middle of the seventeenth century, just when the Puritans were in power. It is worthy of note that the new musical enthusiasm was not directed to the old liturgical and religious music, which had largely predominated until the madrigal period, neither did it seem to have much in common with the works of the Elizabethans. It was an entirely new thing—the beginning of the practice and publication of music for all and sundry—for the tavern, the home, the musical club, the theatre and anywhere else; and it was not confined to any type or class of music—vocal or instrumental—secular or sacred —for the professional or the amateur.

The person who was largely responsible for seizing this great opportunity for providing the people with what they wanted in this new uprising of a popular musical culture, was John Playford, who from 1650 until 1686 was the most important music publisher in England. He was, besides, a musician, author, Clerk to the Temple Church, a man of culture, a friend of

Pepys; but it is as a publisher that we are concerned with him here. His first musical work was *The English Dancing Master*, dated 1651, but issued in 1650, and from the second edition onwards, entitled *The Dancing Master*. It went through seven editions in Playford's lifetime, and many more afterwards. In 1654 he published *A Breefe Introduction to the Skill of Musick*, subsequently, as *An Introduction to the Skill of Musick*, which went through at least ten numbered editions and several others in his lifetime, and many more by his successors. To mention these two epoch-making works is to indicate the great change that had come over English music since the end of the madrigal period; but when it is pointed out that Playford published more than forty song books or collections of secular vocal music, including catches and glees, a number of books of lessons for the cithren and gittern, the lyra viol, flageolet, virginals, and a host of other miscellaneous works, it will be apparent that the changing taste in music—its popular, intimate and friendly appeal, in contrast to the formality of the earlier days—synchronized with the genius and character of a publisher who was ready and able to take advantage of this new movement, and give it impetus and drive, by making accessible to the public copies of the music they were beginning to appreciate, understand and perform.

An interesting connection between Playford as the publisher of the new kinds of music and the music of the madrigal period, is shown in a single sheet catalogue which he issued in 1653.[1] It is headed *A Catalogue of all the Musick-Bookes That have been Printed in England, either for Voyce or Instruments* (B.M. Harl. 5936/421). The first section of the catalogue includes practically all of the music of the Elizabethan period, and the second section, headed *Musick Bookes lately Printed*, consists of eleven of Playford's own publications. Obviously, the first section referred to works he was selling as a bookseller, and which were doubtless still in demand, as distinct from his own publications. This first portion of the catalogue was doubtless based on one, which Rimbault tells us, was issued by Thomas Este in 1609.[2]

John Playford was not a music printer, but engaged others to

---

[1] *See* frontispiece.

[2] William C. Smith, "Playford: some hitherto unnoticed catalogues of early music." (*Musical Times*. July 1, August 1, 1926.)

print his publications—Thomas Harper, William Godbid, Anne Godbid and John Playford the younger. Except in a few instances of engraved music, his works were printed from movable type—the well known lozenge shaped notes each standing separately with its portion of the stave, the lines being unconnected, the quavers and semi-quavers not tied.

He was succeeded by his son Henry, and Richard Carr, to whom he handed the control of his business in 1684, although John Playford's name appeared on some imprints until his death in 1686. Henry Playford who published in association with his father from 1680-86, and also issued during that time a few works in his own name, continued in business on his own account from 1686 until 1707. He published and sold works in conjunction with John and Richard Carr, Samuel Scott, John Church, John Young, John Hare, Daniel Browne, John Sprint, John Cullen and James Woodward. His printing was done by John Playford the younger, Charles Peregrine, Benjamin Motte, Edward Jones, John Heptinstall and William Pearson. When he ceased business, some of his stock was acquired by John Cullen and John Young.

Henry Playford continued the kind of publications which his father had made popular, printed from the same style of lozenge shaped note type as a rule, except for some engraved works, and until the introduction of the tied note in 1687.

Although Henry Playford produced one or two works from engraved plates—Henry Purcell's *A Choice Collection of Lessons for the Harpsichord or Spinnet* (1696) and *The A'lamode Musician* (1698), besides some sheet songs, etc.—he was not seriously concerned with this increasingly popular and cheap method, and did not attempt to compete against the fine engraved productions of Thomas Cross and the widely advertised and less artistically engraved works of John Walsh and John Hare.

It is clear that the Playfords, in addition to their work as publishers, held considerable stocks of other music, both English and foreign, and as indicated in the catalogue of John Playford, already mentioned, they were particularly interested in the sale of the available copies of the Elizabethan publications. Three other sale catalogues, of Henry Playford (B.M. Harl. 5936/ 419-420; 147; 422-428) cover a wide range of items, and give a comprehensive summary of the music available in England at the time, besides indicating quite clearly the lessening interest in Elizabethan music. Obviously the Playfords had the London music business of the seventeenth century, as the Walshes had that of the eighteenth. These catalogues have been dealt with more fully elsewhere,[1] but some details are recorded here.

The catalogues were issued c. 1690, 1691 and c. 1697, and from them it is clear that Henry Playford's business was beginning to decline, and that he was overstocked with works which he was anxious to sell off. The first catalogue (4 pp., containing one hundred and thirty items) is that of an intended auction sale of music, which did not take place, and this priced catalogue was issued instead. It reads:

> A Curious Collection of Musick-Books, Both Vocal and Instrumental (and several Rare Copies in Three and Four Parts, Fairly Prick'd) by the Best Masters, Formerly designed to have been sold by way of Auction: But the Reason of its being put off, was, That several Gentlemen, Lovers of Musick, living remote from London, having a Desire for some of this Collection, and could not be there, they are here set down in Order, with the Rates, being lower than could be afforded otherwise. The Collection is to be sold by Henry Playford, at his House at the Lower-End of Arundel-Street, in the Strand, etc.

Some of the items in this catalogue appear to be quite unknown to-day, and most of them are extremely rare. The prices at which the lots were offered suggest that there was little interest taken in collecting music in those days. *Mr. Gamble's Airs and Dialogues in 2 books* . . . 4s. 0d.; *Mr. Douland's Introduction for singing* . . . 2s. 0d.; *Parthenia* . . . 2s. 6d., were some of the offers, and certain selected items (obviously in no demand) in lots of twenty, fifty or one hundred copies at special rates: "Fifty of *Mr. Farmers first Consort of Musick in 4 parts*, at 2s. a set"; "One hundred, 50 of a sort of the two sets of Mr. Deerings, at 4s. both sets." This catalogue has also a short section headed "Musick-Books printed for John Carr," and an advertisement of "Books lately printed with large Additions, and sold by Hen. Playford." As we know, Carr was closely associated with the Playfords; and he has to his credit the

[1] William C. Smith, "Playford: some hitherto unnoticed catalogues of early music." (*Musical Times*. July 1, August 1, 1926.)

publication of Locke's *Melothesia: or Certain General Rules for Playing upon a Continued-Bass* (1673), one of the earliest works of this nature published in England, and he was the selling agent of another popular instruction book of the period, Mace's *Musick's Monument* (1676), which was "printed by T. Ratcliffe and N. Thompson for the Author."

It should be pointed out that the Playfords, like many other publishers, issued on their various works lists of their other publications, and while details of these Playford lists are not recorded in this dictionary some other lists have been entered as catalogues under the names of the respective publishers. In the last decade of the seventeenth century, Henry Playford took increasing advantage of advertisement in the press.

The 1691 catalogue is without Henry Playford's name, but is attributed to him because of an advertisement on it of the *2d Book of Apollo's Banquet*, which he published. This catalogue appears to be that of one of the earliest auction sales of music of which we have record. It is an octavo, of sixteen pages, containing three hundred and thirty-eight music items, and one hundred and thirty of "Divinity, Physic, Law," etc. The title-page reads:

> A Catalogue Of Ancient and Modern Musick Books, both Vocal and Instrumental, with Divers Treatises about the same, and Several Musical Instruments . . . which will be Sold at Dewing's Coffee-House in Popes-Head Alley near the Royal Exchange, on Thursday, December the 17th, 1691.

In addition to the many English rarities offered were a considerable number of foreign works: Peri's *Euridice*, Caccini's *Euridice*, etc., and some quite unknown or unidentified items. "20 of the 2d setts of Mr. Farmer's tunes printed in 4to" (i.e. *Second Consort of Musick*) were amongst the lots. No copy of this work is in the British Museum.

The title of the third catalogue (c. 1697) reads:

> A General Catalogue of all the Choicest Musick-Books in English, Latin, Italian and French, both Vocal and Instrumental, Compos'd by the Best Masters in Europe, that have been from these Thirty Years past, to the present Time: With all the plainest and easiest Instructions for Beginners on each particular Instrument. Sold for Henry Playford at his Shop in the Temple-Change, Fleetstreet; and are to be

had here, and in most of the Cities and Publick Places in England, Ireland and Scotland.

⸱ It contains ninety-five priced items, besides Anthems, Services, paper, etc. The Museum copy has been cut up, but it appears to have been originally a large single sheet folio, suitable as a display bill, and contains like the other catalogues a number of works, no copies of which appear to have survived.

Henry Playford's music business seems to have declined rapidly from 1700, partly perhaps because of his other interests. He established series of concerts in London and in Oxford, and became more interested in picture and print dealing; but doubtless he was feeling the competition from the production by the cheaper method than musical typography, namely engraved plates. In November 1699 (*The Post Boy*, Nov. 28-30) he advertised another sale of a collection of music books, this time at half price; and the following notice of a late attempt to recover his position as a publisher and music dealer is of interest. It occurs as an advertisement attached to a play, *The Tragedy of King Saul Written by a Deceas'd Person of Honour . . . London, Printed for Henry Playford . . . 1703*, and reads:

Whereas Henry Playford has always made it his Business, and Endeavoured to serve the Publick as well as his Father before him, In Printing and Publishing the best Instrumental and Vocal Musick, both English and Foreign, and is still going on, but finding it very Chargeable by Reason of the Dearness of Good Paper, and the Scandalous Abuse of Musick by selling single Songs at a Penny a Piece, which hinders good Collections: He humbly proposes, with the Advice and Promise of, and Assistance from most of our best Masters, to the Nobility, Gentry, and all other Lovers of Musick, to go on with the Monthly Collections, not only of Songs but Instrumental Musick, by way of Subscription at his House in *Arrundel-Street*, where the Book and Proposals are kept, and where all that Subscribe One Guinney a Year and enter their Names into the same Book, will for the Value of the said Guinney, so paid yearly, Receive in Books to the Value of thirty Shillings; which will not be sold under to none but the Subscribers. A New Catalogue will be speedily Published, of all best Old and New Musick for these twenty Years last past to this time. If any Gentlemen or others, have a mind to Exchange any Choice old Musick for new, they may (if approv'd of) have new at the aforesaid place.

In addition to the printers, publishers and music sellers already mentioned, the following were also contemporaries of John or Henry Playford: Samuel and Benjamin Sprint, John Hudgebut, John Clarke, Thomas Cross and John Crouch. Some of these, together with others, are also listed in the later section dealing with engraved works; and John Hare, John Walsh, John Young and John Cullen, who all started business before Henry Playford ceased, come more particularly in the period of John Walsh.

John Playford did not price his works in his early lists, but later on he adopted this practice, which was continued by his son; the prices remaining fairly constant throughout the period of the firm. Some examples taken from lists or works are the following: R. Dering's *Canticum* [*sic*] *Sacra. First Sett*, four volumes, three shillings and sixpence; *The Treasury of Musick*, three volumes, bound together, ten shillings; *The Musical Companion*, two volumes, bound in one, three shillings and sixpence; *Introduction to the Skill of Musick*, bound, two shillings; *The Dancing Master*, bound, two shillings and sixpence; *Musick's Recreation*, stitched, two shillings and sixpence; *Apollo's Banquet*, one shilling and sixpence; *The Pleasant Companion*, bound, one shilling and sixpence; *Thesaurus Musicus*, Third Book, one shilling and sixpence. Examples of priced works by other publishers of the period are: *A Choice Collection of 180 Loyal Songs* (1685), printed by N. T., bound, two shillings; *A Collection of Twenty Four Songs* (1685), printed by F. Leach, one shilling; *The Songs to the New Play of Don Quixote* (1694), printed by J. Heptinstall, two shillings; *Twelve New Songs*, by Dr. Blow, Dr. Turner, etc. (1699), printed in William Pearson's new London character, one shilling and sixpence.

In 1687 a collection of songs, *Vinculum Societatis*, was published which had far reaching effects on British music typography. It introduced to this country the tied note, and changed the shape of the heads of the notes to oval—thus supplanting the previously used separate lozenge shaped notes. The work was "Printed by F. Clark, T. Moore and J. Heptinstall," but who was the actual inventor of the new type is not known. As far back as 1532 Étienne Briard had produced in France oval shaped notes, having a fixed time relation to each other, in place of the old system of ligatures, and further improvements were made by Robert Granjon and others, although the older form of notes still remained generally in use.

William Pearson published *Twelve New Songs* (by Blow and others) in 1699, "Chiefly to encourage William Pearson's New London Character," which was an improvement on the tied notes with oval heads, introduced in 1687; and Pearson's type was used for some of the later Henry Playford publications. Indeed, Pearson, who was in business from 1699 until 1735, can be considered one of the best music printers of the time, and the quality of his workmanship did much to establish the style of musical typography. He was succeeded by Alice Pearson, presumbably his widow.

The use of engraved plates for music printing was first applied on the Continent in 1586 or earlier,[1] but the practice did not spread to England, as far as we know, until some twenty years later. Probably the first engraved English work was Orlando Gibbons's *Fantazies of III. Parts*, issued without imprint, about 1606-10. It was followed by *Parthenia* (c. 1613), and Angelo Notari's *Prime musiche nuove* (c. 1613), both engraved by William Hole, and *Parthenia In-violata* (c. 1614), engraved by Robert Hole. These four famous works constitute a group by themselves, and no serious attempt was made to continue this form of music printing in England for the next twenty-five years or so, until James Reave produced William Child's *The First Set of Psalmes of III. Voyces*, in 1639, afterwards reissued by John Playford in 1656 as *Choise Musick to the Psalmes of Dauid*. From then until the end of the century (omitting publications by Thomas Cross from 1683, by Walsh and Hare from 1695 and by John Young from 1699), probably not more than forty works, excluding sheet songs, were printed from engraved plates, and the Playfords were concerned in a dozen or so of these. Some of the notable examples of this

[1] Hugo Riemann suggested that Petrus Sambonettus may have printed his collection of *Canzone, Sonetti, Strambotti et Frottole* (Sienna, 1515) from engraved plates. (Festschrift zur 50 Jährigen Jubelfeier des Bestehens der Firma C. G. Röder, Leipzig. 1896, pp. 76-77.)

period are Christopher Simpson's *The Division Violist* (1659, etc.); *Musicke's Hand-maide* (1663); Thomas Greeting's *The Pleasant Companion* (c. 1668, 1673, etc.); *Ayrs for the Violin*, by Nicola Matteis (c. 1675, etc.); Henry Bowman's *Songs for 1 2 & 3 Voyces* (1677, etc.); *Songs set by Signior Pietro Reggio* (1680); Humphrey Salter's *The Genteel Companion* (1683); and *Musica Oxoniensis* (1698). Bowman's and Reggio's *Songs* have finely designed illustrated title-pages, that of the latter being amongst the most beautiful of its kind.[1] The work by Matteis has some title-pages by T. Greenhill, who presumably engraved the music, which is finely executed and has in some of the parts accompanying notes in a faint dotted notation with the principal melody in a larger black notation. *Musica Oxoniensis* (Oxford, 1698), published by Francis Smith and Peter de Walpergen, was "Cut on Steel and Cast . . . Printed by Leon. Lichfield . . . And . . . sold by the Widow Howell"; another issue having Walsh and Hare in the imprint. Walpergen, a Dutchman, settled in Oxford (c. 1672), cut sets of type (punches) which were used as late as 1899 for *The Yattendon Hymnal*.

Other music engravers of the period (omitting for the moment Thomas Cross, John Walsh, etc.) were Robert Thornton and R. Brett, and the printers or publishers of engraved works included an anonymous publisher "At the Bell in St. Paul's Church Yard" (Thomas Adams?), John Clarke, John Pyper (Piper), William Godbid, Henry Brome, Thomas Bowman (Oxford), Richard Hunt, John Crouch, Francis Leach, Walter Davis and Samuel Briscoe.

Before the end of the seventeenth century, music printing from engraved metal plates had become the generally accepted method, and this lasted well on into the nineteenth century when music printing from type took a new lease of life; not that the latter method ever went out of use. It was retained for certain kinds of publications—hymn and psalm books, some song books, etc. and was also used exclusively by some publishers and printers. The metal plate was changed in course of time from copper to pewter, zinc and alloys, and the artist engraver gave place to the more mechanical puncher of plates.

Thomas Cross was more responsible than anyone else for the establishment of music engraving in England. Not only did he

[1] Day and Murrie. Figs. 24, 25.

[14]

popularize the method, but he set a standard of artistic workmanship that was rarely equalled by his contemporaries and
successors. He turned out a considerable amount of work
between 1683 and 1733, nearly all of the very best quality in
design and execution. He is said to have been the son of
Thomas Cross (c. 1644-85), an engraver of portraits and other
works. If so, he probably owed much of his skill and artistic
ability to the training he received from his father. The latter
engraved the portrait of John Gamble in his *Ayres and Dialogues*
(1656), and Kidson suggests that he may have been responsible
for some of the frontispieces to music issued by John Playford.
Whether Cross senior engraved music is not known. Evidence
for the suggestion that he was the father of the music engraver
is found in the fact that the latter, particularly in his early days,
signed his works as T. Cross junior. He is considered by some
writers to have engraved on zinc or pewter, and probably to have
used the etching needle and acid; but from his advertisements
it is quite clear that his usual medium was copper. He also
refused to adopt the less artistic method of partly punching the
plates, a practice introduced to this country probably by John
Walsh and John Hare in the early part of the eighteenth
century. The following interesting extract is from one of
Cross's works, *Dear Sally, a new Song* (c. 1710):

> Engraved by T. Cross in Compton Street Clerkenwell near
> the Pound, who is arriv'd to such perfection in Musick that
> Gen[t]. may have their Works fairly Engraved, as cheap as
> Puncht & Sooner; he having good hands to assist him,
> Covenanted for a term of Years; He can cut Miniture [*sic*],
> without having it writ with ungum'd Ink, to take off upon
> the Plate, as they do for other People. Printed for D. Pratt
> at y[e] Printing Office, y[e] Crown & Bible against York house
> in y[e] Strand, where may be had all y[e] Musick y[t] comes out
> from this time, very reasonable, & Engrav'd by T. Cross.

Kidson refers to the warning on one of Cross's sheet songs,
"Beware of ye nonsensical puncht ones." It is a great pity that
the high standard of Cross's work was not maintained by other
publishers. Cross published for himself and worked for others,
particularly Richard Meares. He popularized the publication
of single sheet songs, of which he issued a considerable number.
One of these, *Bury delights my roving eye*, a two-part song,

was issued as "Set to Musick, & engrav'd by Tho: Cross Junr.",
so that it can be accepted that he was something of a musician.
There is a reference to Cross in a poem by Henry Hall of
Hereford to Dr. Blow, included in the latter's *Amphion Anglicus*
(1700):

> "Music of many Parts has now no force,
> Whole Realms of single Songs become our Curse.
>
> .   .   .   .
>
> While from the shops we daily dangling view
> False Concord, by Tom Cross Engraven true."

The earliest known work of Cross's is Henry Purcell's
Sonnata's of III. Parts, published by John Playford and John
Carr for the Author in 1683. It is a finely executed work,
showing the sure hand of the engraver in his earliest days, and
includes a portrait of Purcell at the time. *The Most Celebrated
Aires in the Opera of Tom Thumb*, by T. A. Arne, printed for
Benjamin Cooke (1733), has Cross's name on the title-page and
has been considered to be one of his last works, but the title-page
is from a plate used for an earlier work, and the music is apparently not engraved by him. The magnificent score of Handel's
Radamisto (with supplement of additional songs), published by
the Composer in 1720, and printed and sold by Richard Meares
and by Christopher Smith, was engraved throughout by Cross.
It is one of the finest productions of the period. Other important
works by Cross are *A Collection of Songs* by Henry Purcell and
John Eccles (c. 1696), with an illustrated title-page; *Fugues
for the Organ* (1704), *The Morning Hymn* from "Paradise
Lost" (1729) and Songs by Philip Hart; *VI Sonatas for a Flute,
& a Through Bass*," by J. E. Galliard (1711), with a very fine
illustrated title-page; *Six Cantatas* by Daniel Purcell, Printed
for J. Cullen (1713), with an illustrated title-page; *Sonate a
Violino, Violone, e Cembalo* by F. Geminiani (1716), the work
which Hawkins wrongly stated had stamped plates; *The Opera
Miscellany*, Printed and sold by John Browne (1725), a small
pocket volume of opera songs issued in competition with a
similar work by Cluer; *A Book of Psalmody* by Matthew
Wilkins (c. 1730); and editions of Corelli's Sonatas, etc.,
Printed for B. Cooke (1732).

With the establishment of John Walsh and John Hare in 1695, music printing, publishing and marketing were revolutionized. John Walsh, whose publishing history before 1695 is not known, no doubt saw the significance of the work of Cross, but he did not generally employ him as his engraver, although one or two works show that Walsh and Cross had some slight business association.[1] Walsh was a shrewd man and from the beginning of his career recognized the value of wide advertisement. The great majority of his works were announced in the press, on other works, and in the various catalogues which he issued. Whether he was a practical engraver or printer himself is uncertain. He must have employed a number of engravers, judging from the many variations in style found in his works, and we know that he had a number of apprentices, among whom were Luke Pippard and William Smith, who later went into business for themselves. Walsh is credited with having cheapened the engraving of music by the use of pewter as a softer metal than copper, and at some time to have introduced the quick method of partly stamping plates. He kept his eye on the foreign market and watched the importation of foreign music, some of which he appears to have been agent for, and which in other cases he pirated. Indeed, musical piracy became very common (the existing protective legislation being quite ineffective, as pointed out later), and Walsh was by no means the only or chief offender. It was frequent enough in the early years of the eighteenth century to find music issued with the imprint, "Sold at the Musick Shops" or variations of this, and it is quite impossible to say in many of these cases who was the printer or publisher. Two hundred years later, history repeated itself in the wide circulation of thousands of unofficial copies of ballads and other popular pieces, which were sold in the streets of London at twopence or so a copy, until the legitimate publishers and composers organized a campaign against the offenders, which resulted in new copyright Acts (1902, 1906).

Walsh, starting with cheap instructors for the flute, violin, etc., and single songs, soon turned his attention to collections of songs, harpsichord books, theatre music, operas, sonatas and other instrumental music, works by Corelli (of which he issued many editions), musical periodicals (*The Monthly Mask of*

[1] William C. Smith, *A Bibliography of the Musical Works published by John Walsh*, etc. Nos. 25, 379, and 539.

Vocal Music, Harmonia Anglicana), and by 1703 had many works to his credit. In his catalogue[1] of that year, which was not his first, there are ninety-two items, and in later catalogues the number was considerably increased. In the first twenty-five years of his business he issued more than six hundred works and editions. But it was his association with Handel in the publication of "Rinaldo" (after which for a number of years he published little of the master) that laid the foundation of much of the firm's success, and entitles Walsh to the praise and admiration of Handelians. The fuller story of his work is told elsewhere,[2] but some further details may be mentioned here— his use of what are known as "passe-partout" title-pages, which meant great economy in plates—his illustrated title-pages—his practice of numbering his publications from about 1727 or a year or two later—his habit of using items from other works, with paginations and alterations which are the despair of musicologists, collectors and librarians. From brief references in the Treasury Papers, and from two documents in Harvard University Library recently brought to notice, it seems that he was opposed to the duties imposed on paper by the Act of May 22, 1712, which were levied on some of his publications. Apparently for his refusal to pay, he was imprisoned in the Marshalsea in 1726, and two pleas were lodged against him in the Court of King's Bench, in the Michaelmas term of that year. He and the plaintiff for the Crown asked for the cases to go before a jury, but the results of these applications are not known.[3]

Walsh did publish a few works from type, but the printing of these was done by others. Some examples are: *The Dancing Master . . . The 13th Edition . . . done in the New Ty'd Note . . . Printed for J. Walsh*, etc. (1706); *Twenty four New Country Dances for the Year 1713 . . . Printed in the New Capital Character of Musick* (1712); *The Merry Musician . . . Printed by H. Meere . . . 1716*; *The Complete Country Dancing-Master . . . printed in the London Capital Character . . . by H. Meere. . . . 1718* (1719), 2 books. The last three works were from a fine clear broken type, roughly tied.

One especially interesting and quaint style of work issued

[1] William C. Smith, *Walsh Bibliography*. No. 140.
[2] William C. Smith, *Walsh Bibliography*.
[3] William C. Smith, "New Evidence concerning John Walsh and the Duties on Paper, 1726." (*Harvard Library Bulletin*. Vol. VI, No. 2. Spring 1952. pp. 252-255.)

particularly by Walsh, but also by others, was a series of Figure Dances, in which the steps are shown in engravings under the tunes (B.M. h. 993). They were modelled on similar works by R. A. Feuillet, a dancing-master of Paris.

Walsh priced his works, as a rule, either on the copies or in the advertisements and catalogues, typical prices being: sixpence for *The Monthly Mask of Vocal Music*; one shilling for small tutors, etc.; one and sixpence for sets of airs and small collections of songs; two and six to three shillings for harpsichord books; four to six shillings for sonatas and concertos for violins and bass; nine shillings for vocal scores of operas, which contained, as a rule, the overture and songs only. His son did not vary these prices greatly, except for sets of larger instrumental works (nine to fifteen shillings or so) and vocal scores of oratorios at ten shillings and sixpence.

During the period of John Walsh the elder (1695-1736), a number of new firms came into existence to share in the widening market for printed music. It is only necessary to mention the most important of them—John Hare and his successors (who had close, probably family, associations with Walsh), John Young, Mickepher Rawlins, Francis and Isaac Vaillant, John Cullen, Richard Meares the elder, and the younger, Luke Pippard, I. D. Fletcher, Daniel Wright the elder, and the younger, John Cluer and his successors, Bezaleel Creake, William Smith, Benjamin Cooke, Richard Cooper (Edinburgh), John Watts and John Simpson. Fuller details of these firms can be found under their respective headings, but some deserve particular mention here, for one reason or another, and it is of interest to note how some of the firms were related to others.

John Hare may have taken over the premises of John Clarke, who was established in 1681. Elizabeth Hare the elder, Hare's widow, had as assistant John Simpson, whose widow, Ann Simpson, married John Cox, and when Cox gave up in 1764, Maurice Whitaker, who had been manager for Mrs. Simpson, succeeded Cox, while at the same time Robert Bremner purchased some of the plates of Cox's stock-in-trade, and when Robert Bremner died in 1789, the stock-in-trade of his London business was purchased by Preston and Son, this business being continued by Thomas Preston until 1834; thus these firms were linked up over about 150 years.

Francis and Isaac Vaillant were the musical agents for the

works engraved and published by Estienne Roger of Amsterdam, and made known for the first time in this country many important foreign musical works.

The Wrights were the most prolific musical pirates of the time, and they had the audacity to publish a catalogue of their publications containing fifty or so items, many of which were also published by Walsh.[1]

John Cullen took over some of the stock of Henry Playford, but there is no evidence that he occupied Playford's premises, although his business was in Fleet Street. His works were usually engraved on copper plates, frequently by Cross. Among his publications were Bassani's *Harmonia Festiva*, the songs in *Thomyris*, *Camilla*, and *Pyrrhus and Demetrius*, Keller's *Thorough Bass* and Daniel Purcell's *Six Cantatas*, which has an illustrated title-page by Cross, afterwards adapted and used by Walsh, who also issued editions of some of the works of Cullen, he in turn pirating some of Walsh's.

Richard Meares and his son Richard were important printers and publishers of music whose records are intermixed and confusing, their names appearing together only in 1722. Prior to that, Richard the elder was associated with the printing, publishing or selling of some distinctive works. He employed Thomas Cross to do some of his engraving, including the fine score of Handel's *Radamisto* previously mentioned. His name appears in the imprints of sonatas by Geminiani, Pietro Castrucci, Corelli, etc. Croft's *Musicus Apparatus Academicus*, engraved by Thomas Atkins, an exceptionally fine work, may have been printed by Meares. It seems that he was frequently guilty of piracy like other publishers of the time, as he issued songs from Handel's operas, Babell's *Suits of Harpsicord and Spinnet Lessons*, Keller's *Rules to play a Thorow Bass* and the rare *The Bird Fancyer's Delight*, all in competition with editions by Walsh, although it is not always easy to decide in some cases who was the pirate.

I. D. Fletcher is only known to us through one work, Johann Mattheson's *Pieces de Clavecin*, published in London with the French title in 1714, and in 1715 with a German title superimposed on the illustrated title-page: *Matthesons Harmonisches Denckmahl/Aus Zwölf erwählten Clavier-Suiten*, etc. Why this work was published in England is not known. It is a superb

[1] *See* G. Taglietti's *Concerti e Sinfonie . . . Opera Seconda.* c. 1734. (B.M. g. 679.)

folio (two volumes, continuous pagination), with a finely illustrated title-page by Van der Gucht, the music being engraved throughout (having no engraver's name) in a style and manner so superior to that of contemporary works as to entitle it to a special place in any history of the subject. In the preface Fletcher refers to "favours received in this country," so it is possible that he was a foreigner and known to Mattheson in Hamburg. An edition, presumably of this work, was advertised in *The Post Boy*, March 17-19, 1720, as *A Choice Book of Lessons, in two volumes, for the Harpsichord or Spinnet; composed by J. Mattheson . . . All engraven on Copper Plates . . . Price 5s. Printed by Richard Meares.*

John Cluer was for a time the most formidable rival of Walsh. His earliest advertisements (1715) are as a printer of labels for perfumers, apothecaries and distillers, shopkeepers' signs, prints, etc. "either in Gold, Silver or other Colours. Done after an entire new Method, known to no others . . . nicely Cut or Engrav'd on Wood or Copper." In one advertisement (*The Weekly Journal*, January 4, 1718) he announced that "all Dealers in black and white and coloured Prints may be now furnished with most Sorts extant . . . And Country Chapmen are desired to take notice that as the above said Company are both the real Cutters and Printers of them, they may and shall be better served than by those who put out both the Cutting and Printing." This referred to the chap-books for which Cluer and his successors, the Diceys, were famous, and to which an interesting reference is made in *Boswell's London Journal 1762-63* (p. 299). The Diceys were the well known family of printers at Northampton and elsewhere, Mrs. Cluer being a sister of William Dicey, who subsequently purchased (1736) the Cluer London business from Thomas Cobb, who had married Mrs. Cluer (c. 1730) after Cluer's death.

From 1721, or earlier, Cluer interested himself very considerably in the marketing, and later on, the preparation of various patent medicines and specifics: "Daffey's Elixir Salutis," "The True Antidote against Bugs," "Hungary Water," and "Dr. Bateman's Pectoral Drops." In this respect he was following in the steps of John Playford, who advertised "The true and right Sympathetical Powder" on *Choice Songs and Ayres*, 1673, and other specifics on some editions of *The Dancing Master*.

[21]

From 1720 onwards Cluer became increasingly occupied with the engraving and printing of music, although a number of sheet songs have been attributed to him before that date. His first major work was Handel's *Suites de Pieces* (1720), which he engraved and printed but did not publish. He experimented in new methods of printing music from engraved plates, and invented new music types, which, however, were not very successful.[1] All of his engraved work was extremely good, much of it being done by Thomas Cobb, who was employed by Cluer. In 1724 Cluer published his first small book of opera songs, *A Pocket Companion for Gentlemen and Ladies*, which was published by subscription, a method then generally unknown in connection with music, and adopted by him for other works. It was an original and beautifully produced book, for which there were four hundred and sixty-six subscribers, taking between them one thousand and four copies; surely a record for an eighteenth century musical work. He followed it up with a second volume in 1725, which had three hundred and ninety subscribers for nine hundred and fifty copies. The originality and success of these works stimulated others to copy him, and John Browne's *The Opera Miscellany* (1725) and Peter Fraser's *The Delightfull Musical Companion* (1726) were obviously modelled on Cluer's work. He acquired the right to publish a number of Handel's operas from *Julius Cæsar* (1724) onwards. The first of these was large pocket size, an innovation for works of that kind; the succeeding operas being rather larger (quarto), but even so, much more convenient than the established folio size of the time. Among other original productions of the firm were packs of playing cards, each card having a song printed on them, a kind of publication copied by others, including John Bowles, who issued a pack of cards containing songs from *The Beggar's Opera*, in 1728, and Longman and Lukey, who issued two packs containing cotillons and country dances, about 1775. Other features of Cluer's work worth recording are the illustrations with which he adorned some of his newspaper advertisements, and the fine, illustrated title-pages and frontispieces to the editions of Handel's operas and the small books of songs.

It is probable that the practice of issuing music from engraved

---

[1] *The London Journal*, July 13 etc., 1728; *The Pedigree of a Fidler.* (B.M. G. 15 . (66.))

plates, instead of from type, gave rise to the use of the description "music printer" by Walsh, Cluer, Meares and others who specialized in engraved music.[1]

Richard Cooper, a music engraver and printer in Edinburgh (c. 1725-64), engraved among other works *Musick for Allan Ramsay's Collection of Scots Songs Set by Alex^r. Stuart* c. 1725), a small delicate production, and also provided the portrait of Ramsay that appears in the latter's *Poems*, 1727.

Some of Benjamin Cooke's plates were acquired by John Johnson (c. 1743), and in 1777 Robert Bremner purchased the greater part of Johnson's stock from his widow.

John Watts, a bookseller and printer, took advantage of the popular ballad-opera movement, and issued a great number of these with the text and music of the airs, the latter from wood blocks. He also issued *The Musical Miscellany*, the finest pocket song-book of the period, in six volumes (1729-31), the whole work being beautifully designed and ornamented, with the music from finely cut blocks. As already pointed out, wood blocks were used in the early days of music printing, and John Cluer advertised that he "cut or engraved on wood and copper." The use of the wood block persisted during the eighteenth century. *The Muses Delight*, published by John Sadler at Liverpool in 1754, is a fine specimen of this method, which was frequently used for music in literary magazines and for some psalm and hymn books, etc.

Prior to the existence of the Copyright Act of 1709, the various licensing acts nominally governed the printing and publishing of books and music, but they ceased to be effective from about 1680, and nothing was done to protect the owner of a work until the Act of 1709, which, as Plomer [2] says, "was a well-meaning one, and it had the effect of making trade in copyrights a feature of the book trade in the eighteenth century, but it did little to stop piracy," which was common enough as pointed out previously.[3] Licences or privileges to print and publish continued to appear in many of the musical works

---

[1] William C. Smith, "The Meaning of the Imprint." (*The Library*. Fifth Series, Vol. VII, No. 1. March 1952. pp. 61-63.)

[2] Plomer II, Introduction, p. viii.

[3] For legislation *see* "Copyright in Music" (Grove's Dictionary); "Copinger and Skone James on the Law of Copyright," eighth edition, Sweet and Maxwell, London, 1948; Edward Cutler, "A Manual of Musical Copyright Law," Simpkin, Marshall, Hamilton, Kent & Co., London, 1905.

published after the Copyright Act of 1709. Handel's *Radamisto*, *Suites de Pieces*, *Flavio*, *Ottone*, *Julius Cæsar*, *Tamerlano*, etc., included one granted to Handel for fourteen years, dated June 14, 1720; *Joshua*, *Samson*, *Susanna*, *Judas Maccabæus*, etc., one granted to John Walsh (the younger) under Handel's authority for fourteen years, dated October 31, 1739, and *A Third Set of Six Concertos*, one granted to John Walsh (the younger), dated August 19, 1760. Other examples from other composers' and publishers' works could be quoted. The existence of such privileges has often led to the incorrect dating of works in catalogues and elsewhere. A significant example is that of *Rule Britannia*. This was apparently first published by H. Waylett with Arne's *The Music in the Judgment of Paris*, some time after September 21, 1745, but has usually been attributed to January 1741, because of the licence to print, dated January 29, 1740-41, which was issued with the work in 1745.

John Walsh the elder was succeeded in 1736 by his son John, who carried on the business until his death in January 1766. The father, as pointed out, in addition to the wide range of miscellaneous works which he published, took advantage of the demand for the operas of Handel and others. The son kept his father's publications continually in front of the public, but extended the scope of the business as musical taste and practice developed. His catalogue, issued in 1747-48, contains about 400 items, including the oratorios of Handel, of which as a rule he did not publish full scores. His successors, Randall and Abell, Randall alone, Wright and Wilkinson, etc., largely developed that form of publication. Walsh the younger was able to acquire, or at least to publish, much foreign music, particularly instrumental; but the expanding market at home and abroad brought some serious rivals into the field. Some of the most important of these were William Smith, John Wilcox, John Simpson and his successors (who have been mentioned earlier), John Johnson, Henry Waylett, Peter Thompson, James Oswald and Robert Bremner.

William Smith was a good engraver as well as a printer and publisher from 1720-63. He served his apprenticeship with Walsh and was employed by Arne to engrave his early works (c. 1740-45), which Arne published himself. Smith was one of the few publishers to date his publications, a practice unfortunately not generally adopted.

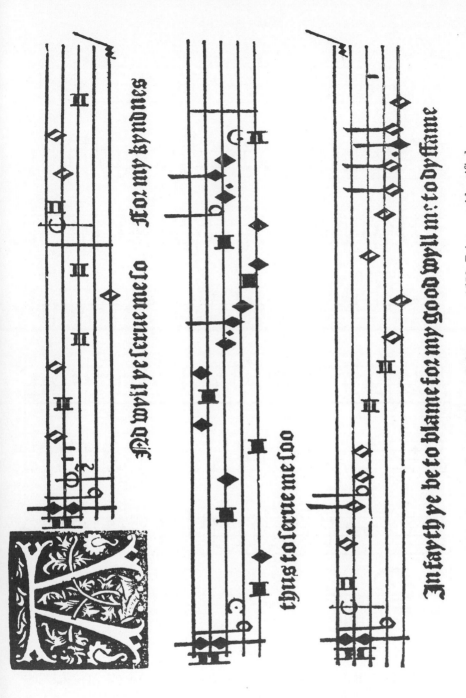

Book of twenty Songs of four and three parts. 1530. Printer unidentified.
The staves from metal blocks, notes from type

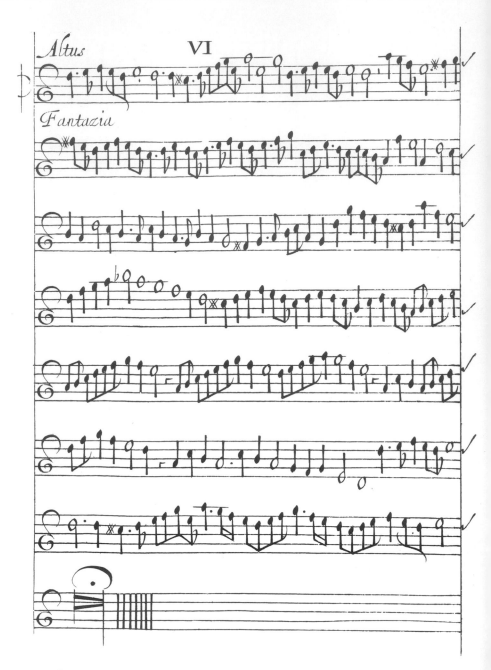

Orlando Gibbons, "Fantazies of III. Parts". c. 1606-10. Probably the earliest engraved English music. Engraver unidentified

Henry Waylett, as previously pointed out, issued Arne's *Judgment of Paris* (1745), which contains the first edition of *Rule Britannia*. It was probably engraved by William Smith. Waylett's publications were uniformly good. Francis Waylett, presumably a relative of Henry's, also issued a little music.

John Wilcox, a music publisher at Virgil's Head in the Strand from c. 1737-43, published three famous musical treatises of the period: J. F. Lampe's *A Plain and Compendious Method of teaching Thorough Bass* (1737), J. Grassineau's *Musical Dictionary* (1740), and P. F. Tosi's *Observations on the Florid Song* (1742). He may have been related to J. Wilcox of Little Britain who published a revised edition of W. Holder's *A Treatise of the Natural Grounds, and Principles of Harmony* (1731).

James Oswald, a dancing-master in Dunfermline in 1734, came to London in 1741, and at first probably worked for John Simpson. His output as a composer was considerable, and he is also particularly remembered as a distinguished member of a group of musicians, "The Society of the Temple of Apollo," [1] He published many works, and his business may have been acquired by Straight and Skillern.

The firm of Thompson, under one name or another, went on from 1746 until well into the nineteenth century.

John Johnson, who founded a most successful business in 1749 or earlier, took over some of the stock of Daniel Wright the elder and the younger, and of Benjamin Cooke, and reissued some works from their plates. In 1777, Robert Bremner acquired the greater part of the music plates and books when Johnson's widow gave up business.

Robert Bremner was one of the most prosperous publishers from 1754 until his death in 1789. He started in Edinburgh, opened his London branch in 1762, and, as the entry under his name indicates, acquired stocks of a number of other publishers. From the following notice in the *Morning Post and Daily Advertiser*, July 25, 1789, we get an idea of his financial success:

To be Sold by Auction,

If not previously Disposed of by Private Contract, The following ESTATES, the property of the late Mr. ROBERT BREMNER, Music-Printer, in the Strand:

[1] Frank Kidson, "James Oswald, Dr. Burney, and the Temple of Apollo." (*The Musical Antiquary*. Oct. 1910, pp. 34-41.)

I. A particularly eligible FREEHOLD ESTATE delightfully situated at BATTERSEA-RISE, near Clapham, Surrey, commanding an elegant and extensive prospect of the Cities of London and Westminster, and the County of Middlesex, known by the name of LAVENDER-HILL; consisting of two substantial modern-built brick Dwelling Houses, stabling, &c. and about two acres of meadow land to each; also two acres of land, lying between the houses, particularly well adapted for building upon.

II. A very desirable FREEHOLD ESTATE, situate in the pleasantest part of BRIGHTHELMSTONE, bounded by the Sea in the South, and the Steyne in the West; consisting of two new-built houses fronting the Steyne, and also a parcel of ground, part Freehold, part Leasehold, adjoining, admirably calculated for building upon.

III. The LEASE of the Deceased's HOUSE, opposite Somerset-Place, in the Strand, with the HOUSEHOLD FURNITURE, and STOCK in TRADE, consisting of Plates, Music, Musical Instruments, &c.

Any person inclined to treat for any of the above, will be pleased to apply to James Mainstone, Esq., Essex-street in the Strand.

As will be seen later, music publishing must have been very lucrative in the last quarter of the eighteenth century, judging from the number of firms who carried on successfully for many years.

The cheap, and in many cases poor quality engraved plate, partly punched, became the recognized medium for printing music by the larger publishers until the end of the century and after. But from time to time attempts were made by various engravers and small firms to produce something more artistic. It was during the period of Walsh the younger (1736-66) that some commendable efforts were made in this direction; but the cheaper and less worthy productions soon made it difficult for the better publishers to survive. The period has also to its credit, not only some attempts at better engraved miscellaneous works, but a number of finely illustrated song-books, usually issued in parts; a type of publication rarely attempted since then: George Bickham's *The Musical Entertainer* (in parts, 1737-39); Henry Roberts's *Calliope* (in parts, 1737-46) and *Clio and Euterpe* (in parts, 1736-59, and a third volume, 1762); William Rayner's *The Universal Musician* (1738); Benjamin Cole's *British Melody* (in parts, 1738-39), and *Orpheus Britannicus* (1760); Jacob Bickerstaff's *The Agreeable Amusement* (1743-44); Thomas Kitchin's *The English Orpheus* (1743); John Newbery's *Universal Harmony* (in parts, 1744-45); John Tyther and Mary Cooper's *Amaryllis* (1746).

Other engravers of the period were B. Fortier, John and Sarah Phillips, Michael Broome (Birmingham), R. Denson, Thomas Bennett, James Read (Edinburgh), Thomas Phinn (Edinburgh), Richard Alderman, Thomas Baker and Frances Pasquali.

B. Fortier engraved one of the finest executed musical works of the eighteenth century: Domenico Scarlatti's *Essercizi per Gravicembalo* (1739). It is generally stated that it was produced abroad, but there is every reason for believing that London should have the credit for it. Fortier did other works here from 1736-38 or later, and the "Essercizi" was advertised and marketed in London by Adamo Scola, a music-master, in Vine Street, Piccadilly. Moreover, Amiconi, the designer of the title-page, was also living in England at the time. A superlative example of Fortier's title-pages is that of Guerini's *Sonate a Violino con Viola di Gamba ó Cembalo . . . Opera Prima*, which has been attributed to 1760, but was probably issued about 1740, and gives Fortier's address as "Castel (i.e. Castle) Street, Leicester Fields."

Thomas Bennett, in addition to other works, printed a number for Lewis Granom which were engraved in a delicate and most attractive style, some with fine title-pages.

R. Denson, an engraver whose output of music was small, deserves special mention for the quality of his productions. He was employed to engrave and sell some of the works of Charles Avison.

Edmund Chapman, who published a few musical works, employed as engraver Richard Alderman. These publications are a model of what could be done by the artistic craftsman and a small publisher. The title-pages of some have a delightful illustration of instruments, cherubs, etc., the music being in a most attractive and bold style, others have fine ornamental borders to the titles. (T. Prota, *Sei Sonate*; N. Dothel, *Six Duetts for 2 German Flutes.*) Alderman also worked for other publishers, and issued some works himself.

Thomas Baker's work was extremely good, with fine ornamental title-pages and the music beautifully engraved in an attractive and clear style. (G. Clari, *Sei Madrigali.*)

Frances Pasquali engraved, printed and published a few works including a beautiful small oblong octavo volume of *Sei Canzonette a due*, by John Christian Bach, Op. IV (c. 1765), a similar volume to which, Op. VI, was engraved by Caulfield, an apprentice of John Walsh the younger.

From what has been said, it is obvious, that for a period of thirty years or so, British music publishing and engraving by a few firms reached a standard superior to anything that had preceded it, but was soon forgotten in the flood of inartistic and cheaply produced works which followed in the next fifty years.

During the eighteenth century little attempt was made to use music type in preference to engraved plates, but there are some commendable examples of the former method. Henry Fougt, a Laplander, who settled in London about 1765, produced a year or two later a beautiful music type for which he obtained a patent in 1767, and which received the commendation of the Society of Arts in 1768 in the following terms:

> The Resolution of the Society for the Encouragement of Arts, Manufactures and Commerce in London. December 28th, 1768, The Society took into Consideration the Specimen of Mr. Henry Fougt's New-invented Type for Printing Music;
>
> Resolved
>
> That Mr. Fougt's Method of Printing Music is an Improvement superior to any before in Use in Great-Britain; and That it appears to answer All the Purposes of Engraving in Wood, Tin, or Copper, for that end, and can be performed with much less Expence. (G. Sarti, *Three Sonatas.* B.M. h. 60. b. (5.))

It is not unlikely that Fougt obtained some of his technical ideas from J. G. Breitkopf, who had, some ten years earlier, revolutionized musical typography and laid down the foundations for its use in the future. Although Fougt's beautiful works were sold at a penny a page, or eighteen pages for a shilling, the use of music engraving predominated over attempts to make type popular. Fougt's title-pages were adorned with a delightful design embodying an owl, a reference to his address "at the Lyre and the Owl." Robert Falkener acquired Fougt's plant and type (c. 1770) and carried on music printing from a type very similar to Fougt's with some success up to about 1780.

Bigg and Cox (c. 1769-76) used a distinctive music type as evidenced in *Modesty's Cap*, a song by Philip Hodgson of Newcastle.[1]

With the death of John Walsh the younger, in 1766, and the continuance of the business in turn by Randall and Abell, Randall alone, Elizabeth Randall, Wright and Wilkinson, etc., the firm made no effort to capture the growing market, but largely contented themselves with advertising and selling previous publications, and producing Handel's oratorios in full scores, a commendable enterprise. These were usually issued by subscription, at two guineas, but had only a moderate number of subscribers (*Messiah* had ninety-two for one hundred and twenty-nine copies and *Judas Maccabæus* one hundred and forty-eight for two hundred and three copies), so the works could not have been very lucrative. The vocal scores of the oratorios and operas, which only included the overtures and songs, etc., were sold at ten shillings and sixpence or less. An examination of Randall's catalogue of 1776 shows no marked changes in prices over the whole range of works since publication by the Walshes; although the alteration in money values from the early days of Walsh to 1776 may have made the works relatively cheaper.

It is evident that before Walsh the younger died in 1766, new vigorous firms were coming into existence. The first financial and cultural effects arising from the Industrial Revolution were being felt in music as in the other arts. A new middle class, with money to spend, was rapidly expanding, and the entrants into it were anxious to educate their children and give them the advantages of culture and refinement. The flood of

[1] William C. Smith collection.

songs by Arnold, Dibdin, Hook, Hudson, Shield and others, provided for the amateur, as well as for the professional, a wide range to select from. The literary magazines of the day (*The Lady's Magazine, The Gentleman's Magazine, The London Magazine, The Universal Magazine, The New Universal Magazine*, etc.) very often included a musical number. Vauxhall and the other gardens were centres of musical attraction, and the subsequent development of the pianoforte gave a great impetus to the production of keyboard music for performance in public and private.

Handel was still popular, and the remarkable celebrations in 1784 and later could not have taken place so successfully without a large supporting musical public. It has been pointed out that full scores and vocal scores of his works were not in circulation at popular prices. James Harrison (Harrison and Co.) was one of the first to see the advantage to be derived from cheaper editions, although in this respect he had been anticipated by John Bland, who claimed to be the first printer to publish singly the works of Handel and other celebrated composers. Bland issued *Songs in Messiah* at three shillings and sixpence, and *The Overture and Songs in . . . Acis and Galatea* at three shillings. He is also to be remembered for a number of thematic catalogues, details of some of which are recorded under his entry. Harrison's first musical work *The New Musical Magazine* was first advertised in 1783. It consisted of works by Handel, Arne, Arnold, Greene, Howard and others, and was issued at one shilling and sixpence a part of sixteen large oblong folio pages, which meant that the complete vocal score of *Messiah* was sold for seven shillings and sixpence, as against Randall and Wright's editions of the full score at two guineas. Harrison pointed out that the first sixteen numbers of his magazine cost one pound four shillings against other sellers' prices of five pounds twelve shillings and sixpence. With each number of *The New Musical Magazine* he gave a sheet of letterpress (4 pp.) of the same size as the music, as part of *An Universal Dictionary of Music . . . and a General History of Music*, a most interesting and ambitious undertaking. He also issued *The Songs of Handel* in four volumes (1786-87) containing twenty-five oratorios, commencing with *Messiah*, the first volume of which had a designed ornamental title-page by E. F. Burney. Harrison, followed by Harrison, Cluse and Co., issued another work in parts, *The Piano-Forte Magazine* (1797-

1802) at half-a-crown a number, and in the prospectus dated May 1, 1797, it was announced as "A Hundred Guineas worth of Musick and a Piano-Forte, worth Twenty-Five Guineas Gratis." There were 250 weekly numbers each with "Note of Hand, signed by Mr. Harrison, entitling Bearer of all the Notes published with every Sett, to an exquisite Brilliant-toned and Elegant Piano-Forte, far superior to many Instruments Sold for Twenty-Five Guineas each."

Samuel Arnold was associated with Harrison in his first two enterprises, and no doubt copied from him the idea of issues in parts, with the part numbers at the bottom of the pages. This practice he adopted in his monumental collected edition of Handel's works, the forerunner of later collected editions (Gesammtausgaben) of Beethoven and others, which appeared on the Continent in the nineteenth century. Arnold also experimented with type, and patented a process in 1784, but his edition of Handel's works was from engraved and stamped plates; Thomas (?) Straight, R. T. Skarratt and probably the Caulfields being among the engravers he employed.

The following firms are the principal ones that took advantage of, and contributed to, the growing popularity of music during the last half of the eighteenth century: Thompson, 1746-98; Wheatstone, 1750 to the present time; Bremner (Edinburgh and London), 1754-89; Stewart (Edinburgh), 1759-1805; Fentum, 1762-1844; Thorowgood and Horne, followed by Thorowgood alone, 1761-80; William Forster the elder and younger, 1762-1824; Welcker, 1762-85; Straight and Skillern and successors, 1766-1826; John Johnston, 1767-78; James Longman and Co. and successors, 1767-1822; Babb, 1770-86; Falkener, 1770-80; William Napier, 1772-1809; James Johnson and successors (Edinburgh), 1772-1815; Preston, 1774-1834; John Bland, 1776-95; John Corri and relatives (Edinburgh and London), 1779-1822; Harrison and Co., followed by Harrison, Cluse & Co., 1779-1803; Birchall and Beardmore and successors, 1783-1824; Dale, 1783-1823; Anne Bland and successors, 1784-1820; Goulding, 1786-1834; Monzani, 1787-1845; Hime Liverpool), 1790 or earlier to 1879; John McFadyen (Glasgow), 1790-1837; George Walker (Edinburgh), 1790-1848; Watlen (Edinburgh and London), 1791-1829; George Walker (London), 1795-1830; Lavenu, 1796-1844; Broderip and Wilkinson and successors, 1798-1810. Many of these publishers issued with their works sheet catalogues of their publications, details of some of which are mentioned under their entries in the dictionary.

The surprising thing about this list is the long range of years over which most of the firms operated. Comments on some are necessary. Henry Thorowgood served his apprenticeship with John Cox. Straight and Skillern learnt their business with John Walsh the younger. John Bland's stock of twelve thousand engraved plates was in 1795 taken over by Lewis, Houston and Hyde, and advertised by them for sale in March 1797. Bland issued many catalogues of his publications, including from 1790 some thematic ones. Birchall's had a circulating library. The circulating musical library of Babb consisted of upwards of twenty thousand music books in 1778, and when purchased by Joseph Dale in 1786 contained more than one hundred thousand books. Anne Bland purchased Dibdin's copyrights and musical stock. William Napier, John McFadyen and the Lavenus also had circulating musical libraries.

Domenico Corri published through his son John, *A Select Collection of the Most Admired Songs, Duetts, &c. From Operas of the highest esteem*, etc. (c. 1779), a work conspicuous for some new ideas in the printing of musical signs and the harpsichord accompaniment, with directions to singers and instrumentalists, illustrations of musical instruments, and thematic indexes—one of the earliest examples of thematic lists in this country.

Kidson suggested that George Walker probably started the practice of marking music at double the price at which it was sold.

The firm of Preston, established by John Preston, c. 1774, had a long and important place among the publishers of the time. They purchased the stock and plates of the equally famous business of Robert Bremner in 1789, and also the stock of plates of H. Wright (who advertised as the successor to Walsh the younger) some time after 1803. By the latter purchase they acquired the oratorios and other works of Handel formerly published by the Walshes, Randalls and Wright; editions of which Thomas Preston subsequently issued. The plates of these works passed to Coventry and Hollier when they succeeded Thomas Preston (c. 1834). One series of works for which the Prestons are to be especially remembered are the various collections of national songs edited by George Thomson, some of which they published for the editor from 1793 onwards until

Coventry and Hollier took their place and continued as Thomson's publishers; John Moir of Edinburgh printing some of the collections from 1802. All of these volumes have beautifully designed and illustrated title-pages.[1]

Benjamin Goodison, a lawyer and amateur musician, is worthy of note for his ambitious scheme to publish, in addition to other works, a complete edition of Henry Purcell's by subscription from about 1790 onwards, of which only a few numbers appeared.[2]

Evidently the music publishers of the day did well out of the composers, who were not satisfied with their returns, judging from the following notice in the *Morning Herald and Daily Advertiser*, March 2, 1781:

New favourite advertisement.

The Composers of music, in London, most respectfully acquaint the nobility and gentry, that henceforth their new music will be sold at their own dwelling houses; the reason for this is, because the music-shop keepers take so much advantage over the composers, viz. 1st when a set of music sells for 10s 6d the music shops take half a crown for their trouble of selling it. I think sixpence or a shilling profit is sufficient for a copy, as the only trouble is to sell it to the person that asks for it in the shop.—N.B. As it is customary with the booksellers. 2dly, the music-shop keepers take the seventh copy for their profit, which they call allowance; consequently there remains only 6s 3d out of the half guinea to the composer for his performance, and he is obliged to pay the engraving, printing, paper and other expences. The composers of music will refer to the impartial judgment of a generous public, if it is just, that when a good composition appears, and is accepted by the public, that the music-shop keepers, take the money, and for the composer remains only the honour, by which he is to live. Consequently the shop keepers live by the sweat and labour of the composers, and are, into the bargain, very insolent and impertinent towards them.

Thus much from
APPOLO.

---

[1] Cecil Hopkinson and C. B. Oldman, "Thomson's Collections of National Song." (*Edinburgh Bibliographical Society Transactions.* Vol. II, Pt. 1, 1940.)
[2] A. Hyatt King. "The First 'Complete Edition' of Purcell." (*The Monthly Musical Record.* March-April 1951, pp. 63-69.)

Engravers of the period were the Caulfields, John the elder and younger, Joseph and Henry; James Johnson (Edinburgh), James Kempson (Birmingham), Thomas Skillern the elder, Thomas Straight, J. B. Scherer, S. Straight, Robert T. Skarratt, and R. Wells, who did a fine edition of *Eighteen Songs Composed by M*ʳ. *Handel, Adapted for a Violoncello Obligato, with a Figured Bass for the Harpsichord; By Henry Hardy. Oxford* (c. 1795), the title-page having a portrait of Handel after Hudson.

In 1784 appeared a *Review of New Musical Publications. Printed by T. Williams, No. 43 nearly opposite Hatton Street Holborn*, the first volume of which (Nos. I-IX) complete with index, is in the British Museum (P.P. 1945. ma.). This journal, extremely rare of its kind, is devoted entirely to short criticisms and announcements of musical works. Williams also printed and published some music.

From 1801 onwards the increase in the number of music publishing firms was considerable, and it is only possible to mention here the most important, with the dates of establishment: Muzio Clementi and Co. and successors, 1801-64; Michael Kelly, 1802-11; Button and Purday, 1807-24; James Power, followed by his widow, 1807-38; Charles Mitchell, 1808-25; William Mitchell, 1811-27; Robert Purdie, followed by his son John (Edinburgh), 1808-87; Lucy Williams, 1808-44, succeeded by Joseph Williams, 1844 to the present time; Chappell and Co., 1811 to the present time; Robert William Keith, followed by Keith, Prowse & Co., 1815 to the present time; Metzler and Son, etc., 1816-1930; Paterson, Mortimer and Co., etc. (Edinburgh), 1819 to the present time; Alexander Robertson (Edinburgh), 1820-70; Addison and Beale, etc., Cramer, Addison and Beale, Cramer and Co., 1823 to the present time; Wessel and Stodart, Wessel and Co., etc., 1823-60; Robert Cocks and Co., 1823-98; T. C. Bates, etc., 1812-63; William Goodwin, 1826-76; J. A. Novello, followed by Novello and Co., 1829 to the present time; Coventry and Hollier, 1834-51; Charles Jefferys, 1835-99; Charles Ollivier and successors, 1837-92; Alexander Glen and successors (Edinburgh), 1840 to the present time; John Alvey Turner, 1843 to the present time.

[34]

Mitchell had a musical library; Chappell was previously employed by Birchall; Wessel and Stodart became large importers of foreign music, and the firm published most of Chopin's pianoforte works in England; Coventry and Hollier succeeded Preston, and a great number of their music plates (including those of Handel's works) were subsequently acquired by J. A. Novello.

Engraved and punched metal plates continued to be the method employed for music printing from 1801 onwards, but the discovery of lithography by Senefelder (c. 1796) introduced a revolution in printing and was soon applied to music. Senefelder was associated with Philipp H. André in the establishment of a lithographic business in London, and G. J. Vollweiler, André's successor, printed a small amount of music from stone at the Polyautographic Press (c. 1806-07). Lithography was adopted by a number of small firms, some of which were: "The Lithographic Press," Westminster (c. 1811), who advertised their works as "Printed from English stone"; William Hawkes Smith, Birmingham (1820 or earlier-c. 1835); Charles Hullmandel's Lithographic Establishment (c. 1820); The Lithographic Press, London (1822); Anthony Fleetwood, Liverpool (c. 1825); T. and J. Allman (1825); The Banff Lithographic Press (1832); and W. Hall, Belfast (c. 1840). In 1847 there appeared the first volume of *Jullien's Album*, a monumental and outstanding example of lithography as applied to music printing, which went on until 1857. It was magnificently designed and executed, with beautiful chromo lithographic frontispieces and title-pages, including several Baxter prints. It was a composite work by Michael and Nicholas Hanhart and William Cornish (chromo lithographic printers), Isaac Davis (lithographic printer of the music) and T. Moody (music engraver).

The first British firm to use lithography for music printing in a large and general way was Augener and Co., who from their establishment in 1853 adopted this method. Other firms also used lithography, which after its early days, as time went on, was modified and improved by the use of metal plates, and chemical and photo mechanical processes.

Stereotyping, invented and patented by William Ged of

Edinburgh in 1725, was applied to music by Carl Tauchnitz of Leipzig (*b.* 1761, *d.* 1836), and by Clowes and others in London; but later, electrotyping took the place of stereotyping.

During the first half of the nineteenth century a few determined efforts were made to bring back into popular favour musical typography—which had never ceased to be used, but only to a comparatively small extent.

One of its most ardent advocates was William Clowes, who effected considerable improvements in this method. *The Harmonicon* (1823-33), *The Musical Library* (1834-37) and *Sacred Minstrelsy* (1834-35) contain excellent specimens of his work. In the first number of Charles Knight's *Musical Library* (printed by Clowes) is an interesting description of the various processes applied to music printing, in which we are told that the publisher had purchased at considerable expense a secret process of printing music, invented by M. Duverger of Paris; and mention is also made of Edward Cowper's double process method of musical typography (1827), which was used by Samuel Chappell and others, but soon abandoned.

J. A. Novello, who was established as a music seller and publisher as early as 1829, published his early works printed from the popular engraved plate methods of the day; but in 1847 he established his own printing business especially for the purpose of printing music from some fine new movable types. His pamphlet on the subject, *Some account of the Methods of Musick Printing* (1847), is of particular interest, and *A Short History of Cheap Music*, published by Novello, Ewer and Co. in 1887, with a preface by George Grove, deals in detail with the history of the firm and gives much information about the musical events and the publishing of music in London. About fifty years ago Novello and Co. reverted to the earlier and cheaper method of music engraving for many of their publications.

Broadly speaking, the three methods—engraved and punched metal plates, movable type, and lithography—are all in use to-day, modified and improved by modern processes, which are adequately treated by Gamble, Kathi Meyer and other writers. Details of such technical improvements, and particulars of the many British firms who, since the middle of the nineteenth century, have carried on with great success and credit the printing, publishing and marketing of music, are outside the scope of the present work; and having covered in this general outline the period with which it is particularly concerned, it now only remains to give some explanatory notes and to provide a short bibliography.

The present dictionary is in no sense a revised edition of Kidson's work, but is an entirely new publication, based in the main upon original research by the authors over the many years of their long association together in the music section of the Department of Printed Books, British Museum.

Kidson's information is in many cases necessarily incomplete and needing revision; moreover, he omitted many firms, as he was quite unable to make an exhaustive search of the early newspapers, etc., or to range over the works on the British Museum shelves. Neither did he have the assistance of Barclay Squire's *Catalogue of Printed Music published between 1487 and 1800 now in the British Museum*, issued in 1912, and the supplements to that work.

The present writers have endeavoured to go to original sources for their information, as far as possible. While not claiming to have searched all the newspapers covering the period of the dictionary, most of them up to the end of the eighteenth century have been examined for advertisements of music, as these notices—apart from the works themselves—provide much of what is now known about many of the firms.

The other major source, from which much important material has been gained first hand, is the music in the British Museum (B.M.), thousands of volumes of which have been examined. Catalogues of other libraries and collections, sale catalogues, publishers' and booksellers' lists, postal and other directories, the *Term Catalogues* (T.C.), *The Dictionary of National Biography* (D.N.B.), dictionaries of music, musical publications and periodicals, have been invaluable aids towards completeness and accuracy. Extensive use has also been made of the various publications of The Bibliographical Society, and many other bibliographical works have been consulted. Particulars collected from all these and other sources have been collated with information brought together by the authors from the newspapers, the musical works and elsewhere.

The British Museum catalogue of music, for the first half of

the nineteenth century, does not, as a rule, give the publishers'
names, as in Squire's catalogue; and as it has been quite impossible to examine all the available music after the year 1800,
a number of the later less important London and provincial
publishers may have been omitted. Apart from such omissions,
the dictionary does present as full a list as possible of the names
of every person and firm known to have been engaged in any
way in the printing, engraving, publishing, selling and advertising of music in the British Isles up to about the middle of the
nineteenth century, including some musical instrument makers
and general booksellers who are known to have sold or issued
music, little or much. The names of engravers of title-pages or
frontispieces, otherwise not concerned with the production of
the music, have been included in a few cases only, more particularly some of those before 1800. With a few exceptions,
printers, publishers, etc. of treatises, literary works, magazines
and periodicals containing some music have been omitted, and
also as a rule, composers and others who only issued or sold
their own works.

The descriptions—publisher, printer, engraver, bookseller,
etc.—have been assigned from evidence on the works, or in
advertisements, etc.; but in many cases it is quite impossible to
say whether a publisher was his own printer or engraver, to
what extent the printing was put out to other individuals or
firms, or whether the engraving was done on the publisher's or
printer's premises by employees or journeyman craftsmen.
Practical engravers, as distinct from publishers and printers,
have been indicated whenever possible. The names are arranged
in one alphabetical list, irrespective of the nature of the work of
the person or firm (printer, publisher or music seller, etc.) or
their place of business, followed by an index of firms under their
respective towns, other than London, and a list of those firms
who are recorded as having been engaged also in the manu-
facture or repair of musical instruments. Entries have been
made for every named member of a firm as well as for the
firm itself.

A simple, short form has been adopted, as a rule, for the
presentation of material under each heading, although it has
been necessary in some cases to deal with a particular firm in a
special way. The address or location is followed by the period
when the firm was at that address, this being indicated by the

years only; but if addresses are not known the working period of the firm has been given if possible. As the dates in many cases have been approximated from the first and last known publications at, or the earliest and latest advertisements from, a particular address, it is most likely that in many instances the period of working was longer than that given, although no evidence to that effect has been traced. Changes of address, or alterations in the name or names of a firm are treated as beginning a new period; but where alternative forms of address were used they are included in the same period, usually in brackets. At the end of each entry, when a firm was continued by others, the name of the succeeding firm is given, the particulars of which are recorded under their respective names; similarly predecessors of firms are also entered separately. Archaic forms of the spelling of shop signs and streets have been retained sometimes, but otherwise, the correct or generally accepted forms have been adopted.

Under the entries for the larger firms no mention is made of the works published, as examples are easily accessible, but where a firm is only known by one or two works, especially if they are of particular importance, short titles of these works have been included, but not always in strict bibliographical form as to capitals, punctuation, etc. Detailed documentation throughout has not been attempted for a number of reasons. Music, as a rule, was not dated, so the period of a firm's working cannot be arrived at from the dates of first and last publications, as it can be done frequently when dealing with the literary publications of publishers and booksellers. The dates given to musical works have to be approximated from various sources—time and order of a composer's works, dedications, lists of other works, internal evidence from the typography, watermarks, names of engravers, etc. Many of the firms did not advertise, or only occasionally, and the files of newspapers for some years are very incomplete. Consequently, advertisements are only a rough guide to the period of working. Directories are of no practical value until the latter part of the eighteenth century, and the information in them is incomplete and often contradictory. Moreover, the first appearance in a directory does not make it certain when the firm first started. In the majority of cases, therefore, the dates supplied have been arrived at by considering all the available evidence, and even then it has only been possible to give approximate dates; but it can be taken for granted that, generally, there is no evidence to prove that the firms were in existence before or after the dates given. To have attempted detailed documentation of the thousands of dates, and many changes of address, would have meant the addition of an explanatory paragraph to most entries, listing the sources examined, and giving reasons for the conjectural dates and other details.

As previously pointed out, many firms issued catalogues of their works from time to time. It was also very common, from the days of John Playford, for publishers to give on their works lists of other publications. Under the respective firms, details are given of some of these catalogues and lists, the latter only in exceptional cases or when a list has been traced separated from the work with which it was originally issued. Many more of such catalogues and lists exist than those enumerated.

Only some 400 or so of the firms mentioned are included in Kidson. Other works, listed in the bibliography—*Grove's Dictionary*; The Bibliographical Society's publications by Duff, McKerrow, and the three volumes by Plomer; Steele's *The Earliest English Music Printing*; Day and Murrie's *English Song Books, 1651-1702*—are important source books, containing information about many firms besides those listed by Kidson. In all cases, therefore, of names which appear in any of these standard works, references are given to them at the end of the respective entries by the letters K. (Kidson), G. (Grove), D. (Duff), M. (McKerrow), P. I, II, III. (Plomer, 1641-67; 1668-1725; Plomer, etc., 1726-75), S. (Steele), D. & M. (Day and Murrie), although these are not the only works that have been consulted in compiling the entries in question. Where it has been considered necessary to indicate that material (usually addresses and over-all dates) has been taken without modification from any of the above mentioned authorities, this is indicated in the body of the entries concerned; but it should be pointed out that the publications of The Bibliographical Society contain a great deal of detailed information about the addresses and activities of many of the firms, other than as printers, publishers, etc. of music, which it has not been considered necessary, as a rule, to incorporate in the present work. The entries that appear in the earlier editions of *Grove's Dictionary* have all been revised, and additional entries have been written for the forthcoming new edition of that work, in keeping with the information given in the present publication.

Kidson, Grove, Steele and Day and Murrie, all provide titles and other details of various works issued by the respective firms, which it has not been considered necessary to repeat in this dictionary. Steele, Day and Murrie, Gamble and Smith (Walsh Bibliography) give many specimens of music types, engravings and title-pages. Examples of the work of the larger and more important firms, particularly in the last seventy or eighty years of the survey, are well known and easily obtainable, and as previously pointed out, in those cases of music firms with a small output, and also of general letterpress printers, publishers, etc., who issued only an occasional musical work, details of such works are given in the entries, thus providing all that is known of the musical activities of the firms in question.

Of the two thousand two hundred or so names listed, many do not appear in any earlier reference work, and it is the identification and placing of firms, particularly the less important ones, that has often been hitherto a source of difficulty to those engaged in musical librarianship and research. A form of imprint, a publisher's address, the changes in the members constituting a firm or partnership, are very often of vital importance in the accurate dating of a work; and it is hoped that the dictionary will justify its existence, in spite of its errors and omissions, if it helps to throw light on some of the obscure pages of the story of music and music publishing in the British Isles.

It is necessary to say how much the authors owe to the inspiration of their distinguished predecessor, Frank Kidson, without whose work it is hardly likely that the present volume would have been undertaken. They would also like to put on record that the late Miss Ethel M. Kidson and her brother, Mr. Alfred Kidson of Liverpool, have expressed their interest in, and approval of, this work, and granted the use of their uncle's material as necessary.

Thanks are especially due to Harold Reeves for the use of his two copies of Kidson's *British Music Publishers* (one of which formerly belonged to Dr. Cummings) containing many additional notes added to them over many years by Harold Reeves, which have proved invaluable. The Rev. Maurice Frost also kindly submitted for use and extract his annotated copy of

[41]

Kidson, which formerly belonged to Alfred Moffat. The late Paul Hirsch, Cecil Hopkinson, A. Hyatt King, Richard Newton, C. B. Oldman, C.B., Miss E. Schnapper, Hugh Mellor, Leonard Hyman, Adam Carse, George Smith (formerly of Ellis and Co.), L. W. Hanson, F. C. Francis, Margaret Dean-Smith and J. S. Hall, O.B.E., F.R.C.S., of Walmer have all been helpful in various ways. Finally the authors are particularly indebted to The Bibliographical Society for the use of material from their invaluable publications, and to the Trustees of the British Museum for permission to use the illustrations, which have all been taken from works in the Department of Printed Books.

It has been impossible for the authors to visit the many libraries in the country where additional information may exist and the names of other firms are recorded. Much of this material will no doubt appear in *The Union Catalogue of Music* now in preparation; but as it stands, it is hoped that this dictionary will encourage private owners and librarians to examine their collections and thus bring to notice any supplementary material, as a work of this kind can never be complete, and can hardly be expected to be free from error.

BIBLIOGRAPHY

In addition to the main general sources of information mentioned in the introduction, the following is a selected list of important works on the subject, which have been consulted and have provided corroborative and useful evidence on many points.

ARBER (EDWARD)
A Transcript of the Registers of the Company of Stationers of London; 1554-1640. Edited by Edward Arber. Vol. 1-4, London, 1875-77; Vol. 5, Birmingham, 1894.

ARBER (EDWARD)
The Term Catalogues, 1668-1709 A.D., with a number for Easter Term, 1711 A.D. 3 vols. Privately printed. Published by Professor Edward Arber, London, 1903-06

BAPTIE (DAVID)
Musical Scotland, Past and Present. Being a dictionary of Scottish musicians from about 1400 till the present time. To which is added a bibliography of musical publications connected with Scotland from 1611. Compiled and collected by D. Baptie. J. and R. Parlane, Paisley, 1894.

BROWN (JAMES D.) AND STRATTON (STEPHEN S.)
British Musical Biography: a Dictionary of musical Artists, Authors and Composers, born in Britain and the Colonies. S. S. Stratton, Birmingham. Printed by Chadfield and Son, Ltd., Derby, 1897.

CALKIN AND BUDD
A Catalogue of a miscellaneous Collection of Music, ancient and modern. Together with treatises on music, and on the history of music, on sale at the prices affixed to each article. Calkin and Budd, London, 1844.

CHRYSANDER (FRIEDRICH)
"A Sketch of the History of Music Printing, from the fifteenth to the nineteenth century." (*The Musical Times*, London. Vol. 18, June-August, October-December, 1877.)

CUMMINGS (WILLIAM H.)
"Music Printing." (*Proceedings of the Musical Association*, London. May 4, 1885, pp. 99-116.)

DAY (CYRUS L.) AND MURRIE (ELEANORE B.)
English Song-Books, 1651-1702. A Bibliography. Oxford University Press, for The Bibliographical Society, London, 1940. (Referred to in the present work as "D. & M.")

[43]

DAY (CYRUS L.) AND MURRIE (ELEANORE B.)

"English Song-Books, 1651-1702, and their publishers." (*The Library. Fourth Series.* Vol. XVI. No. 4. March, 1936, pp. 355-401. Oxford University Press, for The Bibliographical Society, London.) (This and the preceding work are invaluable, and contain many specimens of title-pages, types, etc.)

DEAKIN (ANDREW)

Musical Bibliography. A catalogue of the musical works . . . published in England during the fifteenth, sixteenth, seventeenth and eighteenth centuries, chronologically arranged . . . by Andrew Deakin. Stockley and Sabin, Birmingham, 1892.

DEAKIN (ANDREW)

Outlines of Musical Bibliography: a catalogue of early music and musical works printed or otherwise produced in the British Isles. Part I. Andrew Deakin, Birmingham, 1899.

DUFF (E. GORDON)

A Century of the English Book Trade. Short notices of all printers, stationers, book-binders, and others connected with it from the issue of the first dated book in 1457 to the incorporation of the Company of Stationers in 1557. Printed for The Bibliographical Society, by Blades, East & Blades, London, 1905. (Referred to in the present work as "D.")

FARMER (HENRY GEORGE)

A History of Music in Scotland. Hinrichsen Edition Limited, London. [1948.]

   (Contains a chapter on "The Publishers," pp. 292-299.)

FLOOD (W. H. GRATTAN)

"Dublin Music Printing from 1685 to 1750." (*The Bibliographical Society of Ireland. Publications.* Vol. II. No. 1, pp. 7-12. 1921. John Falconer, Dublin.)

FLOOD (W. H. GRATTAN)

"Dublin Music Printing from 1750 to 1790." (*The Bibliographical Society of Ireland. Publications.* Vol. II. No. 5, pp. 101-106. 1923. John Falconer, Dublin.)

FLOWER (DESMOND)

"On Music Printing: 1473-1701." (*The Book-Collector's Quarterly.* No. IV. October-December, 1931, pp. 76-92. Cassell and Co., London.)

FLOWER (DESMOND)

"Handel's Publishers." (*The English Review*, London. January, 1936, pp. 66-75.)

GAMBLE (WILLIAM)

Music Engraving and Printing. Historical and technical treatise. Sir Isaac Pitman & Sons, London, 1923. (Deals with the technical side in great detail.)

GLEN (JOHN)

The Glen Collection of Scottish Dance Music, Strathspeys, Reels, and Jiggs . . . Arranged . . . by John Glen. Containing . . . sketches of musicians and music sellers, etc. 2 vols. Published at 2 North Bank Street, Edinburgh, 1891, 1895.

GLEN (JOHN)

Early Scottish Melodies including examples from MSS. and early printed works, along with a number of . . . biographical notices, etc. written and arranged by John Glen. J. & R. Glen, Edinburgh, 1900.

GROVE (SIR GEORGE)

Dictionary of Music and Musicians. Edited by J. A. Fuller Maitland. 5 vols. 1904-10; Third Edition, edited by H. C. Colles. 5 vols. 1927-28; Fourth edition, edited by H. C. Colles. 6 vols. 1940. Macmillan & Co., London. (Many articles by Frank Kidson. Revised and rewritten, with many new entries by William C. Smith in the new edition now in preparation, edited by Eric Blom. Referred to in the present work as "G.")

HADER (KARL)

Aus der Werkstatt eines Notensteckers. Waldheim-Eberle, Vienna, 1948.

KIDSON (FRANK)

British Music Publishers, Printers and Engravers. W. E. Hill & Sons, London, 1900. (Referred to in the present work as "K.")

KIDSON (FRANK)

"English Magazines containing Music, before the early part of the nineteenth century." (*The Musical Antiquary*, London. January, 1912, pp. 99-102.)

KIDSON (FRANK)

"Some Illustrated Music-Books of the seventeenth and eighteenth centuries: English." (*The Musical Antiquary*, London. July, 1912, pp. 195-208.)

KIDSON (FRANK)

"John Playford and 17th century Music Publishing." (*The Musical Quarterly*, New York. October, 1918, pp. 516-534.)

KIDSON (FRANK)

"Handel's Publisher, John Walsh, his successors and contemporaries." (*The Musical Quarterly*, New York. July 1920, pp. 430-450.)

LITTLETON (ALFRED HENRY)

"Some Notes on early Printed Music." (*English Music (1604 to 1904)* *being the Lectures given at the Music Loan Exhibition of the Worshipful Company of Musicians. June-July 1904*, pp. 478-496. Part of the *Music Story Series*. The Walter Scott Publishing Co., London, 1906. Second edition, 1911.)

LITTLETON (ALFRED HENRY)

A Catalogue of one hundred Works illustrating the history of Music Printing from the fifteenth to the end of the seventeenth century, in the Library of Alfred Henry Littleton. Novello and Co., London, 1911. (With illustrations.)

MCKERROW (R. B.) *Editor*

A Dictionary of Printers and Booksellers in England, Scotland and Ireland, and of Foreign Printers of English Books 1557-1640. By H. G. Aldis; Robert Bowes; E. R. McC. Dix; E. Gordon Duff; Strickland Gibson; G. J. Gray; R. B. McKerrow; Falconer Madan; and H. R. Plomer. General Editor: R. B. McKerrow. Printed for The Bibliographical Society, by Blades, East & Blades, London, 1910. (Referred to in the present work as "M.")

MEYER (KATHI)

"The Printing of Music, 1473-1934." By Kathi Meyer in collaboration with Eva Judd O'Meara. (*The Dolphin*. Number Two, 1935, pp. 171-207. The Limited Editions Club, New York.)
    (With a bibliography and illustrations.)

MORTIMER (CHARLES)

"Leading Music Publishers." (*Musical Opinion*, London. September, 1938-March, 1942.)

NOVELLO (JOSEPH ALFRED)

Some account of the Methods of Musick Printing, with specimens of the various sizes of Moveable Types; and of other matters. J. A. Novello, London, 1847.

NOVELLO, EWER AND CO.

A Short History of Cheap Music as exemplified in the records of the House of Novello, Ewer & Co., etc. Novello, Ewer and Co., London and New York, 1887.

NOVELLO AND CO.

"Soho and the House of Novello." (*The Musical Times*, London. December, 1906, pp. 797-802.)

NOVELLO AND CO.

"The Novello Centenary, 1811-1911." (*The Musical Times*, London. June, 1911, Supplement.)

Pattison (Bruce)

"Notes on Early Music Printing." (*The Library*. Fourth Series. Vol. XIX. No. 4. March, 1939, pp. 389-421. Oxford University Press, for The Bibliographical Society, London.)

Plomer (Henry R.)

A Dictionary of the Booksellers and Printers who were at work in England, Scotland and Ireland from 1641-1667. Printed for The Bibliographical Society, by Blades, East & Blades, London, 1907. (Referred to in the present work as "P.I.")

Plomer (Henry R.), etc.

A Dictionary of the Printers and Booksellers who were at work in England, Scotland and Ireland from 1668 to 1725. By Henry R. Plomer. With the help of H. G. Aldis, E. R. McC. Dix, G. J. Gray, and R. B. McKerrow. Edited by Arundell Esdaile. Printed for The Bibliographical Society, at the Oxford University Press, 1922. (Referred to in the present work as "P.II.")

Plomer (Henry R.) etc.

A Dictionary of the Printers and Booksellers who were at work in England, Scotland and Ireland from 1726 to 1775. Those in England by H. R. Plomer. Scotland by G. H. Bushnell. Ireland by E. R. McC. Dix. Printed for The Bibliographical Society at The Oxford University Press, 1932 (for 1930). (Referred to in the present work as "P.III.")

Smith (William C.)

"Playford: Some hitherto unnoticed catalogues of early music." (*The Musical Times*, London. Vol. 67. July, August, 1926.)

Smith (William C.)

A Bibliography of the Musical Works published by John Walsh during the years 1695-1720. Oxford University Press, for The Bibliographical Society, London, 1948. (With illustrations and details of catalogues, etc.)

Smith (William C.)

"John Walsh, Music Publisher. The first twenty five years." (*The Library*. Fifth Series. Vol. I. No. 1. June, 1946, pp. 1-5. Oxford University Press, for The Bibliographical Society, London.)

Smith (William C.)

"John Walsh and his successors." (*The Library*. Fifth Series. Vol. III. No. 4. March, 1949, pp. 291-295. Oxford University Press, for The Bibliographical Society, London.)

Smith (William C.)

"The Meaning of the Imprint." (*The Library*. Fifth Series. Vol. VII. No. 1. March, 1952, pp. 61-63. Oxford University Press, for The Bibliographical Society, London.)

SMITH (WILLIAM C.)

" New Evidence Concerning John Walsh and the Duties on Paper, 1726." (*Harvard Library Bulletin*. Vol. VI. No. 2. Spring, 1952, pp. 252-255.)

SQUIRE (WILLIAM BARCLAY)

"Notes on early Music Printing." (*Bibliographica*. Vol. III, pp. 99-122. Kegan Paul, Trench, Trübner and Co., London, 1897.)

STEELE (ROBERT)

The Earliest English Music Printing. A description and bibliography of English printed music to the close of the sixteenth century. The Chiswick Press, for The Bibliographical Society, London, 1903. (This work contains a valuable short bibliography on music printing and many illustrations of types. Referred to in the present work as "S.")

The authors have also had access to the late Robert Steele's manuscript and notes on English Music Printing from 1601-40, a similar work which he was unable to complete, the manuscript of which is in the possession of A. Hyatt King.

WALSH (JOHN)

A Catalogue of Music published by John Walsh and his successors. With a preface by William C. Smith. The First Edition Bookshop Limited, London, 1953.

A Guide to the Exhibition in the King's Library (British Museum) illustrating the history of printing, music-printing and bookbinding. London, 1939. (With illustrations.)

"On the various Processes applied to printing Music." (*Musical Library*. Monthly Supplement. No. 1. April, 1834. Charles Knight, London.)

DICTIONARY

---

a. "Printed and sold at the a," or, "at the little a," 41 Leadenhall Street, London. *See* Bailey or Bayley (William).
    K.

A., E. *See* Allde (Edward).

ABELL (JOHN). *See* Randall & Abell.

ACKERMANN (RUDOLPH). Print and book seller, London; at "R. Ackermann's Repository of Arts," 101 Strand, c. 1799-1827; 96 Strand, c. 1827-33. Became Ackermann and Co., 96 Strand, c. 1833-1856; 36 Strand, c. 1856-57; 106 Strand, c. 1857-59. Published a small amount of music.

ADAM (ALEXANDER). Printer, Glasgow. Printed "The Psalms of David in Metre, newly translated . . . With 23 select Psalm tunes . . . 1773"; "The Musical Repository: a collection of favourite Scotch, English, and Irish Songs set to music. 1799."
    K.

ADAMS (ELIZABETH). *See* Adams (Thomas).

ADAMS (THOMAS). Bookseller and publisher, London; at the White Lion, St. Paul's Churchyard, 1591-1611; The Bell, St. Paul's Churchyard, 1611-20, where he succeeded George Bishop. Published a number of musical works. When Adams died in 1620 the business was carried on by his widow, Elizabeth Adams (M.) for a few years, up to c. 1630 or later. Adams, or his widow, are assumed to have published two editions of "Fantazies of III. Parts," by Orlando Gibbons, both with "London, At the Bell in St. Pauls Churchyard" on the title and dedication page; the second and later edition also having an outer letterpress title-page: "Fantasies of Three Parts," etc., with imprint "London, At the Bell in St. Pauls Church-yard." These editions were from the plates of an earlier edition 1606 or later, issued without imprint or indication of printer or publisher. The imprint "At the Bell in St. Paul's Churchyard," in exactly similar, but smaller type and set-up to that of Gibbon's "Fantasies," occurs on John Legatt's edition of "A Paraphrase upon the Divine Poems. By George Sandys," 1638, which includes "A Paraphrase upon the Psalmes of David. By G. S. Set to new Tunes . . . by Henry Lawes," etc. Probably Legatt took over the business of Mrs. Adams.
    K. G. M.

ADDISON & BEALE.   Music and musical instrument sellers, and publishers, London;   120 New Bond Street, c. 1823 to June 1824; 201 Regent Street, June 1824 to c. November 1824.   Robert Addison and T. Frederick Beale were joined by Johann Baptist Cramer about November 1824, and the firm became Cramer, Addison and Beale.

ADDISON & HODSON.   Music sellers and publishers, 210 Regent Street, and 47 King Street, Golden Square, London, c. 1844-48. Succeeded L. [i.e. L. H.] Lavenu, formerly Mori and Lavenu.   Robert Addison previously a partner in Addison and Beale, and Cramer, Addison and Beale; continued the business as Robert Addison and Co., in 1848.

ADDISON & HOLLIER.   *See* Addison (Robert) & Co.

ADDISON.   *See* Hime and Addison.

ADDISON (ROBERT).   *See* Addison & Beale; Addison & Hodson; Addison (Robert) & Co.; Cramer, Addison & Beale.

ADDISON (ROBERT) & CO.   Music sellers and publishers, 210 Regent Street, and 47 King Street, Golden Square, London, 1848-51.   Succeeded Addison and Hodson; became Addison and Hollier 1851.

AGUTTER (RALPH).   Musical instrument maker, over against York Buildings, in the Strand, London.   Advertised, September 1695, "Twelve Sonatas (newly come over from Rome) in 3 parts: Composed by Signeur Arcangelo Corelli . . . are to be had . . . at Mr. Ralph Agutter's," etc.

AIRD (JAMES) *Junior*.   Music seller and publisher, Glasgow; in the Candleriggs, c. 1778; New Street, c. 1779-95.   For some time also had a shop in King Street.   On trade cards his addresses were given as "At his Music Warehouse opposite the Sugar house in Candleriggs" and "At his shop near McNair's land, New Street".   On his death in 1795 his plates were sold to McGoun and McFadyen, who both reprinted from them.   (Kidson.)
   K.

ALBANI, *Sigr*.   189 Oxford Street, London.   Published c. 1775, "Twelve Minuets for Two Violins & a Bass and six Venetian Ballads composed by Sigr. Nassari."

ALDAY (PAUL).   Music seller and publisher, Dublin; 16 Exchange Street, c. 1810-15; 10 Dame Street, c. 1815-35.   Succeeded Francis Rhames.
   K.

ALDER (DANIEL). Bookseller, 1 Promenade, Cheltenham. Published c. 1848, "The Amaranth Polka . . . Composed . . . by G. E. A."

ALDERMAN (RICHARD). Engraver and publisher, Buckingham Street, York Buildings, London. Published "Six Sonatas for two Violins, a Violoncello, or Harpsichord, composed by Christopher Wagenseil," c. 1760; engraved "Sei Sonate . . . composte dal Sigr. Tomaso Prota di Napoli," etc., 1760; "Six Concerto's for the Organ or Harpsichord, &c. by Thomas Saunders Dupuis," etc., c. 1760; "The Monthly Melody . . . Composed by Dr. Arne . . . MDCCLX."; "Six Duetts for German Flutes, or Violins. Compos'd by Signr. Dothel, Junr.," etc., 1762; "Six Sonatas . . . by Charles Frederick Abel. Op. III," etc., c. 1765.
    K.

ALDRIDGE (JOHN). Music and musical instrument seller, 2 Dame Street, Dublin, c. 1821-22. Succeeded Edmund Lee; succeeded by M. Aldridge and Co.

ALDRIDGE (MARIA) & CO. Music and musical instrument sellers, 2 Dame Street, Dublin, c. 1822-24. Their label appears on a number of works; succeeded John Aldridge.

ALDRIDGE (WILLIAM HENRY). Music and musical instrument seller and publisher, London; 264 Regent Street, c. 1831-40; 25 Holles Street, c. 1840-43.

ALEXANDER (JAMES). Musical instrument maker, music seller and publisher, London; 70 Leadenhall Street, c. 1807-13; 101 Leadenhall Street, c. 1813-51.
    K.

ALLAN (D.). Bookseller? Dickson's Close, Edinburgh. His name appears in the imprint of "The Gentle Shepherd; a Pastoral Comedy; By Allan Ramsay. Glasgow: Printed by A. Foulis, and sold by D. Allan . . . MDCCLXXXVIII."

ALLCROFT (WILLIAM). Music seller and publisher, 15 New Bond Street, opposite Grafton Street, London, c. 1836-53.

ALLDE (EDWARD). Printer, London, various addresses, 1584-1628, (M.) or later. Printed a few musical works from 1610-15 for William Barley, Laurence Lisle and Thomas Adams, including "A Briefe Discourse . . . By Thomas Ravenscroft . . . 1614." His address is given on "Sacred Hymns . . . by John Amner . . . 1615" as "dwelling neere Christ-Church." Only the initials E. A. appear in some imprints.
    K.   G.   M.   S.

[51]

ALLEN (GEORGE). Engraver, copper plate printer and publisher of sacred music, Dublin; 39 Fishamble Street, c. 1808-22; 3 Smock Alley, c. 1822-30; 6 Parliament Street, c. 1830-36; 3 Crane Lane, c. 1836-37; 12 Grafton Street, c. 1837-40; 22 Wicklow Street, c. 1840-41; 28 Wicklow Street, c. 1841-42; 16 Wicklow Street, c. 1842-44; Rear of 32 Wicklow Street, c. 1844-47.
K. G.

ALLEN (WILLIAM). Printer and bookseller, Grantham. Printed and sold "A Select Set of Psalms and Hymns . . . as they are appointed to be sung in the Parish Church of Grantham. By John Hutchinson, late Clerk of the Parish. Third edition . . . 1792."

ALLESTREY (JAMES). *See* Martin (John) and Allestrey (James).

ALLMAN (T.) & (J.). Booksellers, 55 Great Queen Street, Lincoln's Inn Fields, London. Published "Songs of the Greeks . . . 1825." Music and illustrations are lithographed.

AMICONI or AMIGONI (JACOPO). *See* Scola (Adamo).

ANDERSON & BRYCE. Printers, Foulis Close, Edinburgh. Printed "The Sacred Minstrel, a collection of original Church Tunes," c. 1820.
K.

ANDERSON (J.). Music seller and publisher, George Street, Perth, c. 1793-1810. His publications include "The Aberdeen Psalmody," by John Anderson, c. 1802.
K.

ANDERSON (J.). 19 Picardy Place, Edinburgh. Printed and sold, c. 1810, "Oranje-Booven. A favourite air with variations for the piano forte. Composed by John Anderson. Edinburgh."

ANDERSON (JOHN). Music engraver, North Gray's Close, Edinburgh, c. 1809-11. Served apprenticeship with James Johnson; in partnership with Johnson's widow as Johnson and Anderson, 1811-15; joined with George Walker and became Walker and Anderson, 1815-26.
K.

ANDERSON (WILLIAM). Bookseller, Stirling. Published "The Musical Repository: A collection of favourite Scotch, English, and Irish Songs, set to music. Edinburgh: Printed by C. Stewart and Co. for William Anderson, Stirling. 1802."

ANDRE (GUSTAVUS). Importer of foreign music and publisher, London; 79 Cheapside, 1838; 70 Berners Street, July 1838-February 1839; 24 East Street, Red Lion Square, February and March 1839; 29

Newman Street, Oxford Street, March 1839-September 1839. Gave up business owing to ill health; disposed of stock to Messrs. J. J. Ewer and Co.

ANDRÉ (PHILIPP H.). *See* Vollweiler (Georg Johann).

ANDREWS. *See* Ward & Andrews.

ANDREWS (FRANCES). Bookseller, Sadler Street, Durham. Published "The Birthday Quadrilles. Composed for the Durham Assemblies, by the late Francis Wetherell, and arranged for the Piano Forte, by his brother Henry Wetherell. Durham. F. Andrews . . . & H. Wetherell," etc., c. 1842; "Psalms & Hymns, as sung at the Sunday Evening Lectures . . . arranged . . . by Thomas Brown," etc., c. 1842.

ANDREWS (HUGH). Music seller and publisher, London; 129 New Bond Street, 1789-c. 1793; 11 London Road, St. George's Fields, c. 1793-1800; 11 Kendall Place, Lambeth Walk, c. 1800-04; 11 Little Canterbury Place (Kendall Place re-named), Lambeth Walk, c. 1804-12. At one time published in conjunction with G. Verey; was a partner in the firm of Birchall and Andrews 1783-89.
    K.

ANDREWS (JOHN). Bookseller, 167 New Bond Street, London, c. 1831-1842; as Andrews and Co., c. 1842-57. Published a small amount of music.

ANDREWS (R.). Music seller and publisher, Manchester; London Piano Forte and Harp Bazaar, 4 Palatine Buildings, c. 1843-49; 4 Palatine Buildings, and 84 Oxford Street, c. 1850-51; 84 Oxford Street, c. 1852-66. Richard Hoffman Andrews, proprietor of the business, was a composer and teacher of music.

ANDREWS (RICHARD HOFFMAN). *See* Andrews (R.).

ANDREWS (W.). Music seller, engraver, printer and publisher, 12 London Road, Southwark, London, c. 1810-12, or later. In the imprint of "A Selection of Psalms, as sung at the Chapel of the Philanthropic Society," c. 1812, his addresses appear as "12 London Road, Southwark, and No. 11 Little Canterbury Place, Lambeth." The latter address was that of Hugh Andrews.
    K.

ANGUS (ALEXANDER). Bookseller, printer and publisher, Aberdeen, 1744-1802. (P.) His name appears as seller in the imprint of "Fifty Favourite Scotch Airs for a Violin, German-Flute and Violoncello, with a Thorough Bass for the Harpsichord . . . by Francis Peacock,"

c. 1762; A. Angus and Son is given on the title-page as sellers of "The Songster's Favourite . . . By Laurence Ding," c. 1785.
   K. P. III.

ARCHDEACON (JOHN). Printer to the University of Cambridge, 1766-1795. (P.) Printed "Llyfr Gweddi Cyffredin," etc. ("Llyfr y Salmau, wedi eu cyfieithu, a'u cyfansoddi ar fesur cerdd, yn Cymraeg . . . Caer-Grawnt: Printiedig gang J. Archdeacon . . . MDCCLXX.")
   P. III.

ARIS (THOMAS). Printer and bookseller, High Street, Birmingham, 1741-61. (P.) Printed "Six Sonatas, for two Violins and two Basses. Several of which may be perform'd upon the German Flute, or Hautboy. Out of the several Parts may be taken proper Lessons for the Harpsichord by James Lyndon. 1742"; his name appears in the imprint of "Divine Harmony; or, a Collection of fifty-five double and single chants for four voices, as they are sung at the Cathedral of Lichfield; compos'd by John Alcock . . . Printed for the author, and M. Broome . . . in Birmingham, and sold by them . . . T. Aris . . . in Birmingham, 1752." Aris died July 1761.
   P. III.

ASCOUGH (ANNE). See Ayscough.

ASHDOWN & PARRY. See Wessel & Co.

ASHFIELD, Mr. Bookseller? In the Old Change, London. His name appears in the imprint of "An Introduction to Singing, or the Rudiments of Music . . . By James Hewett. Sold by the Author . . . Mr. Buckland . . . Mr. Ashfield in the Old Change . . . MDCCLXV."

ASHLEY (JOHN). London. Published "Cathedral Music: being a collection in score of the most valuable and useful compositions for that service by the several English masters of the last two hundred years . . . Selected and . . . revis'd by Dr. William Boyce . . . Second edition . . . MDCCLXXXVIII."

ASHLEY (JOHN). Composer, vocalist and music seller, at his Music Warehouse, Wade's Passage, Bath, c. 1798-1812, or later. Published c. 1810, "The Celebrated Quakers Song, sung . . . by Mr. Edwin, at the Theatres Royal, Bath and Bristol. Printed for the Author, J. Ashley," etc.

ASHTON (JOSEPH). Stationer and music seller, 36 Bishopsgate Within, London, c. 1800-18. Published a small amount of music.

ASKEY (J.). Music seller, Birmingham. Reissued (? date) "The Chorus's (with the proper cues to each) in the Oratorio of Messiah," originally published by James Kempson in 1780.

[54]

ASSIGNES OF GEORGE WITHER. *See* Wither (George).

ASSIGNES OF JOHN BILL. *See* Bill (John).

ASSIGNES OF RICHARD DAY. *See* Day (Richard).

ASSIGNES OF WILLIAM BARLEY. *See* Barley (William).

ASTLEY (THOMAS). Bookseller, London, 1726-59; Dolphin and Crown, changed in 1742 to The Rose, St. Paul's Churchyard. (P.) Published "A Compendium: or, Introduction to practical Musick . . . By Christopher Sympson. The Seventh edition . . . MDCCXXVII."; "The Mock Lawyer . . . Written by Mr. Phillips . . . To which is added, the musick engraved on copper plates . . . 1733"; his name appears in the imprint of "A Sett of new Psalms and Anthems in four Parts . . . By William Knapp. The Third edition, corrected . . . Printed for T. Astley . . . 1747"; also in the fourth edition, 1750, and sixth edition, 1754.
    P. III.

ASTOR & HORWOOD. Musical instrument makers, music sellers and publishers, 79 Cornhill, London, c. 1814-21. Succeeded George Astor and Co.; when the partnership was dissolved, c. 1821, Astor joined C. Gerock in a business which became Gerock, Astor and Co.
    K.

ASTOR (GEORGE). Musical instrument maker, music seller and publisher, London; 26 Wych Street, c. 1793-98; 79 Cornhill and 27 Tottenham Street, Fitzroy Square, c. 1798-1814; also had an organ manufactory at Sun Street, Bishopsgate Street, c. 1807-11. Became George Astor and Co. or, Astor and Co., c. 1801, and Astor and Horwood, c. 1814; he was in partnership with C. Gerock as Gerock, Astor and Co., c. 1821-31.
    K.

ATKINS (THOMAS). Engraver, London. Engraved the title-page and perhaps the music of John Reading's "A Book of new Songs," c. 1710; engraved "Musicus Apparatus Academicus, being a composition of two Odes with vocal & instrumental musick perform'd in the Theatre at Oxford Monday July the 13th 1713 . . . set to musick by William Croft . . . London. Printed for the Author," etc., 1720; "The Hymn of Adam and Eve, out of the Fifth Book of Milton's Paradise-Lost; set to musick by Mr. Galliard. 1728"; "Cantate da Camera . . . Da Carlo Arrigoni. Londra. 1732."
    K.

ATTWATER (WILLIAM). *See* Blagrove (William M.) & Attwater (Willliam).

ATTWOOD (ELIZABETH). Music and musical instrument seller, 4 Nassau Street (near Grafton Street), Dublin, c. 1817-31. Her stamp, or label, appears on a number of musical publications.
K.

AUSTEN (STEPHEN). Bookseller and publisher, London, 1730-50; Angel and Bible, in St. Paul's Churchyard; Newgate Street. (P.) His name appears in the imprint of "The Psalms of David in Metre: With the tunes used in Parish-Churches. By John Patrick. The Eighth edition. London: Printed for J. Walthoe . . . S. Austen . . . MDCCXLII."
P. III.

AUSTIN (R.). Bookseller, Hertford. His name appears in the imprint of "The Hertfordshire Melody; or, Psalm-singers Recreation . . . By John Ivery . . . London: Printed for J. Wheble . . . R. Austin, in Hertford . . . MDCCLXXIII."

AUSTIN (RICHARD). Bookseller, Ripon. His name appears in the imprint of "The Spiritual-Man's Companion. Containing great variety of chants and anthems . . . The Second Edition with additions. By Israel Holdroyd . . . London: Printed by William Pearson . . . For William Dyson . . . and sold at his shops in Hallifax, and Huddersfield. And by Richard Austin . . . in Ripon," c. 1730.

AUSTIN (STEPHEN). Bookseller and printer, Hertford. Printed and sold, c. 1825, "A Selection of Psalms and Hymns; the melodies adapted and part composed by T. W. Luppino . . . Second edition."

AYLMER (BRABAZON) the Elder & the Younger. Booksellers, at the Three Pigeons in Cornhill, London, 1670-1710. The elder's name presumably appears in the imprints of "A Collection of Ayres, compos'd for the Theatre, and upon other Occasions. By the late Mr. Henry Purcell . . . London, Printed by J. Heptinstall, for Frances Purcell, Executrix of the Author; And are to be sold by B. Aylmer . . . W. Henchman . . . and Henry Playford . . . 1697 "; "Ten Sonatas in Four Parts. Compos'd by the late Mr. Henry Purcell. London, Printed by J. Heptinstall, for Frances Purcells Executrix of the Author; And are to be sold by B. Aylmer . . . 1697 "; "A Book of new Songs (after the Italian manner) with Symphonie, & a Through-Bass fitted to the Harpsichord &c. . . . Compos'd by Mr. John Reading . . . London. Printed for ye Author and are to sold by him . . . and by Brabazon Aylmer" (presumably the younger), etc., 1710.
P. II.

AYRE (R.) & MOORE (G.). Printers, 5 Bridges Street, Covent Garden, London. Printed "Music made easy to every capacity, in a series of

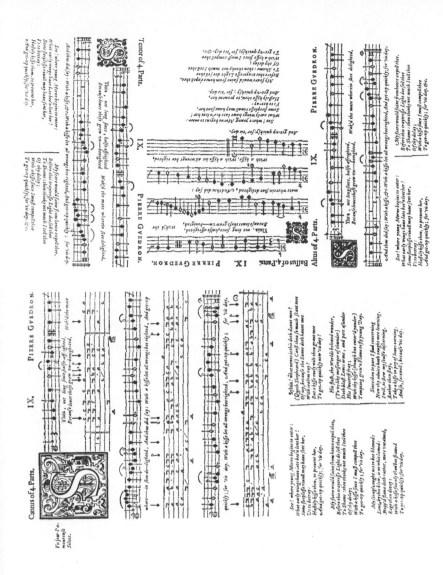

Edward Filmer, "French Court-Aires". Printed by William Stansby. 1929

11

On Womens Inconstancy.

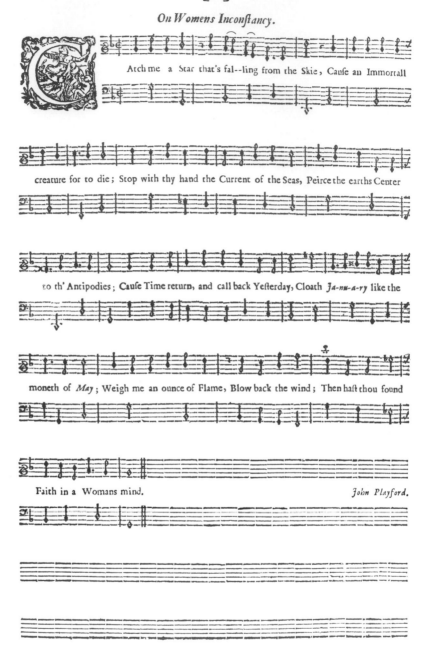

Atch me a Star that's fal--ling from the Skie, Cause an Immortall

creature for to die; Stop with thy hand the Current of the Seas, Peirce the earths Center

to th' Antipodies; Cause Time return, and call back Yesterday, Cloath Ja-nu-a-ry like the

moneth of *May*; Weigh me an ounce of Flame, Blow back the wind; Then hast thou found

Faith in a Womans mind. *John Playford.*

John Wilson and others, "Select Ayres and Dialogues". Printed by
W. Godbid for John Playford. 1659

Dialogues; being practical lessons for the harpsichord . . . by Monsieur Bemetzrieder . . . London: Printed by R. Ayre and G. Moore . . . MDCCLXXVIII." Parts 2 and 3 are dated 1779.

AYSCOUGH (ANNE). Bookseller, Nottingham, 1719-32, or later. (P.) Her name appears in the imprints of "A Book of Psalm-Tunes, with Variety of Anthems in Four Parts, with Chanting-Tunes for the Te Deum, Benedictus, Magnificat . . . By James Green. The Fifth edition . . . London. Printed by William Pearson . . . and sold by . . . Ann Ayscough, in Nottingham . . . 1724."; "A Choice Collection of Psalm-Tunes . . . By John Birch . . . London: Printed by William Pearson, for the Author, and sold by Anne Ascough . . . 1728." Succeeded her husband William Ayscough; succeeded by her son George.
P. III.

AYSCOUGH (GEORGE). Printer, bookseller and publisher, Nottingham, 1734-46. (P.) Printed and sold in conjunction with Richard Willis, "The Excellent Use of Psalmody. With a course of singing Psalms . . . to which is added, a collection of choice hymns . . . By R. W. a Lover of Divine Musick. Nottingham: Printed and sold by George Ayscough and Richard Willis . . . MDCCXXXIV." Son of Anne Ayscough, whom he succeeded in business.
P. III.

AYSCOUGII (WILLIAM). Printer, Bridlesmith Gate, Nottingham, 1710-19. (P.) Printed "A Collection of choice Psalm Tunes in Three and Four Parts: with New & Easie Psalm-Tunes, Hymns, Anthems, and Spiritual Songs, composed by the best Masters . . . By John and James Green. The Third Edition, with large Additions . . . Nottingham: Printed by William Ayscough for Joseph Turner, Bookseller in Sheffield, Yorkshire: and sold by J. Sprint . . . London. 1715." Succeeded by his widow, Anne Ayscough.
P. II.

B., A.   *See* Browne (Alice).

B., I.   *See* Bland (John).

B., J.   *See* Browne (John).

B., R.; Be., Rd.   *See* Bride (Richard).

B., R.; Br., Rt.   *See* Bremner (Robert).

B., R. & W., H.   *See* Bonion (Richard) & Walley (Henry).

B., S.   *See* Babb (Samuel).

C

B., T.   *See* Bennett (Thomas).

BABB (SAMUEL). Music seller and publisher, 132 Oxford Street, facing Hanover Square, London, c. 1770-86. Had an extensive Musical Circulating Library; catalogue in 1778, claimed to consist of upwards of twenty thousand music books; Joseph Dale purchased Babb's stock-in-trade and Musical Circulating Library 1786, and advertised that it consisted of one hundred thousand books and upwards; some single sheet songs bear only the initials S. B.
> K.   G.
> Catalogues:—Vocal and Instrumental Music. c. 1770. 1 p. fol. (B.M. Hirsch M. 1371.); c. 1775. 1 p. fol. (B.M. g. 455. (1.)); c.1785. 1 p. fol. (B.M. g. 625. (4.))

BACK (JOHN). Bookseller, at the Black Boy on London Bridge, near the Drawbridge, 1682-1703. (P.) His name appears in the imprints of a number of ballads with music published by P. Brooksby, J. Deacon, J. Blare and J. Back.
> P. II.

BADGER (RICHARD). Printer, London, 1602-42. (P.) Printed "The Whole Booke of Psalmes. Collected into English meeter by Thomas Sternhold, Iohn Hopkins and others . . . With apt notes to sing them with all . . . London, Printed by R. Badger for the Company of Stationers. 1632."
> K.   P. I.

BAGSTER (SAMUEL). Bookseller, 81 Strand, London. His name appears in the imprint of "Amatory and Anacreontic Songs set to music by Wm. Kitchiner . . . London. Published for the Author by Bagster . . . Preston and Bland & Weller," etc., c. 1809.

BAILEY (RICHARD). Bookseller, Lichfield, 1729-53. (P.) His name appears in the imprint of "Divine Harmony; or, a Collection of fifty-five double and single chants for four voices, as they are sung at the Cathedral of Lichfield; compos'd by John Alcock . . . Printed for the author, and M. Broome . . . in Birmingham, and sold by them . . . Mr. Bailey, Lichfield . . . 1752."
> P. III.

BAILEY or BAYLEY (WILLIAM). Printer, music seller and publisher, at the a, or, at the little a, 41 Leadenhall Street, London, c. 1770-85. Many of his publications are without his name, and have imprints "printed and sold at the a," or, "at the little a, 41 Leadenhall Street."
> K.

BAILLIE (ALEXANDER). Music engraver and printer, Edinburgh. Engraved "Airs for the Flute, with a Thorough Bass for the Harpsichord." The preface is signed by Baillie and dated December 1735; printed "A Collection of old Scots Tunes, with the Bass for Violoncello or Harpsichord . . . by Francis Barsanti," c. 1742.

    K.

BAIN (W.). Glasgow. Published "An Easy Introduction to the Principles of Music: with a Collection of Church-Tunes . . . By John Bain, late teacher of vocal music in Glasgow. The fifth edition . . . Glasgow: Printed for, and sold by, William Bain. MDCCLXXXVI." (*From copy in the possession of the Rev. Maurice Frost.*) The fourth edition was published by the author, 1779.

BAINBRIDGE & WOOD. Musical instrument makers, 35 Holborn Hill, London, c. 1808-20. Published a small amount of music, principally for the flute and flageolet.

    K.

    See also Bainbridge (William).

BAINBRIDGE (WILLIAM). Musical instrument maker, London; 2 Little Queen Street, c. 1802-04; 35 Holborn Hill, c. 1804-31. For a time, c. 1808-20, became Bainbridge and Wood. Published a small amount of music, principally for the flute and flageolet.

    K.

BAKER & GALABIN. Printers, Callum Street, London. Printed for Robert Horsfield, two editions of "Vocal Music, or the Songster's Companion containing a new and choice Collection of the greatest variety of Songs, Cantatas &c.," 1772 and 1775.

BAKER (J.). Bookseller, Black Boy, Paternoster Row, London, 1680-1710. (P.) Advertised May 1710, "Two New Songs, the one entitl'd The Moderate Man, written by Mr. Durfey, to a pleasant new tune, the other The True use of the Bottle, to a dance tune of Mons. Duthels. Printed by J. Cullen . . . and sold by J. Baker in Paternoster Row."

    P. II.

BAKER (THOMAS). Engraver, London? Engraved "Twenty six Concertos . . . Divided into four Books in Score . . . by Charles Avison . . . Newcastle. Printed for the Author . . . 1758 "; "Six Sonatas, for the Harpsichord, with accompanyments, for two Violins, & a Violoncello, composed by Charles Avison . . . Opera Settima. Newcastle. Printed for the Author . . . MDCCLX."; "Fifty Favourite Scotch Airs for a Violin, German-Flute and Violoncello with a Thorough Bass for the Harpsichord . . . by Francis Peacock. London. Printed for the publisher in Aberdeen, and sold by Mrs. Johnson in Cheapside," etc., c. 1762; "Sei Madrigali . . . dal Sigr: Gio. Carlo Maria Clari . . . Parte Prima . . . London," c. 1765; "Elegies, Songs and an Ode of Mr. Pope's, with Instrumental Parts . . . The music by Edward

Miller of Doncaster. Opera Terza. London. Printed for the Author, & sold at Bremner's Music Shop in the Strand," etc. Advertised May 1770.
 K.

BAKER (THOMAS). Bookseller and printer, Southampton, 1767-76. (P.) His name appears in the imprint of "The Psalms of David . . . By I. Watts . . . A new edition, corrected. (Tunes in the Tenor Part fitted to the several Metres.) Salisbury: Printed and sold by Collins and Johnson. Sold also by . . . Baker, at Southampton; Smith, at Marlborough; Maynard, at Devizes; Noyes, at Andover . . . MDCCLXXVI."
 P. III.

BAKER (W.). Bookseller? London. Name appears in the imprint of "The Psalms of David in Metre: With the tunes used in Parish-Churches. By John Patrick. The Eighth edition. London: Printed for J. Walthoe . . . W. Baker . . . MDCCXLII."

BALBIRNIE (WILLIAM). Music engraver and printer, 105 High Street, Edinburgh, c. 1821-23. Previously in partnership with William Hutton as Hutton and Balbirnie, music engravers; engraved and printed some volumes of George Thomson's "The Select Melodies of Scotland" and "Thomson's Collection of the Songs of Burns."

BALDWIN (ANN) Mrs. Bookseller, Oxford Arms in Warwick Lane, London. Widow of Richard Baldwin. Her name appears in an advertisement, August 1699, "An Introduction to the singing of Psalms . . . The Second edition . . . By Wm. Webb . . . Printed for Eben. Tracy. Sold by Mrs. Baldwin," etc.
 P. II.

BALDWIN (RICHARD). Bookseller, bookbinder and printer, London, 1681-98. (P.) Printed and published "The Gentleman's Journal: or the Monthly Miscellany . . . Consisting of news, history, philosophy, poetry, musick, translations, &c. . . . London Printed; And are to be sold by R. Baldwin, near the Oxford Arms, in Warwick-lane, 1692." The parts for 1693 were printed and sold by R. Parker, at the Unicorn under the Piazza at the Royal Exchange in Cornhill; and by R. Baldwin, near the Oxford Arms in Warwick Lane, and at the Black Lyon in Fleet Street, between the Two Temple Gates. Succeeded by his widow, Ann Baldwin.
 K. P. II. D. & M.

BALDWIN (RICHARD) Junior. Bookseller, at the Rose, Paternoster Row, London, c. 1747-70. His name appears in the imprints of a number of sacred music works.
 K.

BALL. *See* Holdsworth & Ball.

BALL (EDWARD). *See* Ball (James).

BALL (JAMES). Pianoforte maker, music seller and publisher, London;
1 Duke Street, Grosvenor Square, c. 1789-1802; for a short time,
c. 1794, became Motta and Ball; 26 Duke Street, c. 1802-08; 27
Duke Street, c. 1808-15; as James Ball and Son, c. 1815-35. The son
was presumably Edward Ball, whose name appears alone in one
directory for 1825.
K. G.

BALLANTYNE (JAMES) & CO. Printers, Paul's Work, Canongate,
Edinburgh. Printed "A Collection of Scottish Airs, harmonized for
the Voice & Piano Forte, with . . . Symphonies; and Accompaniments
for a Violin & Violoncello by Joseph Haydn . . . Edinburgh, Published
by the Proprietor, William Whyte," etc., 1806-07. As Ballantyne
and Co. printed a new edition of George Thomson's "The Melodies
of Scotland, 1831," and other volumes of his collections.

BALLARD (SAMUEL). Bookseller, at the Blue Ball, Little Britain,
London, 1706-33. (P.) His name appears in the imprint of "The
Compleat French Master, for Ladies and Gentlemen . . . The Fourth
edition . . . Printed for R. Sare . . . J. Nicholson . . . and Sam. Ballard,"
1707. Contains the music of "A Collection of new French Songs, &c.";
his name also appears on the fifth edition, 1710, the seventh, 1717,
the eighth, 1721, and the tenth, 1729.
P. II.   D. & M.

BALLS & SON. *See* Balls (James).

BALLS (ELIZA) & CO. Music sellers and publishers, 408 Oxford Street,
London, c. 1852-55. Succeeded Herbert Ingram Balls; succeeded
by George Emery.

BALLS (GEORGE). *See* Balls (James).

BALLS (HERBERT INGRAM). Music seller and publisher, 408 Oxford
Street, London, c. 1850-52. Succeeded James Balls and Son: succeeded by Eliza Balls and Co.

BALLS (JAMES). Music engraver, music seller and publisher, London;
8 Middle Scotland Yard, Whitehall, c. 1803-07; 12 Castle Street,
c. 1807-09; 408 Oxford Street, c. 1809-33; for a time, c. 1811-25,
became James and George Balls; as James Balls and Son, or Balls
and Son, 408 Oxford Street, c. 1833-50. Succeeded by Herbert Ingram
Balls. An edition of James Hook's "Six Sonatas. Op. 54" bears the

imprint, "London, Engraved, printed & sold by J. Balls . . . & to be had of Messrs. Balls & Danjue, Norfolk, Virginia," c. 1811.
K. G.

BALLS (JAMES) & (GEORGE).   Music engravers, music sellers and publishers, 408 Oxford Street, London, c. 1811-25.
See also Balls (James).

BANFF LITHOGRAPHIC PRESS.   Printed "Les paysannes. A first set of quadrilles. By a Lady. Printed at the Banff Lithographic Press. 1832."

BANGER.   *See* Clementi, Banger, Collard, Davis & Collard; Clementi, Banger, Hyde, Collard & Davis.

BANISTER (JOHN).   Violinist and composer, Brownlow Street, Drury Lane, London.   Published "A Collection of Musick in Two Parts . . . By Mr. G. Finger. To which is added a Sett of Ayres in Four Parts by Mr. John Banister. Printed by Tho. Moore for Mr. John Banister . . . 1691."   Acted in conjunction with Robert King as selling agent for music published in Rome and Amsterdam, 1700-02, including Corelli's "Sonate . . . Opera Quinta."

BANKS (ALLEN).   Bookseller, London; Various addresses 1668-73; Fetter Lane, 1673-82. (P.) Published "Titus Tell-Troth: or, The Plot-Founder confounded. A pleasant new song. To the tune of, Hail to the Myrtle Shade [from H. Purcell's 'Theodosius']. London. Printed for Allen Banks, 1682"; "The Compleat Swearing Master: A rare new Salamanca Ballad. To the tune of, Now, now, the Fight's done . . . 1682 "; "The Protestant Flayl: An excellent new song . . . MDCLXXXII."
P. II.

BANKS (JAMES) & (HENRY).   Musical instrument makers and music sellers, Salisbury; Catherine Street, c. 1791-1811; Liverpool; Church Street, 1811-c. 1830; Bold Street, c. 1830-31.   Published a small amount of music; probably succeeded W. Banks at Salisbury; succeeded Cornelius Ward at Liverpool.   Henry died 1830, and his brother James 1831.

BANKS (W.).   Music seller, Salisbury.   His name appears in an advertisement August 1779, "Twelve Voluntaries, by Dr. Green . . . London: printed and sold by J. Bland . . . sold also by W. Banks at Salisbury; W. Score at Exeter," etc.   Probably succeeded by James and Henry Banks.

BARACLOUGH (JOHN).   Engraver and music printer, Nuneaton. Engraved and printed "A Collection of Anthems & Psalms, for two, three, and four voices: with accompanyments for two violins, two horns, two hoboys, clarinets or flutes, a tenor and an instrumental bass: Composed by Thos. Collins," etc., c. 1790.

BARBE (CAMILLE). Musical instrument maker and music seller, 60 Quadrant, Regent Street, London. Published, c. 1827, "L'Echo, a brillante Rondo, preceded by an Introduction for the Piano Forte with an accompaniment (ad libitum) for the Flute, composed . . . by Silvestre. London, publish'd by C. Barbe, & the Author," etc.

BARBER (ABRAHAM). Bookseller and musician, Wakefield. Published "A Book, of Psalme Tunes in four Parts, collected out of several Authors; with some few directions how to name your notes. By, A. B. P. C. W. [i.e. Abraham Barber, Parish Clerk, Wakefield.] York, Printed by John White, for the Author . . . 1687." Also the 4th edition, 1700; 5th edition, 1703; 6th edition, 1711; 7th edition, 1715. He died 1730, after being Parish Clerk for fifty years.
P. II.

BARBER (JOSEPH). Bookseller, music and copper plate printer, New-castle-on-Tyne, 1740-81. (P.) Printed "Six Concerto's in Seven Parts . . . by Charles Avison . . . Opera Secunda. MDCCXL."; "Two Concerto's. The first for an Organ or Harpsicord, in eight Parts. The second for Violins, in seven Parts . . . Composed by Charles Avison . . . M.DCC.XLII."; "Twelve Concerto's in Seven Parts . . . done from two Books of Lessons for the Harpsichord. Composed by Signr. Domenico Scarletti with additional Slow Movements from Manuscript Solo Pieces, by the same Author . . . by Charles Avison Organist in Newcastle upon Tyne. MDCCXLIV."
P. III.

BARBIER (JEAN). *See* Notary (Julian) and Barbier (Jean).

BARFORD (MORRIS). Music engraver, copper plate printer, music and musical instrument seller, Cambridge. Printed and sold at Curry, c. 1775, "Hellendaal's Celebrated Rondo for the Organ, Harpsichord, or Piano Forte," etc.; at Union Street, c. 1795, printed Barford's Collection of Rondos, Airs, Marches, Songs, Duets, Dances &c.; adapted for the Piano Forte, Violin & Gern. Flute," 4 vols.; at Trumpington Street, "Six Duets for two Violins. Composed by Mr. Leclair," c. 1803; "Drink to me only. A favorite Glee for three Voices. With the original words by Ben Jonson," c. 1810. May have been related to the following, or the same person.
K.

BARFORD (MORRIS). Musical instrument maker, 113 Great Portland Street, Cavendish Square, London. Published, c. 1790, Pleyel's "Three Trios concertants. For a Violin, Viola and a Violoncello.

[63]

Op. 11. Printed & sold by M. Barford," etc. May have been related to the preceding, or the same person.

BARKER (CHRISTOPHER). Draper, bookseller and printer, London, various addresses, 1569-99. (M.) His name appears in the imprint of "The Noble Arte of Venerie or Hunting . . . [By George Turbervile.] Imprinted by Henry Bynneman for Christopher Barker," c. 1575. Contains music of "The Measures of blowing set downe in the notes."
M. S.

BARKER (ROBERT). King's printer, Northumberland House, Aldersgate Street, London, 1599-1645. (P.) He is said to have printed in conjunction with the assignes of John Bill "Llyfr y Psalmau, wedi eu cyfieithu, a' i cyfansoddi ar fesur cerdd, yn Gymraeg . . . A'i printio yn Llundain. 1630."
K. P. I.

BARKER (W.). Printer and bookseller, East Dereham, Norfolk. Printed and sold "A Selection of Psalms, from the New Version, with the Morning and Evening Hymns; for the use of Parish Churches . . . Second edition. Printed and sold by W. Barker . . . Sold also . . . by James Peck . . . Messrs. Rivington . . . J. Deighton, Cambridge, James Philo, Parish Clerk, East Dereham . . . 1813."

BARLEY (WILLIAM). Draper, bookseller, printer and publisher, London, 1591-c. 1614; Newgate Market; Gracechurch (Gratious, Gracious) Street, near Leaden-Hall (against St. Peter's Church). (M.) His printing was done in Little St. Helen's. He issued a number of musical works from 1596, or earlier, some from c. 1598 as the assigne of Thomas Morley. The latter was not a printer, but held a patent for the printing and importation of music, and his address was also Little St. Helen's. Some of Barley's publications were printed by John Windet, Thomas Este, and Thomas Snodham as the assignes of William Barley.
K. G. M. S.

BARLING. *See* Benson & Barling.

BARNES (JOSEPH). Printer and bookseller, Oxford, 1573-1618. (M.) Printed "The Feminine Monarchie or a Treatise concerning Bees . . . By Char: Butler, Magd . . . 1609." Contains some musical notes entitled "The Bees Musicke."
M.

BARNETT (JOHN) & CO. Music sellers and publishers, 162 Regent Street, London, c. 1829-31. Succeeded John Gow and Son.
Catalogue:—New Vocal and Instrumental Music just published. c. 1830. 1 p. fol. (B.M.H. 2832. (7.))

BARREAU, *Mr.* Bookbinder, in Lumbard Court, Seven Dials, London. Sold, "New Collection of Dances . . . That have been performed . . . by the best dancers . . . Recollected, put into characters and engraved by Monsieau Roussau, Dancing Master. To be sold at Mr. Barreau's," etc., c. 1715.

BARRET (JOHN). *See* Barrett.

BARRET (P.). Bookseller, Fleet Street, London. Sold, with others, "A Collection of new Songs . . . by Mr. Anthony Young, Organist of St. Clement's Danes." Printed by William Pearson, June 1707. Barret was probably the same person as Philip Barrett, Stationer, London.

BARRETT (JOHN). Bookseller, at the Harp and Crown, Coventry Street, near the Haymarket, London, 1724-c. 1743. Advertised, collected subscriptions for, and sold a few musical works.

BARRETT (PHILIP). Stationer, London. *See* Barret.

BARROW. *See* Culliford & Barrow; Culliford, Rolfe & Barrow.

BARRY (H.). Engraver, 29 St. Martin's Street, Leicester Square, London. Engraved "The Harmonic Cabinet, or Vocal Harmonist, in miniature . . . London, Published by W. Blackman . . . 1821." This work was also issued as "The Harmonic Cabinet or Kentish Harmony" and as "Kentish Harmony" in the same year.

BARTHELET (THOMAS). London, His name appears in the colophon of "An Exhortacion unto praier, thought mete by the Kynges maiestie . . . Also a Letanie with suffrages to be saied or songe in the tyme of the said processions. Imprinted in London by Richard Grafton for Thomas Barthelet, printer to the Kynges hyghnes, the XVI. day of Iune . . . 1544."
    S.

BASSANDINE (THOMAS). Printer, bookseller and bookbinder, at the Nether Bow, Edinburgh, 1564-77. (M.) Printed "The CL Psalmes of Dauid in English metre with the Forme of Prayers . . . vsed in the Church of Scotland . . . 1575."
    K. M. S.

BASSET (R.). Publisher, at the Mitre, over against Chancery Lane, in Fleet Street, London.
    See Roper (Abel) *the Younger*.

BATES (CHARLES). Bookseller, London, c. 1705-14; next the Crown Tavern, in West Smithfield; at the White Hart, in West Smithfield;

at the Sun and Bible, in Giltspur Street, near Pye Corner. Published
some ballads with music.
P. II.

BATES (E.). Music seller, opposite the Royal Circus, Black Friars Road,
London. Published, c. 1797, "Oh! poor Robinson Crusoe. A
Favorite Chaunt written and Sung by Mr. Cussans, at the Royal
Circus, & Sadlers Wells."

BATES (P.). Engraver, London. Engraved "A Book of new Anthems
Containing a Hundred Plates fairly Engraven with a Thorough Bass
figur'd for the Organ or Harpsichord with proper Retornels by John
Reading," London, c. 1715.

BATES (THEODORE CHARLES). Music engraver, music seller and
publisher, organ and pianoforte manufacturer, London; St. John
Street, Smithfield, c. 1812; 7 Jerusalem Passage, St. John Square,
Smithfield, c. 1813; 20 St. John (John's) Square, Smithfield, c. 1814-
1824, with additional premises at 18 Holywell Street, Strand, c 1820-
1822, and 490 Oxford Street, c. 1822-24. From 1824-c. 1833 he was
a partner in the firm of Longman and Bates (Chappell, Longman and
Bates), 6 Ludgate Hill; in business alone at 6 Ludgate Hill, c. 1833-47;
as T. C. Bates and Son, c. 1847-59; Bates and Son, c. 1859-63.
K. G.

BATES (THOMAS) & (SAMUEL). Printers, 48 Howland Street, Fitzroy
Square, London. Printed "Sixty Tunes, adapted to sixty Psalms &
Hymns, for congregational use . . . London: Printed by T. & S.
Bates . . . for G. Furrian, Hampstead, 1823."

BATHURST (CHARLES). Bookseller and publisher, London, 1737-86.
at the Cross Keys, against St. Dunstan's Church; at the Middle
Temple Gates, Fleet Street. (P.) His name appears in the imprint
of "David's Harp well Tuned: or a Book of Psalmody . . . The Third
edition . . . By Robert Barber, Castleton. London: Printed by
Robert Brown . . . For Charles Bathurst, in Fleet Street; Joseph Heath,
at Nottingham and Mansfield; and John Roe, at Derby. MDCCLIII."
P. III.

BAXTER (THOMAS). Bookseller, in Petergate, York. Published "The
Metre Psalm-Tunes, in Four Parts. Compos'd for the use of the
Parish-Church of St. Michaels of Belfry's in York. By Thomas
Wanless . . . London, Printed by J. Heptinstall for Thomas Baxter
. . . 1702."
P. II.

BAYLEY (WILLIAM). *See* Bailey or Bayley.

BEADNELL. *See* Button, Whitaker and Beadnell.

BEALE (T. FREDERICK). *See* Addison & Beale; Cramer, Addison & Beale; Cramer, Beale & Chappell.

BEALE (THOMAS). Music seller and publisher, Manchester; 8 St. Mary's Gate, c. 1803; 6 St. Mary's Gate, c. 1828; 19 St. Ann's Square, 1834-35. Afterwards became Hime, Beale and Co.

BEARDMORE & BIRCHALL. Music and musical instrument sellers, and publishers, 129 New Bond Street, London, 1783.
   See also Birchall & Beardmore.

BEARDMORE (T.). *See* Beardmore & Birchall; Birchall & Beardmore.

BEAULIEU (J. de). Bookseller, over against St. Martin's Church, near Charing Cross, London. Advertised June 1697, "Albion and Albanus, an Opera, or Representation in Musick, containing 44 sheets of large Paper in Folio, to be sung with 1, 2, 3, 4 voices, and diversifyed with the finest Airs, of this time, which may be likewise played upon all sorts of Instruments . . . to be sold by J. de Beaulieu," etc. Also advertised in March 1698, "Albion and Albanus . . . compleat containing 80 sheets of large Paper in Folio," etc.
   D. & M.

BECKLEY (RICHARD). Bookseller, 42 Piccadilly, London. Published "Christmas Carols, ancient and modern; including the most popular in the West of England . . . With an introduction and notes by William Sandys . . . 1833."

BEDFORD MUSICAL REPOSITORY. An establishment from which music was published bearing the imprint "Published at the Bedford Musical Repository." 45 Southampton Row, Russell Square, London, c. 1825-27; 17 Soho Square, c. 1827-29. Owned or managed by George Walker the younger, who afterwards joined the business carried on by his father at 17 Soho Square.

BEECROFT (JOHN). Bookseller and publisher, Paternoster Row, London, 1740-79. (P.) His name appears in the imprint of "The Psalms of David in Metre: With the tunes used in Parish-Churches. By John Patrick. The Eighth edition. London: Printed for J. Walthoe . . . J. Beecroft . . . MDCCXLII."
   P. III.

BEESLY (MICHAEL). Oxford. Engraved, printed and published "A Book of Psalmody containing instructions for young beginners . . . Collected engrav'd and printed by Mich. Beesly and sold by Edward Doe, bookseller in Oxford," etc., c. 1745; "An Introduction to Psalmody containing Instructions for young Beginners . . . Engrav'd, printed

[67]

and sold by Mich. Beesly and by Ed. Doe Bookseller in Oxford by Cha. Pocock at Reading," c. 1755; "A Collection of 20 New Psalm Tunes Compos'd with veriety of Fuges after a differant manner to any extant. Sold by Ed. Doe at Oxford Jos. Wimpey at Newbury. Collected engrav'd and printed by Mich. Beesly," c. 1760.
    K.

BELL (THE) IN ST. PAUL'S CHURCHYARD, LONDON. *See* Adams (Thomas); Legatt (John).

BELLERBY (HENRY). Bookseller, 11 Stonegate, York. His name appears in the imprint of "Twenty-four Chants: to which are pre-fixed, Remarks on Chanting . . . By Mr. J. Gray, of York. Published for the Author, by Preston . . . London, and H. Bellerby; York . . . 1834."

BENNETT (CHARLES). *See* Dale (Joseph).

BENNETT (RICHARD). Music seller and publisher, London; the corner of Clement's Inn, Butcher's Row, near Temple Bar, c. 1752-55; at Ye Golden Violin, New Round Court in the Strand, 1755-56.

BENNETT (THOMAS). Music engraver, music seller and publisher, London; in Ellit's (Elliott's) Court, in the little Old Bailey, c. 1755-60; 61, four doors above (near) St. Andrew's Church, Holborn, c. 1760-80. Some of his single sheet songs bear only the initials T. B.
    K.

BENNING (WILLIAM). Printer, London. Printed "The Psalm Singers Companion; being a collection of psalm tunes, hymns canons and anthems . . . By Abraham Milner. London: Printed by William Benning, and sold by John Gilbert . . . John Wells . . . Mr. Smith and Abraham Milner . . . 1751."

BENNISON (T. T.). Composer, music seller and publisher, London; 51 Albermarle Street, c. 1802-08; 2 Sloane Street, Chelsea, c. 1808-09.
    K.

BENSKIN (THOMAS). Bookseller, London, 1681-1704. (P.) His name appears in the imprints of "The Newest Collection of the choicest Songs, as they are sung at Court, Theatre, Musick-Schools, Balls, &c. With musical notes. London, Printed by T. Haly, for D. Brown . . . and T. Benskin, in St. Brides Church Yard, Fleet Street; 1683"; "The Psalms of David in Metre: Fitted to the tunes used in Parish-Churches. By J. Patrick . . . London, Printed for L. Meredith: and sold by D. Brown . . . T. Benskin, against Lincoln's Inn back Gate, J. Walthoe and F. Coggan . . . 1701."
    P. II. D. & M.

[68]

BENSON & BARLING. Booksellers, bookbinders, printers and publishers, at the Library, Alpha Place, Weymouth. Printed c. 1844, "The Downs: a Song of Dorset, the words composed by the Rev. W. Marriott Smith Marriott. The music by his sister, Lydia B. Smith. Published by D. Rolls," etc.

BENSON (JOHN). Publisher, book and music seller, London; Chancery Lane, c. 1635-? St. Dunstan's Yard, Fleet Street, c. 1641-58. Was associated with John Playford the elder in the publication of "A Musicall Banquet," 1651, 1658; and Hilton's "Catch that Catch can." 1652. John Playford was apprenticed to Benson in 1640.
    K. P. I. D. & M.

BENT (WILLIAM). Bookseller, Paternoster Row, London. Published "The Psalm-Singers Companion . . . The third edition. By Uriah Davenport . . . MDCCLXXXV."

BENTLEY (RICHARD). Bookseller, at the Post House (Post Office), Russel (Russell) Street, Covent Garden, London, 1682-97. (P.) Published in conjunction with J. Tonson, "The Duke of Guise. A Tragedy . . . Written by Mr. Dryden, and Mr. Lee . . . Printed by T. H. for R. Bentley . . . and J. Tonson . . . MDCLXXXIII."; contains one musical number. Previously in partnership with James Magnes and afterwards with M. Magnes.
    P. II. D. & M.

BENTLEY (RICHARD) & MAGNES (M.). Booksellers, at the Post House (Post Office), Russel (Russell) Street, Covent Garden, London, 1678-82. (P.) Published "Theodosius: or, The Force of Love, a Tragedy . . . Written by Nat. Lee. With the musick betwixt the acts . . . Printed for R. Bentley and M. Magnes . . . 1680." Bentley was previously in partnership with James Magnes; afterwards in business alone.
    P. II. D. & M.

BERCHET (PIERRE). French artist and designer, b.1659–d.1720; worked from time to time in London where he died. His name appears as "Berchet Inventor" on the plate engraved by H. Hulsbergh, and used as a frontispiece to "Mr. Ino. Eccles General Collection of Songs," 1704, and afterwards for "Songs in the new opera, call'd Camilla," 1706, etc., and the various volumes of "Apollo's Feast," 1726, etc.

BERGER (GEORGE). Bookseller and publisher, London; 42 Holywell Street, Strand, c. 1834-37; 19 Holywell Street, Strand, c. 1837-64; 12 Newcastle Street, Strand, c. 1864-68. Published a small amount of music.

BETTESWORTH (ARTHUR). Bookseller and publisher, London, 1699-

1738; at the Red Lion, on London Bridge; Paternoster Row. Published and sold a number of musical works, some in partnership with Charles Hitch, his son-in-law.

P. II, III.

BETTS (ARTHUR) *the Elder*. Musical instrument maker, music seller and publisher, London; 2 North Side (North Piazza), Royal Exchange, c. 1827-38; 47 Threadneedle Street, c. 1838-44; 27 Royal Exchange, c. 1844-66.

Catalogue of new and select Music. c. 1835. 1 p. fol. (B.M. H. 1653. e. (6.).)

BETTS (ARTHUR) *the Younger*. Musical instrument maker, music seller and publisher, 37 Cornhill, London, c. 1830-31. Succeeded Charles Vernon.

BETZ (J.). Music seller, publisher, and importer of foreign music, 21 Rupert Street, London, c. 1775-80. Advertised on "Six Quatuors. Op. 2" by Carl Stamitz, that he had "just imported all the works of C. P. E. Bach of Berlin."

BEUGO (JOHN). Engraver, Edinburgh. His name appears in an advertisement, December 1823, "The New Caliope. No. 1. Being a selection of British, and occasionally, foreign melodies, newly arranged for the Piano-Forte, and engraved on copper by John Beugo. To be continued quarterly . . . Published by Archibald Constable and Co., Edinburgh: and Hurst, Robinson, and Co. London."

BEULER (JACOB). Engraver and music publisher, London; 4 Bury Place, Bloomsbury, c. 1825-53; 42 Bemerton Street, Caledonian Road, 1853-73.

BEW (JOHN). Bookseller and publisher, 28 Paternoster Row, London, c. 1774-95. Published "Vocal Music, or the Songster's Companion, being a complete collection of Songs, Cantatas, &c. . . . Selected from the first & second volumes of a favourite work formerly published under that title; to which is now added a variety of other new & choice songs &c. not inserted in any part of ye foregoing work," etc., c. 1778; also advertised February 1786, an edition of "Vocal Music, or, The Songster's Companion," with an engraved title-page. An earlier edition was published by Robert Horsfield, in two volumes, c. 1771 and 1772.

K. P. III.

BICKERSTAFF (JACOB). Publisher, Next the Black Horse in Fleet Street, near the Old Bailey, London. Published in parts, 1743-44, "The Agreeable Amusement, a Collection of ancient & modern Songs: Composed by the most eminent masters."

BICKHAM (GEORGE) *the Elder* & *the Younger*. Engravers, printers and publishers, London, who together and separately issued a number of finely engraved works, including some musical items. It is difficult to distinguish which of the two is referred to in some of their publications. George the elder engraved for other publishers 1714 or earlier, and his earliest known address was somewhere in Hammersmith. In 1733 he commenced the issue in parts of his most famous work "The Universal Penman," completed in 1741, the 1733 title-page of which has the imprint "London: Printed for the Author, and Sold by John Bickham, Engraver, At the Seven-Stars in King Street, Covent Garden. MDCCXXXIII.", and the 1741 title-page "Printed for, and Sold by the Author, at the Crown in James Street, Bunhill Fields, 1741." This work has engraved pages signed Geo. Bickham, Geo. Bickham senʳ., G. J. Bickham, George John's son, and John Bickham. The probability is that the elder Bickham's name was George John Bickham and John Bickham was his brother, and that George John's son, was the earliest form in which George junior signed his work. In 1740 George Bickham (presumably the elder) was at the Blackmoor's Head in the Strand, from where he issued "The Favourite Songs in the Devil to Pay, with the Scene engrav'd in Picture Work at the top of each Song," etc., and advertised at the same time other works including "The Whole Opera of Flora, with the humorous Scenes of Hob, design'd by Gravelot and the musick proper for all Instruments." The latter was presumably the same work as "Songs in the Opera of Flora," engraved by G. Bickham junior, issued in two parts, 1737-38. In 1752 George the elder was at Featherstone Street, Bunhill Fields. George Bickham junior engraved, printed and sold a number of works apart from the musical ones for which he is especially remembered. In 1737 he was at the corner of Bedford-Bury, New Street, Covent Garden, but from some time after April 1738 to 1754 or later, at his house and shop at May's Buildings, Bedford Court, Covent Garden, where he sold some of the works of his father as well as his own. His principal work was "The Musical Entertainer Engrav'd by George Bickham junʳ. Vol. I. London Printed for & Sold by Geo: Bickham, at his House yᵉ Corner of Bedford-Bury, New-Street, Covent Garden. "G. Bickham dil: Scup 17?" "Bickham's Musical Entertainer. Vol. II. Printed for C. Corbett at Addison's Head, Fleet Street. Publish'd According to Act of Parliament. H. Gravelot Inv: G. Bickham junʳ. sculp." "The Musical Entertainer" was issued in separate numbers, January 1737-December 1739, each containing four songs. Thomas Harper and J. Harper acted as printers, publishers and sellers of the parts of Vol. I, and Thomas Cooper was advertised as the printer, publisher and seller of the parts of Vol. II, the title-page of which (issued at the end of the parts) has, however, the imprint of C. Corbett. Vol. I has Bickham's earlier address as the plate was apparently prepared before he had moved, prior to the completion of the volume. Another edition, corrected by John F. Lampe, was issued in parts 1740-41.

The title-page of Vol. I of this edition was from the plate of the original by Bickham but with the imprint amended to read "London Printed for & Sold by Charles Corbett Bookseller and Publisher at Addison's Head, Fleet-Street"; the title-page of Vol. II being the same as in the earlier edition with Corbett's imprint. A later edition of "The Musical Entertainer" is recorded by Kidson, having the imprint "London; printed for Jno. Ryall, at Hogarth's Head, Fleet Street, 1765." Other musical works engraved by George Bickham junior are "Songs in the Opera of Flora . . . Sold by T. Cooper," issued in two parts 1737-38; "An Easy Introduction to Dancing . . . London: Printed and sold in May's Buildings, near Covent Garden," October 1738; also a later edition, c. 1752. He also provided the illustrated title-pages to "The Delightful Pocket Companion for the Flute," issued by John and Ann Simpson, c. 1746-50. John Bickham, who does not appear to have engraved any music, was at Opposite Fetter Lane, Holborn, c. 1749.
K. G.

BICKHAM (JOHN).   *See* Bickham (George) *the Elder* & *the Younger*.

BIELEFELD.   Music seller, 131 Oxford Street, London.   Advertised March 1781, "Six New English Songs for the Harpsichord, the English Guittar and the Italian Pocket Guittar, the words and music by Cesare Mussolini.   Book Second."   Advertised April 1781, "Twenty four New Tunes for the English and Italian Pocket-Guitar, composed by Sig. Cesare Mussolini.   Book Third."

BIGG & COX.   Music printers, opposite Beaufort Buildings in the Strand, London, c. 1769-76.   Published and printed c. 1770, "Modesty's Cap.   [Song.]   Set to music by Mr. Hodgson of Newcastle," etc. They printed some of the musical supplements to "The Lady's Magazine," 1773-74.   Described themselves as "Successors to Mr. Dryden Leach."
P. III.   (Cox & Bigg.)

BIGG (GEORGE).   Printer, London.   Printed "A Set of new Psalms and Anthems . . . By William Knapp . . . The Eighth edition . . . MDCCLXX."; "Melodia Sacra: or the Devout Psalmists' new Musical Companion . . . By William Tans'ur, Senior . . . 1772"; "The Essex Harmony . . . Vol. II.   The Second edition . . . By John Arnold . . . MDCCLXXVIII."; "The Psalm Singers' Assistant . . . By John Crompton of Southwold, Suffolk . . . 1778 "; "The Complete Psalmodist . . . The Seventh edition . . . By John Arnold . . . 1779 "; "Music made Easy to every Capacity . . . by Monsieur Bemetzrieder . . . Printed by George Bigg, Neal Houses, Chelsea For Messrs. Birchall and Andrews . . . 1785."

BILL (JOHN).   Assignes of, London, 1630-60.   (P.)   The Assignes of John

Bill are said to have printed in conjunction with Robert Barker "Llyfr y Psalmau, wedi eu cyfieithu, a'i cyfansoddi ar fesur cerdd, yn Gymraeg . . . A'i printio yn Llundain. 1630."
P. I.

BINCKES (LITCHFIELD). Music seller and publisher, and pianoforte maker, Musical Repository, Old Kent Road, London, c. 1834-60.

BINGLEY (JAMES). Engraver and publisher, 37 Moneyers Street, Hoxton, London. Engraved and published "Bingley's, Select Vocalist containing Songs, Glees, Duets, &c. by eminent composers. The music and pictorial illustrations." 2 vols. c. 1842; Published with William Strange Nos. 1-78 of "The Musical Bouquet," c. 1846, or earlier; continued from 1855 by Charles Sheard.

BINGLEY (WILLIAM). Bookseller and publisher, London. His name appears in the imprints of "The Musical Magazine, or Compleat Pocket Companion for the Year 1767 (1768) . . . Vol. I (II). Sold by T. Bennett . . . and by W. Bingley opposite Durham Yard in the Strand." Also for the years 1769 and 1770, Vols. III and IV, with the imprint "Sold by T. Bennett . . . and by W. Bingley at No. 31 in Newgate Street, London."
P. III.

BINNEMAN (HENRY). *See* Bynneman.

BINNS & ROBINSON. Booksellers and printers, Bath. Printed "Psalms and Hymns as sung in the Church of Norton St. Philip. Collected and edited by the Rev. R. J. Meade." c. 1820.

BIRCHALL & ANDREWS. Music and musical instrument sellers, and publishers, at Handel's Head, 129 New Bond Street, London, 1783 to May 1789. Robert Birchall issued some publications independently; partnership dissolved in May 1789; both continued in business, Hugh Andrews at the same address and Birchall at 133 New Bond Street; succeeded Birchall and Beardmore.
K.
Catalogues:—Music. c. 1785. 2 pp. fol. (B.M. Hirsch IV. 1111. (3.)); Vocal and Instrumental Music. c. 1786. 4 pp. fol. (First Edition Bookshop, Catalogue 40. No. 119.)

BIRCHALL & BEARDMORE. Music and musical instrument sellers and publishers, 129 New Bond Street, London, 1783. The names are transposed on some of their publications; partners were Robert Birchall and T. Beardmore; Robert Birchall was previously with William and Mrs. Elizabeth Randall; succeeded by Birchall and Andrews.
K.

BIRCHALL & CO. *See* Birchall, Lonsdale & Mills.

BIRCHALL, LONSDALE & MILLS. Music sellers and publishers, London; 133 New Bond Street, 1819-c. 1824; 140 New Bond Street, c. 1824-29. Also published as Birchall and Co.; succeeded Robert Birchall; followed by Lonsdale and Mills.
 K.
 Catalogue:—Vocal and Instrumental Music composed by G. Rossini. 1824. 3 pp. 4°. (Haas, Catalogue 27. No. 45.)

BIRCHALL (ROBERT). Music and musical instrument seller, and publisher, London; issued independently some publications while in partnership with Andrews at 129 New Bond Street, 1783 to May 1789; alone at 133 New Bond Street, May 1789-1819. Previously a partner in Birchall and Beardmore, 1783; after he died in 1819, the business was continued as Birchall, Lonsdale and Mills, or, Birchall and Co.
 K. G.
 Catalogues:—Vocal and Instrumental Music. c. 1783. 1 p. fol. (Wm. C. Smith); Musical Publications. c. 1790. 2 pp. fol. (B.M. h. 3200. (8.)); Vocal and Instrumental Music. c. 1794. 2 pp. fol. (B.M. Hirsch IV. 1111. (1.)); Thematic Index to Bland's (continued by Birchall) Harpsichord Collection. c. 1800. 1 p. fol. (B.M. g. 443. r. (1.)); Musical Publications. c. 1802. 2 pp. fol. (B.M. g. 443. b. (26.)); Piano Forte Music. Plate 1. c. 1806. 1 p. fol. (B.M. Hirsch IV. 1111. (2.)); Piano Forte Music. Plate 2. Duetts &c. c. 1806. 1 p. fol. (B.M. h. 275. (15.)); Music. 1806. 4 pp. 8°. (B.M. 1042. e. 20.); Music. 1809. 8 pp. 8°. (B.M. 1042. e. 21.); Music. 1817. 12 pp. 8°. (B.M. 1042. e. 22.)

BIRD (JOHN). Bookseller, at the Angel and Bible, in Ave Maria Lane, London. His name appears in the imprint of "A Compleat Book of Psalmody . . . The second edition, with additions, set forth, and corrected by James Evison. London: Printed by Robert Brown . . . and sold by John Bird . . . MDCCLI." Also in the third edition, 1754.

BIRD (S.). Bookseller? London. Name appears in the imprint of "The Psalms of David in Metre: With the Tunes used in Parish-Churches. By John Patrick. The Eighth edition. London: Printed for J. Walthoe . . . S. Bird . . . MDCCXLII."

BIRT (SAMUEL). Bookseller and publisher, at the Bible and Ball, Ave-Mary Lane, near Stationers' Hall, London, 1728-55. (P.) Sold "The Wedding: a Tragi-Comi-Pastoral-Farcical Opera . . . By Mr. Hawker . . . To which is prefix'd, the overture, by Dr. Pepusch. With . . . the musick to each song, engrav'd on copper-plates . . . MDCCXXIX.", published by W. Mears, at Temple Bar; published "Heaven on Earth; or, the Beauty of Holiness . . . by William Tans'ur . . . MDCCXXXVIII."
 P. III.

BISHOP. *See* Wigley & Bishop.

BISHOP (RICHARD). Printer, St. Peter's, Paul's Wharf, London, 1631-1653. (P.) Printed "The Whole Books of Psalmes: Collected into English Meeter by Thomas Sternhold, Iohn Hopkins, and others . . . London, Printed by R. Bishop for the Company of Stationers . . . 1640." Took over the business of William Stansby, 1639.
P. I.

BLACKMAN (JOSIAH). Musical instrument maker and music publisher, London; 93 Blackfriars Road, c. 1847-57; 120 Blackfriars Road, c. 1857-82. Probably son of William Blackman, whom he succeeded in business in partnership with his mother.

BLACKMAN (JOSIAH) & (S.). Musical instrument makers and music sellers, 5 Bridge Street, Southwark, London, c. 1845-47. Probably the son and widow of William Blackman whom they succeeded; from c. 1847 Josiah was in business alone.
K.

BLACKMAN (WILLIAM). Music seller and publisher, London; 15 Union Street, Borough (Southwark), c. 1810-22; 5 Bridge Street, Borough (Southwark), c. 1822-45. Business continued by Josiah and S. (Mrs. William) Blackman as music sellers and musical instrument makers. His principal publication was "The Harmonic Cabinet or Kentish Harmony," also issued as "The Harmonic Cabinet or Vocal Harmonist, in miniature" and as "Kentish Harmony," in 1821, from Union Street. A later edition was issued from Bridge Street.
K.

BLACKWELL (I. G.). Music and musical instrument seller, 23 Devonshire Street, Queen Square, Bloomsbury, London, c. 1810. Published some of his own compositions.

BLADON (SAMUEL). Bookseller and publisher, Paper Mill, in Paternoster Row, London. (P.) His name appears in the imprint of "The Beggar's Opera . . . To which is prefixed the overture in score: And the musick to each song. London: Printed for W. Strahan, T. Lowndes, T. Caslon, W. Griffin, W. Nicoll, S. Bladon, and G. Kearsly. MDCCLXXI."; also in two editions published 1777.
P. III.

BLAGROVE (WILLIAM M.). Musician, music seller and publisher, Music Warehouse and Concert Rooms, 71 Mortimer Street, Cavendish Square, London, c. 1847-59. In the later years became W. Blagrove and Co.; previously a partner in the business of W. Blagrove and Attwater; stock-in-trade and private collection of music offered for sale by auction June 17th, 1859.

BLAGROVE (WILLIAM M.) & ATTWATER (WILLIAM). Musicians, music sellers and publishers, 56 Great Portland Street, Portland Place, London, c. 1845-46. Traded as W. Blagrove and Attwater. The partners were William M. Blagrove and William Attwater; Blagrove set up in business on his own account at 71 Mortimer Street, c. 1847.

BLAIKIE (ANDREW). Engraver, Paisley. His name appears on the title-page of "A Collection of Irish Airs and Jiggs, with variations . . . by John Murphy, performer on the Union Pipes at Eglinton Castle . . . engraved by A. Blaikie, Paisley," c. 1810; engraved the music in "Minstrelsy: Ancient and modern . . . By William Motherwell . . . MDCCCXXVII."
    K.

BLAKE. *See* Roy & Blake.

BLANCHARD (WILLIAM). Printer, York. Printed "Psalmody for a single Voice . . . First published with Mr. George Sandys's "Paraphrase of the Psalms of David . . . 1638. By Henry Lawes . . . With a variation of each psalm tune . . . By Matthew Camidge . . . To which are prefixed, some introductory reasons for this publication by W. Mason . . . Precentor of York . . . MDCCXXXIX."

BLAND & WELLER. Pianoforte makers, music sellers and publishers, 23 Oxford Street, London, 1792-c. 1818. Anne Bland previously in business on her own account at same address; in 1805 purchased from Charles Dibdin the copyright of three hundred and sixty songs together with his musical stock; when Bland dropped out, c. 1818, E. Weller carried on alone.
    K. G.
    A Catalogue of New Songs, Duetts, Catches, and Glees. c. 1800. 4 pp. fol. (B.M. 7896. h. 40. (1.))

BLAND (ANNE). Music seller and publisher, 23 Oxford Street, London, 1784-92. Went into partnership with E. Weller in 1792, as Bland and Weller.
    K.

BLAND (JOHN). Engraver, printer, music seller and publisher, London; 114 Long Acre, c. 1776 to early in 1778; 45 Holborn, c. early in 1778-95. Claimed to have been the first music printer to publish singly the works of Handel and other celebrated composers; some single sheet songs bear only the initials I. B. Succeeded by Lewis, Houston and Hyde.
    K. G.
    Catalogues:—Vocal and Instrumental Music. 1781. 1 p. fol. (B.M. g. 222. (14.)); Vocal and Instrumental Music. c. 1781. 1 p. fol. (B.M. g. 274. d. (1.)); Music. 1782. 1 p. fol. (B.M. E. 108. e.

(3.)); Vocal and Instrumental Music. 1782. 1 p. fol. (B.M. E. 111. c. (2.)); Vocal and Instrumental Music. 1782. 1 p. fol. (B.M. G. 808. b. (42.)); Music. 1784. 1 p. fol. (B.M. H. 115.); Instrumental, Harpsichord, Vocal Music. c. 1785. 3 pp. fol. (B.M. g. 221. (5.)); Music. c. 1785. 1 p. fol. (B.M. Hirsch M. 1472. (2.)); Music, Vocal and Instrumental. March 25, 1786. 4 pp. fol. (B.M. Hirsch IV. 1113. (1.)); Music. c. 1786. 1 p. fol. (B.M. Hirsch IV. 24. b.); Music, Vocal and Instrumental. January 1789. pp. 1-8; June 24, 1789. pp. 9, 10; June 25, 1790. pp. 11, 12; May 1, 1791. pp. 13, 14. fol. (R.C.M. XVIII. E. 19. Advertises, Public's Guide or a Catalogue with the subjects, or themes, of all the several musical Works engraved . . . by J. Bland, in three parts, viz. No. 1, Instrumental Music; No. 2, Harpsichord ditto; and No. 3, Vocal ditto.) Music. 1790. 1 p. fol. (B.M. g. 221. (8.)); Catalogue of Subjects or Beginnings of Italian Songs. c. 1790. 1 p. fol. (B.M.E. 601. k. (11.)); Instrumental, Harpsichord, Vocal Music. c. 1791. 3 pp. fol. (B.M. g. 148. (7.)); Theme Catalogue of French Songs. c. 1792. 1 p. fol. (B.M. H. 1601. c. (11.)); Subjects or Beginnings of 2 Periodical Works for the Harpsichord or Piano Forte. 1792. 1 p. fol. (B.M. g. 455. i. (2.)); Instrumental, Harpsichord, Vocal Music. c. 1792. 3 pp. fol. (B.M. Hirsch IV. 807.); Vocal, Harpsichord Music.) (Catalogue of Subjects or Beginnings of Bland's Colln. Divine Music.) c. 1793. 3 pp. fol. (B.M. H. 817.); Instrumental, Harpsichord, Vocal Music. c. 1793. 3 pp. fol. (B.M. g. 148. (8.))

BLAND (THOMAS). Engraver, Rood Lane, London. Engraved "Six Sonatas for the Harpsichord with an Accompanyment for a Violin. Opera Secunda. [By Isaac Heaton.] Engraved from the writing of Mr. Benj. Webb by Thomas Bland. 1766." Engraved the title-page of "Royal Harmony: or, the Beauties of Church Music . . . By A. Williams. London. Printed for J. Johnson. No. 72 St. Paul's Ch: Yard," c. 1770.

BLANSHARD (THOMAS). Bookseller, 14 City Road, and 66 Paternoster Row, London. Published "Sacred Melody. A set of tunes collected by the late Revd. John Wesley . . . An edition carefully revised and corrected by his nephew Charles Wesley . . . Printed for & sold by T. Blanshard . . . 1822."

BLARE (JOSIAH) or (JOSEPH). Bookseller, at the Looking Glass on London Bridge, 1683-1706. (P.) His name appears in the imprints of a number of ballads with music published by P. Brooksby, J. Deacon, J. Blare and J. Back.
　　P. II.

BLOCKLEY (JOHN). *See* Jackson, Blockley and Jackson.

BLOUNT (EDWARD). Bookseller, London, 1594-1632. (M.) His name

appears in the imprint of " Le Premier Livre de Chansons & Airs . . . mis en Musique par le sieur Carles Tessier . . . Imprimes a Londres par Thomas Este . . . 1597 [i.e. 1598]. Les presents Liures se treuuent ches Edouard Blount Libraire demeurant au cimitiere de Saint Paul deuant la gran porte du North dudit S. Paul a Londres."
M.

BLOWER or BLORE (RALPH). Printer, near the Middle Temple Gate, Fleet Street, London, 1595-1618. (M.) Said to have published some music. (Pattison.)
M.

BLUNDELL (JAMES). Music seller and publisher, London; at the Handel's Head, 110 St. Martin's Lane, 1778 to near the end of 1780; at the Handel's Head, 10 Haymarket, 1780-82. Son-in-law and successor to Mrs. Mary Welcker; Haymarket premises previously occupied by his brother-in-law, John Welcker. Music seller to his Royal Highness, the Duke of Cumberland.
K.
A Catalogue of Vocal and Instrumental Music. c. 1781. 3 pp. fol. (B.M. Hirsch IV. 1111. (5.))

BOAG (MARY ANN). *See* Boag (William) *the Younger*.

BOAG (WILLIAM) *the Elder*. Music seller, printer and publisher, 11 Great Turnstile, Holborn, London, c. 1795-1833. "Printed and sold by W. Boag at his Cheap Music Shop" appears on many of his publications; business became William and Norris Boag, c. 1833.
K. G.

BOAG (WILLIAM) *the Younger*. Music seller and publisher, 11 Great Turnstile, Holborn, London, c. 1845-60. Followed William and Norris Boag; probably died c. 1860, when the business was carried on by Mrs. Mary Ann Boag as a music seller; stock-in-trade offered for sale by Puttick and Simpson, July 4, 1864.

BOAG (WILLIAM) & (NORRIS). Music sellers and publishers, 11 Great Turnstile, Holborn, London, c. 1833-45. Succeeded William Boag; succeeded by William Boag, the younger.

BOCHSA & CO. Music sellers and publishers, Argyll Harmonic Saloon, 258 Regent Street, London, c. 1825-30.

BODDINGTON (NICHOLAS). Bookseller, at the Golden Ball, Duck Lane, London, 1687-1717. (P.) His name appears in an advertisement January 1700, "An Introduction to the singing of the Psalms . . . by Wm. Webb. Sold by Ebin. Tracy . . . and N. Bodington," etc.
P. II.

BODINGTON (NICHOLAS). *See* Boddington.

BOGUE (DAVID). Bookseller and publisher, 86 Fleet Street, London, c. 1843-57. Published c. 1846, "The Singing Book. The art of singing at sight taught by progressive exercises. By James Turle . . . and Edward Taylor."

BOITARD (LOUIS PIERRE). Engraver. Designed the head-pieces to the songs in "Orpheus Britannicus; or the Gentleman and Lady's Musical Museum; Consisting of one hundred favourite songs . . . London: Printed and sold by Benjn. Cole . . . MDCCLX."

BOND (J.). Music seller, 64 Dean Street, Soho, London, c. 1819-22. May have published some music.
    K.

BOND (JOHN). 46 Holbourn, London. Published c. 1795, "In the dead of Night. As sung with great applause by Mrs. Jordan in the Wedding Day."

BONE & CO. *See* Boone, Boon or Bone (Thomas) & (William).

BONHAM (GEORGE). Printer and Stationer, Dublin; 42 Dame Street, 1778-84; 68 South Great George's Street, c. 1784-1805. Printed, "Select Psalm and Hymn Tunes, adapted to the use of public congregations and private families. By John Mc.Vity . . . The Second Edition . . . MDCCLXXXVII."
    P. III.

BONION (RICHARD) & WALLEY (HENRY). Booksellers, London; at the Spread Eagle at the great North door of St. Paul's Church, and other addresses. (M.) Published "Pammelia. Musicks Miscellanie, or, Mixed Varietie of Pleasant Roundelayes, and delightfull Catches . . . London Printed by William Barley, for R. B. and H. W. and are to be sold at the Spread Eagle at the great North doore of Paules. 1609."
    M.

BONWICKE (HENRY). Bookseller, at the Red Lyon, St. Paul's Churchyard, London, 1677-1706. (P.) His name appears in an advertisement, March 1678, "Songs for One, Two, and Three Voices, to the Thorow-Bass, with short Symphonies. Collected out of some of the select Poems of the incomparable Mr. Cowley, and others. And composed by Henry Bowman, Philo-musicus. Sold by Henry Bonwicke . . . John Carr . . . and Thomas Bowman Bookseller in Oxford "; published, "A Duke and no Duke. A Farce. As it is acted by Their Majesties Servants. Written by N. Tate. With the several songs set to music . . . 1685." Succeeded by Rebecca and James Bonwicke.
    P. II. D. & M.

BONWICKE (J.) & (J.). Booksellers, London. Their names appear in the imprint of "The Psalms of David in Metre: With the tunes used in Parish Churches. By John Patrick. The Eighth edition. London: Printed for J. Walthoe . . . J. and J. Bonwicke . . . MDCCXLII." Presumably succeeded Rebecca and James Bonwicke.

BONWICKE (REBECCA) & (JAMES). Booksellers, Red Lion, St. Paul's Churchyard, 1706-35. (P.) Their names appear in the imprint of "The Psalms of David in Metre: With the tunes used in Parish-Churches. By John Patrick . . . The Seventh edition. London: Printed for D. Brown . . . R. & J. Bonwicke . . . MDCCXXIV." Succeeded Henry Bonwicke.
    P. II, III.

BOONE, BOON or BONE (THOMAS) & (WILLIAM). Booksellers, 29 New Bond Street, London, 1831-72. Published as Bone and Co., Vol II of John Caulfield's "A Collection of the Vocal Music in Shakespeare's Plays," and a revised edition of the two volumes as T. and W. Boon. Prior to 1831 the firm appears in the directories as T. Boone, 480 Strand, but there is no evidence that they published any other music.

BOOSEY & SONS. *See* Boosey (Thomas) & Co.

BOOSEY (THOMAS) & CO. Musical instrument makers, music sellers and publishers, London. Thomas Boosey, bookseller, of 4 Old Broad Street, c. 1792-1819, set up a music branch, with his son Thomas, then twenty-one years of age, in charge; 28 Holles Street, Oxford Street, 1816-c. 1854. (The bookselling business continued as Boosey and Sons, 4 Old Broad Street, c. 1819-30, and as T. & T. Boosey, c. 1830-32.) Title of music firm changed to Boosey and Sons, 28 Holles Street, c. 1854-64, with additional premises at 24 Holles Street, c. 1857-64. Became Boosey and Co., 28 and 24 Holles Street, c. 1864-74; 295 Regent Street, 1874-1930. Purchased the business of Henry Distin and Co., brass musical instrument makers, in 1868; amalgamated in 1930 with Hawkes and Son, of Denman Street, Piccadilly, and became Boosey and Hawkes, Ltd., at 295 Regent Street, the principal address to-day.
    G.
    Catalogues:—Selection of admired Compositions. c. 1818. 4 pp. fol. (B.M. Hirsch IV. 1113. (2.)); New and classical Music. 1820. 2 pp. fol. (First Edition Bookshop, Catalogue 40. No. 132.)

BOOTH (J.) & (W.). Booksellers, Warrington. Reprinted and sold, c. 1820, "Sixteen Psalm Tunes . . . as sung in the Parish Church of Warrington, composed by the late Edmund Olive Organist. Second edition."

BOOTH (JOHN). Bookseller and stationer, Duke Street, Portland Place,

London. Published c. 1798, "The Mary-le-Bone March. Composed (and arranged for the Piano Forte) by M. P. King."

BOOTH (JOHN) of Halifax. *See* Whitley & Booth.

BOOTH (W.). *See* Booth (J.) & (W.).

BOOTH (WILLIAM). Musical instrument maker and music seller, Leeds. From c. 1809-22 had a shop in Mill Hill, and afterwards at various addresses. In 1837 the firm was Booth and Son. May have published some music.
    K.

BOREMAN (THOMAS). Bookseller and publisher, London, 1733-c. 1745; on Ludgate Hill, near the Gate; The Cock on Ludgate Hill; Guildhall. (P.) Advertised January 1736, "Numb. I of the Third Volume of A Complete Collection of English and Scotch Songs, with their respective Tunes prefix'd . . . to be published the first Saturday in every month . . . Printed for T. Boreman, near Child's Coffee-House in St. Paul's Church-yard, and sold at his shop at the Cock upon Ludgate Hill . . . Where may be had Vol. I & II."
    P. III.

BOUCHER (John). Bookseller, Peterborough. His name appears in the imprint of "The Most Useful Tunes of the Psalms, in Two, and some in Three Parts. Collected and transposed, corrected and composed by Edmund Ireland . . . The Second edition, much improved . . . York, Printed by John White, and are to be sold (for the Author) by . . . John Boucher of Peterborough . . . 1713."

BOURGUIGNON-GRAVELOT (HUBERT FRANÇOIS). *See* Gravelot.

BOW CHURCH YARD. Bow Church Yard, London (The Printing House, The Printing Office in). These forms used at times for works issued by John Cluer, Elizabeth Cluer and Thomas Cobb, without their names.
    K.
    See Cluer (Elizabeth); Cluer (John); Cobb (Thomas).

BOWIE & HILL. Music sellers and publishers, George Street, Perth, 1803-15. Thomas Hill also carried on a separate business as a bookseller and stationer; after the death of John Bowie in 1815, the music business was continued by Hill.
    K.

BOWLES (CARRINGTON). *See* Bowles (John).

BOWLES (JOHN). Book, map and print seller, Mercers Hall, London.

Advertised December 1728, "A New Pack of Musical Cards, consisting of the Songs in the Beggars Opera, neatly engraved on copper, and set to Musick, and many of them transposed for the Flute. Sold by John Bowles," etc. A later edition was "Printed for Carrington Bowles, No. 69 St. Paul's Church Yard, London," 1764 or later. Carrington Bowles was the son of John Bowles, whom he succeeded.
P. III.

BOWMAN (THOMAS). Bookseller, Oxford, 1664-78. (P.) Published "Songs, for one, two & three Voices to the Thorow-Bass . . . Collected out of some of the select poems of the incomparable Mr. Cowley, and others: and composed by Henry Bowman . . . Oxford . . . 1678."
K. P. I, II. D. & M.

BOWN (GEORGE WASHINGTON). Music seller and publisher, London; 11 St. Martin's Church Yard, c. 1815-24; 2 St. Martin's Church Yard, c. 1824-28; 17 Holywell Street, c. 1828-30. Described himself as "Late of H.R.H. the Duke of Gloucester's Band."
K.

BOWYER (JONAH) or (JONAS). Bookseller, Ludgate Street, the corner of St. Paul's Churchyard, or, near the West end of St. Paul's Churchyard, London, 1705-c. 1724. His name appears in the imprint of "The Psalms of David in Metre: Fitted to the tunes used in Parish-Churches. By John Patrick . . . London, Printed for W. Churchill . . . J. Bowyer . . . MDCCXVIII."; also in the seventh edition, 1724.
P. II.

BOYD (GEORGE). See Oliver & Boyd.

BOYS (ANTHONY). Bookseller, St. Albans. His name appears in the imprints of "A Collection of some verses out of the Psalmes . . . Collected by Mr. Daniel Warner . . . Revised by Mr. Henry Purcell . . . In the Savoy, Printed by E. Jones; and sold by . . . Anthony Boys at his shop at St. Albans in Hertfordshire. 1694"; "A Collection of some verses out of the Psalms of David: suited to several occasions. Composed in two parts, Cantus & Bassus . . . Collected for Mr. Henry Hunt . . . The Second edition . . . London, Printed by J. Heptinstall for Henry Playford; and are to be sold by Anthony Boys . . . 1698."

BOYS (DICKINSON). Bookseller? Louth. His name appears in the imprint of "A Collection of Psalm-Tunes; with Great Variety of Hymns and Anthems compos'd by the best Masters . . . By James Green. The Fourth edition . . . London. Printed by William Pearson, for the Author: and sold by . . . Dickinson Boys of Louth. 1718."

BRADLEY (ABRAHAM). Printer and bookseller, Dublin, 1730-59. (P.) Published "The Psalms of David in Metre . . . to which are added

Hymns, particularly designed for the Lord's Supper. Printed by S. Powell, for A. Bradley, at the Two Bibles in Dame's Street, over against Sycamore-Alley, Dublin. MDCCXL."
    P. III.

BRADLEY (JOB). Bookseller and printer, Chesterfield, 1725-98. (P.) His name appears in the imprint of "A Book of Psalmody . . . The Fifth edition . . . By John Chetham. London: Printed by A. Pearson, for Joseph Lord . . . in Wakefield . . . and sold by J. Bradley . . . in Chesterfield . . . MDCCXXXVI." The dates 1725-98 may cover two persons of the same name.
    P. II.

BRANSTON & LAMBERT. Engravers, printers, etc., 31 Frith Street, London. Engraved, printed and published c. 1803, "Ten Easy Lessons for the Piano Forte. Composed . . . by T. G. Williamson. Op. 8 "; "Ten Easy Lessons for the Piano Forte. Composed . . . by T. G. Williamson. Op. 9."

BRANSTON (R.). Engraver, London. Engraved "Six Select Songs and one Cantata, by James Newton," published by John Johnston, opposite Lancaster Court, in the Strand, near Charing Cross, c. 1768. No evidence of connection with the following.
    K.

BRANSTON (R.). Music engraver and printer, 2 China Row, Lambeth, London. Engraved and printed, "A Favorite Sonata arranged as a Duett for two Harps or a Harp and Piano Forte . . . by W. Duchatz . . . Opera 3d," c. 1800; "The Wife's Farewell or No my Love, no. The favorite Ballad as sung by Miss Decamp in the much admired Farce Of Age To-morrow," c. 1800. No evidence of connection with the preceding.
    K.

BRASAN or BRESSAN (PETER). Musical instrument maker and music seller, at the Green Door in Somerset House Yard, in the Strand, London. Advertised some music from 1718-24.
    K.

BREMNER (JAMES). Music seller, 108 New Bond Street, London, c. 1770-75. Branch establishment of Robert Bremner's; published "Sei Duetti per due Violini. Composte del Signor Comte Benevento," etc., advertised September 1770. Author of "Instructions for the sticcato pastorale," published by R. Bremner in London, ? date. George Smart was for a time in the employ of James Bremner.
    See also Bremner (Robert).

BREMNER (ROBERT). Music and musical instrument seller, printer and

publisher, at the Golden Harp, opposite the head of Blackfriars Wynd, High Street, Edinburgh, 1754-59; changed sign to the Harp and Hautboy c. 1755; opposite Cross Well, High Street, Edinburgh, c. 1759-89; Harp and Hautboy, opposite Somerset House in the Strand, London, 1762-89; had a branch establishment at 108 New Bond Street, London, c. 1770-75, from which address some music was published with the name of J. Bremner. Some single sheet songs bear only the initials R. B., or, R^t. B^r. Purchased some music plates at the sale of John Cox's stock-in-trade (Simpson's Music Shop), 1764; the greater part of the music plates and books at the sale of the stock of Mrs. Johnson, of Cheapside, 1777; plates and music of Mrs. Welcker, 1779. When he died in May 1789, the Edinburgh business was taken over by John Brysson. A notice in *The Morning Post* of July 25, 1789, advertised for sale by auction, if not previously disposed of by private contract, Bremner's properties at Battersea Rise and Brighton, the lease of his house in the Strand, household furniture, and stock-in-trade consisting of plates, music, musical instruments, etc. The entire stock-in-trade of the London business was purchased by Preston and Son who issued a catalogue in 1790. (B.M. Hirsch IV. 1113. (8.))
K. G.

Catalogues:—Vocal and Instrumental Music. c. 1764. 1 p. fol. (B.M. G. 230. (2.)); 1765. 1 p. fol. (B.M. Hirsch M. 1424.); 1767. 1 p. fol. (B.M. h. 2910. (7.)); 1768. 1 p. fol. (B.M. G. 200. (4.)); c. 1772. 1 p. fol. (B.M. Hirsch IV. 1111. (6.)); c. 1773. 1 p. fol. (B.M. 7896. h. 40. (2.)); 1774. 1 p. fol. (B.M. I. 510); c. 1775. 1 p. fol. (Wm. C. Smith); c. 1775. 1 p. fol. (B.M. G. 802. a. (1.)); August, 1778. 2 pp. fol. (B.M. Hirsch IV. 1112. (1.)); Vocal and Instrumental Music. (Additional Catalogue . . . formerly property of the late Mrs. Johnson . . . Mrs. Welcker, etc.) March, 1782. 6 pp. fol. (B.M. Hirsch IV. 1112. (2.))

BRENAN. *See* Cooke (T.) & Brenan.

BRENT (JOHN) & POWELL (STEPHEN). Printers, at the back of Dick's Coffee House, in Skinners Row, Dublin. Printed "The Psalms of David in Metre. Newly translated with amendments: By William Barton, M.A. And Sett to the best Psalm-Tunes in two Parts . . . By Thomas Smith," etc., c. 1698.
P. II.

BRESSAN (PETER). *See* Brasan or Bressan.

BRETT (R.). Engraver, London. Engraved "A Consort of Musick of Three Parts. Composed by John Lenton & Tho. Tollett. [London.] 1692."

BRETT (W.). Printer, London. Printed "A New Musical Magazine, entitled British Melody." The first and second numbers were advertised in May 1748.

BREWER (SAMUEL) & CO. Music sellers and publishers, 23 Bishopsgate Within, London, c. 1849-93. Had additional premises at 16-18 Castle Street, City Road, c. 1869-72; 8 Collingwood Street, City Road, 1872-79; 14-15 Poultry, 1875-79; 28, 30 Great Eastern Street, 1879-93; 38 Poultry, 1880-89. Succeeded Halliday and Co.

BREWSTER (EDWARD). Bookseller, the Crane, in St. Paul's Churchyard, London, 1654-99. (P.) His name appears in the imprint of "The Whole Book of Psalms, as they are sung in the Churches: with the singing notes of time and tune set to every syllable . . . London, Printed by R. Everingham for the Company of Stationers, and are sold by E. Brewster in S. Paul's Church-yard and S. Kettle . . . 1688."
P. I.

BRIDE, *Mrs.* *See* Bride (Richard).

BRIDE (RICHARD). Music seller and publisher, at the Black Lyon in Exeter Change, in the Strand, London, c. 1765-75. Succeeded Henry Waylett; composed and published some of the songs sung at Finch's Grotto Gardens; some single sheet songs bear only the initials R. B. or Rd. Be. For some time the business was carried on by Mrs. Bride.
K.

BRIDGE (S.). Printer and bookseller, London, 1699-1724; in Austen Friars, near the Royal Exchange; Little Moor-Fields. (P.) Printed "The Book of Psalms in English Metre. The newest version fitted to the common tunes. By C. Darby . . . London. Printed by S. Bridge, for Tho. Parkhurst . . . MDCCIV."
P. II.

BRIGGS (JOHN). Musical instrument maker and music publisher, London; 14 King's Head Court, Shoe Lane, c. 1812-16; 76 Fetter Lane, c. 1816-24; 75 Parson's Street, Ratcliff Highway, c. 1824-37; 84 Parson's Street, Ratcliff Highway, c. 1837-45.

BRIGHT, *Mr.* At the Blue Peruke, in Spring Garden Passage, London. His name appears in the imprint of "Splenetick Pills or Mirth Alamode. Being a collection of humorous songs . . . The words by the celebrated poet John Rumfish Esq. Set to music by Dr. Merriwag [i.e. Thomas Vandernan]. London Printed for Thos. Vandernan, and sold at Mr. Bright at the Blue Peruke," etc., c. 1750.

BRISCOE (SAMUEL). Bookseller, over against Will's Coffee House, Russell Street, or, at the corner of Charles Street, Covent Garden,

London, 1691-1705. (P.) Published "The Songs to the new Play of Don Quixote. Part the first. Set by the most eminent masters of the age. All written by Mr. D'urfey . . . 1694 "; "The Songs to the new Play of Don Quixote . . . Part the second . . . 1694 "; "New Songs in the Third Part of the Comical History of Don Quixote . . . Being the last piece set to musick by the late famous Mr. Henry Purcell: And by Mr. Courtiville, Mr. Akeroyd, and other eminent masters of the age . . . 1696 "; " A Song in Love's Last Shift, sung by the Boy, set by Mr. Daniel Purcell. 'What ungrateful Devil moves you.' London Printed for S. Briscoe in Covent Garden," c. 1696.
  K. P. II. D. & M.

BRITTAIN (THOMAS). Printer, 39 Grafton Street, East, London. Printed, published and sold c. 1835, "A Selection of Psalms, Hymns, &c. as sung at Fitzroy Chapel, arranged for the Pianoforte or Organ . . . by Joseph Coggins. Second edition."

BROCAS (JOHN). Printer, Dublin, 1696-1707. (P.) Printed "The Psalms of David in Metre, Newly translated. With amendments. By William Barton . . . The second edition, corrected and amended. With the Basses. By Thomas Smith . . . 1706."
  P. II.

BRODERIP & WILKINSON. Music sellers, printers and publishers, 13 Haymarket, London, 1798-1808. Partners were Francis Broderip, who had previously been a partner in the firm of Longman and Broderip, and C. Wilkinson; succeeded by Wilkinson and Co.
  K. G.
  Catalogues:—Music for the Pianoforte by W. A. Mozart. c. 1800. 1 p. fol. (Rosenthal, Chamber Music. List 1. No. 57.) Additional Catalogue . . . 1806. 1 p. fol. (B.M. h. 284. (14.)); Additional Catalogue . . . 1807. 1 p. fol. (B.M. Hirsch IV. 1111. (7.))

BRODERIP (FRANCIS). See Broderip & Wilkinson; Longman & Broderip; Longman, Lukey & Broderip.

BROME (CHARLES). Bookseller and publisher, at the Gun, at the West End of St. Paul's Church (West End of St. Paul's), London, 1684-1711. (P.) Published "The Miser; [A Song] written by the Author of the Old Man's Wish, and set to Music by Mr. Michael Wise. Printed by J. P. for Charles Brome . . . 1685"; "Songs and Ayres. Set by Mr. Blow, Mr. Henry Purcell, Mr. James Hart, Mr. William Turner, Mr. Michael Wise. And several other eminent Masters . . . 1696." Succeeded Joanna Brome, probably his mother.
  P. II. D. & M.

BROME (HENRY). Bookseller and publisher, London; at the Hand, in St. Paul's Churchyard, 1657; the Gun, Ivy Lane, 1660-66; Star,

Little Britain, 1666-69; the Gun, Ludgate Street, at the West end of St. Paul's, 1669; the Gun, at (near) the West end of St. Paul's, 1670-78; the Gun, St. Paul's Churchyard, 1678-81. (P.) Published "The Principles of practical Musick delivered in a compendious, easie, and new method. . . . By Chr. Simpson . . . MDCLXV"; also editions in 1667 and 1678; "Chelys, minuritionum artificio exornata . . . The Division-Viol, or The Art of playing extempore upon a ground. Authore Christopher Simpson. Editio secunda . . . MDCLXVII."; "The Catholic Ballad: or an invitation to Popery, upon considerable grounds and reasons. To the tune of 88 . . . MDCLXXIV."; also editions in 1675 and 1678; "New Ayres and Dialogues composed for Voices and Viols . . . Together with lessons for viols or violins, by John Banister . . . and Thomas Low . . . MDCLXXVIII." Succeeded by his widow Joanna.
    K. P. II. D. & M.

BROME (JOANNA). *See* Brome (Charles); Brome (Henry).

BROOKS (JAMES). Musician, composer and music seller, Music Warehouse, 63 St. James's Street, London, c. 1803-08. Previously resided in Bath.

BROOKS (SAMUEL). Bookseller and publisher, at the Golden Ball, Paternoster Row, London. His name appears in the imprint, in partnership with Henry Woodgate, of "The Psalm-Singer's Pocket Companion . . . The second edition. By Uriah Davenport . . . London: Printed by Robert Brown . . . For Stanley Crowder . . . and Henry Woodgate and Samuel Brooks, at the Golden Ball, in Paternoster Row. 1758."
    P. III.

BROOKS (THOMAS). Music seller and publisher, 17 Hunter Street, Brunswick Square, London, c. 1827-31.

BROOKS (THOMAS). Bookseller and publisher, 8 Baker Street, London, 1843-45. Published 1843, "A Selection of Anthems, Chants, Doxologies, &c. . . . By T. F. Travers," etc.

BROOKSBY (PHILIP). Bookseller, London, 1672-96. (P.) Next door to the Ball, in West Smithfield, near to the Hospital Gate; Golden Ball, West Smithfield, near the Hospital Gate, 1683; Golden Harp and Ball, near the Bore Tavern, in Pye Lane. Published a number of songs with music, some with the imprint of "P. Brooksby, J. Deacon, J. Blare, and J. Back."
    P. II.

BROOME (MICHAEL). Musician, music engraver, printer and publisher, Birmingham; at Purcell's Head, Litchfield Street, c. 1741-51; Colmore (or, Colmer) Row, near St. Philip's Church, c. 1751-75. He was previously a singing master at Isleworth, Middlesex, and collected and published some collections of Psalm tunes, etc., c. 1725-30; on these collections his name appears as Broom. He is said to have moved to Abingdon before settling in Birmingham. Broome was Parish Clerk at Birmingham; died 1775 aged 75.

K.

BROTHERTON (JOHN). Bookseller and bookbinder, at the Bible (in Threadneedle Street), near the Royal Exchange, London. Published, "A Short Explication of such foreign words, as are made use of in Musick Books. (An Account of printed musick, for violins, hautboys, flutes, and other instruments, by several masters.) 1724." Sold "The Dancing-Master . . . Done from the French of Monsieur Rameau, by J. Essex . . . London, printed and sold by him and J. Brotherton, bookseller, 1728"; "The Morning Hymn: from the Fifth Book of Milton's Paradise Lost. Set to musick by Philip Hart. London . . . Sold by John Brotherton . . . 1728-9."

P. II.

BROWN (ALEXANDER). Bookseller, Broad Street, Aberdeen. Published "Sacred Harmony, being a Collection of Psalm and Hymn Tunes . . . by John Knott, teacher of singing, Aberdeen." Preface is dated January 27, 1814.

K.

BROWN or BROWNE (DANIEL). Bookseller and music publisher, at the Black Swan and Bible, without Temple Bar, London, 1672-1729. (P.) Published in conjunction with T. Benskin, "The Newest Collection of the Choicest Songs . . . 1683"; and with Henry Playford "Mercurius Musicus . . . 1700"; also for 1701. His name appears in the imprints of a number of sacred music works. He was probably succeeded by a relative, Daniel Browne, who published "An Antidote against Melancholy. Being a Collection of fourscore merry songs . . . MDCCLIX."

K. P. II. D. & M.

BROWN (J.). Without Temple Bar, London. His name appears in the imprint of "The Merry Musician; or a Cure for the Spleen . . . A Collection of . . . Songs . . . London Printed by H. Meere for J. Walsh . . . J. Hare . . . A. Bettesworth . . . and J. Brown . . . 1716."

BROWN (J.). Printer to the Perth Antiquarian Society, Perth. Printed "The Gentle Shepherd, by Allan Ramsay: with the original music . . . 1786"; "The Musical Miscellany; a select collection of the most approved Scots, English, & Irish Songs, set to music . . . MDCCLXXXVI."

K.

BROWN (JAMES). Music seller and publisher, Glasgow; 35 Wilson Street, c. 1820-27; 75 Wilson Street, c. 1827-34. Business continued

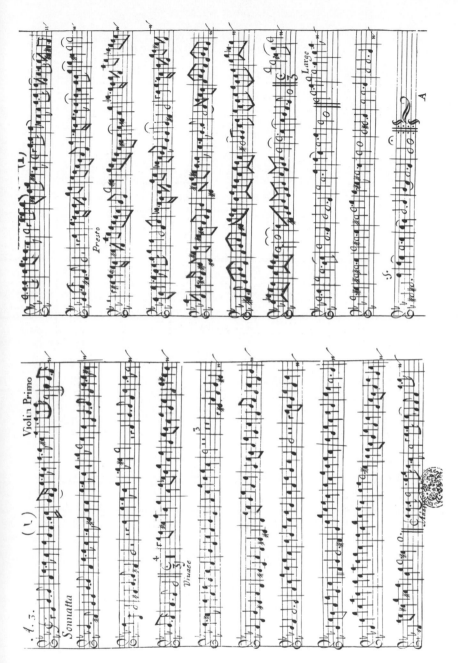

Henry Purcell, "Sonnata's of III. Parts". Engraved by Thomas Cross.
Printed for the Author, and sold by J. Playford and J. Carr. 1683

12

I come to the Waters, &c. Set by Mr. *R. Goodson.*

CUPID's SONG in the Mask of *Orpheus* and *Euridice.*

Come to the Waters, the Woods and the Shades, where the Swains and the Nymphs do all gang: With my Shafts that will go, very swift from my Bow, and a String that shall merrily cry Twang. With my Shafts that will go, very swift from my Bow, and a String that shall merrily, shall merrily, shall merrily, shall merrily, shall merrily cry Twang.

II.

An obstinate Swain
Shall receive twice the Pain,
And my Shaft shall stick up to the Fang:
But who e're courts the Fight
Shall find his Wounds light,
And a String that shall merrily cry Twang

"Musica Oxoniensis". Published by Francis Smith and Peter de Walpergen.
Cut on steel by Walpergen. Printed by Leon. Lichfield. 1698

by his widow at same address from c. 1834-39. Succeeded James Steven.

BROWN or BROWNE (JOHN). Musical instrument maker and publisher, London; at the Black Lyon against the Royal Exchange Gate, Cornhill, or against the Royal Exchange, prior to April 1725; at the Sun near St. Michael's in Cornhill, 1725-c. 1743; the Black Lyon in Cornhill, c. 1743. Published 1725, "The Opera Miscellany. Being a Pocket Collection of Songs, chiefly composed for the Royal Academy of Musick. Consisting of Select Airs in Rodelinda, Julius Cæsar, and other works of Mr. Handel, Airs in Calphurnia & the Great Subscription Book of Mr. Bononcini. Songs of Mr. Attilio Ariosti. Some fine English Airs of that great Master Albinoni and other Authors. The whole Transpos'd for the Flute by Mr. Bolton."
K.

BROWN (R.) & (M.). Printers, London. Printed "The Essex Harmony: Being an entire new collection of the most celebrated Songs and Catches, Canons and Glees ... Vol. II. By John Arnold ... MDCCLXIX."; "The Essex Harmony: Being a choice collection of the most celebrated Songs and Catches . . . Vol. I. The Fourth edition . . . By John Arnold . . . MDCCLXXIV." Succeeded Robert Brown.

BROWN (ROBERT). Printer, London; over against Wright's Coffee House in Aldersgate Street, c. 1742-44; in Windmill Court, Pye Corner, near West Smithfield (or, near Christ's Hospital), 1745-69. Printed a number of music books, principally sacred; succeeded Alice Pearson; succeeded by R. and M. Brown.
K.

BROWN (THOMAS). Bookseller, North Bridge, Edinburgh. His name appears in the imprint of "The Edinburgh Musical Miscellany: a collection of the most approved Scotch, English, and Irish songs, set to music. Selected by D. Sime, Edinburgh. Edinburgh: Printed for W. Gordon, T. Brown . . . Edinburgh . . . MDCCXCII." In volume II the imprint reads "Edinburgh: Printed for John Elder, T. Brown, and C. Elliot, Edinburgh; and W. Coke, Leith. MDCCXCIII."; volume II was reissued as "The New Edinburgh Musical Miscellany . . . Selected by D. Sime. Edinburgh: Printed for J. Elder and T. Brown . . . 1794."

BROWN (W.). Bookseller? Dundee. His name appears in the imprint of "The Edinburgh Musical Miscellany: a collection of the most approved Scotch, English, and Irish songs, set to music. Selected by D. Sime, Edinburgh. Edinburgh: Printed for W. Gordon . . . W. Brown, Dundee. MDCCXCII." In volume II the imprint reads "Edinburgh: Printed for John Elder, T. Brown, and C. Elliot, Edinburgh; and W. Coke, Leith. MDCCXCIII."

BROWN (WILLIAM). Bookseller and publisher, Corner of Essex Street, Strand, London, 1765-97. (P.) His name appears in the imprint of "Sacred Harmony, or A Collection of Psalm Tunes, ancient and modern . . . By R. Harrison. London. Printed for the Author, & sold by T. Williams . . . J. Johnson . . . & W. Brown," etc. [1784.]
   P. III.

BROWN (WILLIAM). Musical string maker, 419 Oxford Street, London, c. 1838-42. Published a small amount of music.

BROWNE (ALICE). Publisher and bookseller, London, Widow and successor of John Browne, 1622. Published in association with M. L. [i.e. Matthew Lownes]: "The Sixt Set of Bookes, wherein are Anthemes . . . Composed by Michaell Est . . . 1624," and "The Second Set of Madrigals and Pastorals . . . Composed by Francis Pilkington . . . 1624." Only her initials A. B. appear in the imprints.
   M. (John Browne.)

BROWNE (DAVID). Musician, music seller and publisher, 12 Upper Sackville Street, Dublin, c. 1818-22.
   K.

BROWNE (I.). *See* Brown or Browne (John).

BROWNE (J.). Bookseller, London. His name appears in the imprint of "The Psalms of David in Metre: Fitted to the tunes used in Parish-Churches. By John Patrick . . . London, Printed by W. Churchill . . . J. Browne . . . MDCCXVIII."

BROWNE (JOHN). Bookseller, publisher and bookbinder, London; St. Dunstan's Churchyard, Fleet Street, and at other addresses, 1598-1622. (M.) Published a number of musical works alone up to 1613, in association with Thomas Snodham and Matthew Lownes (Snodham doing the printing) from 1613, when these three acquired the musical copyrights of William Barley; only the initials J. B. appear in some imprints. Succeeded by his widow Alice Browne.
   K. M.

BRUCE (JAMES). *See* Small, Bruce & Co.

BRYAN (F.). Pianoforte manufacturer, music seller and publisher, London; 36 Southampton Row, Russell Square, Bloomsbury, c. 1800-05; 76 Long Acre, c. 1805.
   K.

BRYCE. *See* Anderson & Bryce.

BRYSON (JAMES). Printer, a little above Kirk Style, at the sign of the Golden Angel, Edinburgh, 1638-42. (P.) Printed and sold "The

Whole Book of Psalmes, in Prose and Meeter . . . (The CL. Psalmes of David . . . With their whole usuall tunes newly corrected & amended.) 1640."

P. I.

BRYSSON (JOHN). Music seller and publisher, Edinburgh; High Street, or South Side of Cross Well, Opposite Cross Well, 1789-c. 1811; 429 High Street, at the head of Bank Street, c. 1811-12; 16 Bank Street, c. 1812-20. Died 1818. Successor to Robert Bremner at his Edinburgh shop, of which he was said to have been manager.

BUCHINGER, BUCKENGER or BUCKINGER & SHARP. Musical instrument makers to his Royal Highness the Duke of Clarence, music sellers and publishers, 443 Strand, London, c. 1805-06. When the partnership ceased, Joseph Buchinger, Buckenger or Buckinger continued at the same address, B. Sharp set up business elsewhere.
See also Buchinger, Buckenger or Buckinger (Joseph).

BUCHINGER, BUCKENGER or BUCKINGER (JOSEPH). Musical instrument maker, music seller and publisher, 443 Strand, London, c. 1785-1811. For a short time, c. 1805-06, became Buchinger, Buckenger or Buckinger & Sharp; previously in partnership with Mrs. Elizabeth Carr, widow of Benjamin Carr, musical instrument maker of Old Round Court, Strand; partnership dissolved Michaelmas, 1782. He advertised in *The Morning Herald*, January 20, 1785, "being the only successor to the late Mr. Rauche, whose Guittars ever justly bore the preference, he continues to make them of the same pattern, having purchased his stock and utensils."

K.

BUCK (JOHN). Printer and bookbinder, Cambridge, 1625-68. (P.) Printed in conjunction with Thomas Buck "The Whole Book of Psalmes: Collected into English meeter, by Thomas Sternhold, John Hopkins, and others . . . Printed by Thomas and John Buck, printers to the Universitie of Cambridge . . . MDCXXIX."; they also printed an edition in 1630.

K. P. I.

BUCK (THOMAS). Printer and bookbinder, Cambridge, 1625-70. (P.) Printed in conjunction with John Buck "The Whole Book of Psalmes: Collected into English meeter, by Thomas Sternhold, John Hopkins, and others . . . Printed by Thomas and John Buck, printers to the Universitie of Cambridge . . . MDCXXIX."; they also printed an edition in 1630. Thomas Buck printed in conjunction with Roger Daniel "The Whole Book of Psalmes: Collected into English metre, by Thomas Sternhold, John Hopkins, and others . . . Printed by Thomas Buck and Roger Daniel, printers to the Universitie of Cambridge. 1637"; they also printed editions in 1638 and 1639.

K. P. I.

[91]

BUCKENGER or BUCKINGER (JOSEPH). *See* Buchinger, Buckenger or Buckinger.

BUCKLAND (JAMES). Bookseller and publisher, at the Buck, Paternoster Row, London, c. 1736-90. Also set up a branch shop in Chelmsford c. 1736. (P.) Printed and published some sacred music from c. 1760.
  K. P. III.

BUDD & CALKIN. *See* Calkin & Budd.

BULKLY or BULKLEY (STEPHEN). Music seller and publisher, at the Bass Violin, Newport Street, near the upper end of St. Martin's Lane, London. Advertised January 1719, "Bulkley's First Collection of Minuets and Rigadoons . . . Printed and sold by Daniel Wright and Stephen Bulkley," etc.; advertised March 1720, "Bulkley's 2d Collection of Minuets and Rigadoons (for the Year 1720) . . . Likewise 24 New Country Dances for the Year 1720 . . . likewise the whole Song of Mad Tom, by Mr. Hayden . . . All printed and sold by Dan. Wright . . . and Stephen Bulkley," etc.; advertised March 1721, "Bulkley's third Collection of the Minuets and Rigadoons for the Year 1721 . . . Likewise . . . Songs in the Opera of Astartus to be sold single. Printed for Ste. Bulkley by Daniel Wright . . . N.B. There is a new Country Dance Book for the Year 1721, and a new Book of Minuets, Rigadoons and Sebels, by Mr. Thomas Jones."

BULL (THOMAS). Musical instrument maker and music publisher, London; 34 Windmill Street, Finsbury Square, c. 1833-68; 23 Tabernacle Walk, Finsbury, c. 1868-69. Published a number of instruction books for musical instruments.

BULMER (W.) & CO. Printers, London. Printed "Anecdotes of George Frederick Handel and John Christopher Smith. With select pieces of music, composed by J. C. Smith, never before published. London: Printed by W. Bulmer and Co. Sold by Cadell and Davies . . . E. Harding . . . Birchall . . . and J. Eaton, Salisbury. 1799."

BUNTING, WALSH, PIGOTT & SHERWIN. Music and musical instrument sellers, and publishers, Dublin Harmonic Institution, 13 Westmorland Street, Dublin, c. 1825-27. Succeeded by Pigott and Sherwin.

BURCHELL *Mr.* Toy Shop, the upper end of Long Acre, near Drury Lane, London. His name appears in the imprint of "Six Solos after an easy & elegant taste for the Violoncello with a Thorough Bass for the Harpsichord. Compos'd by Sigr. Salvador Lancetti. Printed for Claudius Heron, at Mr. Burchells Toy Shop," etc., c. 1760.

BURKE (M. A.). 22 Southampton Street, Strand, London. For a few years prior to c. 1824 was an agent for the London trade of Isaac Willis, Dublin.

BURNS & LAMBERT. *See* Burns (James).

BURNS (JAMES). Bookseller and publisher, London; 1 Duke Street, Manchester Square, c. 1834-35; 17 Portman Street, Portman Square, c. 1835-51. Published a number of sacred music works. Became Burns and Lambert c. 1851.

BURTON (WILLIAM). Printer, London. Printed "A New Version of the Psalms of David, fitted to the Tunes used in Churches. By N. Brady . . . and N. Tate . . . London. Printed by W. Burton, for the Company of Stationers, 1733," etc.
    P. III.

BURY (SAMUEL) & CO. Pianoforte makers and organ builders, 113 Bishopsgate Street Within, London, c. 1787-93. Their name and address, or address only, appeared in the imprints of some of George Goulding's publications in 1788.

BUSSELL (HENRY). Music seller and publisher, Dublin, 7 Westmorland Street, c. 1852-79. Had additional premises at 39 Fleet Street, c. 1857-79; 20 Fleet Street, c. 1860-79. Became H. Bussell and Co. c. 1874: succeeded Robinson and Bussell.

BUSSELL (JAMES). Music seller, 214 Tottenham Court Road, London. Published c. 1815, "This Rose to calm my Brother's Cares. A Ballad, the poetry from Lord Byron's celebrated poem The Bride of Abydos, the music composed . . . by Louis Jansen." Thomas Phillips was afterwards at the same address.

BUTLER (RICHARD). Music seller and publisher, London; 6 Hand Court, High Holborn, c. 1842-1909; 424 Old Kent Road, c. 1909-17. Published principally sacred music. Business presumably carried on by more than one of the same name.

BUTT (RICHARD). Bookseller, London, 1681-96. (P.) Bear and Orange Tree in Princes Street, near Drury Lane; Princess Street in Covent Garden. Printed and sold in Princess Street in Covent Garden, "A Collection of One Hundred and Eighty Loyal Songs, all written since 1678 . . . The Fourth Edition with many additions. 1694."
    K. P. II. D. & M.

BUTTERWORTH, LIVESLEY & CO. Engravers, Leeds. Engraved "Sacred Harmony . . . by B. Clifford," c. 1810. Christopher Livesley was previously in business on his own account.

BUTTERWORTH (JOHN). Music engraver, London? Engraved "Dell' Arte armonica or A Treatise of the Composition of Musick . . . By Giorgio Antoniotto. Vol. the II. Engrav'd by Jnº. Butterworth. London. Printed by John Johnson . . . 1760."

BUTTON & CO. *See* Button, Whitaker & Beadnell.

BUTTON & PURDAY. Music sellers and publishers, 75 St. Paul's Church Yard, London, 1807-08. Formerly as Purday and Button 1807; Purday dropped out c. 1808, and his place taken by John Whitaker, the firm becoming Button and Whitaker.

BUTTON & WHITAKER. Music sellers and publishers, 75 St. Paul's Church Yard, London, 1808-14. Succeeded Button and Purday; became Button, Whitaker and Beadnell, or, Button, Whitaker and Co., and Button and Co., c. 1814. John Whitaker was a composer and organist.
K. G.

BUTTON, WHITAKER & BEADNELL. Music sellers and publishers, 75 St. Paul's Church Yard, London, c. 1814-19. Also as Button, Whitaker and Co. and Button and Co.; followed Button and Whitaker; succeeded by Whitaker and Co.

BUTTON (S. J.). *See* Button & Purday; Button & Whitaker; Button, Whitaker & Beadnell; Purday & Button.

BUTTON (SIMON). Music seller and publisher, Anglesey Street, Dublin. Advertised July 1713, "Vocal and Instrumental Musick." Published "the Birthday Ode for Queen Anne, composed by John Sigismund Cousser, and performed at the Dublin Castle Concert on February 6th, 1712, and the King's Birthday Ode, May 28, 1719." (Grattan Flood.) Also published some sheet songs.

BUTTS (THOMAS). Rattcliff Row, Old Street, London. Published two editions, c. 1760 and c. 1765, of "Harmonia-Sacra, or A Choice Collection of Psalm and Hymn Tunes, in three Parts, for the Voice, Harpsichord, and Organ," etc.
K.

BYE & LAW. Printers, St. John's Square, Clerkenwell, London. Printed "Select Psalms for the use of Portman-Chapel, near Portman Square. MDCCCIV."

BYNNEMAN (HENRY), Printer, London, various addresses, 1566-83. (M.) Printed "The Noble Arte of Venerie or Hunting . . . [By George Turbervile.] Imprinted by Henry Bynneman, for Christopher

Barker," c. 1575. Contains music of "The Measures of blowing, set downe in the notes."
 M. S.

BYRD (WILLIAM). Composer; obtained with Thomas Tallis, January 1575, patent from Queen Elizabeth for printing and selling music and music paper for twenty-one years. They imported a fount of type from Johann Petreius of Nuremberg and employed Thomas Vautrollier, Blackfriars, London, to print for them "Cantiones, quæ ab argumento sacræ vocantur . . . 1575." The type then remained unused until after the death of Vautrollier in 1587, when it passed into the possession of Thomas Este (East), some of whose imprints describe him as the assigne of William Byrd. Tallis died in Nov. 1585, after which Byrd held the patent alone.
 G. S.

C., M. *See* Clark (Mary).

C., R. *See* Carr (Richard).

C., R. *See* also Cayley (Robert).

C., R. *See* also Cotes (Richard).

C., T. *See* Cotes (Thomas).

C., W.; C¹., W. *See* Campbell (William).

CADELL & DAVIES. Booksellers, 144 Strand, London. Their names appear in the imprint of "Anecdotes of George Frederick Handel and John Christopher Smith. With select pieces of music, composed by J. C. Smith, never before published. London: Printed by W. Bulmer and Co. Sold by Cadell and Davies . . . E. Harding . . . Birchall . . and J. Eaton, Salisbury. 1799."

CAHUSAC & SONS. *See* Cahusac (Thomas) *the Elder*.

CAHUSAC (THOMAS) *the Elder*. Musical instrument maker, music seller and publisher, at the sign of the Two Flutes and Violin, opposite St. Clement's Church in the Strand, afterwards 196 Strand, London, c. 1755-94. Took his sons into the business which became Cahusac and Sons, c. 1794-98; after his death in 1798, the business was continued by Thomas and William M. Cahusac.
 K. G.

CAHUSAC (THOMAS) *the Younger*. Musical instrument maker, music seller and publisher, London; 4 Great Newport Street, c. 1781-94; with the firm of Cahusac and Sons, 196 Strand, c. 1794-98; partner

in T. and W. M. Cahusac, 196 Strand, 1798-August, 1800; alone at 41 Haymarket, August 1800-c. 1805; 114 New Bond Street, c. 1805-1808; 42 Wigmore Street, c. 1808-14.
K. G.

CAHUSAC (THOMAS) *the Younger* & (WILLIAM MAURICE). Musical instrument makers, music sellers and publishers, 196 Strand, London, 1798-August 1800. Partnership dissolved August, 1800, and each continued in business independently; previously with Cahusac and Sons.
K. G.

CAHUSAC (WILLIAM MAURICE). Musical instrument maker, music seller and publisher, London; 196 Strand, August 1800-c. 1811; 79 High Holborn, c. 1811-16. Previously with Cahusac and Sons, and T. and W. M. Cahusac.
K. G.

CALCUT, *Mr.* Banbury. His name appears in the imprint of "A Choice Collection of Church Music; containing sixteen Anthems, set by different authors . . . with a select number of Psalm Tunes . . . The whole collected and enlarged by Joseph Watts, of Fennycompton. Sold by Joseph Watts . . . and by Mr. Calcut, in Banbury, Oxon, 1749."

CALDER (THOMAS). Engraver, Edinburgh? Engraved "The Common Tunes; or, Scotland's Church Musick made plain. By Mr. Thomas Bruce Schoolmaster in Edinburgh. Edinburgh: Printed for the Author . . . M.DCC.XXVI."

CALKIN & BUDD. Book and music sellers, 118 Pall Mall, London, c. 1828-53. Published a number of musical works; Joseph Calkin, a violinist, married in 1813 the widow of John Budd the bookseller; the business was carried on as Budd and Calkin until c. 1828, when the names were transposed to Calkin and Budd; stock of music offered for sale by Puttick and Simpson April 7, May 19, August 27, 1852, and August 17, 1853.
Catalogue of a miscellaneous Collection of Music . . . 1844. pp. 202. 8º. (B.M. 011904. aaa. 82.)

CALKIN (WILLIAM). Dealer in music and musical instruments, Arundel, Sussex. Printed and sold c. 1820, "A Set of New Quadrilles and a Waltz for the Piano Forte . . . By William Calkin, Organist of Arundel Sussex."

CALLCOTT (JOHN HUTCHINGS). Music seller and publisher, 22 Great Marlborough Street, London, 1826-c. 1830.

CAMBRIDGE, PRINTERS TO THE UNIVERSITY OF. *See* Buck (Thomas); Daniel (Roger).

CAMERON (DUNCAN). Copper plate engraver and printer, Edinburgh. Printed "A Collection of Scots Reels, or Country Dances and Minuets . . . Composed by John Riddle at Ayr, and sold by Himself there; likewise by Mr. Robt. Bremner in Edinr. also at his shope . . . in the Strand, London . . . Wm. Edward, Sculpt. Dun Cameron prints it, Edinr.", c. 1766.
P. III.

CAMPBELL (ALEXANDER). Printer, at the Westminster Printing Office, near New Palace Yard, London, c. 1725-28. His name appears in the imprint of "The Tonometer . . . By Ambrose Warren . . . 1725," in conjunction with those of John Cluer and B. Creake. He also acted as selling agent for Cluer's other musical publications.
P. III.

CAMPBELL (WILLIAM). Musician, music seller and publisher, London; 93 Berwick Street, Soho, c. 1778-82; 11 New Street, Covent Garden, c. 1782-95; 8 Dean Street, Soho, c. 1795-1802; between c. 1802- c. 1815 his addresses were 4 Market Row, East Street, St. James's Market; 37 New Compton Street, Soho; 31 King Street, Soho; 32 Dean Street, Soho. Some single sheet songs bear only the initials W. C., or, W. C¹.
K.

CANTRELL (WILLIAM). Bookseller, Derby, 1718-27. (P.) His name appears in the imprint of "A Collection of Psalm-Tunes; with Great Variety of Hymns and Anthems compos'd by the best Masters . . . By James Green. The Fourth edition . . . London. Printed by William Pearson, for the Author: and sold by . . . W. Cantrell in Derby . . . 1718."
P. II.

CARD (WILLIAM). Musical instrument maker and music publisher, London; 98 Quadrant, Regent Street, c. 1825-43; 29 St. James's Street, 1843-62.

CARDON (P. H.). Music seller? 1 Lisle Street, Leicester Square, London. Sold "Three Quartetts for two Violins, Tenor & Violoncello. Composed & dedicated to Dr. Haydn by W. A. Mozart," c. 1796.

CARLETON (OSWELL). See Carlton (Oswald).

CARLTON (OSWALD). Bookseller and publisher, Gainsborough. His name appears in the imprint of "A Collection of Psalm-Tunes; with Great Variety of Hymns and Anthems compos'd by the best Masters . . . By James Green. The Fourth edition . . . London. Printed by William Pearson, for the Author: and sold by . . . Oswell Carleton in Gainsborough . . . 1718"; also in the Fifth edition "London. Printed by William Pearson, for Oswald Carlton . . . 1724," and Sixth edition "London: Printed by William Pearson . . . for the Author; and sold by . . . O. Carlton," etc., c. 1730.

P. III.

CARMICHAEL (RICHARD). Engraver, Back of the Guard, Edinburgh. His name appears in the imprint of "A Collection of Lessons for the Harpsichord or Piano & Forte. Composed by Ferdinando Tenducci . . . Printed for the Author & to be gott at his Lodgings . . . & Rich^d. Carmichael," etc., c. 1768.

CARNAN (THOMAS) & NEWBERY (FRANCIS). Booksellers, St. Paul's Churchyard, London. Their names appear in the imprint of "A Set of new Psalms and Anthems . . . By William Knapp . . . The Eighth edition . . . London: Printed by George Bigg, for J. and F. Rivington, T. Carnan and F. Newbery, Jun. . . . MDCCLXX." Thomas Carnan was in business as a bookseller and publisher at 65 St. Paul's Churchyard 1737-88. (P.) On the death of John Newbery in 1767, he continued the business in partnership with Francis Newbery, son of John Newbery; Francis Newbery was at the Crown, Paternoster Row, 1765 or earlier, and in St. Paul's Churchyard 1767-76.

P. III.

CARPENTER (JAMES) & (THOMAS). Booksellers, book and music publishers, 14 Old Bond Street, London. Published some music for Thomas Moore and his friends c. 1802-06; James Carpenter was alone in business in 1803 and after.

K.

CARR (BENJAMIN). *See* Carr (Elizabeth) & Buchinger, Buckenger or Buckinger (Joseph).

CARR (ELIZABETH) & BUCHINGER, BUCKENGER or BUCKINGER (JOSEPH). Musical instrument makers, Old Round Court, Strand, London. Published "Six Sonatas for the Piano Forte or Harpsichord with an Accompaniment for a Violin and Violoncello by G. G. Lang," c. 1780. They dissolved partnership Michaelmas 1782; Buchinger afterwards set up in business at another address; Elizabeth Carr was the widow of Benjamin Carr, musical instrument maker. Benjamin Carr, singer, composer etc., probably a relative of Elizabeth Carr, opened a music publishing business in New York, 1793, and another branch at High Street, Philadelphia, the same year. The New York branch was sold to James Hewitt in 1797. Carr died in 1831.

CARR (J.). Music seller, Middle Row, Holborn, London. Published "Come Britannia," c. 1770; "Sing old Rose and burn the Bellows. A favourite Glee for 3 voices. Sung by Mr. Bannister &c in the Suicide," c. 1778; "Twelve Voluntaries for the Organ or Harpsichord selected

from the Works of several Eminent Masters (never before published),"
c. 1780. May have been the same person as Joseph Carr who opened
a music publishing business in Baltimore, U.S.A., in 1794.

CARR (JOHN). Bookseller, publisher, music seller and musical instrument
maker, London; at (or, near) the Middle Temple Gate, near Temple
Bar, Fleet Street, c. 1672-95; under the King's Head Tavern in
Chancery Lane End, 1684, probably a temporary address while
premises at Middle Temple Gate were being rebuilt. One work, 1692,
gives the address Inner Temple Gate, probably in error. Carr's name
appears as music seller on some works together with the name of his
friend John Playford the elder, 1681-84; from 1685 with the name
of Henry Playford, and from 1687 with the name of Samuel Scott,
who had at first a shop of his own near Temple Bar. In 1689 Carr
and Scott were together at Middle Temple Gate, Scott taking over the
business c. 1695.
K. G. P. II.

CARR (RICHARD). Music publisher, at the Middle Temple Gate, London,
1685-87. Son of John Carr and musician in Charles the Second's
band; published some works in association with Henry Playford; in
1684 John Playford the elder handed over the active control of his
business to his son Henry Playford and Richard Carr; issued some
works bearing only the initials R. C.
K. D. & M.

CARRICK (A.). Bookseller, Saltmarket, Glasgow. Published "The
Musical Repository: a collection of favourite Scotch, English, and
Irish Songs set to music . . . 1799."

CARTE (RICHARD). See Rudall, Carte & Co.; Rudall, Rose, Carte & Co.

CARTIER, Mr. Music seller? Spur Street, Leicester Fields, London.
His name appears in the imprint of "Six Sonatas for the Forte Piano
or Harpsichord with a Violin & Violoncello accompagnem^t. Composed by J. C. Moller. London Printed for the Author & sold at
Mr. Cartiers . . . and by J. Betz," etc., c. 1775.

CARUSO, Mr. Music seller, Coventry Court, Haymarket, London. His
name appears in the imprint of "Six Sonatas for the Harpsichord
with an Accompanyment for a Violin or German Flute. Dedicated to
Miss Blosset. Composed by Sig^r. Mattia Vento. London. Printed by
the Author, and sold at M^r. Caruso's Music Shop," etc., c. 1765.

CASLON (THOMAS). Bookseller and publisher, Stationers' Court, Ludgate Street, London, c. 1750-83. (P.) His name appears in the
imprints of "The Beggar's Opera . . . To which is prefixed the overture
in score: And the musick to each song. London: Printed for W.
Strahan, T. Lowndes, T. Caslon, W. Griffin, W. Nicoll, S. Bladon, and

[99]

G. Kearsly. MDCCLXXI."; also in two editions published 1777; "The Mock Doctor: or the Dumb Lady cur'd. A Comedy . . . With the musick prefix'd to each song. A new edition. With additional songs and alterations. Printed for T. Caslon . . . 1771 "; "The Whole Book of Psalms . . . by John Playford. The Twentieth Edition . . . London: Printed by R. Brown . . . For . . . T. Longman, and T. Caslon in Paternoster-Row . . . 1757."
    P. III.

CAULFIELD (HENRY). *See* Caulfield (John) *the Younger* & (Henry).

CAULFIELD (JOHN) *the Elder*. Music engraver and printer, London, c. 1765-90. At 5 Piccadilly, near the Haymarket, c. 1780-90; was apprenticed to John Walsh the younger.
    K.

CAULFIELD (JOHN) *the Younger* & (HENRY). Music engravers, printers and publishers, 36 Piccadilly, London, c. 1799 or earlier - 1808, after which John Caulfield continued the business alone. He compiled and published at 7 Fountain Court, Strand, "A Collection of the vocal music in Shakespeare's Plays," which was first issued in parts c. 1825 and afterwards in 2 volumes, 1864, by Caulfield, with later editions by other publishers.
    K.

CAULFIELD (JOSEPH). Music engraver, printer and publisher, 436 Strand, London. Published, "The Favorite March, now performing by the Duke of York's Band and the Royal Westminster Volunteers, composed by Mrs. Bland," c. 1802; "The Little Butcher Boy. A new song, written and sung by Mr. Newitzer of the Theatre Royal Drury Lane," c. 1802.

CAYLEY (ROBERT). Printer, London. "R. C.," identified by Steele as the mark of Robert Cayley, is in the border of "Manuale ad vsum per celebris ecclesie Sarisburiensis. Londini noviter Impressum Anno Domini. M.D.Liiii."
    S.

CELLINI (N.). Music publisher, 315 Oxford Street, nearly opposite Holles Street, London, c. 1836.

CHALLONER (NEVILLE BUTLER). *See* Skillern & Challoner.

CHALMERS' MUSIC PRESS. *See* Chalmers (James) *the Younger*.

CHALMERS (JAMES) *the Elder*. Printer, Aberdeen, 1736-64. (P.) Printed and sold, "A New and correct Set of Church Tunes . . . The Third edition, collected by Andrew Tait Organist. 1753."
    P. III.

CHALMERS (JAMES) *the Younger*. Printer, Chalmers' Music Press, Aberdeen, 1764-1810. (P.) Printed "A Collection of Church Tunes in Three and Four Parts together with the Chants used in Episcopal Congregations. Aberdeen. Printed at Chalmers' Music Press," c. 1790, or a few years later.
P. III.

CHALMERS (JAMES). Bookseller, printer and musical instrument dealer, Castle Street, Dundee. Published c. 1844, "The Widow Malone. A favourite song, the words from Charles O'Malley The Irish Dragoon . . . The symphonies and accompaniments by John Daniel."

CHALONER (GEORGE). Bookseller, Church Street, Sheffield. Printed and published c. 1827, "Sacred music: consisting of original Psalm and Hymn Tunes, Anthems, Chorusses, etc., composed and arranged for four voices . . . By Isaac Barraclough, Derby."

CHAMBERLAINE, *Mr.* Bookseller? Milk Street, Cheapside, London. His name appears in the imprint of "An Introduction to Singing, or the Rudiments of Music . . . By James Hewett. Sold by the Author . . . Mr. Buckland . . . and by Mr. Chamberlaine in Milk Street, Cheapside. MDCCLXV."

CHAMPANTE & WHITROW. Wholesale stationers, Jewry Street, Aldgate, London. Published "The Apollo: or, Harmonic Miscellany: containing English, Scotch, & Irish Songs, Ducts, Ballads, &c. &c. with the music, accurately printed for the Voice, Violin, German Flute, &c. &c. . . . 1814."

CHAPMAN (EDMUND). Music publisher, Dukes Court, Bow Street, Covent Garden, London. Published "Six Solos for the German-Flute, Hautboy, or Violin, with a Thorough Bass for the Harpsichord. Compos'd by Sigr. Alessandro Bezozzi," 1759; "Sei Sonate . . . Composte dal Sigr. Tomaso Prota di Napoli," 1760; "Six Duetts for German Flutes, or Violins. Compos'd by Signr. Dothel, Junr.," 1762. Subscriber to Thomas Sanders Dupuis's "Six Concertos for the Organ or Harpsichord," c. 1760.

CHAPPELL & CO. Music and musical instrument sellers and publishers, London; 124 New Bond Street, 1811-c. 1819; 50 New Bond Street, c. 1819-26. Partners at the commencement of the business were Samuel Chappell (previously employed by Robert Birchall), Johann Baptist Cramer and Francis Tatton Latour. Cramer withdrew after a few years, and Latour set up his own business, c. 1826, taking over the premises at 50 New Bond Street. Name of firm became Samuel Chappell, at 135 New Bond Street, c. 1826-30; 50 New Bond Street, c. 1830-34, having taken over the premises and stock of F. T. Latour. Samuel Chappell died 1834; business continued at 50 New Bond

Street by his widow, Emily Chappell, and his two sons, Thomas Patey and William, who published as "Chappell's." In 1844 William went into partnership with Cramer and Beale as Cramer, Beale and Chappell; Mrs. Chappell and Thomas Patey Chappell remained in the old firm, which became Chappell and Co. in 1856, under which name it has continued until the present time at 50 New Bond Street, with additional premises at 49 New Bond Street ,c. 1857-c. 1906; 51 New Bond Street, c. 1869-98; 52 New Bond Street, c. 1877-98; 15 Poultry, c. 1879-90; 14 Poultry, c. 1885-90.

K. G.

See also Chappell (Samuel).

CHAPPELL, LONGMAN & BATES. *See* Longman & Bates.

CHAPPELL (EMILY), *Mrs. See* Chappell & Co.

CHAPPELL (SAMUEL). Music seller and publisher, London; 135 New Bond Street, c. 1826-30; 50 New Bond Street, c. 1830-34. Sometimes described as Samuel Chappell and Co.; previously a partner in Chappell and Co.; took over premises and business of F. T. Latour at 50 New Bond Street; for a short time in 1829 was a partner in Chappell, Longman and Bates; died in 1834; business continued by his widow, Emily Chappell, and his two sons, Thomas Patey and William.

K.

See also Chappell & Co.; Longman & Bates.

CHAPPELL (THOMAS PATEY). *See* Chappell & Co.

CHAPPELL (WILLIAM). *See* Chappell & Co.; Cramer, Beale & Chappell.

CHAPPLE (CLEMENT). Bookseller and stationer, 66 Pall Mall, London. Published for the author, "The Musical Mentor, or St. Cecilia at School: consisting of short and single essays and songs . . . the whole written and composed by Mr. Dibdin"; in 26 numbers, c. 1805. Printed for and sold "The Boat Song or Gallant & Gaily on the Waves riding. The melody by an Amateur, arranged for 3 voices . . . by Wm. Hawes," etc., c. 1805.

CHARNLEY (WILLIAM). Bookseller and publisher, Newcastle-on-Tyne, 1749-1803. (P.) At the Bridge End; The Great Market. Published c. 1753, "The Psalms of David . . . by I. Watts . . . The Eighteenth edition . . . (Tunes in the Tenor Part fitted to the several metres.) Printed for W. Charnley, at the Bridge End Newcastle."

P. III.

CHARTERIS (HENRY). Bookseller and printer, Edinburgh, 1568-99. (M.) Printed "The Psalmes of David in Metre according as they are sung in the Kirk of Scotland . . . 1595"; also an edition 1596.

K. M. S.

CHAUKLIN, *Mrs.* Bookseller, Taunton. Her name appears in the imprint of "A Sett of new Psalm-Tunes and Anthems . . . By William Knapp . . . London: Printed by W. Hutchinson, for the Author, and sold by him in Poole; Mr. George Torbuck in Winbourn . . . Mrs. Chauklin in Taunton . . . MDCCXXXVIII."

CHESTER (CHARLES). Music and book seller, Newcastle-under-Lyme. Printed and sold, c. 1810, "A Collection of Psalm and Hymn Tunes, as sung at Newcastle Church . . . with a copious Selection of Chaunts the chords express'd in notes for the Piano Forte or Organ, by J. Wardle, Organist."

CHEYNE (N. R.). Bookseller, Edinburgh. His name appears in the imprint of "The Edinburgh Musical Miscellany: a collection of the most approved Scotch, English, and Irish songs, set to music. Selected by D. Sime, Edinburgh. Edinburgh: Printed for W. Gordon . . . N. R. Cheyne . . . Edinburgh . . . MDCCXCII." In volume II the imprint reads, "Edinburgh: Printed for John Elder, T. Brown, and C. Elliot, Edinburgh; and W. Coke, Leith. MDCCXCIII."

CHILD (EBENEZER). Music seller, 4 High Street, Hereford. Published "The Ivy Wreath; three original Waltzes . . . Composed by Mrs. Spozzi." c. 1838.

CHISWELL (RICHARD). Bookseller, London, 1666-1711; Two Angels and Crown, Little Britain; Rose and Crown, St. Paul's Churchyard. (P.) His name appears in the imprint of "The Psalms and Hymns, usually sung in the Churches and Tabernacles of St. Martins in the Fields, and St. James's Westminster. London, Printed by R. Everingham for Ric. Chiswell, at the Rose and Crown, in St. Paul's Churchyard. 1688."
P. I.

CHRISTIAN. *See* Tedder & Christian.

CHRISTMAS (CHARLES). Music seller and publisher, London; 36 Pall Mall (Opera and Music Saloon), 1816-19; 15 New Bond Street, 1819-c. 1820. Previously partner in the firm of Falkner & Christmas. K.

CHRISTY (J.). Dublin. Published the second edition of Joseph C. Walker's "Historical Memoirs of the Irish Bards," 1818. K.

CHURCH (JOHN). Music publisher, London. Published works in conjunction with Henry Playford 1695-96. D. & M.

CHURCHILL (AWNSHAM) & (JOHN). Booksellers, at the Black Swan, Paternoster Row, London, 1690-1714. (P.) Published in conjunction with L. Meredith "The Psalms of David in Metre: Fitted to the tunes used in Parish-Churches. By John Patrick. London, Printed for A. & J. Churchill . . . and L. Meredith . . . 1698." May have published earlier editions of the Psalms.
P. II.

CHURCHILL (WILLIAM). Bookseller, London, 1688-1736. (P.) His name appears in the imprint of "The Psalms of David in Metre: Fitted to the tunes used in Parish-Churches. By John Patrick . . . London, Printed for W. Churchill . . . MDCCXVIII."
P. II.

CHURNSIDE & WILSON. Printers, Royal Bank Close, Edinburgh. Their names appear in the imprint of "The Songster's Favourite: or, a new collection, containing forty . . . songs, duets, trios &c. Adapted to the voice, harpsichord, or German flute . . . By Laurence Ding . . . Edinburgh: Printed for the compiler, and sold by him at Churnside and Wilson's Printing Office," etc., c. 1785.

CIANCHETTINI & SPERATI. Publishers and importers of classical music, 5 Princes Street, Cavendish Square, London, c. 1807-11. Partners were Francis Cianchettini and B. Sperati; continued in business independently after partnership was dissolved.

CIANCHETTINI (FRANCIS). Importer and publisher of classical music, 123 New Bond Street, London, c. 1811-12. Published c. 1811, "Fantasie pour le piano forte, composée . . . par J. L. Dussek. Op. 76." Previously a partner in Cianchettini and Sperati. Notice of his bankruptcy appeared in *The London Gazette*, Mar. 17-21, 1812, where he was described as a "music seller, dealer and chapman."

CIMADOR (GIAMBATTISTA). An Italian whose real name was Cimadoro. *See* Monzani & Cimador.

CITTADINI (GIACOMO PINCHIORI). Music publisher, 57 Poland Street, Oxford Street, London, c. 1815-20.

CLARE COURT. Some music was issued c. 1815-20 bearing the imprint "London, printed and sold at No. 1, Clare Court, Drury Lane."
K.

CLARK (ANDREW). Printer, Aldersgate Street, London, 1670-78. (P.) His name appears in the second title of "New Ayres and Dialogues composed for Voices and Viols, of two, three, and four Parts: Together with Lessons for Viols or Violins, by John Banister . . . and Thomas Low . . . London: Printed by M. C. for H. Brome . . . MDCLXXVIII."

The second title reads "New Ayres, Dialogues, and Trialogues, composed to be sung either to the Theorbo-Lute, or Bass-Viol. By sundry Authors. London, Imprinted by Andrew Clark, for Henry Brome . . . MDCLXXVIII." Succeeded by his widow Mary Clark.

    K. P. II. D. & M.

CLARK or CLARKE (FRANCIS). Printer, London, 1687-88. Printed in conjunction with others, "Vinculum Societatis, or The Tie of good Company. Being a choice collection of the newest songs now in use. With thorow bass to each song for the harpsichord, theorbo, or bass-viol. The first book of this character. London, Printed by F. Clark, T. Moore, and J. Heptinstall, for John Carr, and R. C. . . . 1687."

    P. II. D. & M.

CLARK (J.). Plate and seal engraver, The first forestair, below the head of Forrester's Wynd, Edinburgh. Published "Flores Musicæ, or the Scots Musician, being a general collection of the most celebrated Scots Tunes, Reels, and Minuets . . . 1st of June, 1773," etc.

    K.

CLARK or CLARKE (JOHN) *Junior*. Bookseller, London, 1646-78. (P.) Published "Parthenia, or The Mayden-Head of the first Musicke that ever was printed for the Virginalls. Composed By three famous Masters: William Byrd, D^r. John Bull, and Orlando Gibbons, Gentlemen of his Majesties Chappell . . . Printed for John Clark Junior, and are to be sold at his Shop, in the Porch entring into Mercers Chappell. 1646." He also issued editions in 1651 and 1655 with the imprint "Printed for John Clarke, at the lower end of Cheapside, entring into Mercers Chappell."

    K. P. II.

CLARK or CLARKE (JOHN). Bookseller, at the Bible and Crown, in the Poultry, and at various addresses, London, 1697-1723. (P.) His name appears in the imprints of "A Collection of Tunes, suited to the various metres in Mr. Watts's imitation of the Psalms of David, or Dr. Patrick's version . . . London: Printed by W. Pearson . . . for John Clark, at the Bible and Crown, and R. Ford in the Poultry, and R. Cruttenden . . . 1719"; "The Psalms of David . . . By I. Watts . . . (Tunes in the Tenor part fitted to the several metres.) London: Printed for John Clark . . . and Richard Ford . . . MDCCXXII."; also the seventh edition, "Printed for John Clark, and Richard Hett, at the Bible and Crown; and Richard Ford . . . both in the Poultry. MDCCXXIX."

    P. II.

CLARK (MARY). Printer, Aldersgate Street, London, 1677-96. (P.) Widow and successor of Andrew Clark. Her initials appear in the imprints of "New Ayres and Dialogues composed for Voices and Viols, of two, three, and four Parts: Together with Lessons for Viols or

Violins, by John Banister . . . and Thomas Low . . . London: Printed by M. C. for H. Brome . . . MDCLXXVIII." On a second title the imprint reads "London, Imprinted by Andrew Clark, for Henry Brome . . . MDCLXXVIII."; "A Compendium of practical Musick . . . The third editio. By Christopher Simpson . . . London, Printed by M. C. for Henry Brome . . . MDCLXXVIII."
P. II. D. & M. (C., M.)

CLARKE (FRANCIS). *See* Clark or Clarke.

CLARKE (J.). Music seller, St. Martin's Court, Leicester Square, London. Published c. 1785, "The Sweets of Love. A favorite Song for the Voice, Hapsichord [sic], Violin, German Flute, or Guittar. London Printed for J. Clarke at his Music Shop," etc.

CLARKE (JOHN). Music seller and publisher, The Golden Viol, St. Paul's Church Yard, London, c. 1681-95. Premises probably taken over by John Hare, August, 1695.
K. P. II. D. & M.

CLARKE (JOHN). Bookseller, at the Bible, under the Royal Exchange, Cornhill, London. Published 1729, "The Patron: or, The Stateman's Opera, of two acts . . . To which is added the musick to each song . . . London: Printed by W. Pearson, for John Clarke," etc.

CLARKE (JOHN). Bookseller, at the Bible and Crown, in the Poultry, London.
See Clark or Clarke (John).

CLARKE (JOHN) *Junior*. Bookseller, in the Porch entering Mercers' Chapel, London.
See Clark or Clarke (John) *Junior*.

CLAVELL (ROBERT). Bookseller, London; Stags Head, near St. Gregory's Church in St. Paul's Churchyard, 1658-60; Stag in Ivy Lane, 1665-?; Cross Keys Court, Little Britain, 1670-74; at the Peacock, at the West end of St. Paul's Churchyard, 1674-1711. (P.) Published "The Psalter, or Psalms of David paraphrased into verse, set to new tunes, the 3rd edition . . . By Richard Goodridge . . . Printed for R. Clavell . . . 1685"; "A Short Discourse Upon the Doctrine of our Baptismal Covenant . . . By Thomas Bray, D.D. (An Appendix to the Discourse.) London, Printed by E. Holt, for Rob. Clavell . . . 1697." The appendix contains five psalm tunes.
K. P. I.

CLAVELL (ROGER). Bookseller, at the Peacock, Fleet Street, London, 1695-98. (P.) His name appears in the imprint of "The Psalms of David, in English Metre; translated from the original, and suited to all

[106]

the tunes now sung in Churches: With the additions of several new. By Luke Milbourne . . . London, Printed for W. Rogers . . . R. Clavill . . . B. Tooke . . . J. Lawrence . . . and J. Taylor . . . 1698."
P. II.

CLAVILL (R.). *See* Clavell (Roger).

CLAYTON (WILLIAM). Bookseller, Manchester, c. 1700-c. 1719. (P.) His name appears in the imprint of "The Psalm Singer's Compleat Companion." By Elias Hall. "Printed for D. Midwinter . . . and sold by W. Clayton . . . 1708."
P. II.

CLEAVER (WILLIAM JONES). Bookseller and publisher, London; 30 King Street, Portman Square, c. 1832-35; 80 Baker Street, Portman Square, c. 1835-48; 46 Piccadilly, c. 1848-53. Published a small amount of music.

CLEMENTI & CO., or, MUZIO CLEMENTI & CO.
See Clementi, Banger, Collard, Davis & Collard; Clementi, Banger, Hyde, Collard & Davis; Clementi, Collard & Collard; Clementi, Collard, Davis & Collard.

CLEMENTI, BANGER, COLLARD, DAVIS & COLLARD. Musical instrument makers, music sellers and publishers, 26 Cheapside, and 195 Tottenham Court Road, London, c. 1810-18. Also known as Clementi and Co. Succeeded Clementi, Banger, Hyde, Collard and Davis; Banger withdrew c. 1818 and the firm became Clementi, Collard, Davis and Collard.
K. G.

CLEMENTI, BANGER, HYDE, COLLARD & DAVIS. Musical instrument makers, music sellers and publishers, 26 Cheapside, London, c. 1801-10. From c. 1806 had additional premises at 195 Tottenham Court Road; also published as Muzio Clementi and Co., and Clementi and Co.; Hyde withdrew c. 1810 and another Collard came into the business, which became Clementi, Banger, Collard, Davis and Collard. Clementi had previously been a partner in the firm of John Longman, Clementi and Co.
K. G.

CLEMENTI, COLLARD & COLLARD. Musical instrument makers, music sellers and publishers, 26 Cheapside and 195 Tottenham Court Road, London, c. 1822-30. Also known as Clementi and Co. Succeeded Clementi, Collard, Davis and Collard; Clementi withdrew c. 1830 and the firm continued as Collard and Collard.
K. G.

CLEMENTI, COLLARD, DAVIS & COLLARD. Musical instrument makers, music sellers and publishers, 26 Cheapside and 195 Tottenham Court Road, London, c. 1818-22. Also known as Clementi and Co. Succeeded Clementi, Banger, Collard, Davis and Collard; Davis dropped out c. 1822 and the firm became Clementi, Collard and Collard.
K. G.

CLEMENTI (MUZIO).
See Clementi, Banger, Collard, Davis & Collard; Clementi, Banger, Hyde, Collard & Davis; Clementi, Collard & Collard; Clementi, Collard, Davis & Collard; Longman (John), Clementi & Co.

CLEMENTS (HENRY). Bookseller, Half Moon, St. Paul's Churchyard, London, 1707-19. (P.) His name appears in the imprint of "The Psalms of David in Metre: Fitted to the tunes used in Parish-Churches. By John Patrick . . . London, Printed for W. Churchill . . . H. Clements . . . MDCCXVIII."
P. II.

CLEMENTS (J.). 15 Mealcheapen Street, Worcester. Printed and published c. 1828, "I do not love thee, the words by Mrs. Opie, the music composed by G. A. Barker."

CLIFFORD (W.). Leeds. Published c. 1810, "Sacred Harmony. Being an entire new Set of Psalm Tunes . . . figured & adapted for the Organ or Piano-Forte &c. by B. Clifford. Late 1st West York Militia."

CLIPSHAM (JOHN). Market Harborough, Leicester. Published "The Divine Psalmist's Companion. Being, in three parts, a collection of the best and most usefull tunes now extant . . . 1753."

CLOWES (WILLIAM). Music and general printers, London; 20 Villiers Street, Strand, 1803-c. 1813, or before; 6 Northumberland Court, Strand, c. 1813, or before, –1826; Duke Street, Stamford Street, Blackfriars, and 14 Charing Cross, c. 1826-April 1835. Continued as William Clowes and Sons, with principal places of business at Duke Street, Stamford Street, Blackfriars, May 1835-1936, afterwards renamed Duchy Street, 1937-41; 6 Arlington Street, 1941-46; 2 New Street Square, 1946-47; Little New Street, 1947 to present time. Had additional premises at 14 Charing Cross, May 1835-c. 1901; 28 Great Windmill Street, c. 1901-36, also with No. 27 from c. 1902; 51, 52 and 53 Brewer Street, Regent Street, c. 1901-31. Printers of "Hymns Ancient and Modern," with publishing offices at 21 Charing Cross, c. 1869-71; 13 Charing Cross, c. 1871-92; 13 and 14 Charing Cross, c. 1892-1901; 34 and 35 Southampton Street, Strand, c. 1901-1902; 23 Cockspur Street, Charing Cross, c. 1902-13; 31 Haymarket,

c. 1913-20; 94 Jermyn Street, 1920-40; Axtell House, Warwick Street, c. 1941-46; continued at the principal place of business. Also had offices for the publications of the Council of Law Reporting, and were code publishers and compilers at various addresses; with printing works at Beccles, Suffolk. The business was turned into a limited liability company in 1881. One of William Clowes's first musical works was C. F. Abel's "Adagios in score & J. B. Cramer's Specimens in the Fugue style," 1820 (Haas, Catalogue 20, No. 6), and he effected considerable improvements in music typography; other principal works being John Parry's "A Selection of Welsh Melodies," published by J. Power, 1822; "The Harmonicon," 1823-33, "The Musical Library" (Charles Knight) 1834-37, and "Sacred Minstrelsy," 1834-35. "The Musical Library" has an excellent introduction on the subject of music printing. Later the firm carried out other improvements in musical typography.

CLUER (ELIZABETH). Printer, publisher, etc., at Widow Cluer's Printing Office (Cluer's Printing Office, The Printing Office), in Bow Church Yard, London, October 1728-c. 1730. Succeeded her husband, John Cluer, and continued to issue bills, labels, pictures, music, etc., and Dr. Bateman's Pectoral Drops. Married Thomas Cobb, her late husband's foreman, c. 1730, who thus succeeded to the business.
K. G. P. III.

CLUER (JOHN). Printer and publisher of labels, titles, ballads, chap-books, music etc., at the Printing-house in Bow Church Yard, Cheapside, London, 1715, or earlier-October 1728. The address was variously given as Cluer's Printing Office etc.; Cluer's Printing Office at the Maidenhead, etc.; The Printing Office, etc.; The Printing and Engraving Office, etc. Publications were engraved and also printed from type, and included Handel's "Suites de Pieces" and some of his operas, musical playing cards, etc. Published a number of works in conjunction with Bezaleel Creake. Cluer also had an interest, with others, in the preparation and sale of Dr. Bateman's Pectoral Drops, and other specifics. Succeeded by his widow Elizabeth Cluer.
K. G. P. III.

CLUNCH. See Lunch (C.).

CLUSE. See Harrison, Cluse & Co.

COBB & WATLEN. Music and musical instrument sellers and publishers, London; 19 Tavistock Street, Covent Garden, c. 1800-05; 186 Piccadilly, c. 1805-06. John Watlen previously in business in Edinburgh; continued on his own account after the partnership with Cobb was dissolved.
K.
See also Watlen (John).

[109]

COBB (THOMAS). Printer, engraver and publisher, at the Printing Office in Bow Church Yard, or, The Printing House at the Maidenhead, the lower end of Bow Church Yard, against the South Door of Bow Church, London, c. 1730-36. Married Elizabeth Cluer, widow of John Cluer (both of whom had employed him), and carried on the business; issued music, engraved and from type, musical playing cards, bills, labels, pictures, etc., and sold Dr. Bateman's Pectoral Drops. Assigned and sold the business to his brother-in-law, William Dicey of Northampton, c. October 1736, who had been associated with him in it.
 K. (Cluer). P. III.
 See also Dicey (William).

COCHRAN (JAMES). *See* Sands, Donaldson, Murray, & Cochran.

COCHRANE (JAMES) & CO. Booksellers and publishers, 11 Waterloo Place, London. Published "Polish Melodies; the poetry and music by J. Augustine Wade, Esq. . . . 1831."

COCK (JAMES LAMBORN). *See* Leader & Cock.

COCKS (ROBERT) & CO. Music sellers and publishers, London; 20 Princes Street, Hanover Square, 1823 to December 1844; 6 New Burlington Street, January 1845 to December 1898. Purchased some copyrights and plates at the sale of Paine and Hopkins, 1836; business transferred to Messrs. Augener, 1898.
 K. G.
 Catalogues:—Foreign Melodies for the Flute. c. 1827. 1 p. fol·
(B.M. h. 2120.); New Violin Music. c. 1840. 1 p. 8º. (B.M. b. 290. (1.))

COGGAN (FRANCIS). Bookseller, Inner Temple Lane (In the Temple), London, 1699-1707. (P.) His name appears in the imprint of "The Psalms of David in Metre: Fitted to the Tunes used in Parish-Churches By J. Patrick . . . London, Printed for L. Meredith; and sold by D. Brown . . . T. Benskin . . . J. Walthoe and F. Coggan . . . 1701."
 P. II.

COGGAN or COGAN (FRANCIS). Bookseller and publisher, Middle Temple Gate, London, 1730-54. (P.) His name appears in the imprint of "The Female Parson: or, Beau in the Sudds. An Opera . . . By Mr. Charles Coffey . . . London. Printed for Lawton Gilliver . . . and Fran. Cogan . . . MDCCXXX." With the tunes of the songs. Possibly son of the preceding.
 P. III.

COGHLAN (JAMES PETER). Printer and bookseller, 37 Duke Street, Grosvenor Square, London, c. 1782-1800. Printed and published a number of sacred music works.

COKE (WILLIAM). Bookseller and stationer, Leith, 1764-1819. (P.) His name appears in the imprint of "The Edinburgh Musical Miscellany: a collection of the most approved Scotch, English, and Irish songs, set to music. Selected by D. Sime . . . Edinburgh: Printed for W. Gordon . . . Edinburgh; W. Coke, Leith . . . MDCCXCII." In volume II the imprint reads "Edinburgh: Printed for John Elder, T. Brown, and C. Elliot, Edinburgh; and W. Coke, Leith. MDCCXCIII." P. III.

COLBORN (HENRY). Bookseller and publisher, 13 Great Marlborough Street, London, Published "Songs and Ballads, written and set to music by their Royal Highnesses Albert and Ernest, Princes of Saxe Coburg-Gotha . . . Translated from the original German, by G. F. Richardson . . . 1840."

COLBURN (HENRY). Bookseller and publisher, 8 New Burlington Street, London. Published "The Traveller's Oracle; or Maxims for Locomotion . . . With seven songs for one, two, and three voices composed by William Kitchiner . . . 1827."

COLE (BENJAMIN). Engraver, printer and publisher of some head-pieces of maps, music, etc., London. Engraved "The Ancient Hunting Notes of England," etc. [London], c. 1725; the notes being represented by rhythmical signs; "Songs and Duetto's in the Burlesque Opera call'd, The Dragon of Wantley. Composed . . . by Mr. J. F. Lampe . . . London. Printed for John Wilcox. MDCCXXXVIII."; "British Melody; Or, the Musical Magazine . . . English and Scotch Songs . . . one fourth part of them set to musick by John Frederick Lampe . . . Printed for & sold by ye Proprietor Benjn. Cole Engraver, at ye corner of Kings-Head Court, Holbourn. MDCCXXXIX."; issued in parts 1738-39, head-pieces designed by Sig. Marini. Cole engraved some music in "The New Universal Magazine; or Gentleman and Lady's Polite Instructor," 1751-59; "Orpheus Britannicus; or the Gentleman and Lady's Musical Museum . . . each song set to musick & embellished wᵗʰ. a curious head-piece . . . design'd . . . by the late celebrated Mr. Boitard . . . London: Printed and sold by Benjn. Cole, the corner of Kings-Head Court, near Fetter Lane, Holborn. MDCCLX." Cole may have been the Benjamin Cole who engraved a view of Trinity Church, Leeds, for Ralph Thoresby's "Vicaria Leodiensis," (1724), and soon afterwards a plan of Leeds with the address St. Paul's Church Yard.
K. G.

COLE (JAMES). Engraver, worked in London c. 1720-43. His name appears as J. Cole on the title-page of the first edition of Handel's "Suites de Pieces pour le Clavecin . . . London printed for the Author, And are only to be had at Christopher Smith's in Coventry Street . . . and by Richard Mear's . . . in Sᵗ. Pauls Church Yard," 1720. He

[111]

also engraved Peter Fraser's "The Delightfull Musical Companion," 1726, his address at the time being Great Kirby Street, London.

COLES. *See* Fitzpatrick & Coles.

COLLARD & COLLARD. Musical instrument makers, music sellers, printers and publishers, 26 Cheapside, and 195 Tottenham Court Road, London, c. 1830-34. Succeeded Clementi, Collard and Collard. Thomas E. Purday took over the music publishing side of the business c. 1834; Collard and Collard continued as pianoforte makers. One member of the family, W. Collard, was an engraver.

COLLARD (FREDERICK W.). *See* Clementi, Banger, Collard, Davis & Collard; Clementi, Banger, Hyde, Collard & Davis; Clementi, Collard & Collard; Clementi, Collard, Davis & Collard; Collard & Collard.

COLLARD (W.). Engraver. *See* Collard & Collard.

COLLETT (J.). Music seller, 20 Broad Court, Long Acre, London. Engraved, printed and published c. 1806, "Poor little Jane, a new Ballad, sung by Miss Meadows . . . at the Theatre Royal Covent Garden, composed by Percival Mann."

COLLETT (THOMAS). Musical instrument maker, at the Sign of the Violin and French Horn, Little Russel Street, Covent Garden, London. Published by subscription "Twenty four new Country Dances, the first six made at Althrop [i.e. Althorp] House in Northampton Shire on the occasion of the Honourable John Spensor's coming of Age, the 19th of December last, 1755"; also published by subscription "Twenty-four New Country Dances, for Harwich, Ipswich, Colchester, and Bury assemblies. Composed by . . . Thomas Collett." Advertised December 1758. Previously at the Sign of the French Horn and Violin opposite the Wax Work, Fleet Street.

COLLIER & DAVIS. Music publisher, 7 Fish Street Hill, opposite the Monument, London. Published c. 1787, "The much admired new Four and twenty Fiddlers as sung by Mr. Palmer at the Royalty Theatre," and a number of other sheet songs.

COLLIN. *See* Cullen (John).

COLLINS (BENJAMIN). Printer, bookseller and publisher, Salisbury. His name appears in the imprints of a number of sacred music works. In 1737 collected subscriptions for Bickham's "The Musical Entertainer." For some time, 1776 or earlier, he was in partnership as Collins and Johnson, on the Canal, Salisbury.
P. III.

COLLINS (I.), (J.), or (JAMES). Engraver who worked in London. His name as "I: Collins. Sculp" appears on the illustrated title-page of "Songs for One, Two and Three voices . . . By R. King," etc., c. 1690-92, the plate of which was acquired and adapted by John Walsh for use with many other works, from 1698 onwards, being the most frequently used of Walsh's illustrated passe-partout title-pages. Collins probably engraved the music and words of King's "Songs," and may have done other unsigned work for Walsh.

COLLINS (THOMAS). Printer, Harvey's Buildings, Strand, London. His name appears on the letterpress of "The Beauties of Handel . . . Selected . . . with a separate accompaniment for the Piano Forte . . . by Jos. Corfe . . . Printed & sold for the Author, by Preston, 97 Strand," etc. 2 vols. 1803-04.

COLSON (W.). Bookseller, Winchester. His name appears in the imprint of "A Set of New Psalm Tunes in Four Parts By John Bishop . . . Printed by W. Pearson . . . and sold by J. Walsh . . . J. Hare . . . and W. Colson in Winchester." 1710.
P. II.

CONDER (THOMAS). Bookseller, 31 Bucklersbury, London. Published in conjunction with Charles Logan, "A Second Volume to the Revd. Dr. Addington's Collection of Psalm and Hymn Tunes," etc., c. 1797. Published "A New Edition of the Revd. Dr. Addington's Psalm & Hymn Tunes . . . now much enlarged . . . in three volumes," etc., c. 1802.

CONSTABLE (ARCHIBALD) & CO. Booksellers and publishers, 10 and 11 Princes Street, Edinburgh. Their name appears in an advertisement, December 1823, "The New Caliope. No. 1. Being a selection of British, and occasionally, foreign melodies, newly arranged for the Piano-Forte, and engraved on copper by John Beugo. To be continued quarterly . . . Published by Archibald Constable and Co. Edinburgh; and Hurst, Robinson and Co. London."

CONYERS (JOSHUA). Bookseller, London, 1662-89; at the Black Raven, in the Long Walk, near Christ Church; at the Black Raven, Duck Lane. (P.) Published c. 1683, "The Rose of Delight, or, An excellent new song in the praise of His Grace James D. of Monmouth."
P. I, II.

COOK (JOHN). Bookseller and publisher, Sherborne, Dorset, 1713-46. (P.) His name appears in the imprint of "A Sett of new Psalm-Tunes and Anthems . . . By William Knapp . . . London: Printed by W. Hutchinson, for the Author, and sold by him in Poole; Mr. George Torbuck in Winbourn; Messrs. John and Joshua Cook in Sherbourn . . . MDCCXXXVIII."; also in an advertisement May 1745, "A New

Set of Anthems and Psalm Tunes for the use of Parish Churches, compos'd by John Broderip . . . Engrav'd and printed for the Author, and sold by him at Wells; Mr. John Cook, at Sherbourn; Mr. King at Yeovil; and by the printer, John Simpson," etc.
P. II.

COOK or COOKE (JOHN). Bookseller and publisher, Uppingham and Stamford, 1729-c. 1754. His name appears in the imprints of "The Voice of Melody . . . Printed for William East . . . and sold by Mr. Cooke at Uppingham," etc., c. 1748; "The Sacred Melody . . . Collected and publish'd by William East . . . Likewise Mr. Wightman . . . Grantham . . . Mr. Cook Uppingham . . . 1754."
P. III.

COOK (JOSHUA). Bookseller, Sherborne, Dorset. His name appears in the imprint of "A Sett of new Psalm-Tunes and Anthems . . . By William Knapp . . . London: Printed by W. Hutchinson, for the Author, and sold by him in Poole; Mr. George Torbuck in Winbourn; Messrs. John and Joshua Cook in Sherbourn . . . MDCCXXXVIII."
P. III.

COOKE (BARTHOLOMEW) or (BARTLETT). Musical instrument maker, music seller and publisher, 4 Sackville Street, Dublin, c. 1794-98. Business and premises taken over by George Gough c. 1798.

COOKE (BENJAMIN). Music seller and publisher, at the Golden Harp, New Street, Covent Garden, London, 1726-43 Some of his plates were acquired by John Johnson, who reissued copies from them.

COOKE (J.). Printer, Lithographic Office, 12 Pitt Street, Dublin. Printed "When yon pale Moon, a much admired Ballad as sung by Miss Mc Ghie at the Theatre Belfast, composed by W. McGhie," c. 1818.

COOKE (JOHN). Bookseller and publisher, Uppingham and Stamford. *See* Cook or Cooke.

COOKE (T.) & BRENAN. Music and musical instrument sellers and publishers, 45 Dame Street, Dublin, c. 1806-12. Thomas Simpson Cooke, one of the partners, son of Bartholomew or Bartlett Cooke, was also a composer of music; business continued as T. Cooke and Co. at the same address from c. 1812.

COOKE (T.) & CO. Music and musical instrument sellers, and publishers, 45 Dame Street, Dublin, c. 1812-17. Also had Pianoforte warerooms at 13 Fownes Street, c. 1814-17; Thomas Simpson Cooke was one of the partners; succeeded T. Cooke and Brenan.

COOKE (THOMAS SIMPSON). *See* Cooke (T.) & Brenan; Cooke (T.) & Co.

COOPER. *See* Dykes & Cooper.

COOPER (J.). Music engraver, music seller and publisher, London;
8 Winchester Court, Monkwell Court, Wood Street, c. 1801; 16 Fleet
Lane, Old Bailey, c. 1805; 19 Fleet Lane, Old Bailey, c. 1806-10.

COOPER (JAMES). Music engraver, printer, music seller and publisher,
London; 39 Whitcomb Street, near Coventry Street, c. 1786-87;
Cheap Music Repository, 7 Gerrard Street, Soho, c. 1787-95. J. Cooper
and Co. appears on some publications issued from Gerrard Street.
　　A Catalogue of Vocal and Instrumental Music. c. 1790. 1 p. fol.
(B.M. Hirsch IV. 15.a.)

COOPER (JOSEPH). Music seller, 18 Southampton Row, Russell Square,
London, c. 1835-37. Published a small amount of music; also as
J. Cooper and Co. had a pianoforte manufactory at 53 Southampton
Row c. 1834-36 and 48 Southampton Row c. 1836-49.

COOPER (MARY). Publisher, at the Globe in Paternoster Row, London,
c. 1742-61. (P.) Widow of Thomas Cooper, printer and publisher.
Published "The Decoy: An opera . . . MDCCXLIV."; contains the
music to the airs; "Hymns on the Great Festivals, and other occasions
. . . 1746"; "The New Universal Magazine; or Gentleman and
Lady's Polite Instructor," 1751-59, which contains some pages of
music engraved by Benjamin Cole; published in conjunction with
John Tyther "Amaryllis. Being a collection of such songs as are most
in vogue . . . at the public theatres & gardens . . . London. Published
. . . by John Tyther . . . & M. Cooper . . . 1746." Her name appears
in the imprint of "Amaryllis . . . London. Publish'd . . . by T. J. and
sold by M. Cooper . . . J. Wood . . . and I. Tyther," etc., c. 1750;
and in a second edition a little later.
　　P. III.

COOPER (RICHARD). Music engraver and printer, Edinburgh, c. 1725-
1764. Engraved "Musick for Allan Ramsay's Collection of Scots
Songs Set by Alex^r. Stuart," c. 1725; Adam Craig's "A Collection of
the Choicest Scots Tunes . . . Edinburgh . . . 1730"; "A Collection
of Minuets . . . composed by James Oswald . . . Edinburgh . . . 1734";
"Sonatas for two German Flutes . . . Compos'd by Willm. McGibbon
. . . 1734," and other works.
　　K. G. P. III.

COOPER (THOMAS). Printer and publisher, at the Globe in Paternoster
Row, London, 1732-c. 1742. Issued a number of musical works; was
associated with George Bickham, junior, in the publication and sale
of some of his works, including some numbers of "The Musical
Entertainer."
　　P. III.

[115]

COOTE (J.). Bookseller and publisher, at the King's Arms, in Paternoster Row, London. Published "The Musical Magazine. By Mr.
Oswald, and other celebrated Masters." Advertised January 1760,
that the first number would be published on 1st February, and continued the first of each month.
K. P. III.

COOTE (J.). 14 Red Lion Street, Clerkenwell, London. Published
"The Psalms of David . . . By I. Watts . . . (Tunes in the Tenor Part,
fitted to the several metres.) MDCCLXXVII."

COPE. Music engraver, London. At 46 Rathbone Place, engraved
"A Set of six Songs of the wild Flowers of Spring . . . Written by
John William Leslie Esqre. Composed . . . by J. M. Jolly. London.
Published for the Author & sold by R. Hack, 4 Gray's Inn Passage,
Red Lion Square," etc., c. 1834; at Frith Street, Soho, engraved
"Victoria the pride of our Land. A patriotic Solo and Chorus written
by G. W. Bell Esqr. . . . The music composed by J. M. Jolly. London.
Published for the Author by J. Keegan, 3 Burlington Arcade," c. 1837.

COPE (W. P. R.). Music and musical instrument seller and publisher,
22 Mount Street, near the Asylum, Westminster Road, London, 1796.
Published some of his own compositions from 13 Chester Place,
Lambeth, c. 1801, and 2 Great Moore Place, Lambeth, 1812. For
many years organist of St. Saviour's Church, Southwark.
K.
Catalogue. Musical Publications. No. 1. 1796. 1 p. fol. (B.M. g.
140. (2.))

CORBET (CHARLES). Book and music seller, at the Oxford Arms, in
Warwick Lane, London. Published a small number of musical works
between 1682-85, one political song at least under the pseudonym,
C. Tebroc: "Advice to the City or the Wiggs Loyalty explain'd,"
music by Opdar.
P. II. D. & M.

CORBETT (CHARLES). Bookseller and publisher, Addison's Head, next
the Rose Tavern Without Temple Bar, or Addison's Head, over
against St. Dunstan's Church in Fleet Street, London, 1732-52. (P.)
Published in conjunction with John Torbuck, "The Devil of a Duke:
or, Trapolin's Vagaries. A (Farcical Ballad) Opera . . . London:
Printed for Charles Corbett, at Addison's Head, Without Temple Bar;
and John Torbuck, in Clare Court, Drury Lane. MDCCXXXII.";
published "Bickham's Musical Entertainer, Vol. II," 1740, and a
later edition of Vols. I and II, issued in parts, July 1740-41. Advertised
for subscriptions and published "Lyra Britannica, being a Collection
of Ballads and Arietta's . . . Musick . . . by J. F. Lampe," 1740. Succeeded his father Thomas Corbett.
K. P. III.

CORBETT (THOMAS). Bookseller and book auctioneer, London, 1715-32; Corner of Ludgate, next Fleet Bridge; The Child's Coat, down the Ditch side near Bridewell Bridge, or, by Fleet Ditch; Addison's Head, next the Rose Tavern, without Temple Bar, 1719-32. His name appears in an advertisement, June 1728, "This Day is published. Mr. W. Corbet's Bizzaria's or Concerto's, proper for all Instruments or the new Guito's of Italy. The subscribers may have their books by sending the rest of the money to Mr. J. Walsh . . . and Mr. Tho. Corbett at Addison's Head without Temple-Bar, where they are sold," etc. Succeeded by his son Charles Corbett.
P. II.

CORNISH (WILLIAM). Chromo and lithographic printer, London; 62 Bartholomew Close, c. 1847-49; 63 Bartholomew Close, c. 1849-86. Printed some illustrations in colour in "Jullien's Album for 1853."

CORRI & CO. Music sellers and publishers, Edinburgh, 37 North Bridge Street, 1790-1801, with additional premises at 8 South St. Andrew Street, c. 1796-1801. Natale Corri, younger brother of Domenico Corri, was connected with the business. Published in conjunction with Domenico Corri, and afterwards with Corri, Dussek and Co. in London; succeeded Corri and Sutherland.
K. G.
A Catalogue of Music. Vocal and Instrumental. c. 1790. 1 p. fol. (B.M. g. 272. v. (3*.))

CORRI & SUTHERLAND. Music sellers and publishers, Edinburgh, 1780-90; at 37 North Bridge Street, c. 1783-90. Partners were John or Domenico Corri and James Sutherland; partnership dissolved in 1790 when Sutherland died. Domenico Corri having commenced business in London in 1789, the Edinburgh business was continued as Corri and Co., with Natale Corri, younger brother of Domenico, as one of the principals; succeeded John Corri.
K. G.

CORRI, DUSSEK & CO. Music sellers and publishers, London, 67 Dean Street, Soho, January 1794-c. 1801. Additional premises at 68 Dean Street, c. 1795-96, and 28 Haymarket, c. 1796-1801, which became the principal place of business; continued by Domenico Corri alone. Jan Ladislav Dussek was a son-in-law of his partner Domenico Corri. Corri, Dussek and Co. published in conjunction with Corri and Co. in Edinburgh.
K. G.
Catalogues:—New Music. 1795. 1 p. fol. (B.M. Hirsch III. 800.); 1795 & 1796. 1 p. fol. (B.M. G. 806. h. (1.)); For the years 1796 & 1797. 1 p. fol. (B.M. g. 141. (15.))
See also Corri (Domenico).

CORRI, PEARCE & CO. Music and musical instrument sellers, and publishers, at the Apollo Library, 28 Haymarket, London, c. 1805-06. Succeeded Montague P. Corri, M. Hall and Co.; succeeded by Pearce and Co.
> K. G.

CORRI (DOMENICO). Musician and singing master, music seller and publisher, London; 67 Dean Street, Soho, c. 1789-94; from January 1794-1801 joined with J. L. Dussek and became Corri, Dussek and Co. at 67 Dean Street and other addresses; in business alone at 28 Haymarket, c. 1801-04; published some music in conjunction with Corri and Co. in Edinburgh where he was established in 1771 as a musician; imprints of some publications bear only the address of 28 Haymarket; succeeded by Montague P. Corri and Co.
> K. G.
> *See* also Corri & Co.; Corri & Sutherland; Corri (John).

CORRI (JOHN). Music seller, Edinburgh, c. 1779-80. The firm of John Corri was established by Domenico Corri in the name of his son, and published some of Domenico Corri's works. Succeeded by Corri and Sutherland in which he may have been a partner.
> K. G.

CORRI (MONTAGUE P.) & CO. Music and musical instrument sellers, and publishers, 28 Haymarket, London, c. 1804-05. M. P. Corri was a son of Domenico Corri, whom he succeeded in the business; became Montague P. Corri, M. Hall and Co. c. 1805.
> K. G.

CORRI (MONTAGUE P.), HALL (M.) & CO. Music and musical instrument sellers, and publishers, 28 Haymarket, London, c. 1805. Succeeded Montague P. Corri and Co.; succeeded by Corri, Pearce and Co.
> K. G.

CORRI (NATALE). Music and musical instrument seller, and publisher, Edinburgh, c. 1801-22; South St. David Street, c. 1803; 41 Princes Street, ?–1812; Front of his Concert Rooms, head of Leith Walk, c. 1803-22. Younger brother of Domenico Corri; formerly connected with Corri and Co.
> K. G.
> A Catalogue of Vocal and Instrumental Music. c. 1810. 2 pp. fol. (First Edition Bookshop, Catalogue 40. No. 127.)

CORTICELLI, *Mrs.* At the upper end of Suffolk Street, near the Haymarket, London. Her name appears on the title-page of "Divertimenti da Camera traddotti pel cembalo da quelli composti pel violino, o flauto da Giovanni Bononcini. Londra MDCCXXII. Sold onely at Mrs. Corticelles's House," etc. Advertised January 1722, "Bononcini's Book of Cantata's and Duetti's, is now Publish'd and will be deliver'd to Subscribers at Mrs. Corticelli's House," etc. Also advertised February 1722, "A Sett of new Sonata's, compos'd for the Violin or Flute by Bononcini. Sold only at Mrs. Corticelli's House . . . N.B. In a few days will be published, the same Sonata's transpos'd for the Harpsichord. To be had only at the same place."

COTES (RICHARD). Printer, Barbican, Aldersgate Street, London, 1635-1652. (P.) Only the initials R. C. appear in the imprint of the work, presumed to have been printed by Richard Cotes, "The Whole Booke of Davids Psalmes, both in prose and meeter. With apt notes to sing them withall. London, Printed by R. C. for the Company of Sationers [sic] 1643." In partnership with his brother Thomas until the latter's death in 1641.
    P. I.

COTES (THOMAS). Printer, Barbican, Aldersgate Street, London, 1620-1641. (P.) Only the initials T. C. appear in the imprint of the work, presumed to have been printed by Thomas Cotes, "The Whole Booke of Davids Psalmes, both in prose and meeter. With apt notes to sing them withall. London, Printed by T. C. for the Company of Stationers 1635." In partnership with his brother Richard for a time.
    P. I.

COVENTRY & HOLLIER. Music sellers and publishers, 71 Dean Street, Soho, London, c. 1834-48. Succeeded Thomas Preston; John Hollier dropped out c. 1848 and the business was carried on by Charles Coventry; some of the music plates were acquired by Joseph Alfred Novello in 1849.
    G.

COVENTRY (CHARLES). Music seller and publisher, 71 Dean Street, Soho, London, c. 1848-51. Was previously in partnership with John Hollier as Coventry and Hollier. At the sale of Coventry's stock-in-trade in 1851, Joseph Alfred Novello purchased 4,780 plates of sacred works, having previously purchased other plates from the stock of Coventry and Hollier in 1849.

COWPER (EDWARD). Engineer and patentee of printing machinery, etc., Streatham Place, Brixton Hill, and at Clowes's Printing Office, Stamford Street, Blackfriars, London. Invented in 1827 a beautiful, but expensive process of printing music. The notes, made of copper, were set up separately, and the stave lines printed afterwards. This method was used by Samuel Chappell, Goulding, D'Almaine and Co., and Isaac Willis, but was soon abandoned.

COWSE (BENJAMIN). Bookseller, Rose and Crown, St. Paul's Churchyard, London, 1714-c. 1724. His name appears in the imprint of

"The Psalms of David in Metre; With the tunes used in Parish-Churches. By John Patrick . . . The Seventh edition. London: Printed for D. Brown . . . B. Cowse . . . MDCCXXIV."
P. II.

COX. *See* Bigg & Cox.

COX (D.). 12 Nassau Place, Commercial Road, London. Published c. 1815, "The Ship wreck'd Lascar, a Narrative founded on fact, by The Revd. G. C. Smith. Illustrated in poetic verse, by Miss Jane Taylor of Ongar. The music by Thomas Walker."

COX (J.). Langtoft, near Bourn, Lincolnshire. Printed and sold c. 1770, "The Modern Catch-Club. Being a choice Collection of Catches, Glees, Canons & two-part Songs."

COX (JOHN). Musical instrument maker, music seller and publisher, at Simpson's Music Shop, Sweeting's Alley, opposite the East Door of the Royal Exchange, London, 1751-64. Married Mrs. Ann Simpson, widow of John Simpson, probably early in 1751, and continued the business with her as Simpson's Music Shop or John Cox at Simpson's Music Shop until June 1764, when Maurice Whitaker, who had been manager for Mrs. Simpson and Cox prior to 1760, advertised that owing to the state of Mrs. Cox's health, "carries on the same business in every branch thereof at his Music shop, the Sign of the Violin, under the North Piazza of the Royal Exchange." Robert Bremner purchased some of the plates at the sale of the stock-in-trade of Simpson's Music Shop in 1764.
K. G.
Catalogues:—Vocal and Instrumental Music. 1751. 2 pp. fol. (B.M. Hirsch III. 225.); New Music. c. 1755. 2 pp. fol. (B.M. 7896. h. 40. (3.))

COX (T.). At the Lamb, under the Royal Exchange, London. His name appears in the imprint of "Psalmody Epitomiz'd: Being a brief collection of plain and useful psalm-tunes . . . The second edition with additions. By Ely Stansfield. London: Printed by W. Pearson, for T. Cox . . . and M. Fielding . . . in Hallifax. 1731."

CRACE (WILLIAM). Printer, 40 Long Acre, London. Printed and sold "A Selection of Psalms and Hymns with favorite & approved Tunes for the use of Bedford Chapel near Bedford Square," etc. Preface dated November 1791. A reprint of certain pages only of the original edition was issued c. 1805.

CRAMER, ADDISON & BEALE. Music and musical instrument sellers, and publishers, 201 Regent Street, London, 1824-44. Had additional premises at 67 Conduit Street, c. 1841-44; Robert Addison and T.

A single SONG.

Oung *Cory—don, A---minta* Lov'd, the Brighteſt Nymph of all, all,

all, the Plain; But ſhe by no in—trea--ties mov'd, re—fus'd his Courtſhip

with diſ—dain: With Songs and Pre—ſents, all that Witt or Beau—ty

cou'd de——viſe, the A——-mo--rous Shepherd ſtrove to get, in——to his

Hands the Prize.

II.

He try'd in vain, all Arts he knew,
To eaſe his wretched, wretched, wretched State;
Then running to thick Woods ſhe flew,
And curs'd her Beauty and his Fate:
But ſoon return'd, for then his pains
Grew faſter than before;
Yet ſtill Obdurate ſhe remains,
And bid him never ſee her more.

F

Vaughan Richardson, "A Collection of New Songs". Printed by
William Pearson. 1701

Johann Mattheson, "Pieces de Clavecin". Printed for I. D. Fletcher.
1714. Engraver unidentified

Ouverture of Radamiſtus.

Handel's "Radamisto". Printed and sold by Richard Mears and
Christopher Smith. Engraved by Thomas Cross. 1720

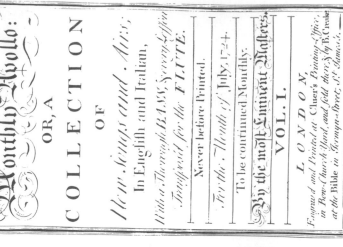

THE
Monthly Apollo:

OR, A

COLLECTION

OF

New Songs and Airs,

In English and Italian,

With a Thorough BASS, Sonata-Lesson
Transpos'd for the FLUTE.

Never before Printed.

For the Month of July, 1724.

To be continued Monthly.

By the most Eminent Masters.

VOL. I.

LONDON,

Engrav'd and Printed at Cluer's Printing-Office,
in Bow-Church-Yard, and sold there; & by B. Creake
at the Bible in Jermyn-Street, St. James's.

"The Monthly Apollo". 1724. Probably engraved by Thomas Cobb

Frederick Beale were previously in partnership together; Johann Baptist Cramer previously a partner in the firm of Chappell and Co.; in early part of 1844, Addison withdrew and set up in business with Hodson; William Chappell entered in his place and the firm became Cramer, Beale and Chappell, or, Cramer, Beale and Co.

 K. G.

CRAMER & CO. *See* Cramer, Beale & Chappell.

CRAMER, BEALE & CHAPPELL. Music and musical instrument sellers, and publishers, London, 201 Regent Street and 67 Conduit Street, 1844-61. Had additional premises at 55 King Street, Golden Square, c. 1845-61; 199 Regent Street, c. 1853-61; and 167 North Street, Brighton, c. 1854–?; also known as Cramer, Beale and Co. Johann Baptist Cramer had previously been a partner in the firms of Chappell and Co., and Cramer, Addison and Beale; T. Frederick Beale previously connected with Addison and Beale, and Cramer, Addison and Beale; William Chappell had previously been in business with Chappell and Co. Succeeded in 1861 by Cramer, Beale and Wood, in 1863 by Cramer and Co. (from 1871 also as Cramer, Wood and Co.), in 1872 by J. B. Cramer and Co., at various addresses, including 199 and 201 Regent Street until 1894, and premises at 207 and 209 Regent Street from 1862-1902, when the firm (since 1897 as J. B. Cramer and Co. Ltd.) moved its headquarters to 126 Oxford Street, the present principal address being 139 New Bond Street.

 K. G.

CRAMER, BEALE & CO. *See* Cramer, Beale & Chappell.

CRAMER, BEALE & WOOD. *See* Cramer, Beale & Chappell.

CRAMER (JOHANN BAPTIST). *See* Chappell & Co.; Cramer, Addison & Beale; Cramer, Beale & Chappell.

CRAMER (JOHN). Military Musical instrument maker, Pimlico Road, London. Printed and sold "Six Favorite Pieces for the Piano Forte, composed by an illustrious Personage . . . Publish'd . . . by M. Stohwasser, Music Master of the Royal Horse Guards Blues," c. 1815.

CRASK (JOHN). *See* Gray (J.) & Crask (John).

CREAKE (BEZALEEL). Bookseller, stationer and publisher, London; The Bible, Jermyn (Jermain, Jerman) Street, St. James's, 1719-c. 1740: opposite York Buildings in the Strand, c. 1740; at the Rose in Jermyn Street, c. 1750. Published a few musical works, some in association with John Cluer, 1723-28, with Thomas Cobb, 1728-36. In 1731 married the widow of Robert Whitledge, printer, bookseller and bookbinder, and removed to the Red Bible in Ave Mary (Maria)

Lane, Ludgate Street, near St. Paul's, London, but still continued his business at The Bible, Jermyn Street; remained at the Red Bible until December 1735 or later, where he sold bibles, prayer-books, school books, music, etc.

K. P. III.

CROALL (GEORGE). Composer, pianist, music seller and publisher, 27 Hanover Street (South Hanover Street), Edinburgh, c. 1840-48. Published some of his own compositions.

CROCKER (JOHN) & (EDMUND). Printers, Frome. Published c. 1823, "Psalms and Hymns for Divine Service. Collected and edited by the Rev. R. J. Meade. Second edition."

CROOKE (WILLIAM). Bookseller, at the Green Dragon, without Temple Bar, London, 1667-94. Published "Peppa: or, The Reward of constant Love. A novel. Done out of French. With several songs set to musick, for two voices. By a Young-Gentlewoman . . . 1689."

P. I, II. D. & M.

CROSBY (B.) & CO. Booksellers and publishers, Stationers' Court, Paternoster Row, or, Ludgate Street, London, c. 1802-15. Published a number of song-books with music, some in conjunction with Oliver and Boyd, Edinburgh.

K.

CROSS (RICHARD). Music publisher? London? c. 1714. Address and details not known. His name appears on a sheet song, "Sung by Mr. Pack acting a Quaker in the Richmond Heiress, the words by Mr. Durfey" (Maiden fresh as a Rose), which has at the bottom "Done for Richard Cross."

CROSS (THOMAS). Music engraver, music seller and publisher and composer, London, c. 1683-1733; at Three Horse-Shoe Court in Pye Corner, near West Smithfield, c. 1692-93; Katherine (Catherine) Wheel Court (on Snow Hill), near Holbourn Conduit (Snow Hill Conduit), 1693-99; Compton Street, Clerkenwell, near the Pound, c.?-1720; his later address not being known. Worked for various publishers (Cullen, Meares, B. Cooke, D. Wright, etc.), and also engraved, published and sold music on his own account; frequently signed himself as Tho. Cross, junior, and is assumed to have been the son of Thomas Cross, engraver of portraits and frontispieces to some works issued by John Playford the elder, and who may have also engraved some music, c. 1644-85.

K. G. D. & M.

CROSS (WILLIAM). Music seller, Oxford. His name appears in the imprint of "A Cantata and Six Songs; set to Musick by a Gentleman of Oxford. London, Printed by John Johnson, and by Wm. Cross in

[122]

Oxford," c. 1750; "Divine Harmony; or, a Collection of fifty-five double and single chants for four voices, as they are sung at the Cathedral of Lichfield; compos'd by John Alcock . . . Printed for the author, and M. Broome . . . in Birmingham, and sold by them; Mr. Cross . . . at Oxford . . . 1752."

CROSSE (THOMAS). *See* Cross.

CROUCH (JOHN). Music seller and publisher, London; at the Three Lutes, Drury Lane, c. 1683-87; at the Three Lutes in Princes Street, near (in) Drury Lane, or, near Covent Garden, c. 1687-1704.
> P. II. D. & M.

CROWCH (J.). *See* Crouch (John).

CROWDER (STANLEY). Bookseller and publisher, London; The Golden Ball, Paternoster Row (in partnership with Henry Woodgate), c. 1755; at the Looking Glass (over against St. Magnus's Church) on London Bridge, c. 1755-60; 12 Paternoster Row, c. 1760-84. His name appears in the imprints of a number of musical works. He was for a time in partnership with Henry Woodgate and the firm was then known as S. Crowder and Company.
> P. III.

CROWLEY (ROBERT). Printer, Ely Rents, Holborn, London. Printed a number of books between 1549 and 1551 (D.), including "The Psalter of Dauid . . . Translated and imprinted by Robert Crowley . . . M.D.XLIX. the xx. daye of September. And are to be solde in Eley rentes in Holburne."
> D. S.

CROWN. At the sign of the Crown, Paul's Church Yard.
> *See* Waterson (Simon).

CRUTTENDEN (R.). Bookseller, at the Bible and Three Crowns in Cheapside, London. His name appears in the imprint of "A Collection of Tunes, suited to the various Metres in Mr. Watts's imitation of the Psalms of David, or Dr. Patrick's version . . . London: Printed by W. Pearson, for John Clark . . . R. Ford . . . and R. Cruttenden . . . 1719."
> P. II.

CRUTTWELL (RICHARD). Printer, Bath. Printed "Psalms and Hymns, appointed to be sung by the congregation assembled at Christ's-Church, Bath . . . 1801."

CRUTTWELL (WILLIAM). Printer and stationer, Sherborne, Dorset, 1764-1804. (P.) His name appears in the imprint of "The Psalms of David . . . By I. Watts . . . A new edition, corrected. (Tunes in the

Tenor Part fitted to the several Metres.) Salisbury: Printed and sold by Collins and Johnson. Sold also by . . . Cruttwell, at Sherborne . . . MDCCLXXVI."
P. III.

CULEN (I.). *See* Cullen (John).

CULLEN (JOHN), CULEN (I.) or COLLIN. Printer, musical instrument and music seller, publisher and stationer, London; at the Roebuck between the two Temple Gates, Fleet Street (near Temple Bar; at the Buck between the two Temple Gates; at the Buck in Fleet Street), 1702-10; at the Buck without (or, just without) Temple Bar, April 1710-13. Works issued by Cullen were usually engraved on copper plates, and he seems to have taken over some of the stock of Henry Playford; but there is no evidence that he took over the premises formerly occupied by Henry Playford or John Carr and Richard Carr, as suggested by Kidson. Issued some works in conjunction with John Young.
K. G. P. II. D. & M.
Catalogue:—Books printed for and sold by John Cullen. 1707. 1 p. fol. (B.M. K. 2. i. 22.)

CULLIFORD & BARROW. Pianoforte and tambourine manufacturers, 172, Corner of Surrey Street, Strand, London. Published, "Six Rondos for the Harp or Piano Forte with an Accompaniment for the Tamborino; composed by James Platts," advertised March, 1798. Previously partners in Culliford, Rolfe & Barrow.

CULLIFORD, ROLFE & BARROW. Musical instrument makers, music sellers and publishers, 112, opposite Bow Church, Cheapside, London, 1795 to end of 1797. Also had a manufactory at 13 Red Lion Court, Watling Street. When the partnership was dissolved at the end of 1797, William Rolfe continued at the Cheapside address, and Culliford and Barrow went into business together.

CUNNINGHAM (J. T.). Professor of Dancing from the King's Theatre, 21 Argyle Street, London. Published and sold c. 1821, "A New Set of Quadrilles, with improved figures . . . by J. T. Cunningham."

CURRELL (W.). Engraver, London. Engraved "The Modern Violin Preceptor . . . By J. Jousse. London, Printed by Goulding, Phipps, D'Almaine and Co.," etc., c. 1808.

CURRY (WILLIAM) *Junior* & CO. Booksellers and publishers, 9 Upper Sackville Street, Dublin. Their name appears in the imprint of "The Psaltery; a Collection of Psalm and Hymn Tunes, carefully selected from the works of the most eminent composers . . . Dublin: Published for John Kirkwood . . . By W. Curry, Jun. and Co. . . . 1835."

CURWEN (ISAAC) & CO. Music sellers and publishers, 15 Westmoreland ·Street, Dublin, c. 1825-31.

CUTHBERT, *Mr*. Music seller, in Russell Street, Covent Garden, London. His name appears in an advertisement March 1702, "The Useful Instructor on the Violin . . . By John Lenton . . . and are to be sold by Mr. Playford . . . Mr. Salter . . . Mr. Crouch . . . and by Mr. Cuthbert," etc.

D., J. *See* Day (John).

DALE, COCKERILL & CO. Music sellers and publishers, 19 Poultry, London, c. 1832-37. Succeeded Elspeth Dale; succeeded by G. Gange and Co.

DALE (CHRISTOPHER). Music and musical instrument seller, 12 King's Road, near Sloane Square, Chelsea, London. Printed and sold c. 1813, "The Sisters, three favorite Waltzes for the Piano Forte, composed . . . by William Grosse."

DALE (ELSPETH). Music seller and publisher, 19 Poultry, London, c. 1827-32. Succeeded William Dale, probably her husband; succeeded by Dale, Cockerill and Co.
    K.
    A Catalogue of new Music. c. 1830. 1 p. fol. (B.M. H. 2835. a. (13.))

DALE (JAMES). *See* Dale (Joseph).

DALE (JOSEPH). Musician, music and musical instrument maker and seller, and publisher, London; published from his house, 19, opposite the Six Clerks Office, Chancery Lane, 1783-January 1786; 132 Oxford Street, opposite Hanover Square, January 1786 to early in 1791; 19 Cornhill, and 132 Oxford Street, opposite (or, facing) Hanover Square (or, the corner of Holles Street, also given as 29 Holles Street, Oxford Street), early in 1791-c. 1802; 19 Cornhill, 132 Oxford Street (or, the corner of Holles Street, Oxford Street), and 151 New Bond Street, opposite Clifford Street, c. 1802-05. As Joseph Dale and Son (or, Joseph and William Dale), 19 Cornhill, the corner of Holles Street, Oxford Street, and 151 New Bond Street, c. 1805-09; his son William went into business on his own account at another address, c. 1809. Joseph Dale continued alone at 19 Cornhill, opposite the Royal Exchange, the corner of Holles Street, Oxford Street, and 151 New Bond Street, c. 1809-10; 19 Cornhill and the corner of Holles Street, Oxford Street, c. 1810-17; 25 Cornhill, c. 1817-19; 10 Cornhill, c. 1819-21. In 1785 he issued a catalogue of music in which he stated that he had purchased some plates, copyrights, and copies of the books, from William Napier, music seller in the Strand, for £540; also some from Charles Bennett, Temple, once the property of John Welcker, music seller, Haymarket, for £682. He purchased the stock-in-trade and Musical Circulating Library of Samuel Babb at 132 Oxford Street in 1786, and advertised that it consisted of one hundred thousand books and upwards. Joseph Dale took out Letters Patent for his improvements on the Tambourine, an instrument in which J. Dale junior (presumably son of Joseph) was interested. Joseph Dale was organist of St. Anthony and St. John Baptist, Watling Street, London, in 1805. James Dale, perhaps a brother of Joseph, composed, printed and published some pianoforte sonatas, etc., at 16 Bowling Green Place, Kennington, about 1800 and a little later.

K. G.

Catalogues:—Favorite Music. (Includes music purchased from W. Napier and C. Bennett.) 1785. 1 p. fol. (B.M. g. 131. (1.)); Favorite Music. c. 1785. 1 p. fol. (B.M. D. 293. c.); Music. c. 1786. 1 p. fol. (B.M. g. 245. (2.)); Vocal and Instrumental Music. c. 1787. 1 p. fol. (B.M. h. 32. a.); Vocal and Instrumental Music. c. 1790. 1 p. fol. (B.M. Hirsch 555.); Music. c. 1790. 1 p. fol. (B.M. Hirsch IV. 1111. (8.)); Music. 1791. 1 p. fol. (B.M. g. 161. f. (1.)); Music. c. 1792. 2 pp. fol. (B.M. g. 270. r. (14.)); Music. c. 1795. 1 p. fol. (B.M. E. 100. b. (6.)); Music. 1799. 2 pp. fol. (B.M. h. 270. (11.)); Music. c. 1800. 1 p. fol. (B.M. g. 301. (3.)); Music. c. 1802. 1 p. fol. (B.M. h. 270. (10.)); Music. 1809. 1 p. fol. (B.M. h. 270. (12.))

DALE (JOSEPH) & SON. See Dale (Joseph).

DALE (JOSEPH) & (WILLIAM). See Dale (Joseph); Dale (William).

DALE (WILLIAM). Music and musical instrument seller, and publisher, London; 8 Poultry, c. 1809-23; 19 Poultry, c. 1823-27. Son of Joseph Dale with whom he was in partnership as Joseph Dale and Son, and occasionally given as Joseph and William Dale, c. 1805-09. Succeeded by Elspeth Dale, probably his widow.

K. G.

D'ALMAINE & CO. Musical instrument makers, music sellers, printers and publishers, London; 20 Soho Square, c. 1834-58; 104 New Bond Street, c. 1858-66. Had additional premises at 10 Sutton Place, Sutton Street, Soho Square, c. 1850-57; 16 Soho Square, c. 1851-52; Burwood Mews, Edgware Road, c. 1854-66. For a time in the early 1840's Thomas Mackinlay joined the firm and some music was issued with the imprint of D'Almaine and Mackinlay. Succeeded Goulding and D'Almaine; Thomas D'Almaine died in 1866; stock-in-trade offered for sale May 1867, and realised nearly £12,000; name and goodwill of the firm purchased by Joseph Emery, who continued the business as a pianoforte manufacturer at other addresses.

K. G. (Goulding & Co.)

A Select Catalogue of Music. c. 1837. 22 pp. 8°. (Haas, Catalogue 27. No. 45.)

D'ALMAINE & MACKINLAY. *See* D'Almaine & Co.

D'ALMAINE (THOMAS). *See* D'Almaine & Co.; Goulding & D'Almaine; Goulding, D'Almaine, Potter & Co.; Goulding, Phipps D'Almaine.

DANIEL (JAMES). Engraver, Aberdeen. Engraved, printed and published "A Collection of Scotch Airs, Strathspeys, Reels . . . adapted for the pianoforte, or violin and violoncello; by a Citizen, Aberdeen." Date unknown, probably c. 1800.
    K.

DANIEL (ROGER). Printer and bookseller, London and Cambridge, c. 1627-66. (P.) His name appears on "The Whole Booke of Psalmes: Collected into English Meeter, with apt notes to sing them withall . . . Printed by the Printers to the University of Cambridge, and are to be sold at London by R. Daniel, at the Angel in Lumbard-Street. 1628"; printed with Thomas Buck "The Whole Book of Psalmes: Collected into English Metre, by Thomas Sternhold, John Hopkins, and others . . . Printed by Thomas Buck and Roger Daniel, printers to the Universitie of Cambridge. 1637", also editions in 1638 and 1639; Roger Daniel alone, "The Whole Book of Psalmes . . . Printed by Roger Daniel, printer to the Universitie of Cambridge . . . 1645"; printed with William Dugard "The Book of Psalms in Metre . . . translated by W. Barton . . . London: Printed by Roger Daniel, and William Du-gard, and are to be sold by Francis Eglesfield, and Thomas Underhill . . . and Francis Tyton . . . 1654."
    P. I.

DANNELEY (JOHN FELTHAM). Music seller and publisher, 13 Regent Street, London, c. 1831-34. Published some of his own compositions.

DAVENHILL (MARY). Bookseller, 30 Cornhill, London, c. 1778-83. Her name appears in the imprint of "A Collection of Psalm Tunes in three Parts . . . to which are added 2 Anthems & 2 Canons by Is. Smith. London. Sold by Mrs. Davenhill . . . and Mr. Buckland," etc., c. 1780. Succeeded her husband William Davenhill.

DAVENHILL (WILLIAM). Bookseller and publisher, London; 103 Leadenhall Street, c. 1766-67; 8 Cornhill, c. 1768-72; 19 Cornhill, c. 1773-75; 30 Cornhill, c. 1776-78. His name appears in the imprints of a number of musical works; succeeded by his widow Mary Davenhill.
    P. III.

DAVENPORT (JAMES). Music seller, High Street, Oxford, c. 1800-10. Printed and sold c. 1803, "Duetto, for a Violin & Violoncello and a favorite Scotch Tune with Variations by Joseph Reinagle."

DAVEY (P.). Bookseller and publisher, Ave Mary Lane, London, c. 1756-1760. His name appears in the imprints of "The Whole Book of Psalms . . . By John Playford. The Twentieth Edition . . . London: Printed by R. Brown . . . For P. Davey and B. Law, in Ave-Mary-Lane. 1757"; "Sacra Concerto: or the Voice of Melody . . . By Benjamin West . . . London: Printed by R. Brown . . . for P. Davey and B. Law . . . and J. Lacy at Northampton. MDCCLX."
    P. III.

DAVIDS (W. S.). 35 South Audley Street, Grosvenor Square, London. Published c. 1832, "Reforms, or 'What will Mistress Grundy say.' The words and music by Lledder Yeldah Caasi Esqr." [i.e. Isaac Hadley Reddell.]

DAVIDSON (GEORGE HENRY). Stereotype printer, music printer and publisher, London; 6 Tudor Street, New Bridge Street, c. 1833-44; 25 Water Street, New Bridge Street, c. 1844-47; 19 Peter's Hill, Doctors' Commons, c. 1847-60. Business continued as The Music Publishing Co., 19 Peter's Hill (or, St. Peter's Hill), 1860-66; 167 High Holborn, 1867-81, with additional premises at 60 Museum Street, 1867-68.
    G.

DAVIE & MORRIS. Music sellers and publishers, Musical Repository, Union Street, Aberdeen, c. 1810-20. By 1820 the partnership between James Davie and Michael Morris had been dissolved, and both were carrying on business independently.
    K.

DAVIE (JAMES). Musician, music seller and publisher, Aberdeen; Broad Street, c. 1820; 55 Castle Street, c. 1825-30. Previously a partner in the business of Davie and Morris.
    K.

DAVIES. See Cadell & Davies.

DAVIES (CHARLES). See Davis.

DAVIES (JOHN). Music engraver, printer and publisher, at the Musical Printing Office, 90 High Holborn, London, c. 1800-10. For some time at 61 Red Lion Street, Holborn.
    K.

DAVIES (JOHN). Music seller and engraver, 446 Strand, London. Printed and sold c. 1806, "The Complete Preceptor, for Davies's new invented Syrrynx or Patent Pandean Harmonica . . . Arranged & composed by the inventor I. Davies."

DAVIS. *See* Collier & Davis.

DAVIS (CHARLES). Bookseller, London, 1723-55; Covent Garden; Hatton Garden; Holbourn, opposite Gray's Inn; against Gray's Inn Gate in Holbourn; Paternoster Row. (P.) His name appears in the imprint of "Penelope, a Dramatic Opera, as it is acted at the New Theatre in the Hay-Market. London: Printed, and sold by Tho. Green . . . and Charles Davis, in Paternoster Row. 1728 "; with the music to the overture and the songs. Advertised in May 1728, "Penelope . . . the overture . . . and the musick to each song, by Mr. Roseingrave. Printed for Charles Davies . . . J. Green . . . and sold by A. Dodd . . . and E. Nutt," etc.
    P. III.

DAVIS (D.). *See* Clementi, Banger, Collard, Davis & Collard; Clementi, Banger, Hyde, Collard & Davis; Clementi, Collard, Davis & Collard.

DAVIS (ISAAC). Lithographer and music printer, London; 2 Leicester Street, Leicester Square, c. 1834-35; 13 Leicester Street, Leicester Square, c. 1835-37; 25 Berwick Street, Soho, c. 1837-55. Printed the music in "Jullien's Album for 1850," also for 1851.

DAVIS (JOSEPH). Musical instrument maker, London; 11 Catherine Street, Strand, c. 1810-30; 92 Blackfriars Road, c. 1828-43. Published a small amount of music from the Catherine Street address.

DAVIS (RICHARD). Bookseller, Oxford, 1648-88. (P.) Published "Cheerfull Ayres or Ballads. First composed for one single voice and set for three voices by John Wilson, Dr. in Musick . . . MDCLX."; "A Short Direction for the performance of Cathedrall Service . . . By E. L. [i.e. Edward Lowe.] 1661 "; Edward Lowe's "A Review of some short Directions in the performance of Cathedral Service . . . Second edition . . . 1664 "; "Songs, for one, two, & three Voyces to the Thorow-Bass . . . Collected out of some of the select poems of the incomparable Mr. Cowley, and others. And composed by Henry Bowman, Philo-Musicus. The Second edition, corrected and amended by the Authour . . . MDCLXXIX."; also an edition in 1683.
    P. I. D. & M.

DAVIS (RICHARD) & (WILLIAM). Musical instrument makers, 31 Coventry Street, London, c. 1822-36. Published a small amount of music. Richard Davis previously in business alone; William continued the business on his own account c. 1836-46.

DAVIS (WALTER). Bookseller and bookbinder, Amen Corner, London, 1676-87. (P.) Published "A Collection of Twenty Four Songs, written by several Hands. And set by several masters of musick. With the tunes engraven on copper-plates . . . London, Printed by

F. Leach, for Charles Corbet, and published by W. Davis . . . MDCLXXXV." Probably the same work as "A Collection of thirty one Songs," etc. (Lowndes, "The Bibliographer's Manual," vol. III. No. 2444. 1863.)
P. II. D. & M.

DAVIS (WILLIAM). *See* Davis (Richard) & (William).

DAWSON (THOMAS). Printer, London, 1568-1620. (M.) Some editions of the Sternhold and Hopkins versions of the Psalms, issued by the Company of Stationers 1611-17, have been attributed to Dawson.
M.

DAY (JOHN). Printer, London, 1546-84. Printed a number of religious and musical works; began to print in 1546 in partnership with William Seres, at the sign of the Resurrection, above the Conduit in Holborn, and later they had another shop by the Conduit in Cheapside; Day ceased the partnership and moved to "Over Aldersgate, beneath Saint Martin's" in 1549; additional shop taken in St. Paul's Churchyard 1572; was granted a number of privileges to print various works, including the Sternhold and Hopkins versions of the Psalms, which had many editions. The reversion of his patent passed to his son Richard, who succeeded him when he died in 1584.
K. G. D. S.

DAY (RICHARD). London. Printer in association with his father John Day and for some time at The Long Shop at the West End of St. Paul's. (M.) In 1584 succeeded to the patent granted to his father under which he had printed the Sternhold and Hopkins versions of the Psalms, etc. Richard Day assigned his interest to others and the works were issued with the imprint "Assignes of Richard Day," 1585-1603.
K. M. S.

DEACON (JOHN). Bookseller, London; at the Rainbow, Holborn, a little above St. Andrew's Church, 1682-c. 1694; at the Angel, in Giltspur Street, without Newgate, c. 1694-1701. (P.) His name appears in the imprints of a number of ballads with music published by P. Brooksby, J. Deacon, J. Blare and J. Back.
P. II.

DEAN & MUNDAY. Printers and publishers, London; 35 Threadneedle Street, c. 1810-37; 35 and 40 Threadneedle Street, c. 1837-42. Published "The London Minstrel: a collection of esteemed English, Irish, and Scotch songs . . . written, selected, and arranged by a professional gentleman. London. Printed for Dean and Munday . . . and A. K. Newman and Co. . . . 1825 "; "The Beauties of Melody; a collection of the most popular Airs, Duets, Glees, &c. . . . compiled, composed, selected, and arranged, by W. H. Plumstead," 1827.

DEAN (J.). Bookseller, London; Cranborn Street, in Leicester Fields, near Newport House, 1679-85; at the Queen's Head, between the Royal Grove and Helmet in Drury Lane, 1685. (P.) Published a number of single songs.
> P. II.

DEAN (JOHN). Music and musical instrument seller, printer and publisher, 148 New Bond Street, opposite Conduit Street, London, c. 1831-1837. The name is given as "J. Dean & Co." in the imprint of some publications. Succeeded by Morton and Co.

DEIGHTON (JOHN). Bookseller, Cambridge. His name appears in the imprint of "A Selection of Psalms, from the New Version, with the Morning and Evening Hymns; for the use of Parish Churches . . . Second edition. Printed and sold by W. Barker, Bookseller, East Dereham. Sold also . . . by . . J. Deighton, Cambridge . . . 1813."

DELANY (JOHN). Musical instrument maker, Great Britain Street, Dublin. Published c. 1800, "The Compleat Tutor for the German Flute containing the best and easiest Instructions for Learners to obtain a proficiency," etc.

DENHAM (HENRY). Printer, London, 1560-89. (M.) At White Cross Street, Cripplegate, 1564; at the sign of the Star (Starre), Paternoster Row, 1565-83 or later; at the Star, Aldersgate Street, c. 1587-89. William Seres assigned his patent to print psalters, etc., to Henry Denham c. 1574, who was succeeded at his death, c. 1589, by Richard Yardley and Peter Short, at the Star, on Bread Street Hill. Denham printed "Seuen Sobs of a Sorrowfull Soule for Sinne: Comprehending those seuen Psalmes of . . . Dauid, commonlie called Pœnitentiall: framed into a forme of familiar praiers, and reduced into meeter by William Hunnis . . . 1583 "; another edition in 1587, and probably one in 1589.
> K. M. S.

DENSON (R.). Engraver and music seller, at the Harp and Laurel, Long Acre, London. Advertised, August 1743, "This Day are publish'd. Two Concertos: The first for a Harpsichord, &c. in eight Parts; the second for Violins, &c. in seven Parts. Compos'd by Charles Avison," etc.; Engraved, "Twelve Concerto's in Seven Parts . . . done from two Books of Lessons for the Harpsichord. Composed by Signr. Domenico Scarletti with additional Slow Movements from Manuscript Solo Pieces, by the same Author . . . by Charles Avison . . . MDCCXLIV." Previously published two other concertos of Avison.

DE VINE. *See* Guernsey & De Vine.

DE WALPERGEN (PETER). *See* Walpergen.

DIBDIN (CHARLES). Composer, music seller and publisher, London; 411 Strand, opposite the Adelphi, March 1790-96; 2 Leicester Place, Leicester Square, 1796-1805. Retired from business and sold stock-in-trade to Bland and Weller, 1805; resumed business at 125 Strand, 1808-c. 1810.
    K.

DICEY & CO., or DICEY & OKELL. *See* Dicey (William).

DICEY (CLUER). *See* Dicey (William).

DICEY (WILLIAM). Printer and publisher, St. Ives, Huntingdonshire, and Northampton, c. 1719-56; also associated with his brother-in-law Thomas Cobb in the music publishing business, at the Maidenhead, the lower end of Bow Church Yard, in Cheapside, London. About October 1736 Dicey purchased Cobb's business for himself and his son, Cluer Dicey, who managed it, William Dicey continuing the Northampton business, which apparently printed a little music. The London firm advertised as William and Cluer Dicey, at the Printing Office and Picture Warehouse, the lower end of Bow Church Yard, 1738, and later as Dicey and Co., Dicey and Okell, and Cluer Dicey. They engraved and printed little music, but principally sign-plates, bills, trade cards, chapbooks, etc., as well as advertising and selling Dr. Bateman's Pectoral Drops, of which John Cluer and his successors, including William and Cluer Dicey, had an interest, and which were on sale at the Northampton and London premises. (Sometimes known as Dicey and Company's Warehouse, at the King's Arms and Boar's Head directly facing the south door of Bow-Church.) In 1764 Cluer Dicey went into partnership with Richard Marshall at Aldermary Church Yard, London, as printers of chapbooks, etc., Cluer Dicey having taken these premises a year or two earlier, although retaining some interest in the old premises in Bow Church Yard, where the medicine business was continued as Dicey, Beynon and Co., etc., for a number of years.
    K. G. (Cluer). P. II.

DICKINSON (JOSEPH). Print seller, 114 New Bond Street, London. Published "The London Spring Annual, lyrical & pictorial for 1834 . . . Edited by William Ball."

DIETHER (JOHN). Composer, music seller and publisher, London; 27 New Lisle Street, c. 1807-15; 29 Lisle Street, Leicester Square, c. 1815-30.
    K.

DILLY (CHARLES). Bookseller, 22 Poultry, London, c. 1779-1800. His name appears in the imprint of "The Psalms of David . . . By I. Watts . . . (Tunes in the Tenor Part.) London: Printed for J. F. and C. Rivington, J. Buckland, T. Longman, T. Field, C. Dilly, and

W. Goldsmith. MDCCLXXX." Charles Dilly was previously a partner in Edward and Charles Dilly.
    P. III.

DILLY (EDWARD). Bookseller, in the Poultry, London, c. 1758-65. His name appears in the imprint of Martin Madan's "A Collection of Psalm and Hymn Tunes, never published before. To be had at the Lock Hospital near Hyde Park Corner, and of E. Dilly in the Poultry," c. 1765. Edward Dilly was joined by his brother Charles c. 1765 and the business was continued as Edward and Charles Dilly.
    P. III.

DILLY (EDWARD) & (CHARLES). Booksellers and publishers, in the Poultry, near the Mansion House, London, c. 1765-79. Their names appear in the imprints of a number of sacred music works; Edward was previously in business alone; business continued by Charles Dilly.
    P. III.

DING (LAURENCE). Musician, music seller and publisher, Edinburgh. Published "The Songster's Favourite: or, a new collection, containing forty . . . songs, duets, trios . . . By Laurence Ding . . . Edinburgh: Printed for the compiler, and sold by him at Churnside and Wilson's Printing Office, Royal Bank Close," etc., c. 1785; "The Beauties of Psalmody . . . By Laurence Ding . . . Edinburgh, Printed for and sold by the Editor at his house, first entry within the Netherbow, 1792." Had a music shop 4 Parliament Square, c. 1793; 19 Parliament Square, c. 1794-1801.
    K.

DISTIN & CO. *See* Distin (Henry).

DISTIN & SONS. Music and musical instrument sellers and publishers, 31 Cranbourn Street, Leicester Square, London, c. 1845-49. Succeeded by Henry Distin.

DISTIN (HENRY). Music seller and brass musical instrument manufacturer, London; 31 Cranbourn Street, Leicester Square, c. 1849-57; 31 Cranbourn Street, Leicester Square, and 9 Great Newport Street, Long Acre, c. 1857-59; 9 Great Newport Street, Long Acre, c. 1859-1868, with additional premises at No. 10 from c. 1861-68 and No. 11, c. 1866-68. Became Henry Distin and Co. c. 1862. Boosey and Co. purchased the business in 1868 and until 1874 continued to use the name of Distin and Co. at 9-11 Great Newport Street. Succeeded Distin and Sons.
    G.

DIXON (WILLIAM). Musician, music engraver and printer. Engraved and printed a number of his own compositions; at Guildford, "Psalmodia Christiana . . . Harmonized, & . . . composed by William Dixon," c. 1789; at 6 Borough Road, St. George's Fields, London, "Six Anthems in Score," c. 1790; "Four Services in Score," c. 1790; "A New Anthem in Score," c. 1795; at Cambridge, "Moralities," c. 1800. Also at Cambridge engraved and printed for the editor, "A Second Collection, of Glees, Rounds, & Canons . . . Composed by the members of the Harmonic Society of Cambridge, and publish'd by Charles Hague," c. 1800.

DOBSON or DOPSON (ELIPHAL). Bookseller, Castle Street, Dublin, 1682-c. 1720. (P.) His name appears in the imprint of "The Psalms of David in Metre, Newly translated. With amendments. By William Barton . . . The Second edition, corrected and amended. With the Basses. By Thomas Smith. Dublin. Printed by J. Brocas, for Elip. Dopson, Tho. Servant Booksellers in Castle Street and P. Lawrence . . . 1706."
P. II.

DOD or DODD (ANNE), *Mrs.* Book and pamphlet seller, London, 1726-1743; Without Temple Bar; Peacock, near Temple Bar; Near Essex Street in the Strand. (P.) Advertised and sold a number of musical works.
P. II, III.

DODD (T.). Musical instrument maker, 11 New Street, Covent Garden, London. Published "Twenty Four Country Dances for the Year 1795 . . . With proper Tunes and Directions to each Dance . . . Set for the Violin German Flute or Hautboy."

DODSLEY (ROBERT). Bookseller and publisher, at Tully's Head, Pall Mall, London, 1735-64. (P.) Published "Colin's Kisses. Set to musick by Mr. Oswald. Neatly engrav'd on copper, with a curious frontispiece. Printed for R. Dodsley in Pall Mall and sold by T. Cooper in Paternoster Row"; advertised December 1742. Advertised November 1744 and March 1745 that he took in subscriptions for "A Proposal for printing by subscription, Six Odes of Horace, set to musick, vocal and instrumental . . . in five volumes . . . by Sig. Gioseppo Antonio Paganelli."
P. III.

DOE (EDWARD). Bookseller, Oxford. His name appears in the imprints of "A Book of Psalmody . . . Collected engrav'd and printed by Mich. Beesly and sold by Edward Doe Book-seller in Oxford," etc., c. 1745; "An Introduction to Psalmody containing Instructions for young Beginners . . . Engrav'd printed and sold by Mich. Beesly and by Ed. Doe," etc., c. 1755; "A Collection of 20 New Psalm Tunes Compos'd with veriety of Fuges after a differant manner to any extant. Sold by Ed. Doe," etc., c. 1760.

DOIG (SILVESTER). Bookseller? Edinburgh. His name appears in the imprint of "The Edinburgh Musical Miscellany: a collection of the most approved Scotch, English, and Irish songs, set to music. Selected by D. Sime, Edinburgh. Edinburgh: Printed for W. Gordon . . . Silvester Doig, Edinburgh . . . MDCCXCII." In volume II the imprint reads "Edinburgh: Printed for Elder, T. Brown, and C. Elliot, Edinburgh; and W. Coke, Leith. MDCCXCIII."

DOLLIFE (FRANCIS). Bookbinder, book and music seller, Oxford. His name appears in the imprint of "Deliciæ Musicæ: Being, a Collection of the newest and best Songs . . . The First Book of the Second Volume. London, Printed by J. Heptinstall, for Henry Playford . . . and for John Church, sold by Daniel Dring . . . And also sold at Oxford by Francis Dollife . . . 1696"; also "The Second Book of the Second Volume. London, Printed by J. Heptinstall, for Henry Playford . . . And sold at Oxford by Francis Dollife . . . 1696."
    P. II. D. & M.

DONALDSON (JAMES). *See* Sands, Donaldson, Murray, & Cochran.

DONALDSON (JOHN). Bookseller, 195 Strand, corner of Arundel Street, London. Published "The Gentle Shepherd: a Scots Pastoral Comedy. Adorned with cuts, the overtures to the songs, and a complete glossary By Allan Ramsay . . . MDCCLXXV."
    P. III.

DOPSON (ELIPHAL). *See* Dobson or Dopson.

DOVER & HENDERSON. Music and musical instrument sellers, and publishers, 68 Chancery Lane, London, c. 1825-28. William Dover was previously in business alone.

DOVER (WILLIAM). Music and musical instrument seller, and publisher, London; Lincoln's Inn Fields, leading to Great Turnstile, c. 1805-20; 5 (or 6) Newman's Row, c. 1820-24; 68 Chancery Lane, c. 1824-25. Joined by Henderson c. 1825 and became Dover and Henderson.
    K.

DOWNING (M.). Bookseller, Bartholomew Close, London, 1735-53. (P.) Name appears in the imprint of "The Psalms of David in Metre: With the tunes used in Parish-Churches. By John Patrick. The Eighth edition. London: Printed for J. Walthoe . . . M. Downing . . . MDCCXLII."
    P. III.

DRAPER (S.). Music seller, at his Musical Repository, 246 High Street, Shoreditch, London. Printed and published "Siege of Algiers, Divertimento for the Pianoforte by Mr. Thorley," c. 1805.

DRAPER (SOMERSET). Bookseller and publisher, London, 1743-54.
See Tonson (Jacob) *third of the name* & (Richard) *the Younger*.

DRING (DANIEL). Bookseller, at the Harrow and Crown, at the corner
of Clifford's Inn Lane, Fleet Street, London, 1695-96. (P.) His
name appears in the imprints of "Joyful Cuckoldom, or the Love of
Gentlemen and Gentlewomen," c. 1696?; "Thesaurus Musicus:
Being a Collection of the newest Songs performed at His Majesties
Theatres . . . The Fourth Book . . . 1695,"; also The Fifth Book. 1696;
"Deliciæ Musicæ: Being a Collection of the newest and best Songs
. . . The First Book of the Second Volume . . . 1696." Probably a son
of Thomas Dring whom he succeeded at this address.
    P. II. D. & M.

DRING (THOMAS). Bookseller, at the Harrow, at Clifford's Lane end
in Fleet Street, London, and other addresses, 1668-95. (P.) His
name appears in the imprint of "The Songs in the Indian Queen:
As it is now compos'd into an Opera. By Mr. Henry Purcell . . .
London, Printed by J. Heptinstall; and are to be sold by John May
. . . And for John Hudgbutt at Tho. Dring's . . . 1695."
    P. II. D. & M.

DROUET (LOUIS FRANÇOIS PHILIPPE). Flautist, flute maker and
music seller, London, c. 1815-19, first at his Flute Manufactory and
Music Warehouse, 23 Conduit Street, Bond Street, afterwards at 358
Oxford Street. Published some of his own compositions.
    G.

DUCKWORTH (J.). At his house, 9 Oakley Street, near the Asylum,
Lambeth, London. Printed and sold, c. 1795, "Spanish Dollars, a
favourite song by Mr. Astley, senior, sung by Mr. Connell, and
introduced in the representation of the situation of Lieutenant Rion
in the Guardian Frigate, when surrounded by an island of ice, and
now performing at Astley's, Westminster Bridge," etc. May have
been John Duckworth, musician, 6 Paradise Row, Lambeth, 1805.
    K.

DUCKWORTH (JOHN). Music engraver, printer and publisher, 1
Catherine Street, Strand, London, c. 1777-80.

DUFF & HODGSON. Music sellers and publishers, London; 65 Oxford
Street, c. 1837-62; 20 Oxford Street and 51 Hanway Street, c. 1862-66.
Succeeded John Duff and Co.; succeeded by Duff and Steward.

DUFF & STEWARD. *See* Duff & Hodgson.

DUFF (JOHN) & CO. Music seller and publisher, 65 Oxford Street,
London, c. 1831-37. Became Duff and Hodgson, c. 1837.

DUFF (S.). Music seller, 79 Swallow Street, Hanover Square, London. Advertised June 1787, "Three Sonatas for the Harpsichord, or Piano Forte, with an accompaniment for the Violin, composed . . . by George Baker . . . Printed by S. Duff, Music-seller," etc.

DUFFY (JAMES). Bookseller, 23 Anglesea Street, Dublin. Published "The Spirit of the Nation. Ballads and songs by the writers of 'The Nation,' with original and ancient music, arranged for the voice and piano-forte . . . 1845"; also an edition in 1846.

DUFOUR (WILLIAM). Stationer, music seller and publisher, 33 Piccadilly, London, c. 1842-45.

DUGARD (WILLIAM). Schoolmaster and printer, London, 1644-62. (P.) Printed in conjunction with Roger Daniel "The Book of Psalms in Metre . . . translated by W. Barton. To be sung in usuall and known tunes . . . London: Printed by Roger Daniel, and William Du-Gard, and are to be sold by Francis Eglesfield, and Thomas Underhill . . . and Francis Tyton . . . 1654."
    P. I.

DUKE (RICHARD). Musical instrument maker and music seller, opposite Great Turnstile, Holborn, afterwards 53 High Holborn, London, c. 1760-83. Had a high reputation among English violin makers; published a small amount of music, some in conjunction with Henry Thorowgood; died 1783; business carried on by his daughter Mrs. A. Paris assisted by her brother.
    G.

DUKES COURT, BY THE MEUSE. *See* Scouler (J.).

DUNCAN. *See* Lyon & Duncan.

DUNCOMBE & MOON. Music sellers, printers and publishers, 17 Holborn Hill, London, c. 1848-53. Partners were John Duncombe, previously in business alone, and Frederick Moon; stock-in-trade offered for sale by Puttick and Simpson 20th December 1853.

DUNCOMBE (JOHN). Music seller, printer and publisher, London; at his cheap music warehouse, 14 St. Martin's Court, c. 1810-15; 19 Little Queen Street, c. 1815-35; 10 Middle Row, Holborn, c. 1835-48. Became John Duncombe & Co., c. 1840; Duncombe and Moon, c. 1848.

DUNOYER (PETER). Bookseller, at the sign of Erasmus's Head, near the Fountain Tavern, in the Strand, London. Advertised March 1711, "Six Sonata's for a Flute and a Thorough Bass by Mr. Gaillard [i.e. Galliard]. Sold by Peter Dunoyer," etc.; advertised January 1725,

"A New System of Music, both theorical and practical, and yet not mathematical; containing a scale of twelve notes with the abolishing of all flats and sharps, and those great puzzlers the clefs, &c. . . . Sold by William Meadows . . . and Peter du Noyer," etc.
    P. III.

DUPREE (GEORGE). Stationer, 22 Bucklersbury, London. Published c. 1843, "The Indian Woman's Death Song, a Ballad, the words by Mrs. Hemans, the music composed . . . by a young Friend."

DUSSEK (JAN LADISLAV). *See* Corri, Dussek & Co.

DYKES & COOPER. Booksellers, 33 Piccadilly, London. Published, c. 1841, "The Star of the Realm or, The Princess Royal, Song, the music composed by Mrs. Brent, the words by Æ. M. G."

DYSON (WILLIAM). Bookseller, Halifax and Huddersfield. Published, "The Spiritual-Man's Companion. Containing great variety of chants and anthems, and also tunes fitted to all the different measures of the Psalms. . . By Israel Holdroyd . . . London. Printed by Wm. Pearson," etc., c. 1724; also the second edition, c. 1730.

E., P. *See* Evans (P.).

E., T. *See* Este, Est, East, or Easte (Thomas).

EAST (LUCRETIA). *See* Este, Est, East, or Easte (Thomas).

EAST or EASTE (THOMAS). *See* Este, Est, East, or Easte.

EAST (WILLIAM). Printer, Waltham, near Melton Mowbray, Leicestershire, 1748-54. (P.) Printed and sold "Musarum Britannicanarum Thesaurus: or, A Choice Collection of English Songs, Dialogues, and Catches . . . Collected, printed and sold by William East . . . 1748 "; "The Voice of Melody, Or: A Choice Collection of Psalm-Tunes in Four Parts . . . Printed for William East", etc., c. 1748; "The Second edition of the first Book of the Voice of Melody. With great additions . . . Collected, printed and sold by William East . . . 1750 "; "The Second Book of the Voice of Melody . . . Collected, printed, and sold by William East . . . 1750 "; "The Sacred Melody. Being the newest and choicest collection of Church-musick now extant . . . Collected and publish'd by William East . . . 1754."
    P. III.

EASTLAND (GEORGE). Musician, whose address is given as "Hanging Sword Court, near to the Green Dragon and Sword in Fleet Street." (M. Dowling. *The Library*, 4th Series. XII. No. 4, March 1932.) Acquired the manuscript of John Dowland's "Second Booke of Songs or

Ayres, 1600, which was printed by Thomas Este, but "Published by George Eastland, and are to be sold at his house neere the greene Dragon and Sword in Fleetstreete."
K.

EASTON (JAMES). Bookseller, Salisbury. His name appears in the imprint of "Anecdotes of George Frederick Handel and John Christopher Smith. With select pieces of music, composed by J. C. Smith, never before published. London: Printed by W. Bulmer and Co. Sold by Cadell and Davies . . . E. Harding . . . Birchall . . . and J. Eaton [i.e. Easton], Salisbury. 1799."

EAVESTAFF (WILLIAM). Music seller, publisher and pianoforte maker, 66 Great Russell Street, London, 1823-51, with additional premises at 17 Sloane Street, c. 1844-51.
K.

EBBLEWHITE (W.). Music seller, 14 Tottenham Court Road, London. From Collard and Collard, late Clementi and Co. Published, c. 1835, "Sing the Song and join the Chorus. A song, written by A. F. Westmacott Esqr. The music composed . . . by N. J. Sporle."

EDLIN (THOMAS). Printer and bookseller, Prince's Arms, opposite Exeter Exchange, in the Strand, London, 1721-28. (P.) Published "Recueil d'airs françois, serieux & à boire. A une, deux, & trois parties, composé en Angleterre, par Mr. Jean Claude Gillier . . . 1723"; "Di Canzonette e di Cantate libri due di Paolo Rolli . . . MDCCXXVII."
K. P. II, III.

EDMUND (JOHN). Winchester. His name appears in the imprint of "A Book of Psalmody . . . Collected engrav'd and printed by Mich. Beesly and sold by . . . John Edmund at Winchester," c. 1745.

EDWARD (WILLIAM). Engraver, Edinburgh. Engraved "Six Solos for a Violin with a Bass for the Violoncello and Thorough Bass for the Harpsichord" for Neil Stewart, c. 1765; "A Collection of Scots Reels or Country Dances and Minuets . . . Composed by John Riddle at Ayr, and sold by Himself there; likewise by Mr. Robt. Bremner in Edinr. also at his shope . . . in the Strand, London . . . Wm. Edward, Sculpt. Dun Cameron prints it, Edinr.", c. 1766.
K.

EGERTON (JOHN). Bookseller, Whitehall, London. His name appears in the imprint of "Scottish Song in Two Volumes. [Edited, with an historical essay, by Joseph Ritson.] London: Printed for J. Johnson, in St. Paul's Churchyard; and J. Egerton . . . MDCCXCIV." Related to Thomas Egerton with whom he was in business in 1792.

[139]

EGERTON (THOMAS). Bookseller, Whitehall, London. His name appears in the imprint of "Robin Hood: A collection of all the ancient poems, songs, and ballads, now extant, relative to that celebrated English outlaw . . . In two volumes. [With some tunes. Edited by Joseph Ritson.] London: Printed for T. Egerton, Whitehall, and J. Johnson, St. Paul's Churchyard. MDCCXCV." Related to John Egerton with whom he was in business in 1792.

EGLESFIELD (FRANCIS). Bookseller, at the Marigold, St. Paul's Church-yard, London, 1637-67. (P.) His name appears in the imprint of "The Book of Psalms in Metre . . . translated by W. Barton. To be sung in usuall and known tunes . . . London: Printed by Roger Daniel and William Du-Gard, and are to be sold by Francis Eglesfield, and Thomas Underhill . . . and Francis Tyton . . . 1654."
P. I.

EKIN or EKINS (NATHANIEL). Bookseller, at the Gun in St. Paul's Church Yard, London, 1641-73. (P.) Published "Ayres and Dialogues For One, Two, and Three Voyces; To be Sung either to the Theorbo-Lute or Basse-Viol. Composed by John Gamble . . . The Second Book. London, Printed by W. Godbid for Nathaniel Ekin at the Gun in St. Pauls Church-yard: 1659."
P. I, II. D. & M.

ELDER (JOHN). Bookseller, Edinburgh. His name appears in the imprint of Volume II of "The Edinburgh Musical Miscellany: a collection of the most approved Scotch, English, and Irish songs, set to music. Selected by D. Sime, Edinburgh. Edinburgh: Printed for John Elder, T. Brown, and C. Elliot, Edinburgh; and W. Coke, Leith. MDCCXCIII."; the above volume was reissued as "The New Edinburgh Musical Miscellany . . . Selected by D. Sime. Edinburgh: Printed for J. Elder and T. Brown . . . 1794."

ELLARD (ANDREW). Musical instrument maker, music seller and publisher, Dublin; 27 Lower Sackville Street, c. 1819-22; 47 Lower Sackville Street, c. 1822-38. Was the Dublin agent for Phillips, Mayhew and Co., London.
K.

ELLIOT (CHARLES). Bookseller and publisher, Parliament Close, or, Parliament Square, Edinburgh, 1770-93. Published "The Gentle Shepherd: a Scots pastoral Comedy. Adorned with cuts, the overture to the songs, and a complete glossary . . . By Allan Ramsay . . . MDCCLXXVI." His name also appears in the imprints of a number of musical works; he was a partner in the firm of C. Elliot and T. Kay, booksellers, 332 Strand, London, 1787-91.
P. III.

ELLIOT (CHARLES) & KAY (T.). Booksellers and Stationers, 332 Strand, opposite Somerset Place, London, 1787-91. Published, "Calliope: or, The Musical Miscellany. A select collection of the most approved English, Scots, and Irish Songs, set to music . . . MDCCLXXXVIII." Charles Elliot was also in business as a bookseller and publisher in Edinburgh, 1770-93.
P. III.

ELLIS (THOMAS WILLIAM). Music seller and publisher, London; 102 St. Martin's Lane, 1842; 41 Greek Street, Soho, 1843. Published some of his own compositions.

ELLISTON. Music seller? Leamington. His name appears in the imprint of "Washing Day, a proper new Ballad, for wet weather. Birmingham, Printed at the Lithographic Press, by W. Hawkes Smith. Sold also by . . . — Elliston, Leamington", etc., c. 1820.

EMBERY, *Mr.* Bookseller? In St. Martin's Street, Leicester Fields, London. Advertised May 1757, "Twelve Odes of Horace, translated into Italian verse by Signor Bottarelli, and set to music by the most eminent English Masters . . . Printed for, and sold by, Mr. Embery", etc.

EMERY (GEORGE). *See* Balls (Eliza) & Co.

EMERY (JOSEPH). *See* D'Almaine & Co.

ENGLEFIELD (E.). Printer and publisher, at the Bible, West Street, London. Printed and sold "The Spiritual Psalmodist's Companion; being a choice collection of psalms, and hymns with tunes. . . . London: Printed and sold by E. Englefield . . . and W. Kent . . . MDCCLXXII."

ESSEX (JOHN). Dancing Master, Rood Lane, Fenchurch Street, London. His name appears in the imprint of "The Dancing Master . . . Done from the French of Monsieur Rameau, by J. Essex . . . London, printed and sold by him and J. Brotherton . . . 1728." Composed and wrote in characters Country Dances in "A Treatis of Chorography . . . Translated from the French of Mon^{sr}. Feuillet . . . London, Sold by I. Walsh . . . & by ye Author at his house in Rude-lane Fanchurch-street, 1710"; and another edition, "A Treatise of Chorography", etc., c. 1715.

ESTE, EST, EAST, or EASTE (THOMAS). Printer, bookseller, music printer and publisher, London, c. 1566-1609; at Fleet Street, near St. Dunstan's Church, c.1566-70; at Bread Street, at the nether end, 1568; at London Wall, by the sign of the Ship, 1571-77. (M.) Issued some musical works from c. 1587, when his address was "by Paules Wharfe, Thames Street, where he was from 1577-88; in Aldersgate

Street over against the Sign of the George, 1589; in Aldersgate Street at the sign of the Black Horse, 1589-c. 1605 or later, but many of his imprints merely give London; issued some works bearing only the initials T. E.; he died in 1609 and his business apparently passed to Thomas Snodham a former apprentice, to whom Este's widow Lucretia, made over some of her husband's copyrights in 1609 and others to John Browne in December, 1610. Este issued works from 1587 as the assigne of William Byrd, from 1600 as the assigne of Thomas Morley, and from 1606 as the assigne of William Barley; for some time up to 1572 he was in partnership with Henry Middleton. "Lucretia East the assignee of William Barley" issued in 1610 an edition of Byrd's "Songs of sundry natures", etc., previously issued by her husband in 1589.

K. G. M. S.

EUANS (DORETHIE). *See* Evans.

EVANS & LUCAS. Music sellers and publishers, 53 Cheapside, London, c. 1821. Business afterwards carried on by R. W. Evans.

EVANS (DOROTHY). Her name appears on the title-page of "Parthenia or The Maydenhead of the first musicke that euer was printed for the Virginalls Composed By three famous Masters William Byrd, D^r: Iohn Bull, & Orlando Gibbons . . . Ingrauen by William Hole. Lond: print: for M^{ris} Dor: Euans . . . Are to be sould by G: Lowe print^r in Loathberry," c. 1613; also two slightly later issues with modified title-pages, bearing the names of William Hole, Dorethie Euans and G. Lowe.

K. (William Hole).

EVANS (P.). Music seller and publisher, 102 High Holborn, London, 1776-c. 1786. Previously with Longman, Lukey & Co.; some single sheet songs bear only the initials P. E.

K.

EVANS (ROBERT WILLIAM). Composer, musician, music seller and publisher, London; 17 Charles Street, Covent Garden, c. 1815; 53 Cheapside, c. 1821-22; 146 Strand, c. 1824-27. Was partner in Evans and Lucas, 53 Cheapside, c. 1821, and Ware and Evans, 146 Strand, c. 1823; on one of his compositions he states that he was late of the King's Theatre, Haymarket.

EVANS (THOMAS). Bookseller and publisher, Paternoster Row, London, 1770-1803. (P.) His name appears in the imprint of "Hymns for Three Voices, accompanied with Instruments; to which is added an Anthem by William Flackton. London. Printed & sold by S. & A. Thompson . . . and Thomas Evans", etc., c. 1778.

P. III.

EVANS (WILLIAM) & CO.   Printers, booksellers and publishers, London;
22 Warwick Square, Paternoster Row, c. 1848-87; 19 Warwick
Square, Paternoster Row, c. 1887-91.   Published some songs with
music on single sheets.

EVERINGHAM (ROBERT).   Printer, Seven Stars, Ave Mary Lane,
London. 1680-1700.   (P.)   Printed "The Whole Book of Psalms, as
they are now sung in the Churches: with the singing notes of time
and tune set to every syllable . . . London, Printed by R. Everingham
for the Company of Stationers, and are to be sold by E. Brewster . . .
and S. Kettle . . . 1688.";   "The Psalms and Hymns, usually sung
in the Churches and Tabernacles of St. Martins in the Fields, and
St. James's Westminster.   London, Printed by R. Everingham for
Ric. Chiswell . . . 1688."
    P. II.

EWER & JOHANNING.   Music sellers and publishers, London;   1 Bow
Church Yard, Cheapside, c. 1825-29.   Had additional addresses at
263 Regent Street, c. 1825-26, and 20 Titchbourne Street, Piccadilly,
c. 1826-29.
    K. (Ewer & Co.).
    See also Ewer (John Jeremiah) & Co.; Johanning & Whatmore.

EWER (JOHN) & CO.   Music sellers and publishers, London;   1 Bow
Church Yard, Cheapside, c. 1823-25, with additional premises at
263 Regent Street, end of 1824-25.   From c. 1825-29 business
became Ewer and Johanning at 1 Bow Church Yard, Cheapside, with
other addresses at 263 Regent Street, c. 1825-26, and 20 Titchbourne
Street, Piccadilly, c. 1826-29.   Johanning withdrew c. 1829 and
firm became J. J. Ewer and Co.;   1 Bow Church Yard, c. 1829-41;
69 Newgate Street, c. 1841-43;   72 Newgate Street, c. 1843-52;
390 Oxford Street, c. 1852-59; 87 Regent Street, c. 1859-67.   Merged
with Novello and Co. in 1867 and became Novello, Ewer and Co.;
purchased stock-in-trade of G. Andre 1839.
    K. G.

EYRES (JOHN).   Printer and bookseller, next door to the White Bull,
in the Horse Market, Warrington, 1731-c. 1756.   (P.)   His name
appears in the imprint of "A Book of Psalmody . . . The Second edition
. . . By Robert Barber.   London: Printed by W. Pearson . . . for the
Author; and for John Eyres, Bookseller, in Warrington, and Josiah
Rathbone, Bookseller in Macclesfield.   MDCCXXXIII."
    P. III.

F., I.;   F., Ino.;   F—m, I.   *See* Fentum (Jonathan) or (John).

F., M.   *See* Fletcher or Flesher (Miles).

F—m, Ka. *See* Fentum (Catherine).

F., W. *See* Forster (William) *the Elder*.

FADEN (WILLIAM). Printer, London. Printed "A Small Collection of Psalms to the old Tunes, sung by the Charity Children of the City of Chichester. Published for general use . . . 1761."

FALKENER (ROBERT). Music printer, music seller and publisher, London; published from his houses, 45 Salisbury Court, Fleet Street, c. 1770-75; 3 Peterborough Court, Fleet Street, c. 1775-80; also had a shop at 159, near Somerset House, in the Strand, c. 1775; Is said to have purchased the plant and improved type of Henry Fougt, c. 1770; printed and sold music at one penny per page.
K.

FALKNER & CHRISTMAS. Music sellers and publishers, London; Opera Music Warehouse, 9 Pall Mall, c. 1811-14; 36 Pall Mall, c. 1814-16. Succeeded Michael Kelly. Partnership between Henry Falkner and Charles Christmas dissolved 1816, and both carried on business independently.
K.

FALKNER (HENRY). Music seller and publisher, Opera Music Ware-house, 3 Old Bond Street, London, 1816-44. Previously partner in the firm of Falkner & Christmas.
K.
Select Catalogue of new and popular Piano-forte Music. c. 1822. 1 p. fol. (B.M. g. 271. b. (45.))

FARMER (HENRY). Music seller, High Street, Nottingham. Published "The Adrienne Polka. Composed . . . by Arthur S. H. Lowe", c. 1846; "The Review Polka, composed . . . by Frank M. Ward", c. 1849.

FARN (CHARLES JOSEPH). Musical instrument maker, music seller and publisher, 72 Lombard Street, London, c. 1831-33. Previously in the employ of Charles Vernon.

FARNSWORTH (B.). Bookseller, Newark, 1715-19. (P.) His name appears in the imprint of "A Collection of Psalm-Tunes; with Great Variety of Hymns and Anthems compos'd by the best Masters . . . By James Green. The Fourth edition . . . London. Printed by William Pearson, for the Author: and sold by . . . B. Farnsworth in Newark . . . 1718."
P. I.

FARTHING (A. C.). Printer, 23 Corn Street, Bath. Printed for the Author, Vol. II of "A Periodical Collection of Vocal Music (never before printed) consisting of Italian and English Songs . . . Composed by Venanzio Rauzzini . . . In two volumes," c. 1797; printed for the composer, "A Collection of Church Music; consisting of a Te Deum, Jubilate, and twelve Psalms or Hymns . . . as performed . . . at St. James's Church, and the Countess of Huntingdon's Chapel, in the City of Bath . . . MDCCXCVIII."; composed by A. Loder.

FELLOWS.   *See* Hart & Fellows.

FENTUM (CATHERINE).   Music seller and publisher, 417, later at 416, near Bedford Street, Strand, London, c. 1780-85.   Some single sheet songs bear only the letters "Ka. F—m."
  K.

FENTUM (HENRY).   Musician, music seller and publisher, 78 Strand, London, c. 1844-59.   Succeeded Mary Ann Fentum.
  G.

FENTUM (JOHN).   *See* Fentum (Jonathan).

FENTUM (JONATHAN).   Music engraver, music seller and publisher, London; 22 Exeter Exchange in the Strand, 1763-c. 1765; the corner of Salisbury Street, near Southampton Street, in the Strand, c. 1765-70; as J. Fentum, Corner of Salisbury Street, near Cecil Street in the Strand (or, 78 Corner of Salisbury Street), c. 1770-81; as Fentum's Music Shop, 78 Corner of Salisbury Street, near Cecil Street in the Strand, c. 1781-84; as John Fentum (who had succeeded Jonathan 1784, or earlier), 78 Strand, 1784-1835, with additional premises at 2 St. George's Place, near Camberwell Green, 1810. Some single sheet songs bear only the abbreviations or initials "Ino. F."; "I. F."; "I. F—m." John Fentum was succeeded by Mrs. Mary Ann Fentum.
  K. G.
    Catalogues:—Vocal and Instrumental Music.   1784.   1 p. fol. (B.M. g. 421. v. (1.)); Music.   c. 1790.   1 p. fol. (B.M. Hirsch IV. 1112. (3.))

FENTUM (MARY ANN).   Music seller and publisher, 78 Strand, London, c. 1835-44.   Mrs. Fentum succeeded Jonathan Fentum; succeeded by Henry Fentum.
  G.

FIELD (THOMAS).   Bookseller and publisher, London, 1755-c. 1775; near St. Paul's; at the White Sheaf, the corner of Paternoster Row. (P.) His name appears in the imprints of a number of sacred music works.
  P. III.

FIELDEN (MARTIN). *See* Fielding or Fielden.

FIELDING (JOHN). Bookseller, 23 Paternoster Row, London. Published "The Convivial Songster, being a select collection of the best Songs in the English language . . . 1782"; "The Vocal Enchantress, presenting an elegant Selection of the most favourite Hunting, Sea, Love, & miscellaneous Songs," etc., 1783; "Music, Poetry & Painting, presenting an elegant Selection of the most approv'd Songs, Sonatas &c. With a thorough bass for the Harpsichord, under the inspection of Mr. Joseph Olive . . . 1785," only the first part of which, containing six songs, appears to have been published.
    K.

FIELDING or FIELDEN (MARTIN). Bookseller, Halifax. His name appears in the imprints of "Psalmody Epitomiz'd . . . The second edition with additions. By Ely Stansfield. London: Printed by W. Pearson, for T. Cox . . . and M. Fielding . . . in Hallifax. 1731"; "The Spiritual Man's Companion. The third edition . . . By Israel Holdroyd . . . London: Printed by W. Pearson . . . for the Author, and sold by him and by Mr. Hammond . . . in York, and by Martin Fielden, Bookseller, in Hallifax. MDCCXXXIII."; "A Book of Psalmody . . . The Fifth edition . . . By John Chetham. London: Printed by A. Pearson, for Joseph Lord . . . in Wakefield . . . and sold by . . . Martin Fielding . . . in Hallifax . . . MDCCXXXVI."

FILMER (EDWARD). Published "French Court-Aires, with their Ditties Englished, Of foure and fiue Parts. Together with that of the Lute . . . Collected, Translated, Published by Ed: Filmer, Gent: London, Printed by William Stansby. 1629."
    K.

FIRTH (RICHARD). Music seller and publisher, Oxford, c. 1785-1805, or later.

FISHER (THOMAS). Stationer, in Cornhill, near the Royal Exchange, London. His name appears in an advertisement December 1676, "The famous and long expected Musicks of Two Parts, by Nicola Matteis are now published; consisting of Ayres of all sorts, fitted for all hands, and capacities, and 190 Copper-plates; cut at the Desire, and Charge of certain Well-wishers to the Work. They are to be sold by John Carr . . . Thomas Fisher . . . And also by the Author," etc.

FITZPATRICK & COLES. Music sellers and publishers, 177 High Holborn, London, c. 1815-25.

FITZWILLIAM (JAMES) & CO. Music sellers and publishers, London; 8 New Street, Covent Garden, c. 1820-24; 44 King Street, Soho, c. 1824.
    K.

FLEETWOOD (ANTHONY). Lithographic printer, stationer and bookseller, 44 Ranelagh Street, Liverpool. Printed from stone at A. Fleetwood's Lithographic Press c. 1825, "God save the King, arranged with Variations, for the Piano Forte by D. M°Pherson."

FLEETWOOD (EDWARD). Bookseller? At the foot of the Parliament Stairs in Westminster Hall, London. His name appears in the imprint of "A Book of new Songs (after the Italian manner) with Symphonies & a Through-Bass fitted to the Harpsichord &c. . . . Compos'd by Mr. John Reading . . . London. Printed for ye Author and are to be sold by him . . . and by Brabazon Aylmer . . . Edward Fleetwood," etc., c. 1710.

FLEMING (R.). Music seller, at the Cross, Edinburgh. Sold, "Lessons in the practice of Singing, with an addition of the Church Tunes, in four parts, and a collection of Hymns, Canons, Airs, and Catches . . . by Cornforth Gilson, teacher of music in Edinburgh . . . 1759."
K.

FLESHER (MILES). *See* Fletcher or Flesher.

FLETCHER (I. D.). London. Published, "Pieces de Clavecin en Deux Volumes Consistant des Ouvertures, Preludes, Fugues, Allemandes, Courentes, Sarabandes, Giques, et Aires. Composées par I. Mattheson, Secr. 1714"; also an edition with a German title-page: "Mattheson Harmonisches Denckmahl/Aus Zwölf erwåhlten Clavier-Suiten/ Bestehend in Ouverturen/Symphonien/Fugen/Boutaden/Præludien/ Allemanden/Couranten/Sarabanden/Giquen/Arien und Menuetten/ nebst ihren Doublen oder Variationen,Von Arbeitsamer und ungemeiner Structur errichtet . . . 1714", preface is dated February 1715. Given as I. D. Fletcher in the imprints, but probably meant for J. D.

FLETCHER (JAMES). *See* Rivington (James) & Fletcher (James).

FLETCHER or FLESHER (MILES). Printer, Little Britain, London, 1611-64. (P.) Only the initials M. F. appear in the imprint of the work presumed to be printed by Miles Fletcher, "The Whole Booke of Psalmes: collected into English Meter, by Tho. Sternhold, John Hopkins, W. Whittingham, and others . . . with apt notes to sing them withall . . . London. Printed by M. F. for the Company of Stationers. 1641"; also an edition in 1642.
P. I.

FLETCHER or FLESHER (MILES). Printer, London. Printed "A Psalm of Thanksgiving, to be sung by the Children of Christ's Hospital, on Monday, Tuesday, and Wednesday in Easter Week . . . 1688."

FLETCHER (THOMAS) & HODSON (FRANCIS). Printers, Market

Hill, Cambridge, 1762-77. (P.) Their names appear in the imprint of "The Psalms of David . . . By I. Watts . . . A new edition, corrected. (Tunes in the Tenor Part fitted to the several Metres.) Salisbury: Printed and sold by Collins and Johnson. Sold also by Fletcher and Hodson, at Cambridge . . . MDCCLXXVI."
    P. III.

FLETCHER (WILLIAM). Music seller, Bull Street, Birmingham. Printed and sold for the author, "Odes, Cantatas, Songs &c, Divine, moral, entertaining set to music by Mr. Pixell. Opera Seconda. 1775."

FLIGHT & ROBSON. Organ builders, 101 St. Martin's Lane, London, c. 1806-33. Published "A Selection of Psalms & Hymns as set on the Organ, in the Parish Church of Sutton on the Forest in York-shire . . . 1809"; "A Selection of Psalms and Hymns, as set on the Organ, in the Chappel of Aberystwith", etc., c. 1811; "A Selection of Psalms & Hymns as set on the Organ, the gift of . . . the Marquis of Buckingham, to the Parish Church of Stowe, Bucks," c. 1817; "A Selection of Psalms & Hymns as set on the Organ, the gift of . . . the Duke of Bedford to the Parish Church of Milton Abbot," c. 1818.

FORBES (JOHN). Bookseller and printer, above the Meal Market at the sign of the Towns Armes, Aberdeen, 1656-1704. (P.) Printed "Cantus, Songs and Fancies to Thre, Foure, or Five Partes, both apt for Voices and Viols. With a briefe introduction of musick, as is taught in the Musick-Schole of Aberdene by T. D. Mr. of Musick . . . MDCLXII."; "Cantus, Songs and Fancies . . . With a brief introduction to musick, as is taught by Thomas Davidson, in the Musick-School of Aberdene. Second edition, corrected and enlarged . . . MDCLXVI."; "Cantus, Songs and Fancies . . . The third edition, exactly corrected and enlarged. Together also, with severall of the choisest Italian-Songs, and new English ayres . . . 1682"; Psalm Tunes to four voices, issued without title-page, but with colophon: "Aberdene, printed by Iohn Forbes, and are to be sold at his shop, 1666."
    K. P. I. D. & M.

FORD (JOHN). Bookseller and stationer, at the Middle Temple Gate, Fleet Street, London, 1671-73. (P.) His name appears in the imprint of "Choice Songs and Ayres for one Voyce to sing to a Theorbo-Lute, or Bass-Viol . . . Composed by several Gentlemen of His Majesties Musick. The First Book. London, Printed by W. G. and are sold by John Playford . . . and John Ford . . . 1673."
    P. II. D. & M.

FORD (RICHARD). Bookseller and publisher, at the Angel in the Poultry, near Stocks Market, London, c. 1719-40. His name appears in the imprints of a number of sacred music works.
    P. III.

FORSTER & SON. *See* Forster (William) *the Elder*.

FORSTER (WILLIAM) *the Elder*. Musical instrument maker, music seller and publisher, London; Corner of Duke's Court, St. Martin's Lane, or, 133 St. Martin's Lane, c. 1762 to early in 1785; 348 Strand, near Exeter Change, early in 1785 to early in 1786. Continued as W. Forster and Son at the same address early in 1786-c. 1800; some works advertised as by W. Forster and Son bear the imprint of W. Forster only, and some single sheet songs bear only the initials, W. F. Forster reissued some works from John Kerpen's plates. Business continued by his son William.
    K. G.
    Catalogues:—Music. c. 1780. 1 p. fol. (B.M. Hirsch III. 364.); c. 1784. 1 p. fol. (B.M. g. 420. c. (7.)); 1784. 1 p. fol. (B.M. g. 420. c. (6.)); c. 1784. 1 p. fol. (B.M. g. 443. b. (1.)); W. Forster and Son. c. 1786. 1 p. fol. (B.M. g. 417. d. (3.)); 1786. 1 p. fol. (B.M. g. 421. l. (3.))

FORSTER (WILLIAM) *the Younger*. Musical instrument maker, music seller and publisher, London; 348 Strand, near Exeter Change, c. 1800-03; 22 York Street, Westminster, c. 1803-16; 87 Strand, c. 1816-21; 41 Lisle Street, c. 1821-24. Continued the business established by his father and reissued a number of his publications.
    K.
    A Catalogue of Music. c. 1800. 1 p. fol. (B.M. g. 161. j. (2.))

FORTIER (B.). Music engraver and printer, Castel (i.e. Castle) Street, Leicester Fields, London. Engraved N. Porpora's "Sinfonie da Camera a tre istromenti . . . Opra. II . . . Londra MDCCXXXVI."; E. Duni's "Arie composte per il Regio Teatro, Cantate dal Signor Carlo Broschi Farinello . . . Londra nel MDCCXXXVII."; A Song, "Osscquioso Ringraziamento per Le cortesissime Grazie ricevute nella Britannica Gloriosa Nazione dall' . . . umilissimo . . . servo Carlo Broschi Farinello", c. 1737; "VI Concerti grossi con due violini, alto-viola, è violoncello obligati; è due violini è basso di rinforzo: composti da Giuseppe St. Martini. Opra. II. . . . Londra. MDCCXXXVIII." "Essercizi per Gravicembalo di Domenico Scarlatti", advertised in London, February 1739; engraved and printed "Sonate a violino con viola di gamba ó cembalo . . . da Francesco Guerini. Opera prima . . . Londra", etc., c. 1740. This last work is the only one bearing the Castel Street address.
    G.

FOUGT (HENRY). Music printer and publisher, at the Lyre and Owl, St. Martin's Lane, near Long Acre, London, c. 1765-70. Described as "Musical Typographer." Printed music from his improved metal types, for which he obtained a patent in 1767; sold his single sheet songs at one penny per page. Is said to have sold his plant and type to Robert Falkener, c. 1770.

 K. G.

  Catalogue:—New Music. [5 items.] 1769. 1 p. fol. (B.M. g. 222. (13.))

FOULIS (ANDREW). Printer, Glasgow. Printed "The Gentle Shepherd; a Pastoral Comedy; By Allan Ramsay. Glasgow: Printed by A. Foulis, and sold by D. Allan . . . Edinburgh, also by J. Murray . . . and C. Elliot . . . London. MDCCLXXXVIII."; with the music of the songs; also an edition in 1796 with the imprint "Glasgow: Printed and sold by Andrew Foulis."

FOX (SAMUEL). Bookseller, Derby, c. 1754-58. His name appears in the imprint of "The Sacred Melody . . . Collected and publish'd by William East . . . Likewise Mr. Wightman . . . Grantham . . . Mr. Fox Derby . . . 1754."

 P. III.

FRANCIS (G.). Music seller and publisher, 25 King Street, Covent Garden, London, 1824.

FRANCIS (JOHN). Music engraver, 41 St. John's Square, Clerkenwell, London. Published "Out of Sight out of Mind, sung by Mr. Robinson, written by E. C. Snelson, composed by Thomas Scarsbrook, c. 1838"; "The Vestal. Recitative & Air sung by Manon in the Musical Drama of the Portrait . . . The opera by E. C. Snelson. Published for the Author . . . by J. Francis," c. 1838.

FRASER & CO. Booksellers, 54 North Bridge, Edinburgh. Their name appears in the imprints of "The Psaltery; a Collection of Psalm and Hymn Tunes, carefully selected from the works of the most eminent composers . . . Dublin: Published for John Kirkwood . . . By . . . Fraser and Co. Edinburgh. 1835"; "Popular Airs and Sacred Melodies, adapted for social singing. With hymn tunes and anthems . . . Dublin: Hardy & Walker . . . London: Richard Groombridge . . . Edinburgh: Fraser and Company. 1839."

FRASER (PETER). King's Arms Court, Ludgate Hill, London. Published 1726, "The Delightfull Musical Companion for Gentlemen and Ladies, being a choice collection out of all the latest Operas, composed by Mr. Handel, Sigr. Bononcini, Sigr. Attilo, &c. Vol. 1; Curiously engraven for ye Publisher, Peter Fraser," etc. Proposals for a second volume were announced by Fraser in March 1726, but it was never published.

 K.

FREDERICA, *Mr.* Near Meard's Court, in Wardour Street, Soho,

London. Advertised February 1755, "Twelve Sonatas or Lessons for the Harpsichord. Dedicated to her Royal Highness the Lady Augusta. By Sig. Paradies. Printed for and sold by the Author, at Mr. Frederica's . . . and by John Johnson", etc.

FREDERICK (WILLIAM). Bookseller and publisher, 18 The Grove, Bath, c. 1742-76. (P.) His name appears in the imprint of "Twelve English Songs with their Symphonies. The words by Shakespeare and other celebrated poets. Set to musick by M[r]. Thomas Chilcot, organist of Bath. London Printed and sold by John Johnson . . . M[r]. Leak and M[r]. Fredrick Booksellers in Bath", etc., 1744.
P. III.

FREDRICK, *Mr.* *See* Frederick (William).

FREEMAN (J.). Bookseller? London. Published "The Merry Medley; or, a Christmas-Box, for gay gallants, and good companions . . . Containing . . . celebrated and jovial songs, set for the voice, violin, and modish country dances . . . by C. F. President of the Comical Club in Covent Garden . . . Vol. II. London, printed for J. Freeman, 1745."

FREEMAN (JAMES). Engraver, music seller and publisher, 5 Little Warwick Street, Charing Cross, London, c. 1782-92.
K.

FRENCH (JOHN). Bookseller and publisher, London; 28 Poultry, c. 1775; 47 Holborn, opposite Hatton Garden, c. 1775-78. Issued a few musical publications.
K. P. III.

FRENCH (THOMAS). Music seller, Rochester. Published c. 1823, "The Russian Quadrilles, the subjects from admired Russian Airs, adapted and arranged for the Piano Forte . . . by T. Brotherson. Music Master, Royal Marines."

FRYER & THOMSON. Pianoforte and music sellers, and publishers, Edinburgh; 12 South St. David Street, c. 1848-53; 7 South St. Andrew Street, c. 1854; 7 and 11 South St. Andrew Street, c. 1855-58.

FURRIAN (G.). Hampstead, London. Published "Sixty Tunes, adapted to sixty Psalms & Hymns, for congregational use . . . London: Printed by T. & S. Bates . . . for G. Furrian, Hampstead. 1823."

G., A. *See* Godbid (Anne) & Playford (John) *the Younger*.

G., A. *See* also Griffin (Anne).

G., E. *See* Griffin (Edward).

[151]

G., S. *See* Griffin (Sarah).

G., W. *See* Gawler (William).

G., W. *See* also Godbid (William).

GALABIN. *See* Baker & Galabin.

GALABIN (HENRY LOUIS). Printer, Ingram Court, Fenchurch Street, London, c. 1795-1800. Printed a small number of sacred music books; succeeded John William Galabin.

GALABIN (JOHN WILLIAM). Printer, Ingram Court, Fenchurch Street, London, c. 1785-95. Printed a small number of sacred music books; succeeded by Henry Louis Galabin.
    K.

GALBRAITH (J. MURRAY). *See* Gow & Galbraith.

GALES (JOSEPH). Bookseller and stationer, Sheffield. Printed and published "The Musical Tour of Mr. Dibdin . . . Sheffield: Printed for the Author by J. Gales . . . MDCCLXXXVIII." Contains music of some songs by Charles Dibdin.
    K.

GALLOWAY (DANIEL). Music seller and publisher, 37 Great Pulteney Street, London, c. 1816-19; previously in partnership with William Galloway.
    K.

GALLOWAY (WILLIAM). Music and musical instrument seller, and publisher, London; 12 Great Pulteney Street, c. 1816-19; 21 Wigmore Street, c. 1819-28; 4 Lower Seymour Street, 1828-31; previously in partnership with Daniel Galloway.
    K.

GALLOWAY (WILLIAM) & (DANIEL). Music sellers and publishers, 12 Great Pulteney Street, London, c. 1814-16. For a time had additional premises at 37 Great Pulteney Street; afterwards carried on business independently.

GANER (CHRISTOPHER). Pianoforte maker and music publisher, 48 Broad Street, Soho, London, c. 1781–1811. From c. 1806 had additional premises at 47 Broad Street.
    K.

GANGE (GEORGE) & CO. Pianoforte manufacturers and music sellers, 19 Poultry, London, c. 1837-43. George Gange was formerly with

Richard Neale, "A Pocket Companion for Gentlemen and Ladies . . . :
Opera Songs & Airs". Engraved and printed at Cluer's Printing Office.
1724. Probably engraved by Thomas Cobb

THE HYMN

OF

ADAM and EVE;

Out of the Fifth Book of

MILTON'S Paradise Lost;

Set to Musick by

Mr GALLIARD.

1728.

J.Pine sine N.Sculp.

"The Hymn of Adam and Eve". Published by subscription through Joseph Hare and others. Music engraved by Thomas Atkins

Messrs. Broadwood; succeeded Dale, Cockerill and Co.; succeeded by John Alvey Turner.

GARDNER (HENRY). Bookseller and publisher, 200, opposite St. Clement's Church, in the Strand, London, c. 1774-86. Published "Select Portions of the Psalms of David . . . The music from the most approved compositions. The Second edition . . . MDCCLXXXVI."
  P. III.

GARDOM (GEORGE). Music and musical instrument seller and publisher, 23 St. James's Street, London, c. 1772-91, or later.
  K.

GARTHWAITE (TIMOTHY). Bookseller, various addresses, London, 1650-69. (P.) His name appears in the imprint of "Musica Deo Sacra & Ecclesiæ Anglicanæ . . . by Thomas Tomkins. London. Printed by William Godbid . . . and are to be sold by Timothy Garthwait in Little S. Bartholomews Hospital. MDCLXVIII."
  P. I.

GAWLER (WILLIAM). Musician and publisher, London; 17 Walcot Place West, Lambeth, c. 1794; 19 Paradise Row, Lambeth, c. 1795-1800. Some single sheet songs bear only the initials W. G.; at one time organist to the Asylum for Female Orphans.
  K.

GAY'S (MR.) HEAD IN TAVISTOCK STREET, COVENT GARDEN, LONDON. *See* Heney.

GENT (THOMAS). Printer, London, and Coffee Yard, York, 1710-78. (P.) Printed and sold c. 1744, "The Delightful new Academy of Compliments. Being the rarest and most exact art of wooing a maid or widow, by way of dialogue and complimentary expressions . . . Whereunto are added, fifteen of the newest songs sung at court and city. Set to the newest tunes, by the best wits of the age. York, printed and sold by Thomas G[e]n[t]." (Huntington Library, 529.)
  P. II.

GEORGE & MANBY. Music sellers and publishers, 85 Fleet Street, London, c. 1830-41, with additional premises at 8 Church Row, Upper Street, Islington, c. 1830-35. William George was previously in business alone; partnership dissolved c. 1841, and Charles William Manby continued at the same address.

GEORGE (JAMES). Musician, Bath. Engraved and printed by the Author c. 1750, "Six Concerto's in seven Parts, four for Violins, one for a German Flute, one for a Violoncello, a Tenor, & Thorough Bass for the Organ, or Harpsichord. Composed by James George."

F

GEORGE (WILLIAM). Music seller and publisher, London; 85 Fleet Street (Corner of St. Bride's Avenue), and 8 Church Row, Upper Street, Islington, c. 1828-30. Joined by Charles William Manby and became George and Manby c. 1830.

GEROCK & WOLF. Musical instrument makers, music sellers and publishers, 79 Cornhill, London, c. 1831-32. Succeeded Gerock, Astor and Co.; succeeded by C. Gerock and Co.

GEROCK, ASTOR & CO. Musical instrument makers, music sellers and publishers, London; 76 Bishopsgate Street Within, c. 1821-27; 79 Cornhill, c. 1821-31. Both had previously been in business on their own account; succeeded by Gerock and Wolf.
K.

GEROCK (CHRISTOPHER). Musical instrument maker, music seller and publisher, London; 76 Bishopsgate Street Within, c. 1804-21; with additional premises at 1 Gracechurch Street, c. 1815-21. Joined by George Astor and became Gerock, Astor and Co.
K.

GEROCK (CHRISTOPHER) & CO. Musical instrument makers, music sellers and publishers, 79 Cornhill, London, c. 1832-37. Succeeded Gerock and Wolf; succeeded by Robert Wolf and Co.

GIBSON (WILLIAM). Musical instrument maker, music teacher and publisher, Dublin; College Green, 1766-74; 6 Grafton Street, 1774-1790. In partnership with Robert Woffington from 1775 to 1778.

GILBERT (JOHN). Mathematical instrument maker, in Postern Row, Tower Hill, London. His name appears in the imprint of "The Psalm Singers Companion; being a collection of psalm tunes, hymns canons and anthems . . . By Abraham Milner. London: Printed by William Benning, and sold by John Gilbert . . . 1751."

GILES (W.). Publisher, London. Published "Loyalty triumphant; or A Looking-Glass for Deceivers . . . [Song, to the tune of 'Let the Critticks adore.'] Printed for W. Giles, 1682." (Huntington Library, 1175.)

GILLIES (JAMES). Bookseller and stationer, Glasgow. His name appears in the imprint of "The Edinburgh Musical Miscellany: a collection of the most approved Scotch, English, and Irish songs, set to music. Selected by D. Sime, Edinburgh. Edinburgh: Printed for W. Gordon . . . J. Gillies, Glasgow . . . MDCCXCII." In volume II the imprint reads "Edinburgh: Printed for John Elder, T. Brown, and C. Elliot, Edinburgh; and W. Coke, Leith. MDCCXCIII."

GILLIVER (LAWTON). Bookseller and publisher, London, c. 1728-38. (P.) Homer's Head, against St. Dunstan's Church in Fleet Street; Westminster Hall. His name appears in the imprint of "The Female Parson: or, Beau in the Sudds. An Opera . . . By Mr. Charles Coffey . . . London. Printed for Lawton Gilliver, over against St. Dunstan's Church; and Fran. Cogan . . . MDCCXXX.''; with the tunes of the songs; "The Tragedy of Chrononhotonthologos: being the most tragical Tragedy, that ever was tragediz'd by any Company of Tragedians. Written by Benjamin Bounce, Esq. [i.e. Henry Carey.] London: Printed for J. Shuckburgh, and L. Gilliver, in Fleet Street, J. Jackson . . . and sold by A. Dodd . . . and E. Nutt", etc., c. 1734; with the tunes of the songs.
    P. III.

GILLRAY (JAMES). Caricaturist and engraver, b. 1757–d. 1815. In the early part of his career was employed as a music engraver, and his name appears on several title-pages.
    K.

GLADMAN (T.). Music seller and publisher, 24 Middle Row, Holborn, London, c. 1795-1815.
    K.

GLASS (JOHN). Printer, 44 South Bridge, Edinburgh. Published c. 1827, "A Few of the easiest learned Psalm & Hymn Tunes, (with appropriate words to each tune) for Beginners By William Smith."

GLEN (ALEXANDER). Bagpipe maker, Edinburgh; 30 West Register Street, c. 1840-47; 30 St. Andrew Square, c. 1847-69; At his house, 16 Calton Hill, c. 1869-73. Elder brother of Thomas Macbean Glen; published a small amount of music for the bagpipe; succeeded by his son David.
    G.

GLEN (DAVID). Bagpipe maker and music publisher, 8 Greenside Place, Edinburgh, c. 1873-1911; as David Glen and Sons, c. 1911 to present time. Son of Alexander Glen whom he succeeded in business.
    G.

GLEN (JOHN) & (ROBERT). Musical instrument makers and music publishers, Edinburgh; 2 North Bank Street, 1866-c. 1870; 2 and 3 North Bank Street, c. 1870-1911; 497 Lawnmarket, c. 1911 to present time. Original partners were sons of Thomas Macbean Glen whom they succeeded in the business. John was an authority on early Scottish music and collected a valuable library, which is now in the National Library of Scotland, Edinburgh.
    G.
    See Bibliography for works by John Glen.

GLEN (ROBERT). *See* Glen (John) & (Robert).

GLEN (THOMAS MACBEAN). Musical instrument maker, Edinburgh; 265 Cowgate, 1827-36; 2 North Bank Street, 1836-66. Brother of Alexander Glen; published a small amount of music for the bagpipe; succeeded by his sons John and Robert.

GLOVER (HURST). Blandford. His name appears in the imprint of "A Sett of new Psalm-Tunes and Anthems . . . By William Knapp . . . London: Printed by W. Hutchinson, for the Author, and sold by him in Poole; Mr. George Torbuck in Winbourn . . . and Mr. Hurst Glover in Blandford . . . MDCCXXXVIII."

GODBID (ANNE) & PLAYFORD (JOHN) *the Younger*. Printers, at Little Britain, Aldersgate Street, London, c. 1679-83, the business continued by John Playford alone c. 1683-85. Anne Godbid, the widow of William Godbid, succeeded to his business at his death; John Playford was nephew of John Playford the elder, and presumably served his apprenticeship with William Godbid; Anne Godbid and John Playford printed works for John and Henry Playford, Charles Brome and others; John Playford's house and plant were advertised for sale by his sister Ellen or Eleanor, May 6th, 1686; they issued some works with the initials A. G. and J. P.
D. & M.

GODBID (WILLIAM). Printer of music from movable type, at Little Britain (over against the Anchor Inn), Aldersgate Street, London, c. 1656-79, during which period he printed works for John Playford, the elder. Issued some works bearing the initials W. G.; business continued by his widow Anne Godbid and John Playford the younger.
K. G. P. I. D. & M.

GOLDSMITH (WILLIAM). Bookseller and publisher, London; 20 Paternoster Row, 1772; 24 Paternoster Row, 1773-90; 1 Warwick Court, Warwick Lane, 1791-96. His name appears in the imprints of a number of sacred music works.
P. III.

GOODISON (BENJAMIN). Lawyer, London; James Street, Westminster; afterwards at Kensington Square and Chelsea. Proposed to publish by subscription all the available works of Henry Purcell, but only issued a few, besides some works of Handel, Pergolesi, Sarti and Steffani, 1787-90.

GOODWIN (JACOB). Music seller and publisher, Dublin; 20 Sackville Street, c. 1805-06; 47 Henry Street, c. 1806-11.

GOODWIN (ROBERT FELIX). *See* Goodwin (William).

GOODWIN (WILLIAM). Music seller and publisher, London; 12 York Street, Covent Garden, c. 1826-32; 31 Bow Street, Covent Garden, c. 1832-39; 4 Charles Street, Covent Garden, c. 1839-44; 4 Upper Wellington Street (Charles Street re-named), Covent Garden, c. 1844-1860; 39 Wellington Street, Strand, c. 1860-63; 15A Leicester Place, Leicester Square, c. 1863-76. Died 1876. At one time librarian to the Royal Academy of Music, and copyist to the Society of British Musicians; business continued by Goodwin and Tabb, in which his son Robert Felix Goodwin was a partner.

GORDON (WILLIAM). Bookseller, Parliament Close, Edinburgh, 1773-1793. (P.) His name appears in the imprint of "The Edinburgh Musical Miscellany: a collection of the most approved Scotch, English, and Irish songs, set to music. Selected by D. Sime, Edinburgh. Edinburgh: Printed for W. Gordon, T. Brown . . . Edinburgh . . . MDCCXCII." In volume II the imprint reads "Edinburgh: Printed for John Elder, T. Brown, and G. Elliot, Edinburgh; and W. Coke, Leith. MDCCXCIII."
P. III.

GORE (JOHN). Bookseller and stationer, Dale Street, Liverpool, 1762-76. (P.) His name appears in the imprint of "A Set of Hymns and Psalm Tunes . . . Composed by Ed. Harwood. London. Printed for the Author & sold by Joh. Johnson . . . and Jn. Gore Liverpool," c. 1765.
P. III.

GOSLING (FRANCIS). Bookseller and publisher, Mitre and Crown, over against Fetter Lane, London, 1741-57. His name appears in the imprint of "The Psalms of David in Metre: With the tunes used in Parish-Churches. By John Patrick. The Eighth edition. London: Printed for J. Walthoe . . . F. Gosling . . . MDCCXLII." Son of Robert Gosling.
P. III.

GOSLING (ROBERT). Bookseller, London, 1707-41; at the Mitre (or Mitre and Crown), against St. Dunstan's Church in Fleet Street; at the Middle Temple Gate. (P.) His name appears in the imprint of "The Psalms of David in Metre: Fitted to the tunes used in Parish-Churches. By John Patrick . . . London, Printed for W. Churchill . . . R. Gosling . . . MDCCXVIII.'; also in the seventh edition, 1724.
P. II.

GOUGH (GEORGE). Music seller and publisher, Dublin, 4 Sackville Street, c. 1798-1807. Took over business and premises from Bartholomew or Bartlett Cooke. Also published some music with the address, probably earlier, of 29 Capel Street.
K.

GOUGH (JOHN). Stationer and printer, London. Began business on his own account in Fleet Street, 1526. (D.) By the summer of 1533 he had removed to Cheapside, at the sign of the Mermaid, which was apparently sublet to Gough by John Rastell. (F. Isaac: "English and Scottish Printing Types.") Gough shares with John Rastell the credit for introducing into England the system of printing music in one impression. Printed Coverdale's "Goostly psalms and spirituall songes drawen out of the holy Scripture . . . Imprynted by me Johan Gough", etc., c. 1539. "A new interlude and a mery of the nature of the iiij. elements," etc., variously dated between 1519 and 1539, has been attributed to Gough and to John Rastell. In 1540 Gough was living in Lombard Street, at the sign of the Mermaid, against the Stocks Market. (D.) He died in 1543.
D. S.

GOULD (SAMUEL). Bookseller and publisher, Dorchester, 1733-83. (P.) His name appears in the imprint of "A Sett of new Psalm-Tunes and Anthems . . . By William Knapp . . . London: Printed by W. Hutchinson, for the Author, and sold by him in Poole . . . Mr. Gould in Dorchester . . . and Mr. Hurst Glover in Blandford . . . MDCCXXXVIII."
P. III.

GOULDING & CO. *See* Goulding, D'Almaine, Potter & Co.; Goulding, Phipps & D'Almaine.

GOULDING & D'ALMAINE. Music sellers and publishers, 20 Soho Square, London, c. 1823-34. Succeeded Goulding, D'Almaine, Potter and Co.; succeeded by D'Almaine and Co.
K. G.
Catalogue:—Select Vocal Music. 1831. 1 p. fol. (B.M. H. 1238.)

GOULDING, D'ALMAINE, POTTER & CO. Music sellers and publishers, London; 124 New Bond Street, c. 1810-11; 20 Soho Square, c. 1811-1823. Had a branch establishment at 7 Westmoreland Street, Dublin, c. 1810-16. Also known as Goulding and Co. and occasionally c. 1813, as Goulding, D'Almaine, Potter and Wood; succeeded Goulding, Phipps, D'Almaine and Co.; Potter dropped out c. 1823 and the firm became Goulding and D'Almaine. Succeeded at Dublin by Isaac Willis.
K. G.
Catalogues:—c. 1810. 1 p. fol. (Haas, Catalogue 21. No. 39.); Country Dances. c. 1810. (Haas Catalogue 18. No. 6.); Instrumental Music. Part 1. c. 1820. 50 pp. 8º. (B.M. Hirsch IV. 1106.); New and popular Piano Forte Music. c. 1823. 1 p. fol. (B.M. h. 726. d. (4.))

GOULDING, D'ALMAINE, POTTER & WOOD. *See* Goulding, D'Almaine, Potter & Co.

GOULDING, KNEVETT & CO. Music sellers and publishers, 7 West-moreland Street, Dublin, c. 1803-06. The Irish branch of Messrs. Goulding, Phipps, and D'Almaine, of London, who continued the Dublin business when Knevett withdrew, c. 1806.
K.

GOULDING, PHIPPS & D'ALMAINE. Military musical instrument makers, music sellers and publishers, London; 45 Pall Mall, 1798-c.1804, with additional premises at 76 St. James's Street, 1800-04; 117 New Bond Street, c. 1804-08; 124 New Bond Street, c. 1808-10. From c. 1806 became Goulding, Phipps, D'Almaine and Co., or Goulding and Co. Had a branch establishment at 7 Westmoreland Street, Dublin, under the name of Goulding, Knevett and Co., c. 1803-06, and as Goulding, Phipps, D'Almaine and Co., c. 1806-10. Phipps withdrew c. 1810, and the business became Goulding, D'Almaine, Potter and Co.; succeeded George Goulding.
K. G.
A Complete Catalogue of the works of Joseph Mazzinghi. 1798. 1 p. fol. (B.M. Hirsch M. 1471. (4.))

GOULDING (GEORGE). Musical instrument maker, music seller and publisher, London; 25 James Street, Covent Garden, c. 1786-87; The Haydn's Head, 6 James Street, Covent Garden, c. 1787-98. Had additional premises at 17 Great Turnstile, Holborn, 1787, and a selling agency at Samuel Bury and Co., Pianoforte makers and organ builders, 113 Bishopsgate Street within, in 1788. Became Goulding, Phipps and D'Almaine early in 1798.
K. G.
Catalogue of new Music. 1791. 1 p. fol. (B.M. H. 1174.).

GOW & GALBRAITH. Music sellers and publishers, 60 Princes Street, Edinburgh, February-October 1826. Partners were Nathaniel Gow, previously in business as Nathaniel Gow and Son at same address, and J. Murray Galbraith formerly a tuner with Messrs. Broadwood, London.
K. G.
See also Gow (Nathaniel).

GOW & SHEPHERD. Music sellers and publishers, Edinburgh; 41 North Bridge Street, 1796-c. 1801; 16 Princes Street, c. 1801-11; renumbered 40 Princes Street, c. 1811-14. Partners were Nathaniel Gow and William Shepherd. Shepherd died January 1812; Gow carried on until the beginning of 1814; stock-in-trade sold by auction on 1st March 1814, and following days.
K. G.
Catalogue. c. 1801. 1 p. fol. (B.M. 7692. tt. 8. (2.))
See also Gow (Nathaniel).

[159]

GOW (ANDREW).   *See* Gow (John) & (Andrew).

GOW (JOHN).   Musician, music seller and publisher, London; 31 Carnaby
   Street, c. 1803-15; 31 Great Marlborough Street, c. 1815-23. Son of
   Niel Gow, the violinist and composer; joined by son John H., and
   became John Gow and Son, 162 Regent Street, c. 1823-29. Died
   1827; previously in partnership with his brother Andrew; succeeded
   by John Barnett and Co.
      K. G.
      Catalogue:—Music published by John Gow & Son. c. 1823. 1 p.
   fol. (B.M. g. 272. s. (4.))

GOW (JOHN) & (ANDREW).   Musicians and music sellers, 60 King Street,
   Golden Square, London, c. 1787-1803. Sons of Niel Gow the violinist
   and composer; agents for their father's publications, also for their
   brother Nathaniel. After the death of Andrew in 1803, John continued
   at another address.
      K. G.

GOW (JOHN) & SON.   *See* Gow (John).

GOW (JOHN H.).   *Son of John.*   *See* Gow (John).

GOW (NATHANIEL).   Musician, music seller and publisher, Edinburgh.
   Son of Niel Gow, the violinist and composer.   His name appears as
   "Nath. Gow within the head of Halkerston's Wynd" as one of the
   music sellers of the Second Collection of his father's Strathspey Reels,
   1788. (H. G. Farmer.) Commenced business as partner in Gow and
   Shepherd, at 41 North Bridge Street, 1796-c. 1801; and at 16 Princes
   Street, c. 1801-11; afterwards renumbered 40 Princes Street, c. 1811-
   1814. Resumed business with his son Niel as Nathaniel Gow and Son,
   60 Princes Street, August 1818-23; 7 Hanover Street, 1823-May 1824;
   60 Princes Street, May 1824-February 1826; his son died in 1823.
   Went into partnership with J. Murray Galbraith as Gow and Galbraith,
   60 Princes Street, February-October 1826. Gow's bankruptcy was
   advertised May 1827 and in the following month an advertisement
   announced the sale of the stock of music and his property at 2 Hanover
   Street, where he carried on his music teaching.
      K. G.
      See also Gow & Galbraith; Gow & Shepherd; Gow (Nathaniel)
   & Son.

GOW (NATHANIEL) & SON.   Music sellers and publishers, Edinburgh;
   60 Princes Street, August 1818-23; 7 Hanover Street, 1823-May
   1824; 60 Princes Street, May 1824-February 1826. Neil Gow, the
   son, died in 1823. Succeeded by Gow and Galbraith.
      K. G.
      See also Gow (Nathaniel).

GOW (NIEL). Violinist and composer of dance music, 1727-1807. Did not publish any music.
    See Gow (Nathaniel).

GOW (NIEL). *Son of Nathaniel.*
    See Gow (Nathaniel); Gow (Nathaniel) & Son.

GRAFTON (RICHARD). Printer, London. Lived for some time from 1540 in the house of the Grey Friars, Newgate Street, after the order had been dissolved. Printed "An Exhortacion unto praier, thought mete by the Kynges maiestie . . . Also a Letanie with suffrages to be saied or songe in the tyme of the said processions. Imprinted in London by Richarde Grafton for Thomas Barthelet, printer to the Kynges hyghnes, the XVI. day of Iune . . . 1544." Grafton probably printed another edition in 1544. Also printed "The Booke of Common praier noted. (John Merbecke.) 1550"; with colophon, "Imprinted by Richard Grafton Printer to the Kinges Maiestie. 1550."
    G. D. S.

GRAHAM (WILLIAM). Bookseller, High Street, Oxford. Published "The Psalms and Hymns taken from the Morning and Evening Service . . . and the Chants to which they are sung in the Church of St. Peter-in-the-East, Oxford. Oxford; Printed by J. Munday, jun. Published by W. Graham. 1838."

GRANT & MOIR. Printers, Paterson's Court, Edinburgh. Printed "The Edinburgh Musical Miscellany: a Collection of the most approved Scotch, English, and Irish Songs, set to music. Selected by D. Sime, Edinburgh . . . MDCCXCII." Vol. II is dated 1793.
    K.

GRAVELOT, or rather BOURGUIGNON-GRAVELOT (HUBERT FRANÇOIS). French engraver and designer, 1699-1773, lived in London c. 1732-45. Executed title-pages and pictorial designs for "The Musical Entertainer," 1737-39, "Songs in the Opera of Flora," 1737-38, which were engraved by George Bickham junior; besides other works, including the ornamental design for the Houbraken portrait of Handel, issued as a frontispiece to "Alexander's Feast," 1738.

GRAY & PETER. Booksellers, in the Exchange, Edinburgh. Published "A Collection of Psalm-Tunes in four Parts. Neatly engraved on copper . . . Edinburgh: Printed by Sands, Donaldson, Murray and Cochran. For Gray and Peter, in the Exchange. MDCCLVIII." William Gray, one of the partners, wrote the preface.

GRAY (HENRY). Engraver and printer, 23 Red Cross Square, Cripplegate, London. Published "Addington's Selection of Psalm & Hymn Tunes. With additions. London, Published June 11, 1807 by H. Gray . . . & sold also by L. Higham," etc.

GRAY (J.) & CRASK (JOHN). Engravers and printers, Bury St. Edmunds.
Engraved and printed "Gray's and Crask's Occasional Polite Repertory
of Dances. No. 1." Continued as "Gray's and Crask's Occasional
Polite Repertory of Waltzs, Reels, & Dances for the Piano Forte, Harp
or Violin. With their proper Figures. No. 2 and 3," c. 1808-09.
Gray alone afterwards printed and sold "Augustine. The celebrated
German Waltz, arranged with Variations for the Piano Forte by
L. Spindler." c. 1810; "The True Sportsman. A favorite song
written and composed by J. N. Plummer," c. 1810.

GREEN. *See* Yaniewicz & Green.

GREEN (HENRY). Bookseller? Westerham, Kent. His name appears in
an advertisement December 1752, "The Second edition of The
Psalmist's New Companion . . . By Abraham Adams, of Shoreham in
Kent. Printed for the Author; and sold by Peter Thompson . . . and
by Henry Green," etc.

GREEN (JOHN). Composer, music agent, music seller and publisher,
London; 28 Norfolk Street, Strand, c. 1815-20; 33 Soho Square,
c. 1820-48. Inventor and sole manufacturer of the Royal Seraphine;
stock-in-trade offered for sale by Puttick and Simpson during 1848,
1849 and 1852.
K.

GREEN (THOMAS). Bookseller and publisher, London, 1728-35, at the
corner of Spring Garden, near Charing Cross; near, or At Charing
Cross; against Falstaffe's Head, near Charing Cross; over against
the Mew's Gate, near Charing Cross. (P.) His name appears in the
imprint of "Penelope, a Dramatic Opera, as it is acted at the New
Theatre in the Hay-Market. London: Printed, and sold by Tho.
Green, at the corner of Spring-garden, near Charing Cross, and
Charles Davis . . . 1728," with the music to the overture and the songs.
Advertised in May 1728, "Penelope . . . the overture . . . and the
musick to each song, by Mr. Roseingrave. Printed for Charles Davies
. . . J. Green . . . and sold by A. Dodd . . . and E. Nutt", etc.
P. III.

GREEN (W.). Printer and bookseller, Chelmsford, 1731-55; Bury St.
Edmunds, 1755-69. (P.) Printed "A Choice Collection of Church
Music . . . to which is added a compleat introduction to Psalmody.
By Robert Catchpole, of Bury St. Edmund's Suffolk . . . Bury: Printed
by W. Green, for the Author . . . 1761."
P. III.

GREENHILL (T.). Engraver. His name appears on the title-pages of
works by Nicola Matteis: "Ayres for the Violin . . . The Third and
Fourth Parts . . . 1685"; "Ayres for the Violin. Att two, three and

four parts . . . 1685". Presumably also engraved the music of these and other similar works of this series by Matteis c. 1675-1688.

GREENSHIELDS, BROTHERS. Pianoforte and music sellers, and publishers, Glasgow; 114 West Nile Street, c. 1845-46; 19 Argyle Arcade, c. 1846-51; 28 Buchanan Street, c. 1851-54.

GRIERSON (HUGH BOULTER PRIMROSE). Printer, Dublin; at the King's Arms in Dame's Street; at the King's Arms in Parliament Street, 1758-70. (P.) Issued a few musical works between the years 1765-68, including "Two Essays on the Theory and Practice of Music . . . by the Rev. John Trydell . . . 1766."; he was the King's Printer for Ireland.
    K. P. III.

GRIFFIN (ANNE). Printer, Old Bailey, St. Sepulchre's parish, London, 1634-43. (P.) Widow of Edward Griffin, printer, whose business she continued, taking her son Edward Griffin the younger into partnership in 1638. Printed "The Whole Booke of Psalmes. Collected into English Meeter, by Thomas Sternehold, Iohn Hopkins and others . . . with apt notes to sing them withall . . . London, Printed by A. G. for the Company of Stationers. 1635"; also an edition in 1637.
    P. I.
    See also Griffin (Edward) *the Younger*.

GRIFFIN (EDWARD) *the Elder*. *See* Griffin (Anne).

GRIFFIN (EDWARD) *the Younger*. Printer, Old Bailey, St. Sepulchre's parish, London, 1638-52. (P.) At first in association with his mother Anne Griffin. Printed in conjunction with J. Raworth, "The Whole Booke of Psalmes. Collected into English Meeter by Thomas Sternehold, John Hopkins and others . . . London, Printed by E. Griffin and I. Raworth, for the Company of Stationers, 1638"; Printed "The First Book of selected Church Musick . . . Collected . . . by John Barnard . . . London. Printed by Edward Griffin, and are to be sold at the Signe of the Three Lutes in Pauls Alley. 1641"; "Psalmorum Davidis Paraphrasis Poetica Georgii Buchanani Scoti . . . Londini, Apud Edw. Griffinum. 1648 (1647)"; "The Psalmes of David . . . To be sung after the old tunes used in the churches. London, Printed by Ed. Griffin, and are sold by Humphrey Moseley, at the Princes Armes in St. Paul' Church-yard. 1651." In addition, some Psalters "printed by E. G. for the Company of Stationers," 1639, etc., are presumed to have been by E. Griffin. Succeeded by his widow, Sarah Griffin.
    K. P. I.
    See also Griffin (Anne); Wilson (William).

GRIFFIN (SARAH). Printer, Old Bailey, St. Sepulchre's parish, London, 1652-73. (P.) Widow and successor of Edward Griffin the Younger.

Only the initials S. G. appear in the imprint of the work presumed to be printed by Sarah Griffin, "The Whole Booke of Psalmes collected into English Meeter by Thomas Sternhold, John Hopkins, and others . . . with apt notes to sing them withall . . . London, S. G. for the Company of Stationers. 1661."
P. I.

GRIFFIN (WILLIAM). Bookseller, printer and publisher, London, c. 1764-76; Fetter Lane; Garrick's Head, Catherine Street, Strand. (P.) His name appears in the imprint of "The Beggar's Opera . . . To which is prefixed the overture in score: And the musick to each song. London: Printed for W. Strahan, T. Lowndes, T. Caslon, W. Griffin, W. Nicoll, S. Bladon, and G. Kearsly. MDCCLXXI." W. Griffin appears in the imprint of Luke Heron's "A Treatise on the German Flute . . . Sold . . . by Luke Heron . . . Dublin . . . London: W. Griffin. 1771." (Dayton Miller collection.)
P. III.

GRIFFITH (WILLIAM). Printer, London, at the Sign of the Griffin in Fleet Street a little above the Conduit, 1552. (D.) Printed "A Godly Psalme, of Marye Queene . . . By Rychard Beeard. Imprinted at London in Fleete-streete, at the sygne of the Faucon against saint Donstans Church by Wylliam Griffith: and are to be solde at his shoppe a lytle above the Conduit . . . 1553"; "A Newe Ballade of a Louer Extollinge his Ladye. To the tune of Damon and Pithias. Imprinted in London in Fletstrete at the sign of the Faucon, by Wylliam Gryffith. 1568."
D. S.

GRIGGS (W.). Publisher, London. Published "Tony's lamentation: or Potapski's City-Case . . . [Song, to the tune of 'Let Oliver now be forgotten.'] Printed for W. Griggs, in the year 1682." (Huntington Library, 2230.)

GRIST (B. F.). Music engraver, 15 Dean Street, Soho, London. "Up among the Mountains, Ballad à la suisse . . . Composed . . . by Madame F. Warlich. London, George Warne, 103 Great Russell Street, Bloomsbury," c. 1838; "My Birthday, a Ballad, written by Mrs. George Warne, composed . . . by G. Warne, late organist of the Temple. London. Published by the Author at Olliver's, 41 New Bond Street," etc., c. 1847.

GROOMBRIDGE (RICHARD). Bookseller, 6 Panyer Alley, Paternoster Row, London. His name appears in the imprints of "The Psaltery; a Collection of Psalm and Hymn Tunes, carefully selected from the works of the most eminent composers . . . Dublin: Published for John Kirkwood . . . By . . . R. Groombridge, London . . . 1835"; "Popular Airs and Sacred Melodies, adapted for social singing. With hymns and anthems . . . Dublin: Hardy & Walker . . . London: Richard Groombridge . . . Edinburgh: Fraser and Company. 1839."

GROSSÉ (WILLIAM). Music seller, teacher of music and composer, London; Music Repository, 14 Princes Row, Pimlico, c. 1815-26; Musical Academy, 20 Shaftesbury Terrace, Pimlico, c. 1826-30.

GRUA, RICORDI & CO. Music and musical instrument sellers, and publishers, 2 Albemarle Street, Piccadilly, London, c. 1825-28.

GRYFFYTH (WYLLIAM). *See* Griffith (William).

GUCHT (MICHIEL VAN DER). Engraver, b. 1660, Antwerp, d. 1725, London. Engraved the illustrated title-page to Daniel Purcell's "The Judgment of Paris" issued by John Walsh, June 1702, the plate being adapted for John Eccles's work of the same name issued by Walsh also in 1702. In 1706 the plate, further modified, was used for "Songs in the new opera, call'd The Temple of Love Compos'd by Sign^r. Gioseppe Fedelli Saggione," and was used again for "The Monthly Mask of Vocal Musick" by Walsh in 1717. Gucht also engraved the Hugh Howard portrait of Corelli which appeared in some Walsh editions of that composer's works. Johann Mattheson's "Pieces de Clavecin" issued by I. D. Fletcher, London, 1714, has an illustrated title-page engraved by Gucht.

GUERNSEY & DE VINE. Music sellers, Nassau Music Saloon, 20 Nassau Street, Dublin. Published c. 1844, "The Tree that in Childhood I planted. Ballad, composed . . . by William Mc Ghie." Wellington Guernsey was also a composer.

GUICHARD (C.). Music seller and publisher, London; at Bossange and Masson, 14 Great Marlborough Street, c. 1814-15; 100 New Bond Street, c. 1816-17.

GURNEY (JOSEPH). Bookseller and publisher, 54 Holborn, London, 1769-72. (P.) His name appears in the imprint of "The Psalm Singers Help, being a Collection of Tunes, in three parts . . . With a thorough bass for the harpsichord or organ . . . By Thomas Knibb. A new edition. London; Printed for George Pearch . . . and Joseph Gurney," etc., c. 1770.
　　P. III.
　　See also Knibb (Thomas).

GUTHRIE (ALEXANDER). Bookseller, 25 South Bridge Street, Edinburgh. His name appears in the imprint of "Tom of Bedlam as sung by Mr. Incledon, in the Wandering Melodist. London Printed by Goulding, Phipps & D'Almaine . . . Likewise may be had of . . . A. Guthrie, Edinburgh," etc., c. 1803.

H., I.   *See* Haviland (John).

H., P.   *See* Hodgson (Peter).

H., S.   The initials S. H. appear in the imprints of "Orpheus Britannicus
. . . Compos'd by Mr. Henry Purcell . . . The Second Book . . . The
Second edition . . . London: Printed by William Pearson, for S. H.
Sold by J. Young . . . J. Cullen . . . 1711"; also the Second Book, the
Second edition, "Printed by William Pearson, for S. H. and sold by
John Young . . . MDCCXII.'; the third edition of both books, "Printed
by William Pearson, for S. H. and sold by J. Young . . . MDCCXXI.";
"Harmonia Sacra: or Divine Hymns and Dialogues . . . Composed
by the best masters of the last and present age . . . The First Book.
The 3d edition . . . London: Printed by William Pearson, for S. H.
and sold by John Young . . . MDCCXIV."; also Book II, the second
edition, 1714.
D. & M.

H., T.   Printer, London.   Printed "The Scotch Lasses Constancy: or,
Jenny's lamentation for the death of Jockey . . . Being a most pleasant
song, to a delightful new tune.   Printed by T. H. for P. Brooksby . . .
1682"; "The Duke of Guise.   A Tragedy . . . Written by Mr.
Dryden, and Mr. Lee . . . London, Printed by T. H. for R. Bentley
. . . and J. Tonson . . . MDCLXXXIII.", which contains one musical number.
D. & M.

H., T.   *See* also Harper (Thomas).   Printer, Little Britain, London.

H—d, H.   *See* Holland (Henry).

HABERKORN (JOHN).   Printer and bookseller, Grafton Street, Soho,
London, 1755-65.   (P.)   His name appears in the imprint of "Psalm-
odia Germanica or the German Psalmody, translated from the High
German together with their Proper Tunes and Thorough Bass.
London Printed for A. Hummel . . . I. Haberkorn," etc., c. 1760;
also an edition with the imprint "London: Printed and Sold by
J. Haberkorn . . . M.CCC.LXV."
P. III.

HABGOOD (THO.).   Music seller, King Street, Golden Square, London.
Published 1759, "A Pocket Companion For the Guittar Containing XL
of the newest and most favourite Minuets Country-Dances Jiggs Airs
&c.   All carefully Transposed & properly adapted to that Instrument,
To which is added the Prussian March in two parts And favourite
Hymn for Easter."   British Museum copy of "Six Concertos for the
Organ by Thomas Sanders Dupuis", c. 1760, has Habgood's name added
in ms. to list of subscribers.

HACK (ROBERT). Musical instrument maker, music seller and publisher, London; 4 Gray's Inn Passage, Red Lion Square, c. 1834-37, and c. 1840-42; 5 Bedford Street, Bedford Row, c. 1837-40; 174 Fleet Street, c. 1842-59; 36 Great College Street, c. 1859-63. Had additional premises at 9 Portland Row, Camberwell Road, c. 1845-50.

HAGUE (WILLIAM). Music seller, Petty Cury, Cambridge. His name appears in the list of subscribers in "Six Songs with an accompanyment for the Harpsichord, or two Violins and a Violoncello. Composed by Mr. King. London Printed by Longman and Broderip", c. 1786; published in conjunction with John Peppercorn, "A Collection of Psalm & Hymn Tunes some of which are new & others by permission of the authors with six Chants and Te Deums . . . The whole revis'd & harmonized by Dr. Randall. And published by Wm. Hague and Jno. Peppercorn. Cambridge. Printed by A. Macintosh for the publishers. 1794." Hague published a second edition c. 1800.

HALE (CHARLES). Music seller and publisher, Cheltenham, c. 1815-61; at 340 High Street, c. 1815; in the later years at Promenade House and Montpellier Walk. Traded as C. Hale and Son c. 1845-61.
   K.

HALL (M.). *See* Corri (Montague P.), Hall (M.) & Co.

HALL (W.). Lithographic printer, Belfast. Lithographed "The Belfast Rifle Club Quadrilles, or McFadden's Second Set, composed & arranged for the Piano Forte . . by A. McFadden," c. 1840.

HALL (WILLIAM). Printer, Oxford, 1652-72. (P.) Printed for Richard Davis, "Cheerfull Ayres or Ballads. First composed for one single voice and since set for three voices by John Wilson . . . MDCLX.";
"A Short direction for the performance of Cathedrall Service . . . By E. L. [i.e. Edward Lowe.] 1661"; Edward Lowe's "A Review of some short Directions in the performance of Cathedral Service . . . Second Edition . . . 1664"; Printed for the Author, "Poems of Mr. Cowley and others. Composed into Songs and Ayres with a Thorough Basse to the Theorbo, Harpsecon or Base-violl; by William King, Organist of New-College in the Universtiy of Oxon . . . 1668."
   K. P. I. D. & M.

HALL (WILLIAM) & SONS. London. Published Charles Nicholson's "A School for the Flute. Being a new practical instruction book. 1836."

HALLIDAY & CO. Music sellers and publishers, 23 Bishopsgate Street Within, London, c. 1804-49. Succeeded Thomas Jones; succeeded by Samuel Brewer and Co.
   K.

HALY (THOMAS). Printer, London, c. 1677-83. Printed "The Newest Collection of the choicest Songs, as they are Sung at Court, Theatre, Musick-Schools, Balls, &c. with musical notes. London, Printed by T. Haly for D. Brown, at the Black Swan and Bible without Temple-Bar, and T. Benskin, in St. Brides Church-Yard, Fleet Street; 1683."
P. II. D. & M.

HAMILTON & KINCAID. Booksellers? Edinburgh. Their names appear in the imprint of "A Collection of old Scots Tunes, with the Bass for the Violoncello or Harpsichord . . . by Francis Barsanti. Edinburgh, Printed by Alexander Baillie, & sold by Messrs Hamilton & Kincaid, c. 1742."
K. (Alexander Baillie).

HAMILTON & MÜLLER. Musical instrument and music sellers, and publishers, 116 George Street, Edinburgh, c. 1840-89. Both partners, David Hamilton and Johann Martin Müller, were organists and composers.

HAMILTON (ALEXANDER). Bookseller, music seller, publisher and musical instrument dealer, London; 5 Russel Court, Covent Garden, c. 1790-93; 18 Holborn, near Gray's Inn Gate, c. 1793-95; 221 Piccadilly, c. 1795-1808. Business continued by James Alexander Hamilton.
K.
Catalogues:—Instrumental and Vocal Music. c. 1802. 2 pp. fol. (B.M. h. 2910. b. (4.)); c. 1802. 1 p. fol. (B.M. g. 421. (4.)); Vocal and Instrumental Music. 1806. 4 pp. fol. (B.M. 7896. h. 40. (4.))

HAMILTON (JAMES ALEXANDER). Music seller and publisher, London; 201 Piccadilly, c. 1806-08; 221 Piccadilly, c. 1808-17; 121 Wardour Street, c. 1817-23; 123 Wardour Street, c. 1823-26; 24 King Street, Holborn, c. 1826-27; 40 Berwick Street, Soho, c. 1827. Author of a number of books on music theory; succeeded Alexander Hamilton.
K.

HAMILTON (JOHN). Music seller and publisher, 24 North Bridge Street, opposite the Post Office, Edinburgh, c. 1795-1810. Author of many Scotch songs.
K.

HAMILTON (JOHN). Music seller and publisher, 26 Princes Street, Edinburgh, c. 1812-13.
K.

HAMILTON (WILLIAM). Music printer and publisher, and stationer, Glasgow; 88 Stockwell, c. 1834; 139 Renfield Street, c. 1835-60; 33 Bath Street, c. 1860-87.

HAMMOND (THOMAS). Bookseller and publisher, York, c. 1713-40. His name appears in the imprints of "The Most Useful Tunes of the Psalms, in Two, and some in Three Parts. Collected and transposed, corrected and composed by Edmund Ireland . . . The second edition, much improved . . . York, Printed by John White, and are to be sold (for the Author) by . . . Thomas Hammond . . . 1713"; "The Spiritual Man's Companion. The Third edition . . . By Israel Holdroyd . . . London: Printed by W. Pearson . . . for the Author, and sold by him and Mr. Hammond . . . in York, and Martin Fielden . . . in Hallifax. MDCCXXXII."
P. III.

HANHART (MICHAEL) & (NICHOLAS). Chromo and lithographic printers, London; 64 Charlotte Street, Fitzroy Square, c. 1840-66; 83 Charlotte Street, Fitzroy Square, c. 1866-94; 42 Tottenham Street, Fitzroy Square, c. 1894-97; 48 Charlotte Street, Fitzroy Square, c. 1897-1903. Printed some illustrations in colour in "Jullien's Album des bals de la cour," c. 1848; also "Jullien's Album," for 1847-57.

HANNAM (HENRY). Music seller and publisher, London; Musical Circulating Library, 4 London Road, St. George's Fields, near the Obelisk, c. 1816-28; 34 Bridgehouse Place, Southwark, c. 1828-30, or later. Afterwards at 62 Newington Causeway.
K.

HANNAM (JOHN). Music seller and publisher, 162 Sloane Street, London, c. 1801-10.
K.

HANSARD (LUKE). Printer, 6 Great Turnstile, Lincoln's Inn Fields, London. Printed "A Selection of Psalms and Hymns, for use of the Parish Church of Chislehurst in Kent . . . London, Printed for the Author: And sold by G. Wilkie . . . and J. Hatchard . . . 1803."

HARBOUR (JACOB). Musician, musical instrument maker and music seller, London, issued three books of Country Dances. The second book for the year 1784 was issued from 25 Duke Street, Lincoln's Inn Fields; third book published c. 1797 from 15 Lamb's Conduit Street.
K.

HARDING (EDWARD). Print seller, Pall Mall, London. His name appears in the imprint of "Anecdotes of George Frederick Handel and John Christopher Smith. With select pieces of music, composed by J. C. Smith, never before published. London: Printed by W. Bulmer and Co. Sold by Cadell and Davies . . . E. Harding . . . Birchall . . . and J. Eaton, Salisbury. 1799."

HARDING (SAMUEL). Bookseller and publisher, on the Pavement in St. Martin's Lane, London, c. 1726-55. (P.) In 1737 collected subscriptions for Bickham's "The Musical Entertainer." Published January, 1741, "Lyric Poems; being twenty four Songs (Never before printed;) by the late Matthew Prior Esqr.; set to music by several eminent masters."
    P. III.

HARDMAN (WILLIAM). Musical instrument maker, music seller, etc., 36, afterwards 37, Coney Street, York, August 1829-November 1855. Published a small amount of music; succeeded Samuel and Philip Knapton.

HARDY & WALKER. Booksellers and publishers, 4, Lower Sackville Street, Dublin. Their names appear in the imprint of "Popular Airs and Sacred Melodies, adapted for social singing. With hymn tunes and anthems . . . Dublin: Hardy & Walker . . . London: Richard Groombridge . . . Edinburgh: Fraser and Company. 1839."

HARDY (HENRY). Music seller, printer and publisher, High Street, Oxford, c. 1790-1805. Republished many of the publications issued by William Mathews whom he succeeded.
    K.

HARDY (J.). Music seller, at the Lamb & Harp, at the lower end of St. Martin's Lane, near ye Strand, London. Published 1754, "Six Sonatas for two German-Flutes, Violins, or Hautboys, with a Bass for the Harpsichord or Violoncello composed by Sigrs. Pla's."; his name appears in the imprint of "The Favourite Songs in the new Opera call'd Antigono, by Sig. Conforti. Printed and sold for the Proprietor, and to be had at Mr. Taylor's . . . at Mr. Hardy's Musick shop in St. Martin's Lane opposite Northumberland House, and at Mr. Francis Waylet's", etc, 1757.

HARE (ELIZABETH) *The Elder*. *See* Hare (John).

HARE (ELIZABETH) *the Younger*. Music printer and publisher, London; at the Viol and Hautboy (or, Viol and Hoboy), in Cornhill opposite Birchin Lane, July 1733-c. January 1743; The Viol and Hautboy, in Birchin Lane, opposite the old shop, near the Royal Exchange, c. January 1743-March 1748, when the premises were destroyed by fire; The Viol and Hautboy, opposite the Mansion House (over against the Mansion House, Cheapside), January 1749-July 1752; widow of Joseph Hare, and carried on the business after his death.
    K. G.
    Information about Elizabeth Hare is included in works on John Walsh by Frank Kidson and William C. Smith. (*See* Bibliography.)

HARE (JOHN). Musical instrument maker and seller, music printer and publisher, London; Freeman's Yard in Cornhill, near the Royal Exchange, July 1695; at the Golden Viol (or, Golden Violin), in St. Paul's Church Yard (premises probably taken over from John Clarke), and at his shop in Freeman's Yard in Cornhill, near the Royal Exchange, August 1695-April 1706; at the Golden Viol and Flute (or, Viol and Flute, Violin and Flute), in Cornhill, near the Royal Exchange, April 1706-December 1721. Joseph Hare joined his father, and the business was John and Joseph Hare at the Viol and Flute (or, Golden Viol and Flute), in Cornhill, near the Royal Exchange, January 1722-September 1725, when John Hare died; Joseph Hare carried on the business in his name at the same address, probably on behalf of his mother Elizabeth Hare, September 1725-June 1728, when he set up for himself at the Viol and Hautboy (or, Viol and Hoboy), in Cornhill, near the Royal Exchange (three doors further over against Birchin Lane), and carried on there until July 1733, when he died. Elizabeth Hare the elder, widow of John Hare, apparently retained possession of the business at the Viol and Flute in Cornhill, near the Royal Exchange, July 1728-July 1734, when she sold out and retired to Islington, where she died in 1741. Apparently John Simpson assisted Elizabeth Hare in her business, as after her retirement in 1734 he started on his own account at the Viol and Flute in Swithen's (Swithin's or Sweeting's) Alley near the Royal Exchange, taking her sign for his premises, and announcing that he was "from the Widow Hare's in Cornhill." There must have been a close association between John Walsh senior and John and Joseph Hare from July 1695-November 1730, as nearly all the publications of the Hares were issued in conjunction with John Walsh and have the names and addresses of both firms in the imprints in the respective forms as in use at the time of issue, but there is no evidence what the business relationship between them was.

K. G. P. II. D. & M.

Information about John Hare is included in works on John Walsh by Frank Kidson and William C. Smith. (*See* Bibliography.)

HARE (JOHN) & (JOSEPH). *See* Hare (John).

HARE (JOSEPH). Musical instrument maker and seller, music printer and publisher, London. In business with his father as John and Joseph Hare, at the Viol and Flute (or, Golden Viol and Flute), in Cornhill, near the Royal Exchange, January 1722-September 1725; when John Hare died, Joseph Hare carried on the business in his name at the same address, probably on behalf of his mother Elizabeth Hare, September 1725-June 1728, when he set up for himself at the Viol and Hautboy (or, Viol and Hoboy), in Cornhill, near the Royal Exchange (three doors further over against Birchin Lane), and continued there until his death in July 1733; succeeded by his widow Elizabeth Hare the younger; his mother, Elizabeth Hare the elder, continued

[171]

the business at the Viol and Flute in Cornhill, near the Royal Exchange, July 1728-July 1734.
K. G.
Information about Joseph Hare is included in works on John Walsh by Frank Kidson and William C. Smith. (*See* Bibliography.)
See also Hare (John).

HARFORD (ROBERT). Bookseller, at the Angel in Cornhill, near the Royal Exchange, London, 1677-81. (P.) Published a work by Giovanni Francesco Loredano, "The Ascents of the Soul . . . being paraphrases on the fifteen Psalms of Degrees . . . Render'd into English . . . London, Printed by A. G. and J. P. for Robert Harford . . . 1681."
P. II.

HARGREAVES. *See* Hime & Hargreaves.

HARPER (J.). Publisher, at the Angel in Fleet Street, London. Published Nos. XXIII-XXV? of Vol. 1 of Bickham's "The Musical Entertainer," 1738, earlier numbers of which were published by Thomas Harper.
See also Harper (Thomas) Copper plate printer.

HARPER (THOMAS). Printer and music printer from movable type, Little Britain, London, 1614-56. (P.) Printed Ravenscrofts "The Whole Booke of Psalmes," 1633, etc., and musical works for John Playford, the elder, 1650-55, including the first edition of "The English Dancing Master"; issued some works bearing only the initials T. H.
K. G. P. I. D. & M.

HARPER (THOMAS). Copper plate printer, in Dogwell Court, White Fryar's, London. Printed, published and sold Nos. I-XVI, or after, of Vol. I of Bickham's "The Musical Entertainer", January 1737-38? May have moved to the Angel in Fleet Street, where J. Harper continued the publication of "The Musical Entertainer."
See also Harper (J.).

HARRINGTON, *Mr.* 32 Princes Street, Leicester Square, London. Printed and sold c. 1785, "A Minuetto con XII Variazioni per il Piano Forte con Accompagnamento d' un Violino. Composti dal Sigr. I. Pleyel."

HARRIS (BARTHOLOMEW). Stationer, 66 Hatton Garden, London. Published "God save Victoria, Great Britain's Queen, a coronation melody. Composed & arranged for the Piano Forte by W. Dodd. 1838."

HARRIS (BENJAMIN). Bookseller and printer, next the Golden Boar's Head, against the Cross Keys Inn, in Gracechurch Street, and at

various addresses, London, 1673-1708. (P.) Advertised June 1701, "The Psalms of David in Metre. Fitted to the Tunes used in Parish-Churches. By John Patrick. Sold by B. Harris. Next the Golden Boar's head against the Cross Keys Inn in Grace-church-street."
P. II.

HARRIS (THOMAS). Bookseller and publisher, at the Looking Glass and Bible, on London Bridge, London, 1741-45. (P.) His name appears in the imprint of "A Collection of Tunes, Set to Music, As they are commonly sung at the Foundery. London: Printed by A. Pearson, and sold by T. Harris . . . MDCCXLII."
P. III.

HARRISON & CO. Music publishers and booksellers, London; Paternoster Row, 1779-98; with a second address at Dr. Arne's Head, 141 Cheap-side, corner of the New London Tavern, 1788, etc. James Harrison, founder of the firm, may have been associated with Joseph Wenman, 144 Fleet Street, 1778 or earlier, some of whose publications he continued; the firm's principal musical publications were "The New Musical Magazine" (which included oratorios, etc., by Handel, ballad operas, etc.), 1783, etc.; "The Songs of Handel", 1786-87; "The Pianoforte Magazine," 1797-1802; these were engraved works at popular prices designed to compete with the more expensive editions of Randall, Wright and Co. etc.; firm became Harrison, Cluse and Co., 1798.
K. G.
Catalogue:—c. 1786. 4 pp. obl. fol. (?) (First Edition Bookshop, Catalogue 25. No. 72.)

HARRISON, CLUSE & CO. Music publishers, London, 78 Fleet Street, 1798-1802; 108 Newgate Street, 1802-c. 1803. Succeeded Harrison and Co.
K. G.

HARRISON (JAMES). *See* Harrison & Co.

HARROD (WILLIAM). Printer and stationer, Stamford. Printed by and for W. Harrod, "Select Psalms of David, in the Old Version, set to music in two parts, Tenor and Bass . . . MDCCLXXXIX."

HARROT (JOHN). Teacher of Psalmody, Great Bowden, Leicestershire. His name appears in the imprints of "The Sacred Melody . . . Collected and publish'd by William East . . . Likewise Mr. Wightman . . . Grantham . . . and by Mr. John Harrot . . . Great Bowden. 1754."

HART & FELLOWS. Music sellers and publishers, London; Sacred Music Repository, 71 Fetter Lane, c. 1818-26; 2 Hatton Garden, c. 1826-30. Joseph Hart carried on the business alone c. 1830.

[173]

HART (ANDRO). Bookseller, bookbinder and printer, a little beneath the Cross, High Street, Edinburgh, 1587-1621. (M.) Printed "The CL. Psalmes of David in Meeter, with diuers notes and tunes augmented to them . . . At Edinburgh, Printed by Andro Hart, and are to be sold at his owne shoppe, a little beneath the Crosse. Anno 1611." He also printed editions in 1614 and 1615; editions were printed "by the heires of Andro Hart" in 1632, 1633, 1634 and 1635.
K. G. M.

HART (JOSEPH). Engraver, printer and publisher, London; 2 Hatton Garden, c. 1830-34; 109 Hatton Garden, c. 1834-58. Previously a partner in Hart & Fellows; published principally engraved sacred music.

HART (JOSEPH BINNS). Musician, composer and music seller, Hastings, 1829-44; at 1 Castle Terrace, c. 1831-34; Musical Repository, 2 Wellington Place, c. 1838-40. Published some of his own compositions.
G.

HART (PHIL.). London. His name appears in an advertisement July 1716, "Melodies proper to be sung to any of the versions of the Psalms of David . . . Published by Phil. Hart and sold by R. Smith . . . and R. Meers", etc.

HARWARD (SAMUEL). Printer and bookseller, Tewkesbury and Cheltenham, 1760-1809. (P.) His name appears in the imprint of "Six Favorite Minuets for two Violins and a Violoncello, Harpsichord or Piano Forte. By J. Leon. London, S. A. & P. Thompson, and Cheltenham, S. Harward," c. 1785.
P. III.

HARWOOD (JOHN) & (FREDERICK). Stationers, 26 Fenchurch Street, London. Published in conjunction with Collard and Collard c. 1834, "A Complete Collection of Haydn's Quartetts. Being a corrected copy of the Paris edition. London. Collard & Collard . . . J. & F. Harwood," etc.

HATCHARD (JOHN). Bookseller, 190 Piccadilly, London. His name appears in the imprint of "A Selection of Psalms and Hymns, for use of the Parish Church of Chislehurst in Kent . . . London, Printed for the Author: And sold by G. Wilkie . . . and J. Hatchard . . . 1803."

HAVILAND (JOHN). Printer, in the Old Bailey, London, 1613-38. (M.) Printed "The Feminine Monarchie: or the Historie of Bees . . . by Charles Butler, Magd. . . . London, Printed by Iohn Haviland, for Roger Iackson . . . 1623"; contains four pages of music. "The Principles of Musik, in singing and setting . . . By Charles Butler,

Magd. . . . London, Printed by John Haviland, for the Author, 1636";
"The Whole Book of Psalmes. Collected into English Meeter by
Thomas Sternhold, Iohn Hopkins, and others . . . London, Printed
by I. H. for the Company of Stationers. 1638."
 K. M.

HAWES (L.). Bookseller, at the Red Lion, Paternoster Row, London,
 1750-76. (P.) In partnership with Charles Hitch published "A Book
 of Psalmody . . . The Eleventh edition . . . By James Green. London:
 Printed by Robert Brown, for C. Hitch and L. Hawes . . . MDCCLI."
 P. III.

HAWES (WILLIAM). Bookseller, London, 1698-1709; at the Rose,
 Ludgate Street, 1698-1704; Golden Buck, Fleet Street, over against
 St. Dunstan's Church, 1705; Bible and Rose, Ludgate Street, 1706;
 Rose and Crown, next the Dog Tavern on Ludgate Hill, 1709. (P.)
 Published "A Short Discourse Upon the Doctrine of our Baptismal
 Covenant . . . By Thomas Bray, D.D. (An Appendix to the Discourse.)
 London, Printed for Will. Hawes . . . 1699"; the appendix contains
 ten psalm tunes; "A Collection of Psalms, proper to be sung at
 Churches . . . The whole collected out of the New Version, and set
 to the most approved tunes. London: Printed by S. Holt, for Will.
 Hawes at the Rose, Ludgate Street, 1704."
 P. II.

HAWES (WILLIAM). Musician, music seller, printer and publisher,
 London; 7 Adelphi Terrace, c. 1828-30; 355 Strand, c. 1830-46. One
 of the promoters of the Regent's Harmonic Institution, afterwards
 Royal Harmonic Institution; in partnership with Thomas Welsh
 c. 1826-28.

HAWKES & CO. Music sellers and publishers, London; 33 Soho Square,
 1865-76. Partners were William Henry Hawkes and Jules Prudence
 Rivière, the latter acting as manager. Continued as Rivière and
 Hawkes at 28 Leicester Square, 1876-89. Partnership was dissolved
 at close of year 1884; Oliver Hawkes, only son of W. H. Hawkes,
 entered into partnership with his father. Title of firm changed to
 Hawkes and Son, 28 Leicester Square, 1889-96; Denman Street,
 Piccadilly Circus, 1896-1930. Amalgamated in 1930 with Boosey and
 Co., and became Boosey and Hawkes, Ltd. at 295 Regent Street.

HAWKINGS (RICHARD). See Hawkins.

HAWKINS (RICHARD). Bookseller, in Chancery Lane, near Sergeant's
 Inn, London, 1613-36. (M.) His name appears in the imprint of
 "Canzonets. Or Little Short Songs To Three Voyces: Published by
 Thomas Morley . . . Now Newly Imprinted with some Songs added by

[175]

the avthor. London. Printed by William Stansby, Richard Hawkings, George Latham, 1631."
M.

HAWTHORN (PETER). Music seller, 9 Marylebone Street, near the Haymarket, London. Published "Six Sonatinos for the Piano Forte or Harpsichord, with an Accompanyment for a Violin. Composed by J. W. Callcott, M.B. Op. III.", c. 1786; "A Favorite Air with Variations, composed by J. Pleyel, adapted for the Harpsichord or Piano Forte," etc., c. 1786.

HAXBY (THOMAS). Musical instrument maker and music seller, at the Organ, Blake Street, York, c. 1763-97. Published "Six Easy Lessons for the Harpsichord composed by John Camidge, Organist of York Minster," c. 1770; "Six Lessons for the Guittar. Composed by Thomas Thackray of York," c. 1770. In 1770 took out a patent for some improvements in harpsichords; succeeded by Samuel Knapton.
K.

HAYS (ALFRED). *See* Lonsdale (Christopher).

HAZARD (JOSEPH). Bookseller, at the Bible, near (against) Stationers' Hall, London, c. 1712-35. His name appears in the imprints of a number of musical works; succeeded by Robert and James Hazard, who issued several collections of songs, words only, 1737-39.
P. II.

HAZARD (SAMUEL). Printer and bookseller, Bath, 1772-1806; Cheap Street; King's Mead Square. (P.) Published "Selection of Hymns of Peculiar Metre intended for the use of the Congregation meeting in Argyle Chapel. By Rev. Jay. Bath: printed and sold by Samuel Hazard . . . 1791"; "Carmina Christo or Hymns to the Saviour . . . By . . . T. Haweis. Part 1," etc., c. 1792.
P. III.

HEATH (JOSEPH). Bookseller and publisher, Nottingham and Mansfield, 1744-60. (P.) His name appears in the imprint of "David's Harp well Tuned: or a Book of Psalmody . . . The Third edition . . . By Robert Barber, Castleton. London: Printed by Robert Brown . . . For Charles Bathurst . . . Joseph Heath, at Nottingham and Mansfield; and John Roe, at Derby. MDCCLIII."; "The Sacred Melody . . . Collected and publish'd by William East . . . Likewise . . . Mr. Heath junr. Nottingham, and . . . in Mansfield . . . 1754."
P. III.

HEBNER (JONATHAN). Engraver, printer, stationer, etc. to the Royal Family, 15 Maddox Street, London. Printed "A New Set of Quadrilles, with improved figures . . . by J. T. Cunningham. Professor of Dancing from the King's Theatre. Published & sold at his Academy, 21 Argyle Street, London," c. 1821.

HEDGLEY (JOHN). Music seller and publisher, 12 Ebury Street, Pimlico, London, c. 1830-59. Stock-in-trade offered for sale by auction January 28-30, 1863.

HEHL (FREDERICK). Music publisher, 81 Wells Street, Oxford Street, London, c. 1844-45. Previously with Joseph Alfred Novello.

HELLENDAAL (PIETER). Musician and music seller, Cambridge. Printed and sold at the author's house, in Trompington Street, opposite St. Peter's Colledge, c. 1770, "Eight Solos for the Violoncello with a Thorough Bass, composed . . . by . . . Peter Hellendaal. Op. Vta."; printed and sold by the author and son opposite Peterhouse College, c. 1785, "Two Glees for four Voices with full accompanyments in score. Composed . . . by . . . Peter Hellendaal"; printed and sold by the editor at his music shop opposite Peterhouse College, c. 1790, "A Collection of Psalms for the use of Parish Churches . . . the music compos'd & harmoniz'd by Peter Hellendaal Senr., selected and arrang'd by Peter Hellendaal Junr.", etc.

HENCHMAN (WILLIAM). *See* Hensman, Henseman, Henchman, or Hinchman (William).

HENDERSON. *See* Dover & Henderson.

HENEY. Fan painter, Mr. Gay's Head, or Gay's Head, Tavistock Street, Covent Garden, London. Advertised July 1728, "The new and entertaining Fan, consisting of 14 Songs taken out of the Beggars Opera, publish'd some time since in this paper, meeting with a general approbation, has induced the contriver to engrave a second plate for the other side, which contains 15 more, making together 29 of the most celebrated songs out of the said diverting opera, all within the compass of the Flute. Sold by the Author at Mr. Gay's Head . . . and at Mr. Rawlinson's, at the Blue Canister and Fan, the upper end of Castle Street, Leicester Fields." Advertised April 1729, "This day is publish'd, in Quarto, Polly, an Opera: Being the second part of the Beggars Opera . . . With the songs and basses engraven on copper plates. Printed for the Author, and sold by Mr. Heney," etc.

HENSEMAN (WILLIAM). *See* Hensman, Henseman, Henchman, or Hinchman (William).

HENSMAN, HENSEMAN, HENCHMAN, or HINCHMAN (WILLIAM). Bookseller, King's Head, Westminster Hall, London, 1671-1700. (P.) His name appears in the imprints of "A Collection of Ayres, compos'd

for the Theatre, and upon other Occasions. By the late Mr. Henry
Purcell . . . London, Printed by J. Heptinstall, for Frances Purcell,
Executrix of the Author; And are to be sold by B. Aylmer . . . W.
Henchman . . . and Henry Playford . . . 1697"; "Ten Sonatas in
Four Parts. Compos'd by the late Mr. Henry Purcell. London,
Printed by J. Heptinstall, for Frances Purcell, Executrix of the Author;
And are to be sold by B. Aylmer . . . W. Henchman . . . and Henry
Playford . . . 1697." In an advertisement, June 1697, his name
appears as Henseman.
P. II.

HEPTINSTALL (JOHN). Printer, London, 1671-1717. Printed some
musical works in conjunction with Francis Clark, or Clarke, and
Thomas Moore 1687-91; printed works for Henry Playford 1692-98,
and works by Henry Purcell, also editions of "The Whole Book of
Psalms" by John Playford, for the Company of Stationers, 1697-1717.
K. G. P. II. D. & M.
See also Clark or Clarke (Francis).

HERON (CLAUDIUS). London. His name appears in the imprint of
"Six Solos after an easy & elegant taste for the Violoncello with a
Thorough Bass for the Harpsichord. Compos'd by Sigr. Salvador
Lancetti. Printed for Claudius Heron, at Mr. Burchell's Toy Shop,
the upper end of Long Acre, near Drury Lane and sold at the music
shops", c. 1760.

HERRON (JAMES). *See* Longman & Herron.

HETT (RICHARD) Bookseller and publisher, at the Bible and Crown, in
the Poultry, London, 1726-66. (P.) His name appears in the imprint
of "The Psalms of David . . . By I. Watts . . . The Seventh edition . . .
London: Printed for John Clark . . . Richard Hett . . . and Richard
Ford . . . MDCCXXIX."; also in the ninth edition, 1734, and the eleventh
edition, 1737, both printed for Richard Ford and Richard Hett.
P. III.

HEWETT (JOHN). Bookseller, Library, Leamington. Published 1843,
"O how that Sound. Song, written, composed . . . by Mrs. Hyde
Clarke."

HEYBOURN (CHRISTOPHER). Associated in some way with the Patent
to print musical works granted to Thomas Morley, September 28, 1598.

HICKFORD, *Mr.* Concert Room, Panton Street, London. His name
appears in an advertisement June 1732, "This Day is published. Six
Concerto's in seven parts. Composed by Mr. Francis Geminiani,
(three of which are for the German Flute) and are to be had at Mr.
Hickford's in Panton Street (where subscriptions for his Concerts next

year are taken in) and at the musick shops, at 12s 6d per set. N.B. These are not the Concerto's published by Mr. Walsh; but are those which were perform'd at Mr. Geminiani's Concerts last winter, and were never before printed." Hickford, a dancing-master whose premises were used for concerts from 1713 onwards, was not generally interested in the sale of music.

HICKS (FRANCIS). Bookseller, Cambridge, 1682-99. (P.) His name appears in an advertisement June 1691, "A Collection of choice Ayres for 2 and 3 Treble Flutes. Composed by the best masters of musick. Sold by Thomas Jones . . . John May . . . and Fr. Hicks in Cambridge."
    P. II.

HIGHAM (L.). Bookseller, 6 Chiswell Street, London. His name appears in the imprint of "Addington's Selection of Psalm & Hymn Tunes. With additions. London, Published June 11, 1807, by H. Gray . . . & sold also by L. Higham", etc.

HILDYARD (FRANCIS). Bookseller, at the Bible in Stonegate, York, c. 1680-1731. (P.) His name appears in the imprint of "The Most Useful Tunes of the Psalms, in Two, and some in Three Parts. Collected and transposed, corrécted and composed by Edmund Ireland . . . The Second edition, much improved . . . York, Printed by John White, and are to be sold (for the Author) by Francis Hildyard . . . 1713." He was succeeded by his son John.
    P. II.

HILDYARD (JOHN). Bookseller, at the Bible in Stonegate, York, 1731-57. (P.) Published, "Anthems: for Two, Three, Four, Five, Six, Seven, and Eight Voices. As they are now perform'd, in the cathedrals in York, Durham, and Lincoln. With the additions of fifteen new anthems. By Thomas Ellway . . . 1753." Son of Francis Hildyard whom he succeeded in the business.
    P. II.

HILL (HENRY). Musical instrument maker, music seller and publisher, London; 28 Regent Street, c. 1829-44; 3 Old Bond Street, c. 1844-45. Described on some imprints as Hill and Co., also as Hill and Sons c. 1838; previously a partner in the business of Monzani and Hill; died January 1839, aged 57; stock-in-trade sold by auction May 1845.

HILL (JOSEPH). Music seller, in the Minories, near Aldgate, London, 1731-34.

HILL (JOSEPH). Musical instrument maker, London; at the Harp and Hautboy, Piccadilly; in High Holborn; at the Violin, Angel Court, Westminster; and from 1762 at the Harp and Flute, in the Hay Market, where he published: "Six Easy Lessons for the Harpsichord.

Compos'd by Sigr: Binder-Mazzinghi-Ritstchel Sigr: Legne-Galuppi-Zamperelli. Book I.", c. 1765; with "James Turpin Sculpt," at the end of the music; "A Set of Easy Lessons for the Harpsichord . . . Opera Trentesima Prima," preface signed J. M., advertised November 1766. Founder of the firm of W. E. Hill and Sons, Violin makers, now at 140 New Bond Street.
    K.

HILL (JOSEPH). Printer, music seller and publisher, Dublin; 8 Mary Street, c. 1789-93; 36 Denmark Street, c. 1793-96; 51 Abbey Street, c. 1796-99.
    K.

HILL (NICHOLAS). Printer, London. Came from the Low Countries to England in 1519. (D.) Printed "The Actes of the Apostles, translated into Englyshe metre . . . by Christopher Tye . . . wyth notes to eche chapter, to synge and also to play vpon the Lute . . . 1553. Imprynted at London by Nycolas Hyll, for Wyllyam Seres." This was a second issue, the first being "Imprynted at London by Wyllyam Seres dwellynge at the signe of the Hedghogge."
    D. S.

HILL (THOMAS). Bookseller, stationer and music seller, George Street, Perth. Partner in the firm of Bowie and Hill, 1803-15; continued the business after the death of John Bowie in 1815.
    K. (Bowie & Hill).
    See also Bowie & Hill.

HILL (W.). 4, near the Westminster Hospital, Bridge Road, Lambeth. Advertised, October 1811, "Flute and Flageolet—Just published, complete in 9 numbers, Hill's Magazine of Music, for the Flute and Flageolet."

HIME & ADDISON. Music and musical instrument sellers, and publishers, Manchester; 19 St. Ann's Square, c. 1847-70; 30 Victoria Street, c. 1870-85; 30 and 32 Victoria Street, c. 1885-1909; 195 and 197 Deansgate, c. 1909-35; 37 John Dalton Street, c. 1935 to present time. Succeeded Hime, Beale and Co.

HIME & HARGREAVES. Music sellers, 14 St. Ann's Square, Manchester. Published c. 1827, "Farewell thou fair Day . . . The words by Robt. Burns, the music composed . . . by B. Hime." Benjamin Hime was in business alone at the same address c. 1828.

HIME & SON. See Hime (Humphrey).

HIME, BEALE & CO. Music sellers and publishers, 19 St. Ann's Square, Manchester, c. 1835-47. Benjamin Hime and Thomas Beale were previously in business independently; succeeded by Hime and Addison.

HIME (BENJAMIN). Musician, music seller and publisher, Manchester; 14 St. Ann's Square, c. 1828; 20 St. Ann's Square, c. 1834-35. Previously a partner in the firm of Hime and Hargreaves; afterwards joined with Thomas Beale and became Hime, Beale and Co.

HIME (HUMPHREY). Music seller and publisher, 14 Castle Street, Liverpool, c. 1790-1805. Continued as Hime and Son, Castle Street and Church Street, c. 1805-40; imprints of early publications are without numbers of their premises; later numbers are 56 (c. 1825-27) and 53 Castle Street, and 32 (c. 1825-27) and 23 Church Street; 57 Church Street, c. 1840-79; Humphrey Hime was previously in partnership with his brother Morris, or Maurice.
    K. G.

HIME (MORRIS) or (MAURICE). Musical instrument and music seller, and publisher, Dublin; 40 College Green, c. 1790; 34 College Green, c. 1791-1811; 29 College Green, c. 1811-14; 26 Dame Street, c. 1814-1817; 3 Westmoreland Street, c. 1817-19; 14 Eustace Street, c. 1819-1820. Previously in partnership with his brother Humphrey in Liverpool.
    K. G.

HIME (MORRIS) or (MAURICE) & (HUMPHREY). Music sellers and publishers, 15 Castle Street Liverpool, for a few years prior to 1790. Partnership ceased c. 1790; Morris set up in business in Dublin, Humphrey continued in Liverpool.
    K. G.

HINCH (S.). Printer, London. His name appears in the imprint of a song "Wonderful News from the River of Thames. To a pleasant new tune. Printed on the frozen Thames, by the loyal young printers, viz. E. and A. Milbourn, S. Hinch, J. Mason . . . 1683."
    P. II.

HINCHMAN (WILLIAM). *See* Hensman, Henseman, Henchman or Hinchman (William).

HINDMARSH (JOSEPH). Bookseller, London; at the Black Bull in Cornhill, 1678-85; at the Golden Ball over against the Royal Exchange in Cornhill, 1685-96. (P.) Published some music which included "Choice New Songs never before Printed. Set to several new Tunes by the best Masters of Music. Written by Tho. D'Urfey . . . 1684"; "A Third Collection of New Songs, never Printed before. The words by Mr. D'Urfey. Set to Music by the best Masters in that Science . . . 1685."
    K. P. II. D. & M.

HINTON (JOHN). Bookseller and publisher, various addresses, London,

c. 1739-81. (P.) His name appears in the imprints of "The Psalms of David in Metre: With the tunes used in Parish-Churches. By John Patrick. The Eighth edition. London: Printed for J. Walthoe . . . J. Hinton . . . MDCCXLII."; "The Spiritual Man's Companion . . . The Fifth edition . . . By Israel Holdroyd . . . London: Printed by Robert Brown . . . for J. Hinton, at the King's Arms in Newgate Street. MDCCLIII."
P. III.

HITCH (CHARLES). Bookseller, at the Red Lion, Paternoster Row, London, 1732-64. Published and sold a number of musical works, some in partnership with his father-in-law Arthur Bettesworth, and later with L. Hawes.
P. III.

HODGES & SMITH. Booksellers and publishers, Dublin. Published "The Ancient Music of Ireland, arranged for the Piano Forte. To which is prefixed a dissertation on the Irish Harp and Harpers including an account of the old melodies of Ireland. By Edward Bunting . . . 1840."

HODGES (CHARLES). Music seller, 28 Clare Street, Bristol, c. 1800-1830 or later. Published a small amount of music.

HODGES (*Sir* JAMES). Bookseller, at the Looking Glass on London Bridge, or, over against St. Magnus's Church, London Bridge, London, c. 1730-58. (P.) Published and sold a number of musical works.
P. III.

HODGSON (CHARLES). *See* Duff & Hodgson.

HODGSON (PETER). Engraver, music seller and publisher, Maiden Lane, Covent Garden, London, c. 1776-81. Some single sheet songs bear only the initials P. H.
K.

HODSOLL (WILLIAM). Music seller and publisher, Sevenoaks, 1794. (K.) 45 High Holborn, London, 1798-1831. Succeeded Francis Linley; succeeded by Zenas T. Purday.
K. G.
Catalogues:—Vocal Music. c. 1806. 1 p. fol. (William C. Smith); Instrumental Music. 1814. 1 p. fol. (B.M. h. 283. (15.)); Catalogue thematique, of Symphonies and Overtures by Mozart, Haydn, Rossini, Pleyel &c. Arranged . . . by S. F. Rimbault. c. 1824. 1 p. fol. (B.M. h. 276. (3.)); c. 1824. 1 p. fol. (B.M. h. 276. (8.)); c. 1825. 1 p. fol. (B.M. h. 276. (12.)); No. 1. Catalogue thematique, of Symphonies and Overtures, by Mozart, Haydn, Beethoven, Himmel, Weber and Mehul. Arranged . . . by S. F. Rimbault. c. 1827. 1 p.

fol. (B.M. h. 276. (9.)); No. 2. Catalogue thematique of Symphonies and Overtures, by A. Romberg, Pleyel, Winter, Rossini, Kreitzer [i.e. Kreutzer], Handel, Paer and Mozart. Arranged . . . by S. F. Rimbault. c. 1827. 1 p. fol. (B.M. 276. (10.))

HODSON. *See* Addison & Hodson.

HODSON (FRANCIS). *See* Fletcher (Thomas) & Hodson (Francis).

HODSON (GEORGE ALEXANDER). Music seller and publisher, at the Dublin Musical Repository, 108 Grafton Street, Dublin, c. 1827-31; At the Bedford Musical Repository, 12 Store Street, London, c. 1835. Composed some music.

HOEY (JAMES). Printer, Dublin, 1730-74, in Christ Church Yard; at the Pamphlet Shop in Skinner's Row opposite to the Tholsel, or simply, in Skinner Row; at the sign of the Mercury, in Skinner's Row. (P.) Printed for the Author c. 1748, "Ladies Amusement: Being a new Collection of Songs, Ballads, &c. with Symphonies and Thorough-Bass. The music by John Frederick Lampe." Also printed some Handel libretti. Hoey is said to have been originally in partnership with George Faulkner, printer of "The Dublin Journal" ("Faulkner's Journal").
G. P. III.

HOFFMAN (A.). *See* Hoffman (John Andrew).

HOFFMAN (FRANCIS). Engraver, London? Engraved the music in "Lyra Davidica: or, A Collection of Divine Songs and Hymns . . . London, Printed for J. Walsh . . . 1708"; "Hymns and Spiritual Songs . . . By Simon Browne . . . London: Printed for Emanuel Matthews . . . MDCCXX."; "The Psalms of David . . . By I. Watts . . . . London . . . MDCCXXII."; also the seventh edition, 1729; ninth, 1734; eleventh, 1737 and fifteenth, 1748.

HOFFMAN (JOHN ANDREW). Musician, music seller and publisher, London; 124 Oxford Street, c. 1795-99; 9 Princes Street, Cavendish Square, c. 1799-1808; 21 Manchester Street, Manchester Square, c. 1808-22.
K.

HOLBECHE (A.). Bookseller, at the Bible and Crown, in Barbican, London. His name appears in the imprint of "The Merry Mountebank; or, the Humourous Quack Doctor . . . In a choice collection of old and new songs; and compiled . . . By Timothy Tulip . . . Vol. I. London: Printed by W. Pearson for A. Holbeche . . . F. Jefferis . . . and C. Pickman . . . 1732."
P. III.

HOLDEN (SMOLLET). Composer, music seller and publisher, 26 Parliament Street, Dublin, c. 1800-18.
K.

HOLDSWORTH & BALL. Booksellers and publishers, London; 18 St. Paul's Church Yard, c. 1828-33; 1 Amen Corner, c. 1833-36. Published "Original Psalmody . . . Composed by William Bird, Watford, Herts. Printed for the Author & sold by Messrs. Holdsworth and Ball," etc; preface dated January 27, 1829. An edition was also published c. 1830.

HOLE (ROBERT). Engraver, London. Engraved "Parthenia Inviolata. Or Mayden-Musicke for the Virginalls and Bass-Viol Selected out of the Compositions of the most famous in that Arte By Robert Hole . . . Printed at London for John Pyper, and are to be sold at his shopp at Pauls gate next unto cheapside at the crosse keies," c. 1614.
K. G.

HOLE (WILLIAM). Engraver, London. Engraved "Parthenia or The Maydenhead of the first musicke that euer was printed for the Virginalls Composed By three famous Masters: William Byrd, Dr: Iohn Bull, & Orlando Gibbons . . . Ingrauen by William Hole. Lond: print: for Mris Dor: Euans . . . Are to be sould by G: Lowe printr in Loathberry," c. 1613; also two slightly later issues with modified title-pages, but bearing the names of William Hole, Dorethie Euans and G. Lowe. Hole also engraved "Prime musiche nuove di Angelo Notari à una, due, e tre voci, per cantare con la tiorba, et altri strumenti, nouamente poste in luce," etc., c. 1613.
K. G.

HOLLAND & JONES. Musical instrument makers, music sellers and publishers, 23 Bishopsgate Street Within, London, c. 1797-1800. Henry Holland was previously in business on his own account; T. Jones carried on alone when Holland dropped out, c. 1800.

HOLLAND (HENRY). Organ builder, music seller and publisher, London; Music and musical instrument warehouse, facing Bedford Row, near Gray's Inn, 1782 to January 1789, with additional premises at 48 St. James's Street (The corner of St. James's Street), Piccadilly, c. 1786-January 1789; 48 St. James's Street (The corner of St. James's Street), Piccadilly, only, January 1789-c. 1793; Newgate Street, c. 1793-97. Nephew of and successor to Mr. Pyke; some single sheet songs bear only the initials H H—d.; became partner in Holland and Jones, c. 1797.
K.

HOLLAND (JAMES). Bookseller, at the Bible and Ball, at the West end of St. Paul's, or in St. Paul's Churchyard, London, 1705-c. 1717.

[184]

The REPROOF.

Charming is— your Shape and Air, And your

Face as Morn--ing fair! As Morn--ing fair! Coral

Lips, and Neck of Snow; Cheeks, where op'ning

Rofes blow! When you fpeak, or

fmile, or   move,   All is Rapture, all is Love.

But thofe Eyes, alas, I hate!
Eyes, that heedlefs of my Fate,
Shine with undifcerning Rays;
On the Fopling idly gaze;
Watch the Glances of the Vain;
Meeting mine with cold Difdain.

For

For the F L U T E.

"The Musical Miscellany". Printed by John Watts from wood blocks. 1729-31

Published "A Supplement to the New Version of Psalms by Dr. Brady and Mr. Tate . . . The Sixth edition . . . With the addition of plain instructions . . . near 30 new tunes, composed by several of the best masters . . . Printed by John Nutt; and sold by James Holland . . . MDCCVIII." His name also appears in the imprints of the seventh edition, 1712, and the eighth edition, 1717.
P. II.

HOLLIER (JOHN). *See* Coventry & Hollier.

HOLLOWAY & CO. Wholesale music sellers, musical instrument makers, and publishers, 40 Hart Street, Bloomsbury, London, c. 1805-20.
K.

HOLLOWAY (THOMAS). Music seller and publisher, London; 5 Hanway Street, c. 1821-59; 41 Hanway Street, c. 1859-68. Sometimes styled Holloway & Co.; previously a partner in Phipps and Holloway; retired from business in 1864; sale of stock by Puttick and Simpson, 6th July, 1864; 30th March, 2nd and 4th May, 1868.
K.

HOLST (M.). Musician, music and musical instrument seller, and publisher, 126 Great Portland Street, London, c. 1814-25.

HOLT (E.). Printer, London. Printed "A Short Discourse Upon the Doctrine of our Baptismal Covenant . . . By Thomas Bray, D.D. (An Appendix to the Discourse.) London, Printed by E. Holt, for Rob. Clavel . . . 1697." The appendix contains five psalm tunes.

HOLT (S.). Printer, London. Printed "A Collection of Psalms, proper to be sung at Churches . . . The whole collected out of the New Version, and set to the most approved tunes. London: Printed by S. Holt, for Will. Hawes . . . 1704."

HOLY LAMB IN DRURY LANE. Appears in an advertisement March 1747, "The Music in score of the Thanksgiving Anthem, perform'd at the Protestant-Lutheran-German-Church in the Savoy, on Thursday the 9th of October 1746. Compos'd by John Frederick Lampe. The words to the musick both English and German. Printed for the Author, at the Holy Lamb in Drury Lane, near Long-Acre", etc.

HOME (ROBERT). Engraver, 10 High Terrace, Edinburgh. Engraved on copper "The Sacred Harmony of the Church of Scotland . . . Edited and chiefly arranged by R. A. Smith. Second edition. Published by Alexr. Robertson . . . Edinburgh ", c. 1825.

HONE (WILLIAM). Writer, bookseller and publisher, b.1780–d.1842. Published at 67 Old Bailey, London, c. 1817, "Great gobble gobble

G

gobble, and twit twittle twit; or Law, versus Common Sense . . . A new Song with original music by Lay Logic, Esqre. Student in the law of Libel."

HOOPER (SAMUEL). Bookseller and publisher, various addresses, London, 1756-93. (P.) Published c. 1770, "The New Musical Pocket Companion to the Magdalen Chapel . . . by Adam Smith . . . Printed for S. Hooper at the East Corner of the New Church in the Strand."
P. III.

HOPKINS. *See* Paine & Hopkins.

HOPKINS (FREDERICK SAMUEL). Stationer and music seller, London; 42 Bishopsgate Street Within, c. 1813-24; 5 Bishopsgate Street, Within, c. 1824-47. Published a small amount of music.
K.

HOPKINSON (JOHN) & (JAMES). Pianoforte manufacturers, music sellers and publishers, Leeds and London. Leeds; 6 Commercial Street, 1835-c. 1860; as Hopkinson Brothers, 5 and 6 Commercial Street, c. 1860-70; as Hopkinson Brothers and Co., 5 and 6 Commercial Street, c. 1870-1904; continued as Hopkinsons' Successors Ltd. at same premises. London; 70 Mortimer Street, Cavendish Square, 1846-December 1847; 27 Oxford Street, January 1848-51; 18 Soho Square, 1851-56; 235 Regent Street, 1856-82; 95 New Bond Street, 1882-92; 34-36 Margaret Street, Cavendish Square, 1892-1900; 84 New Bond Street, 1900-10; 52 Wigmore Street, 1910-19; also a manufactory at Fitzroy Road, Regent's Park, c. 1866-1948. From about 1895 the firm were solely pianoforte makers.
G.

HORN (T.). Bookseller? London. Name appears in the imprint of "The Psalms of David in Metre: Fitted to the tunes used in Parish-Churches. By John Patrick . . . London. Printed for W. Churchill . . . T. Horn . . . MDCCXVIII."

HORN (WILLIAM). Music seller and publisher, London; 21 Oxendon Street, Haymarket, c. 1817-24; 13 Tichborne Street, Piccadilly, and 8 Borough Road, c. 1824-25; 8 Borough Road, only, c. 1825-28; 28 Aldermanbury, c. 1828-31; 3 Welbeck Street, Cavendish Square, c. 1831-33; 6 Adelaide Street, Strand, c. 1833-35; 16 Lowther Arcade, Strand, c. 1835-36.
K.

HORNE. *See* Thorowgood & Horne.

HORNE (E.). Bookseller? London. Name appears in the imprint of

"The Psalms of David in Metre: With the tunes used in Parish-Churches. By John Patrick. The Seventh edition . . . London: Printed for D. Brown . . . E. Horne . . . MDCCXXIV."

HORSFIELD (ROBERT). Bookseller and publisher, London; the Crown, 22 Ludgate Street, c. 1763-73; 5 Stationers' Court, c. 1773-78. Published "Vocal Music, or the Songster's Companion containing a new and choice Collection of the greatest variety of Songs, Cantatas &c.", in two volumes, c. 1771 and 1772. Further editions, printed by Baker and Galabin, were published in 1772 and 1775; an edition in three volumes was printed in 1778 by James Bew.
K. P. III.

HORWOOD. *See* Astor & Horwood.

HOSKINS (WILLIAM). Printer and bookseller, London; Fetter Lane; Middle Temple Gate; c. 1575-1600. (M.) An entry of William Hoskins appears in the Registers of the Company of Stationers, March 1597 (Arber III, 81.), "A playne and perfect Instruction for learnynge to play on ye virginalles by hand or by booke by notes and letters or Tabliture neuer heretofore sett out by any &c."
M. S.

HOUBRAKEN (JACOBUS). Engraver of portraits, b. 1698–d. 1780, worked principally in Amsterdam. Engraved the plate containing Handel's portrait issued by John Walsh, junior, with his edition of "Alexander's Feast," 1738. The portrait may have been an original work by Houbraken, the decorative work in the design, including the scene from Alexander's Feast was by Hubert François Gravelot. The plate was used again and again with many issues of Handel's scores by W. Randall and others from c. 1768-69 to well on into the nineteenth century.

HOULSTON & SON. Booksellers and publishers, 65 Paternoster Row, London, c. 1826-38. Published a small number of sacred musical works. Succeeded by Houlston and Stoneman.

HOULSTON & STONEMAN. Booksellers and publishers, 65 Paternoster Row, London, c. 1838-57. Published a small number of sacred musical works. Succeeded Houlston and Son.

HOUSTON. *See* Lewis, Houston & Hyde.

HOW & PARSONS. Publishers, Fleet Street, London, Published "The Songs of Charles Dibdin, chronologically arranged, with notes, historical, biographical, and critical; and the music of the best and most popular of the melodies, with new piano-forte accompaniments. To which is prefixed a memoir of the author, by George Hogarth, Esq . . . MDCCCXLII." The partners were Jeremiah How and John Parsons.

[187]

HOWE (W.). 1 Alfred Place, London Road, St. George's Fields, London, c. 1795-1805. Published some music in conjunction with Riley and Willis.

HOWELL (JAMES). Music seller and publisher, 27 King William Street, Strand, London, c. 1833-37.

HOWELL (MARY). Bookseller, Oxford. Her name appears in the imprint of "Musica Oxoniensis. A Collection of Songs: for One and Two Voices, with the Thorough-Bass. Publish'd by Francis Smith, and Peter de Walpergen Letter-Founder, by whom 'twas Cut on Steel, and Cast, by the Directions of the former. Oxford: Printed by Leon. Lichfield . . . And are to be sold by the Widow Howell, 1698."
P. II. D. & M.

HOWELL (THOMAS). Music seller and teacher of the pianoforte, Clare Street, Bristol, c. 1790 until 1830 or later. At No. 12, c. 1790-1818; No. 13, c. 1825-30. Published a small amount of music. Also said to have lived in St. John's Street.
K.

HUBERT (H.). 402 Strand, opposite Salisbury Street, London. Published "Four Songs being the leading subject in Canto the first, section the 15th to 24th from the Lady of the Lake, the music composed by A. Radiger," c. 1811; "Allen bane the Harper, the words from the Lady of the Lake, set to music by A. Radiger," c. 1812.

HUDGEBUT (JOHN). Book and music seller and publisher, London, 1679-99; at the Golden Harp and Hoboy in Chancery Lane; St. Paul's Churchyard; later near Charing Cross, or near St. Martin's Lane, in the Strand. (P.) In the later imprints given as Hudgebutt. He was author of "A Vade Mecum for the Lovers of Musick, shewing the Excellency of the Rechorder . . . MDCLXXIX."
K. G. P. II. D. & M.

HUGHES (GEORGE). Music seller to H.R.H. the Princess of Wales, 221 Tottenham Court Road, London. Published c. 1815, "La Bouton de rose; a favorite divertisement consisting of an introductory Movement & Rondo. Composed . . . by J. A. Parrin."

HULLMANDEL (CHARLES). Lithographic printer, 51 Great Marlborough Street, London. Printed at C. Hullmandel's Lithographic Establishment, "Dernière sonate pour le piano forte, avec accompaniment de violon; composée expressément pour Madame la Maréchade Moreau: par le celebre Jos: Haydn. À Paris publiée par Naderman, à Londres par Clementi & Co. 26 Cheapside," c. 1820.

HULSBERGH (HENRY). Engraver, died in London, 1729. Engraved a number of illustrated title-pages and also the characters for figure dances in musical works published by John Walsh and others c. 1702-24.

HULTON (R.). Bookseller, corner of Pall Mall, London. One of a number of booksellers etc. who collected subscriptions for Bickham's "The Musical Entertainer," January 1737, etc.

HUME (JOHN). Printer, Westgate Street, Bath. Printed "Sacred Harmony. Hymns and Psalms appointed to be sung at Laura Chapel, Bathwick; the music composed by eminent masters, ancient and modern, adapted for the harp or piano-forte (by Thomas White) . . . 1808."

HUMMELL (A.). Music seller, printer and publisher, facing Nassau Street, in King Street, St. Ann's, Soho, London, c. 1760-70.
    K.

HUMPHREYS, *Mr.* Bookseller? In St. Paul's Churchyard, London. His name appears in an advertisement October 1741, "Neatly printed, the second edition, with very large additions of, The Divine Musick Scholars Guide . . . By John Sreeve . . . Printed for James Hodges . . . and sold by Mr. Johnson . . . and Mr. Humphreys", etc.

HUNT (RICHARD). Musical instrument maker and music seller, at the Lute in St. Paul's Church Yard, London. Published in conjunction with Humphry Salter, "The Genteel Companion; being exact directions for the Recorder: With a collection of the best and newest tunes and grounds extant. Carefully composed and gathered by Humphry Salter . . . 1683."; his name appears in the imprint of "The Circle: or Conversations on Love & Gallantry; originally in French. Now Englished. And since augmented with several new songs, illustrated with musical notes, both treble & bass. By Nath. Noel, Gent . . . 1676."
    K. P. II. D. & M.

HURST, ROBINSON & CO. Booksellers, London; 90 Cheapside and 8 Pall Mall, c.1818-25; 6 Pall Mall and 5 Waterloo Place, c. 1825-27. Published "The Loyal and National Songs of England, for one, two, and three voices, selected from original manuscripts and early printed works in the library of William Kitchener. 1823." The firm is mentioned in an advertisement, December 1823, "The New Caliope. No. 1. Being a selection of British, and occasionally, foreign melodies newly arranged for the Piano-Forte, and engraved on copper by John Beugo. To be continued quarterly . . . Published by Archibald Constable and Co., Edinburgh; and Hurst, Robinson and Co. London." The firm were also selling agents for some issues of George Thomson's "The Select Melodies of Scotland," 1823.

HURST (HENRY). Publisher, 27 King William Street, West Strand, London. Published "The Illustrated Musical Almanack . . . for 1847. Edited, and the songs written, by F. W. N. Bayley . . . MDCCCXLVII."

HUTCHINSON (W.). Printer, London. Printed for the Author, "A Sett of New Psalm Tunes and Anthems, in four parts. By William Knapp. MDCCXXXVIII."

HUTTON & BALBIRNIE. Music engravers, 105 High Street, Edinburgh, c. 1819-21, or later. Partners were William Hutton and William Balbirnie.
     K.
     See also Balbirnie (William); Hutton (William).

HUTTON (WILLIAM). Music engraver, 105 High Street, Edinburgh, c. 1815-19. Became Hutton and Balbirnie at same address, c. 1819-21; previously in partnership with George Walker as Walker and Hutton, Foulis Close, c. 1811-15.
     K.

HYATT. *See* Kauntze & Hyatt.

HYDE. *See* Lewis, Houston & Hyde.

HYDE (FREDERICK AUGUSTUS). *See* Clementi, Banger, Hyde, Collard & Davis; Lewis, Houston & Hyde.

HYLL (NYCOLAS). *See* Hill.

INNYS (JOHN). *See* Innys (William).

INNYS (WILLIAM). Bookseller, Prince's Arms, St. Paul's Churchyard, London, 1711-56. (P.) Joined by John Innys and became William and John Innys for a time; names appear in the imprints of a number of sacred music works.
     P. II, III.

INNYS (WILLIAM) & (JOHN). *See* Innys (William).

IRELAND (JOHN). Bookseller, Leicester. His name appears in the imprint of "The Sacred Melody . . . Collected and publish'd by William East . . . Likewise Mr. Wightman . . . Mr. Ireland Leicester . . . 1754."

IRELAND (WILLIAM). At the Golden Stirrup, near Leisterfields, London. His name appears in the imprint of "The Most Useful Tunes of the Psalms, in Two, and some in Three Parts. Collected and transposed, corrected and composed by Edmund Ireland . . . The

Second edition . . . York, Printed by John White, and are to be sold (for the Author) by . . . and William Ireland . . . London, 1713."

IRONMONGER (DAVID). Music importer and publisher, 18 Whitfield Street, Leonard Square, Finsbury, London. Published c. 1840, "David Ironmonger's Instructions for the Double & Single Harmonicon Glasses", etc.

ISAAC (MAYHEW) & CO. Booksellers and publishers, at the Office of the National Library of Standard Works, 14 Henrietta Street, Covent Garden, London. Published c. 1835, "National Library of Standard Music. The Beggar's Opera, arranged from a very scarce Edition . . . with new Symphonies and Accompaniments for the Pianoforte by John Barnett," etc.

ISLIP (ADAM). *See* Wolfe (John).

IVY. *See* Wood & Ivy.

J., J. *See* Johnston (John).

J., T. *See* Jefferys (Thomas).

JACKSON & SMITH. 409 Oxford Street, London. Published c. 1790, "Sonata pour le Clavecin ou Forte Piano que represente La Bataille de Rosbach. Composées par Mr. Bach."

JACKSON, BLOCKLEY & JACKSON. Music sellers and publishers, London; 96 New Bond Street, c. 1842-44, 21 Orchard Street, Portman Square, c. 1844-45. Partners were Thomas Jackson, John Blockley and Joseph Jackson.

JACKSON (J.). Bookseller and publisher, London, 1728-61; Pall Mall, near St. James's House; bottom of St. James's Street; St. James's Street, near the Palace. (P.) His name appears in the imprint of "The Tragedy of Chrononhotonthologos: being the most tragical Tragedy, that ever was tragediz'd by any Company of Tragedians. Written by Benjamin Bounce, Esq. [i.e. Henry Carey.] London: Printed for J. Shuckburgh, and L. Gilliver . . . J. Jackson, in Pall Mall, and sold by A. Dodd . . . and E. Nutt", etc., c. 1734; with the tunes of the songs.
    P. III.

JACKSON (JOSEPH). *See* Jackson, Blockley & Jackson.

JACKSON (ROGER). Bookseller, in Fleet Street over against the Conduit, London, 1601-25. Published "The Feminine Monarchie: or the Historie of Bees . . . by Charles Butler, Magd. . . . London, Printed by Iohn Haviland, for Roger Iackson and are to be sold at his shop in Fleetstreet, ouer against the conduit. 1623"; contains four pages of music.

M.

JACKSON (THOMAS). *See* Jackson, Blockley & Jackson.

JACOBS (E.). Printer and bookseller, near the new Market, Halifax. Published, "The Yorkshire Musical Miscellany, comprising an elegant selection of the most admired songs in the English language, set to music . . . 1800"; "Sacred Music, consisting of a new book of Psalmody . . . by the Rev. John Chetham . . . the whole carefully corrected and revised by Mr. Stopford, organist of Halifax . . . 1811."

K.

JAMES (JOHN). Letter Founder, Bartholomew Close, London. Issued a large folio single sheet, "A Specimen of Musick by John James, Letter Founder in Bartholomew Close, London, 1748. Purcell's, Fairest Isle all Isles excelling."

JAMES (W. N.). 38 Foley Place, London. Published c. 1830, "Adagio & Rondo, for the Flute & Piano Forte . . . by L. Drouet."

JAUNCEY (JOHN). Music engraver and printer, 4 Cross Street, Islington, London. Engraved and printed "The New Harmonic Magazine, or Compendious Repository, of Sacred Music, in full score. By John Beaumont. 1801. Published "As I wander'd one Morn, a favorite Song with an accompaniment for the Piano-Forte, composed by Mr. Ross, Aberdeen," c. 1805; "I'll gang nae mair to yon Town. The Prince Regent's favorite Scottish Tune . . . Arranged as a Rondo for the Piano Forte . . . by Louis Jansen", c. 1810; "The Pupils' Lesson by Charles James Jones," c. 1810.

JEEB (ROBERT). Bookseller, in the Pavement in York. His name appears in the imprint of "The Psalm Singer's Guide . . . Collected and compos'd by Edm. Ireland, and taught by J. Hall, E. Micklewhait, and R. Sowerby. The Third edition . . . York: Printed for the Author, and are sold by Robert Jeeb . . . in York; and Arthur Bettesworth . . . London. 1719."

JEFFERIS (F.). *See* Jeffries or Jeffris (Francis).

JEFFERYS & NELSON. Composers, music sellers and publishers, 21 Soho Square, Soho, London, c. 1840-43.
See also Jefferys (Charles).

JEFFERYS (CHARLES). Composer, music seller and publisher, London; 5 Carlton Cottages, St. George's Road, c. 1835; 31 Frith Street, Soho,

c. 1836-40; 21 Soho Square, c. 1840-43 as Jefferys and Nelson, c. 1843-68 as Charles Jefferys; 57 Berners Street, c. 1868-74; 67 Berners Street, c. 1874-98; 70 Berners Street, c. 1898-99. Died 1865; in later years business was carried on as C. Jefferys and Co., Jefferys and Son, and Jefferys Ltd.

JEFFERYS (THOMAS). London. Published "Amaryllis; Consisting of such Songs as are most esteemed for Composition and Delicacy, and Sung, at the Publick Theatres or Gardens; All chosen from the Works of the Best Masters . . . London. Publish'd . . . by T. J. and sold by M. Cooper in Paternoster Row, J. Wood, at the Royal Exchange, and I. Tyther music seller in Moorfields," 2 vols., c. 1750; a second edition with the same imprint was issued a little later.

JEFFES (ABEL). Printer, Fore Street, without Cripplegate, etc., London, 1584-99. (M.) Printed "An introduction to the true arte of musicke . . . by William Bathe . . . 1584"; Thacker's "A godlie Dittie to be song for the preseruation of the Queenes most excelent Maiesties raigne. Imprinted at London by Abell Ieffes, dwelling in the fore streete without Creeple-gate. 1586."
  K. M. S.

JEFFRIES or JEFFRIS (FRANCIS). Bookseller, at the Bible and Crown, Ludgate Street, London. His name appears in the imprint of "The Merry Mountebank; or, the Humourous Quack Doctor . . . In a choice collection of old and new songs; and compiled . . . By Timothy Tulip . . . Vol. I. London: Printed by W. Pearson for A. Holbeche . . . F. Jefferis . . . and C. Pickman . . . 1732."
  P. III.

JENKINSON (J.). Musical instrument maker, 39 Fashion Street, Spittal-fields, London. Printed c. 1797, "Come Slumbers steal me soft away. A Favourite Song. Composed by J. A. Parrin."

JOHANNING & CO. See Johanning & Whatmore.

JOHANNING & WHATMORE. Music and musical instrument sellers, and publishers, London; 126 Regent Street, c. 1831-35; 6 John Street, Oxford Street, c 1835-37; 122 Great Portland Street, c. 1837-1843; 9 Newman Street, Oxford Street, c. 1843-49; 2 Marylebone Street, Piccadilly, c. 1849-50. Had a "Circulating Library for Foreign Music." Also described as Johanning and Co.; Julius Johanning was a partner in the firm of Ewer and Johanning c. 1825-29.

JOHANNING (JULIUS). See Ewer & Johanning; Johanning & Whatmore.

JOHNSON & ANDERSON. Music engravers and printers, Edinburgh;

G *

475 High Street, 1811-12; North Gray's Close, 1812-15. Partners were Mrs. Johnson, widow of James Johnson, and John Anderson.

JOHNSON & CO. *See* Johnson (James).

JOHNSON. 96 Cheapside, London. *See* Lewis & Johnson.

JOHNSON, *Mr.* Music seller, near the Royal Exchange, London. Advertised works by G. B. Marella, February 1758; not otherwise identified. May have been connected with, or a reference to, John Johnson of the Harp and Crown, Cheapside.

JOHNSON. Printer and bookseller, Salisbury. Name appears in the imprint of "The Psalms of David . . . By I. Watts . . . A new edition, corrected. (Tunes in the Tenor Part fitted to the several Metres.) Salisbury: Printed and sold by Collins and Johnson. Sold also by Fletcher and Hodson, at Cambridge . . . MDCCLXXVI." Published some libretti with Benjamin Collins, as Collins and Johnson, on the Canal, Salisbury.

JOHNSON, *Mrs.* *See* Johnson (John).

JOHNSON (JAMES). Music engraver and music seller, Edinburgh, c. 1772-1811. At Bell's Wynd 1787-c. 1790; as Johnson and Co. at shop in the Lawnmarket, at the head of Lady Stair's Close c. 1790-1811. After his death in 1811, business carried on by his widow and John Anderson as Johnson and Anderson.
    K. G.

JOHNSON (JOHN). Musical instrument maker, music seller, printer and publisher, London; at the Harp and Crown, facing Bow Church (near Wood Street) in Cheapside, 1740 or earlier-May 1748; removed to other premises, at the Harp and Crown, in Cheapside, "exactly facing Bow Church," where he remained June 1748-c. 1762. Johnson may have taken over some of the stock of Daniel Wright the elder and the younger, and of Benjamin Cooke, as he issued some works from plates of these publishers. Succeeded (c. 1762) by his widow Mrs. Johnson (or R. Johnson), opposite (or facing) Bow Church, Cheapside, from c. 1770 numbered 110 Cheapside, with no mention of the Harp and Crown. James Longman and Co. apparently obtained the right c. 1767, to use Johnson's sign, the Harp and Crown, for their premises at 26 Cheapside, on the south side, west of Johnson's shop. Mrs. Johnson published in her own name, but occasionally from 1763-70 the old name of John Johnson appeared in the imprints, which may have referred to her late husband, or to another relative; she probably continued business until c. 1777, as in November of that year Robert Bremner advertised that he had "purchased the greater part of the music plates and books that belonged to the late Mrs. Johnson."
    K. G.

Catalogues:—Vocal and Instrumental Musick. c. 1754. 2 pp. fol. (B.M. Hirsch IV. 1111. (9.)); Vocal and Instrumental Music. 1770. 2 pp. fol. (B.M. Hirsch IV. 1111. (10.))

JOHNSON (MRS. JOHN). *See* Johnson (John).

JOHNSON (JOSEPH). Bookseller and publisher, London; Paternoster Row, 1760-70; 72 St. Paul's Churchyard, 1770-1809. (P.) Published a number of musical works.
P. III.

JOHNSON (JOSEPH). At Mead's Head, opposite the Monument, London. Published "The Universal Psalmodist . . . by A. Williams, Teacher of Psalmody in London. 1763"; second edition, 1764; also third edition, 1765.

JOHNSON (R.). Music seller? New Bond Street, London. Published c. 1810, "Three Waltzes for the Pianoforte, by Mozart," etc.
K.

JOHNSON (R.) *Mrs. See* Johnson (John).

JOHNSON (THOMAS). Clerk of the Charlotte Street and Bedford Chapels, London. Published and sold "An Abridgment of the new version of the Psalms, for the use of Charlotte Street and Bedford Chapels: With proper tunes adapted to each psalm," etc. The preface is dated September 29, 1777.

JOHNSTON. *See* Newland & Johnston.

JOHNSTON (ALEXANDER). Grass Market, Edinburgh. His name appears in the imprint of "A Select Collection of Psalm & Hymn Tunes. Adapted to a variety of measures published for a Society in Edinburgh. Sold by Alexr. Johnston . . . & W. Whyte, music seller," etc., c. 1800.

JOHNSTON (JOHN). Music seller, printer and publisher, London; at the Apollo in the Strand opposite the New Exchange Coffee Rooms (Coffee House), January-August 1767; opposite Lancaster Court in the Strand (or, Near Charing Cross, or, near Northumberland House), August 1767 to near the end of 1768; 11 York Street, Covent Garden, or, The Corner of York Street, end of 1768 to August 1772; between the new Exhibition Room and Exeter Change, or, near Exeter Change, Strand, August 1772-c. 1776; 97 Drury Lane, c. 1776-78. Some single sheet songs bear only the initials J. J. Published some works in conjunction with Longman, Lukey and Co. Some of Johnston's stock and plates were acquired by Longman and Broderip when Johnston ceased business.
K. G.

JOLLIE (FRA.). Bookseller, Carlisle. Published "A Collection of Anthems in two, three, four, and six Parts: with a Hymn for Christmas-Day . . . The third edition . . . By Josiah Street . . . MDCCLXXXV."

JONES & CO. Publishers, London; Warwick Square, c. 1820-23; 3 Acton Place, Kingsland Road, c. 1823-28; Temple of the Muses, Finsbury Place, c. 1828-41. Published a number of music books.
K.

JONES & CO. 23 Bishopsgate Street, London.
See Jones (Thomas).

JONES (CHARLES). Music seller, opposite Staples Inn, near Holborn Bars, London. Published 1759, "All the Tunes in the Beggar's Opera, transposed into easy and proper keys for the Guittar." His name appears in the list of subscribers to A. Bezozzi's "Six Solos for the German-Flute, Hautboy, or Violin, with a Thorough Bass for the Harpsichord," 1759.
K.

JONES (CHARLES). Music seller, in Russel Court, near Catherine Street in the Strand, London. Published "Six English Songs as sung by Mr. Lowe & Mrs. Lampe Junr. at Mary-bone Gardens. Set to music by Mr. Chas. Lampe. 1764."

JONES (EDWARD). King's Printer, in the Savoy, London, 1687-1706. Printed for Henry Playford, "The Banquet of Music." 6 books. 1688-92; "Harmonica Sacra." Book I. 1688. Book 2. 1693; "The Dancing Master." Eighth edition, 1690; Ninth edition, 1695; "Apollo's Banquet." Sixth edition, 1690; First book. Seventh edition, 1693; Second book, 1691; "An Introduction to the Skill of Musick." Twelfth edition, 1694; Thirteenth edition, 1697. Printed for Jos. Knight and Fran. Saunders, "New Songs sung in The Fool's Preferment, or the Three Dukes of Dunstable . . . 1688"; printed "A Collection of some Verses out of the Psalmes . . . Collected by Mr. Daniel Warner . . . Revised by Mr. Henry Purcell . . . 1694."
K. G. P. II. D. & M.

JONES (JOHN). Musical instrument maker, music printer and publisher, at the Golden Harp, New Street, Covent Garden, near St. Martin's Lane, London, c. 1716-20.

JONES (THOMAS). Music seller, at the White Horse without Temple Bar, London. His name appears in an advertisement June 1691, "A Collection of choice Ayres for 2 and 3 Treble Flutes. Composed by the best masters of musick. Sold by Thomas Jones . . . John May . . . and Fr. Hicks," etc.

[196]

JONES (THOMAS). Music seller and publisher, 23 Bishopsgate Street Within, London, c. 1800-04. Sometimes styled T. Jones and Co.; succeeded Holland and Jones; succeeded by Halliday and Co.
    K.

JONES (WILLIAM). Printer, 18 Green Street, Dublin. Printed some single sheet songs engraved by Graham Stewart, including "The Double Mistake" and "The Merry Christ'ning," c. 1780.

JOSELIN (WILLIAM SANDERS). Music engraver, London. Engraved "The Mountain Rover, La caccia tirolese. The poetry by Charles Mackay Esqe. The music, composed . . . by H. Lee. London. Published by H. Wray, 37 Haymarket," c. 1833.

JULLIEN (LOUIS ANTOINE). Music seller and publisher, London; 3 Little Maddox Street, New Bond Street, c. 1842-45; at his dépôt général de musique dansante, 214 Regent Street and 45 King Street, Golden Square, c. 1845-48. He became bankrupt in April 1848; business continued as Jullien and Co. at the latter addresses 1848-c. 1858; Jullien was a conductor and composer of dance music.
    G.

JUNG (PHILIP). Music seller and publisher, Oxford, c. 1790-95. Among his publications, which were few in number, were the songs "The Knave's Necklace . . . To the Tune of To Anacreon in Heaven"; "Delia's Complaint"; "The Virtue of Snuff"; "Oh stay my sweet Pilgrim" and "Canticum Potatorium . . . composed by Mr. Schulz . . . and adapted . . . by Dr. Hayes."
    K.

K., F. *See* Kingston (Felix).

KAUNTZE & HYATT. Music sellers, publishers and music teachers, London; 376 Strand, c. 1800-01; 2 St. James Street, 1802. George Kauntze was previously in business on his own account.
    K.

KAUNTZE (GEORGE). Music seller and publisher, opposite the Admiralty, Whitehall, London, c. 1795-1800. On one of his own compositions states, "late of his Royal Highness the Duke of York's Band and taught the Violin, Flute, Clarinet and Violoncello." Afterwards became a partner in the business of Kauntze and Hyatt.
    K.

KAY (T.). *See* Elliot (Charles) & Kay (T.).

KEARNS (JOSEPH). Music seller and publisher, 44 Grafton Street, Dublin, c. 1794-1803. Succeeded Henry Mountain.

[197]

KEARSLEY or KEARSLY (GEORGE). Bookseller and publisher, London; at the Golden Lion, Ludgate Street, 1758-73; Fleet Street, opposite Fetter Lane, or 46 Fleet Street, 1773-92. Published "The Monthly Melody: or Polite Amusement for Gentlemen and Ladies. Being a collection of vocal and instrumental music composed by Dr. Arne . . . MDCCLX."; his name appears in the imprint of "The Beggar's Opera . . . To which is prefixed the overture in score: And the musick to each song. London: Printed for W. Strahan, T. Lowndes, T. Caslon, W. Griffin, W. Nicoll, S. Bladon, and G. Kearsly. MDCCLXXI."; also in two editions published 1777. Succeeded Jacob Robinson.
K. P. III.

KEEGAN (JOHN). Music seller and publisher, 3 Burlington Arcade, London, c. 1836-52. Sale of stock-in-trade by Puttick and Simpson March 5, 1852.

KEELER (HENRY). Music and musical instrument seller, Bristol; Beethoven House, 18 Lower Arcade, c. 1845-60; additional premises at 17 Lower Arcade, c. 1848-60; 20 Queen's Road, c. 1860-65. Published a small amount of music.

KEITH, PROWSE & CO. Music sellers and publishers, London; 131 Cheapside, 1829-32; 48 Cheapside, 1832-46. R. W. Keith previously in business on his own account, died 1846; from 1846-c. 1865 William Prowse carried on the business in his own name; from c. 1865 reverted to the old title of Keith, Prowse and Co. when H. Bryan Jones joined Prowse. The firm later became opera, theatre and concert ticket agents, and established a large number of branches in London. The musical instrument and music publishing side of the business was carried on at 48 Cheapside, c. 1865-1940; 162 New Bond Street, c. 1908-22; 159 New Bond Street, c. 1922-27; Music Publishing Depot, 42 Poland Street, c. 1903-24; 42 and 43 Poland Street, c. 1924 to present time.
Catalogue of Music publications. c. 1830. (Haas, Catalogue 22. No. 795.)

KEITH (GEORGE). Bookseller and publisher, London, 1749-75; in Mercers' Chapel, Cheapside; Bible and Crown, in Gracechurch Street. (P.) His name appears in the imprint of "The Psalm Singers Help, being a Collection of Tunes in three parts . . . London, printed for and sold by Thomas Knibb . . . also by G. Keith, Gracechurch Street, and at Messrs. Straight & Skillern's music shop," etc., c. 1775.
P. III.

KEITH (ROBERT WILLIAM). Musical instrument maker, music seller and publisher, London; 91 Aldersgate Street, c. 1815-22; 131 Cheapside, c. 1822-29. Succeeded Longman and Herron at latter address; became Keith, Prowse and Co., c. 1829.

KELLY (IGNATIUS). Printer, Mary's Lane, Dublin. Published December 1747, "The Merry Medley," containing Jovial Songs and Country Dances. (Grattan Flood.)

KELLY (MICHAEL). Singer, composer, acting manager of the King's Theatre, music seller and publisher, London; published some of his compositions from his house, 9 New Lisle Street, Leicester Square, up to the end of 1801; opened The Music Saloon (The Saloon, Kelly's Opera Saloon), 9 Pall Mall, January 1, 1802, with another house at 4 Pall Mall. Occupied both premises until he moved to 13 Great Russell Street after his bankruptcy, September 1811, when Falkner and Christmas succeeded him as publishers at 9 Pall Mall. (Kelly, "Reminiscences.")
    K. G.
    Catalogue of Italian Music. c. 1806. 1 p. fol. (B.M. G. 809. (47.))

KELLY (THOMAS). Bookseller and publisher, 17 Paternoster Row, London. Published "The New Musical and Vocal Cabinet, 1820." 2 vols.
    K.

KELWAY, *Mr.* London. His name appears in advertisements. In April 1739, "Twelve Sonata's for a Violin, with a Thorough Bass for the Harpsichord, or Bass Violin. Composed by Sig. Francesco Geminiani. The subscribers to which work are desired to send to Mr. Kelway's near Depuis's Coffee-house in Conduit Street," etc.; In May 1747, "Six Solos for a Violoncello, with a Thorough Bass for the Harpsichord. By Signor Francesco Geminiani. Opera V. The same Six Solos transpos'd and adapted with proper alterations for the Violin by the Author. To be had of Mr. Kelway, at his house in Kings Row, Upper Grosvenor-Street." Kelway may have been Joseph Kelway, the organist, who was a pupil of Geminiani.

KEMP (JOSEPH). Musician, composer and music seller, at his Music Warehouse, 43 Old Bond Street, London, c. 1806-09. Published a small amount of music, including some of his own compositions; organist of Bristol Cathedral 1802; had a music college in Exeter c. 1810.

KEMPSON (JAMES). Engraver, Great Charles Street, Birmingham. Engraved in 1774, "Odes, Cantatas, Songs &c . . . by Mr. Pixell. Opera Seconda. Birmingham. Printed and sold for the author by William Fletcher, Bull Street. 1775 "; Engraved and sold, "The Chorus's (with the proper cues to each) in the Oratorio of Messiah . . . MDCCLXXX."; reissued by J. Askey, date unknown.

KENT (W.). Bookseller? Corner of Kingsgate Street, Holborn, London. His name appears in the imprint of "The Spiritual Psalmodist's Companion; being a choice collection of psalms, and hymns with tunes . . . London: printed and sold by E. Englefield . . . and W. Kent . . . MDCCLXXII."

KERPEN (JOHN). Music seller, printer and publisher, 19 Wardour Street, Soho, London, c. 1782-85, or later. William Forster the elder, reissued some works from Kerpen's plates.

KETTLE (JOHN). Bookseller, 117 High Holborn, London. Published c. 1833, "The Night is closing round Mother, the words by permission of Barry Cornwall, the music composed . . . by S. W. Ketell."

KETTLE (S.). Bookseller, near the Temple Gate, London. His name appears in the imprint of "The Whole Book of Psalms, as they are now sung in the Churches: with the singing notes of time and tune set to every syllable . . . London, Printed by R. Everingham for the Company of Stationers, and are sold by E. Brewster . . . and S. Kettle . . . 1688."

KEY (THOMAS). Military musical instrument maker, 20 Charing Cross, London. Published c. 1815, "Six Waltzes composed for a Military Band, by an Officer of Dragoons, arranged by permission for the Piano Forte, by J. Salmon, Pianist." Key was previously at 2 Pall Mall.

KEYMER (WILLIAM). Bookseller and publisher, Colchester, 1750-1813. (P.) His name appears in the imprint of "The Psalmodists Exercise, or a Set of Psalm Tunes & Anthems . . . composed . . . by William Cole. London Printed for the Author by J. Johnson . . . & sold by . . . W. Keymer at Colchester," etc., c. 1760; also another edition, c. 1768. Printed for and sold by "When bending o'er the lofty Yard: a favourite Song in the Man of Enterprise. Set to music and sung by Mr. Fisher of the Theatre Royal, Norwich," c. 1789; "An Ode to Charity, written for the use of the Sunday Schools throughout England. Set to music by Mr. Fisin. August, 1790."
P. III.

KHULL. *See* Niven, Napier & Khull.

KIALLMARK (G.). Music seller, Bedford Musical Saloon, 47 Southampton Row, Russell Row, London. Printed and sold c. 1810, "Air religieux, et pastorelle; for the Piano Forte composed . . . by L. von Esch."

KINCAID. *See* Hamilton & Kincaid.

KING, *Mr.* Bookseller? Yeovil. His name appears in an advertisement May 1745, "A New Set of Anthems and Psalm Tunes for the use of Parish Churches, compos'd by John Broderip . . . Engrav'd and printed for the Author, and sold by him at Wells; Mr. John Cook, at Sherbourne; Mr. King at Yeovil; and by the printer, John Simpson," etc.

KING (CHARLES). In London House Yard, near St. Paul's, London. Published in conjunction with John Young and John Hare, "Choice Lessons for the Harpsichord or Spinett. Being the works of the late famous Mr. Jeremiah Clarke . . . Carefully corrected by himself. Being what he design'd to publish . . . 1711." King was presumably the organist, and brother-in-law of Jeremiah Clarke.

KING (ROBERT). Musician and composer, York Buildings, near the Strand, London. Acted in conjunction with John Banister as selling agent for music published in Rome and Amsterdam, 1700-02, including Corelli's "Sonate . . . Opera Quinta."

KINGSTON (FELIX). Printer, London, 1597-1651; over against the sign of the Checker, Paternoster Row, 1603; in Paternoster Row, at the Signe of the Gilded Cock, 1644. Son of John Kingston, whom he succeeded in 1615. (P.) A number of editions of the Sternhold and Hopkins versions of the Psalms, issued from 1612-24 have been attributed to him, some of which bear only the initials F. K.
P. I.

KINGSTON (JOHN). Printer, London, 1553-c. 1584. For some time his address was "at the West Door of St. Paul's," but from 1554-55 issued Manuals, Processionals and Hymnals in conjunction with Henry Sutton, whose business was in St. Paul's Churchyard. Kingston printed for James Rowbotham "A Briefe and easye instrution to learne the tableture to conducte and dispose thy hande vnto the Lute [by A. le Roy] englished by J. Alford . . . 1568," and a later edition of the same work "A briefe and plaine Instruction . . . for the Lute . . . translated into English by F. Ke. Gentleman . . . 1574."
K. D. M. S.

KINLOCH (ALEXANDER MONRO). Dancing Master and music seller, Newcastle-on-Tyne. Published c. 1815, "One hundred Airs, (principally Irish) selected & composed by Lieut. Gen: Dickson, arranged for the Piano Forte, Violin, Flute, &c. by Mr. Thomson, Organist of St. Nicholas, Newcastle-upon-Tyne . . . London, Printed by Messrs. Goulding & Co. for Mr. Kinloch, at his Music Saloon, Newcastle."
K.

KIRKWOOD (JOHN). Engraver and printer, 11 Crow Street, Dublin. Engraved and printed "The Psaltery; a Collection of Psalm and Hymn Tunes, carefully selected from the works of the most eminent composers . . . Dublin: Published for John Kirkwood . . . By W. Curry, Jun. and Co. and J. Robertson and Co. Dublin; R. Groombridge, London, and Fraser and Co. Edinburgh. 1835."

KITCHIN (THOMAS). Engraver, London. Published c. 1743, a volume of engraved songs with illustrated headings entitled "English Orpheus", in Bartlett's Court, near St. John's Gate, Clerkenwell; engraved the title-page and probably some of the music plates of "Universal Harmony or, the Gentleman and Ladie's Social Companion," published by John Newbery in 1745, and a later edition in 1746; engraved the title-page of "The Land of Cakes, Book the first. Containing six songs . . . To which is added The Tears of Scotland. London. Printed for R. Williams," c. 1750; engraved "A Small Collection of Psalms to the old Tunes, sung by the Charity Children of the City of Chichester. Published for general use . . . 1761"; his address on this work is "Star. Holborn Hill."
    K.

KNAPLOCK (ROBERT). Bookseller, London, 1696-1737; Angel and Crown, St. Paul's Churchyard; Bishop's Head, St. Paul's Churchyard. (P.) His name appears in the imprint of "The Psalms of David in Metre: Fitted to the tunes used in Parish-Churches. By John Patrick . . . London, Printed for W. Churchill . . . R. Knaplock . . . MDCCXVIII."; also in the seventh edition, 1724.
    P. II.

KNAPTON, WHITE & KNAPTON. Musical instrument makers, music sellers and publishers, Coney Street, York, c. 1820-21. Succeeded Samuel Knapton; became Samuel and Philip Knapton c. 1821.
    K.

KNAPTON (JAMES). Bookseller, London, 1687-c. 1730; Queen's Head, St. Paul's Churchyard; at the Crown, St. Paul's Churchyard. (P.) His name appears in the imprint of "The Psalms of David in Metre: Fitted to the tunes used in Parish-Churches. By John Patrick . . . London, Printed for W. Churchill . . . J. Knapton . . . MDCCXVIII."; also in the seventh edition 1724. Succeeded by James and John Knapton.
    P. II.

KNAPTON (JAMES) & (JOHN). Booksellers, at the Crown, in St. Paul's Churchyard, London, c. 1730-35. Published "The Beggar's Wedding. A New Opera . . . To which are added the new prologue and epilogue, and the musick to all the songs . . . The Fourth edition . . . MDCCXXXI." Succeeded James Knapton; succeeded by John and Paul Knapton.

KNAPTON (JOHN) & (PAUL). Booksellers and publishers, London, 1735-c. 1770; at the Crown, St. Paul's Churchyard; Crown, in Ludgate Street. Their names appear in the imprint of "The Psalms of David in Metre: With the tunes used in Parish-Churches. By John Patrick. The Eighth edition. London: Printed for J. Walthoe

. . . J. and P. Knapton . . . MDCCXLII." Succeeded James and John Knapton.
> P. II.

KNAPTON (PAUL). *See* Knapton (John) & (Paul).

KNAPTON (PHILIP). *See* Knapton (Samuel) & (Philip).

KNAPTON (SAMUEL). Musical instrument maker, music seller and publisher, York; Blake Street, c. 1797-1805; Coney Street, c. 1805-20. Succeeded Thomas Haxby; became Knapton, White and Knapton, c. 1820; afterwards in business as Samuel and Philip Knapton.
> K.

KNAPTON (SAMUEL) & (PHILIP). Musical instrument makers, music sellers, 36 Coney Street, York, c. 1821-August 1829. Published a small amount of music; Philip Knapton, son of Samuel, was also a pianist and composer; succeeded Knapton, White and Knapton; succeeded by William Hardman.
> K.

KNEVETT. *See* Goulding & Knevett.

KNIBB (THOMAS). Editor of Hymnals and publisher, London. Published at Opposite Skinners Street, Bishopsgate Without, "A Collection of Tunes in three Parts, that are now us'd in the several dissenting Congregations in London . . . together with an introduction for the use of Learners," c. 1745; "The Psalm Singers Help, being a Collection of the Tunes in three Parts, that are now us'd in the several Churches & dissenting Congregations in London with a Thorough Bass for the Harpsicord or Organ . . . Together with an introduction for the use of learners," c. 1765; another edition was issued by George Pearch and Joseph Gurney, c. 1770; a later edition was issued c. 1775 with the imprint "London, printed for and sold by Thomas Knibb, near Spital Square, Bishopsgate Without; also by G. Keith, Gracechurch Street, and at Messrs. Straight & Skillern's music shop," etc.
> K.

KNIGHT, *Mrs.* Bookseller, Lincoln. Her name appears in the imprint of "A Book of Psalm-Tunes, with Variety of Anthems in Four Parts, with Chanting-Tunes for the Te Deum, Benedictus, Magnificat . . . By James Green. The Fifth edition . . . London. Printed by William Pearson . . . and sold by . . . Mrs. Knight . . . Lincoln. 1724." Succeeded her husband John Knight.

KNIGHT (CHARLES). Bookseller and publisher, London; 13 Pall Mall East, c. 1824-33; 22 Ludgate Street, and 13 Pall Mall East, c. 1833-35; 22 Ludgate Street, c. 1835-37; as Charles Knight and Co., 22 Ludgate

Street, c. 1837-48. Published a number of editions of "The Musical Library," from 1834.

KNIGHT (JOHN). Bookseller, Lincoln, 1696-1718. His name appears in the imprint of "A Collection of Psalm-Tunes; with Great Variety of Hymns and Anthems compos'd by the best Masters . . . By James Green. The Fourth edition . . . London. Printed by William Pearson, for the Author: and sold by . . . J. Knight in Lincoln . . . 1718." The business was continued by his widow.
    P. I.

KNIGHT (JOSEPH) & SAUNDERS (FRANCIS). Booksellers, at the Blue Anchor in the Lower Walk of the New Exchange in the Strand, London. Published "A Fool's Preferment, or The Three Dukes of Dunstable. A Comedy. As it was acted at the Queens Theatre in Dorset-Garden, by Their Majesties Servants. Written by Mr. D'urfey. Together, with all the Songs and Notes to 'em, excellently compos'd by Mr. Henry Purcell . . . 1688."
    P. II. D. & M.

KOHLER (JOHN). Musical instrument maker, 89 St. James Street, London. Published c. 1800, "Six favorite Duets, for two Clarinets never before Published. Composed by Mr. Michell. Opera XII." At one time Master of the Band to His Majesty's Royal Lancaster Volunteers.

KYNGESTON (JOHN). *See* Kingston.

KYNGSTON (JOHN). *See* Kingston.

L. & B. *See* Longman & Broderip.

L., H. *See* Lownes (Humfrey) *the Elder*.

L., I. *See* Legatt (John).

L. L.; L. L. & CO. *See* Longman, Lukey & Co.

L. L. & B. *See* Longman, Lukey & Broderip.

L., M. *See* Lownes (Matthew).

LACY (J.). Bookseller and publisher, in the Drapery, Northampton. His name appears in the imprint of "Sacra Concerto: or the Voice of Melody . . . By Benjamin West . . . London: Printed by R. Brown . . . for P. Davey and B. Law . . . and J. Lacy at Northampton. MDCCLX."; also in the second edition "Printed by Dryden Leach, for B. Law . . . and J. Lacy at Northampton. MDCCLXIX."
    P. III.

LADIES MUSICAL REPOSITORY. Princes Row, corner of Warwick Row, Pimlico, London. Published c. 1817, "The Dialogues, Solos & Chorusses, of a Musical Show, now performing . . . at all the principal & notorious Fairs in England, Scotland, & Ireland . . . Words & music by Mr. Ehrlich, German organist . . . London. Pubd. at the Ladies Musical Repository . . . & Phillips & Co. No. 17 Old Bond Street."

LAMBERT. *See* Branston & Lambert.

LAMPSON (J.). Dancing Master, at the Hand and Pen, the Field end of King Street, Bloomsbury, London. Published some French and Country Dances, advertised 1730.

LANCASHIRE (J.). Printer and bookseller? Huddersfield. Printed and sold c. 1814, "The Musical Cabinet, being a selection of the most admired English, Scotch, and Irish Songs, with the Music."
K.

LANE, DARLING & CO. *See* Lane, Newman & Co.

LANE, NEWMAN & CO. Booksellers, 33 Leadenhall Street, London, c. 1802-07. Published a number of song books with music, some in conjunction with Oliver and Boyd, Edinburgh; William Lane previously in business alone; afterwards became Lane, Darling and Co.
K.

LATHAM (GEORGE). Bookseller and printer, at the Brazen Serpent, afterwards at the Bishop's Head, St. Paul's Church Yard, London, 1622-58. (P.) His name appears in the imprints of "Ayres, or Fa La's for Three Voyces. Newly composed and published by Iohn Hilton, Bachelor of Musicke. London, Printed by Humfrey Lownes, and are to be sold by George Lathum at the Bishops Head in Pauls Churchyard. 1627"; "Canzonets. Or Little Short Songs To Three Voyces: Published by Thomas Morley . . . London, Printed by William Stansby, Richard Hawkings, George Latham. 1631"; "The Seventh Set of Bookes . . . Lately set out by Michael East . . . London, Printed for William Stansby, and George Latham, 1638." The Bishop's, Head, St. Paul's Churchyard was formerly the address of Matthew Lownes.
K. P. I.

LATHUM (GEORGE). *See* Latham.

LATOUR (FRANCIS TATTON). Music seller and publisher, 50 New Bond Street, London, c. 1826-30. Previously partner in the firm of Chappell and Co. c. 1811-c. 1826; died in 1845; business and premises taken over by Samuel Chappell c. 1830.
K.

LAURENCE or LAWRENCE (PETER). Bookseller, Dublin. His name appears in the imprints of "The Psalms of David in Metre. Newly translated with amendments: By William Barton, M.A. And sett to the best Psalm-Tunes in two Parts . . . With brief instructions . . . By Thomas Smith . . . Dublin. Printed by J. Brent and S. Powell . . . and are to be sold by Peter Laurence at his shop in Bridge Street, near the Old Bridge." c. 1698; "The Psalms of David in Metre . . . The Second edition, corrected and amended . . . Dublin. Printed by J. Brocas, for Elip. Dopson, Tho. Servant . . . and P. Lawrence Bookseller on the Merchants-Key, 1706."

LAVENU & MITCHELL. Music sellers, printers and publishers, London; 29 New Bond Street (at their Musical Circulating Library), c. 1802-05; 26 New Bond Street, c. 1805-08. Partnership dissolved c. 1808, Lewis Lavenu remained at 26 New Bond Street until c. 1811, and Charles Mitchell opened up at 51 Southampton Row, Russell Square.
K. G.
Catalogues:—Musical Publications. Plate I. c. 1805. 1 p. fol. (B.M. 7896. h. 40. (5.)); New Music. 1806. 8 pp. fol. (B.M. 7896. h. 40. (6.)); A Collection of Periodical Duetts for two performers on one Piano Forte. 1806. 1 p. fol. (B.M. h. 278. (2.))
See also Lavenu (Lewis).

LAVENU (ELIZABETH). Music seller and publisher, London; 28 New Bond Street, c. 1819-21; and c. 1827-28; 24 Edwards Street, Manchester Square, c. 1821-27. Presumably the widow of Lewis Lavenu; she married Nicholas Mori in 1819 and the business was continued as Mori and Lavenu from c. 1828.
K. G.

LAVENU (LEWIS). Music seller and publisher, London; 23 Duke Street, St. James's, c. 1796 to November 1798; 29 New Bond Street, c. November 1798-1805; 26 New Bond Street, c. 1805-11; 28 New Bond Street, c. 1811-19. For a time c. 1802-08, became Lavenu and Mitchell; business continued by Elizabeth Lavenu c. 1819, presumably widow of Lewis Lavenu.
K. G.

LAVENU (LOUIS HENRY). Composer, violoncellist, music seller and publisher, 28 New Bond Street, London, c. 1839-44. Presumably son of Lewis and Elizabeth Lavenu; succeeded to the business of Mori and Lavenu; business taken over by Addison and Hodson, but the premises were acquired by Sidney Nelson. Lavenu published as L. Lavenu.
K. G.

LAVO (JOHN). London. His name appears in the imprint of "Six Sonatas or Trio's for two Violins or German Flutes with the Thorough Bass for the Harpsichord. Compos'd by Signor Domenico Ferrari.

To be had of John Lavo at Mr. Paisan's at the Half Moon in Compton Street, Soho, London"; advertised October 1757.

LAW. *See* Bye & Law.

LAW (BEDWELL). Bookseller and publisher, 13 Ave Mary Lane, London, 1756-98. (P.) His name appears in the imprints of "The Whole Books of Psalms . . . By John Playford. The Twentieth Edition . . . London: Printed by R. Brown . . . For . . . P. Davey and B. Law, in Ave-Mary-Lane. 1757"; "Sacra Concerto: or the Voice of Melody . . . By Benjamin West . . . London: Printed by R. Brown . . . for P. Davey and B. Law . . . and J. Lacy at Northampton. MDCCLX."; also in the second edition "Printed by Dryden Leach, for B. Law . . . and J. Lacy at Northampton. MDCCLXIX."
P. III.

LAWRENCE (JOHN). Bookseller, at the Angel in the Poultry, London, 1681-1711. (P.) His name appears in the imprints of "A Proposal to Perform Musick, in Perfect and Mathematical Proportions . . . By Thomas Salmon. London: Printed for John Lawrence . . . 1688"; "The Psalms of David, in English Metre; translated from the original, and suited to all the tunes now sung in Churches: With the additions of several new. By Luke Milbourne . . . London, Printed for W. Rogers . . . R. Clavill . . . B. Tooke . . . J. Lawrence . . . and J. Taylor . . . 1698."
P. II.

LAWSON (HENRY). Pianoforte manufacturer, London; 29 John Street, Fitzroy Square, c. 1800-14; Nassau Street, Cavendish Square, c. 1814-1824. Published c. 1815, "Six Anthems in Score, figured for the Organ & Piano Forte. Composed . . . by Samuel Chapple, Organist Ashburton, Devon. Opera 4."
K.

LAWSON (JAMES). Music seller and publisher, 42 Rathbone Place, Oxford Street, London, c. 1839-42.

LAWSON (JOSEPH). Musical instrument maker, music seller and publisher, 198, Tottenham Court Road, London, c. 1815-45.
K.

LEACH (DRYDEN). Printer, London, 1759-69. Printed "Sacra Concerto: or The Voice of Melody. Containing an introduction to the grounds of music; also, forty-one psalm-tunes, and two anthems . . . By Benjamin West, of Northampton. The second edition; with the addition of two new anthems . . . MDCCLXIX."; "The Complete Psalmodist: or the Organist's, Parish-Clerk's and Psalm-Singer's

Companion . . . The Sixth edition . . . By John Arnold . . . 1769."
Succeeded by Bigg and Cox.
    P. III.

LEACH (FRANCIS). Printer, Elliot's Court, Little Old Bailey, London,
    1673-1707. (P.) Printed "A Collection of Twenty Four Songs,
written by several Hands. And set by several masters of Musicke.
With the tunes engraven on copper-plates with great care . . . London,
Printed by F. Leach, for Charles Corbet, and published by W. Davis
. . . MDCLXXXV."; "A Psalm of Thanksgiving to be sung by the
Children of Christ's Hospital . . . in Easter Week . . . 1706. Composed
by Mr. Barrett, Master of the Musick School. Printed by Fr. Leach,
printer to Christ's Hospital. 1706."
    P. II. D. & M.

LEACH (JOHN). Bookseller and printer, High Street, Wisbech. Printed
and sold "Hymns: Selected from approved authors, sung in the Church
of Wisbech Saint Peter, by the choir and congregation . . . 1841."

LEADER & COCK. Music sellers and publishers, 63 New Bond Street,
London, 1843-62. Had additional premises at 61 Brook Street, 1857-
1862, and at 62 New Bond Street, 1860-62. The partners were
Frederick C. Leader and James L. Cock. Leader was previously in
business alone.

LEADER (FREDERICK CHRISTOPHER). Music seller and publisher,
63 Old Bond Street, London, 1842-43. Afterwards Leader and Cock.

LEAK, *Mr.* *See* Leake (James).

LEAKE, *Mr.* Bookseller, Bath. His name appears in the imprint
of "Nancy or the Parting Lovers. A Musical Interlude. As Performed
at ye Theatre Royal in Covent Garden. The Words & Musick by
M^r. Carey. London printed for the Author and sold at the Musick
Shops and at the Theatre, also by M^r. Leake at Bath," c. 1740. The
"Mr. Leake" may have been James Leake.

LEAKE (JAMES). Bookseller and publisher, Bath, c. 1724-64. (P.) His
name appears in the imprint of "Twelve English Songs with their
Symphonies. The words by Shakespeare and other celebrated poets.
Set to musick by M^r. Thomas Chilcot, organist of Bath. London
Printed and sold by John Johnson . . . M^r. Leak and M^r. Fredrick
Booksellers in Bath", etc. 1744.
    P. III.

LEAKE (JOHN). Printer, Angel Street, St. Martin's-le-Grand, London,
    c. 1741-48. Printed "A Sett of Psalm-Tunes and Anthems, in four

Parts . . . By William Knapp. The Second edition corrected . . .
Printed by J. Leake . . . for the Author", etc., c. 1741.
P. III.

LEE (ALEXANDER) & LEE. Music sellers and publishers, 86
Regent Quadrant, London, c. 1830-34.

LEE (ANNE). Music seller and publisher, 2 Dame Street, Dublin, 1776-
1788. Succeeded her husband Samuel Lee; was assisted by her son
Edmund, who afterwards carried on the business.
K.

LEE (EDMUND). Musical instrument maker, music seller and publisher,
2 Dame Street, Dublin, c. 1788-1821. Son of Samuel and Anne Lee,
who carried on the business established by them; issued many
publications in conjunction with his brother John, usually with the
imprint of John and Edmund Lee, Dame Street. Succeeded by John
Aldridge.
K.

LEE (HENRY). Music seller and publisher, London; 59 Frith Street,
c. 1836-40; 13 Lisle Street, Leicester Square, c. 1840-46. The Frith
Street premises were previously occupied by H. Wray.

LEE (JOHN). Musical instrument maker, music seller and publisher,
Dublin; 64 Dame Street, c. 1776-78; 70 Dame Street, c. 1778-1803.
Son of Samuel and Anne Lee; issued many publications in conjunc-
tion with his brother Edmund, usually with the imprint of John and
Edmund Lee, Dame Street.
K.

LEE (LEONI). Music seller and publisher, London; 17 Old Bond Street,
c. 1831-36; 48 Albemarle Street, c. 1836-63. For a time, c. 1845-53,
became Leoni Lee and Coxhead. Previously a partner in Mayhew
and Lee c. 1830-31.

LEE (LEONI) AND COXHEAD. Music sellers and publishers, 48
Albemarle Street, London, c. 1845-53.
See also Lee (Leoni).

LEE (SAMUEL). Music seller, printer and publisher, Dublin; published
from his house at the Little Green, 1752-63; at the Harp and
Hautboy, Fownes Street, January 1764-December 1768; 2 Dame
Street, 1769-76. After his death in 1776 the business was carried on
by his widow Anne Lee.
K. G.

LEGATT (JOHN). Printer, London and Cambridge, 1620-58. (P.)
Printed in London from 1633 onwards several editions of "The Booke

[209]

of Psalmes, collected into English Meeter, by T. Sternhold, I. Hopkins, and others," etc., with the imprints "I. L. for the Company of Stationers"; and in 1638 "A Paraphrase upon the Divine Poems. By George Sandys. London, At the Bell in St. Pauls Church-yard", which includes "A Paraphrase upon the Psalmes of David. By G. S. Set to new Tunes for private Devotion: And a thorow Bass, for Voice, or Instrument. By Henry Lawes," etc., with colophon at the end of the whole work "London, Printed by Iohn Legatt. 1637". Thomas Adams was previously "at the Bell in St. Pauls Church-yard", 1611-20, where he was succeeded by his widow, Elizabeth Adams 1620-c. 1630 or later. Legatt printed for Ralph Mab, William Barriffe's "Mars, his triumph. Or, the description of an exercise performed the XVIII. of October, 1638. in Merchant-Taylors Hall by certain gentlemen of the Artillery Garden London, printed by I. L. for Ralph Mab. 1639," which contains some musical examples for use with artillery exercises. Legatt was appointed printer to the University of Cambridge in 1650, his patent being cancelled in 1655, after which he appears to have settled at Little Wood Street, London, until 1658.

M. P. I.

LEGGE (CANTRELL). Printer, Cambridge, 1606-c. 1629. (M.) Printed "The Whole Booke of Psalmes: collected into English metre, with apt notes to sing them withall . . . Cambridge: Printed by Cantrell Legge Printer to the University. 1623."

M.

LEIGH & SOTHEBY. Booksellers, 9 York Street, Covent Garden, London. Their names appeared in the list of firms who received subscriptions for and sold the works of Purcell and others issued by Benjamin Goodison, 1787-90. The partners were George Leigh and John Sotheby.

LEIGH (SAMUEL). Bookseller and publisher, 18 Strand, London. Published c. 1820, "The Beauties of Mozart, Handel, Haydn, Beethoven, etc. Adapted to the words of popular psalms & hymns for one or two voices with an accompaniment & symphonies for the piano forte, organ or harp. By an eminent Professor. Printed for S. Leigh", etc.

LEKPREVIK (ROBERT). Printer and bookbinder, Edinburgh, Stirling and St. Andrews. At one time his address was in the Netherbow, Edinburgh. (M.) Printed "The Forme of Prayers and ministration of the Sacraments &c. vsed in the English Church at Geneua, approued and receiued by the Churche of Scotland . . . with the whole Psalmes of Dauid in English meter . . . Printed at Edinburgh . . . 1564"; also printed an edition in 1565.

K. M. S.

LEMARE (FREDERICK) & SON. Music sellers, High Street, Guildford, and High Street, Godalming. Published c. 1845, "Select Harmony, of Psalm and Hymn Tunes, and Cathedral Chants arranged . . . by Frederick Lemare," etc.

LEONARD (WILLIAM). Music seller, at his Music Saloon, 62 Judd Street, Brunswick Square, London, c. 1816-20. Published some of his own compositions.

LEONE (GABRIEL). London. Printed and sold c. 1765, "Six Duets for two Violins . . . Composed by Sigr. Emanuele Barbella."

LE ROUSSAU (F.). Dancing master, musician and engraver, London. His name appears as composer, engraver, etc. of "New Collection of Dances, containing a great number of the best Ball and Stage Dances; That have been performed . . . by the best dancers . . . Recollected, put in characters and engraved by Monsieau Roussau, Dancing Master. To be sold at Mr. Barreau's, Bookbinder in Lumbard Court, Seven Dials; and at Mr. Roussau's in York Street, near St. James's Square"; c. 1715; "A Chacoon for a Harlequin . . . Compos'd writt in Characters and engraved by F. Le Roussau, Dancing-master. Sold by ye Author in St. Alban's-Street and att Mr. Barrett's Musik-shop at the Harp & Crown in Pickadily," c. 1730.

LEVINSTON (ALEXANDER). *See* Livingston.

LEWER (JAMES). Musical instrument maker, music printer and publisher, facing New Broad Street, Moorfields, London, c. 1760-75. Succeeded John Tyther; Longman, Lukey and Broderip purchased some of Lewer's stock c. 1775.
    K.

LEWIS & CO. Music sellers and publishers, London; 96 Cheapside, c. 1850-53; 509 Oxford Street, 1853-57. Succeeded Lewis and Johnson.
    See also Lewis (Thomas Crump).

LEWIS & JOHNSON. Pianoforte, print and music sellers, and music publishers, 96 Cheapside, London, c. 1848-50. Thomas Crump Lewis had previously been a partner in the business of Tregear and Lewis, and from c. 1844-48 was at same address on his own account. Succeeded by Lewis and Co.

LEWIS, HOUSTON & HYDE. Music sellers and publishers, 45 Holborn, London, 1795-97. Succeeded John Bland; advertised the business for sale, with about 12,000 engraved plates, March 1797; purchased by Francis Linley. Hyde may have been Frederick Augustus Hyde, later in partnership as Clementi, Banger, Hyde, Collard and Davis.

He compiled "A Miscellaneous Collection of Songs," etc., issued by Longman and Broderip, for F. A. Hyde, F. W. Collard and D. Davis, c. 1797-98.
Catalogue of Subjects or Beginnings of Italian Songs, etc. c. 1796. 1 p. fol. (B.M. G. 811. (3.))
K.

LEWIS (GEORGE HERBERT). Music engraver, Exeter. Engraved "Hurrah! for the Hearts of true blue. Song, the music composed by Lady Adams, the words by William R. Neale," c. 1835.

LEWIS (THOMAS CRUMP). Print and music seller, and music publisher, 96 Cheapside, London, c. 1844-48. Previously a partner in Tregear and Lewis c. 1842-44; succeeded by Lewis and Johnson c. 1848-50; afterwards became Lewis and Co. c. 1850-57.

LICHFIELD (LEONARD). Printer, Oxford, 1687-1749. (P.) Printed "Musica Oxoniensis. A Collection Of Songs: For One and Two Voices, With The Thorough-Bass. Publish'd by Francis Smith, and Peter de Walpergen Letter-Founder, by whom 'twas Cut on Steel, and Cast, by the Directions of the former. Oxford: Printed by Leon. Lichfield . . . And are to be Sold by the Widow Howell, 1698"; also issued the same work with the imprint "Oxford: Printed by Leon Lichfield: And are to be Sold by John Walsh . . . And John Hare . . . London, 1698."
P. II. D. & M.

LIDDELL (M.). Music seller, 109 Pilgrim Street, Newcastle on Tyne. Published c. 1841, "The Knill Court Waltzes, composed and arranged for the Piano Forte . . . by S. W. Ketelle."

LIESSEM (REN). Music seller and printer, Compton Street, St. Ann's, Soho, London. Advertised October 1757, "Il Passa tempa della guitarra in twelve Italian Airs for the Voice, accompanied by the Guitar or Harpsichord. Composed by Sig. Santo Lapis. M.D. of Italian music" (Published as "The Amusement of the Guitar", etc.); advertised April 1758, "Guittar in Fashion; containing twelve double Sonatas for all Sorts of Guittars, with Minuets, and six Duettos and [i.e. for] two Guittars, and an Italian Song, compos'd by Santo Lapis. Sold by R. Liessem", etc.; printed and sold "Miss Mayer. A new Guittar Book in 4 parts viz Italian, French, English Airs, and Duets for the voice accompanied with the Guittar and a Thorough Bass for the Harpsicord. Composed by Santo Lapis . . . Opera XVI. MDCCLIX."; "A libro aperto. Light Airs with Minuets for the Harpsicord and for all sorts of Guittars . . . Composed by Mr. Santo Lapis . . . Opera XVII . . . MDCCLX."

LIMBIRD (JOHN). Stationer, book and music publisher, London; 143

Strand, c. 1823-52; 11 Exeter Change, Strand, c. 1852-54; 344 Strand, c. 1854-68.

LINDSAY (THOMAS). Flute maker, music seller and publisher, London; 217 Regent Street, c. 1825-27; 35 High Holborn, c. 1827-28; 32 East Street, Red Lion Square, c. 1828-33.

LINLEY (FRANCIS). Composer, music seller and publisher, London; at some time music agent for John Watlen of Edinburgh at 42 Penton Street, Pentonville; 45 Holborn, 1797-98. Was blind from his birth; at one time organist of Pentonville Chapel; succeeded Lewis, Houston and Hyde whose business and stock he purchased; succeeded by William Hodsoll.
    K. G.

LINTERN (JAMES) & (WALTER). Musical instrument makers, music sellers and publishers, Bath, c. 1782-1817; first at Abbey Yard; afterwards at 3 Abbey Church Yard, up to c. 1810, where the business was continued by James Lintern alone, until he removed a year or two later to 13 Grove (now Orange Grove), where he remained until c. 1817. Agents for the Cahusac family.
    K. G.

LINTERN (WALTER). *See* Lintern (James) & (Walter).

LINTOT (BERNARD). Bookseller and publisher, at the Cross Keys in St. Martin's Lane, and elsewhere, London, 1698-1736. (P.) Published Philip Hart's "An Ode in the Praise of Musick set for Variety of Voices and Instruments. Written by J. Hughes . . . 1703." Published with Jacob Tonson, first of the name, "Daphnis and Chloe. A Ballad," c. 1719, his address being at this time, "between the Temple Gates in Fleetstreet."
    P. II.

LISLE (LAURENCE). Bookseller, at the sign of The Tiger's Head, St. Paul's Churchyard, London, 1607-26. (M.) Published "The Description of a Maske: Presented in the Banqueting roome at Whitehall . . . . at the mariage of the . . . Earle of Somerset and the . . . Lady Frances Howard. Written by Thomas Campion. Whereunto are annexed diuers choyse Ayres composed for this Maske that may be sung with a single voyce to the Lute or Basse-Viall. (Ayres made by seuerall Authors; And Sung in the Maske . . . Set forth for the Lute and Base Violl, and may be exprest by a single voyce, to eyther of these Instruments.) London, Printed by E[dward]. A[llde]. for Laurence Li'sle, dwelling in Paules Church-yard, at the signe of the Tyger's head. 1614."
    K. M.

LISTON (EDWARD). Music seller and publisher, 10 Princes Street, Edinburgh, c. 1806. Previously a partner in the business of Urbani and Liston.
See also Urbani & Liston.

LITHOGRAPHIC PRESS, 10 King Street, Westminster, London. Printed a Song, c. 1811, "Tell me where is the Stream. Printed from English stone, at the Lithographic Press . . . Sold by I. Power."

LITHOGRAPHIC PRESS, 5 Bond Street, Walbrook, London. Printed "Sprigs of Cypress; to the memory of Miss, C. H. . . . The poetry by Sir George Dallas Bart. The music by Mr. William Abington . . . Printed and published by the Composer . . . 1822."

LITTLE a. "Printed and sold at the little a", or "at the a", 41 Leadenhall Street, London.
See Bailey or Bayley (William).

LITTLETON (HENRY). See Novello (Joseph Alfred).

LIVESLEY (CHRISTOPHER). Engraver, Leeds, c. 1790-1810. Engraved a number of musical compositions of Henry Hamilton; joined another engraver named Butterworth and became Butterworth, Livesley and Co., c. 1810.
K.

LIVINGSTON (ALEXANDER). Music and musical instrument seller, at the Violin and Hautboy, Birchin Lane, London. His name appears in the imprints of a number of music works c. 1699-1712.

LIZARS (WILLIAM HOME). Engraver and printer, 3 James's Square, Edinburgh. Engraved and printed some volumes of George Thomson's "The Select Melodies of Scotland," 1822-23, and "Collection of the Songs of Burns," in 1824 and 1828.

LLOYD (EDMUND). Bookseller, 57 Harley Street, Cavendish Square, London. Published "Original Compositions in Prose and Verse; to which is added some vocal and instrumental music . . . MDCCCXXXIII."

LLOYD (WILLIAM). Bookseller? Next the King's Arms Tavern, Chancery Lane, near Fleet Street, London. Published "The Universal Musician; or, Songster's Delight. Consisting of the most celebrated English and Scotch Songs, favourite Cantata's, &c . . . Vol. I . . . 1738"; issued in parts 1737-38; some of the illustrations at the head of the songs bear the name of J. Smith. An edition of "The Universal Musician" with illustrations by J. Smith was also published by William Rayner, 1738, and another anonymously, with the imprint "London. Printed and sold by the Booksellers and at the Musick Shops in Towne

and Country." Some of the plates were reissued in "The Lady's Curiosity: or Weekly Apollo", 1752.
  P. III.

LOBB (R.). *See* Toft (Timothy) & Lobb (R.).

LOCKE (W.). 12 Red Lion Street, Holborn, London. Published "The Anacreontic Magazine; or, Songster's Musical Companion. Containing Songs, Cantatas, Catches, Glees, Duets, Trios, &c. &c. . . . Volume the First. 1792"; "The Divine Harmonist, or Sunday Associate . . . arranged and conducted, selected and the new music composed by Thomas Busby. London: Printed for the Conducter; and sold by W. Locke . . . 1792."

LODER (ANDREW). Music seller and publisher, 4 Orange Grove, Bath, c. 1820-26, or later.
  K.

LODER (JOHN DAVID). Violinist, music and musical instrument seller, printer and publisher, 46 Milsom Street, Bath, c. 1820-35. He was the father of Edward J. Loder, and related to Andrew Loder.
  K.

LOGAN & CO. Aberdeen. Published "A Collection of Ancient Piobaireachd or Highland Pipe Music . . . by Angus Mackay . . . 1838."

LOGAN (CHARLES). Bookseller, 71 Chancery Lane, London. Published in conjunction with Thomas Conder c. 1797, "A Second Volume to the Revd. Dr. Addington's Collection of Psalm and Hymn Tunes," etc.

LOGIER (JOHANN BERNARD). Music seller and publisher, Dublin; 76 Lower Sackville Street, corner of Abbey Street, 1809-11; 27 Lower Sackville Street, July 1811-c. 1817; resumed business and had a shop at 46 Upper Sackville Street, c. 1829-41. From 1842-44 had a "Musical Academy" at 28 Westmorland Street, and at 45 St. Stephen's Green, 1845-46.
  K. G.

LONDON SACRED MUSIC WAREHOUSE.
  See Novello (Joseph Alfred).

LONGHURST (JAMES). Organ builder, 23 Commerce Row, Blackfriars Road, London. Printed and published c. 1806, "The Hero of the Sea, or Nelson immortal, written by Mr. Upton. The music composed by H. B. Schroeder."

LONGMAN & BATES. Musical instrument makers, music sellers and publishers, 6 Ludgate Hill, London, 1824-c. 1833. In 1829 Samuel Chappell joined the firm which became Chappell, Longman and Bates;

partnership dissolved c. 1833; George Longman carried on business at 131 Cheapside, and Theodore C. Bates continued at Ludgate Hill; Bates had previously been in business at St. John's Square.

See also Chappell (Samuel).

LONGMAN & BRODERIP. Musical instrument makers, music sellers, engravers, printers and publishers, 26 Cheapside, London, 1776-98. Additional premises at 13 Haymarket, were taken in December 1782; advertised in September 1789 "that they have . . . during the watering season opened a shop at Margate and Brighthelmstone for the sale of musical instruments"; succeeded Longman, Lukey and Broderip; became bankrupt and partnership dissolved in 1798; John Longman went into partnership with Muzio Clementi at 26 Cheapside, and Francis Broderip with C. Wilkinson at 13 Haymarket. Some single sheet songs bear only the initials L. & B. Acquired some of the stock and plates of John Johnston when he ceased business. On some catalogues Longman and Broderip's address is given as "At the King's Arms and Apollo, No. 26 Cheapside" (1781) or, "At the Apollo, No. 26 Cheapside and No. 13 Haymarket" (c. 1782-92). Johnston's address at one time was "At the Apollo in the Strand."

K. G.

Catalogues:—New Music. c. 1780. 4 pp. fol. (B.M. 7896. h. 40. (7.)); Printed and sold. (Catalogue.) c. 1780. 1 p. fol. (B.M. Hirsch IV. 1111. (11.)); Longman and Broderip, Music-sellers . . . MDCCLXXXI. (Catalogue, Instruments and Music) 16 pp. 8°. (B.M. Hirsch IV. 1110. (1.)); New Music. Published in London, and imported . . . 1781. 4 pp. 8°. (B.M. Hirsch IV. 1110. (2.)); Longman and Broderip, Music-sellers . . . MDCCLXXXII. (Catalogue, Instruments and Music.) 16 pp. 8°. (Adam Carse.); Musical Publications III. c. 1782. 1 p. fol. (B.M. h. 726. p. (8.)); New Music. 1785. 1 p. obl. fol. (B.M. E. 108. e. (1.)); Musical publications. c. 1785. 1 p. fol. (B.M. g. 421. i. (2.)); A Complete Register of all the new Musical Publications . . . imported from . . . Europe. August 1786. 4 pp. 8°. (B.M. Hirsch IV. 1110. (3.)); 1786. 4 pp. 4°. (B.M. 7896. h. 40. (9.)); Musical Publications. c. 1788. 4 pp. fol. (B.M. Hirsch IV. 1112. (4.)); Musical Publications. 1788. 4 pp. fol. (Haas, Catalogue 3. No. 32.); Musical Publications III. c.1789. 1 p. fol. (B.M. h. 61. (7.)); Printed and sold, &c. (Catalogue.) c. 1790. 4 pp. fol. (First Edition Bookshop, Catalogue 40. No. 121.); Longman and Broderip (Catalogue). 1792. 4 pp. 8°. (Hirsch IV. 1110. (4.)); Musical Publications II. 1792. 1 p. fol. (B.M. D. 280. (1.)); Musical Publications III. c. 1795. 2 pp. fol. (First Edition Bookshop, Catalogue 40. No. 122.)

LONGMAN & HERRON. Musical instrument makers, music sellers and publishers, 131 Cheapside, London, c. 1816-22. Partners were Giles Longman and James Herron; succeeded John Longman. R. W. Keith occupied the premises from c. 1822.

"The Musical Entertainer". Engraved by George Bickham junior.
Vol. I. Printed for and sold by George Bickham. Vol II. Printed for
C. Corbett. 1737-39

SONATE

a VIOLINO con VIOLA di GAMBA ó CEMBALO

Dedicate all Eccellenza Di

MADAMA ELISABETTA RUSSEL

CONTESSA di ESSEX

da

FRANCESCO GUERINI

Opera Prima .

sculp.é é stamp.é in Londra, da J.B. Fortier, in Castel street Leicester fields .

Engraved and printed by B. Fortier, c. 1740, the engraver of
Domenico Scarlatti's ''Essercizi per Gravicembalo'', 1739

LONGMAN & LUKEY. *See* Longman, Lukey & Co.

LONGMAN, CLEMENTI & CO. *See* Longman (John), Clementi & Co.

LONGMAN, LUKEY & BRODERIP. Musical instrument makers, music seller, engravers, printers and publishers, 26 Cheapside, London, c. September 1775-76. Succeeded Longman, Lukey and Co.; Lukey withdrew in 1776 and the business was continued as Longman and Broderip; some single sheet songs bear only the initials L. L. & B.; they purchased some of the stock of James Lewer c. 1775.
>   K.
>   Catalogue:—Music. c. 1775. 4 pp. fol. (B.M. H. 879. a. (3.))

LONGMAN, LUKEY & CO. Musical instrument makers, music sellers, engravers, printers and publishers, 26 Cheapside, London, c. 1769-75. Sometimes as Longman and Lukey. Succeeded James Longman and Co.; in December 1771, advertised that they had removed to 45 St. Paul's Church Yard till their house at 26 Cheapside is rebuilt; a few imprints give "Engraved printed & sold by Longman, Lukey & Co."; the firm became Longman, Lukey and Broderip c. September 1775; some single sheet songs bear only the initials L. L. & Co., or L. L. Published some works in conjunction with John Johnston.
>   K.

LONGMAN, REES & CO. Booksellers, 39 Paternoster Row, London. Their names appear in the imprint of "Musical and Poetical Relicks of the Welsh Bards . . . By Edward Jones . . . The Third edition . . . The first volume. London: Printed for the Author . . . 1808. And sold by Longman, Rees, and Co.", etc.

LONGMAN (GEORGE). Music and musical instrument seller, and publisher, 131 Cheapside, London, c. 1833-39. Previously a partner in Longman and Bates.

LONGMAN (GILES). *See* Longman & Herron.

LONGMAN (JAMES) & CO. Musical instrument makers, music sellers and publishers, at the Harp and Crown, 26 Cheapside, London, c. 1767-69. Joined by Lukey in 1769 and the firm became Longman, Lukey and Co. Longman's premises were on the south side of Cheapside, between Friday Street and Mitre Court. John Johnson's premises on the north side of Cheapside were also known as the Harp and Crown until Longman used this sign.
>   K.

LONGMAN (JOHN). Musical instrument maker, music seller, printer and publisher, 131 Cheapside, London, c. 1801-16. Sometimes John

Longman and Co.   Previously a partner in the firm of John Longman, Clementi and Co.;   succeeded by Longman and Herron.
K.
A Catalogue of Songs.   Printed by John Longman & Co.   c. 1810. 3 pp. fol. (B.M. 7896. h. 40. (10.))

LONGMAN (JOHN), CLEMENTI & CO.   Musical instrument makers, music sellers and publishers, 26 Cheapside, London, 1798-c. 1801. Longman had previously been a partner in the firm of Longman and Broderip;   partnership dissolved in 1801;   John Longman went into business alone at 131 Cheapside, and Muzio Clementi entered into partnership with others at 26 Cheapside.
K.
Catalogues:—Musical Publications.   I.   1799.   1 p. fol. (B.M. h. 1747. (2.))   Musical Publications.   II.   c. 1800.   1 p. fol. (B.M. h. 383. e. (6.))

LONGMAN (THOMAS).   Bookseller, Ship and Black Swan, Paternoster Row, London, 1726-75.   (P.)   His name appears in the imprints of a number of sacred music works;   the firm continued under the same name after the death of the founder.
P. II, III.

LONSDALE & MILLS.   Music sellers and publishers, 140 New Bond Street, London, c. 1829-34.   Christopher Lonsdale and Richard Mills succeeded Birchall, Lonsdale and Mills;   partnership dissolved 1834; Mills continued in business at same address, and Lonsdale at 26 Old Bond Street.
K.

LONSDALE (CHRISTOPHER).   Music seller and publisher, 26 Old Bond Street, London, 1834-80.   Previously a partner in Birchall, Lonsdale and Mills, and Lonsdale and Mills;   died 1877;   firm continued under the same name until succeeded by Alfred Hays, 1880.

LORD (HENRY).   Bookseller, at the Duke of Monmouth's Head, Westminster Hall, London, 1680-82.   (P.)   His name appears in an advertisement December 1680, "The Book of Songs with a thorough Basse to them for Instrument [sic], Set and composed by Signior Pietro Reggio, Engraven in copper, in a very large folio, most of them out of Mr. Abraham Cowley's excellent Poems, are to be had only at Mr. Thomas Norman's, at the Popes Head right against the Castle Tavern in Fleetstreet, and at Mr. Lord's Shop", etc.   (D. & M. No. 52.)
P. II.

LORD (JOSEPH).   Bookseller and publisher, Wakefield, Barnsley and Pontefract.   Published "A Book of Psalmody . . . The fourth edition . . . By John Chetham . . . 1731"; also the fifth edition 1736; sixth

edition 1741; seventh edition 1745; eighth edition 1752; "A Book containing great variety of Anthems, in two, three, and four parts . . . The second edition . . . By Josiah Street . . . 1746."
K. P. III.

LOW (SAMPSON). Bookseller and stationer, 42 Lambs Conduit Street, London. Published "Gems of Sacred Melody; being a choice collection of psalm and hymn tunes, chants . . . Selected, arranged, and composed by George Worgan . . . 1841."

LOWE (GEORGE). Printer, in "Loathberry," London. Printed and sold "Parthenia or The Maydenhead of the first musicke that euer was printed for the Virginalls Composed By three famous Masters: William Byrd, D^r: Iohn Bull, & Orlando Gibbons . . . Ingrauen by William Hole. Lond: print: for M^{ris} Dor: Euans . . . Are to be sould by G: Lowe print^r in Loathberry," c. 1613, and two slightly later issues with modified title-pages, but bearing the names of William Hole, Dorethie Euans and G. Lowe. Lowe may also have printed "Prime musiche nuove di Angelo Notari à una, due e tre voci, per cantare con la tiorba, et altri strumenti . . . In Londra Intagliate da Guglielmo Hole", c. 1613.
M.

LOWE (JOHN). Bookseller, Gainsborough. His name appears in the imprint of "A Book of Psalm-Tunes, with Variety of Anthems in Four Parts, with Chanting-Tunes for the Te Deum, Benedictus, Magnificat . . . By James Green. The Fifth edition . . . London. Printed by William Pearson, for . . . John Lowe . . . Gainsborough . . . 1724."

LOWNDES (THOMAS). Bookseller and publisher, Fleet Street, London, 1756-84. (P.) His name appears in the imprint of "The Beggar's Opera . . . To which is prefixed the overture in score: And the musick to each song. London: Printed for W. Strahan, T. Lowndes, T. Caslon, W. Griffin, W. Nicoll, S. Bladon, and G. Kearsly. MDCCLXXI."; also in two editions published 1777. Did not generally publish music, but issued and sold a number of libretti, some in conjunction with W. Lowndes.
P. III.

LOWNES (HUMFREY) the Elder. Bookseller and printer, London, 1587-1629 (M.); first at the West Door of St. Paul's Church; from 1604 at the sign of the Star, on Bread Street Hill, premises formerly occupied by Peter Short, whose widow Lownes married in 1604. Printed a few musical works 1606-27, including "The First Booke of Songs or Aires of foure parts . . . Composed by John Dowland . . . 1606"; "A Plaine and Easie Introdvction to Practicall Musicke . . . By Thomas Morley . . . 1608"; "Gradualia . . . Lib. Primus (Secundus).

Authore Gulielmo Byrde . . . 1610"; "Ayres, or Fa La's for Three Voyces . . . by Iohn Hilton . . . 1627," etc. Some works, assumed to have been printed by Humfrey Lownes, have only the initials H. L. Robert Young, who apparently was in partnership with Lownes at the time of his death, carried on the business at the Star, on Bread Street Hill.

K. M.

LOWNES (HUMFREY) *the Younger*. Bookseller and printer, London, 1612-28. (M.) May or may not have issued any musical works, although he is said to have printed "Ayres, or Fa La's for Three Voyces . . . by Iohn Hilton . . . 1627," which was presumably the work of Humfrey Lownes the Elder.

K. M.

LOWNES (MATTHEW). Bookseller, printer and publisher, London, 1591-1625 (M.); first at St. Dunstan's Churchyard, in Fleet Street; at the sign of the Bishop's Head, St. Paul's Churchyard, 1610-25, during which time he printed and published a number of musical works mostly in association with Thomas Snodham, John Browne and Alice Browne. Some works bear only the initials M. L. In 1627 George Latham (Lathum) was at the sign of the Bishop's Head.

K. M.

LUCAS. *See* Evans & Lucas.

LUFF (GEORGE). Pianoforte manufacturer, music seller and publisher, London; (Music and Quadrille Repository) 92 Great Russell Street, Bloomsbury, c. 1833-38; 103 Great Russell Street, Bloomsbury, c. 1838-62. Became George Luff and Co. c. 1837-54, George Luff and Son c. 1854-62.

Catalogue:—New and popular vocal and instrumental music just published. 1834. 1 p. fol. (B.M. H. 1687. (18.))

LUKEY. *See* Longman, Lukey & Co.; Longman, Lukey & Broderip.

LUNCH (C.). Printer, Great Market Street, Dublin. Printed "Douze Nouveaux Quatuors dediés a Son Majesté le Roi de Prusse. Composés par Ignace Pleyel," c. 1790; "Trois Quatuors, Pour deux violons, alto et basses," by I. J. Pleyel, c. 1790; "Trois Sonates pour le Piano forte ou le Clavecin avec accompagnement d'un Violon ad libitum pour les deux premieres, et oblige pour la troisieme . . . composees par Mr. Hullmandel. Op. VI." c. 1795; "Three Sonatas for the Piano Forte or Harpsichord with an Accompaniment for a Flute or Violin & Violoncello. Dedicated to H.M. the Queen of Great Britain," c. 1795.

LYNE (SAMUEL). At ye Globe, in Newgate Street, London. His name appears on the sheets of a volume of engraved songs with illustrated headings entitled "English Orpheus. Publish'd by Tho. Kitchin & sold by Sl. Lyne", etc., c. 1743.

LYON & DUNCAN. Pianoforte manufacturers, London; 82 Wells Street, c. 1810-13; 22 Suffolk Street, c. 1813-14; 22 Nassau Street, c. 1814-15. Published a small amount of music; both were previously with John Broadwood.

    See also Lyon (Samuel Thomas).

LYON (SAMUEL THOMAS). Pianoforte manufacturer, London; 82 Wells Street, c. 1807-10; became Lyon and Duncan, 82 Wells Street, c. 1810-13; 22 Suffolk Street, c. 1813-14; 22 Nassau Street, c. 1814-1815; continued as S. T. Lyon at the latter address, c. 1815-40. Published a small amount of music, including some of his own compositions; previously with John Broadwood.

M. & M. *See* Monro and May.

M., A. *See* Miller (Abraham).

M., G. *See* Miller (George).

M., J. *See* Macock (John).

MAB or MABB (RALPH). Bookseller and publisher, at the Greyhound, St. Paul's Churchyard, London, 1610-42. (P.) His name appears in the imprint of William Barriffe's "Mars, his triumph. Or, the description of an exercise performed the XVIII. of October, 1638. in Merchant-Taylors Hall by certain gentlemen of the Artillery Garden London, printed by I. L. for Ralph Mab. 1639," which contains some musical examples for use with artillery exercises.
    P. I.

MAC or Mc. Names beginning with either of these forms are placed here together.

McCALLEY (JOHN). Music seller and publisher, 33 Moore Street, Dublin, c. 1783-1801. Succeeded by Mary McCalley.
    K.

McCALLEY (MARY). Music seller and publisher, Dublin; 33 Moore Street, c. 1801-14; 36 Moore Street, c. 1814-15. Succeeded John McCalley.
    K.

McCARTHY. *See* Rutter & McCarthy.

McCLARY (HENRY JAMES). Bookseller, 32 St. James's Street, London. His name appears in the imprint of "A Collection of Ancient Piobaireachd or Highland Pipe Music . . . by Angus Mackay. Second edition. Edinburgh. Published by the Editor to be had at McClary's Library . . . London . . . 1839."

McCULLAGH & McCULLAGH. Music and musical instrumental sellers, and publishers, 108 Grafton Street, and 22 Suffolk Street, Dublin, c. 1831-51. Partners were Edward and James McCullagh; succeeded Edward McCullagh.

McCULLAGH (EDWARD). Music and musical instrument seller, and publisher, 1 Arcade, College Green, Dublin, c. 1821-31. Had additional premises at 22 Suffolk Street, c. 1830-31; succeeded by McCullagh and McCullagh.
    K.

McCULLAGH (JAMES). *See* McCullagh & McCullagh.

McDONNELL. Musical instrument and music seller, and publisher, 2 Church Lane, Dublin, c. 1790-1810. Also said to have had a second address, 28 Nassau Street.
    K.

McFADYEN (JOHN). Music seller, publisher and stationer, Glasgow; 30 Wilson Street (or, Corner of Hutcheson and Wilson Street), c. 1790-1826; 63 Wilson Street c. 1826-37. Had a circulating musical library.
    K. (Joseph McFadyen.)

McGLASHAN & GILL. Booksellers and publishers, 50 Upper Sackville Street, Dublin, c. 1856-76. Published some musical works; James McGlashan was previously in business on his own account.

McGLASHAN (JAMES). Bookseller and publisher, Dublin; 21 D'Olier Street, c. 1847-50; 50 Upper Sackville Street, c. 1850-56. Published some musical works; succeeded by McGlashan and Gill.

McGOUAN (A.). *See* McGoun (Archibald) *the Younger*.

McGOUN (ARCHIBALD) *the Elder*. Book and music seller, and publisher, Stockwell, Glasgow, c. 1783-95.
    K.

McGOUN (ARCHIBALD) *the Younger*. Stationer, music seller and publisher, 10 Argyle Street, Glasgow, c. 1796-1810. His name also appears as McGown, McGouan and McGowan.
    K.

McGOWAN (A.). *See* McGoun (Archibald) *the Younger*.

McGOWN (A.). *See* McGoun (Archibald) *the Younger*.

MACHEN (J.). Bookseller and publisher, 8 D'Olier Street, Dublin. Published "The Native Music of Ireland. 1842."

MACINTOSH (A.). Music engraver, Edinburgh. Engraved "Waly, Waly, a favourite old Scots Song, with . . . alterations by Robert Riddell, Esq. of Glenriddell," c. 1790; "A Curious Selection of favourite Tunes with Variations . . . Harmonized by an eminent master. Edinr. Printed for J. Brysson's Music Shop", c. 1791; "Thirty New Strathspey Reels &c. With a bass for the violoncello or harpsichord. Composed by Abrm. Macintosh. Edinburgh Printed for & sold by the Author & by J. Bryson . . . Messrs. Corri & Sutherland, Messrs. Stewart, R. Ross", etc., 1792; "A New Strathspey . . . Dedicated to Miss Barbara Campbell, by J. Thomson, Edinburgh, printed for the author," date unknown.
K.

MACINTOSH (A.). Printer, Cambridge. Printed "A Collection of Psalm & Hymn Tunes some of which are new & others by permission of the authors with six Chants and Te Deums . . . The whole revis'd & harmonized by Dr. Randall. And published by Wm. Hague and Jno. Peppercorn. Cambridge . . . 1794."

McINTYRE. *See* Simms & McIntyre.

MACKINLAY (THOMAS). *See* D'Almaine & Co.

MACLACHLAN & STEWART. Booksellers, South Bridge, Edinburgh. Their names appear in the imprint of "A Collection of Ancient Piobaireachd or Highland Pipe Music . . . by Angus Mackay. Second edition. Edinburgh. Published by the Editor to be had at . . . MacLachlan & Stewart . . . 1839." The first named was J. Mac-Lachlan.

McLEAN (JOHN). Music seller and publisher, Dublin: 19 Anglesea Street, c. 1813-16; 10 Bachelor's Walk, c. 1816-35. Had a circulating musical library.
K.

McMILLAN (BUCHANAN). Printer in ordinary to His Majesty, 6 Bow Street, Covent Garden, London. Printed for the editor, "A Collection of Madrigals and Motetts, Chiefly for four equal Voices, by the most eminent composers of the sixteenth and seventeenth centuries . . . collated . . . by Joseph Gwilt, Architect, F.S.A. . . . 1815"; printed volumes 1 and 2 of "A Collection of Glees, Canons, and Catches, composed by the late John Wall Callcott . . . together with a memoir of the late author, by William Horsley . . . London: Published, for the author's widow, By Birchall, Lonsdale, and Mills, 133 New Bond Street, 1824."

MACOCK (JOHN). Printer, at Addle or Addling Hill, London, 1645-92. (P.) Printed "An Essay to the advancement of Musick . . . By Thomas Salmon . . . Printed by J. Macock, and are to be sold by John Car [i.e. Carr] . . . 1672," with musical examples; "The Whole Book of Psalms. Collected into English Meeter, by Thomas Sternhold, John Hopkins, and others . . . with apt notes to sing them withal . . . London, Printed by J. M. for the Company of Stationers. MDCCLXXXVII."
    K. P. I.

MACPHERSON (JAMES). Bookbinder, bookseller, stationer, and music seller, at the Figure of the Ancient Bard of Cona, Princes Street, Cavendish Square, London. Printed and sold c. 1800, "McPherson's Collection of ancient music, in the poems and songs of Ossian . . . Adapted by Thos. Brabazon Gray. No. 1."

MADELEY (GEORGE EDWARD). Lithographic printer, 3 Wellington Street, Strand, London. Printed the music of "Christmas Carols, ancient and modern; including the most popular in the West of England . . . With an introduction and notes by William Sandys. London: Richard Beckley . . . 1833."

MAGNES (JAMES) & BENTLEY (RICHARD). Booksellers, at the Post Office, Russel (Russell) Street, Covent Garden, London, 1675-78. (P.) Published "The Fool turn'd Critick: a Comedy: As it is acted at the Theatre-Royall. By T. D. Gent . . . Printed for James Magnes and Richard Bentley . . . 1678." Bentley was afterwards in business as Richard Bentley and M. Magnes.
    P. II. D. & M.

MAGNES (M.). *See* Bentley (Richard) & Magnes (M.).

MAINWARING (WILLIAM). Music seller and publisher of engraved music, Corelli's Head, College Green, Dublin, c. 1740-63. Published one or two collections of Songs from Arne's "Comus," Handel's "Athalia," etc., in conjunction with William Neale. After his death in July 1763 the business was continued by his widow. The name also appears as Manwaring.
    K.

MAJOR (R.). Music engraver, printer and publisher, London; at his cheap music warehouse, 43 Bedford Street, Strand, c. 1800-18; at 7 High Holborn, 1820. Many of his publications are without any address.
    K.

MAJOR (RICHARD). Music engraver, 10 Broad Street, Bristol. Printed and published, "Eight Anthems, in four Parts, with an Accompaniment for the Organ or Piano Forte . . . by William Holmes, of Ideford Devon." Preface is dated April 8, 1811.

MAJOR (SAMUEL). Music seller and publisher, 35 Duke Street, West Smithfield, London, c. 1778-1825.
    K.

MALIER (W. T.). Bookseller and stationer, 2 Corn Market, Belfast. Published c. 1840, "The Belfast Rifle Club Quadrilles, or McFadden's Second Set, composed & arranged for the Piano Forte . . . by A. McFadden."

MAN (JAMES). Bookseller, at the Heart and Bible in Cornhill, near the Royal Exchange, London. His name appears with Thomas Cross in the imprints of "Philomela or The Vocal Musitian," etc., 1692; "Synopsis Musicæ . . . 1693"; on one number "A Dialogue . . . in the play . . . the Richmond Heiress" included in "Joyful Cuckoldom," the title-page of which is dated 1671, but which contains items 1690?-1696? He was presumably a son of Samuel Man, publisher, 1616-74.
    D. & M.

MANBY (CHARLES WILLIAM). Music seller and publisher, 85 Fleet Street, London, c. 1841-46. Previously a partner in the firm of George & Manby.

MANWARING (WILLIAM). *See* Mainwaring.

MARCH (JOHN). Bookseller, Exeter, 1713-26, near the Conduit; The Bible, a little below St. Martin's Church in Fore Street. (P.) His name appears in an advertisement January 1726, "Notice is hereby given, That this day, being the 21st inst. Cluer and Creak's Second Pocket Volume of Opera Songs, will be published and delivered to subscribers . . . On Thursday the 27th they will publish their Second Pack of Musical Playing Cards. The words and music composed by Mr. Carey . . . They have just published, The Tonometer . . . All sold at Cluer's Printing Office . . . and at Mr. Creak's . . . and at Mr. John March's, Bookseller in Exon.", etc.
    P. II.

MARINI, *Sig.* Designer, London. His name appeared in advertisements June 1738, as having designed the head-pieces of "British Melody; Or, the Musical Magazine . . . Printed for & sold by . . . Benjn. Cole . . . Holbourn. MDCCXXXIX."; issued in parts 1738-39.

MARSH (THOMAS). Printer, "in fleete streete nighe unto S. Dunstanes churche," London. Printed John Hall's "The Couurte of vertu

H *

contaynynge many holy or spretuall songs sonettes psalmes ballettes
. . . Imprinted at London . . . 1565", etc.
   D. (Marshe.) S.

MARSH (THOMAS). Bookseller, Minster Gates, York. His name appears
   in the imprint of "Twenty-four Chants: to which are prefixed,
   Remarks on Chanting . . . By Mr. J. Gray, of York. Published for the
   Author, by Preston . . . London, and H. Bellerby; York . . . and of
   the following booksellers . . . T. Marsh, York. 1834."

MARSH (WILLIAM). Bookseller, Palace Street, Canterbury. His name
   appears in the imprint of "Resignation. 58th Hymn Lady Huntingdon's Collection Set to Music by William Marsh, Canterbury. Sold
   by W. Marsh Bookseller, Canterbury," etc., c. 1805.

MARSHALL (J.). At the Old Flesh Market, Newcastle on Tyne. Printed
   "Garlands of New Songs", c. 1810.

MARSHALL (J.) & (J.). Booksellers, at the Bible, in Newgate Street,
   London. Published "An Introduction to Psalmody . . . Together
   with a collection of various, easy, and pleasant tunes in two parts.
   To which are added, some divine hymns never before printed . . .
   MDCCXXXVII." Succeeded Joseph Marshall.

MARSHALL (JOSEPH). Bookseller, at the Bible, in Newgate Street,
   London, c. 1709-34. Previously in partnership with his father,
   William Marshall; published editions of two musical works by Daniel
   Warner, "The Singing Master's Guide," and "A Further Guide to
   Parish Clark's"; both works were advertised in January 1719 and
   March 1727, The Singing Master's Guide also in 1728; earlier
   editions were published by William and Joseph Marshall. Succeeded
   by J. and J. Marshall.
   P. II.

MARSHALL (R.). *See* Simpkin (W.) & Marshall (R.).

MARSHALL (RICHARD). *See* Dicey (William).

MARSHALL (WILLIAM). Bookseller and bookbinder, London; Butcher's
   Hall Lane, 1676; at the Bible in Newgate Street, 1679-1702. (P.)
   His name appears in an advertisement March 1702, "A Guide to
   Parish Clerks. Fitted and contrived for common use, for singing
   Psalms . . . Printed for William Marshall and sold by him at the Bible
   in Newgate-street," etc. In 1702 he took his son Joseph into the
   business, and continued as William and Joseph Marshall.
   P. II.

MARSHALL (WILLIAM). Music seller and publisher, High Street,
   Oxford, c. 1810-45.

MARSHALL (WILLIAM) & (JOSEPH). Booksellers, at the Bible, in Newgate Street, London, 1702-c. 1709. Published "A Further Guide to Parish Clerks . . . By Daniel Warner." 1707; "A New Guide to Parish Clerks: Being the treble and bass of the singing psalms . . . By Daniel Warner." 1708. William was previously in business alone; Joseph continued on his own account c. 1709.
P. II.

MARTIN & CO. Music importers, music sellers and publishers, London; 87 Piccadilly, opposite the Green Park, 1844-October 1845; 3 Old Bond Street, October 1845-46.

MARTIN (ANDREW). Bookseller, in the Parliament Close, Edinburgh, c. 1728-38. (P.) His name appears in the imprint of "Twelve Solo's or Sonata's for a Violin and Violoncello, with a Thorough Bass for the Harpsicord . . . Composed by Charles Macklean. Opera Prima . . . Edinburgh. Printed by R. Cooper, for the Author, and sold by him and Mr. And. Martin, Bookseller in the Parliament Close. 1737."
P. III.

MARTIN (CHARLES). Stationer, Greenwich. Printed and sold c. 1795, "In airy Dreams, a favourite Song and Duet."
K.

MARTIN (JOHN) & ALLESTREY (JAMES). Booksellers, at the Bell, in St. Paul's Churchyard, London. Published "Psalterium Carolinum. The devotions of His Sacred Majestie in his solitudes and sufferings, rendred in verse. Set to musick for 3 voices and an organ, or theorbo, by John Wilson Dr. and musick professor of Oxford . . . 1657."
P. I.

MARTIN (R.). Music seller, Edinburgh. Published c. 1832, "A Selection of Scots, English and Irish Songs with accompaniments for the Piano-Forte. From the most eminent composers," etc. 2 vols.

MASON (ISAAC). Music seller, publisher and musical string manu-facturer, London; 58 Great Russell Street, c. 1836-38; 20 Hanway Street, c. 1838-41; 14 Hanway Street, c. 1841-42; 4 Gray's Inn Passage, Holborn, c. 1842-44.

MASON (J.). Printer, London. His name appears in the imprint of a song "Wonderful News from the River of Thames. To a pleasant new tune. Printed on the frozen Thames, by the loyal young printers, viz. E. and A. Milbourn, S. Hinch, J. Mason. 1683."
P. II.

MASSEY (ROBERT). Music seller, Manchester. His name appears in the imprint of "A New Sett of Hymns and Psalm Tunes . . . Composed by J. Leach, Rochdale. London. Printed for the Author, sold by Preston & Son . . . R. Massey, Music seller, Manchester," etc.; preface dated June 29, 1789; also on "A Second Sett of Hymns and Psalm Tunes," c. 1797.

MATHER (J.). Music seller, at his musical repository, 9 Green Side Place, Head of Leith Walk, Edinburgh. Published c. 1810, "The Legacy, An Irish Melody arranged as a Rondo for the Piano-Forte, composed . . . by J. Mather."

MATHEWS (JAMES). Music seller and publisher, Bath, c. 1790-1800; High Street, c. 1790; Milsom Street, c. 1794; 3 George Street, c. 1795-1800. Published some of his own compositions.

MATHEWS (WILLIAM). Music seller, High Street, Oxford, c. 1775-90. Published a small amount of music; succeeded by Henry Hardy.
  K.

MATTHEWS & CO. Pianoforte manufacturers, music sellers and publishers, 30 Brydges Street, Covent Garden, London, c. 1846-55.

MATTHEWS (EMANUEL). Printer and bookseller, at the Bible in Paternoster Row, London, 1700-26. (P.) His name appears in the imprints of "Hymns and Spiritual Songs . . . By Simon Browne . . . MDCCXX.";
"The Psalms of David in Metre: With the tunes used in Parish-Churches. By John Patrick . . . The Seventh edition . . . London: Printed for D. Brown . . . Em. Matthews . . . MDCCXXIV."
  P. III.

MAUND (CHARLES). Music engraver and printer, music seller and publisher, 5 Stephen Street, Rathbone Place, London, c. 1833-47.

MAUND (G.). Music engraver, London? Engraved "Sacred Harmony: or a choice collection of psalms and hymn tunes, in two or three parts, for the voice, harpsicord, & organ." Edited by John Wesley. London, 1788.

MAY (CHARLES). Musical instrument maker and music seller, 87 Blackman Street, Southwark, London, 1788-c. 1799. Previously employed by Longman and Broderip; published a small amount of music; succeeded by Richard Watts.

MAY (HARRY). Music seller and publisher, 11 Holborn Bars, London, 1848-62. Previously a partner in the firm of Monro and May.

MAY (JOHN). Music seller, London. His name appears in an advertisement June 1691, "A Collection of choice Ayres for 2 and 3 Flutes. Composed by the best masters of musick. Sold by Thomas Jones . . .

John May at the Sugar Loaf near the Temple Gate . . . and Fr. Hicks,"
etc.; his name appears in the imprint of "The Songs in the Indian
Queen: As it is now compos'd into an Opera. By Mr. Henry Purcell
. . . London, Printed by J. Heptinstall; and are to be sold by John
May, at his shop under St. Dunstan's Church: And for John Hudge-
butt at Tho. Dring's . . . 1695."
    D. & M.

MAYHEW & CO. Music sellers and publishers, 17 Old Bond Street,
London, c. 1822-30. Thomas Mayhew was the principal partner;
succeeded Phillips, Mayhew and Co.; advertised in December 1824
that they had purchased some of John Whitaker's copyrights; succeeded by Mayhew and Lee.
    K.

MAYHEW & LEE. Music sellers and publishers, 17 Old Bond Street,
London, c. 1830-31. Succeeded Mayhew and Co.; Thomas Mayhew
dropped out and business was continued by Leoni Lee c. 1831.
    K.

MAYNARD, *Mrs.* Bookseller, Devizes. Her name appears in the imprint of "The Psalms of David . . . By I. Watts . . . A new edition,
corrected. (Tunes in the Tenor Part fitted to the several Metres.)
Salisbury: Printed and sold by Collins and Johnson. Sold also by
. . . Maynard, at Devizes . . . MDCCLXXVI."
    P. III.

Mc. For names beginning with this form, *see* Mac.

MEAD (E.). Printer, London. Printed "Devotions in the ancient Way
of Offices . . . Reformed by a Person of Quality . . . The III. edition
. . . (The Tunes to the Hymns.) London: Printed by E. Mead, for
John Nicholson . . . and John Sprint . . . 1706"; succeeded T. Mead.

MEAD (T.). Printer, London. Printed "Devotions in the ancient Way
of Offices . . . Reformed by a Person of Quality . . . The Second edition
. . . (The Tunes to the Hymns.) London: Printed by T. Mead, for
John Nicholson . . . and John Sprint . . . 1701"; succeeded by
E. Mead.

MEADOWS (WILLIAM). Bookseller and publisher, at the Angel, in
Cornhill, London, 1719-53. (P.) Advertised January 1725, "A New
System of Music, both theorical and practical, and yet not mathe-
matical; containing a scale of twelve notes with the abolishing of all
flats and sharps, and those great puzzlers the clefs, &c . . . Sold by
William Meadows . . . and Peter du Noyer," etc.
    P. II, III.

MEARES (RICHARD) *the Elder*. Musical instrument maker, music printer, publisher, stationer, retailer of cutlery wares, London; Without Bishopsgate near Sir Paul Pindar's (opposite The Catherine Wheel Inn), c. 1669-?; at the Golden Viol in Cornhill (or in Leadenhall Street, which may, or may not, have been the same premises), 1699-?; at the Golden Viol and Hautboy (sometimes given as "the Golden Viol," only, or "the Viol and Hautboy," or "the Golden Ball and Hautboy") on the North side of St. Paul's Church Yard, 1706 or earlier-c. 1722. For a short period in 1722 the advertisements and imprints give Richard Meares senior and junior; Corelli's "Sonate a tre," 1722, have the imprint "Imprime per Richard Meares Seg^r. et Iun^r. A L'ensign de la Bass de Viole Dor dans le Cemetiere de S^t. Paul." It is assumed that Meares the elder died in 1722 and was succeeded by his son, but the latter was probably in partnership with his father from 1717 or earlier and was responsible for the printing side of the business; the evidence on the matter being incomplete it is difficult to identify whether Meares *senior* or *junior* is referred to in the various notices. The name also appears as Meers and Mears.
K. G.
See also Meares (Richard) *the Younger*.

MEARES (RICHARD) *the Younger*. Musical instrument maker, music printer and publisher, at the Golden Viol and Hautboy (or The Golden Viol, or The Viol and Hautboy, or The Golden Ball), on the North side of St. Paul's Church Yard, London, c. 1722-c. 1727. Formerly in partnership with his father Richard Meares at this address, and is assumed to have been responsible for the printing side of the business from 1717 or earlier. Hawkins says that he moved in due course from St. Paul's Churchyard to Birchin Lane, where he remained about two years, and then removed to London House Yard in St. Paul's Churchyard where he died about 1743. The available records do not clearly indicate in most cases which of the two Meares is referred to.
K. G.
See also Meares (Richard) *the Elder*.

MEARS (RICHARD). *See* Meares (Richard) *the Elder*.

MEARS (W.). Bookseller, at the Lamb without Temple Bar, London, c. 1713-34. Published "The Contrivances: with the Songs, and other additions, as now acted at the Theatre-Royal in Drury-Lane . . . As also the tunes of the songs, neatly engraven on copper-plates. Written by Mr. Carey. The second edition . . . MDCCXXIX."; "The Wedding: a Tragi-Comi-Pastoral-Farcical Opera. As it is now acting at the Theatre-Royal in Lincoln's Inn Fields . . . By Mr. Hawker . . . To which is prefix'd, the overture, by Dr. Pepusch. With an addition of the musick to each song, engrav'd on copper-plates . . . London. Printed for W. Mears, at Temple-Bar and sold by S. Birt. . . .

MDCCXXIX.''; also a second edition, 1734. His name appears in the imprint of ''The Psalms of David in Metre: Fitted to the Tunes used in Parish-Churches. By John Patrick . . . London, Printed for W. Churchill . . . W. Mears . . . MDCCXVIII.''; also on the seventh edition, 1724.
P. III.

MEERE (H.). Printer, London, c. 1706-24; at the Black Fryar, in Black-friars; Old Bailey. (P.) Printed for the Author, ''Orchesography or, The Art of Dancing, by Characters and demonstrative figures . . . being an exact and just translation from the French of Monsieur Feuillet by John Weaver . . . 1706.'' Printed for J. Walsh, ''The Merry Musician; or, A Cure for the Spleen . . . Vol. I . . . 1716''; ''The Compleat Country Dancing-Master . . . 1718''; ''The Second Book of the Compleat Country Dancing-Master . . . 1719.''
K. P. II.

MEERS (R.). *See* Meares (Richard) *the Elder.*

MELVILL (DAVID). Bookseller, Aberdeen, 1622-43. (P.) Published ''The Psalms of David, in Prose and Metre: With the whole forme of Discipline and Prayers, according to the Church of Scotland . . . Aberdene, Printed by Edward Raban, 1633. For David Melvill.''
P. I.

MENZIES (ROBERT). Printer, Lawnmarket, Edinburgh. Published ''A Collection of original Strathspeys and Reels, arranged for the Piano Forte, Violin, & Violoncello . . . by D. McKercher,'' etc.; preface is dated March 10, 1824.

MEREDITH (LUKE). Bookseller, London; King's Head, West end of St. Paul's Churchyard, 1684-86; at the Angel, Amen Corner, 1687-92; at the Star, St. Paul's Churchyard. (P.) 1692-1701. Published in conjunction with A. & J. Churchill ''The Psalms of David in Metre. Fitted to the Tunes used in Parish-Churches. By J. Patrick . . . 1698''; published another edition in 1701 with the imprint ''London, Printed for L. Meredith, and sold by D. Brown . . . T. Benskin . . . J. Walthoe and F. Coggan . . . 1701.'' May have published editions of the Psalms before 1698.
P. II.

MERRIDEW (JOHN). Music seller, Warwick. His name appears in the imprint of ''Washing Day, a proper new Ballad, for wet weather. Birmingham, Printed at the Lithographic Press, by W. Hawkes Smith. Sold also by . . . Merridew, Warwick,'' etc., c. 1820.

METZLER & CO. Musical instrument makers, music sellers and pub-lishers, London; 105 Wardour Street, c. 1833-42; 37 Great Marl-borough Street, c. 1842-81; 42 Great Marlborough Street, c. 1881-95;

40-43 Great Marlborough Street, c. 1895-1909. Re-formed as Metzler and Co. (1909) Ltd., 40-43 Great Marlborough Street, c. 1909-11; 42 Great Marlborough Street, c. 1911-20; again re-formed as Metzler and Co. (1920) Ltd., 142 Charing Cross Road, 1920-29; 14 Rathbone Place, c. 1929-30. Succeeded Metzler and Son. The original principal partner, George Richard Metzler, was previously with Metzler and Son. He retired from the business 1866, which was continued by his son George Thomas Metzler and Frank Chappell.
  G.

METZLER & SON. Musical instrument makers and music publishers, 105 Wardour Street, London, c. 1816-33. Valentin Metzler, the father, commenced business as a musical instrument maker 1788; after his death the business was continued by his son, George Richard, as Metzler and Co.
  G.

MICKLEBOROUGH, *Mr.* New Bond Street, near Union Street, London. His name appears in the imprint of "Antient British Music; or, a Collection of tunes, never before published . . . Part I . . . London: Printed for, and sold, by the Compilers, John Parry at his house . . . and Evan Williams at Mr. Mickleborough's in New Bond Street . . . MDCCXLII."

MIDDLETON (HENRY). *See* Este, Est, East, or Easte (Thomas).

MIDGLEY (RO.). London. His name appears in the imprint of "A Collection of the Choyest and newest Songs. Sett by severall Masters with a Thorow Bass to each Song for yᵉ Harpsichord Theorbo or Bass-Violl The Second Book. Printed for and Sold by Iohn Crouch who is lately removed out of Drury Lane to the three Lutes in Princes Street nere Covent-Garden. Licenced Mar. 26. 1687 Ro: Midgley."
  D. & M.

MIDWINTER (DANIEL) *the Elder.* Bookseller and publisher, London; at the Rose and Crown, St. Paul's Churchyard, 1698-c. 1707; at the Three Crowns, St. Paul's Churchyard, c. 1707-25. (P.) Published "The Psalm Singer's Compleat Companion." By Elias Hall. "Printed for D. Midwinter . . . and sold by W. Clayton, bookseller, in Manchester, 1708"; his name appears in the imprint of "The Psalms of David in Metre: Fitted to the Tunes used in Parish-Churches. By John Patrick . . . London, Printed for W. Churchill . . . D. Midwinter . . . MDCCXVIII."; also on the seventh edition, 1724. Succeeded by his son Daniel, the younger.
  K.   P. II.

MIDWINTER (DANIEL) *the Younger.* Bookseller and publisher, St. Paul's Churchyard, London, 1726-57. (P.) His name appears in the imprint of "The Psalms of David in Metre: with the tunes used in

Parish-Churches. By John Patrick. The Eighth edition. London: Printed for J. Walthoe . . . D. Midwinter . . . MDCCXLII." Succeeded his father Daniel the elder.

P. III.

MIDWINTER (EDWARD). Bookseller, London, at the Three Crowns, St. Paul's Churchyard, and Looking Glass, on London Bridge. His name appears in the imprint of "The Dancing-Master. Vol. the First . . . The 18th edition . . . London, Printed by W. Pearson and sold by Edward Midwinter, at the Three Crowns and Looking Glass, and John Young," etc., c. 1725.

K.

MILBOURN (ALEXANDER). Printer, London, 1683-93. His name appears in the imprint of a song "Wonderful News from the River of Thames. To a pleasant new tune. Printed on the frozen Thames, by the loyal young printers, viz E. and A. Milbourn, S. Hinch, J. Mason. 1683."

P. II.

MILBOURN (E.). Printer, London. His name appears in the imprint of a song "Wonderful News from the River of Thames. To a pleasant new tune. Printed on the frozen Thames, by the loyal young printers, viz. E. and A. Milbourn, S. Hinch, J. Mason. 1683." Related to the preceding.

P. II.

MILHOUSE (WILLIAM). Military musical instrument maker, printer and publisher, London; 100 Wardour Street, Soho, c. 1789-97; 337 Oxford Street, c. 1797-1825; as William Milhouse and Son, c. 1825-37.

K.

MILLAR (ANDREW). Bookseller and publisher, London, 1728-68; Buchanan's Head, near St. Clement's Church; opposite Catherine Street, Strand. (P.) Published a number of Ballad Operas with the music to the songs; his name appears in the imprint of "The Psalms of David in Metre: With the tunes used in Parish-Churches. By John Patrick. The Eighth edition. London: Printed for J. Walthoe . . . A. Millar . . . MDCCXLII."

P. III.

MILLER (ABRAHAM). Printer, Blackfriars, London, 1645-53. (P.) Only the initials A. M. appear in the imprints of the works presumed to have been printed by Abraham Miller, "The Whole Book of Psalmes: collected into English Meeter by Thomas Sternhold, Iohn Hopkins, and others . . . with apt notes to sing them withall . . . London, Printed by A. M. for the Companie of Stationers . . . 1647"; also editions in 1648 and 1653. Succeeded his father George Miller.

P. I.

MILLER (ELIZABETH). Music and musical instrument seller, at the sign of the Violin and Hautboy (Violin), on London Bridge, 1707-c. 1727. Widow of John Miller; her name appears in the imprints of a number of musical works.
>   K. (John Miller.)

MILLER (GEORGE). Printer, Blackfriars, London, 1601-46. (P.) Only the intials G. M. appear in the imprints of the works presumed to have been printed by George Miller, "The Whole Booke of Psalmes: collected into English Meeter, by Thomas Sternhold, Iohn Hopkins, and others . . . with apt notes to sing them withall . . . London, Printed by G. M. for the Companie of Stationers . . . 1632 "; also editions in 1633, 1634, 1636, 1637, 1638, 1639, 1640, 1641, 1642, 1645 and 1646. Succeeded by his son Abraham.
>   P. I.

MILLER (GEORGE). Music and musical instrument seller, near the Royal Exchange, London. His name appears in the imprint of "The Circle: or Conversations on Love & Gallantry; Originally in French. Now Englished. And since Augmented with several New Songs . . . By Nath. Noel, Gent . . . London, Printed for the Author, and are to be sold by John Carre [i.e. Carr] . . . Richard Hunt . . . George Miller . . . 1676."
>   D. & M.

MILLER (J.). Music seller, at his shop in Birchin Lane, London. Sold the "Compleat Musick Master," 1707.

MILLER (JOHN). Music and musical instrument seller, and publisher, at the sign of the Violin and Hautboy (or, Golden Violin), on London Bridge, 1695-1707. Business was carried on by his widow, Elizabeth Miller, in 1707.
>   K.

MILLER (ROBERT). Engraver, printer and bookseller, 24 Old Fish Street, St. Paul's, London. Published c. 1820, "The Lyre. A Selection of popular Psalm & Hymn Tunes, with appropriate vignetts."

MILLER (WILLIAM). Bookseller to His Royal Highness the Duke of Clarence, 5 Old Bond Street, London. Published "The Psalms of David for the use of Parish Churches . . . The music selected, adapted & composed by Edward Miller Mus. Doc.," etc.; preface is dated March 1790; "Three Quartetts for a Flute, Violin, Tenor, and Violoncello; composed . . . by G. Weiss. Opera 5," c. 1790; "6 Quartetts for a Flute, Violin, Tenor & Violoncello by G. Weiss. Opera 6. London, Published for the Author, and sold by W. Miller," etc., c. 1790; "Psalm Tunes. Composed in four parts for choirs or singers . . . By Edward Miller. Printed and published by W. Miller," etc., c. 1805.

MILLER (WILLIAM). Bookseller and publisher, 49 Albemarle Street, London. His name appears in the imprint of "Musical and Poetical Relicks of the Welsh Bards . . . By Edward Jones . . . The Third edition . . . The first volume. London: Printed for the Author . . . 1808. And sold by William Miller," etc.

MILLN (GEORGE). Bookseller, Dundee. His name appears in the imprint of "The Edinburgh Musical Miscellany: a collection of the most approved Scotch, English, and Irish songs, set to music. Selected by D. Sime, Edinburgh. Edinburgh: Printed for W. Gordon . . . G. Milln . . . Dundee. MDCCXCII." In volume II the imprint reads "Edinburgh: Printed for John Elder, T. Brown, and C. Elliot, Edinburgh; and W. Coke, Leith. MDCCXCIII."

MILLS (RICHARD). Music seller and publisher, 140 New Bond Street, London, 1834-c. 1868. Continued as Richard Mills and Sons at same address, c. 1868-96; 57 Great Marlborough Street, 1897-1900; 16 Wells Street, Oxford Street, 1901-03. Richard Mills was a nephew of Robert Birchall; previously a partner in Birchall, Lonsdale and Mills, and Lonsdale and Mills.

MILSOM (CHARLES). Music seller, Argyle Street, Bath, c. 1825-50; at No. 14, c. 1825-29; at No. 2, c. 1840-50. Published a small amount of music; afterwards became C. Milsom and Sons.

MITCHELL (CHARLES). Music seller and publisher, London; 51 Southampton Row, Russell Square, c. 1808-14; 13 Southampton Row, c. 1814-25. Previously a partner in Lavenu and Mitchell, c. 1802-08; published in association with William Mitchell.
        K.

MITCHELL (JOHN). Bookseller, 33 Old Bond Street, London, c. 1831-89. Published a small amount of music.

MITCHELL (WILLIAM). Music seller and publisher, London; Mitchell's Musical Library and Instrument Warehouse, 159 New Bond Street, opposite Clifford Street, c. 1811-21; 28 New Bond Street, c. 1821-27. Published in association with Charles Mitchell.

MITCHISON (WILLIAM). Musician, music seller and publisher, Glasgow; 28 Buchanan Street, c. 1839-40; 42 Buchanan Street, c. 1840-1847; 112 Buchanan Street, c. 1847-50; 37 West Nile Street, c. 1850-1853. From c. 1849 traded as William Mitchison and Co.

MOIR. See Grant & Moir.

MOIR (JOHN). Printer, Edinburgh; Royal Bank Close, afterwards at 21 West Register Street. Printed between 1802 and 1828 a number of George Thomson's Collections of Scottish Songs, etc.

MONEY (JOHN). Stationer, at the Mitre in Mitre Court, Fleet Street, London. His name appears in the imprint as the seller of "Thesaurus Musicus: being a Collection of the newest Songs . . . To which is annexed a Collection of Aires, composed for two Flutes, by several Masters. The First Book . . . 1693 "; also the second book, 1694; the third book, 1695. His name appears in an advertisement, January 1695, "A Collection of new Ayres: Composed for two Flutes, with Sonatas. By some ingenious masters of the age. The First collection. Printed for J. Hudgebutt . . . J. Carr . . . and J. Money," etc.
  D. & M.

MONRO & MAY. Music and musical instrument sellers, and publishers, 11 Holborn Bars, near Middle Row, London, c. 1823-48. About 1839 called the "Western City Musical Repository"; John Monro was previously in business on his own account; partnership dissolved early in 1848, business continued by Harry May alone. Stock of music and music plates offered for sale by auction April 17, 1848. Some publications bear only the letters M. & M.
  K.
  Catalogue:—New Music. c. 1823. 1 p. fol. (Wm. C. Smith.)

MONRO (HENRY). Music seller and teacher of music, Pilgrim Street, Newcastle on Tyne. Published c. 1817, "A Set of Strathspeys, Allemandes &c. Arranged for the Piano Forte."

MONRO (JOHN). Music seller and publisher, 60 Skinner Street, Snow Hill, Holborn, London, c. 1815-23. Published some of his own compositions and other music; joined by Harry May and became Monro and May, c. 1823.
  K.

MONZANI & CIMADOR. Music sellers and publishers, London; 2 Pall Mall, early in 1800-c. 1803; 3 Old Bond Street, c. 1803-05. The partners were Tebaldo, or Theobald Monzani and Giambattista Cimador, whose real name was Cimadoro; also appeared incorrectly in the directories as Cringdon, Cundon and Cungdor.
  K. G.

MONZANI & CO. *See* Monzani & Hill; Monzani (Tebaldo) or (Theobald).

MONZANI & HILL. Musical instrument makers, music sellers and publishers, London; 3 Old Bond Street, c. 1807-13; 24 Dover Street, 1813-c. 1819; 28 Regent Street (Regent Circus), c. 1819-29. Had additional premises at 100 Cheapside; c. 1808-14. The firm also known as Monzani and Co.; T. Monzani was previously in business on his own account; partnership dissolved c. 1829 and business continued by Henry Hill.
  K. G.

Catalogues:—Flute Music. c. 1810. 1 p. fol. (B.M. g. 521. No. 1.);
Violin, Tenor, Violoncello Music. c. 1815. 1 p. fol. (B.M. g. 421.
(2.)); Flute Music. c. 1815. 2 pp. fol. (B.M. g. 521. No. 10.); Flute
Music. c. 1815. 2 pp. fol. (B.M. g. 521. No. 24.); Violin, Tenor,
Violoncello Music. c. 1820. 1 p fol. (B.M. Hirsch IV. 1111. (12.));
Catalogue thematique of L. V. Beethoven's Works. For the Piano
Forte. 2 pp. fol. c. 1820-25. (B.M. Hirsch IV. 1112. (5.))

MONZANI (TEBALDO) or (THEOBALD). Musical instrument maker
and musician, music seller and publisher, London. Published some
of his own compositions and other music from his various residences:
10 Princes Street, Cavendish Square, 1787-88; in 1789 and 1790
his publications were printed and sold for him by James Ball,
1 Duke Street, Grosvenor Square; 6 Coventry Street, corner of
Coventry Court, Haymarket, 1792; 6 Great Marlborough Street,
1793; 16 Down Street, Piccadilly, 1795; 5 Hamilton Street, Piccadilly, 1796 to February 1798; 2 Pall Mall, February 1798 to early in
1800. Became Monzani and Cimador, 2 Pall Mall, early in 1800-
c. 1803; 3 Old Bond Street, c. 1803-05. Partnership dissolved and
Monzani continued the business alone at 3 Old Bond Street (The Opera
Music Warehouse) c. 1805-07, when it became Monzani and Co.
afterwards Monzani and Hill. Died June, 1839, aged 77.
K. G.
Catalogues:—Music. c. 1799. 2 pp. fol. (B.M. g. 521. a. (2.)
No. 5.); Catalogue thematique of Mozart's Works. c. 1805. 2 pp.
fol. (B.M. 7896. h. 40. (12.)); Vocal Italian Music. c. 1806. 6 pp.
fol. (B.M. 7896. h. 40. (11.)); Flute Music. c. 1807. 1 p. fol. (B.M.
g. 521. No. 22.); Instrumental Music. Monzani & Co. c. 1807.
6 pp. fol. (B.M. 7896. h. 40. (11a.))

MOODY (T.). Music engraver, London? Engraved "Julliens' Album
for 1848."

MOON (FREDERICK). See Duncombe & Moon.

MOORE, *Mr.* 2 Bridgewater Square, Barbican, London. His name appears
in the imprint of "Six Easy Lessons for the Harpsichord. Compos'd
by Bartholomew Davis. Opera Primo. London. Printed for and
sold by the Author, at Mr. Moore's," etc., c. 1775.

MOORE (G.). See Ayre (R.) & Moore (G.).

MOORE (THOMAS). Printer, London. c. 1685-91. Printed a small
number of musical works, some in conjunction with Francis Clark or
Clarke and John Heptinstall.
P. II. D. & M.

MORELAND. See Smart & Moreland.

MORGAN (I.).   Engraver and printer, Bristol.   Engraved and printed "A Grand March . . . of the Bath Volunteer Association by . . . C. Henry Seine.   To be had at the Authors . . . Bath . . . Engrav'd & printed for the Author by I. Morgan, Bristol," c. 1805.

MORGAN (JOHN).   Half-Moon Alley, the third House from Bishopsgate Street, London.   His name appears in the imprint of "The Divine Musical Miscellany.   Being, a Collection of Psalm, and Hymn Tunes: great part of which were never before in Print.   London.   Printed by Wm. Smith and sold at Mr. John Morgan's in Half-Moon Alley, the 3ᵈ. House from Bishopsgate Street," c. 1740; another edition was printed by R. Williamson, 1754.

MORGAN (WILLIAM C.).   Bookseller and Stationer, 20 Henrietta Street, Cavendish Square, London.   Published c. 1840, "So oder so, German Ballad, with English translation, edited by Edward Clare."

MORI & LAVENU.   Music sellers and publishers, 28 New Bond Street, London, c. 1828-39.   The partners were Elizabeth Lavenu and Nicholas Mori.   When Nicholas Mori died in 1839, Louis Henry Lavenu, the son of Elizabeth, continued the business.
K. G. (Lavenu.)

MORI (NICHOLAS).   *See* Mori & Lavenu.

MORLEY (THOMAS).   Musician, Little St. Helen's, London.   Acquired from Queen Elizabeth a monopoly patent September 28, 1598, for printing and importation of music, with which in some way Christopher Heybourn was also concerned.   Morley was not a printer although one work, Richard Carlton's "Madrigals to Fiue Voyces" 1601, has the imprint "Printed by Thomas Morley, dwelling in Little Saint Helens."   William Barley, Thomas Este and Peter Short printed a number of works as the assignes of Thomas Morley, including Morley's own works.   Barley, who had a shop in Gracechurch (Gracious) Street, printed under Morley's direction at the latter's address in Little St. Helen's, the works being sold at Barley's shop in Gracechurch Street.   Morley died in 1603.   Barley continued printing until c. 1614.
K. G. S.

MORRIS (MICHAEL).   Music seller and pianoforte maker, 55 Union Street, Aberdeen, c. 1820-30.   Previously a partner in the business of Davie and Morris.

MORTELLARI (MICHELE C.).   Music seller and publisher, 51 Oxford Street, London.   Published "Twelve Italian Vocal Pieces, for one and two voices, composed . . . by A. Mortellari", c. 1803; "Twelve Arrietts . . . by Sig. Antonio Mortellari", c. 1805; "A Day and a Night, a ludicrous Anecdote by Mr. Melodioso . . . The music . . .

composed and arranged for the piano forte . . . by F. Fiorillo. Op. 33. London Published for the Author . . . and M. C. Mortellari ", etc., c. 1805.

MORTIMER. *See* Paterson, Mortimer & Co.

MORTON & CO. Music printers and publishers, 148 New Bond Street, opposite Conduit Street, London, c. 1837-?. Succeeded John Dean.

MOSELEY or MOSLEY (HUMPHREY). Bookseller, at the Princes Arms, St. Paul's Churchyard, London, 1630-61. (P.) His name appears in the imprint of "Choice Psalmes put into Musick for Three Voices . . . Compos'd by Henry and William Lawes . . . London, Printed by James Young, for Humphrey Moseley . . . and for Richard Wodenothe . . . 1648 "; published "Ayres and Dialogues. (To be sung to the Theorbo-Lute or Bass-Viol.) By John Gamble . . . London, Printed by W. Godbid for Humphry Mosley . . . 1657 "; "The Psalmes of David, from the new translation of the Bible turned into Meter: To be sung after the old tunes used in the churches. London, Printed by Ed. Griffin, and are sold by Humphrey Moseley . . . 1651."
    P. I. D. & M.

MOSES (MARCUS). Music and musical instrument seller and publisher, Dublin; 4 Westmoreland Street, c. 1831-60. Had additional premises at 60 and 61 Fleet Street, c. 1840-45; 5 Westmoreland Street, c. 1845-1860; 40 and 41 Fleet Street, c. 1845-60. Succeeded William Power.

MOTT (ISAAC HENRY ROBERT). Composer, music seller and teacher of the pianoforte, Music Saloon, New Steine, 141 North Street, Brighton, c. 1813-18. Continued as Mott and Co., pianoforte makers, London; 95 Pall Mall, c. 1818-20; 92 Pall Mall, c. 1820-42, with additional premises at 135 Oxford Street, c. 1830-35; 76 Strand, c. 1842-55. Mott published some of his own compositions; was inventor and patentee of the "Sostenente Piano Forte."

MOTTA & BALL. Pianoforte makers, music sellers and publishers, 1 Duke Street, Grosvenor Square, London, c. 1794. The partners were Domenico Motta and James Ball.
    See also Ball (James).

MOTTA (DOMENICO). *See* Motta & Ball.

MOTTE (BENJAMIN). Printer and bookseller, London, c. 1687-1738; Aldersgate Street; Middle Temple Gate, Fleet Street. (P.) Printed for Henry Playford, "The Theater of Music: or, A Choice Collection of the newest and best Songs sung at the Court, and Public Theaters . . . The fourth and last book . . . 1687."
    P. II. D. & M.

MOUNTAIN (HENRY). Violinist, music seller and publisher, Dublin; 20 Whitefriar Street, c. 1784-90; 44 Grafton Street, c. 1790-94. Succeeded by Joseph Kearns.
K. G.

MUFF (JOSHUA). Music seller, Commercial Street, Leeds; at No. 17, c. 1810-25; at No. 12, c. 1825-30; at No. 16, c. 1830-46. Published a small amount of music.
K.

MUIR, WOOD & CO. Musical instrument makers, music sellers and publishers, Edinburgh; 16 George Street, c. 1798-1803; 7 Leith Street, c. 1803-10; 13 Leith Street, c. 1810-18. Principal partners were John Muir and Andrew Wood; succeeded James Muir; succeeded by Wood, Small and Co.
K.

MUIR (JAMES). Music seller and publisher, 16 George Street, Edinburgh, c. 1796-98. Succeeded by Muir, Wood and Co.

MUIR (JOHN). *See* Muir, Wood & Co.

MÜLLER (JOHANN MARTIN). *See* Hamilton & Müller.

MUNDAY. *See* Dean & Munday.

MUNDAY (J.) *Junior*. Printer, Oxford. Printed "The Psalms and Hymns taken from the Morning and Evening Service . . . and the Chants to which they are sung in the Church of St. Peter-in-the-East, Oxford. Oxford: Printed by J. Munday, jun. Published by W. Graham . . . 1838."

MUNDELL & SON. Printers, Edinburgh. Printed by and for, "The Edinburgh Musical Miscellany: a collection of the most approved Scotch, English, and Irish Songs, set to music. The second edition . . . 1804."

MURGATROYD (JOSEPH). Bookseller, 73 Chiswell Street, London. Published "A Collection of Psalm Tunes for publick Worship. Adapted to Dr. Watts's Psalms and Hymns . . . By Stephen Addington. D.D. The eleventh edition; corrected & enlarged (Supplement, etc.) . . . 1792"; also published the twelfth edition in 1797, and thirteenth edition in 1799. His name is in the imprint of "A Collection of approved Anthems, selected from the most eminent Masters; by Stephen Addington. The second edition. Printed for the Author, and sold by him . . . also by J. Murgatroyd . . . 1795."
K.

MURRAY (ALEXANDER). *See* Sands, Donaldson, Murray, & Cochran.

MURRAY (JOHN). Bookseller and publisher, The Ship, 32 Fleet Street, London, 1768-93. (P.) His name appears in the imprint of "The Gentle Shepherd; a Pastoral Comedy; By Allan Ramsay. Glasgow: printed by A. Foulis, and sold by . . . J. Murray . . . London. MDCCLXXXVIII."
P. III.

MUSIC PUBLISHING CO. *See* Davidson (George Henry).

N., T. Printer, London. Printed "The Whole Booke of Psalms collected into English Meeter by Thomas Sternhold, John Hopkins, and others . . . with apt notes to sing them withall . . . London, T. N. for the Company of Stationers, 1669."

N., W. *See* Napier (William).

NAISH (T.). Goldsmith, cutler and music seller, Bristol. His name appears in the imprint of "Twenty Psalm Tunes in three Parts . . . Composed by the late Mr. Coombes and other eminent Masters. London. Engraved and printed by Longman, Lukey & Co. for T. Naish, Goldsmith, Cutler and Music seller in Bristol", c. 1775.

NAPIER. *See* Niven, Napier & Khull.

NAPIER (GUGLIELMO). *See* Napier (William).

NAPIER (WILLIAM). Music seller and publisher, London; the corner of Lancaster Court, 474 Strand, c. 1772-March, 1791; 49 Great Queen Street, March, 1791-c. 1800 ; 8 Lisle Street, Leicester Square, c. 1800-1809; Princes Street, Leicester Square, c. 1809. His name appears as "Guglielmo Napier" in the imprint of "Sei Divertimenti per due violini . . . da Luigi Borghi. Op. IIIª.", c. 1780; established a circulating musical library early in 1784; Joseph Dale issued a catalogue of music c. 1785 in which he stated that he had purchased some plates, copyrights and copies of the books from William Napier for £450. Napier became bankrupt in 1791; some single sheet songs bear only the initials W. N. George Smart was for a time employed by Napier.
K.
Catalogues:—c. 1778. 2 pp. fol. (B.M. H. 348. d. (3.)); c. 1780. fol. (Haas, Catalogue 20. No. 590.)

NEALE or NEAL (JOHN). Musical instrument maker, music printer, music seller and publisher of engraved music, Christ Church Yard, Dublin, 1721-34. In 1729, or earlier, his son, William, was taken into partnership, and continued the business on the death of John Neale in 1734.
K. G.

NEALE or NEAL (WILLIAM). Music seller and publisher of engraved music, Christ Church Yard, Dublin, 1734-41. He was previously in partnership with his father, John Neale, or Neal and continued the business commenced by his father; gave up publishing in 1741 and became the managing director and treasurer of "The Musick Hall" in Fishamble Street, Dublin, in which Handel's Messiah was performed for the first time on 13th April (Rehearsal 8th April), 1742; Neale died December 18, 1769. Published one or two works in conjunction with William Mainwaring, c. 1740.
> K. G.

NEILSON (JOHN). Printer, Paisley. Printed "The Psalm Singer's Assistant. Being a collection of the most approved Psalm and Hymn tunes, mostly in four parts. Selected from the best authors . . . By Robert Gilmour, Teacher of music, Paisley. The second edition, with improvements. MDCCXCIII."

NELSON (SIDNEY). Composer, music seller and publisher, London; 61 Greek Street, Soho, c. 1843 to September 1844; 28 New Bond Street, September 1844-47, premises formerly occupied by L. H. Lavenu. Was a partner in the business of Jefferys and Nelson, c. 1840-43.

NETHERWOOD (R.) Printer, Gloucester. Printed c. 1750, "Six Canzonets. For three voices. With a figured base for the organ or harpsichord. By Benjamin Thomas. Printed by R. Netherwood for the Author, Gloucester."

NEWBERY (FRANCIS). *See* Carnan (Thomas) & Newbery (Francis).

NEWBERY (JOHN). Bookseller, Reading, 1730-44. (P.) London; at the Bible and Crown, Without Temple Bar, 1744-45; at the Bible and Sun, St. Paul's Churchyard, 1746-67. Published "Universal Harmony or, the Gentleman and Ladie's Social Companion . . . 1745," issued in parts, 1744-45; later edition published with the imprint "London, Printed for the Proprietors, & sold by J. Newbery . . . 1746"; advertised June 1747, "The Temple of Apollo; or, The Theatre of the Muses. For the month of April, 1747. By a Society of Gentlemen . . . Printed for the Society, and sold by J. Newbery," etc.; his name appears in the imprint of "A Sett of New Psalms and Anthems . . . By William Knapp . . . The Third edition . . . London . . . 1747"; also in the fourth edition, 1750; the sixth edition, 1754; the seventh edition, 1762. On his death in 1767, the business was continued by Thomas Carnan in partnership with Francis Newbery, son of John Newbery.
> K. P. III.

NEWBOROUGH (THOMAS). Bookseller, London, 1686-1707; at the Star, St. Paul's Churchyard; at the Golden Ball, St. Paul's Church-

yard. (P.) Published "The Christians Daily Manual of Prayers and Praises. In two parts . . . The Second containing a course of select psalms and hymns, with their proper tunes . . . London, Printed by J. Heptinstall for Tho. Newborough at the Golden Ball in St. Paul's Church Yard, 1703."
P. II.

NEWLAND & JOHNSTON. Music sellers and publishers, 36 Southampton Row, London, c. 1818-20.
K.

NEWLAND (R.). 6 Pall Mall, London. Printed and sold c. 1820, "La Biondina in gondoleta. A favourite Venetian canzonett . . . by Geo. F. Cooke."

NEWMAN. See Lane, Newman & Co.

NEWMAN (ANTHONY KING) & CO. Booksellers, 32 and 33 Leadenhall Street, London. Published with Dean and Munday "The London Minstrel: a collection of esteemed English, Irish, and Scotch Songs . . . written, selected, and arranged by a professional gentleman. London. Printed for Dean and Munday . . . and A. K. Newman and Co . . . 1825."

NEWMAN (DORMAN). Bookseller, at the King's Arms in the Poultry, and at other addresses, London, 1665-94. (P.) Published "Synopsis of Vocal Musick: containing the rudiments of singing rightly any Harmonical Song . . . Whereunto are added several Psalms and Songs of three parts. Composed by English and Italian authors . . . By A. B. Philo-Mus . . . 1680."
P. II. D. & M.

NEWTON (T.). Music seller? The Corner of Maiden Lane, London. His name appears in an advertisement June 1759, of "Eight Sonatas, or Lessons for the Harpsichord. By Mr. Gillier, Junior. Opera Terza. Printed for the Author . . . likewise of . . . T. Newton," etc.

NIBERT (J. P.). Penzance. Published c. 1825, "The First Set of Cornish Quadrilles . . . Composed by William Harrison, late Master in the band of the Cornish Yeomanry Cavalry."

NICHOLLS (GEORGE). Musician, Cambridge. His name appears in the imprint of "Hymn performed during a Service for the Benefit of the British Prisoners in France, the words & melody by the Revd. Edward Daniel Clarke . . . with an organ part by John Clarke . . . London Printed for Geoe. Nicholls Cambridge by Wilkinson & Co. (Late Broderip & Wilkinson)," etc., c. 1810.

[243]

NICHOLSON (GEORGE). Bookseller and printer, Stourport. Published "The British Orpheus; being a Selection of two hundred and seventy Songs and Airs, adapted for the Voice, Violin, German Flute, Flagelet," c. 1810; "The Young Musician, or the Science of Music, familiarly explained . . . By N. Swaine," 1818. In 1799 Nicholson was at Ludlow, and in 1801-02 at Ploughmill, near Ludlow, from which places he issued many daintily printed volumes of ballads, songs, etc., generally illustrated with charming engravings and woodcuts of the Bewick School.
    K.

NICHOLSON (JOHN). Bookseller, at the King's (Queen's) Arms, Little Britain, London, 1686-1715. (P.) His name appears in the imprint of "The Compleat French Master, for Ladies and Gentlemen . . . The Second edition . . . London, Printed for R. Sare . . . and John Nicholson . . . 1699"; contains the music of "A Collection of new French Songs, &c."; his name also appears on the fourth edition, 1707; the fifth in 1710, and the seventh in 1717. Published with John Sprint "Devotions in the ancient Way of Offices . . . Reformed by a Person of Quality . . . The Second edition. (The Tunes to the Hymns.) London: Printed by T. Mead . . . 1701"; also the third edition. 1706.
    P. II. D. & M.

NICOLL (W.) Bookseller, London, 1761-c. 1777, Paper Mill, in St. Paul's Churchyard; 51 St. Paul's Churchyard. (P.) His name appears in the imprint of "The Beggar's Opera . . . To which is prefixed the overture in score: And the musick to each song. London: Printed for W. Strahan, T. Lowndes, T. Caslon, W. Griffin, W. Nicoll, S. Bladon, and G. Kearsly. MDCCLXXI."; also in two editions published 1777.
    P. III.

NIVEN, NAPIER & KHULL. Printers, Trongate, Glasgow. Printed "A Collection of Psalm Tunes, Hymns and Anthems . . . carefully selected and arranged by Allan Houston", etc., c. 1808.

NORMAN, *Mrs.* Music seller, St. Paul's Churchyard, London. Her name appears in the list of subscribers to Volume 1 and 2 of "A Pocket Companion for Gentlemen and Ladies", engraved and printed by Cluer, 1724-25. Her name also appears in an advertisement March 1730, "To be sold by Auction, This Day the 23rd instant, at the Church Coffee-House in St. Paul's Church-Yard, A Choice Collection of Musical Instruments, being the stock of the late Mr. Barak Norman . . . Catalogues to be had at the Widow Norman's in St. Paul's Church Yard," etc.
    K.

NORMAN (BARAK). Musical instrument maker and music seller, London. His name appears in an advertisement April 1699, "The Compleat Violist; or, An Introduction to the playing on the Bass-Viol . . . Also several lessons, composed . . . by . . . Benjamin Hely. Sold by J. Hare . . . and by B. Norman at the Bass-Viol in St. Paul's Alley", etc.; also March 1730, "To be sold by Auction, This Day the 23rd instant, at the Church Coffee-House in St. Paul's Church-Yard, A Choice Collection of Musical Instruments, being the stock of the late Mr. Barak Norman . . . Catalogues to be had at the Widow Norman's in St. Paul's Church Yard", etc. His widow had taken over the business by 1724.
    K.

NORMAN (THOMAS). Bookseller, at the Pope's Head, against the Castle Tavern, Fleet Street, London. His name appears in an advertisement December 1680, "The Book of Songs with a thorough Basse to them for Instrument [sic], Set and composed by Signior Pietro Reggio, Engraven in copper, in a very large folio, most of them out of Mr. Abraham Cowley's excellent Poems, are to be had only at Mr. Thomas Norman's . . . and at Mr. Lord's Shop at the Duke of Monmouth's Head, in Westminster Hall." (D. & M. No. 52.)
    P. II.

NORTH (R.). Engraver and printer, Charlotte Street, Fitzroy Square, London. Engraved and printed "L'Orpheline. Romance with an Accompaniment for the Piano Forte composed . . . by Mlle. Annette de Lihu, c. 1817."

NORTON (JOHN). Printer, London, 1621-45. (P.) Printed "Siren Coelistis centum harmoniarum, duarum, trium, & quatuor vocum. Quam . . . in lucem dedit, Georgius Victorinus Monachij. Eandem, methodo docendi, et discendi musicam longè facillima . . . Willihelmus Bray-thwaitus Anglus . . . communicavit, & commendavit. Editio altera correctior & melior. Londini. Ex typographeo Iohannis Norton. 1638."
    P. I.

NOTARY (JULIAN) & BARBIER (JEAN). Printers, London, various addresses. (D.) In 1498 printed at Westminster for Wynkyn de Worde a Sarum Missal containing staves from blocks, leaving notes to be filled in by hand.
    D. S.

NOTT (WILLIAM). Bookseller, at the King and Queen's Arms, turning into St. James's Square, Pall Mall, London. Sold "Albion and Albanius: an Opera. Or, Representation in Musick. Set by Lewis Grabu . . . 1687"; "A Collection of several Simphonies and Airs in three Parts; composed for Violins Flute and Hoe-boys. Printed for all lovers of musick . . . 1688."

    P. II. D. & M.

NOVELLO & CO. Music sellers, printers and publishers, successors to Joseph Alfred Novello, London; 69 Dean Street, Soho, 1861-67; 1 Berners Street, December 1867-near the end of 1906, where the printing was also done for a short time after removal, but was soon transferred to the old publishing house at 69 Dean Street, 70 Dean Street being acquired later in addition; from 1898 to the present day printing works have been in Hollen Street. The publishing business has been carried on at 160 Wardour Street from 1906 to the present time. The firm retained the additional premises formerly occupied by Joseph Alfred Novello at 35 Poultry from November 1861-June 1876, and had premises at 80 and 81 Queen Street, Cheapside, June 1876-1905. The bindery was from 1878 at 111 and 113 Southwark Street, No. 115 being added a little later. In 1871 a new music store was opened at 751 Broadway, New York. In 1884 a branch under the firm's own direction was established at 129 Fifth Avenue, New York. In 1867 the firm of Ewer and Co. was acquired and the name became Novello, Ewer and Co., until 1898, when it reverted to Novello and Co. In 1906 the New York business was handed over to H. W. Gray and Co.

    K. G.

    See Bibliography for works dealing with the firm of Novello and Co.

NOVELLO, EWER & CO. *See* Novello & Co.

NOVELLO (JOSEPH ALFRED). Music seller, printer and publisher, son of Vincent Novello, London; 67 Frith Street, Soho, 1829-34; 69 Dean Street, 1834-61, the firm being occasionally known up to 1845 as "The Sacred Music Warehouse". In 1847 Novello established his own printing house at 69 Dean Street, the address of which was given in his "Some account of the Methods of Musick Printing" as "Dean's Yard, over against Dean Street, near Soho Square." Had additional premises at "The Golden Crotchet," 24 Poultry, May 1845-July 1856, the firm being known at both addresses as "The London Sacred Music Warehouse"; 35 Poultry, corner of Grocer's Hall, July 1856-61. In August 1852 established a branch at 389 Broadway, New York, the American business having been conducted previously through agencies. In 1859 the New York branch was at Clinton Hall, Astor Place. J. A. Novello took Henry Littleton into partnership November 1861, the firm becoming Novello and Co. In 1866 Henry Littleton became sole proprietor, retiring from active direction at the beginning of 1887. In 1849 purchased plates of musical works from the stock of Coventry and Hollier, and in 1851, 4780 plates of sacred works at the sale of the stock-in-trade of Charles

Coventry, besides some 1427 plates of the newly engraved edition of Mozart's pianoforte works, edited by Cipriani Potter.

K. G.

See also Novello & Co.

NOVELLO (VINCENT). Organist, London, edited and arranged various collections of sacred music, some of which he published himself from 1811-28. In 1829 his son Joseph Alfred commenced business as a music seller and publisher at 67 Frith Street, Soho, his first important work being a continuation of "Purcell's Sacred Music," begun by his father, December 1828 and completed in October 1832.

See also Novello (Joseph Alfred).

NOYER (PETER du). *See* Dunoyer.

NOYES. Bookseller? Andover. Name appears in the imprint of "The Psalms of David . . . By I. Watts . . . A new edition, corrected. (Tunes in the Tenor Part fitted to the several Metres.) Salisbury: Printed and sold by Collins and Johnson. Sold also by . . . Noyes, at Andover . . . MDCCLXXVI."

NUTT (EDWARD). Bookseller, Royal Exchange, London, 1725-c. 1730. (P.) Advertised and sold a number of musical works.

P. III.

NUTT (ELIZABETH). Printer, in the Savoy, London, c. 1717-38. (P.) Printed "A Supplement to the New Version of Psalms by Dr. Brady and Mr. Tate . . . and tunes . . . The Seventh edition. In the Savoy. Printed by Eliz. Nutt . . . 1717"; also the Eighth edition, 1717. Presumably widow of John Nutt and his successor.

P. III.

NUTT (JOHN). Printer and bookseller, London; near Stationers Hall, c. 1690-1706; in the Savoy, c. 1707-10 or later. (P.) Printed, published and sold a number of musical works. Presumably succeeded by Elizabeth Nutt.

P. II. D. & M.

O., N. *See* Okes (Nicholas).

OAKLEY (THOMAS). Bookseller, Blandford. Published "English Melodies . . . The Airs, symphonies & accompaniments, composed by Miss Smith of Down House, Blandford. Blandford, Published by T. Oakley; and London, by Mori & Lavenu," etc. c. 1834. He also issued a second edition.

OGG (JAMES). Bookseller, stationer, and music seller, 12 South St. Andrews Street, Edinburgh. His name appears in the imprint of "Lady Cathcarts Reel and The Lake of Killarney. Two favorite airs arranged as rondo's for the piano forte by T. H. Butler. Edinburgh. Publish'd by the Author and sold by Mr. Ogg, Bookseller, stationer, and music seller", etc. c. 1805.

OGLE (JOSEPH). Bookseller, Leeds. His name appears in the imprint of "A Book of Psalmody . . . The Fifth edition . . . By John Chetham. London: Printed by A. Pearson, for Joseph Lord . . . in Wakefield . . . and sold by . . . Joseph Ogle . . . in Leeds . . . MDCCXXXVI."

OKELL (BENJAMIN). *See* Dicey (William).

OKES (JOHN). Printer, Little St. Bartholomews near Smithfield, London, 1636-44. (P.) Son of Nicholas Okes; printed "The Whole Book of Psalmes. Collected into English Meeter by Thomas Sternhold, Iohn Hopkins, and others . . . with apt notes to sing them withall . . . London Printed by I. Okes, for the Company of Stationers. 1640."
P. I.

OKES (NICHOLAS). Printer, London, 1606-39; at the sign of the Hand, near Holborn Bridge, 1613; in Foster Lane. (M.) Printe d"The Triumphs of Truth. A Solemnity . . . at the confirmation . . . of . . . Sir Thomas Middleton . . . in the . . . office of . . . Lord Maior of . . . London October 29, 1613 . . . Directed, written, and redeem'd into forme, from the ignorance of some former times . . . By Thomas Middleton . . . 1613"; contains the music of one song; "The Triumphs of Truth . . . Shewing also his Lordships Entertainment upon Michaelmas day last . . . 1613"; contains the music of one song; "The Maske of Flowers. Presented by the Gentlemen of Graies-Inne at the Court of Whitehall, in the Banquetting House, upon Twelfe Night, 1613. Being the last of the solemnities . . . which were performed at the marriage of . . . the Earle of Somerset and the Lady Francis daughter of the Earle of Suffolke, Lord Chamberlaine. London Printed by N. O. for Robert Wilson . . . 1614"; contains the music; "Tes Irenes Trophæa. Or, The Tryumphs of Peace. That celebrated the Solemnity of the right Honorable Sr Francis Iones Knight, at his Inauguration into Maioraltic of London . . . the 30. of October, 1620," etc.; contains the music of a two-part song.
M. S.

OLIVER & BOYD. Printers and publishers, Edinburgh. Partners were Thomas Oliver and George Boyd. Printed and published a number of song books with music, including "The Caledonian Musical Repository," 1811; "The Scottish Minstrel," c. 1812, also editions in 1813 and 1814; "Albyn's Anthology . . . Collected and arranged by Alexander Campbell," Vol. 1, 1816. Vol. 2, 1818; "The English Minstrel," c. 1825. Also printed for, and published in conjunction with Lane, Newman and Co., and B. Crosby and Co., both of London, a small number of song books with music.
K.

"Clio and Euterpe". Engraved and sold by Henry Roberts. 1756-62

NANCY, *The words by Mr. Robinson.* 1

Vivace

No Nymph who grac'd *Arcadia's* plains as love-fick Bards declare, In-

voking *Phœbus* melting ftrains, with *Nancy* can compare; with *Nancy* can com-

pare; Bright *Nancy's* graces who can fee and

not a_dore her more Than *Jove Olympus Queen* when fhe the *Paphian* Girdle

wore. the *Paphian* Girdle wore.

2

That magic *Zone,* whofe mighty fpells
Enhanc'd her radiant charms;
And raptur'd funk, as *Homer* tells,
Heav'n's Thund'rer in her Arms;
But when the Gods all piercing Eye
The cheat divine explor'd,
His indignation fhook the Sky,
And he no more ador'd.

3

Had *Nancy* with her matchlefs fway
The Goddefs place fupply'd;
Troys Tow'rs had fall'n in duft that day,
And Godlike *Hector* dy'd:
E'en *Mars* had he my *Nancy* feen,
Tranfported with her charms,
For her had left the Cyprian Queen,
Prefering *Nancy's* Arms.

Edward Miller, "A Collection of New English Songs and a Cantata.
Printed and sold by John Johnson. c. 1760

OLLIVIER & CO. *See* Ollivier (Robert Wilby).

OLLIVIER (CHARLES). Music and musical instrument seller and publisher, 41 New Bond Street, London, 1837-53. Had additional premises at 42 New Bond Street, 1844-53; for a time c. 1848-51, became Charles and Robert Ollivier.

OLLIVIER (CHARLES) & (ROBERT). Music and musical instrument sellers and publishers, 41 and 42 New Bond Street, London, c. 1848-51. Robert withdrew c. 1851 and went into business on his own account.

OLLIVIER (JOHN). Bookseller, publisher and stationer, 59 Pall Mall, London, c. 1839-55. Published a small amount of sacred music.

OLLIVIER (ROBERT WILBY). Music seller, publisher and concert agent, London; 19 Old Bond Street, c. 1851-70; 39 Old Bond Street, c. 1870-72; 38 Old Bond Street, c. 1872-92. Some publications bear the imprint "Ollivier & Co."; previously with the firm of Charles and Robert Ollivier; during the later years became solely a concert and theatre ticket agent.

ONELY (WILLIAM). *See* Onley.

ONLEY (WILLIAM). Printer, London, c. 1694-1709; Little Britain; Bond's Stables, near Chancery Lane. (P.) His name appears in the imprint of "A Collection of French Songs to the Newest and best French and English Tunes. London: Printed by W. Onely, for T. Salusbury," which forms part of "The Compleat French-Master, for Ladies and Gentlemen . . . By A. Boyer . . . London: Printed for Tho. Salusbury . . . 1694."
P. II. D. & M.

ORTON. *See* Smith (William Hawkes).

OSBORN (JOHN). Bookseller and publisher, London, 1711-39; Oxford Arms in Lombard Street (P.); at the Golden Ball, Paternoster Row, 1734 or earlier. His name appears in the imprints of a number of sacred music works; advertised November 1734 and December 1737, "Lately published; curiously printed in six neat pocket volumes . . . The Musical Miscellany. Being a collection of choice songs and lyrick poems. Set to musick by the most eminent masters with the basses to each tune, and transposed to the flute," etc. This was presumably the work originally issued by John Watts, 1729-31.
P. II.

OSBORN or OSBORNE (THOMAS). Bookseller, Gray's Inn, London, 1702-43. (P.) His name appears in the imprint of "A Treatise of the Natural Grounds, and Principles of Harmony. By William

I

Holder . . . To which is added, by way of appendix: Rules for playing a Thorow-Bass . . . By the late Mr. Godfrey Keller . . . London: Printed by W. Pearson . . . for J. Wilcox . . . and T. Osborne . . . 1731." Published "The Decoy: an Opera. As it is acted at the New Theatre in Goodman's Fields . . . London: Printed for, and sold by T. Osborn . . . MDCCXXXIII."; with the music of the airs.

P. II.

OSWALD (JAMES). Musician, music seller and publisher. In 1734 he was a dancing master at Dunfermline where he published "A Collection of Minuets . . . Composed by James Oswald, Dancing Master"; from 1736-40 was in Edinburgh where he published "A Curious Collection of Scots Tunes," etc. Removed to London early in 1741, gave music lessons and probably worked for John Simpson, who published some of his compositions; Oswald was in business for himself as music seller and publisher at St. Martin's Churchyard (on the Pavement St. Martin's Churchyard, St. Martin's Church, at the Corner of St. Martin's Lane), 1747-c. 1762 or a few years later, and the business may have been acquired by Straight and Skillern, who republished some of Oswald's works at 17 St. Martin's Lane, 1769-c. 1778. Oswald was one of a small group of musicians known as "The Society of the Temple of Apollo." He died in January 1769 and was buried at Knebworth.

K. G.

Frank Kidson:—James Oswald, Dr. Burney and the Temple of Apollo. (*The Musical Antiquary*. October, 1910. pp. 34-41.)

OSWALD (JOHN). Bookseller and publisher, London, 1726-53; White's Alley, Chancery Lane; Rose and Crown, in the Poultry. (P.) Published in conjunction with J. Buckland "The Psalms of David . . . By I. Watts . . . The Fifteenth edition . . . (Tunes in the Tenor part fitted to the several metres.) London. Printed for J. Oswald, in the Poultry, and J. Buckland . . . MDCCXLVIII."

P. III.

OULTON (RICHARD). Printer, near Christ Church, [Newgate Street,] London, 1633-43. (P.) Printed "A Psalme of Thanks-giving to be sung by the Children of Christs Hospitall, on Monday in the Easter Holy-dayes, at S. Maries Spittle, for their Founders and Benefactors . . . 1641 "; "A Psalme of Thanks-giving to be sung by the Children of Christs Hospitall on Tuesday in the Easter Holy-dayes at S. Maries Spittle, for their Founders and Benefactors . . . 1641."

P. I.

OWEN (WILLIAM). Book and music seller, and publisher, Homer's Head, between the Temple Gates, Fleet Street, afterwards numbered 11 Fleet Street, London, 1748-93. (P.) Published a small amount of music.

K. P. III.

P., A. *See* Portal (Ab.).

P., E. *See* Paxton (Edmund).

P., I.; P., J. *See* Preston (John).

P., J. *See* Godbid (Anne) & Playford (John) *the Younger*.

P., T. *See* Purfoot (Thomas).

P., W. *See* Pearson (William).

PAINE & HOPKINS. Music and musical instrument sellers, and publishers, 69 Cornhill, London, c. 1821-36. Robert Cocks and Co.
purchased some of their copyrights and plates in 1836.
K.

PAINE (JOHN). Musician and musical instrument maker, 23 Tichborne
Street, top of the Hay Market, London. Published "John Paine's
Annual Collection of twenty-four Country Dances, for 1807."

PAISAN, *Mr.* At the Half Moon, Compton Street, Soho, London. His
name appears in the imprint of "Six Sonatas or Trio's for two
Violins or German Flutes with the Thorough Bass for the Harpsichord.
Compos'd by Signor Domenico Ferrari. To be had of John Lavo
at Mr. Paisan's", etc., advertised October 1757.

PALMER (JOHN B.). Music seller, 16 Bold Street, Liverpool. Published
c. 1835, "Serenade, Dearest Love I watch for thee . . . Composer
James May."

PANORMO (LOUIS). Musical instrument maker and music seller, High
Street, St. Giles, Bloomsbury, London, c. 1820-47. Published a
small amount of music.

PARAMORE (G.). North Green, Worship Street, London. Printed,
"Four Anthems adapted for Public Worship . . . To which are added
sixteen Psalm or Hymn Tunes . . . By John Beaumont "; preface is
dated Dec. 3, 1793.

PARKER (EDMUND). Bookseller, London, 1704-39; at the Bible and
Crown in Lombard Street, near St. Mary Wolnoth's Church, or, near
Stocks Market; under the Royal Exchange. (P.) His name appears
in the imprint of "The Devout Singer's Guide; containing all the
common tunes now in use, with select portions of the psalms adapted
to each tune, and rules for singing treble and bass . . . Recommended
by Daniel Warner . . . London, Printed for S. S. and sold by Edmund
Parker, at the Bible and Crown in Lombard Street, and John Hare

. . . 1711 "; also advertised the fourth edition with directions by
S. Shenton.
P. II, III.

PARKER (HENRY). In Bull Head Court, Jewin Street, London. Published "The Jealous Clown: or, The Lucky Mistake. An Opera (of one act) . . . By Thomas Gataker, Gent. To which is annex'd the musick . . . 1730."

PARKER (JOHN WILLIAM). Publisher, 445 West Strand, London, c. 1832-51. Published a number of musical works; continued as John W. Parker and Son, c. 1851-61.

PARKER (RICHARD). Bookseller, at the Unicorn under the Piazza of the Royal Exchange, Cornhill, London, 1692-c. 1725. (P.) Published the numbers for February 1692 to December 1693 of "The Gentleman's Journal: or the Monthly Miscellany . . . Consisting of news, history, philosophy, poetry, musick, translations, &c."
P. II. D. & M.

PARKER (WILLIAM). Music engraver, London. Engraved at 15 Hertford Street, Fitzroy Square, "Sonata, O Nanny wilt thou gang with me to which is added a Capriccio à la russe for the Piano Forte . . . Composed by John Watlen. Op. 13. Printed for the Author . . . London," c. 1808; at 4 Warren Street, Fitzroy Square, "He's dear dear to me tho' he's far far away. A favorite antient Ballad. The music composed by Mr. Watlen, set with Variations for the Pedal Harp by J. T. Craven. London. Printed by J. Watlen . . . 5 Leicester Place," c. 1815.

PARKHURST (THOMAS). Bookseller, at various addresses, London, 1653-1711. (P.) Published "The Book of Psalms in English Metre. The newest version fitted to the common tunes. By C. Darby . . . London. Printed by S. Bridge, for Tho. Parkhurst at the Bible and Three Crowns in Cheapside near Mercers Chapel. MDCCIV."
P. II.

PARRY (D.). Music seller and musician, 3 Paddington Street, near High Street, Marylebone, London, c. 1800-16. Published some of his own compositions and a few other works.

PARRY (HENRY JOHN). See Wessel & Co.

PARSONS (JOHN). See How & Parsons.

PASQUALI (FRANCES). Music engraver, printer and publisher, Poland Street, near Great Marlborough Street, London. Engraved "Six Sonatas for the Harpsicord with Accompanyments for a Violin or German Flute, and Violoncello . . . Compos'd by Charles Frederick

Abel. Opera II. London. Printed for the Author," etc., c. 1760; "Sei Arie messe in musica da Felice Giardini. Dedicate all'il^{ma} Sig^{ra} la Signora Francesca Pelham. Londra"; preface dated April 3, 1762; published "Six Concertos for the Harpsichord, in Five Parts . . . Composed by Frances Xaverio Richter," c. 1765; engraved "Sei Canzonette a due composte da Giovanni Cristiano Bach . . . Londra. Opera IV.", c. 1765; "Six Concertos . . . to which is added a Harpsichord Sonata: composed by Phil: Hayes, Bac: Mus: London, Published for the Author"; preface dated July, 1769; "Six Canzonets for two voices, composed by Thomas Morley. London. Printed by Welcker," c. 1775.

PATERSON & ROY. Musical instrument makers, music sellers and publishers, Edinburgh; 43 Hanover Street, c. 1826-30; 27 George Street, c. 1830-50. Partners were Robert Paterson and Peter Walker Roy; succeeded Paterson, Mortimer and Co.; succeeded by Paterson and Sons.

PATERSON & SONS. Musical instrument makers, music sellers and publishers, 27 George Street, Edinburgh, c. 1850 to present time; 152 Buchanan Street, Glasgow, c. 1857 to present time. Also set up branch establishments, or agencies, at Perth, Ayr, Dundee, Dumfries, Paisley, Kilmarnock, Aberdeen, Oban and London. Robert Paterson, original senior partner, previously a partner in Paterson, Mortimer and Co., and Paterson and Roy, died in 1859 and his second son, Robert Roy Paterson, became senior partner. In later years firm became Paterson, Sons and Co. Ltd.; succeeded Paterson and Roy.
    G.

PATERSON, MORTIMER & CO. Musical instrument makers and music sellers, Edinburgh; 18 North Bridge, c. 1819; 51 North Bridge, c. 1820-26. Had additional premises at 370 Castle Hill, c. 1824-26; when partnership was dissolved c. 1826, Robert Paterson was joined by P. W. Roy and became Paterson and Roy.
    G.

PATERSON (ROBERT). *See* Paterson & Roy; Paterson & Sons; Paterson, Mortimer & Co.

PATTON (MATTHEW). Music seller, Bath. Known to have been at 4 St. Andrew's Terrace, c. 1812-19; 28 Milsom Street, c. 1826-30. Published, "Spanish Theme. National Air . . . with variations for the Guitar," etc., by R. L. Dounes.

PAWLETT (ROBERT). Bookseller, at the Bible in Chancery Lane, near the Inner Temple Gate, London, 1641-67. (P.) His name appears in the imprint of "Directions for the Flagellett wth 20 severall lessons

fitted to the same Instrument. Written & engraven by Tho: Swain gent: 1667. Sold by Robert Pawlett att the Bible in Chancery lane."
P. I, II.

PAXTON (EDMUND). Printer, London. Only the initials E. P. appear in the imprint of the work presumed to have been printed by Edmund Paxton, "The Whole Book of Psalmes. Collected into English meeter by Thomas Sternhold, Iohn Hopkins, and others . . . with apt notes to sing them withall . . . London, Printed by E. P. for the Company of Stationers, 1636."

PAYNE (THOMAS). Bookseller, 88 Pall Mall, London. His name appears in the imprint of "Musical and Poetical Relicks of the Welsh Bards . . . By Edward Jones . . . The Third edition . . . The first volume. London: Printed for the Author . . . 1808. And sold by . . . T. Payne," etc.

PAYNE (THOMAS) & SONS. Booksellers, at the Mews Gate, Castle Street, Leicester Fields, London. Their name appears in the imprint of "Historical Memoirs of the Irish Bards . . . and an appendix . . . with select Irish melodies. By Joseph C. Walker . . . London. Printed for T. Payne and Son . . . and G. G. J. and J. Robinson . . . MDCCLXXXVI."

PEACHEY (GEORGE). Pianoforte manufacturer and music seller, London; 31 Wormwood Street, Bishopsgate, c. 1828-32; 73 Bishopsgate Street Without, c. 1832-82. Published a small amount of music.

PEARCE & CO. Music and musical instrument sellers and publishers, London; 28 Haymarket, c. 1806-09; 70 Dean Street, c. 1809-12; 24 Panton Street, c. 1812-15. Succeeded Corri, Pearce and Co.
K.

PEARCE or PEARCH (GEORGE). Bookseller and publisher, 12 Cheapside, London, 1768-71. (P.) His name appears in the imprint of "The Psalm Singers Help, being a Collection of Tunes, in three parts . . . With a thorough bass for the harpsichord or organ . . . By Thomas Knibb. A new edition. London; Printed for George Pearch . . . and Joseph Gurney," etc., c. 1770.
P. III.
See also Knibb (Thomas).

PEARCH (GEORGE). *See* Pearce or Pearch (George).

PEARSON (ALICE). Printer, over against Wright's (Sutton's) Coffee House, in Aldersgate Street, London, c. 1735-42. Printed a number of music books; succeeded William Pearson, presumably her husband; succeeded by Robert Brown.
K. (William Pearson.)

Catalogue:—Books printed by and for A. Pearson. 1 p. 8°. In "The Spiritual Man's Companion . . . By Israel Holdroyd." Printed and sold by Robert Brown, London, 1746. (B.M. B. 639. c.)

PEARSON (WILLIAM). Printer, London; next door to the Hare and Feathers, in Aldersgate Street, 1699-1700; in Red Cross Alley, in Jewin Street, 1700-24; over against Wright's Coffee House, in Aldersgate Street, 1724-35. Printed a number of musical works, including many for Henry Playford 1699-1707; printed some works with the imprint "Printed by W. P."; succeeded by Alice Pearson, presumably his widow.
K. G. P. II. D. & M.

PECK (J.) & (J.). Music engravers, music sellers and publishers, London; 32 Noble Street, Falcon Square, c. 1832-34; 44 Newgate Street, c. 1834-36. Partners were presumably James Peck and his son John, who continued the business alone. Succeeded James Peck.
K.

PECK (JAMES). Composer, music engraver, printer, music seller and publisher, London; 9 Westmoreland Buildings, Aldersgate Street, c. 1797-1800; 61 Newgate Street, 1800-c. 1804; 47 Lombard Street, c. 1804-24; 52 Paternoster Row, c. 1824-26; 3 Ball Alley, Cornhill, c. 1826-32. Published principally engraved sacred music. Succeeded by J. and J. Peck.
K.

PECK (JOHN). Music engraver, music seller and publisher, 44 Newgate Street, London, c. 1836-50. Succeeded J. and J. Peck.
K.

PEMBERTON (E.). Dancing Master and engraver? London. Author of "An Essay to the further Improvement of Dancing . . . London Printed and Sold by J. Walsh . . . J. Hare . . . and at the Author's next the Fire-Office in St. Martin's Lane, 1711." The "characters and figures" of a number of Dances by Anthony L'Abbe and others issued between 1713-33, are described as "writ by Mr. Pemberton," which may mean that he was responsible for the engraving as well as the designing of the figures of the dances.

PENROSE (JOHN). Bookseller, Leeds. His name appears in an advertisement July 1700, "The Psalm-Tunes in 4 Parts . . . The 4th edition, corrected and revised by A. Barber . . . Sold by Abr. Barber . . . and John Penrose . . . and by Eben. Tracy," etc.

PENSON, ROBERTSON & CO. Music engravers, music sellers and publishers, 47 Princes Street, Edinburgh, c. 1810-20. Also known as Penson and Robertson. Partners were William Penson and Alexander

Robertson, both teachers of music; partnership dissolved c. 1820; Robertson continued the business alone at the same address.
    K.
    Catalogue of Vocal & Instrumental Music. c. 1815. 2 pp. fol. (B.M. h. 1480. p. (6.))

PEPPERCORN (JOHN). Mott's Yard, Bridge Street, Cambridge. Published in conjunction with William Hague, "A Collection of Psalm & Hymn Tunes some of which are new & others by permission of the authors with six Chants and Te Deums . . . The whole revis'd & harmonized by Dr. Randall. And published by Wm. Hague and Jno. Peppercorn. Cambridge. Printed by A. Macintosh for the publishers. 1794."

PEREGRINE (CHARLES). Printer, London. Printed for Henry Playford, "An Introduction to the Skill of Musick . . . Eleventh edition, corrected and enlarged . . . 1687."
    K. D. & M.

PETER. *See* Gray & Peter.

PETREIUS (JOHANN). *See* Byrd (William).

PETTET (ALFRED). Music seller and publisher, London; 154 Oxford Street, 1828-30; 18 Hanway Yard, Oxford Street, 1830-33.

PHILIPS, *Mr.* Music seller, Oxford. His name appears in the imprint of "Divine Harmony; or, a Collection of fifty-five double and single chants for four voices, as they are sung at the Cathedral of Lichfield; compos'd by John Alcock . . . Printed for the author, and M. Broome . . . in Birmingham and sold by them . . . Mr. Philips . . . at Oxford . . . 1752."

PHILIPS (JOHN). *See* Phillips or Philips (John) & (Sarah).

PHILIPS (SARAH). *See* Phillips or Philips (John) & (Sarah).

PHILLIPS & CO. Pianoforte makers, music sellers and publishers, 17 Old Bond Street, London, c. 1817-20. Afterwards became Phillips, Mayhew and Co.
    K.

PHILLIPS, MAYHEW & CO. Music sellers and publishers, 17 Old Bond Street, London, c. 1820-22. Also known as Phillips and Mayhew. Succeeded Phillips and Co.; became Mayhew and Co., c. 1822.
    K.

PHILLIPS or PHILIPS (JOHN) & (SARAH). Music engravers, printers and publishers, London, at the Harp, in St. Martin's Court, near

Leicester Fields, c. 1740-65. After the death of John Phillips, his widow Sarah, who was also a music engraver, continued the business from c. 1766-75. She had a music shop in Bedford Court, and printed and sold some music in Great Earl Street, Seven Dials.

    K. G.

PHILLIPS (RICHARD). Bookseller, 71 St. Paul's Church Yard, London. Published "The Monthly Musical Journal. Consisting of original British and of new foreign music vocal & instrumental. Collected by Dr. Busby," advertised 1801.

PHILLIPS or PHILIPS (SARAH). *See* Phillips or Philips (John) & (Sarah).

PHILLIPS (THOMAS). Musical instrument maker, 214 Tottenham Court Road, London. Printed and published 1816, "Arise thou bright Sun. The much admired Song written in honor of the Royal nuptials between Princess Charlotte of Wales & Prince Leopold of Saxe Cobourg, by J. W. Lake, Esq . . . the music composed by J. Addison." James Bussell was previously at the same address.

PHILLIPS (WILLIAM). Music and musical instrument seller, and publisher, 3 Manor Row, Little Tower Hill, London, 1793-c. 1827. Previously in the employ of Longman and Broderip.

    K.

PHILO (JAMES). Parish Clerk, East Dereham, Norfolk. His name appears in the imprint of "A Selection of Psalms, from the New Version with the Morning and Evening Hymns; for the use of Parish Churches . . . Second edition. Printed and sold by W. Barker . . . Sold also . . . by . . . James Philo . . 1813."

PHINN (THOMAS). Music engraver, Edinburgh. Engraved "Thirty Scots Songs for a Voice & Harpsichord"; published by R. Bremner, Edinburgh, 1757; "A Collection of Airs &c. for the Violin or German Flute, with a Bass for the Violincello or Harpsichord taken from the best masters and published in six numbers . . . to be had at the shop of Thos. Phinn, engraver, Luckenbooths," c. 1767.

    K.

PHIPPS & CO. Music and musical instrument sellers, and publishers, 25 Duke Street, Grosvenor Square, London, c. 1810-18. Phipps was previously a partner in the firm of Goulding, Phipps and D'Almaine prior to opening his own business; joined by Thomas Holloway c. 1818, and became Phipps and Holloway.

    K.

PHIPPS & HOLLOWAY. Music sellers and publishers, London; 95 New Bond Street, c. 1818-20; 5 Hanway Street, c. 1820-21. Phipps

I *

previously partner in the firm of Phipps & Co.; Thomas Holloway carried on the business alone c. 1821.
K.

PHIPPS. *See* Goulding, Phipps & D'Almaine; Phipps & Co.; Phipps & Holloway.

PICKERING (JOHN). Music seller, 16 St. Ann's Square, Manchester, c. 1830-44. Published a small amount of music.

PICKMAN (C.). Bookseller, Ratcliff Highway, London. His name appears in the imprint of "The Merry Mountebank; or, the Humourous Quack Doctor . . . In a choice collection of old and new songs; and compiled . . . By Timothy Tulip . . . Vol. I. London: Printed by W. Pearson for A. Holbeche . . . F. Jefferis . . . and C. Pickman . . . 1732."

PIGOT (JAMES). Engraver and copper plate printer, 11 Fountain Street, Manchester. Engraved and printed c. 1815, "The Minstrel to his Harp, a Ballad written by Miss F. D. Browne, composed & arranged with an Accompaniment for the Piano Forte or Harp . . . by T. Barford."

PIGOTT & SHERWIN. Music and musical instrument sellers, and publishers, Dublin Harmonic Institution, 13 Westmorland Street, Dublin, c. 1827-29. Succeeded Bunting, Walsh, Pigott and Sherwin; partners were S. J. Pigott and J. F. Sherwin; partnership dissolved c. 1829, Pigott continued at same address and Sherwin set up in business at 32 Grafton Street.

PIGOTT (SAMUEL J.). Music and musical instrument seller, and publisher, Dublin; Harmonic Institution, 13 Westmorland Street, c. 1829-36; Harmonic Institution, 112 Grafton Street, c. 1836-66; continued as Pigott and Co. from c. 1866 to present time at the latter address, with additional premises in Suffolk Street. Previously a partner in the business of Bunting, Walsh, Pigott and Sherwin, c. 1825-27, and Pigott and Sherwin, c. 1827-29.

PIGUENIT (C. D.). Bookseller, Berkeley Square, London. Advertised, June 1778, "This day is published . . . Six Canzonets, with an Accompaniment, for the Harpsichord, the Piano Forte, or the Harp. Composed by Samuel Arnold, Mus. Doc. Opera 13. Printed for C. D. Piguenit, Berkeley Square; and Longman and Broderip, Cheapside."
P. III (Piquenit).

PILBROW (TYCHO). Music and musical instrument seller, High Street, Exeter. Published for the Author c. 1835, "Hurrah! for the Hearts of true blue. Song, the music composed by Lady Adams, the words by William R. Neale."

PINE (JOHN). Engraver and a man of letters, 1690-1756. He engraved the title-page of "The Hymn of Adam and Eve, out of the fifth book of Milton's Paradise-Lost; set to Musick by M^r. Galliard. 1728."

PINNOCK (WILLIAM). Music and musical instrument seller, and publisher, 267 St. Clement's Church Yard, Strand, London, c. 1821-26.
Catalogue:—New and popular Music. c. 1821. 1 p. fol. (B.M. h. 1480. c. (7.))

PIPER or PYPER (JOHN). Bookseller, "at Pauls Gate next unto Cheapside at the Crosse Keies," London. Published c. 1614, "Parthenia In-violata. Or Mayden-Musicke for the Virginalls and Bass-Viol Selected out of the Compositions of the most famous in that Arte By Robert Hole . . . Printed at London for John Pyper," etc.
K.

PIPPARD (LUKE). Musical instrument maker, music engraver and publisher, London; at the Golden Flute and Hautboy, opposite to Will's and Tom's Coffee Houses, Russell Street, Covent Garden, 1709-10; at the sign of Orpheus (or, the Orpheus), opposite to Tom's Coffee House (or, next door to Bickerstaff's Coffee House), Russell Street, Covent Garden, December 1710-c. 1712; at Orpheus, next door to Button's Coffee House, Russell Street, Covent Garden, c. 1712-1713. Presumably Pippard occupied the same premises 1709-13, although the form of his address was modified from time to time; formerly an apprentice of John Walsh the elder.
K.

PLATTS (CHARLES). Music seller and publisher, 9 John Street, Oxford Street, London, c. 1834-38. Succeeded James Platts.

PLATTS (FREDERICK). Engraver and stationer, 3 New Church Street, Edgware Road, London. Published "Jim Crow, arranged with an accompaniment for the Spanish Guitar," c. 1839; "No. 1-4 of Popular Songs, sung in The Tempest, arranged with accompaniments for the Spanish Guitar by Jane Taylor," c. 1839.

PLATTS (JAMES). Music seller, printer and publisher, London; published at his house, 9 Lovel's Court, Paternoster Row, Cheapside, c. 1790-97; 6 St. John's Court, Fleet Street, c. 1797-1800; 21 Portland Street, Soho, c. 1800-05; 83 Berwick Street, Oxford Street, c. 1805-16; 320 Oxford Street, near Hanover Square, c. 1816-20; 340 Oxford Street, near the Pantheon, c. 1820-22; 9 John Street, Oxford Street, c. 1822-34. Succeeded by Charles Platts.
K.
Catalogues:—Instrumental & Vocal Music. c. 1800. 1 p. fol. (B.M. g. 139. (1.)); c. 1802. 1 p. fol. (B.M. g. 422. c. (8.)); c. 1805. 1 p. fol. (B.M. g. 301. (4.)); Airs for the Harp. c. 1811. 1 p. fol. (B.M. g. 661. (24.)

PLAYFORD (HENRY).   Book and music seller, music publisher, editor
of various works, dealer in musical instruments, prints and paintings;
also established concerts of music in London and Oxford.   Son of John
Playford.   Was in association with his father "near the Temple
Church," London, 1680-86, during which period he issued a few
works in his own name from the same address.   In 1684, with Richard
Carr, he took over the active control of his father's business, which he
conducted in his own name "near the Temple Church," 1686-95,
sometimes using in addition the address of his house (formerly his
father's) over against the Blue Ball in Arundel Street in the Strand, this
address appearing alone on some works in 1695-96.   From 1696
his shop was in the Temple Change (over against St. Dunstan's Church;
near Temple Bar), Fleet Street, when he gave up these premises
c. 1705, he continued business at his house in Arundel Street until
1707.   In July of that year he is given as "At his Rooms in Queen's
Head Tavern Passage, over against the Middle Temple Gate in Fleet
Street (up one pair of stairs next the Queen's Head Tavern), after
which he appears to have ceased business, John Cullen and John Young
acquiring some of his stock.   He died probably in 1709.   From 1701,
or earlier, Playford dealt in prints and paintings.   He published and
sold works in conjunction with John and Richard Carr, 1685-86;
with Samuel Scott, 1691-96; with John Church, 1695-96; with John
Young, 1699; with John Hare, 1699-c. 1702; with Daniel Browne
(or Brown) 1700; with John Sprint, 1703-06; with John Cullen,
1705; and with James Woodward, July 1707.   Playford was not a
printer or engraver, his musical works being printed by John Playford
the Younger 1685; by Charles Peregrine 1687; by Benjamin Motte
1687; by Edward Jones 1687-97; by John Heptinstall 1692-98; by
William Pearson 1699-1707.
    K. G. D. & M.
    Works on John Playford by Frank Kidson and William C. Smith.
(See Bibliography); L. M. Middleton:—John Playford.   D.N.B.;
Notes and Queries. Ser. VIII. Vol. VII. pp. 449-51, 494.

PLAYFORD (JOHN) the Elder.   Bookseller, musical instrument seller,
book and music publisher, composer, author, editor of various works,
stationer, and from 1653-1686 Clerk to the Temple Church, London.
He was apprenticed to John Benson in March 1640.   His business
was carried on at his shop in the Inner Temple (the Temple), near
the Church Door (near the Temple Church), 1648-86, but during
that period, he was living at various addresses.   In 1653 or earlier,
he resided at Three Leg Alley, Fetter Lane, next door to the Red
Lion, but at the time of his marriage or when he was appointed
Clerk to the Temple Church he moved to his business premises in the
Inner Temple, where he resided from 1653-c. 1662, when he moved
to Islington with Mrs. Playford who had opened a boarding school in
a large house "over against the Church," which she carried on until
her death in October 1679.   Playford continued to reside there until

late in 1680 when he moved to a private house in Arundel Street near the Thameside, the lower end over against the George, given in 1686 as over against the Blue Ball in Arundel Street. Playford handed over the control of his business to his son Henry and Richard Carr in 1684, but his name still appeared in imprints up to some time in 1686, the year of his death. Published some musical works in conjunction with John Benson, 1651-58; in partnership with Zachariah Watkins at the shop in the Temple, 1663-65; with his son Henry from 1680; and sold some musical works in conjunction with John Carr 1681-84. Playford was not a printer or engraver, his musical works being printed by Thomas Harper 1650-55; by William Godbid c. 1658-c. 1679; by Anne Godbid and John Playford the younger, c. 1679-83; by John Playford the younger, c. 1683-85. In 1649 John Playford published some pamphlets, two or three of which were entered in the Registers of the Stationers Company to Henry Playford, identified as gentleman of St. Giles's Cripplegate, whose relation and association with John Playford is not clear; he was one of the godfathers of Henry the son of John Playford, but there is no evidence that he was a printer or bookseller.

K. G. P. I. D. & M.

Works on John Playford by Frank Kidson and William C. Smith. (*See* Bibliography); L. M. Middleton:—John Playford. D.N.B.; Notes and Queries. Ser. VIII. Vol. VII. pp. 449-51, 494. Some details supplied by Margaret Dean-Smith.

PLAYFORD (JOHN) *the Younger*. *See* Godbid (Anne) & Playford (John) *the Younger*.

POCOCK (CHARLES). Bookseller? Reading. His name appears in the imprint of "An Introduction to Psalmody containing Instructions for young Beginners . . . Engrav'd printed and sold by Mich. Beesly and by . . . Cha. Pocock at Reading," c. 1755.

POHLMAN (HENRY). Music seller and publisher, 22 Waterhouse Street, Halifax. Published "Greenwood's Psalmody, harmonized in score . . . by the late John Greenwood . . . 1838"; "The First Part of the Yorkshire Harmonist . . . by Thomas Parker", c. 1845; "A New and enlarged edition of Cheetham's Psalmody. Harmonized in score with an arrangement for the organ or piano-forte by J. Houldsworth. Eighth edition . . . 1845"; also ninth edition, 1848; as H. Pohlman and Son, twelfth edition, 1853; sixteenth edition, 1859; eighteenth edition, 1861; as Pohlman and Son, twentieth edition, 1868.

POLE (JOHN FREDERICK). Teacher of music, music and musical instrument seller, and publisher, Edinburgh; Music and Musical Instrument Repository, 95 Princes Street, c. 1827; 69 Princes Street, 1828. Published "Original Lyrics, arranged to Scotish Melodies. The poetry by Wm. Magee. 1828."

POLYHYMNIAN COMPANY. *See* Walker (George) *the Elder*.

PORTAL (AB.). Music publisher, 163, opposite the New Church, Strand, London, c. 1775-80. Some single sheet songs bear only the initials A. P.
    K.

PORTER (EDWARD). Music and book seller, Leeds; Briggate, c. 1790-1798; at various numbers in Lowerhead Row, c. 1798-1837. His name, and name stamp appears on some music.

PORTEUS. 90 Strand, London. Published c. 1831, "A British Man-o-War, a patriotic Song . . . the poetry by Robert Manners White, the music by Leigh Smith."

POTTER. *See* Goulding, D'Almaine, Potter & Co.

POTTER (SAMUEL). Musical instrument maker, 20 King Street, Parliament Street, Westminster, London. Published c. 1815, "A New Sett of Duetts, for two Violins, by Ignace Pleyel. Arranged expressly for juvenile performers."

POWELL (J. H.) Musical instrument seller, 3 St. John's Lane, St. John's Street, West Smithfield, London. Published by the Author at his Musical Instrument Warehouse, c. 1825, "I'll buy thy Heart. In answer to 'Who'll buy a Heart' . . . written & composed . . . by J. H. Powell."

POWELL (SAMUEL). Printer, Dublin; Crane Lane, c. 1728-62; Dame Street, 1762-72. (P.) Son of Stephen Powell. Printed "Les Psaumes de David mis en vers françois . . . Nouvelle edition . . . MDCCXXXI."; "The Psalms of David in Metre. Collected out of principal versions now in use. To which are added Hymns, particularly designed for the Lord's Supper. Printed by S. Powell, for A. Bradley . . . Dublin. MDCCXL."; "Cantiques sacrez pour les principales solemnitez chretiennes à Dublin . . . 1748"; "A Collection of Hymns and Sacred Poems . . . MDCCXLIX."; "Select Psalms for the use of the Parish-Church of New St. Michan's in Dublin. MDCCLII."
    K. P. III.

POWELL (STEPHEN). *See* Brent (John) & Powell (Stephen).

POWER (JAMES). Military musical instrument maker, music seller and publisher, 34 Strand, London, c. 1807-38. For a number of years had additional premises at 3 Burlington Arcade; published in conjunction with his brother William, of Dublin, with whom he was previously in partnership; died 1836; business carried on by his widow until c. 1838.
    K. G.

Catalogues:—Vocal Music by Thomas Moore and Sir John Stevenson. (J. and W. Power.) 1815. 3 pp. fol. (B.M. Hirsch IV. 1112. (7.)); Vocal Music by Thos. Moore and Sir J. Stevenson. c. 1815. 1 p. fol. (B.M. H. 1650. b. (33.)); Vocal Music by Thomas Moore and Sir John Stevenson. (J. and W. Power.) 1816. 3 pp. fol. (B.M. Hirsch IV. 1113. (7.)); Vocal and Instrumental Music. 1822. 8 pp. fol. (B.M. I. 387. b.); Vocal and Instrumental Music. 1828. 11 pp. fol. (B.M. G. 402.)

POWER (WILLIAM) & CO. Musical instrument makers, music sellers and publishers, 4 Westmoreland (Westmorland) Street, Dublin, c. 1802-31. James Power was in partnership with his brother William until c. 1807, when he established a business in London; many publications were issued with their joint names; the "& Co." was dropped c. 1810. Succeeded by Marcus Moses.
K. G.
Catalogues:—*See* Power (James).

PRATT (DANIEL). Bookseller, at the Printing Office, the Crown and Bible, against York House in the Strand, London. Published c. 1710, "Dear Sally. A new Song. Engraved by T. Cross in Compton Street, Clerkenwell."
P. II.

PRATT (JONAS). Music seller and music teacher, Cambridge, during the latter half of the eighteenth century. In 1791 the business was being carried on by his widow.
G.

PRATT (WILLIAM). Bookseller and printer, Stokesley, Yorks. Printed "A Selection of Psalms, as set on the Organ in the Parish Church, of Stokesley, together with the Morning and Evening Hymns . . . 1824."

PRESTON & SON. *See* Preston (John).

PRESTON (JOHN). Musical instrument maker, music printer, music seller and publisher, London; 9 Banbury Court, Long Acre, c. 1774-1775; 105 Strand, near Beaufort Buildings, c. 1775-78; 97 Strand, near Beaufort Buildings (or simply 97 Strand), c. 1778-87; 97 Strand and Exeter Change, c. 1787-89. His son Thomas joined the business and it became Preston and Son, 97 Strand, and Exeter Change, c. 1789-98. Some single sheet music bears only the initials I. P. or J. P.; Preston and Son purchased the stock and plates of Robert Bremner in 1789. In an advertisement of 1778, John Preston claimed to be the original inventor of the method for tuning the guitar with a watch key. Business of Preston and Son was carried on by Thomas Preston, c. 1798-c. 1834.
K. G.

Catalogues:—New Music. 1782. 1 p. obl. fol. (B.M. E. 111. c. (3.)); New Music. 1783. 1 p. fol. (B.M. h. 64. (7.)); New Music. c. 1783. 1 p. obl. fol. (B.M. g. 276. g.); New Music. 1784. 1 p. fol. (B.M. h. 64. (5.)); Preston and Son. Musical Publications. (Additional Catalogue of Instrumental and Vocal Music late property of Robert Bremner.) 1790. 10 pp. fol. (B.M. Hirsch IV. 1113. (8.))

PRESTON (THOMAS). Musical instrument maker, music printer, music seller and publisher, London; 97 Strand, and Exeter Change, c. 1798-1810; 97 Strand (only), c. 1810-22; 71 Dean Street, Soho, 1822-34. Carried on the business of Preston and Son commenced by his father John Preston; purchased the stock of plates of Thomas Skillern the elder, and of H. Wright, c. 1803; and of Wilkinson and Co., c. 1810. Succeeded by Coventry and Hollier, c. 1834.
K. G.
Catalogues:—Additional Catalogue of Musical Publications. 1803. 4 pp. fol. (B.M. 7896. h. 40. (13.)); Songs, Duets, Glees, Catches, &c. 1804. 8 pp. fol. (B.M. 7896. h. 40. (13.)); Additional Catalogue of Musical Publications. 1805. 4 pp. fol. (B.M. 7896. h. 40. (13.)); Publications selected from the Catalogue published by Broderip and Wilkinson, lately purchased. c. 1810. 4 pp. fol. (B.M. Hirsch IV. 1113. (11.)); Select Musical Publications. c. 1817. 4 pp. 8°. (B.M. Hirsch IV. 1110. (5.)); Catalogue thematique of Beethoven's Works. 1823, or later. 1 p. fol. (B.M. Hirsch IV. 1112. (8.)); Appendix or additional Catalogue of new Musical Works. 1825. 8 pp. 8°. (B.M. 1042. g. 26. (1.)); Catalogue of new Musical Works. 1830. 16 pp. 8°. (First Edition Bookshop, Catalogue 40. No. 133.).

PRICE (THOMAS). Bookseller, Gloucester. His name appears in the imprint of "A Book of Psalmody . . . Collected engrav'd and printed by Mich. Beesly and sold by . . . Tho. Price Bookseller in Gloucester," etc., c. 1745.
P. III.

PRINTING HOUSE (or PRINTING OFFICE) IN BOW CHURCH YARD, LONDON. These forms sometimes used for works issued by John Cluer, Elizabeth Cluer and Thomas Cobb, without their names.
See Cluer (Elizabeth); Cluer (John); Cobb (Thomas).

PROUD & CO. Music sellers, 25 Duke Street, Grosvenor Square, London. Published c. 1820, "Wake Mary, wake! A ballad . . . Composed by R. Guylott," etc.

PROWSE (JOSEPH). Flute maker from Clementi and Co., 3 Old Jewry, London. Published c. 1836, "Oh! come with me o'er the distant Sea, Ballad . . . written by Miss Bishop, composed by W. R. Baldwin."

PROWSE (THOMAS). Musical instrument maker, music seller and

publisher, London; 13 Hanway Street, Oxford Street, c. 1835-60; 15 Hanway Street, c. 1860-68. Stock-in-trade offered for sale by Puttick and Simpson, January 30, March 30 and September 1, 1868.
Catalogue of Vocal and Instrumental Music. c. 1845. 1 p. fol. (B.M. h. 3213. j. (11.))

PROWSE (WILLIAM). Music seller and publisher, 48 Cheapside, London, c. 1846-65. Partner in the firm of Keith, Prowse and Co. 1829-46; joined by H. Bryan Jones c. 1865 when the business reverted to the old title of Keith, Prowse and Co.; retired 1876; died April 1886, aged 81.
See also Keith, Prowse & Co.

PULLEN (OCTAVIAN). *See* Thomason (George) & Pullen (Octavian).

PURCELL (HENRY). Printer, Handel's Head, Wood Street, London. Published "The Muses Delight. An accurate collection of English and Italian Songs, Cantatas and Duetts, set to music . . . M,DCC,LIV."; "The Compleat Tutor, or Familiar Instructions . . . 1754." Described in W. H. Cumming's copy of Kidson as "A reprint from Prelleur's Modern Musick-Master (1731)."

PURDAY. *See* Button & Purday; Purday & Button.

PURDAY & BUTTON. Music sellers and publishers, 75 St. Paul's Church Yard, London, c. 1805-07. Succeeded Henry Thompson. Name of the firm changed to Button and Purday, 1807. S. J. Button was formerly a bookseller at 24 Paternoster Row.
K. G.
Catalogue:—New Music. c. 1805. 1 p. fol. (B.M. g. 443. q. (17.))

PURDAY (THOMAS) & SON. *See* Purday (Thomas Edward).

PURDAY (THOMAS EDWARD). Music seller and publisher, London; 50 St. Paul's Church Yard, c. 1834-62; 531 Oxford Street, c. 1862-64 as Thomas Purday and Son. Took over the music publishing branch of Collard and Collard c. 1834.
K.

PURDAY (ZENAS TRIVETT). Music seller and publisher, 45 High Holborn, London, 1831-60. Succeeded William Hodsoll; published many humorous songs; sale of stock-in-trade by Puttick and Simpson, July 2-4, 1860.
K. G.

PURDIE (JOHN). Music seller and publisher, 83 Princes Street, Edinburgh, c. 1837-87. Succeeded his father Robert Purdie.

PURDIE (ROBERT). Music seller and publisher, Princes Street, Edinburgh, c. 1808-37; at No. 35, c. 1808-13; No. 71, 1813-c. 1816; No. 70, c. 1816-28; No. 83, c. 1828-37. Was a teacher of music in 1804; reissued some of Nathaniel Gow's publications in conjunction with Alexander Robertson; succeeded by his son John c. 1837.
K. G.

PURFOOT (THOMAS). Printer, London, 1591-1640; at the sign of the Lucrece within the new rents in Newgate Market; over against St. Sepulchre's Church without Newgate. (M.) Printed "The Noble Arte of Venerie or Hunting . . . [By George Turbervile.] At London, Printed by Thomas Purfoot. An. Dom. 1611"; contains music of "The Measures of blowing, set downe in the notes." Editions of the Sternhold and Hopkins versions of the Psalms, 1614, 1635 and 1637 printed by T. P. for the Company of Stationers have been attributed to Purfoot.
M.

PURSER (J.). Printer, 4 Red Lion Court, Fleet Street, London. Printed "The Leicestershire Harmony: Containing a set of excellent Psalm-tunes and Anthems . . . The second edition, with additions. By John Arnold, Organist . . . MDCCLXVII."

PYE (JOHN BRIDGE). Musician, music seller and publisher, opposite the Post Office, Lord Street, Liverpool, c. 1785-96.

PYNSON (RICHARD). Printer, London; ?-1530, first in the parish of St. Clement Danes, outside Temple Bar; from 1500 at the sign of the George or St. George, next door to St. Dunstan's Church, Fleet Street (D.), where he printed Sarum Missals, Sarum Processional, and Sarum Manual, 1500-20.
D. S.

PYPER (JOHN). *See* Piper.

QUADRILLE REPOSITORY & MUSIC WAREHOUSE. 3 Carlton Street, Regent Street, near Waterloo Place, London. Published at the Quadrille Repository and Music Warehouse c. 1825, "Der Frey-schutz, the popular Quadrilles arranged from the Opera of Karl Maria von Weber, with entire new figures and a novel finale to the celebrated Waltz . . . by T. W. Lloyd."

R., I. *See* Rutherford (John).

R., T. *See* Raynald (Thomas).

R., W. *See* Randall (William).

RABAN (EDWARD). Printer, Aberdeen, 1622-59. (M.) Printed "The Psalms of David, in Prose and Metre: With the whole forme of Discipline and Prayers, according to the Church of Scotland . . . Aberdene, Printed by Edward Raban, 1633. For David Melvill." He was the first printer in Aberdeen. Previously in Edinburgh and St. Andrews from 1620 to 1622.

    K. M. P. I.

RAIKES (ROBERT). Printer, St. Ives, Huntingdonshire, 1718-20; Northampton, over against All Saints' Church, 1720-22; Gloucester; against the Swan Inn, 1722-23; Southgate Street, 1723-43; Black-Friars, 1743-57. (P.) Printed at Gloucester "Two Cantata's and six Songs, set to Musick. By B. Gunn, Organist of the Cathedral in Gloucester. 1736." Founded "The Gloucester Journal" with William Dicey in 1722.

    K. P. II.

RAMSAY (ALLAN). Bookseller, Edinburgh, various addresses, c. 1716-1758. (P.) Printed and sold c. 1725, "Musick for Allan Ramsay's Collection of Scots Songs. Set by Alexr. Stuart & engraved by R. Cooper. (Musick for the Scots Songs in the Tea Table Miscellany.)"

    P. II.

RANDAL. Music seller, at the Harp and Hautboy, in May's Build-ings, St. Martin's Lane, London. Published "A New Song, call'd The Invitation to Miss Davies's Benefit." Issued in connection with the Benefit Concert for Miss Davies (10 years of age) at Hickford's Room, February 6, 1754. Randal, not otherwise identified, was probably William Randall, or another member of the family associated with Walsh, or James Randal of Charing Cross, who was a subscriber to Hale's "Social Harmony," 1763.

RANDAL. See also Randall.

RANDALL & ABELL. Music printers, music sellers and publishers, Catharine (Catherine) Street, Strand, London, January 1766-July 1768. Continued the business of John Walsh, junior, under arrangements specified in the Will of John Walsh; John Abell died July 29, 1768, and William Randall carried on alone.

RANDALL (ELIZABETH). Music printer, music seller and publisher, Catharine (Catherine) Street, Strand, London, January 1776-c. April 1783. Advertisements in 1781 and after, give the address as No. 13 Catherine Street. Widow and executrix of William Randall; issued some works with imprints of John Walsh, junior, Randall and Abell, William Randall, in addition to her own; succeeded by Wright and Wilkinson.

    K. G.

A Catalogue of Vocal and Instrumental Music. c. 1782. 4 pp. fol.
(B.M. 1879. cc. 13. (22.)).

Information about Elizabeth Randall is included in works on John
Walsh by Frank Kidson and William C. Smith. (*See* Bibliography.)

RANDALL (PETER). Music publisher, at the Violin and Lute (occasionally, Lute and Violin, Viol and Lute), by Paulsgrave Hand (or Head)
Court (Paulsgrave Court) without Temple Bar in the Strand, London,
November 1706-October 1708, during which period Randall's publications were issued in connection with John Walsh the elder, Catherine
Street, Strand, having both names and addresses in the imprints and
advertisements. J. Walsh and P. Randall published as one firm, at the
Harp and Hoboy, in Catherine Street, Strand, and the Violin and Lute
by Paulsgrave Court, etc., October 1708-July 1709, and from Catherine
Street only, July 1709-December 1710. Randall was presumably the
brother-in-law of Walsh.
    K. G.
    Information about Peter Randall is included in works on John
Walsh by Frank Kidson and William C. Smith. (*See* Bibliography.)

RANDALL (WILLIAM). Music printer, music seller and publisher,
Catharine (Catherine) Street, Strand, London, July 1768-c. January
1776. Previously a partner in the business of Randall and Abell;
was a cousin or second cousin of John Walsh the younger, issued some
works with Walsh imprints in addition to his own; some single sheet
songs bear only the initials W. R.; died c. January 1776; his widow
Elizabeth continued the business.
    K. G.
    Information about William Randall is included in works on John
Walsh by Frank Kidson and William C. Smith. (*See* Bibliography.)
    A Catalogue of Vocal and Instrumental Music, for the Year 1776.
4 pp. fol. (B.M. G. 159. Vol. I.)

RANSFORD (EDWIN). Composer, vocalist, music seller and publisher,
London; 46 Museum Street, Bloomsbury, prior to 1841; 13 Charles
Street, Soho, 1841-48; 461 Oxford Street, 1848-51.

RASTELL (JOHN). Printer, lawyer and member of Parliament, London.
In business, at Fleet Bridge, "at the Abbot of Wynchcomb his place"
(? date); South Side of St. Paul's, before 1519; at the sign of the
Mermaid, next to Paul's Gate, Cheapside, 1519-36. (F. Isaac:
"English and Scottish Printing Types.") His few works include one
or two with music:—A black letter ballad sheet, of which only a
fragment remains, c. 1516 (B.M. 8. k. 8.); "A new interlude and a
mery of the nature of the iiij. elements," etc., which has been variously
dated between 1519 and 1539, and attributed to Rastell and to John
Gough, one of whom was responsible for the introduction into England
of the system of printing music at one impression. John Gough

became Rastell's tenant at the sign of the Mermaid in 1533. (Isaac.)
D. S.

RATCLIFFE (THOMAS) & THOMPSON (NATHANIEL). Printers, London. Printed for the Author, "The English Opera; or The Vocal Musick in Psyche, with the instrumental therein intermix'd. To which is adjoyned the instrumental musick in the Tempest. By Matthew Locke . . . MDCLXXV."; "Musick's Monument; or, A Remembrancer of the best practical Musick, both divine and civil . . . Divided into three parts . . . By Tho. Mace . . . 1676"; "Tripla Concordia: or a Choice Collection of new Airs in three parts. For Treble and Basse Violins: by several Authors . . . 1677." Thompson was also in business on his own account.
K.
See also Thompson (Nathaniel).

RATHBONE (JOSIAH). Bookseller and publisher, Macclesfield, 1723-56. (P.) Published "A Book of Psalmody . . . with several Hymns, and thirteen Anthems . . . By Robert and John Barber. London: Printed by William Pearson . . . for Josiah Rathbone . . . 1723." His name appears in the imprints of "The Psalm Singer's choice Companion: or a plain and easy introduction to musick . . . By Robert Barber . . . London: Printed by W. P. and sold by Josiah Rathbone in Maccles-field and J. Osborn, and T. Longman in Paternoster Row. MDCCXXVII."; "A Book of Psalmody . . . the Second edition . . . By Robert Barber. London: Printed by W. Pearson . . . for the Author; and for John Eyres, Bookseller, in Warrington, and Josiah Rathbone, Bookseller in Macclesfield. MDCCXXXIII."
P. III.

RAUCHE (MICHAEL). Musical instrument maker and publisher, at the sign of the Guittar and Flute, Chandois Street, London, c. 1763-84. Michael Rauche and Co. also appears on some imprints; published principally music for the guitar. An advertisement, January 20, 1785, stated that "Buchinger No. 443 Strand . . . being the only successor to the late Mr. Rauche, whose Guittars ever justly bore the preference, he continues to make them of the same pattern, having purchased his stock and utensils."
K.

RAWLENS (MICKEPHER). *See* Rawlins.

RAWLINGS (MICKEPHER). *See* Rawlins.

RAWLINS (MICKEPHER). Musical instrument maker, music seller and publisher, by Charing Cross (next door to the Greyhound Tavern; near the Gray-Hound Tavern; next door to the Half-Moon and Greyhound Tavern; over against the Globe Tavern), in the Strand,

London, 1699-1728. It is not known whether Rawlins occupied the same premises during the whole period, and simply changed the form of his address from time to time; from 1725, or earlier, the Globe Tavern is mentioned. His name sometimes appears as Rawlens, and Rawlings.

D. & M. (Rawlens.)

RAWLINSON, *Mr.* At the Blue Canister and Fan, the upper end of Castle Street, Leicester Fields, London. His name appears in an advertisement July 29, 1728, "The new and entertaining Fan, consisting of 14 Songs taken out of the Beggars Opera, publish'd some time since in this paper, meeting with a general approbation, has induced the contriver to engrave a second plate for the other side, which contains 15 more, making together 29 of the most celebrated songs out of the said diverting opera, all within the compass of the Flute. Sold by the Author at Mr. Gay's Head . . . and at Mr. Rawlinson's," etc.

RAWORTH (JOHN). Printer, Parish of St. Bennet Paul's Wharf, London. 1638-45. (P.) Printed in conjunction with E. Griffin "The Whole Booke of Psalmes. Collected into English Meeter by Thomas Sternehold, John Hopkins and others . . . London, Printed by E. Griffin and I. Raworth, for the Company of Stationers, 1638."

P. I.

RAYNALD (THOMAS). Printer and physician, London, c. 1540-55. At first as a printer in St. Andrew's Parish, in the Wardrobe. (D.) From 1549-c. 1555 at the Star in St. Paul's Churchyard, from where he is said to have issued two editions of a Sarum Processional and a Sarum Manual 1555, although the Star was apparently occupied by Roger Madeley in 1553. The initials T. R. appear in some imprints.

D. S.

RAYNER (WILLIAM). Printer and publisher, London, next the George Tavern, Charing Cross, 1731; Faulcon Court, near St. George's Church, Southwark, 1736-39. (P.) Published "The Universal Musician, or the Songster's Delight. Consisting of the most celebrated English and Scottish Songs, favourite Cantatas, &c . . . Vol. I . . . 1738"; some of the illustrations at the head of the songs bear the name of J. Smith; some of the plates were reissued in "The Lady's Curiosity: or Weekly Apollo," 1752. An edition of "The Universal Musician," with illustrations by J. Smith was also issued in parts by William Lloyd, 1737-38, and another anonymously with the imprint "London. Printed, and Sold by the Booksellers, London and at the Musick Shops in Towne and Country."

K. P. III.

READ (JAMES). Music engraver, Edinburgh, c. 1756-72. He engraved many of Robert Bremner's Edinburgh publications, including "A

Curious Collection of Scots Tunes," c. 1759, and "Six Duets for two Violins by Messrs. Clagget," c. 1760. Read also worked for Niel Stewart and engraved "A Collection of the newest and best Reels or Country Dances," c. 1761-63.

    K.

REAVE (JAMES). Printer, London. Printed "The First Set of Psalmes of III. Voyces. Fitt for private Chappells or other private meetings with a continuall Base either for the Organ or Theorbo newly composed after the Italian way. By William Childe . . . 1639."

REDMER (RICHARD). Bookseller, London, 1610-32; The Star, at the West door of St. Paul's. (M.) His name appears in the imprints of "Gradualia, ac cantiones sacræ . . . Lib. Primus. Authore Gulielmo Byrde . . . Editio secunda, priore emendatior . . . Londini, Excudebat H. L. Impensis Ricardi Redmeri, Stella aureæ in D. Pauli Cæmeterio. 1610"; "Gradualia, seu cantionum sacrarum . . . Lib. secundus. Authore Gulielmo Byrde . . . Excudebat H. L. Impensis Ricardi Redmeri, ad Insigne Stella aureæ in Divi Pauli Cæmeterio. 1610."

    M.

REES (WILLIAM). Printer, Llandovery. Published "Ancient National Airs of Gwent and Morwganwg; being a collection of original Welsh Melodies . . . Collected and arranged for the Harp or Piano Forte by M. Jane Williams of Aberpergwm. MDCCCXLIV."

REGENT'S HARMONIC INSTITUTION. Lower Saloon, Argyll Rooms, Regent Street, London, c. 1819-20, afterwards named the Royal Harmonic Institution, c. 1820-26. Formed by a number of professors of music with the object of publishing and selling music on a co-operative basis, and for the performance of concerts; taken over by Thomas Welsh and William Hawes, two of their number, c. 1826; after c. 1828 Welsh continued alone.

    K. (Royal Harmonic Institution.) G. (Argyll Rooms.)

    Catalogue of Music composed by W. Hawes. And which may be had at the Royal Harmonic Institution. 1821. 1 p. fol. (B.M. H. 1224. (17.))

RELFE (LUPTON). Bookseller and stationer, 13 Cornhill, London. Published c. 1810, "The Eve of Departure, a favorite Ballad, from Friendship's Offering, composed & arranged . . . by John Relfe, Musician in Ordinary to His Majesty."

REYNES (JOHN). Bookseller, at the sign of Saint George in Paul's Churchyard, London. The edition of Higden's "Polycronicon" printed by Peter Treveris, 1527, has colophon "Imprented in South-

werke by my Peter Treveris at yᵉ expences of Iohn̄ Reynes boke seller at the sygne of saynt George in Poules chyrchyarde," etc.
> S.

REYNOLDS (JAMES).   Copper plate printer, book and music seller, 174 Strand, London, c. 1836-76.   Published a small amount of music; became J. Reynolds and Sons c. 1876.
> K.

RHAMES (BENJAMIN).   Music seller and publisher, Dublin;   Blind Quay, 1756-c. 1764;   at the Sun, 16 Upper Blind Quay, c. 1764-75. Also in business as a haberdasher; succeeded by his widow, Elizabeth Rhames.
> K. G.

RHAMES (ELIZABETH).   Music seller and publisher, Dublin; 16 Upper Blind Quay, c. 1775-76;   16 Exchange Street (Upper Blind Quay renamed), c. 1776-78.   Also carried on business as a haberdasher; succeeded her husband, Benjamin Rhames; succeeded by her son, Francis Rhames, who carried on the business in her name until 1806, afterwards in his own.   Her name appears as "Mrs. Rhimes" in the imprints of volumes 1 and 2 of "A Selection of Scots Songs, harmonized . . . by Peter Urbani," c. 1794.
> K. G.

RHAMES (FRANCIS).   Music seller and publisher, 16 Exchange Street, Dublin, c. 1778-1810.   Succeeded his mother, Elizabeth Rhames and carried on the business in her name until 1806, afterwards in his own. Succeeded by Paul Alday.
> K. G.

RHIMES, *Mrs.*   *See* Rhames (Elizabeth).

RHODES (HENRY).   Bookseller, London, next door to the Bear Tavern, Fleet Street, near Bride Lane;   next door to the Swan Tavern, Fleet Street, at the corner of Bride Lane;   at the Star, at, or near the corner of Bride Lane, Fleet Street, or near Fleet Bridge, 1681-1709.   (P.) The various addresses may describe the same house.   Published the January to July, 1694, numbers of "The Gentleman's Journal: or the Monthly Miscellany . . . Consisting of news, history, philosophy, poetry, musick, translations, &c . . . London, Printed for Henry Rhodes, at the Star, the corner of Bride Lane, in Fleet Street." Published and sold "The Psalm-Singer's necessary Companion: Being, a collection of most single and double Psalm Tunes now in use . . . Composed by able masters . . . The Second edition.   London.   Printed by J. Heptinatall, for Henry Rhodes, at the Star, near Bride Lane in Fleet Street, 1700."
> P. II. D. & M.

RIBOTEAU or RIBOTTEAU (HENRY). Book and music seller, at the Crown, over against Exeter Exchange, in the Strand, London, 1711-15. Succeeded Isaac Vaillant as selling agent for the musical works engraved and printed by E. Roger of Amsterdam; also advertised "New Books in all Faculties."
P. II.

RICE (JOHN). Musical instrument maker, music seller and publisher, Dublin; 13 Dame Street, c. 1775-78; 53 Dame Street, c. 1778-80; 5 College Green, c. 1780-91; 2 College Green, c. 1791-96.
K.

RICH (N.). Bookseller? London. Published 1729, "The Beggar's Wedding: A new opera . . . To which is added, the new prologue and epilogue . . . London, printed for N. Rich." With the tunes.

RICHARDSON (M.). Bookseller and publisher, Paternoster Row, London. The name appears in the imprint of "The Royal Melody Compleat: or The new Harmony of Sion . . . By William Tans'ur, Senior . . . The Third edition . . . London: Printed by R. Brown, for S. Crowder, T. Longman and M. Richardson . . . MDCCLXIV."

RICHARDSON (W.). Bookseller, Royal Exchange, London. Published "Parochial Music corrected: intended for the use of the several Charity-Schools in London, Westminster, &c . . . The whole adapted, written, and composed, by H. Heron, Organist of St. Magnus, London Bridge . . . MDCCXC."

RICHARDSON (WILLIAM). Bookseller, Greenwich. His name appears in the imprint of "Four Anthems composed by an Amateur . . . London, Printed for the Author by Button, Whitaker & Beadnell . . . & sold by W. Richardson, Greenwich," c. 1814.

RICKMAN (THOMAS CLIO). Stationer, 7 Upper Marylebone Street, London. Published c. 1802, "To Arms! To Arms! Or, John Bull's Charge to his Country. The words by James Fisher . . . The music by Mr. Davy."

RICORDI. See Grua, Ricordi & Co.

RIDLEY (J.). Bookseller? Woodbridge. His name appears in the imprint of "The Psalmodists Exercise or A Set of Psalm Tunes & Anthems . . . composed . . . by William Cole. London Printed for the Author, by J. Johnson . . . & sold by . . . J. Ridley at Woodbridge," etc., c. 1760.

RILEY & WILLIS. Music engravers, printers and publishers, London; 23 Commerce Row, Blackfriars Road, c. 1793; 1 Charlotte Street, Blackfriars Road, c. 1797; 291 Strand, 1805. Published some music

in conjunction with W. Howe, 1 Alfred Place, London Road, St. George's Fields, London.
K.

RILEY (EDWARD). Music engraver and printer, music seller and publisher, London; 196 Fleet Street, c. 1795-98; 8 Strand, c. 1798-1803; 11 Bentick Street, Soho, c. 1806.
K.

RIVIERE & HAWKES. *See* Hawkes & Co.

RIVINGTON (ANNE). Printer to Christ's Hospital, St. John's Square, London, 1785-1832, or later. Widow of, and successor to, John Rivington the younger. Printed "A Psalm of Thanksgiving to be sung by the Children of Christ's Hospital on Monday and Tuesday in Easter Week . . . The music by R. Glenn . . . 1825"; also printed the Psalm for Easter 1827, 1828 and 1832.

RIVINGTON (CHARLES) *the Elder*. Bookseller, at the Bible and Crown, St. Paul's Churchyard, 1711-42. His name appears in the imprints of "A Book of Psalmody . . . The Fifth edition . . . By John Chetham. London: Printed by A. Pearson, for Joseph Lord . . . in Wakefield . . . and sold by . . . C. Rivington . . . London. MDCCXXXVI."; "Divine Recreations: Being a collection of Psalms, Hymns, and Canons . . . London, Printed by A. Pearson, and sold by C. Rivington . . . and by T. Cooper . . . MDCCXXXVI. (MDCCXXXVII.)"; in three parts. Succeeded by his sons John the elder, and James.
P. II.
Septimus Rivington. "The Publishing Family of Rivington." Rivingtons, London, 1919.

RIVINGTON (CHARLES) *the Younger*. Printer, London, 1746-90; White Lyon Court; Steyning (Staining) Lane. Son of Charles the elder. Printed "A Psalm of Thanksgiving to be sung by the Children of Christ's Hospital, on Monday and Tuesday in Easter Week, according to ancient custom . . . The musick by Mr. Hudson, M.B. Master of the Musick School . . . Printed by Charles Rivington, in Staining Lane, Printer to Christ's Hospital 1787." He also printed the Psalm for Easter 1789.
P. III.

RIVINGTON (CHARLES) *third of the name* & (JOHN) *third of the name*. Booksellers, London; 62 St. Paul's Churchyard, and 3 Waterloo Place, Pall Mall, 1822-27. Published some musical works. John was nephew of Charles; succeeded Francis, Charles and John Rivington; in 1827 two sons of Charles joined the firm which became Charles, John, George and Francis Rivington.

[274]

RIVINGTON (CHARLES) *third of the name*, (JOHN) *third of the name*, (GEORGE) & (FRANCIS) *the Younger*. Booksellers, London; 62 St. Paul's Churchyard and 3 Waterloo Place, Pall Mall, 1827-31. May have published or sold some musical works. George and Francis, sons of Charles, were brought into the business previously carried on by Charles and his nephew John; Charles died in 1831 and the business was continued by John, George and Francis.

RIVINGTON (FRANCIS) *the Elder* & (CHARLES) *third of the name*. Booksellers, 62 St. Paul's Churchyard, London, February 1792-1810. Published and sold some musical works. Succeeded John, Francis and Charles Rivington when their father, John, died in February 1792; became Francis, Charles and John Rivington in 1810, when John, eldest son of Francis was brought into the business.

RIVINGTON (FRANCIS) *the Elder*, (CHARLES) *third of the name* & (JOHN) *third of the name*. Booksellers, London; 62 St. Paul's Churchyard, 1810-18; 62 St. Paul's Churchyard and 3 Waterloo Place, Pall Mall, January 1819-22. Their names appear in the imprints of a number of sacred music works; John, son of Francis, in 1810 was brought into the business previously carried on by Francis and Charles; Francis died in 1822 and the business was continued by Charles and John.

RIVINGTON (FRANCIS) *the Younger* & (JOHN) *fourth of the name*. Booksellers, London; 62 St. Paul's Churchyard, and 3 Waterloo Place, Pall Mall, 1842-53; 3 Waterloo Place, Pall Mall, only, 1853-59. Published and sold some musical works. Succeeded George, Francis and John Rivington.

RIVINGTON (GEORGE), (FRANCIS) *the Younger* & (JOHN) *fourth of the name*. Booksellers, London; 62 St. Paul's Churchyard, and 3 Waterloo Place, Pall Mall, 1841-42. May have published or sold some musical works. Succeeded John, George, Francis and John Rivington; George retired in 1842 on account of ill health and the firm became Francis and John Rivington.

RIVINGTON (JAMES) & FLETCHER (JAMES). Booksellers, Paternoster Row, London, 1756-60. Published some musical works of Joseph Stephenson, "Church Harmony," 1757; also third edition, 1759; "An Excellent Anthem . . . for the . . . complete victories obtained . . . November 5, and December 5, 1757, by the Army commanded by his Prussian Majesty. And the Third Psalm paraphrased", 1758; "A New loyal Health to the King, Prince, Duke, and the Heroic King of Prussia", 1758. James Rivington, previously in partnership with his brother John, partnership dissolved March 1756; James Fletcher was the son of James Fletcher, bookseller of Oxford; partnership with James Rivington dissolved in 1760, when James Rivington went to America and settled as a bookseller in Philadelphia.

[275]

RIVINGTON (JOHN) *the Elder*.   Bookseller, 62 St. Paul's Churchyard, London, 1756-c. 1768.   His name appears in the imprint of "A Set of new Psalms and Anthems . . . By William Knapp . . . The Seventh edition.   London.   Printed for J. Newbery, and J. Rivington . . . R. Baldwin, and S. Crowder and Co . . . MDCCLXII."   Previously in partnership with his brother James, partnership dissolved March 1756; became J. and F. Rivington c. 1768, when John Rivington brought his son Francis into the business.

RIVINGTON (JOHN) *the Elder* & (FRANCIS).   Booksellers, 62 St. Paul's Churchyard, London, c. 1768-77.   Father and son; their names appear in the imprints of a number of sacred music works; another son, Charles, was brought into the business c. 1777, which became John, Francis and Charles Rivington.

RIVINGTON (JOHN) *the Elder*, (FRANCIS) & (CHARLES) *third of the name*.   Booksellers, 62 St. Paul's Churchyard, London, c. 1777-February 1792.   Father and sons; their names appear in the imprints of a number of sacred music works.   After the father died in February 1792, the business was continued by Francis and Charles.

RIVINGTON (JOHN) *the Elder* & (JAMES).   Booksellers, 62 St. Paul's Churchyard, London, 1742-56.   Sons of Charles Rivington the elder, whom they succeeded in business; partnership dissolved March 1756; John continued at the same address, James went into partnership with James Fletcher; may have published or sold some musical works.

RIVINGTON (JOHN) *the Younger*.   Printer, St. John's Square, Clerkenwell, London, 1780-85.   Son of John the elder.   Printed "Select Psalms for the use of Portman-Chapel near Portman-Square . . . MDCCLXXX."; also an edition in 1784.   When he died in 1785 the business was carried on by his widow, Anne Rivington.
    P. III.

RIVINGTON (JOHN) *third of the name*, (GEORGE) & (FRANCIS) *the Younger*.   Booksellers, London; 62 St. Paul's Churchyard, and 3 Waterloo Place, Pall Mall, 1831-36.   May have published or sold some musical works.   Succeeded Charles, John, George and Francis Rivington; John, son of John, joined the firm in 1836 which became John, George, Francis and John Rivington.

RIVINGTON (JOHN) *third of the name*, (GEORGE), (FRANCIS) *the Younger* & (JOHN) *fourth of the name*.   Booksellers, London; 62 St. Paul's Churchyard and 3 Waterloo Place, Pall Mall, 1836-41.   Published and sold some musical works.   Succeeded John, George and Francis Rivington.   The senior John Rivington died in 1841, and the firm continued as George, Francis and John Rivington.

ROBBENS (THOMAS S.). Music and musical instrument seller, Bath; 5 Chapel Row, c. 1824; 3 Margaret's Buildings, Brock Street, c. 1825-1830. Published a small amount of music including some of his own compositions.

ROBBINS (JAMES). Printer and bookseller, College Street, Winchester. Published "Harmonia Wykehamica, the Original Music in Score of the Graces, used at Winchester College, and at New College in Oxford, also the Hymn Jam Lucis; the Song of Dulce Domum; and the Song of Omnibus Wykehamicis as performed at the Anniversary Meeting of Gentlemen educated at either of the above Colleges. The whole printed under the Direction of the Revd. Gilbert Heathcote. A.M. . . . 1811"; "An English version of Domum set to music by George William Chard, Organist of the Cathedral & College at Winchester," c. 1811.
K.

ROBERTS (HENRY). Engraver, print and music seller, London; at the Star opposite the Vine Tavern in Holborn (in New Turnstile, over against the Vine Tavern in High Holborn), 1737-?; near Hand-Alley, almost opposite Great Turnstile, Holborn, c. 1745-62; later given as No. 56 near Hand Alley, etc. Worked as an engraver until 1765 or later, his best known works are "Calliope or English Harmony, a Collection of the most celebrated English and Scots Songs," etc. 2 vols. 1739-46 (issued in parts 1737, etc.); and "Clio and Euterpe or British Harmony, a Collection of celebrated Songs and Cantatas," etc. 2 vols. 1758-59 (issued in parts 1756, etc.); "Clio and Euterpe" was republished in 1762 when a third volume was added engraved by Roberts, and a fourth volume was published by John Welcker c. 1778, which may or may not have been engraved by Roberts. He engraved the ornamental dedicatory leaf in Giuseppe San Martini's "XII Sonate . . . Opera Terza . . . MDCCXLIII. Londra."
K. G.

ROBERTS (JAMES). Printer, bookseller and publisher, London; near Stationers' Hall, 1706; Warwick Lane, 1713-54. (P.) Published, sold and advertised a number of ballad operas with the music to the songs.
P. II.

ROBERTS (W.). 53 London Wall, London. Printed and published c. 1805, "New Instructions for the Bugle, with Hunting & Military Calls &c. By J. Jones."

ROBERTS (WILLIAM). Book and music seller, and printer, 197 High Street, Exeter. Printed "Twenty Original Tunes for Congregational Psalmody, and private circles, composed by Henry Devenish. Northtawton . . . 1847."

[277]

ROBERTSON (ALEXANDER). Music teacher, music seller, engraver and publisher, Edinburgh; 47 Princes Street, c. 1820-33; 47 and 39 Princes Street, c. 1833-35; 39 Princes Street, c. 1835-70. Previously partner in the business of Penson, Robertson and Co.; in the later years became Alexander Robertson and Co. Reissued some of Nathaniel Gow's publications in conjunction with Robert Purdie.
K. G.

ROBERTSON (DANIEL). Music teacher and music seller, 21 South College Street, Edinburgh, c. 1810-56. Published a small amount of music.
K.

ROBERTSON (JOHN) *Junior*. Bookseller, at Shakespear's Head, in the Saltmercat, Glasgow. Published "The Gentle Shepherd: a Scots pastoral comedy by Allan Ramsay. Adorned with cuts, the overtures to the songs, and a complete glossary . . . MDCCLVIII."

ROBERTSON (JOHN) & CO. Booksellers and stationers, 35 Lower Sackville Street, Dublin. Their name appears in the imprint of "The Psaltery; a Collection of Psalm and Hymn Tunes, carefully selected from the works of the most eminent composers . . . Dublin: Published for John Kirkwood . . . By . . . J. Robertson and Co . . . 1835."

ROBINSON, of Bath. *See* Binns & Robinson.

ROBINSON, of London. *See* Hurst, Robinson & Co.

ROBINSON & BUSSELL. Music and musical instrument sellers and publishers, 7 Westmoreland Street, and 39 Fleet Street, Dublin, c. 1843-52. Succeeded by Henry Bussell.

ROBINSON, BUSSELL & ROBINSON. Music sellers and publishers, 7 Westmoreland Street, Dublin, c. 1836-43. Had additional premises at 39 Fleet Street, Dublin, c. 1842-43. Succeeded Isaac Willis and Co.; succeeded by Robinson and Bussell.

ROBINSON (GEORGE). Music seller and publisher, 18 Duke Street, Grosvenor Square, London, c. 1837-38.

ROBINSON (GEORGE), (GEORGE) & (JOHN). Booksellers, 25 Paternoster Row, London, c. 1793-1801. Their names appear in the imprint of "An Introduction to Harmony by William Shield. London. Printed for the Author & sold by G. G. & J. Robinson . . . 1800." They succeeded George, George, John and James Robinson; succeeded by George and John Robinson.

ROBINSON (GEORGE), (GEORGE), (JOHN) & (JAMES). Booksellers, 25 Paternoster Row, London, c. 1786-93. Their names appear in the imprint of "Historical Memoirs of the Irish Bards . . . and an appendix . . . with select Irish melodies. By Joseph C. Walker . . . London. Printed for T. Payne and Son . . . and G. G. J. and J. Robinson . . . MDCCLXXXVI." Succeeded by George, George and John Robinson.

ROBINSON (GEORGE) & (JOHN). Booksellers, 25 Paternoster Row, London, c. 1801-06. Their names appear in the imprint of "Lyric Airs: consisting of specimens of Greek, Albanian, Walachian, Turkish, Arabian, Persian, Chinese, and Moorish national Songs and Melodies . . . by . . . Edward Jones . . . London: Printed for the Author. 1804. And sold . . . by G. & J. Robinson," etc. Succeeded George, George and John Robinson.

ROBINSON (H.). Musical instrument maker and music seller, London; printed and sold at Trinity Square, Great Tower Hill, c. 1802, "The Thrush. A favorite Rondo for a Military Band . . . also arranged for the Piano Forte, composed by W. Godfrey"; at 2 Crown Street, Finsbury Square, and Catherine Court, Great Tower Hill, "Robinson's Twenty four fashionable Country Dances, for the year, 1807"; at 3 Wilson Street, Finsbury Square, and Catherine Court, Tower Hill, "Robinson's Twenty four fashionable Country Dances, for the year, 1811."

ROBINSON (JACOB). Bookseller and publisher, London; Next the One Tun Tavern, near Hungerford Market in the Strand, 1737; Golden Lyon, in Ludgate Street, 1742-58. (P.) Published "The Merry Medley; or, a Christmas-Box, for gay gallants, and good companions . . . Containing . . . celebrated and jovial songs, set for the voice, violin, and modish country dances . . . by C. F. President of the Comical Club in Covent Garden", etc., c. 1744; "The Divine Companion: or, Davids Harp new-tun'd. Being a choice collection of psalms, hymns, and anthems", etc., c. 1745. Advertised and sold "The Agreeable Amusement", published by Jacob Bickerstaff, 1744; "Universal Harmony", published by John Newbery, 1744-45. Succeeded by George Kearsley or Kearsly.
P. III.

ROBINSON (JOHN). Music seller, 39 Stonegate, York. His name appears in the imprints of "Mozart's Third Motett 'Deus tibi laus et honor,' for four voices . . . Arranged . . . by Vincent Novello. London, Published for the Editor . . . and at Mr. J. Robinson's, York," etc., c. 1825; "Twenty-four Chants: to which are prefixed, Remarks on Chanting . . . By Mr. J. Gray, of York. Published for the Author, by Preston . . . London, and H. Bellerby; York; and to be had also at the music warehouses of . . . Robinson . . . in York . . . 1834."

ROBINSON (RANEW). Bookseller, Golden Lion, St. Paul's Churchyard, London, 1713-26. (P.) His name appears in the imprint of "The Psalms of David in Metre: Fitted to the tunes used in Parish-Churches. By John Patrick . . . London, Printed for W. Churchill . . . R. Robinson . . . MDCCXVIII."; also in the seventh edition, 1724.
    P. III.

ROBOTHAM (JAMES). *See* Rowbotham.

ROBOTHOME (JAMES). *See* Rowbotham.

ROBSON. *See* Flight & Robson.

ROBSON (JAMES). Bookseller, 27 New Bond Street, London. Printed and sold, "A Fifth Set of Six Sonatas for the Harpsichord Piano Forte and Organ with Accompanyments for two Violins and a Violoncello . . . by John Garth. Op. VII.", advertised November 1782.

ROCHEAD & SON. Musical instrument makers, music sellers and publishers, Edinburgh; Castle Hill and 4 Greenside Place, c. 1805-11; 370 Castle Hill, c. 1811-13; 14 Princes Street, c. 1813-16; 370 Castle Hill, c. 1816-18; 378 Castle Hill, c. 1818-22.
    K.

ROCK (WILLIAM). Organist, 27 Parliament Street, Westminster, London. Published 1785, "A Favorite Anthem as performed in Westminster Abbey. Composed by Mrs. Wilbraham & published with her permission by William Rock . . . Opera 1st." Organist of St. Margaret's, Westminster, 1774-1802.

ROE (JOHN). Bookseller? Derby. His name appears in the imprint of "David's Harp well Tun'd: or a Book of Psalmody . . . The Third edition . . . By Robert Barber, Castleton. London: Printed by Robert Brown . . . For Charles Bathurst . . . Joseph Heath, at Nottingham and Mansfield; and John Roe, at Derby. MDCCLIII."

ROGERS (ANDREW). Bookseller and publisher, Stamford, 1744-50. (P.) His name appears in the imprint of "The Voice of Melody . . . Printed for William East . . . and sold by . . . Mr. Rogers of Stamford," etc., c. 1748.
    P. III.

ROGERS (WILLIAM). Bookseller, London; Maiden's Head in Fleet Street, 1678-79; at the Sun, against St. Dunstan's Church, Fleet Street, 1680-1711. (P.) Published "A New and Easie Method to learn to Sing by Book . . . and furnished with variety of Psalm Tunes in Parts . . . 1686"; "The Psalms of David, in English Metre; translated from the original, and suited to all the tunes now sung in

SEI SONATE

OVVERO

DIVERTIMENTI DA CAMERA,

A DUE FLAUTI TRAVERSIERI

O DUE VIOLINI,

CON IL BASSO.

COMPOSTE

dal Sig.r Tomaso Prota

DI NAPOLI.

Printed for & Sold by Edmund Chapman in Duke's Court, near Bow Street, Covent Garden. and at the Music Shops. Price 5.s

Engraver of this title-page unidentified. Richard Alderman engraved
the music. 1760

Engrav'd by Rᵈ Alderman

Tomaso Prota, ''Sei Sonate ovvero Divertimenti da Camera''. Printed for Edmund Chapman. 1760

Churches: With the additions of several new. By Luke Milbourne
. . . London, Printed for W. Rogers . . . R. Clavill . . . B. Tooke . . .
J. Lawrence . . . and J. Taylor . . . 1698."
.K. P. II.

ROLFE (WILLIAM). Music seller and publisher, and pianoforte maker,
112 Cheapside, London, 1797-c. 1806. Afterwards became William
Rolfe and Sons, pianoforte makers; Rolfe was previously a partner
in the firm of Culliford, Rolfe and Barrow.
K.

ROLLS (DANIEL). Music and musical instrument seller, York Buildings,
Weymouth. Published c. 1844, "The Downs: a Song of Dorset, the
words composed by the Rev. W. Marriott Smith Marriott. The music
by his sister, Lydia B. Smith. Published by D. Rolls, at his Pianoforte
and music warehouse . . . Printed by Benson and Barling . . . Weymouth."

ROPER (ABEL) *the Elder*. Bookseller, London, 1638-80; Black Spread
Eagle, over against St. Dunstan's Church, in Fleet Street, 1641; at
the Sun, against St. Dunstan's Church in Fleet Street, c. 1650-80
(P.) Published "A Paraphrase upon the Psalms of David. By George
Sandys. Set to new tunes for private devotion: And a thorough-base
for voice, or instrument. By Henry Lawes . . . revised . . . By John
Playford. London: Printed by W. Godbid, for Abel Roper, at the
Sun against St. Dunstan's Church in Fleet Street, 1676;" forming
part of "A Paraphrase upon the Divine Poems. By George Sandys."
P. I.

ROPER (ABEL) *the Younger*. Nephew of Abel Roper the elder, publisher,
London, 1688-1726. (P.) His name appears together with that of
R. Basset in the imprints of "The Musical Entertainments in the
Virgin Prophetess; or the Fate of Troy. A new Opera. Perform'd
at the Theatre Royal. Composed by Mr. Finger. London: Printed
for A. Roper, over against St. Dunstan's Church; and R. Basset, at
the Mitre over against Chancery Lane in Fleet, 1701"; "Cassandra:
or the True Virgin Prophetess. An Opera, as it is perform'd at the
Theatre Royal . . . The Musical Entertainments being inserted in
their proper places. Printed for A. Roper at the Black Boy, and
R. Basset at the Mitre in Fleet Street," 1702. The British Museum
copies of these works do not contain any music.
P. II.

ROSE (JOHN). *See* Rudall, Rose, Carte & Co.

ROSE (WILLIAM). Music seller, 53 Strand, near Buckingham Street,
London, c. 1825-27. Published a small amount of music.
K.

ROSS (ROBERT). Musician, music seller and publisher, Edinburgh; published at his house in Playhouse Close, Canongate, 1769; at his music shop back of the Fountain Well, 1770-85; at the Head of Carrubber's Close, 1785-1805.
K.

ROUBOTHUM (JAMES). *See* Rowbotham.

ROUSSAU (F. LE). *See* Le Roussau.

ROWBOTHAM (JAMES). Bookseller, London, 1559-80; at the Rose and Pomegranate, Cheapside; at the Lute in Paternoster Row. (M.) Published at the latter address "A Briefe and easye instrution to learne the tableture to conducte and dispose thy hande vnto the Lute [by A. Le Roy] englished by J. Alford. Imprinted at London by Ihon Kynston for Iames Roubothum and are to be solde at hys shop in Paternoster rowe . . . 1568"; "A Briefe and plaine Instruction . . . for the Lute . . . by Adrian Le Roy . . . 1574." Steele (p. 101) records an unidentified work "A briefe and plaine instruction for . . . the Gitterne," c. 1568. His name also appears as Robotham, Robothome, Roubothum, Rowbothome and Rowbothum.
M. S.

ROWBOTHOME (JAMES). *See* Rowbotham.

ROWBOTHUM (JAMES). *See* Rowbotham.

ROWE (PETER ELLISON). Music seller, Royal Musical Repository, 44 Bedford Street, Plymouth. Published "Come away, come away 'tis the Nightingale's Song, Cavatina . . . Composed by Alexander Lee," c. 1840; "Tee Total Society. Sung by Mr. W. A. Chapman," etc., c. 1840.

ROY & BLAKE. Music sellers, 3 Waterloo Place, Edinburgh, c. 1825-26. Peter Walker Roy was previously in business alone.

ROY (PETER WALKER). Music seller, 3 Waterloo Place, Edinburgh, c. 1823-24. Continued as Roy and Blake, c. 1825-26; became a partner in the firm of Paterson and Roy, c. 1826.

ROYAL HARMONIC INSTITUTION. *See* Regent's Harmonic Institution.

RUDALL, CARTE & CO. Musical instrument makers, music sellers and publishers, London; 20 Charing Cross, c. 1871-78; 23 Berners Street, c. 1878 to present time. Succeeded Rudall, Rose, Carte and Co.

RUDALL, ROSE, CARTE & CO. Musical instrument makers, music sellers and publishers, London; 100 New Bond Street, c. 1852-56;

100 New Bond Street and 20 Charing Cross, c. 1856-57; 20 Charing Cross, c. 1857-71. Succeeded G. Rudall; afterwards became Rudall, Carte and Co.

RUDALL (G.). Musical instrument maker and music publisher, London; at Rudall and Rose's Flute manufactory, 7 Tavistock Street, Covent Garden, c. 1823-25; 15 Great Piazza, Covent Garden, c. 1825-37; 1 Tavistock Street, Covent Garden, c. 1837-47; 38 Southampton Street, Strand, c. 1847-52. Succeeded by Rudall, Rose, Carte and Co.

RUSSELL (W.). Music engraver, London; engraved at 8 Duke's Court, St. Martin's Lane, "The Labyrinth. A favorite Dance, arranged as a Rondo, for the Piano Forte, by Saml. Thos. Lyon. London. Printed and sold by S. T. Lyon, 82 Wells Street, Oxford Street," c. 1807; at 5 Heddon Court, Swallow Street, "These Adagio's the Composition of (the late) C. F. Abel, are now published . . . by his . . . pupil, J. B. Cramer . . . London. Printed for the Proprietor, by the Royal Harmonic Institution," etc., c. 1820.

RUTHERFORD (DAVID). Music seller and publisher, at the Violin and German Flute (German Flute and Violin) in St. Martin's Court, near Leicester Fields, London, c. 1745-71; succeeded by John Rutherford.
K. G.

RUTHERFORD (JOHN). Music seller and publisher, at the Violin and German Flute in St. Martin's Court, near Leicester Fields, London, c. 1771-84. Some single sheet songs bear only the initials I. R.; succeeded David Rutherford.
K. G.

RUTTER & McCARTHY. Music and musical instrument sellers, and publishers, 120 New Bond Street, London, c. 1818-23. Premises afterwards occupied by Addison and Beale.
K.

RYALL (JOHN). Publisher, at Hogarth's Head, Fleet Street, London, c. 1755-65. Published an edition of Bickham's "The Musical Entertainer," 1765.
P. III.

RYLAND (EDWARD). Ave Mary Lane, near St. Paul's, London. Published "A Collection of Twelve English Songs set to Musick by Mr. John Stanley M.B. London, Printed for and sold by Edward Ryland . . . 1741."

RYLES (THOMAS). Bookseller, Hull, 1707-36. (P.) His name appears in the imprint of "A Collection of Psalm-Tunes; with Great Variety of Hymns and Anthems compos'd by the best Masters . . . By James

Green. The Fourth edition . . . London. Printed by William Pearson, for the Author: and sold by . . . Tho. Ryles in Hull . . . 1718"; also in the Fifth edition, 1724.

    P. III.

S., G. *See* Smart (George).

S., J. & J. *See* Simpson (James) & (John).

S., P. *See* Short (Peter).

S., S. *See* Shenton (S.).

S., T. *See* Snodham (Thomas).

S., W. *See* Stansby (William).

SACRED MUSIC WAREHOUSE, LONDON. *See* Novello (Joseph Alfred).

SADLER (JOHN). Bookseller and printer, Harrington Street, Liverpool, 1740-65. (P.) Published "The Muses Delight. An accurate collection of English and Italian Songs, Cantatas and Duetts, set to music . . . MDCCLIV."; reissued in two volumes with the title of "Apollo's Cabinet: or the Muses Delight . . . MDCCLVI."; an edition was also published in 1757 bearing the additional words on the title-page "With twelve Duettos for two French Horns, composed by Mr. Charles"; and another in 1758.

    K. P. III.

SAFFERY (JAMES). Music seller, Christ Church Yard, Canterbury. Printed and sold "Lady Harriet Hope's Reel. Arranged as a Rondo by Osmond Saffery," c. 1800; his name appears in the imprint of "An Introduction to Music, with a variety of progressive Lessons, Songs & Preludes . . . on the Piano Forte by Osmond Saffery. London, Printed for the Author, to be had at Goulding & Co's . . . and at J. Saffery's Music Warehouse . . . Canterbury," c. 1816.

SAGG (W.). At the Minster Gates, York. His name appears in the imprint of "A Collection of Psalm-Tunes; with Great Variety of Hymns and Anthems compos'd by the best Masters . . . By James Green. The Fourth edition . . . London. Printed by William Pearson, for the Author: and sold by . . . W. Sagg . . . in York . . . 1718."

SALTER (HUMPHREY). Music seller, at the Lute in St. Paul's Churchyard (North side of St. Paul's Church), London, c. 1683-1705. Published in conjunction with Richard Hunt, "The Genteel Companion;

being exact directions for the Recorder . . . 1683." His name appears as music seller in the imprints of a few works.

K.

SALUSBURY (THOMAS). Bookseller, at the Kings Arms, next St. Dunstan's Church, Fleet Street, and at other addresses, London, 1685-98. (P.) Published "The Compleat French-Master, for Ladies and Gentlemen . . . By A. Boyer . . . London: Printed for Tho. Salusbury . . . 1694"; contains "A Collection of French Songs, to the newest and best French and English Tunes. London: Printed by W. Onely, for T. Salusbury."

P. II. D. & M.

SANDBY (WILLIAM). Bookseller and publisher, at the Ship, Without Temple Bar, Fleet Street, London, c. 1742-68. Advertised August 1743, "A Set of new Psalm Tunes and Anthems, in four Parts . . . The Second edition, corrected. Printed for William Sandby," etc.

P. III.

SANDERS, *Mrs.* 15 Bateman's Buildings, Soho Square, London. Her name appears in the imprint of "Three Sonatas for the Piano Forte, with an Accompaniment for a Violin. Composed by G. F. Pinto. London, To be had at the principal Music Shops, and of Mrs. Sanders," etc., c. 1806.

SANDFORD (JAMES). Music seller, 79 Leadenhall Street, London, c. 1828-33. Published c. 1830, "Alexander's Improved Preceptor for the Flute . . . to which are added a selection of admired airs," etc.

SANDS, DONALDSON, MURRAY & COCHRAN. Printers, Edinburgh. Printed "A Collection of Psalm-Tunes in four Parts. Neatly engraved on copper . . . Edinburgh: Printed by Sands, Donaldson, Murray, and Cochran. For Gray and Peter . . . MDCCLVIII." The partners were William Sands, James Donaldson, Alexander Murray and James Cochran.

SARE (RICHARD). Bookseller, at Gray's Inn Gate, Holborn, London, 1684-1723. (P.) His name appears in the imprint of "The Compleat French Master, for Ladies and Gentlemen . . . The Second edition . . . London, Printed for R. Sare . . . and John Nicholson . . . 1699"; contains the music of "A Collection of new French Songs, &c."; his name also appears on the fourth edition, 1707; the fifth in 1710; the seventh in 1717; and the eighth in 1721.

P. II. D. & M.

SATCHELL (J.). Musical instrument maker, Bedford Court, Covent Garden, London. Advertised, June 1782, "This day are published. Nine Canzonets for two Voices and six Airs with an accompaniment for the Piano Forte; to which is added, the Death Song of the Cherokee Indians, by a Lady . . . Also six favorite Duets, for two Voices with an Accompaniment, composed and published at the request of many ladies of distinction, by the late Aug. John Retzel."

SAULTER (HUMFREY).   *See* Salter.

SAUNDERS (FRANCIS).   *See* Knight (Joseph) & Saunders (Francis).

SAVORY (H.).   Music engraver, 220 Tottenham Court Road, London. Engraved and printed "Angel's Tears, a favourite Ballad . . . The music composed by D. Bruguier", c. 1809; "Six Ballads, with an accompaniment for the Piano Forte or Harp, composed . . . by Mrs. O'Moran," c. 1809.

SAWBRIDGE (THOMAS).   Bookseller, London, 1669-92; next the Anchor, Duck Lane (P.); at the Three Flower-de-Luces, in Little Britain.   Advertised October 1692, "A Choice Collection of Songs set by Signior Pietro Reggio, newly re-printed.   Printed for Tho. Sawbridge at the 3 Flower-de-Luces in Little Britain," etc.
P. II.   D. & M.

SCARMARDINE, *Mr*.   Grantham.   His name appears in the imprints of "Five Concertos the principal Part for the Bassoon or Violoncello, composed by Henry Hargrave . . . London Printed for the Author and sold by Mr. Walsh . . . Mrs. Johnson . . . Mr. Wynne . . . Cambridge, and Mr. Scarmardine in Grantham," c. 1765; "Five Concertos the principal Part for a Bassoon or Violoncello.   The First, Second and Fourth, for a Bassoon, four Violins, a Tenor, Harpsichord and a Part for the Double Bass.   The Third & Fifth, for a Bassoon or Violoncello & Hautboy obligato, composed by Henry Hargrave.   London Printed for the Author, and sold by Mr. Walsh . . . Mrs. Johnson . . . Mr. Wynne . . . at Cambridge, Mr. Scarmardine in Grantham", etc., c. 1765.

SCATES (JOSEPH).   Concertina manufacturer and music publisher, London; 40 Frith Street, c. 1844-47; 32 New Bond Street, c. 1847-49. Published principally music for the concertina.

SCHERER (J. B.).   Music engraver, 47 Haymarket, London.   Engraved some music issued by various publishers c. 1780-1801.

SCHETKY (G.) *Junior*.   6 Great Pulteney Street, Golden Square, London. Published "The Lonely Isle, a Song from the Lady of the Lake; written by Walter Scott Esq.   Set to music by J. G. C. Schetky," c. 1815; "Norman's Song and the Coronach.   From the Lady of the Lake written by Walter Scott Esq.   Set to music by J. G. C. Schetky," c. 1815.

SCHLIMS (F.). Stationer and importer of foreign music, 32 South Moulton Street, Oxford Street, London. His name is in the imprint of "Six Trios for two Violins and a Violoncello . . . Composed by Reichardts . . . Op. 1 . . . Sold by F. Schlims", etc., c. 1780.

SCHMIDT (JOHANN CHRISTOPH). *See* Smith (Christopher).

SCHROEDER (R.). Music seller, at his Music Repository, 7 New Bridge Street, Vauxhall, London. Published "Anxiety for thee Love, a favorite Song . . . written by Chas. Westmacott, Esqr. Composed . . . by J. Watson," c. 1820; "A Celebrated Air, arranged with Variations for the Piano Forte or Harp, by Gelinek. No. 3," c. 1821.

SCHUCHART (CHARLES). Musical wind instrument maker, at the Two Flutes & Hautboy, Chandois Street, London. Published c. 1760, "On Miss Betsy Ball. A new Song."

SCOLA (ADAMO). Music master, Vine Street, near Swallow Street, Piccadilly, over against the Brewhouse, London. Advertised February 1739, "Essercizi per Gravicembalo. Being 30 Sonatas for the Harpsichord . . . from the originals of Domenico Scarlatti . . . To be sold by Mr. Adamo Scola," etc. This work was engraved by B. Fortier, with a frontispiece by Jacopo Amiconi [Amigoni], and is usually assumed to have been published in Venice, but as Scola, Fortier and Amiconi were all in London in 1739, it seems that this beautiful work was produced and published in London.
G.

SCORE (W.). Music seller, Exeter. His name appears in an advertisement August 1779, "Twelve Voluntaries, by Dr. Green . . . London: printed and sold by J. Bland . . . sold also by W. Banks at Salisbury; W. Score at Exeter", etc.

SCOTT & CO. Pianoforte makers and music publishers, London; 15 Margaret Street, Cavendish Square, c. 1805-08; 36 Pall Mall, c. 1808-1810; 37 Pall Mall, c. 1810-13; 29 Mortimer Street, Cavendish Square, c. 1813-28. Published some music from the Pall Mall addresses.
K.

SCOTT, *Mrs*. Music seller, at the Middle Temple Gate, Fleet Street, London, 1699-?. Her name appears in an advertisement February 1700, "A New Collection of Ayres for two Flutes: Composed by Mr. Courteville, Mr. Eccles, Mr. Keen, Mr. Church, Mr. Corbet, and Mr. Cross. Sold by J. Hare . . . also sold for J. Hudgebutt at the Widow Scot's Musick Shop," etc. Succeeded her husband Samuel Scott.

SCOTT (E.). Brunswick Row, Queen Square, London. Published c. 1785, "Sophrosyne. The words from Mr. Hayley's Triumph of Temper. Set to music by Mr. Percy."

SCOTT (SAMUEL). Music seller and publisher, London; at the Miter by Temple Bar, 1687; at his shop in Bell-Yard, near (within) Temple Bar, 1688; in association with John Carr at Carr's shop at the Middle Temple Gate, 1689-c. 1695; alone at Middle Temple Gate, c. 1695-99. Scott published and sold some works in conjunction with Henry Playford; business continued by Scott's widow.
D. & M.

SCOTT (WILLIAM). Engraver, Ashley, near Market Harborough. Engraved "The Voice of Melody, Or; A Choice Collection of Psalm-Tunes in Four Parts . . . Printed for William East, in Waltham, near Melton, Leicestershire . . . Engrav'd by William Scott," etc., c. 1748.

SCOULER (J.). Music seller? In Duke's Court, near the Mews, London. His name appears in an advertisement June 1759, of "Eight Sonatas, or Lessons for the Harpsichord. By Mr. Gillier, Junior. Opera Terza. Printed for the Author . . . and J. Scouler", etc. He probably published "The Wounded Ghizzard. The words by a young lady. Set by Dl. Grant. Sold at the Musick Shop, in Dukes Court, by the Meuse", c. 1760.

SEELEY (LEONARD BENTON). Bookseller, London; 56 Paternoster Row, c. 1795-98; 15 Ave Maria Lane, Ludgate Street, c. 1798-1809; 169 Fleet Street, c. 1809-29. Continued as L. B. Seeley and Sons, 169 Fleet Street, c. 1829-36. Published and sold a number of musical works.

SELMAN (MATHEW). Bookseller, London, 1594-1627; in Fleet Street, next the Inner Temple Gate; in Fleet Street, near Chancery Lane. (M.) Published "The Second Booke of Songs and Ayres, Set out to the Lute, the base Violl the playne way, or the Base by tableture after the leero fashion. Composed by Robert Iones. Printed by P. S. for Mathew Selman by the assent of Thomas Morley, and are to be sold at the Inner temple gate, 1601."
M.

SENEFELDER (ALOIS). See Vollweiler (Georg Johann).

SERES (WILLIAM). Printer, London, c. 1546-77. At first associated with other printers, particularly John Day. Lived in Ely Rents, Holborn, then at Peter College, St. Paul's Churchyard; at the Hedgehog in St. Paul's Churchyard from 1553, or earlier. (D.) Granted licence to print psalters, primers, etc. in 1552, with reversion to his son. His musical works are "Certayne Psalmes . . . by F. S. [i.e.

Francis Seager] . . . 1553," and "The Actes of the Apostles . . . by Christopher Tye . . . 1553," both issued from The Hedgehog. A second edition of Tye's work was "Imprynted at London by Nycolas Hyll, for Wyllyam Seres, 1553". Seres assigned his patent to Henry Denham, c. 1574.
K. G. D. S.

SERVANT (THOMAS). Bookseller, Castle Street, Dublin. His name appears in the imprint of "The Psalms of David in Metre, Newly translated. With amendments. By William Barton . . . The Second edition, corrected and amended. With the Basses. By Thomas Smith. Dublin. Printed by J. Brocas, for Elip. Dopson, Tho. Servant Booksellers in Castle Street and P. Lawrence . . . 1706."
P. I.

SETCHEL (HENRY) & SON. Booksellers, 23 King Street, Covent Garden, London. Published "Messiah", containing the overture, songs and recitatives. 1809.

SHADE (GEORGE). Music seller and publisher, London; 9 Charles Street, Soho, c. 1815-17; East Side, afterwards 21 Soho Square, c. 1817-40. He had a branch establishment or agency at 1 Parliament Street, Dublin, kept by Henry L. Shade.
K.

SHADE (HENRY L.). Music seller, 1 Parliament Street, Dublin, c. 1828-1840. Was agent for George Shade, of London.

SHAND (ROBERT). Book and music seller, 41 Dundas Street, Edinburgh. Published "Love's Delight is Wooing. A Song, the words by N. C. The music by J. M. [i.e. John Moffat.], c. 1848.

SHARP (B.). Music seller, 11 Russell Court, Drury Lane, London. Published c. 1806, "No. 3 Bagatelle for the Piano Forte. Composed by L. Beethoven." Previously a partner in Buchinger, Buckenger, or Buckinger and Sharp.

SHAVE (JOHN). Bookseller, printer and publisher, Stationer's Arms, Butter Market, Ipswich, 1745-93. (P.) His name appears in the imprints of a number of musical works.
P. III.

SHAW (JOHN). Printer, 16 Crow Street, Dublin. Printed "Queen Caroline's Harmonic Trumpet Waltz for the Piano Forte, or Harp. Composed by G. P. Warden," c. 1820; "The Sorrowing Queen, a favorite Air, with Variations for the Piano Forte or Harp. Composed by G. P. Warden," c. 1820.

SHEARD (CHARLES). See Bingley (James).

SHENTON (S.). London. Published under his initials only, "The Devout Singer's Guide; containing all the common tunes now in use, with select portions of the psalms adapted to each tune, and rules for singing treble and bass . . . Recommended by Daniel Warner . . . London, Printed for S. S. and sold by Edmund Parker . . . and John Hare . . . 1711"; the fourth edition was advertised as by S. Shenton, and there may have been others bearing his name.

SHEPHERD & SUTTON. Stationers, 8 Foster Lane, London. Published c. 1830, "The Musical Golconda, or, The Beauties of Melody; a collection of the most popular airs, duets, glees, &c . . . The whole composed, selected, and arranged, by W. H. Plumstead", etc.

SHEPHERD (WILLIAM). *See* Gow & Shepherd.

SHERWIN (JOHN FREDERICK). Music and musical instrument seller, and publisher, 32 Grafton Street, Dublin, c. 1829-32. Previously partner in the business of Bunting, Walsh, Pigott and Sherwin, c. 1825-27, and Pigott and Sherwin, c. 1827-29.

SHERWOOD & CO. Booksellers and publishers, 23 Paternoster Row, London, c. 1829-49. Published a number of musical works, principally for the flute.

SHERWOOD (B.). Music seller, at his house in Old Round Court, near the Strand, or at his shop in Savile Row Passage, near Conduit Street, London. Sold "Arie nove da battelo for the Harpsichord or Guitar", c. 1760.

SHIELD (I.). Engraver, London? Engraved "Six Quartettos, five for two Violins a Tenor & Violoncello and one for a Flute, Violin Tenor, and Violoncello. Composed . . . by Willm. Shield. Op. III. Printed for Wm. Napier," etc., 1782.

SHORT (PETER). Printer, at the sign of the Star, on Bread Street Hill, London, 1589-1603. (M.) Succeeded Henry Denham, whose last place of business was the Star, Aldersgate Street. Printed a number of musical works, including some in 1600 and 1601 as "assigne of Thomas Morley." Up to c. 1593 he was in partnership with Richard Yardley. Issued some works with the imprint "Printed by P. S." His business passed to Humphrey Lownes the elder, who married Short's widow in 1604.
    K. M. S.

SHUCKBURGH (JOHN). Bookseller and publisher, London, c. 1727-61; between the two Temple Gates in Fleet Street; at the Sun, near the Inner Temple Gate in Fleet Street; at the Sun, next to Richard's Coffee House, Fleet Street. (P.) His name appears in the imprints of

"The Morning Hymn: from the Fifth Book of Milton's Paradise Lost. Set to musick by Philip Hart. London, Ingrav'd by Thos. Cross for the Author. Sold by John Brotherton . . . John Shuckburgh . . . John Young . . . & Joseph Hare . . . 1728-29"; "The Tragedy of Chrononhotonthologos: being the most tragical Tragedy, that ever was tragediz'd by any Company of Tragedians. Written by Benjamin Bounce, Esq. [i.e. Henry Carey]. London: Printed for J. Shuckburgh, and L. Gilliver . . . J. Jackson . . . and sold by A. Dodd . . . and E. Nutt", etc., c. 1734; with the tunes of the songs. In January 1739 he advertised the libretto of Handel's "Saul" with the address "at the Inner Temple Gate".
P. III.

SIBBALD (JAMES). Book and music seller, and publisher, Parliament Square, Edinburgh, c. 1780-1803. Some publications bear the name of J. Sibbald and Co.
K. P. III.

SIBBALD (WILLIAM). Musician and music seller, 5 Temple Bar, Liverpool, c. 1770-81, or later. Published c. 1773, "A Choice Collection of XII of the most favourite Songs for the Guittar, sung at Vaux Hall, and in the Deserter, now performing at the Theatre Royal, in Drury Lane . . . with an easy bass throughout, by D. Ritter."
K.

SIBLEY (WILLIAM). Music seller, London; King's Mews Gate, Castle Street, Leicester Square, c. 1818-25; 20 Duke's Court, St. Martin's Lane, c. 1825-30; 42 Whitcomb Street, Haymarket, c. 1830-40. Published a small amount of music; also in business as a carver and gilder.
K.

SIMMS & McINTYRE. Printers and booksellers, High Street, Belfast. Published "A Collection of ancient Irish Airs, adapted for the Harp, Violin, Flute, and Pipes, by John Mulholland," etc. 2 vols. Vol. 2 is dated 1810.
K.

SIMMS (HENRY). Music seller, 31 Gay Street, Bath, c. 1835-83. Published a small amount of music; afterwards became H. Simms and Son.

SIMPKIN (W.) & MARSHALL (R.). Booksellers and publishers, 4 Stationers' Court, Ludgate Hill, London, c. 1815-37. As Simpkin, Marshall and Co. c. 1837-89, at same address which was changed to Stationers' Hall Court, c. 1842. Continued as Simpkin, Marshall, Hamilton and Kent c. 1889. Published a number of musical works.

SIMPSON, *Mr.* Music seller, Cambridge. In 1737 collected subscriptions for Bickham's "The Musical Entertainer."

SIMPSON (ANN). Publisher, Sweeting's Alley, opposite the East Door of the Royal Exchange, London, c. 1749-51. Widow of John Simpson; continued in her own name until she married John Cox, probably early in 1751, after which the business was carried on by both of them as Simpson's Music Shop, or John Cox at Simpson's Music Shop, until 1764.
 G.
 A Catalogue of new Music. c. 1750. 2 pp. fol. (B.M. 7896. h. 40. (21.))
 See also Cox (John).

SIMPSON (J. C.). Sweeting's Alley, Royal Exchange, London. His name appears in the imprint of "Twelve Hymns in Four Parts, the words from Lady Huntingdon's Collection. Set to music by John Frederic Hering. London: Printed for the Author & sold by Messrs. Preston & Son . . . & Mr. J. C. Simpson," etc., c. 1796. May have been the same person as James Simpson junior.
 K.

SIMPSON (JAMES) *Junior.* Music seller, Sweeting's Alley, Royal Exchange, London. Published and sold c. 1799, "Unless with my Amanda blest. A Favorite Song. Composed by S. Porter. The words by the celebrated James Thomson." James Simpson junior, was presumably related to James and John Simpson, who were in business c. 1765-95, and he may have been the same person as J. C. Simpson.
 K. G.

SIMPSON (JAMES) & (JOHN). Musical instrument makers, music printers and publishers, at the Bass Viol and Flute, near the East Door of the Royal Exchange, later 15, Sweeting's Alley, Cornhill, London, c. 1765-95. Some single sheet songs bear only the initials J. & J. S. James and John Simpson were presumably related to John and Ann Simpson who were at Sweeting's Alley 1734-c. 1749, and c. 1749-51 respectively, and also to James Simpson junior.
 K. G.

SIMPSON (JOHN). Musical instrument maker, publisher and engraver, at the Viol and Flute (Bass Viol and Flute), Swithens (Swithin's, or Sweeting's) Alley, near (opposite the East Door of) the Royal Exchange, London, 1734-c. 1749. Previously with Elizabeth Hare, widow of John Hare, at the Viol and Flute in Cornhill; after Simpson's death, business carried on by his widow, Mrs. Ann Simpson, who had as manager, Maurice Whitaker, formerly assistant to her husband.
 K. G.
 A Catalogue of new Musick. c. 1746. 3 pp. 8°. (B.M. d. 56.)

SIMPSON (JOHN). Musical instrument maker, music seller and teacher of the flute, London; 260 Regent Street, c. 1826-30; 266 Regent Street, c. 1830-69. Published a small amount of music.

SIPPEL (C.). 15 New Square, Cambridge. Published c. 1842, "Strains of Solitude, a Fantasia for the Cornopean, with an Accompaniment for the Piano Forte, composed . . . by C. P. Smith."

Sk:; Sk:, T. *See* Skillern (Thomas) *the Elder.*

SKARRATT (ROBERT THOMAS). Music engraver, and composer London; 54 Great Wild Street, c. 1796-1809; 10 King's Place, St. Pancras, c. 1809-11 or later; 9 Platts Terrace, St. Pancras, 1817-18 or later; 11 Terrace, Upper Street, Islington, c. 1821-28 or later; 18 Cloth Fair, c. 1836-38; 1 Pearl Crescent, Lower Road, Pentonville, c. 1839. Presumably the same as the engraver of "Alcides," c. 1791, and maybe other numbers of Arnold's edition of Handel's works.
K.

SKILLERN & CHALLONER. Music sellers and publishers, 25 Greek Street, Soho, London, c. 1806-10. Partners were Thomas Skillern the younger, and Neville Butler Challoner; Skillern was previously in business on his own account; succeeded by Skillern and Co.
K.
Catalogue of New Music. 1807. 1 p. fol. (Haas, Catalogue 29. No. 35.)

SKILLERN & CO. Music and musical instrument sellers, and publishers, London; 25 Greek Street, c. 1810-16; 138 Oxford Street, c. 1816-19; 247 Regent Street, c. 1819-26. Succeeded Skillern and Challoner.
K.
Catalogue of Harp Music. c. 1813. 1 p. fol. (B.M. g. 661. (16.))

SKILLERN (THOMAS) *the Elder.* Music engraver, music seller and publisher, 17 St. Martin's Lane, London, end of 1777 or beginning of 1778-1802. His address was also given as St. Martin's Church Yard, which may have been his private residence, although it was formerly the business address of James Oswald. Some single sheet songs bear only the letters T. Sk: or, Sk: ; previously a partner in the business of Straight and Skillern; at one time an engraver in the employ of John Walsh the younger; entire stock of his music plates purchased by Thomas Preston, c. 1803.
K.
Catalogue of Vocal and Instrumental Music. 1782. 1 p. fol. (B.M. H. 1651. e. (13.))

SKILLERN (THOMAS) *the Younger.* Music seller and publisher, 25 Greek Street, Soho, London, c. 1802-06. Joined by Neville Butler Challoner

c. 1806 and became Skillern and Challoner. Partner in the firm of Skillern and Co., c. 1810-26.

K.

SLAUGHTER. At Slaughter's Coffee House on the paved stones, at the upper end of St. Martin's Lane, London. His name appears in an advertisement March 1732, "Twelve Sonatas for the Chamber, for two Violins and a Bass doubled. Composed by Mr. Bononcini. To be sold at Slaughter's Coffee House . . . at Mr. William Smith's, at Corelli's Head," etc.

SMALL, BRUCE & CO. Musical instrument makers and music sellers, Edinburgh; 54 Princes Street, c. 1830-33; 101 George Street, c. 1833-37, or later. The senior partner, George Small, had previously been a partner in the firm of Wood, Small and Co.; James Bruce was an organ builder.

SMALL (GEORGE). *See* Small, Bruce & Co.; Wood, Small & Co.

SMART & MORELAND. Music sellers and publishers, Music Warehouse, 521(?) Oxford Street, London. Published c. 1810, "Messiah. Overture and Songs in the sacred oratorio of the Messiah adapted for the voice pianoforte and organ by the late Dr. Arnold. Printed at Smart and Moreland's Music Warehouse", etc.

SMART (GEORGE). Musical instrument maker, music seller and publisher, London; the corner of Conduit Street, near Savile Row, c. 1773-December 1774; the corner of Argyll Street, 331 Oxford Street, December 1774-1805. Prior to setting up in business was employed at James Bremner's shop in New Bond Street, and afterwards by William Napier. Some single sheet songs bear only his initials G. S.; father of Sir George Smart the musician; succeeded by William Turnbull.

K.

SMITH & CO. Music sellers and publishers, London; 185 Oxford Street, c. 1834-36; 28 Southampton Row, Russell Square, c. 1836-39.

SMITH. *See* Hodges & Smith.

SMITH, *Mr.* Music seller, at the Harp and Hautboy, in Piccadilly, London. His name appears in the imprint of "An Introduction to the Art of playing on the Violin . . . By Stephen Philpot, of Lewes in Sussex . . . London: Printed and sold for the Author, by Messrs. Randall and Abell . . . Mrs. Johnson . . . Mr. Smith . . . Mr. Charles Thompson . . . and Mr. Bremner," etc; preface is dated December 10, 1766.

[294]

SMITH. Bookseller? Marlborough. Name appears in the imprint of "The Psalms of David ... By I. Watts ... A new edition, corrected. (Tunes in the Tenor Part fitted to the several Metres.) Salisbury: Printed and sold by Collins and Johnson. Sold also by . . . Smith, at Marlborough . . . MDCCLXXVI."

SMITH (ANDREW P.). Music seller, Bristol. His name appears in the imprints of "Washing Day, a proper new Ballad, for wet weather. Birmingham, Printed at the Lithographic Press, by W. Hawkes Smith. Sold also by . . . A. P. Smith, Bristol," etc., c. 1820; "Quad-rilling; a favourite Song, by the Author of 'Rejected Addresses' . . . Birmingham, Printed . . . by William Hawkes Smith. Sold also by . . . A. P. Smith, Bristol," etc., 1822.
K.

SMITH (B.). Printer, Woodbridge, Suffolk. Printed for the Author, "Sacred Harmony, containing two Anthems, fifteen Psalms and Hymn Tunes, and five pieces adapted to different subjects, in two, three, and four parts, with Symphonies, Ground Bass's, &c. By Thomas Barber, Langford," etc., preface is dated June 6, 1814.

SMITH (C.). 43 Mincing Lane, Fenchurch Street, London. Published c. 1829, "Freedom's happy Land, a national Song, the words by Edward Haskew Senr. The Music composed by Edward Haskew Junr."

SMITH (CHRISTOPHER). Music seller, whose real name was Johann Christoph Schmidt. He is said to have been brought to England by Handel whom he assisted in the management of his financial affairs. Was engaged in music selling at the Hand and Musick Book, in Coventry Street, the upper end of the Haymarket, London, 1720-25; at Meard's Court, Wardour Street, Old Soho, 1725-32, or later. Smith seems to have been principally concerned as seller of Handel's works published by John Cluer and Richard Meares.
G.

SMITH (E.) *Mrs.* Pamphlet seller, under the Royal Exchange, London. Her name appears in the imprint of "The Quaker's Opera. As it is perform'd at Lee's and Harper's Great Theatrical Booth in Bartholomew Fair. With the musick prefix'd to each song. London: Printed for J. W. And sold by J. Roberts . . . A. Dodd . . . and E. Watt and E. Smith at the Royal-Exchange. 1728."
P. III.

SMITH (FRANCIS). Oxford? Published "Musica Oxoniensis. A Collection of Songs: For One and Two Voices, With The Thorough-Bass. Publish'd by Francis Smith, and Peter de Walpergen Letter-Founder, by whom 'twas Cut on Steel, and Cast, by the Directions of the former.

Oxford: Printed by Leon. Lichfield . . . And are to be Sold by the Widow Howell, 1698." The same work was also issued with the imprint "Oxford: Printed by Leon. Lichfield: And are to be Sold by John Walsh . . . And John Hare . . . London. 1698."
D. & M.

SMITH (G.). Printer, Princes Street, Spittle Fields, London. Printed "A New Method of learning Psalm Tunes, with an instrument of musick call'd the Psalterer. 1729," by James Leman; "Psalmodia Germanica; or the German Psalmody. Translated from the high Dutch. Together with their proper tunes and thorough bass. The Second edition . . . 1732."

SMITH (JACOB?). Engraver. His name appears on some of the frontispieces of "The Modern Musick-Master . . . Printed . . . at the Printing-Office in Bow-Church-Yard, 1730"; and on some of the illustrations at the head of the songs in "The Universal Musician; or, Songster's Delight," published by William Lloyd, 1737-38; an edition of which was also published by William Rayner in 1738, and another anonymously with the imprint "London. Printed, and sold by the Booksellers, and at the Musick Shops in Towne and Country." Some of the plates of "The Universal Musician" were reissued in "The Lady's Curiosity: or Weekly Apollo", 1752. Smith's name as engraver also appears on one or two flute tutors.

SMITH (JAMES). Music and musical instrument seller, and publisher, Lord Street, Liverpool, c. 1830-65; at No. 67, 1832; No. 58, 1834; No. 64, c. 1838-40; No. 66, c. 1840-59; No. 76, c. 1860-65. Had additional premises at 47 Bold Street, c. 1843-50, afterwards became J. Smith and Son.

SMITH (JAMES TAYLOR). Bookseller, Royal Exchange, Edinburgh. His name appears in the imprint of "A Collection of Psalm Tunes and Hymns. Sung in St. George's Church. Selected . . . by Robert Gale. Edinburgh Sold by Mr. Smith . . . 1815."

SMITH (JOHN). Bookseller, Russel Street, Covent Garden, London. Published "An Heroick Poem to His Royal Highness the Duke of York, on his return from Scotland. With some choice Songs and Medleyes on the Times. By Mat. Taubman, Gent . . . 1682"; published in conjunction with John Crouch, "A New Song, to be sung by a Fop newly come over from France: To an old French tune. London, Printed for John Crouch . . . and John Smith . . . 1685"; "Three new Songs in Sir Courtley Nice. London, Printed for John Crouch . . . and John Smith . . . 1685."
P. II. D. & M.

SMITH (JOHN). Lithographer and engraver, Hanover Street, Edinburgh. Published c. 1845, "A Collection of Strathspeys & Reels, together with a set of Scots Quadrilles selected & arranged for the Piano-Forte, Violin and Violoncello . . . by James Taylor, Teacher of Music, Elgin."

SMITH (M.). At Bishop Beveridge's Head, Paternoster Row, London. His name appears in the imprint of "Psalmodia Germanica; or a Specimen of Divine Hymns, translated from the High Dutch. To-gether with their Proper Tunes and Thorough Bass. London Printed and sold by J. Young . . . M. Smith . . . 1722."

SMITH (RALPH). Bookseller, under the Piazza of the Royal Exchange, Cornhill, London. His name appears in an advertisement July 1716, "Melodies proper to be sung to any of the versions of the Psalms of David . . . Published by Phil. Hart and sold by R. Smith Bookseller, under the Royal Exchange, Cornhill, and R. Meers", etc.

SMITH (THOMAS). Musical instrument maker, in Piccadilly, London. He was a pupil of Peter Walmsley, Wamsley or Warmsley, and succeeded to his business c. 1744. Published "Minuets for His Majesty's Birth Day. As they were perform'd at the Ball at Court. For the Harpsichord, Violin, or German Flute. Printed for T. Smith, Musical Instrument Maker to His Majesty . . . 1766."

SMITH (WILLIAM). Musical instrument maker and seller, music engraver, printer and publisher, London; at the Orange Tree, between Norfolk and Arundel Streets, near St. Clement's Church in the Strand, or, at the Orange Tree, near St. Clement's Church in the Strand, c. 1720-25; at Corelli's Head, against Norfolk Street in the Strand, or, at Corelli's Head, near St. Clement's Church in the Strand, c. 1726-40; at the Golden Bass, in Middle Row, near Holborn Bars (occasionally in French as "a la Basse D'or dans le Middle Row Hol-bourne"), c. 1740-63. Served apprenticeship with John Walsh the elder.
K. G.

SMITH (WILLIAM). Printer and bookseller, Bedford. Printed "Select Psalms and Hymns, for the use of the Parish Church of Cardington, in the County of Bedford . . . MDCCLXXXVII."

SMITH (WILLIAM HAWKES). Printer, at the Lithographic Press, Birmingham, before 1820 to between 1830-35. Published a small number of illustrated songs with music by lithographic process; previously a partner in the firm of Orton and Hawkes Smith which commenced c. 1814, and are not known to have printed any music.
K.

SNAGG (RICHARD). Bookseller and publisher, London; 29 Paternoster Row, c. 1774-75; 129 Fleet Street, c. 1775-76. Published 1774,

Volume 1 of "The New Musical and Universal Magazine "; later volumes were published by John French. Snagg also published some song books without music.

K. P. III.

SNODHAM (THOMAS). Music printer and publisher, London, 1609-24. (1603-25; St. Botolph without Aldersgate. M.) Apprentice to, and son-in-law of, Thomas Este, whose widow made over to him some of her husband's copyrights in 1609, and some of Snodham's works in 1609 have the imprint Tho. Este alias Snodham. Printed works for John Browne, Matthew Lownes and Alice Browne. Issued some works with only his name in the imprint, and others in conjunction with Browne and Lownes. From 1611-13 he printed as the assigne of William Barley. In February 1626 Snodham's widow transferred her late husband's copyrights to William Stansby. Only the initials T. S. appear in some imprints.

K. G. M.

SNOWDEN (ANN). Printer, London. Printed "The Book of Psalms in Metre . . . To be sung in usual and known tunes newly translated, with amendments . . . By William Barton . . . London: Printed by Ann Snowden, for the Company of Stationers, 1705."

SNOWDEN (THOMAS). Printer, London, c. 1678-96. Printed "The Book of Psalms in Metre. Close and proper to the Hebrew: Smooth and pleasant for the metre. To be sung in usual and known tunes. Newly translated by W. Barton . . . London: Printed by Tho. Snowden, for the Company of Stationers. 1696."

P. II.

SOLEMNE or SOLEMPNE (ANTHONY DE). Dutch printer at Norwich, printed 1568-80. Printed "De C.L. Psalmen Dauids Wt den Franchoyschen Dichte in Nederlantschen ouerghesett door Petrum Dathenum. Mitsgaders den Christelicken Catechismo Ceremonien eñ Gebeden . . . Tot Noorvitz, Gheprint von Anthonium de Solemne Anno M.D.LXVIII."

S.

SOTHEBY (JOHN). See Leigh & Sotheby.

SOUTHWELL (JOHN). Music seller and publisher, 17 Earl Street, North, Dublin, c. 1803-06.

K.

SOUTHWELL (NICHOLAS). Musical instrument maker and music seller, at various numbers in Duke Street, Liverpool, c. 1810-32; at No. 99, 1810-11; 101, 1813-17; 105, 1818; 109, 1821; 109 and 110, 1824-27; 117 and 118, 1829; 104 and 105, 1832. Published c. 1817,

"Six Waltzes for the Flute with an accompaniment for the Piano Forte. Composed . . . By Chas. Nicholson. Printed & publish'd by N. Southwell, at his P.Forte manufactory, 101 Duke Street, L'pool", etc.

SPAVAN (R.). Bookseller and publisher, at the Crown, in Ivy Lane, Paternoster Row, London. Advertised as republished, January 1750, "In six volumes . . . The Musical Miscellany. Being a collection of choice songs, set to the violin and flute by the most eminent masters. Sold by R. Spavan", etc. This work was originally published by John Watts, 1729-31.

SPERATI (B.). Music seller, 34 Bury Street, St. James's, London, c. 1811-?. Previously a partner in Cianchettini and Sperati.

SPIERS (WALTER). Stationer and publisher, 399 Oxford Street, London. Published "The Christmas Fête: a literary and musical offering for 1836. Written by the author of 'Clarenswold.' Composed by W. Kirby."

SPRINT (BENJAMIN). Bookseller and publisher, at the Bell, in Little Britain, London, c. 1709-37, in partnership with his brother John until 1729. Published a number of musical works, some while in partnership with his brother.
    K. P. II. D. & M.

SPRINT (JOHN). Bookseller and publisher, at the Bell, in Little Britain, London, 1698-1729, at first in partnership with his father, Samuel Sprint. Published a number of musical works from c. 1701, some in conjunction with John Nicholson, 1701-06, some with Henry Playford, 1703-06, and some in partnership with his brother Benjamin, c. 1709-29.
    K. P. II. D. & M.

SPRINT (SAMUEL). Bookseller and publisher, London; at the Golden Ball, 1670-71; at the Bell (Blue Bell), Little Britain, 1672-1707? (P.) His name appears in the imprint of "The Dancing-Master . . . The Tenth edition . . . Printed by J. Heptinstall, for Samuel Sprint . . . and H. Playford . . . 1698." Took his son John into partnership in 1698, who published alone at the above address from c. 1701, although Samuel Sprint may have retained the business until his death in 1707.
    P. II.
    See also Sprint (John).

STAMMERS (JOSEPH). Managing director of the London Wednesday Concerts Society, 4 Exeter Hall, Strand, London, c. 1849-50. Published a small amount of music.

STANLY (R.). Publisher, Newmarket. His name appears in the imprints of "Six Duets for two Violins . . . By T. A. Hughes. London, Published by R. Hack . . . & R. Stanly, Newmarket," c. 1835; "Hack's Selection of one hundred new & favorite Mazourkas, Quadrilles, Waltzes, Dances &c . . . London, Published by R. Hack . . . & R. Stanly, Newmarket", etc., c. 1840.

STANSBY (WILLIAM). Printer and bookseller, London, 1597-1639. (M). Apprentice to John Windet for seven years; printed a number of musical works from 1610, including editions of the Sternhold and Hopkins versions of the Psalms. In 1611 Windet assigned his copyrights to Stansby, who may have taken over Windet's premises at the Cross Keys, St. Paul's Wharf. Acquired the copyrights of Thomas Snodham from his widow, February 1626. Stansby's business passed to Richard Bishop in 1639.
K. M.

STAPLETON (FREDERIC). *See* Wessel & Co.

STATIONERS' COMPANY. Stationers' Hall, London. Issued many editions of the Psalms, particularly the versions by Sternhold and Hopkins, from 1604 onwards, printed for the Company by John Windet and others, whose names are recorded separately in this dictionary.
M.

STEART (GEORGE). Letter press, copper plate and music printer, 5 Barton Street, Bath. Printed for the Author, Vol. I of "A Periodical Collection of Vocal Music, (never before printed) consisting of Italian and English Songs . . . Composed by Venanzio Rauzzini . . . In two volumes," c. 1797; "Portions of Psalms, selected from the versions of Brady and Tate, and adapted to fifty tunes . . . Composed by the late John Broderip . . . and Robert Broderip "; preface dated August 31, 1798; "Twenty New Psalms, composed by Thomas Shell, and sung at the Rev. Dr. Randolph's Chapel, Laura Place, Bath," c. 1801.

STENT (PETER). Printer and engraver, at the White Horse, Gilt Spur Street, without Newgate, London, 1643-67. (P.) Printed "The Psalmes of David in 4 languages . . . Set to ye tunes of our Church. With corrections by W. S. [i.e. William Slatyer] . . . 1652."
P. I.

STEVEN (JAMES). Music seller, publisher and stationer, Glasgow; King Street, c. 1801; 35 Wilson Street, c. 1802-20. Sometimes referred to in imprints as Stevens; succeeded by James Brown.
K.

STEVENS (JAMES). *See* Steven.

STEVENSON (THOMAS). Bookseller, Trinity Street, Cambridge. His name appears in the imprint of "Twenty-four Chants: to which are prefixed, Remarks on Chanting . . . By Mr. J. Gray, of York. Published for the Author, by Preston . . . London, and H. Bellerby; York . . . and of the following booksellers . . . Stevenson, Cambridge . . . 1834."

STEVENSON (THOMAS GEORGE). Bookseller and publisher, 87 Princes Street, Edinburgh. Published "Minuets &c. Composed by the Right Honourable Thomas Earl of Kelly . . . MDCCCXXXVI."; "Minuets and Songs, composed by The Right Honourable Thomas Earl of Kelly, now for the first time published; with an introductory notice by Charles Kirkpatrick Sharpe, Esq. Second edition . . . MDCCCXXXIX."

STEWART. *See* MacLachlan & Stewart.

STEWART (CHARLES) & CO. Printers, Edinburgh. Printed "The Vocal Magazine containing a Selection of the most esteemed English, Scots, and Irish Songs," etc., 1797-1800; "The Musical Repository: A collection of favourite Scotch, English, and Irish Songs . . . Edinburgh: Printed by C. Stewart and Co. for William Anderson, Stirling. 1802."
K.

STEWART (GRAHAM). Engraver, 23 Green Street, Dublin. Engraved some single sheet songs printed by William Jones, which included "The Double Mistake" and "The Merry Christ'ning", c. 1780.

STEWART (N.) & (M.). *See* Stewart (Neil).

STEWART (NEIL). Musical instrument seller and repairer, music seller and publisher, Edinburgh; at the sign of the Violin and German Flute, in the Exchange, c. 1759-60; opposite the Head of Blackfriars Wynd, c. 1760; at the Violin and Guitar, the Exchange, c. 1765; Milns Square, opposite the Tron Church, c. 1770-73; Parliament Square, or Close, c. 1773-92, with additional premises at 40 South Bridge Street, c. 1788-92; 37 South Bridge Street, c. 1792-1802; 39 South Bridge Street, c. 1802-04; 69 Adam Square, c. 1804; 88 West Side, South Bridge Street, c. 1805. From 1787 the business was carried on under the names of Neil Stewart and Co., or N. and M. Stewart, i.e. Neil and Malcolm Stewart, the sons of Neil, the founder of the firm.
K. G.

STOCKDALE (JOHN). Bookseller, Piccadilly, London, c. 1784-1815. Published with George Goulding, "The Psalms of David for the use of Parish Churches. The words selected by the Rev. Sir Adam Gordon Bart . . . The music selected, adapted, and composed by

[301]

Dr. Arnold . . . assisted by J. W. Callcott . . . London. Printed for John Stockdale . . . & George Goulding "; preface dated November 1, 1791.

STOCKDALE (JOHN JOSEPH). Bookseller, 41 Pall Mall, London, c. 1806-20. Published a small amount of music.

STODART. *See* Wessel & Stodart.

STOKES (JOSHUA). . Music seller and publisher, Dublin; 13 Dame Street, c. 1781; 24 Dame Street, c. 1782-90.
K.

STONEHOUSE. *See* Wallis & Stonehouse.

STONEMAN (JOHN). *See* Houlston & Stoneman.

STORY (JOHN). Bookseller, Newcastle-on-Tyne, 1685-86. His name appears in the imprint of "A Joco-Serious Discourse in two Dialogues, between a Northumberland-Gentleman, and his Tenant a Scotchman, both old Cavaliers . . . By George Stuart . . . London, Printed for Benjamin Tooke, at the Ship in St. Paul's Church-Yard, and John Story, in Newcastle, 1686 "; contains the music of seven songs.
P. II. D. & M.

Str: *See* Straight (Thomas).

Str: & Sk: *See* Straight & Skillern.

STRAHAN (A.). Printer, Printer Street, London. Printed "The Bardic Museum, of primitive British Literature . . . By Edward Jones, Bard to the Prince . . . London: Printed by A. Strahan . . . for the Author; 1802", etc.

STRAHAN (WILLIAM). Printer, London, 1737-85; Bury Court, Love Lane; New Street. (P.) His name appears in the imprint of "The Beggar's Opera . . . To which is prefixed the overture in score: And the musick to each song. London: Printed for W. Strahan, T. Lowndes, T. Caslon, W. Griffin, W. Nicoll, S. Bladon, and G. Kearsly. MDCCLXXI."; also in two editions published 1777.
P. III.

STRAIGHT & SKILLERN. Music engravers, music sellers and publishers, London; opposite Tom's Coffee House in Russell Street (sometimes given as Great Russell Street), Covent Garden, 1766-69; 17 St. Martin's Lane (T. Straight & Skillern, St. Martin's Lane, next the Strand), 1769 to end of 1777 or beginning of 1778. "Str: & Sk:" appears on some of their music where the full imprint is not given.

Thomas Straight and Thomas Skillern were previously music engravers with John Walsh the younger; partnership dissolved at the end of 1777 or beginning of 1778; both carried on business independently, Skillern at 17 St. Martin's Lane, and Straight at 138 St. Martin's Lane. Straight and Skillern may have acquired the business of James Oswald, some of whose works they republished.

    K. G.

STRAIGHT (S.). Music engraver, printer and publisher, London; 4 Green Street, Leicester Square, c. 1790-1800; 14 Green Street, Leicester Square, c. 1800-05; 12 Hemmings Row, Kings Mews, c. 1820. Probably the son of Thomas Straight, as he was sometimes described as Straight, Junior.

STRAIGHT (THOMAS). Music engraver, music seller and publisher, 138 St. Martin's Lane (near Charing Cross), London, end of 1777 or beginning of 1778-c. 1783. At Compton Street, Clerkenwell, engraved "The Psalm Singers Help . . . London. Printed for & sold by Thos. Knibb opposite Skinners Street, Bishopsgate," etc., c. 1765; at 7 Lambeth Walk, Surrey, engraved "A General Collection of the ancient Irish Music . . . adapted for the Piano Forte, with a prefatory introduction by E. Bunting. Vol. 1. London. Printed & sold by Preston & Son, 97 Strand," c. 1796. Presumably the same as the engraver of "Belshazzar," c. 1790, and maybe other numbers of Arnold's edition of Handel's works. Was a partner in Straight and Skillern 1766-77 or 1778; at one time an engraver in the employ of John Walsh the younger; some single sheet songs bear only the letters "Str:".

    K.

STRAKER (D.). Music seller, 15 Great Portland Street, Cavendish Square, London. Published "at his Musical Repository" some of his own compositions, c. 1823.

STRANGE (WILLIAM). Bookseller and publisher, 21 Paternoster Row, London, c. 1831-52. Published with James Bingley Nos. 1-78 of "The Musical Bouquet," c. 1846, or earlier.

STURGE (JOSEPH). Music seller, 28 Park Street, Bristol, c. 1800-13. Published c. 1800, "Twelve Solos for a Violin with a Thorough Bass for the Piano Forte or Violoncello. Composed by Michele Mascitti. Opera Prima and Seconda."

SURMAN (JOSEPH). Music publisher, 9 Exeter Hall, Strand, London, c. 1839-71. Conductor of the Sacred Harmonic Society 1832-48; first conductor of the London Harmonic Society which started in 1848.

SUTHERLAND (JAMES). *See* Corri & Sutherland.

SUTHERLAND (JOHN). Book and music seller, and publisher, Edinburgh; 27 Leith Street, c. 1809-11; 9 Calton Street, c. 1811-32; 12 Calton Street, c. 1832-60. Became John Sutherland and Co. c. 1845.
    K.

SUTTON. *See* Shepherd & Sutton.

SUTTON (HENRY). Printer, London, c. 1552-63, at various addresses; The Black Boy or Moryan, in St. Paul's Churchyard, and sometimes given as in Paternoster Row. (D.) Sutton in conjunction with John Kingston issued Manuals, Processionals and Hymnals, from 1554-55.
    D. S.

SWAIN (THOMAS). Engraver, London? Engraved "Directions for the Flagellett wth 20 severall lessons fitted to the same Instrument. Written & engraven by Tho: Swain gent: 1667. Sold by Robert Pawlett att the Bible in Chancery lane."

SWAIN (THOMAS). Music and musical instrument seller, and publisher, 53 Upper Baker Street, London, c. 1838-53.

SWALE (JOHN). Bookseller, Leeds, 1714-42. (P.) His name appears in the imprints of "A Collection of Psalm-Tunes; with Great Variety of Hymns and Anthems compos'd by the best Masters . . . By James Green. The Fourth edition . . . London. Printed by William Pearson, for the Author: and sold by . . . J. Swale in Leeds . . . 1718"; "A Book of Psalmody . . . The Fifth edition . . . By John Chetham. London: Printed by A. Pearson, for Joseph Lord . . . in Wakefield . . . and sold by . . . John Swale . . . in Leeds . . . MDCCXXXVI."
    P. III.

SWALLOW (JOHN). Letterpress and music printer, Corn Exchange, Leeds, c. 1835-70. Printed and published c. 1845 a small number of compositions by William Jackson of Masham, Yorkshire.
    K.

SYKES & SONS. *See* Sykes (William).

SYKES (JOHN). Music seller and publisher, 30 Boar Lane, Leeds, c. 1845-1861, or later. Succeeded Sykes and Sons.

SYKES (W.) *Junior*. Artist and designer whose name appears on the illustrated title-page of "Songs in the new Opera call'd Rosamond . . . Compos'd by Mr. Tho. Clayton," issued by John Walsh, John Hare and P. Randall in 1707.

SYKES (WILLIAM). Music seller and publisher, Leeds; 18 Burley Gate, c. 1817-25, with additional premises at 16 Burley Gate, c. 1822-25;

became Sykes and Sons, 72 Briggate, and 16 and 18 Burley Gate, c. 1826-36; 21 Boar Lane, c. 1836-45; 30 Boar Lane, c. 1845. Succeeded by John Sykes.

    K.

T
C*S. *See* Thompson (Charles) & (Samuel).

T., H. *See* Thorowgood (Henry).

T., N. *See* Thompson (Nathaniel).

T
S*A. *See* Thompson (Samuel) & (Ann).

T
S P. *See* Thompson (Samuel), (Ann) & (Peter).
A

TALLIS (THOMAS). *See* Byrd (William).

TANS'UR (WILLIAM). Composer of Psalm Tunes, etc. Engraved and printed, at the Golden Ball in Wood's Close, London, "The Oxfordshire Harmony . . . Containing, a select number of Hymns, Anthems, and Chants, Canons . . . By John Sreeve . . . 1741," 3 vols.

TAYLOR, *Mr.* Bookseller, opposite the Opera House, in the Haymarket, London. His name appears in the imprint of "The Favourite Songs in the new Opera call'd Antigono, by Sig. Conforti. Printed and sold for the Proprietor, to be had at Mr. Taylor's," etc., advertised April 1757.

TAYLOR (JOHN). Bookseller, London; at the Globe, at the West End of St. Paul's Churchyard, 1683-87; at the Ship, in St. Paul's Churchyard, 1687-1713. (P.) His name appears in the imprint of "The Psalms of David, in English Metre; translated from the original, and suited to all the tunes now sung in Churches: with the additions of several new. By Luke Milbourne . . . London, Printed for W. Rogers . . . R. Clavill . . . B. Tooke . . . J. Lawrence . . . and J. Taylor . . . 1698." From c. 1700-11 in partnership with his son William, who afterwards went into business on his own account.

    P. II.

TAYLOR (JOHN EDWARD). *See* Taylor (Richard) & (John Edward).

TAYLOR (JOSEPH). Music seller, Glasgow; 18 Hutcheson Street, c. 1805-15; 37 Hutcheson Street, c. 1815-29; 94 Argyle Street, c. 1829-33; 138 Argyle Street, c. 1833-35; 72 Argyle Street, c. 1835-1838. Published a small amount of music.

    K.

TAYLOR (RANDAL). Bookseller, near Stationers' Hall, London. Published a Ballad, "A True Relation of the dreadful combate between Moze of Moze-Hall and the Dragon of Wantley . . . 1685."

TAYLOR (RICHARD). Music seller, 11 Watergate Street, Chester. His name appears in the imprints of "Adieu my Fair. A favorite ballad. Composed by E. Bailey. London. Printed by Broderip and Wilkinson . . . and by Richd. Taylor . . . Chester," c. 1800; "Rule Britannia as a Duet for two Performers and for a Soprano and Bass by the Author of 'The Principles of Music at one View'. London. Printed by Goulding & Co. . . . and by Richard Taylor . . . Chester," c. 1800.

TAYLOR (RICHARD) & (JOHN EDWARD). Printers and publishers, 7 Red Lion Court, Fleet Street, London, c. 1838-51. Published a small amount of music.

TAYLOR (ROBERT). Bookseller and publisher, Berwick on Tweed, 1753-76. (P.) Printed and sold "The Psalms of David . . . By I. Watts . . . The Eighteenth edition . . . (Tunes in the Tenor Part fitted to the several metres.) MDCCLIII."
P. III.

TAYLOR (ROBERT). Music engraver, London. Engraved "The Kiss dear Maid. Song, the words by Lord Byron. The melody by T. Williams. Arranged by Henry Smith. London. Published by T. Williams, music seller, 29 Tavistock Street, Covent Garden," c. 1815.

TAYLOR (WILLIAM). Bookseller, at the Ship, Paternoster Row, London, 1711-23. (P.) His name appears in the imprint of "The Psalms of David in Metre: Fitted to the tunes used in Parish-Churches. By John Patrick . . . London, Printed for W. Churchill . . . W. Taylor . . . MDCCXVIII." From c. 1700-11 in partnership with his father John Taylor.
P. II.

TEBROC (C.) *pseud.* See Corbet (Charles).

TEDDER & CHRISTIAN. Music sellers and publishers, 28 High Street, Newington Butts, London, c. 1849-51.

TEGG (THOMAS). Bookseller and publisher, London; 111 Cheapside, c. 1805-23; 73 Cheapside, c. 1823-32. Became Thomas and James Tegg c. 1832-33; Thomas Tegg and Son c. 1833-38; continued as Thomas Tegg c. 1838-48. Published a number of song books with music.
K.

TEGG (THOMAS) & (JAMES). *See* Tegg (Thomas).

TERRY (GEORGE). One of His Majesty's Musicians in ordinary, Denmark Street, Soho, London. Published and sold c. 1760, "Six Trios for two German Flutes or two Violins with a Thorough Bass for the Harpsichord. Composed by Sigr. Gio. Giacomo Androux."

THOMAS (THOMAS). Printer, Eastgate Row, Chester. Published "Bangor Cathedral Collection: being a selection of anthems and sacred music . . . By the very Rev. the Dean of Bangor [J. H. Cotton] . . . Chester. T. Thomas . . . MDCCCLVIII."

THOMAS (W.). Music seller, 5 Exeter Street, Sloane Street, London. Printed and published c. 1806, "The Celebrated Fairy Dance. (As danced in the first Circles of Fashion.) Arranged as a Rondo for the Piano Forte by M. Holst."

THOMASON (GEORGE) & PULLEN (OCTAVIAN). Booksellers, The Rose, St. Paul's Churchyard, London, c. 1639-43. (P.) Published "The Psalmes of David in 4 languages . . . Set to ye tunes of our Church by W. S. [i.e. William Slatyer.] London. Printed by Tho: Harper for George Thomason & Octauian Pullen . . . 1643." Both were in business on their own account prior to, and after, the partnership, but there is no evidence that they published any other music.
P. I. (Pulleyn.)

THOMPSON & SON. Musical instrument makers, music sellers and publishers, at the Violin and Hautboy, St. Paul's Church Yard, London, c. 1757-61. Widow and son of Peter Thompson; some publications have imprints, Mrs. Thompson and Son, and Charles and Ann Thompson. Succeeded Peter Thompson; followed by Thompson and Sons.
K. G.

THOMPSON & SONS. Musical instrument makers, music sellers and publishers, St. Paul's Church Yard, London, c. 1761-63. Widow and sons of Peter Thompson: succeeded Thompson and Son: succeeded by Charles and Samuel Thompson.
K. G.

THOMPSON, *Mr*. At the Dolphin, in St. Paul's Churchyard, London. His name appears in an advertisement February 1750, "The Morning Hymn, from the Fifth Book of Milton's Paradise Lost. Set to musick by the late Mr. Philip Hart and sold by his nephew William Hart, at the following places, viz At Billingsgate Ward School on St. Mary-Hill, Mrs. Hare, over against the Mansion-House, Cheapside; Mr. Thompson's at the Dolphin in St. Paul's Church Yard; Mr. Smith's Middle Row, Holborn", etc.

THOMPSON (ANN) & (HENRY). Musical instrument makers, music sellers and publishers, 75 St. Paul's Church Yard, London, 1795-c. 1798. Succeeded Samuel, Ann and Henry Thompson; followed by Henry Thompson.
K. G.

THOMPSON (CHARLES) & (ANN). *See* Thompson & Son.

THOMPSON (CHARLES) & (SAMUEL). Musical instrument makers, music sellers and publishers, 75 St. Paul's Church Yard, London, c. 1763-76. Some single sheet songs bear only the initials $\frac{T}{C*S}$; succeeded Thompson and Sons; followed by Samuel Thompson.
K. G.

THOMPSON (HENRY). Musical instrument maker, music seller and publisher, 75 St. Paul's Church Yard, London, c. 1798-1805. Succeeded Ann and Henry Thompson; succeeded by Purday and Button.
K. G.

THOMPSON (M.). London. Published "The Loyal Sherifs of London and Middlesex. Upon their election. To the tune of, Now at last the Riddle is expounded. London. Printed for M. Thompson, 1682."

THOMPSON (NATHANIEL). Printer and bookseller, Dublin and London, 1666-88. (P.) Printed a number of musical works, some bearing only the initials N. T.; for a few years after c. 1673 in partnership with T. Ratcliffe.
P. II. D. & M.
See also Ratcliffe (Thomas) & Thompson (Nathaniel).

THOMPSON (PETER). Musical instrument maker, music printer, music seller and publisher, at the Violin and German Flute (Violin, German Flute and Hautboy) (Viol and Hautboy) (Violin and Hautboy), West end of St. Paul's Church Yard, London, c. 1746-57. Business continued by his widow and son as Thompson and Son.
K. G.
A Catalogue of Musick. c. 1752. 2 pp. fol. (B.M. Hirsch IV. 1111. (14.))

THOMPSON (ROBERT). Musical instrument maker and publisher, London; at the Bass Violin (Bass Viol), near (next) the Chapter House, or, 1 Paul's Alley (in Paul's Alley), St. Paul's Church Yard, 1748-December 1769; 8 Lombard Street, January 1770-85.
K.

THOMPSON (SAMUEL). Musical instrument maker, music seller and publisher, 75 St. Paul's Church Yard, London, c. 1776-77. Succeeded

Charles and Samuel Thompson; Ann Thompson came into the business c. 1777, which continued as Samuel and Ann Thompson.
K. G.

THOMPSON (SAMUEL) & (ANN). Musical instrument makers, music sellers and publishers, 75 St. Paul's Church Yard, London, c. 1777-79. Some single sheet songs bear only the initials $\frac{T}{S*A}$; succeeded Samuel Thompson; became Samuel, Ann and Peter Thompson c. 1779.
K. G.

THOMPSON (SAMUEL), (ANN) & (HENRY). Musical instrument makers, music sellers and publishers, 75 St. Paul's Church Yard, London, c. 1794-95. In some imprints described as Messrs. Thompson, or, Thompsons' Warehouse; succeeded Samuel, Ann, Peter and Henry Thompson; Samuel died August 1795, and business became Ann and Henry Thompson.
K. G.

THOMPSON (SAMUEL), (ANN) & (PETER). Musical instrument makers, music sellers and publishers, 75 St. Paul's Church Yard, London, c. 1779-93. Some single sheet songs bear only the initials $\frac{T}{S\ P}$; A succeeded Samuel and Ann Thompson; Henry Thompson came into the business c. 1793, which continued as Samuel, Ann, Peter and Henry Thompson.
K. G.
Catalogues:—Music. c. 1781. 4 pp. fol. (B.M. Hirsch IV. 1111. (15.)); c. 1782. 4 pp. fol. (B.M. 7896. h. 40. (14.)); New Music. October 1, 1785. 4 pp. 4°. (Haas, Catalogue 21. No. 39.); October 1, 1786. 4 pp. fol. (B.M. 7896. h. 40. (8.)); October 1790. 8 pp. 8°. (B.M. 7900. f. 18.)

THOMPSON (SAMUEL), (ANN), (PETER) & (HENRY). Musical instrument makers, music sellers and publishers, 75 St. Paul's Church Yard, London, c. 1793-94. Sometimes described in their imprints as Messrs. Thompson, or, Thompsons' Warehouse; succeeded Samuel, Ann and Peter Thompson; Peter dropped out c. 1794 and business continued as Samuel, Ann and Henry Thompson.
K. G.

THOMSON. *See* Fryer & Thomson.

THOMSON (GEORGE). Edinburgh and London. Collector of Scotch, Welsh and Irish Airs, which he published in collections at his own expense from 1793 to 1845. The melodies had symphonies and accompaniments by Haydn, Beethoven, Pleyel, Kozeluch, and the

printers were John Moir, Thomas Preston, W. H. Lizars, and Ballantyne and Co., who are entered separately in this dictionary.
K. G.

Cecil Hopkinson and C. B. Oldman: "Thomson's Collections of National Song with special reference to the contributions of Haydn and Beethoven. Printed for the Authors, Edinburgh, 1940." (Reprinted from *Edinburgh Bibliographical Society Transactions*. Vol. II. Part 1. 1940.)

THOMSON (T.). Bookseller? London. Published John Gay's "Polly: An Opera. Being the second part of the Beggar's Opera. Printed for T. Thomson. 1729."

THOMSON (WILLIAM). Book and music seller, Exeter Change, London, c. 1775-80, or later. His name appears in the imprint of "A Collection of Glees Catches and Canons for three, four, five and six voices. Composed by Benjamin Cooke . . . London. Printed for the Author & may be had at his house . . . and of William Thomson," etc., preface dated February 22, 1775; edited, published and sold "Symphonia, or a Collection of Anthems . . . Composed by Messrs. Bird, Tallis, Bull, Mundy, Greene, Travers and Kent. The whole selected from manuscripts . . . by Wm. Thomson," etc., c. 1780. He was at one time librarian to the Academy of Ancient Music, and organist of St. Michael's, Cornhill.
G.

THORNTON (ROBERT). Bookseller and printer, at the sign of the Leather Bottle, in Skinner Row, Dublin, 1682-1701. (P.) Engraved, printed and published some music 1685-86.
K. P. II.

THOROWGOOD & HORNE. Musical instrument makers, music printers and publishers, London; at the Violin and Guitar, opposite Grocers Alley in the Poultry, c. 1761 to mid-1763; at the Violin and Guitar, near Mercer's Chapel, Cheapside, 1763 until near the end of 1764; Henry Thorowgood continued the business alone.
K. G.

THOROWGOOD (HENRY). Musical instrument maker, music printer and publisher, London; at the Violin and Guitar, near Mercer's Chapel, Cheapside, near the end of 1764 to the beginning of 1765; at the Violin and Guitar, under the North Piazza of the Royal Exchange (afterwards numbered 6 North Piazza, Royal Exchange in 1767), beginning of 1765-c. 1780. Served apprenticeship with John Cox; published some music in conjunction with Richard Duke; some single sheet songs bear only the initials H. T. Previously in partnership as Thorowgood and Horne.
K. G.

THREE LUTES IN PAUL'S ALLEY, THE. *See* Griffin (Edward).

TILLEY (S.). Engraver, 2 Booth's Court, Oxford Street, London. Engraved "The Blue Bell of Scotland. With Variations for the Harp or Piano Forte by W. Duchatz. Professor of the Pedal Harp No. 24, Portland Street, Soho," c. 1800; "A Favorite Duett on Peace. Composed by R. Kent. London. Printed by Alexr. Webley, No. 11 Welbeck Street," c. 1805; "Four Pieces of Music in imitation of the Four Seasons of the Year with four analogus and most elegant engravings . . . set for the Piano Forte . . . by Signor Sampieri. Printed for the Author," c. 1806.

TILLEY (THOMAS). Musical instrument maker, 5 Charing Cross, London. Printed for and sold by, c. 1790, "The Favorite Sinfonie as performed at Mr. Kammell's Subscription Concert . . . for two Violins, two Oboes, two Horns, a Tenor and Bass. Composed by Sigr. Carlo Ditters."

TILLMAN (ISAAC). Printer, at the Violin and Woolpack, near the Horn Tavern in Fleet Street, London. Printed for the Author c. 1760, "Six Concerto's for the Organ or Harpsichord. With Instrumental Parts. Composed by Mr. Edwards."

TILT (CHARLES). Bookseller and publisher, 86 Fleet Street, London. His name appears in the imprint of "Musical Souvenir for 1829. London. C. Tilt . . . Chappell . . . and Longman & Bates," etc.

TODD (J.) & (G.). Booksellers, Stonegate, York. Their names appear in the imprint of "Twenty-four Chants: to which are prefixed, Remarks on Chanting . . . By Mr. J. Gray, of York. Published for the Author, by Preston . . . London, and H. Bellerby; York . . . and of the following booksellers . . . J. & G. Todd . . . York. 1834."

TOFT (TIMOTHY) & LOBB (R.). Booksellers and publishers, Chelmsford. Their names appear in the imprint of "The Psalmodists Exercise or A Set of Psalm Tunes & Anthems . . . composed . . . by William Cole. London Printed for the Author, by J. Johnson . . . & sold by . . . Messrs. Toft & Lobb at Chelmsford," c. 1760.
P. III.

TOLKIEN (HENRY). Music seller and publisher and pianoforte manufacturer, London; 64 Great Marlborough Street, c. 1836; afterwards at various numbers in King William Street, London Bridge; No. 26, c. 1837-38; No. 28, c. 1838-49; Nos. 27, 28, 29, c. 1849-76; No. 51, c. 1877-88; No. 28, c. 1889. In the later years he was in business solely as a pianoforte manufacturer.

TOMLINSON & SONS. Music sellers, 28 Blake Street, York. Their name

appears in the imprint of "Twenty-four Chants: to which are prefixed, Remarks on Chanting . . . By Mr. J. Gray, of York. Published
for the Author, by Preston . . . London, and H. Bellerby; York; and
to be had also at the music warehouses of . . . Tomlinson, in York
. . . 1834."

TONSON (JACOB) *first of the name*. Bookseller and publisher, London;
at the Judge's Head, in Chancery Lane, near Fleet Street, 1678-98;
in Gray's Inn Gate, next Gray's Inn Lane, 1700-1710; at Shakespear's Head, against Catherine Street, in the Strand, 1710-20. (P.)
Published a number of musical works. His business was continued by
Jacob Tonson, third of the name.
    P. II. D. & M.
    See also Tonson (M.).

TONSON (JACOB) *second of the name*. Bookseller, London; Gray's Inn
Gate; Shakespeare's Head, opposite Catherine Street in the Strand,
c. 1689-1735. (P.) Son of Richard Tonson the elder (bookseller,
1675-89); was apparently associated in business with his father and
afterwards with his uncle, Jacob Tonson, first of the name, but does
not appear to have published any music.
    P. II.

TONSON (JACOB) *third of the name* & (RICHARD) *the Younger*. Booksellers and publishers, in the Strand, London. Published "The
Beggar's Opera. Written by Mr. Gay. With the ouverture in score,
the songs and the basses, engrav'd on copper plates . . . MDCCLXI.";
also an edition in 1765; "Damon and Phillida. A Ballad Opera . . .
With the musick prefix'd to each song . . . MDCCLXV." Also published
libretti of works by Handel and others, some in conjunction with
Somerset Draper. Jacob Tonson, third of the name, was the son of
Jacob Tonson second of the name. He carried on the business of
Jacob Tonson, first of the name, in the Strand, 1720-67, at first at the
Shakespear's Head, against Catherine Street, and for a few years
before his death at other premises near by. Richard Tonson the
younger's name appears with Jacob's in imprints of libretti from
c. 1740.

TONSON (M). Bookseller, at Gray's Inn Gate, in Gray's Inn Lane,
London. Name appears in the imprint of "Amphitryon; or, The
Two Socia's. A Comedy . . . Written by Mr. Dryden. To which is
added, the musick of the Songs. Compos'd by Mr. Henry Purcel.
London, printed for J. Tonson . . . and M. Tonson . . . 1690"; also
issued an edition dated 1691. M. Tonson was probably the widow of
Richard Tonson the elder, bookseller, 1675-89, who apparently did not
publish any music.
    D. & M.

THREE
SONATAS

FOR THE

HARPSICHORD,

COMPOSED BY

Sig. GIUSEPPE SARTI.

BY HIS MAJESTY'S ROYAL LETTERS PATENT.

LONDON:

PRINTED AND SOLD BY HENRY FOUGT,
AT THE LYRE AND OWL, IN ST. MARTIN'S-LANE, NEAR LONG-ACRE.

[Price Two Shillings.]

An example of Fougt's fine title-pages. 1769

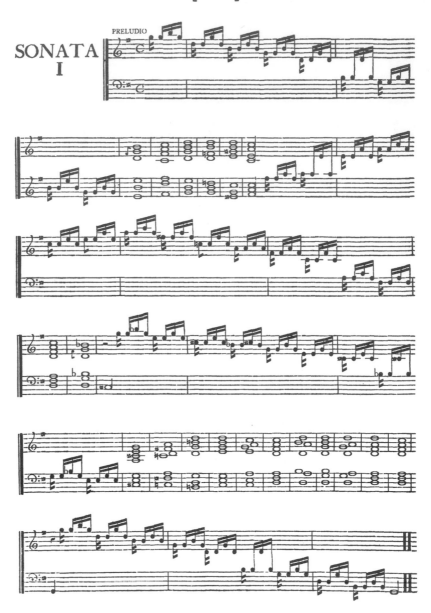

Giuseppe Sarti, "Three Sonatas for the Harpsichord". Printed and
sold by Henry Fougt. 1769

TONSON (RICHARD) *the Elder*. Bookseller, at Gray's Inn Gate, London, 1675-89. (P.) Apparently he did not publish any music. Was succeeded by M. Tonson, presumably his widow.
P. II.

TOOKE (BENJAMIN). Bookseller, London; at the Anchor, Duck Lane, 1669; at the Ship in St. Paul's Churchyard, 1670-87; at the Middle Temple Gate, Fleet Street, 1687-1716. (P.) His name appears in the imprints of "A Joco-Serious Discourse in two Dialogues, between a Northumberland-Gentleman, and his Tenant a Scotchman, both old Cavaliers . . . By George Stuart . . . London, Printed for Benjamin Tooke, at the Ship in St. Paul's Church-Yard, and John Story in New-castle, 1686"; contains the music of seven songs; "The Psalms of David, in English Metre; translated from the original, and suited to all the tunes now sung in Churches: with the additions of several new. By Luke Milbourne . . . London, Printed for W. Rogers . . . R. Clavill . . . B. Tooke at the Middle Temple Gate . . . J. Lawrence . . . and J. Taylor . . . 1698."
P. II. D. & M.

TORBUCK (GEORGE). Bookseller, Wimborne. His name appears in the imprint of "A Sett of new Psalm-Tunes and Anthems . . . By William Knapp . . . London. Printed by W. Hutchinson, for the Author, and sold by him in Poole; Mr. George Torbuck in Wimbourn . . . MDCCXXXVIII."

TORBUCK (JOHN). Printer and bookseller, Clare Court, Drury Lane, London, c. 1732-41. (P.) Published in conjunction with Charles Corbett "The Devil of a Duke: or, Trapolin's Vagaries. A (Farcical Ballad) Opera . . . London: Printed for Charles Corbett, at Addison's Head, without Temple Bar; and John Torbuck, in Clare Court, Drury Lane. MDCCXXXII."
P. III.

TOWNSEND (JOHN). Music seller and musical instrument maker, King Street, Manchester; at No. 73, c. 1825; No. 2, c. 1828; No. 3, c. 1834-60. Published a small amount of music.
K.

TRACY (EBENEZER). Bookseller, at the Three Bibles on London Bridge, 1695-1719. (P.) Published, advertised and sold a number of musical works.
K. P. II.

TREGEAR & LEWIS. Pianoforte, print and music sellers, and music publishers, 96 Cheapside, London, c. 1842-44. Partners were Mrs. Gabriel S. Tregear and Thomas Crump Lewis; succeeded G. S. Tregear; partnership ceased c. 1844, and Lewis continued alone at same address.

TREGEAR (GABRIEL SHIR). Print and music seller, and music publisher, 96 Cheapside, London, c. 1829-41. Business continued by Mrs. Tregear until c. 1842, when she went into partnership with Thomas Crump Lewis as Tregear and Lewis.

TRENKLEE (MICHAEL). Music engraver, 32 St. Martin's Street, Leicester Square, London. Engraved "First Set of Chiverian Quadrilles. By Mr. G. M. S. Chivers . . . London, Published at the Author's Salle de Danse, No. 7, Pickett Place near Temple Bar," c. 1820; "The Original Caledonians, an admired Highland set of Quadrilles. Arranged for the Piano Forte or Harp . . . by G. M. S. Chivers. London Published at the Bedford Musical Repository", etc., c. 1823.

TREVERIS (PETER). Printer, Southwark, London. Printed the 1527 edition of Higden's "Polycronicon" which contains a short fragment of the stave containing eight notes printed from a wood block, which in Wynkyn de Worde's edition, 1495, were printed from rules and quads, and for which a blank space was left in Caxton's edition of 1482 to be filled in by hand. The colophon of the 1527 edition is "Imprented in Southwerke by my Peter Treveris at yᵉ expences of Iohñ Reynes boke seller at the sygne of saynt George in Poules chyrchyarde", etc.
D. S.

TROTTER (T.). Strand on the Green, Kew Bridge. Published c. 1800, "Song. Brittannia's Mandate: The Volunteer's March."

TRYE (THOMAS). Bookseller and publisher, at Gray's Inn Gate, Holborn, London, 1737-c. 1760. (P.) His name appears in the imprint of "A Collection of Tunes, Set to Music, As they are commonly sung at the Foundery. London: Printed by A. Pearson, and sold by . . . T. Trye . . . MDCCXLII."
P. III.

TURNBULL (THOMAS). Printer, Canongate, Edinburgh. Printed "The British Musical Miscellany: being a collection of Scotch, English & Irish Songs, set to music, with proper keys for the Voice, Violin, German-Flute, and Military Fife . . . 1805."

TURNBULL (WALTER). Music seller and publisher, London; 331 Oxford Street, c. 1805-08; 124 Oxford Street, c. 1808-10; 101 Portland Street, c. 1810-11; 59 Portland Street, c. 1811-20. Succeeded George Smart.
K.
Catalogues:—New Music. c. 1805. 1 p. fol. (B.M. g. 272. w. (21.)); c. 1807. 1 p. fol. (B.M. 7896. h. 40. (15.))

TURNER (JOHN). Music and musical instrument seller, London; 79 Leadenhall Street, c. 1833-35; 84 Leadenhall Street, c. 1835-52. Published a small amount of music.

TURNER (JOHN ALVEY). Musical instrument maker and seller, music seller and publisher, London; 19 Poultry c. 1843-59; 19 Cornhill, c. 1859-63; 1a Leadenhall Street, c. 1863-81; 33 Bishopsgate Street Within, c. 1881-92; 33 Bishopsgate Street Within, and 39 Oxford Street, c. 1892-1907; 39 Oxford Street, c. 1907-12; 139 Oxford Street, c. 1912-26; 68 New Oxford Street, c. 1926 to present time. In the later years made a limited company; succeeded G. Gange and Co.

TURNER (JOSEPH). Bookseller, Sheffield, 1701-18, or later. Published "A Collection of choice Psalm Tunes in Three and Four Parts: with New & Easie Psalm-Tunes, Hymns, Anthems, and Spiritual Songs, composed by the best Masters . . . By John and James Green. The Third Edition, with large Additions . . . Nottingham: Printed by William Ayscough for Joseph Turner . . . 1715"; "A Book of Psalmody, containing variety of Tunes . . . and fifteen Anthems . . . By John Chetham . . . 1718."
P. II.

TURNER (WILLIAM). Printer, Oxford, 1624-43. (P.) Printed "The Feminine Monarchie, or the Histori of Bee's . . . By Charles Butler . . . Oxford, Printed by William Turner . . . M.DC.XXXIV."; contains four pages of music, known as the "Bees' Madrigal." The text is printed in Butler's reformed spelling.
K. P. I.

TURPIN (JAMES). Music engraver, London? Engraved "Six Easy Lessons for the Harpsichord. Compos'd by Sigr: Binder-Mazzinghi-Ritschel Sigr: Legne-Galuppi-Zamperelli. Book I. London Printed for, and sold by Joseph Hill," etc., c. 1765.

TYTHER (JOHN). Music seller and publisher, at the Violin, German Flute and Hautboy, facing New Broad Street, Moorfields, London, c. 1745-60. Among other works his name appears in the imprint of the first edition of "Amaryllis. 1746," and in two editions, in two volumes, c. 1750, and a little later. Succeeded by James Lewer.
K.

TYTON (FRANCIS). Bookseller, at the Three Daggers, near the Temple in Fleet Street, London, 1649-67. (P.) His name appears in the imprint of "The Book of Psalms in Metre . . . translated by W. Barton. To be sung in usuall and known tunes . . . London: Printed by Roger Daniel and William Du-Gard, and are to be sold by Francis Eglesfield, and Thomas Underhill . . . and Francis Tyton . . . 1654."
P. I.

UNDERHILL (THOMAS). Bookseller, London, 1641-59; at the Bible in Wood Street; at the Anchor and Bible, St. Paul's Churchyard. (P.) His name appears in the imprint of "The Book of Psalms in Metre . . . translated by W. Barton. To be sung in usuall and known tunes . . . London: Printed by Roger Daniel and William Du-Gard, and are to be sold by Francis Eglesfield, and Thomas Underhill, in S. Paul's Church Yard and Francis Tyton . . . 1654."
P. I.

URBANI & LISTON. Music sellers and publishers, 10 Princes Street, Edinburgh, c. 1795-1806. When the partnership between Pietro Urbani and Edward Liston terminated c. 1806, Liston continued the business for a short time. Urbani was an Italian musician who became eminent in Edinburgh and Glasgow as a singer and music teacher; he was also a composer and arranged a number of Scottish songs and airs; died in Dublin 1816.
K. G.
Catalogue of Scots Music etc. c. 1795. 1 p. fol. (B.M. g. 133. (61.))

V

I. G. *See* Vogler (John) & (Gerard).

VACHE (S.). Perfumer, importer of foreign music and music seller, 36 St. Alban's Street, Pall Mall, London, c. 1780-85. His name appears among others, on a number of publications issued by John Welcker.
K.

VAILLANT (FRANCIS). French bookseller, printer and music seller, in the Strand, three doors from the West Corner of Catherine Street, near Exeter Exchange, London, 1700-06. Vaillant acted as the London agent of Estienne Roger of Amsterdam, whose works he stocked and sold, printing some of them from Roger's plates and importing others printed by Roger; succeeded by Isaac Vaillant.

VAILLANT (ISAAC). Book, map and music seller, near Catherine Street (at the Bishop's Head) in the Strand, London, 1706-11. Continued the business of Francis Vaillant, acting as selling agent for the musical works engraved and printed by Estienne Roger of Amsterdam; succeeded by Henry Riboteau, at the Crown, over against Exeter Exchange, in the Strand.

VALENTINE (HENRY). Musician, Leicester. His name appears in "A Collection of Anthems & Psalms, for two, three, and four voices . . . Composed by Thos. Collins . . . Engrav'd by John Baraclough, N— Eaton." (Sold by Mr. Henry Valentine, Leicester.) c. 1790.

VALIANT (FRANCIS). *See* Vaillant.

VALIANT (ISAAC). *See* Vaillant.

VALLOTTON, *Mrs.* Milliner, James Street, Golden Square, London. Her name appears in the imprints of "Scelta d'Arietta Francesi, Italiane ed Inglesi con accompagnamento di Chitarra. Composte da Giacomo Merchi . . . Opera XV. London Printed for the Author at Mʳˢ. Vallotton's Millener . . . in James Street Golden Square. Where may be had all the said Author's Opera's", etc., advertised 1766; also "Dodici Suonate per la Chitarra, sei a due Chitarre o con accompagnamento di Violino e Sei a solo. Composte da Giacomo Merchi . . . Opera XVI," etc., advertised 1766.

VAN DER GUCHT (MICHIEL). *See* Gucht.

VANDERNAN (THOMAS). Musician, publisher and engraver, London. Published "Splenetick Pills or Mirth Alamode. Being a collection of humorous songs adapted to the modern taste of the choice spirits. The words by the celebrated poet John Rumfish Esq. Set to music by Dr. Merriwag [i.e. Thomas Vandernan]. London Printed for Thos. Vandernan, and sold at Mr. Bright at the Blue Peruke in Spring Garden Passage", etc., c. 1750; "Thirty six Arietta's for a single Voice with a thorough Bass for the Harpsicord and within compass of the German Flute. Compos'd by Signor Alessandro Scarlatti. London. Printed for Thos. Vandernan, and sold by Jno. Cox", etc., c. 1755; engraved and published "Divine Harmony. Being a collection of two hundred and seven double and single chants in score . . . sung at His Majesty's Chapels Royal . . . London Feby. 1770," etc. Vandernan was a Gentleman of the Chapel Royal.

VARNHAM (THOMAS). Bookseller, Lombard Street, London, 1711-c. 1725. (P.) His name appears in the imprint of "The Psalms of David in Metre: Fitted to the tunes used in Parish-Churches. By John Patrick . . . London, Printed for W. Churchill . . . T. Varnham . . . MDCCXVIII."
P. II.

VAUTROLLIER (THOMAS). Printer, bookseller and bookbinder, London and Edinburgh, 1562-87. (M.) Huguenot refugee who settled in London and printed at Blackfriars, Tallis and Byrd's "Cantiones", 1575, and books of "Psalms", 1587. In 1570 he had a licence to print a "boke of musyke" and he is also said to have printed "A Briefe Instruction of Musicke" (or, "A Briefe Introduction to Musicke"), collected by P. Delamotte, 1574. He established a press at Edinburgh in 1584.
K. G. M. S.

VEREY (GEORGE). Book and music seller, Great May's Buildings, St. Martin's Lane, London, c. 1795-1802. Published some music in conjunction with Hugh Andrews.
    K.

VERNON (CHARLES). Musical instrument maker, music seller and publisher, 37 Cornhill, London, c. 1825-30. Succeeded by Arthur Betts the younger.

VIRTUE (GEORGE). Bookseller and publisher, 26 Ivy Lane, Paternoster Row, London, c. 1823-52. As George Virtue and Co. c. 1852-57. Published a small amount of music.

VOGLER (JOHN) & (GERARD). Music sellers and publishers, Glasshouse Street near Swallow Street, London, c. 1777-85. Premises previously occupied by Robert Worman; some single sheet songs bear only the initials $I. \overset{V}{G}.$
    K.

VOKINS (HENRY). Bookseller, Sloane Street, London. His name appears on the title-page of "Lady Gore's Waltz arranged as a Rondo for the Piano Forte or Harp by J. Dale. London, Printed for the Author . . . also sold by H. Vokins", etc., c. 1804.

VOLLWEILER (GEORG JOHANN). Lithographic printer, at the new invented Patent Polyautography (Polyautographic Press), 9 Buckingham Place, Fitzroy Square, London, c. 1806-August 1807. Printed a small amount of music from plates of stone, by the Polyautographic process. The process was invented by Alois Senefelder, who obtained a Patent in England for fourteen years in 1801, and assigned it to Philipp H. André; André left England for Germany in 1805. André did not print any music. After a lapse of eighteen months, Vollweiler succeeded as patentee and further improved the method; he also returned to Germany in August 1807.

W., H. *See* Bonion (Richard) & Walley (Henry).

W., J. *See* Watts (John).

W., M. *See* Whitaker (Maurice).

W., P. *See* Welcker (Peter).

W., T. *See* Williams (T.).

WALKER & ANDERSON. Music engravers, printers and publishers, 42 High Street, Edinburgh, 1815-26. Both previously in business;

partnership between George Walker and John Anderson dissolved
1826; business continued as Walker and Co. at same address.
    K.
    See also Anderson (John); Walker (George).

WALKER & CO. *See* Walker (George).

WALKER & HUTTON. Music engravers, Foulis Close, Edinburgh,
c. 1811-15. When the partnership was dissolved, George Walker
entered into partnership with John Anderson, and William Hutton
went into business on his own account.
    K.
    See also Hutton (William); Walker (George).

WALKER. *See* Hardy & Walker.

WALKER (A.). 31 Frith Street, Soho, London. Published c. 1834,
"Merrily, merrily passes the Day, Glee, for three voices and chorus,
the words & music composed by Mrs. Coll. Stewart."

WALKER (GEORGE). Music engraver, Edinburgh, c. 1790-1848; Head
of Galloway's Close, c. 1793-96; Head of Skinner's Close, c. 1796-
1805; Fountain Well, c. 1805-11; in partnership with William
Hutton as Walker and Hutton, Foulis Close, c. 1811-15; John Anderson joined him and became Walker and Anderson, 42 High Street,
1815-26; business called Walker and Co., 42 High Street, 1826-29;
2 North Bridge, 1829-48; business was carried on by his widow for
a few years prior to 1848.
    K. G.

WALKER (GEORGE) *the Elder*. Book and music seller, music publisher,
London; 106 Great Portland Street, c. 1795-1821; 17 Soho Square,
c. 1821-48. Had additional premises at 9 Brook Street, Bond Street,
c. 1803-05; 105 Great Portland Street, c. 1812-20; 64 Burlington
Arcade, c. 1820-30. About 1829 the business became George Walker
and Son; the son had previously been connected with an establishment with the name of "The Bedford Musical Repository." Walker
the elder's name appears on some publications that have the imprint
"Printed for the Polyhymnian Company and sold wholesale by
G. Walker, 106 Great Portland Street".
    K. G.
    Catalogues:—Books & Music. c. 1805. (First Edition Bookshop,
Catalogue 40. No. 126.); Catalogue of new Music. c. 1807. 1 p. fol.
(B.M. g. 272. q. (16.)); c. 1808. 1 p. fol. (B.M. g. 272. q. (37.)); c.
1809. 1 p. fol. (B.M. g. 272. t. (17.)); New Vocal Music. c. 1820. 1
p. fol. (B.M. H. 1652. h. (21.))
    See also Bedford Musical Repository.

WALKER (GEORGE) *the Younger*. *See* Bedford Musical Repository; Walker (George) *the Elder*.

WALKER (WILLIAM). Music seller and publisher, 116 Portland Street, London, c. 1807-08. Previously in the employ of Corri, Dussek and Co.

WALKER (WILLIAM). Printer, London, "from Thoyts, Morgans & Major Genl. Geo. Warde [Coppersmiths], White Chapel". Printed "When I was a Boy in my Father's Mud Edifice, as sung by Mr. Johnstone," c. 1815.

WALLEY (HENRY). *See* Bonion (Richard) & Walley (Henry).

WALLIS & STONEHOUSE. Publishers and booksellers, Yorick's Head, Ludgate Street, London. Published c. 1775, "The New Merry Companion or Vocal Remembrancer; being a select collection of the most celebrated songs . . . The Second edition . . . London. Printed for Wallis and Stonehouse . . . J. Bew . . . W. Davenhill . . . & Longman Lukey & Broderip", etc. John Wallis was one of the partners.
    P. III.

WALLIS (JOHN). Map, print and bookseller, 16 Ludgate Street, London. Published a Song "Britons to Arms . . . July 30 1803."

WALMSLEY, WAMSLEY or WARMSLEY (PETER). Luthier, who worked in London from c. 1720 at the Golden Harp, afterwards the Harp, in Piccadilly. Collected subscriptions for, and sold, a few musical works at the Harp, c. 1729-44. Business may have been carried on in his name from 1741 by his widow. Thomas Smith, a pupil of Walmsley's, succeeded to the business.
    G.

WALPERGEN (PETER DE). Letter-founder, Oxford. Published "Musica Oxoniensis. A Collection Of Songs: For One and Two Voices, With The Thorough-Bass. Publish'd by Francis Smith, and Peter de Walpergen Letter-Founder, by whom 'twas Cut on Steel, and Cast, by the Directions of the former. Oxford: Printed by Leon. Lichfield . . . And are to be Sold by the Widow Howell, 1698 "; the same work was also issued with the imprint "Oxford: Printed by Leon. Lichfield: And are to be Sold by John Walsh . . . And John Hare . . . London. 1698." Walpergen, a Dutchman who settled in Oxford, in addition to the above work, cut sets of type (punches) which were used as late as 1899 for "The Yattendon Hymnal."
    D. & M.

WALSH, of Dublin. *See* Bunting, Walsh, Pigott & Sherwin.

WALSH (JOHN) *the Elder.* Musical instrument maker, music printer,
music seller and publisher, London, c. 1692-1736; appointed musical
instrument maker to William III, 1692, address unknown; at the
Golden Harp and Hautboy (or Harp and Hautboy, Harp and Hoboy),
Catherine (Catharine, Katherine or Katharine) Street, Strand, 1695-
1736. Most of the works issued by Walsh, from the earliest in July
1695-November 1730, were published in conjunction with the firm
of John Hare and his son Joseph, and have the names and addresses of
Walsh and the Hares in the imprints, with the addresses in the
respective forms as in use at the time of issue:—With John Hare,
1695-December 1721, with John and Joseph Hare, January 1722-
September 1725, with Joseph Hare, September 1725-c. November
1730. There is no evidence that the Hares were directly interested
in the business at Catherine Street. Other publishers whose names
also occur occasionally in the Walsh imprints are entered separately
in this dictionary, but of these, special mention must be made of
Peter Randall who after being in business for himself, joined Walsh
at Catherine Street and published with him as J. Walsh and P. Randall,
at the Harp and Hoboy, in Catherine Street, Strand, and the Violin
and Lute by Paulsgrave Court without Temple Bar, October 1708-
July 1709; at Catherine Street only, July 1709-December 1710.
P. Randall was previously alone at the Violin and Lute by Paulsgrave
Hand (or Head) Court without Temple Bar in the Strand, November
1706-October 1708. Walsh was alone at Catherine Street December
1710-36. Succeeded by his son John, March 1736.
      K. G. D. & M.
      For works on John Walsh by Frank Kidson and William C. Smith;
and "Handel's Publishers" by Desmond Flower, *see* Bibliography.
      Catalogues:—1701. 1 p. fol. (B.M. c. 105. a. (5.)); 1702. 1 p. fol.
(B.M. Hirsch II. 749.); 1703. 2 pp. obl. fol. (Bodleian); c. 1721.
2 pp. fol. (B.M. 7897. y. 12. (1.)); c. 1729. 2 pp. fol. (B.M. Hirsch
IV. 1111. (17.)); c. 1733. 2 pp. fol. (Gerald Coke Collection);
c. 1733. 1 p. fol. (B.M. g. 237.)
      Fuller details of catalogues issued by John Walsh are given in "A
Bibliography of the musical works published by John Walsh" by
William C. Smith.

WALSH (JOHN) *the Elder* & RANDALL (PETER). *See* Randall (Peter);
Walsh (John) *the Elder*.

WALSH (JOHN) *the Younger.* Musical instrument maker, music printer,
music seller and publisher, at the Harp and Hautboy, Catherine
(Catharine) Street, Strand, London, 1736-66. Succeeded his father,
John Walsh the elder; left the business to be carried on in his name
by William Randall and John Abell.
      K. G.

Works on John Walsh the elder by Frank Kidson and William C. Smith, and "Handel's Publishers" by Desmond Flower (*see* Bibliography) give particulars of John Walsh the younger.

Catalogues:—c. 1743; Later issue c. 1744. 1 p. fol. (B.M. Hirsch III. 208.); 1743. 1 p. fol. (B.M. 7897. y. 12. (2.)); c. 1747. 2 pp. fol. (B.M. Hirsch IV. 1111. (16.)); c. 1752. 2 pp. fol. (B.M. 7897. y. 12. (3.)); c. 1752. 1 p. fol. (B.M. R.M. 14. d. 19.)

Fuller details of catalogues issued by John Walsh the younger are given in "A Bibliography of the musical works published by John Walsh" by William C. Smith.

WALTHOE (JOHN). Bookseller, at various addresses, London, 1683-1748. (P.) His name appears in the imprints of a number of sacred music works.
P. III.

WAMSLEY (PETER). *See* Walmsley, Wamsley or Warmsley.

WARD & ANDREWS. Music sellers and publishers, 18, afterwards at 55, Spring Gardens, Manchester, c. 1828-37, or later.

WARD (AARON). Bookseller and publisher, King's Arms, in Little Britain, London, c. 1726-47. (P.) His name appears in the imprint of "The Psalms of David in Metre: With the tunes used in Parish-Churches. By John Patrick. The Eighth edition. London: Printed for J. Walthoe . . . A. Ward . . . MDCCXLII."
P. III.

WARD (CORNELIUS). Music seller, Liverpool; 36 Lord Street, c. 1805; 19 Church Street, c. 1806-11. Published a small amount of music; succeeded by James and Henry Banks.

WARD (GEORGE). Musical instrument seller, London; 1 White Lion Street, Goodman's Fields, c. 1838-40; 90 Leman Street, Goodman's Fields, c. 1840-44. Published a small amount of music.
K.

WARD (THOMAS). Bookseller, Inner Temple Lane, London, 1711-26. (P.) His name appears in the imprint of "The Psalms of David in Metre: With the tunes used in Parish-Churches. By John Patrick . . . The Seventh edition . . . London: Printed for D. Brown . . . T. Ward . . . MDCCXXIV."
P. III.

WARE & EVANS. Music sellers and publishers, 146 Strand, London, c. 1823. Both previously in business, William Henry Ware at same address and R. W. Evans at 53 Cheapside; R. W. Evans carried on the business after the partnership was dissolved.

WARE (CATHERINE). Bookseller and publisher, at the Bible and Sun, in Amen Corner, Ludgate Hill, London, 1756-c. 1760. Her name appears in the imprint of "The Whole Book of Psalms . . . By John Playford. The Twentieth edition . . . London: Printed by R. Brown . . . For C. Ware . . . 1757." Presumably the widow of, and successor to, Richard Ware; after c. 1760 she was in partnership with Richard Ware, presumably her son.
P. III.

WARE (RICHARD). Bookseller and publisher, at the Bible and Sun, in Amen Corner, London, c. 1717-56. (P. Ellic Howe: "A List of London Bookbinders." 1950.) His name appears in the imprints of a number of sacred music works; succeeded by Catherine Ware, presumably his widow.
P. III.

WARE (WILLIAM HENRY). Composer, violinist, music seller and publisher, 146 Strand, London, c. 1822. On one of his composition she stated that he was leader and composer to the Theatre Royal, Covent Garden; afterwards joined by R. W. Evans and became Ware and Evans.

WARMSLEY (PETER). *See* Walmsley, Wamsley or Warmsley.

WARNE (GEORGE). Musician, music seller and publisher, London; 47 Edgware Road, c. 1831-33; 103 Great Russell Street, Bloomsbury, c. 1836-38; 191 Sloane Street, Knightsbridge, c. 1838-44; 48 Holborn Hill, c. 1852-61. Also published some of his own compositions; at one time organist of the Temple Church, London.

WARRELL (WILLIAM). Musical instrument maker, music seller and publisher, London; 35 Tavistock Street, c. 1777-80; New Road, near Westminster Bridge; Surrey Side of Westminster Bridge; or, Near Astley's Theatre, Westminster Bridge; 17 Bridge Road, Lambeth, c. 1780-94 or later. Described as Warrell and Co. on some publications.
K.

WASSELL (H.). Music seller, 64 Charing Cross, London. Published "Annette, the Maid of the Cottage, a favorite Song . . . Composed by Mr. Hook," c. 1810 ; "Three Original Spanish Boleras, for the Piano Forte . . . inscribed to Miss Elphinstone," c. 1810.

WATERSON (SIMON). Bookseller and publisher, at the sign of the Crown, St. Paul's Church Yard, London, 1584-1634. (M.) Published "The Schoole of Musicke: wherein is taught, the perfect method of true fingering of the Lute, Pandora, Orpharion, and Viol de Gamba . . . Newly composed by Thomas Robinson, Lutenist. London: Printed by Tho. Este for Simon Waterson, dwelling at the signe of the Crowne

in Paules Church-Yard, 1603." His name also appears in the imprint of "A Musicall Dreame . . . Composed by Robert Iones . . . London. Imprinted by the Assignes of William Barley, and are to be solde in Powles Church-yeard, at the Signe of the Crowne. 1609."
  M.

WATKINS (ZACHARIAH). Bookseller and publisher, was in partnership with John Playford the elder, at his shop in the Temple, near the Church Door, London, 1663-65.
  K. P. I. D. & M.

WATLEN (JOHN). Musician, music and musical instrument seller and publisher. Published from his house at 17 Princes Street, Edinburgh, 1791; Music Warehouse at 13 North Bridge Street, Edinburgh, 1792-1793; 34 North Bridge Street, Edinburgh, c. 1793-98, during which time he also occupied another shop at 24 North Bridge Street, and had a London agency with Francis Linley, 42 Penton Street, Pentonville, followed by one at 1 Charlotte Row, Long Lane, Southwark. He became bankrupt and his stock-in-trade was advertised for sale by auction, July 1798. Watlen taught music and published some music from his house, The Hermitage, Abbey Hill, near Holyrood, c. 1799. He removed to London and published from 3 Upper James' Street, Golden Square, c. 1800; became partner in Cobb and Watlen, 19 Tavistock Street, Covent Garden, c. 1800-05; 186 Piccadilly, c. 1805-1806. He continued alone at 5 Leicester Place, Leicester Square, c. 1806-18; 13 Leicester Street, Leicester Square, c. 1818-29. Watlen described himself on one of his compositions as being formerly of Salisbury Cathedral; late organist of Bombay, and an officer in His Majesty's Royal Navy. Was for seven years in the employ of Corri and Sutherland.
  K. G.
  Catalogues:—Original Music composed by John Watlen. c. 1800. 1 p. fol. (B.M. g. 272. d. (31.)); The Musical Compositions of John Watlen. c. 1808. 1 p. fol. (B.M. g. 272. d. (32.))

WATSON (A.) & (W.). Booksellers, 7 Capel Street, Dublin, c. 1824-32. Their names appear in the imprints of "The Hymns & Anthems as sung in Protestant Churches & Chapels . . . Arranged by the late David Weyman . . . Dublin. Printed and published by Geo. Allen . . . and may be had at A. & W. Watson's", etc., c. 1830; "The 150 Psalms as authorized and sung in Churches . . . as set in the large edition of the Melodia Sacra. By Mr. Weyman . . . Dublin. Printed & published by . . . Geo. Allen . . . sold at A. &. W. Watson's . . . Second edition", etc., c. 1831. Presumably succeeded William Watson.

WATSON (WILLIAM). Bookseller, 7 Capel Street, Dublin, c. 1805-18. His name appears in the imprint of "Fifty of the Psalms of David . . . Arranged & harmonized by David Weyman . . . Printed by Geo.

Allen . . . and may be had of Willm. Watson . . . Dublin." c. 1810. Presumably succeeded by A. and W. Watson.

WATTS (I.). 16 Mount Street, Grosvenor Square, London. Published c. 1795, "The Gloucester Bumpkin. A favorite Song."

WATTS (JOHN). Printer and bookseller, at the Printing Office, in Wild Court, near Lincoln's Inn Fields, London, ?-1763. From 1728 printed and published a large number of Ballad Operas and Plays, with the music to the airs inserted in the text, besides many libretti of oratorios, etc; also "The Musical Miscellany; being a collection of choice songs, set to the violin and flute, by the most eminent masters", 1729-31. 6 vols. He printed some works which bear only the initials J. W.
    K. G. P. III.

WATTS (RICHARD). Music seller, 87 Blackman Street, Southwark, London, c. 1799-1836. Succeeded Charles May; published a small amount of music.

WAUGH (J.). Bookseller, Lombard Street, London. His name appears in the imprint of "The Psalms of David . . . By I. Watts . . . The Twenty-ninth edition . . . (Tunes in the Tenor Part fitted to the several metres.) London: Printed for J. Buckland . . . J. Waugh . . . MDCCLXV." Connection with the following not clear.

WAUGH (JAMES). Bookseller, at the Turk's Head, Lombard Street, London, 1747-57. Advertised September 1750, "A Collection of Tunes in various Airs, adapted to Psalms taken out of Dr. Watt's imitation of David's Psalms . . . By John Taylor, of Norwich. Printed and sold by J. Waugh", etc. Connection with the preceding not clear.
    P. III.

WAYLETT (FRANCIS). Music seller, music shop opposite Suffolk Street, near Pall Mall (Charing Cross), London. Published "The Muse's Choice, a favourite collection of Songs, set for the Violin, German Flute, and Harpsichord, by Mr. Joseph Bryan. Book 1st, 1756"; his name appears in the imprint of "The Favourite Songs in the new Opera call'd Antigono, by Sig. Conforti. Printed and sold for the Proprietor, to be had at Mr. Taylor's . . . at Mr. Oswald's . . . at Mr. Rutherford's . . . at Mr. Hardy's . . . and at Mr. Francis Waylet's Musick shop in Charing Cross," advertised April 1757; also in a similar imprint of Hasse's "The Favourite Songs in . . . Il Re Pastore," 1757; "Two English Cantatas and four Songs . . . by Christopher Dixon of York. Book 2d. London Printed for Francis Waylett . . . opposite Suffolk Street, Charing Cross," c. 1760. The name is also given as Waylet. Presumably related to Henry and John Waylett.
    K. G.

WAYLETT (HENRY). Musical instrument maker, printer and publisher, at the Black Lyon in Exeter Change (Exchange), in the Strand, London, c. 1743-65. Published the first edition of "Rule Britannia," which appeared with "The Music in the Judgment of Paris," etc., by T. A. Arne, c. 1745. Presumably related to Francis and John Waylett. The name is also given as Waylet. Succeeded by Richard Bride.
K. G.

WAYLETT (JOHN). In Exeter Exchange, in the Strand, London. His name appears (probably a misprint for Henry Waylett) in an advertisement May and June 1745. "A Collection of such Psalm Tunes as are commonly sung in the Churches of London and Westminster, with Basses fitted for the Voice, and figur'd for the Organ. For the use of Ewel in Surrey . . . Engrav'd, printed and sold by [i.e. for] the Author, by Henry Roberts . . . Elizabeth Hare . . . and John Waylett in Exeter Exchange, in the Strand."

WEAVER & CO. Music sellers and musical instrument makers, 2 Spring Gardens, London. Published "Eight Anthems, twelve Psalm Tunes and Gloria Patri . . . adapted for the use of country choirs, by W. H. Burgiss"; preface dated August 1, 1808.

WEAVER (SAMUEL). Music seller, at the Violin and Hautboy on London Bridge. His name appears in the imprint of "VI Sonate a fagoto ò violoncello, col' basso continuo; dal Luidgi Merci . . . Opera terza. London Printed for the Author & sold by Sam[ll]. Weaver . . . John Johnson", etc., c. 1745.

WEBB (WILLIAM). Organist of Windsor. His name appears in the imprint of "Twelve Sonatas for two Violins and a Bass or an Orchestra. Compos'd by Gio. Batta. Pergolese . . . Printed for Mr. Webb Organist of Windsor. And sold by R. Bremner", etc., c. 1780.

WEBLEY (ALEXANDER). Musical instrument maker, music seller and publisher, 11 Welbeck Street, Cavendish Square, London, c. 1800-16.

WEISS (WILLOUGHBY GASPER). See Yaniewicz & Weiss.

WELCKER (JOHN). Music seller, engraver, printer and publisher, London; 9 Haymarket, opposite the Opera House, 1775 to near the end of 1777 when the number was changed to 10; 10 Haymarket, near the end of 1777-July 1780, when he became bankrupt. Stock-in-trade, furniture and other effects were offered for sale on July 6, 1780; advertisement of sale said "The stock comprizes the works of the most eminent and esteemed composers in several thousand engraved plates." James Blundell, brother-in-law of Welcker, afterwards took over the premises at 10 Haymarket. Welcker resumed business at 80 Haymarket, four doors below the Opera House, August 1780 to the end of 1784; 18 Coventry Street, 1784-85. Son of Peter and Mary Welcker. K. G.

Catalogues:—Vocal and Instrumental Music. c. 1775. 4 pp. fol. (B.M. 7896. h. 40. (17.)); 1776. 4 pp. fol. (B.M. g. 415. (1.)); c. 1777. 4 pp. fol. (B.M. 7896. h. 40. (22.)); 1778. 1 p. fol. (B.M. G. 669. a. (2.))

WELCKER (MARY). Music seller and publisher, 17 Gerrard Street, St. Ann's, Soho, London, 1775-78. Widow of Peter Welcker; imprints usually only give the surname and are indistinguishable from those of her late husband; advertisements give her name in full; died 1778; for a few months business carried on by her executors; by July of same year, James Blundell, son-in-law of Mrs. Welcker, had taken over the business, and opened up at 110 St. Martin's Lane, Charing Cross. Robert Bremner purchased some of Mrs. Welcker's plates and music in 1779. K. G.

WELCKER (PETER). Music seller, engraver, printer and publisher, Gerrard Street, afterwards numbered 17, St. Ann's, Soho, London, 1762-75. Published a large amount of music by the leading composers of the day; some single sheet songs bears only the initials P. W.; and "P. W-k-r" appears on some works where the full imprint is not given. Died 1775; his widow Mary, carried on the business at same address. K. G.

Catalogues:—c. 1765. 1 p. fol. (B.M. H. 456. h.); 1767. 1 p. fol. (B.M. I. 347.); c. 1768. 1 p. fol. (B.M. G. 136.); Vocal and Instrumental Music. 1769. 1 p. fol. (B.M. h. 206. h; H. 125.); 1771. 4 pp. fol. (B.M. Hirsch III. 220.); c. 1773. 4 pp. fol. (B.M. 7896. h. 40. (16.)); c. 1775. 4 pp. fol. (B.M. g. 474. a. (1.))

WELLER (E.). Pianoforte maker, music seller and publisher, 23 Oxford Street, London, c. 1818-20. Previously a partner in Bland and Weller. Also published as Weller and Co.

WELLS (JOHN). At the Golden Fish, within Bishopsgate, London. His name appears in the imprint of "The Psalm Singers Companion; being a collection of psalm tunes, hymns canons and anthems . . . By Abraham Milner. London: Printed by William Benning, and sold by . . . John Wells . . . 1751."

WELLS (R.). Engraver, Greenhill's Rents, Smithfield Bars, London. Engraved "Eighteen Songs by Mr. Handel, Adapted for a Violoncello Obligato, with a Figured Bass for the Harpsichord; By Henry Hardy. Oxford. Printed for and Sold by the Editor", etc., c. 1795.

WELSH & HAWES. Musicians, music sellers and publishers, Royal Harmonic Institution, Argyll Rooms, 246 Regent Street, London, c. 1826-28. Thomas Welsh and William Hawes took over the business from the Royal Harmonic Institution; after the partnership was dissolved, Welsh continued at the same address, and Hawes set up in business elsewhere.

A Catalogue of new popular vocal music (A Catalogue of Operas). c. 1828. 2 pp. fol. (B.M. H. 2834. (11.)).

WELSH (THOMAS). Musician, music seller and publisher, Royal Harmonic Institution, Argyll Rooms, 246 Regent Street, London, c. 1828-1838. Premises destroyed by fire, February 1830, and for a time Welsh's address was 234 Regent Street, until the rebuilding of 246 Regent Street. One of the promoters of the Regent's Harmonic Institution, afterwards Royal Harmonic Institution; in partnership with William Hawes at the same address c. 1826-28.

K. (Royal Harmonic Institution.)

Catalogues:—Vocal works. c. 1830. 1 p. fol. (B.M. H. 1652. n. (27.)); Appendix to Catalogue of Music. 1831. 4 pp. fol. (B.M. H. 1300. b.)

See also Regent's Harmonic Institution.

WENMAN (JOSEPH). Bookseller, 144 Fleet Street, London.
See Harrison & Co.

WESSEL & CO. Music sellers and publishers, and importers of foreign music, London; 6 Frith Street, Soho Square, c. 1838-39; 67 Frith Street, corner of Soho Square, c. 1839-46; 229 Regent Street, corner of Hanover Square, c. 1846-56; 18 Hanover Square, c. 1856-60. Frederic Stapleton was in partnership with Christian Rudolph Wessel from 1839 to 1845; business also known as Wessel and Stapleton. Succeeded Wessel and Stodart; Wessel retired in 1860 and transferred his business to Edwin Ashdown and Henry John Parry, who had been his managers.

G.

WESSEL & STAPLETON. See Wessel & Co.

WESSEL & STODART. Music sellers and publishers, and importers of foreign music, London; 1 Soho Square, c. 1823-28; 6 Frith Street, Soho Square, c. 1828-38. Stodart retired in 1838 and Christian Rudolph Wessel continued the business as Wessel and Co.

K.

Catalogue:—Select Publications of foreign Piano Forte & Guitar Music. c. 1830. 1 p. fol. (B.M. h. 124. (13.))

WESTERN CITY MUSICAL REPOSITORY. See Monro & May.

WESTLEY (FRANCIS). Bookseller, 10 Stationers' Court, London, c. 1818-26. Published a small amount of music.

WHATMORE. *See* Johanning & Whatmore.

WHEATLEY (SAMUEL). Dublin. Engraved "Six Sonatas for a Violin and Basse. Dedicated to Aemilia Reb. Forster by G. B. Marella. Op. 1. Dublin 1753 graved by Sam. Wheatley." (Eitner.)

WHEATSTONE. Music seller, Gloucester.
    See Wheatstone (Charles).

WHEATSTONE (CHARLES). Musical instrument maker, music seller, music engraver and publisher, London. Said to have been established in 1750, and was at some time at 83 St. James's Street, and 9 Whitehall. Charles Wheatstone (presumably not the founder of the firm) was at 36 Chandos Street, St. Martin's Lane, c. 1791-93; 31 Newgate Street, c. 1794; 3 Bedford Court, Covent Garden, c. 1795; 14, Corner of Castle Street, Leicester Square, c. 1801; 20 Panton Street, Leicester Square, c. 1803-05; 436 Strand, c. 1805-27, as C. Wheatstone and Co. from c. 1815; 20 Conduit Street, c. 1827-1905; 15 West Street, W.C. 2, 1905 to present time; also had a branch or agency at 2 Wades Passage, Bath, c. 1815-16. Sir Charles Wheatstone (1802-75) son of a Gloucester music seller, was a musical instrument maker in London, associated with C. Wheatstone and Co., and was inventor of the concertina in 1829, the patent for which was held by the Wheatstone firm.
    K. G.
    Catalogues:—Music, Vocal and Instrumental. c. 1805. 4 pp. fol. (B.M. 7896. h. 40. (18.)); Annual Catalogue of new Music. 1806. 1 p. fol. (B.M. 7896. h. 40. (18.))

WHEATSTONE (WILLIAM). Musical instrument maker, music seller and publisher, London; 128 Pall Mall, c. 1813-23; 24 Charles Street, St. James's, c. 1823-24; 118 Jermyn Street, c. 1824-26. Believed to have joined the firm of C. Wheatstone and Co., c. 1826.
    K. G.

WHEBLE (JOHN). Bookseller and publisher, 24 Paternoster Row, and various addresses, London. His name appears in the imprint of "The Hertfordshire Melody; or, Psalm-singers Recreation . . . By John Ivery . . . London: Printed for J. Wheble, in Paternoster Row; R. Austin, at Hertford . . . MDCCLXXIII."; published c. 1775, "The New Merry Companion, or Complete Modern Songster: being a select collection of . . . songs, lately sung at the theatres . . . also a collection of the most esteemed catches and glees . . . London: Printed for John Wheble, No. 24 Pater Noster Row."
    K. P. III.

WHITAKER & CO. Music sellers and publishers, 75 St. Paul's Church Yard, London, c. 1819-24. Succeeded Button, Whitaker and Beadnell; Messrs. Mayhew and Co. advertised in December 1824 that they had purchased some of John Whitaker's copyrights.

WHITAKER (JOHN). *See* Button & Whitaker; Button, Whitaker & Beadnell; Whitaker & Co.

WHITAKER (MAURICE). Musical instrument maker, music printer and publisher, at the Violin under the Piazza next the North Gate of the Royal Exchange, opposite Bartholomew Lane, London, c. 1760-78, or later. At one time assistant to John Simpson in Sweetings Alley, and after Simpson's death was for several years, prior to 1760, chief manager for his widow and John Cox who married Mrs. Simpson. When Cox and his wife ceased business in June 1764, owing to the state of Mrs. Cox's health, Whitaker claimed to be carrying on the same business at his own address. Some single sheet songs bear only the initials M. W.
  K. G.

WHITAKER (R. S.). Music seller and publisher, 24 Thavies Inn, Holborn, London, c. 1825-38.

WHITE. *See* Knapton, White & Knapton.

WHITE (GRACE). Printer, Coffee House Yard, near the Star, in Stonegate, York, 1716-21. (P.) Printed "The Psalm Singer's Guide, being a choice collection of the most useful tunes of the Psalms . . . collected and composed by Edm. Ireland, and taught by J. Hall, R. Sowerby, J. Turner, and others, the 4th edition, with additions . . . 1720." Succeeded her husband, John White.
  K. P. II.

WHITE (HENRY). Book and music seller and publisher, London; 350 Oxford Street, c. 1838-49; 337 Oxford Street, c. 1849-57. Became Henry White and Son c. 1857 and continued the business at 337 Oxford Street and other addresses until after 1900.

WHITE (JOHN). Printer, at the Printing House in Coffee House Yard in Stonegate, York, 1680-1716. (P.) Printed "A Book, of Psalme Tunes in four Parts, collected out of several Authors; with some few directions how to name your notes. By, A. B. P. C. W. [i.e. Abraham Barber. Parish Clerk, Wakefield.] York, Printed by John White, for the Author . . . 1687"; also the 4th edition 1700; 5th edition 1703; 6th edition 1711; 7th edition 1715; "The Most Useful Tunes of the Psalms . . . collected . . . and composed by Edmund Ireland . . . Second edition . . . 1713"; "Psalmody epitomiz'd" by Ely Stansfield, 1714. Succeeded by his widow Grace White.
  P. II.

WHITE (JOHN). Bookseller, at Horace's Head, 63 Fleet Street, London. His name appears in the imprints of "Lyric Airs: consisting of Greek, Albanian, Walachian, Turkish, Arabian, Persian, Chinese, and Moorish national Songs and Melodies . . . by . . . Edward Jones . . . London: Printed for the Author. 1804. And sold . . . by John White", etc.; "Musical and Poetical Relicks of the Welsh Bards . . . By Edward Jones . . . The Third edition . . . The first volume. London: Printed for the Author . . . 1808. And sold by . . . John White", etc.

WHITE (JOHN CHARLES). Music and musical instrument seller, and publisher, 1 Milsom Street and 3 George Street, Bath, c. 1815-45. Published some of his own compositions.
K.
Catalogues:—Catalogue of Music. c. 1817. 1 p. fol. (B.M. h. 125. (38.)); c. 1820. 1 p. fol. (B.M. h. 125. (41.))

WHITE (LUKE). Printer and bookseller, Dublin; 18 Crampton Court, c. 1775-79; 6 Crampton Court, c. 1779-82; 86 Dame Street, c. 1782-1789. Issued a number of musical works.
K.

WHITEHEAD (T.). Music seller, 2 Bond Street, Bath. Advertised, June 1774, "In a few days will be published, Six favourite Minuets In eight parts; as performed at the Assemblies in Bath; dedicated to William Wade Esq. Master of the Ceremonies, by Thomas Shaw, jun."

WHITEMAN, *Mr.* *See* Wightman or Whiteman (Thomas).

WHITFIELD (G.). City Road, London. Sold "Sacred Harmony: or a choice Collection of Psalm and Hymn Tunes, in two or three parts, for the voice, harpsicord, & organ. Sold by G. Whitfield", etc., c. 1789.

WHITLEDGE (ROBERT). Printer, bookseller and bookbinder, London, c. 1695-1717; at the Bible, in Creed Lane within Ludgate; at the Bible and Ball, in Ave Mary Lane. (P.) His name appears in the imprint of "A Supplement to the New Version of Psalms by Dr. Brady and Mr. Tate. Containing the psalms in particular measures; the usual hymns . . . with Gloria Patri's and tunes (Treble and Bass). The Seventh edition . . . Printed by J. Nutt; and sold by J. Holland . . . R. Whitledge at Ave Mary Lane; and J. Hazard . . . 1712"; also in the eighth edition, 1717. In 1731 Bezaleel Creake married the widow of Whitledge and moved to the Red Bible in Ave Mary (Maria) Lane.
P. II.

WHITLEY & BOOTH. Printers, stationers and booksellers, 3 Crown Street, Halifax. Published and sold, "A New and enlarged edition of Cheetham's Psalmody, harmonized in score; with an arrangement

[331]

for the organ, or piano-forte. By J. Houldsworth . . . MDCCCXXXII.";
also the fifth edition, 1840.

WHITLEY (R. B.). Engraver, Bath. Engraved "The New Somerset-
shire March . . . Printed for J. Mathews, Music seller Bath. Compos'd
by J. M. Octr. 11. 1797"; "Benedictio ante Cænam, humbly inscribed to the members of the respectable Harmonic Society at Bath.
1797"; "A Periodical Collection of Vocal Music (never before
printed) consisting of Italian and English Songs Duetts, Terzetts,
recitatives, Canzonetts, Ballads, &c. Composed by Venanzio Rauzzini
. . . Vol. I. Printed for the Author by Geo: Steart, and sold by Messrs.
Lintern's, Bath and at Messrs. Longman & Broderip . . . in London.
Vol. II. Printed for the Author by A. C. Farthing, and sold by Messrs.
Lintern's, Bath and at Messrs. Longman & Broderip . . . in London,"
c. 1797.

WHITROW. *See* Champante & Whitrow.

WHITTAKER (GEORGE B.). Bookseller, 13-16 Ave Maria Lane, London,
c. 1825-29. Published a small amount of music.

WHITTINGHAM (W.). Lynn, Norfolk. Published c. 1836, "Song of
the Fisher's Wife, composed . . . by Josh. F. Reddie."

WHYTE (WILLIAM). Book and music seller, and publisher, Edinburgh;
at the sign of the Organ, 1 South St. Andrew Street, c. 1799-1809;
17 South St. Andrew Street, c. 1809-11; 12 South St. Andrew
Street, c. 1811-26; 13 George Street, c. 1826-58. From c. 1825
traded as William Whyte and Co.
K. G.

WICKSTEED (E.). Bookseller, London, 1735-53; in the Temple; at the
Bible and Bell, in Ave Maria Lane. (P.) His name appears in the
imprint of "The Psalms of David in Metre: With the tunes used in
Parish-Churches. By John Patrick. The Eighth edition. London:
Printed for J. Walthoe . . . E. Wicksteed . . . MDCCXLII."
P. III.

WIGHTMAN or WHITEMAN (THOMAS). Bookseller and stationer,
Grantham. His name appears in the imprints of "The Voice of
Melody . . . Printed for William East . . . and sold by . . . Mr. White-
man of Grantham", etc., c. 1748; "The Second edition of the first
Book of the Voice of Melody . . . Collected, printed, and sold by William
East . . . likewise by Mr. Whiteman stationer in Grantham . . . 1750";
"The Second Book of the Voice of Melody . . . Collected, printed, and
sold by William East . . . likewise, by Mr. Whiteman, stationer in
Grantham . . . 1750"; "The Sacred Melody . . . Collected and

publish'd by William East . . . Likewise Mr. Wightman bookseller in Grantham . . . 1754."
P. III.

WIGLEY & BISHOP.   Music sellers and publishers, adjoining the Academy of Fashion, Spring Gardens, London, c. 1801-04.
See also Wigley (Charles).

WIGLEY (CHARLES).   Musical instrument maker, music seller and publisher, London; Spring Gardens, Charing Cross, c. 1799-1801; became Wigley and Bishop, adjoining the Academy of Fashion, Spring Gardens, c. 1801-04; alone at 204 Strand, c. 1804-11; 151 Strand, c. 1811-16; 84 Strand, c. 1816-24. About 1813 issued some publications with the imprint "London. Published by C. Wigley Panharmonicon Exhibition, Royal Great Rooms, Spring Gardens". He was also a jeweller in business at the Repository of Fashion, 6 Spring Gardens.
K.

WIGLEY (JOHN).   Music and musical instrument seller, London; 15 Coventry Street, Haymarket, c. 1786-1805; 11 Princes Street, Hanover Square, c. 1805-10.
K.

WILCOX (J.).   Bookseller, in Little Britain, London. His name appears in the imprint of "A Treatise of the Natural Grounds, and Principles of Harmony. By William Holder . . . To which is added, by way of appendix: Rules for playing a Thorow-Bass . . . By the late Mr. Godfrey Keller . . . London: Printed by W. Pearson . . . for J. Wilcox . . . and T. Osborne . . . 1731."
P. II.

WILCOX (JOHN).   Music publisher, at Virgil's Head, opposite to the new Church, or, against the new Church, in the Strand, London, c. 1737-43.
K.

WILCOX (W. T.).   Musical instrument warehouse, 91 Aldersgate Street, London. Published "A Select Collection of Country Dances, Waltzes, &c. with their proper figures as performed at Almacks . . . Composed & arranged for the Piano Forte or Harp by W. T. Wilcox. No. 1," c. 1822; "Six Easy and Progressive Duetts, for two Violins. Composed . . . by J. M. Jolly," c. 1830.

WILD (JOSEPH).   Bookseller, at the Elephant, at Charing Cross, 1698-1700. (P.) Advertised March 1700, "A Supplement to the New Version of Psalms by Dr. Tate and N. Brady. Printed and sold at Stationers Hall . . . D. Brown . . . J. Wild . . . 1700."
P. II.

WILKIE (G.). Bookseller, 57 Paternoster Row, London. His name appears in the imprint of "A Selection of Psalms and Hymns, for use of the Parish Church of Chislehurst in Kent . . . London, Printed for the Author: And sold by G. Wilkie . . . and J. Hatchard . . . 1803."

WILKIN (R.). Bookseller and publisher, London. His name appears in the imprint of "The Psalms of David in Metre: With the tunes used in Parish-Churches. By John Patrick . . . The Seventh edition . . . London: Printed for D. Brown . . . R. Wilkin . . . MDCCXXIV."; also in the eighth edition 1742.
    P. III.

WILKINS (ELIZABETH). Great Milton, near Thame, Oxfordshire. Published c. 1745, "A Collection of Church Music. In Two, Three, and Four parts by the best Masters, with a short Introduction to the scale of Musick." Wife of Matthew Wilkins. Elizabeth Wilkins died in 1778.

WILKINS (MATTHEW). Great Milton, near Thame, Oxfordshire. Collected, printed, taught and sold c. 1730, "A Book of Psalmody, containing some easy instructions for young beginners; to wch is added a select number of Psalm Tunes, Hymns & Anthems, in 2, 3, & 4 parts"; a later edition was issued c. 1745. He died in 1773.
    K.

WILKINSON & CO. Music sellers and publishers, 13 Haymarket, London, 1808-10. C. Wilkinson, the principal partner, was previously partner in the firm of Broderip and Wilkinson, who were succeeded by Wilkinson and Co. Entire stock-in-trade purchased by Thomas Preston c. 1810, who issued a catalogue of selected publications. (B.M. Hirsch IV. 1113. (11.))
    Catalogues:—Additional Catalogue of new Music for the Year 1808. 2 pp. fol. (B.M. 7896. h. 40. (20.)); New Music. 1809. 1 p. fol. (B.M. g. 451. (2.))

WILKINSON. *See* Wright & Wilkinson.

WILKINSON (C.). *See* Broderip & Wilkinson; Wilkinson & Co.

WILLIAMS, *Mr.* Music engraver, Baron's Buildings, St. George's Fields, London. His name appears in the list of subscribers to "Twelve Hymns in four Parts . . . by Iohn Frederic Hering. London. Printed for the Author," etc.; preface is dated April 30, 1795.

WILLIAMS (A.). Music engraver, 11 Great Kirby Street, Hatton Garden, Holborn, London. Engraved "Six Easy Lessons for the Harpsichord. Compos'd by Bartholomew Davis. Opera Primo. London. Printed for and sold by the Author, at Mr. Moore's, 2 Bridgewater Square, Barbican," c. 1775.

WILLIAMS (BENJAMIN). Music printer and publisher, London; 19 Cloth Fair, West Smithfield, c. 1834-42; 30 Fountain Court, Cheapside, c. 1842-47; 11 Paternoster Row, c. 1847-68. Had additional premises at 2 Alsop's Buildings, Great Dover Road, c. 1845-46; 170 Great Dover Road, c. 1846-59. Business continued until the end of the century at many other premises in Paternoster Row.
K.

WILLIAMS (EVAN). Bookseller to the Duke and Duchess of York, 11 Strand, London. Published "Sixty of the most admired Welsh Airs, collected principally during his excursions into Wales by the Rev. W. Bingley . . . The basses and variations arranged for the Piano Forte, by W. Russell, Junr. 1803"; also another edition, 1810.

WILLIAMS (JOSEPH) [i.e. Joseph William Williams]. Music printer and publisher, London; 41 Duke Street, Little Britain, 1844; 123 Cheapside 1845-57; 6 Milk Street and 123 Cheapside, 1857-62; 123 Cheapside and 11 Holborn Bars, 1862-68; 24 Berners Street and 123 Cheapside, 1868-83; 24 Berners Street alone, 1883–97; 32 Great Portland Street, August 1897-1939; 29 Enford Street, Marylebone, January 1939 to present time. Succeeded Lucy Williams and Son; the original Joseph Williams died July 1883; business carried on as Joseph Williams by his son Joseph Benjamin Williams, known under the pseudonym of Florian Pascal, until he died in July 1923; since when it has been carried on by his son Florian Williams who had the assistance of his brother Ralph Williams for some years. The business became a family company, Joseph Williams Limited, in 1900.
K. G.

WILLIAMS (LUCY). Music and copper plate printer, London; Fountain Court, Cheapside, 1808-37; 41 Duke Street, Little Britain, 1837-43; as Lucy Williams and Son, 1843-44. Printed music for the firm of Clementi and Co.; succeeded by Joseph Williams.

WILLIAMS (R.). London. Published c. 1750, "The Land of Cakes, Book the first. Containing six Songs set to musick in the true Scots Taste. To which is added The Tears of Scotland."
K.

WILLIAMS (T.). Engraver, printer, print and music seller, and publisher, London; 43 Holborn, c. 1783-85; 146 Borough High Street, Southwark, c. 1786-90. Some single sheet songs bear only the initials T. W. Published the "Review of New Musical Publications." Vol. I. 1784.

WILLIAMS (THOMAS). Music engraver and printer, 18 Clerkenwell Green, London. Printed and sold, "Instructions in Miniature for learning Psalmody . . . By T. Williams . . . 1778"; "Harmonia

Cœlestis or The Harmony of Heaven imitated: a Collection of Scarce
. . . Anthems . . . also six New Anthems . . . composed by the late
Mr. A. Williams . . . 1780"; engraved "A Collection of Psalm Tunes in
three Parts . . . to which are added 2 Anthems & 2 Canons by Is.
Smith. c. 1780"; printed and sold, "Psalmody in Miniature in V.
books . . . By A. Williams. The third edition . . . to which is now
added a complete index to the five books . . . 1783."

WILLIAMS (THOMAS). Music seller and publisher, London; 29
Tavistock Street, Covent Garden, c. 1814-18; 2 Strand, Charing Cross,
c. 1818-47.
   K.

WILLIAMSON (R.). Printer, London. Printed "The Divine Musical
Miscellany. Being, a Collection of Psalm, and Hymn Tunes: great
part of which were never before in Print. London. Printed by
R. Williamson and sold at Mr. John Morgan's in Half-Moon Alley,
the 3^d. House from Bishopsgate Street. 1754."; an earlier edition
was printed by William Smith, c. 1740; "Harmonia Sacra, or Divine
and Moral Songs with Hymns and Anthems, by several eminent
masters. Adapted to the German Flute, with a thorough Bass, for
the Harpsichord or Organ, and an easy introduction to singing.
London. Printed by R. Williamson, and sold at Lewer's Music Shop
facing New Broad Street, Moorfields, London," c. 1770.

WILLIAMSON (RICHARD). Bookseller and publisher, near Gray's Inn
Gate, Holborn, London, 1723-37. (P.) His name appears in the
imprint of "The Compleat French Master, for Ladies and Gentlemen
. . . The Tenth edition . . . London: Printed for Samuel Ballard . . .
and Richard Williamson . . . MDCCXXIX."; contains the music of "A
Collection of new French Songs, &c."; his name also appears on the
eleventh edition, 1733.
   P. III. D. & M.

WILLIAMSON (T. G.). Composer, music seller and publisher, at his
Music, Print and Fancy Warehouse, 20 Strand, London, c. 1797-1802.
   K.

WILLIS & CO. *See* Willis (Isaac) & Co.

WILLIS. *See* Riley & Willis.

WILLIS (ISAAC) & CO. Music and musical instrument sellers and
publishers, Royal Harmonic Saloon, 7 Westmoreland Street, Dublin,
c. 1816-36; London; 55 St. James's Street, c. 1824-27, and c. 1829-36;
Royal Musical Repository, Egyptian Hall, Piccadilly, c. 1827-29;
75 Lower Grosvenor Street, 1836-48; as Isaac Willis, 119 New Bond
Street, c. 1849-62. Prior to opening in London, M. A. Burke, 22

Southampton Street, Strand, was the agent for the London trade; also had an agency at 4 bis, Rue de la Paix, Paris, c. 1830. Commenced business in Dublin as Isaac Willis and became Willis and Co. in London; at the Dublin address succeeded Goulding, D'Almaine, Potter and Co., and were succeeded there by Robinson, Bussell and Robinson.

K. G.

Catalogue:—New and admired publications for the Piano Forte. 1836. 1 p. fol. (B.M. h. 124. (31.))

WILLIS (RICHARD). Bookseller, Bearwood Lane, Nottingham. His name appears in the imprint of "The Excellent Use of Psalmody. With a course of singing Psalms . . . To which is added, a collection of choice hymns . . . By R. W. a Lover of Divine Musick. Nottingham: Printed and sold by George Ayscough and Richard Willis . . . MDCCXXXIV."

P. III.

WILSON. *See* Churnside & Wilson.

WILSON (JOHN). Music and musical instrument seller and publisher, 34 Great Russell Street, Bloomsbury, London, c. 1805-13.

WILSON (ROBERT). Bookseller, at various addresses, London, c. 1610-1639. (M.) Published "The Maske of Flowers. Presented by the Gentlemen of Graies-Inne, at the Court of White-hall, in the Banquetting House, vpon Twelfe Night, 1613. Being the last of the solemnities . . . which were performed at the marriage of . . . the Earle of Somerset and the Lady Francis, daughter of the Earle of Suffolke, Lord Chamberlaine. London Printed by N. O. for Robert Wilson, and are to be sold at his shop at Graies-Inne, new gate. 1614"; with the music.

K. M.

WILSON (WILLIAM). Printer, at the Three Foxes, Long Lane, London, 1640-65. (P.) His name appears in the colophon of "The Whole Booke of Psalmes. Collected into English Meetre by Thomas Sternhold, Iohn Hopkins, and others . . . with apt notes to sing them withall . . . Printed by I. L. for the Company of Stationers. 1646", with colophon "London, Printed by W. Wilson, for the Company of Stationers, 1646"; also another edition of "The Whole Booke of Psalmes . . . London, Printed by E. G. for the Company of Stationers . . . 1646", with colophon "London, Printed by W. Wilson, for the Company of Stationers, 1646."

P. I.

WILSON (WILLIAM). 4 King Street, St. James's Square, London. Published c. 1812, "Lewie Gordon by T. H. Butler."

WIMPEY (JOSEPH). Bookseller and publisher, Newbury. His name appears in the imprint of "A Collection of 20 New Psalm Tunes Compos'd with veriety of Fuges after a differant manner to any yet extant. Sold by Ed. Doe at Oxford Jos. Wimpey at Newbury", etc., c. 1760.
  P. III.

WINDET (JOHN). Printer, London, 1584-1611. (M.) At the White Bear in Adling Street, near Baynard's Castle (? dates); at the Cross Keys at Paul's Wharf, from c. 1594-?. Richard Alison's "An Howres Recreation in Musicke . . . 1606," was printed by Windet and sold at the Golden Anchor in Paternoster Row, which may or may not have been an address of Windet's. Printed a considerable number of editions of the Sternhold and Hopkins versions of the Psalms, 1591-1604, for the assignes of Richard Day, and from 1604-10 for the Company of Stationers; also from 1604 a number of other musical works, some as the assigne of William Barley. In 1611 he assigned his copyrights to a former apprentice, William Stansby.
  K. G. M. S.

WITHER (GEORGE). Printed by the Assignes of George Wither appears in the imprint of "The Hymnes and Songs of the Church . . . Translated and composed, by G. W. [i.e. George Wither. With music by Orlando Gibbons.] London, Printed by the Assignes of George Wither. 1623"; an edition was also published c. 1624; another 1623 edition of this work has imprint, "Printed for G. W."

W-k-r (P.). *See* Welcker (Peter).

WOAKES (W. H.). Music seller, professor of music, organist and composer, Music Warehouse, St. Owen's Street, Hereford. Known to have been at this address 1817-25, and probably longer. Published some of his own compositions.

WODENOTHE (RICHARD). Bookseller and haberdasher, London, 1645-1656; at the Star, under St. Peter's Church, in Cornhill; Leadenhall Street, next to the Golden Heart. (P.) His name appears in the imprint of "Choice Psalmes put into Musick for Three Voices . . . Compos'd by Henry and William Lawes . . . London, Printed by James Young, for Humphrey Moseley . . . and for Richard Wodenothe, at the Star under S. Peters Church in Cornhill. 1648."
  P. I.

WOFFINGTON (ROBERT). Organist, publisher, etc., Dublin. In partnership with William Gibson, musical instrument maker, etc., from 1775-78.
  See also Gibson (William).

WOGAN (PATRICK). Bookseller, 15 Lower Ormond Quay, Dublin, c. 1807-16. Printed "High Mass, and Sundays Vespers, as sung in most of the different Roman Catholic Chapels throughout the United Kingdom. The Second edition, with considerable additions . . . 1808."
K.

WOLF. *See* Gerock & Wolf.

WOLF (ROBERT) & CO. Pianoforte makers, London; 79 Cornhill, c. 1837-40; 45 Moorgate Street, c. 1840-41; 20 St. Martin's le Grand, c. 1841-45. Published a small amount of sheet music: succeeded C. Gerock and Co.

WOLFE (JOHN). Printer and publisher, London, 1579-1601; in Distaff Lane, near the sign of the Castle, 1582-88; at Stationers' Hall, 1588-1591; in Paul's Chain, over against the South Door of St. Paul's, 1592-1601; with a shop in Pope's Head Alley, off Lombard Street, 1598. (H. R. Hoppe: "John Wolfe." *The Library*. 4th Series. XIV. pp. 241-288.) Musical works include "Musicke of Six, and Fiue partes . . . By John Cosyn. London Imprinted by Iohn Wolfe. 1585"; "The Lamentations of Ieremie . . . with apt notes to sing them withall . . . translated . . . into English by Christopher Fetherstone . . . London Printed by Iohn Wolfe, dwelling in Distaffe-lane, neere the signe of the Castle 1587"; and a number of issues of the Sternhold and Hopkins versions of the Psalms, without any address except London, some for the Assignes of Richard Day. At his death in 1601, his printing business and stock were transferred to Adam Islip; there is no evidence that Islip printed any music.
K. G. M. S.

WOOD & CO. Musical instrument makers, music sellers and publishers, Edinburgh; 12 Waterloo Place, c. 1830-c. 1854; 18 Waterloo Place, c. 1854-60; 49 George Street, c. 1858-1909; 83 Princes Street, c. 1909-29. Succeeded Wood, Small and Co.
K. G. (Muir Wood.)

WOOD & IVY. Musical instrument makers, 50 New Compton Street, Soho, London, c. 1837-47. Published a small amount of music; George Wood was previously in business on his own account.

WOOD, SMALL & CO. Musical instrument makers, music sellers and publishers, Edinburgh; 13 Leith Street, c. 1818-22; 12 Waterloo Place, c. 1822-30. Principal partners were Andrew Wood and George Small; when the partnership ceased, Small became a partner in the firm of Small, Bruce and Co. Succeeded Muir, Wood and Co.; succeeded by Wood and Co.

WOOD. *See* Bainbridge & Wood.

WOOD. *See* Goulding, D'Almaine, Potter & Co.

WOOD (ANDREW). *See* Muir, Wood & Co.; Wood, Small & Co.

WOOD (B.). Music engraver, London; at 22 Hyde Street, Bloomsbury,
published c. 1785, "The Rush-Light an additional Song, introduced
and sung by Mr. Bannister, Junr. in Peeping Tom, the words by
G. Colman, Esq. Compos'd by Dr. Arnold."; at 60 Chandos Street,
Covent Garden, published c. 1789, "My Daddy O. A favorite Scotch
Song sung by Mrs. Martyr at Vauxhall Gardens. Composed by Mr.
Hook. The words by Mr. O'Keefe."

WOOD (GEORGE). Musical instrument maker, 50 New Compton Street,
Soho, London, c. 1832-37. Published a small amount of music;
became Wood and Ivy c. 1837.

WOOD (J.). Music seller? At the Royal Exchange, London. His name
appears in the imprint of "Amaryllis; Consisting of such Songs as
are most esteemed for Composition and Delicacy, and Sung, at the
Publick Theatres or Gardens; All chosen from the works of the Best
Masters, and rightly Adapted for the Voice, Violin, Hautboy, Flute
and German Flute. With a figured Base for the Harpsichord . . .
London. Publish'd according to Act of Parliament, by T. J. and sold
by M. Cooper . . . J. Wood . . . and I. Tyther," etc., c. 1750. 2 vols.;
a second edition was issued a little later.

WOOD (JOHN MUIR) & CO. Musical instrument and music sellers,
and publishers, 42 Buchanan Street, Glasgow, 1848-99. Had additional
premises at 15 Princes Square, c. 1859-65; John Muir Wood, elder
son of Andrew Wood, died in 1892.
G.

WOOD (THOMAS). Bookseller and printer, Little Britain, London.
Published a number of Ballad Operas with the music to the songs,
including "Flora . . . Being the farce of the Country-Wake, alter'd
after the manner of the Beggar's Opera . . . MDCCXXIX."; also the
second edition 1729; "The Cobbler's Opera . . . MDCCXXIX."; published in conjunction with A. Bettesworth and C. Hitch, "A Sequel
to the Opera of Flora . . . MDCCXXXII."

WOOD (WILLIAM). Bookseller, Lincoln. His name appears in the
imprint of "A Book of Psalm-Tunes, with Variety of Anthems in Four
Parts, with Chanting-Tunes for the Te Deum, Benedictus, Magnificat
. . . By James Green. The Fifth edition . . . London. Printed by
William Pearson . . . and sold by . . . Mr. Wood . . . Lincoln. 1724."
P. III.

WOODFALL (HENRY). Bookseller, London. His name appears in the imprint of "The Psalms of David . . . By I. Watts . . . The Twenty eighth edition . . . (Tunes in the Tenor Part fitted to the several metres.) London: Printed for H. Woodfall . . . 1768."
P. III.

WOODGATE (HENRY). Bookseller and publisher, at the Golden Ball, Paternoster Row, London. He was for a time in partnership with Stanley Crowder, and afterwards with Samuel Brooks. His name appears in the imprints of "The Psalm-Singer's Pocket Companion . . . By Uriah Davenport . . . London: Printed by Robert Brown . . . For Stanley Crowder and Henry Woodgate, at the Golden Ball, in Paternoster Row," c. 1755; "The Psalm-Singer's Pocket Companion . . . The Second edition. By Uriah Davenport . . . London: Printed by Robert Brown . . . for Stanley Crowder . . . and Henry Woodgate and Samuel Brooks, at the Golden Ball, in Paternoster Row. 1758."
P. III.

WOODWARD (JAMES). Bookseller and publisher, in St. Christopher's Churchyard, Threadneedle Street, near Stocks Market, London. Published in conjunction with Henry Playford the second edition of Playford's "The Divine Companion", advertised July 1707.
P. II.

WOODWARD (MICHAEL). Musical instrument maker and music seller, Birmingham, c. 1790-1829, or later; 7 New Street, c. 1790-1809; Union Street, c. 1814-15; 17 Bull Street, c. 1822-23; 7 Church Street, c. 1828-29. Printed and sold c. 1805, "Six Canzonets, with an Accompaniment for the Piano Forte. Composed . . . by Geo. Fred. Pinto."
K.

WOODWARD (WILLIAM). Bookseller, Portsea. Published "A Selection from the Psalms and Hymns, now used in the different Churches of the Establishment, in the Parishes of Portsmouth and Portsea . . . By Thomas Edward Bell . . . 1836."

WORDE (WYNKYN DE). Printer, assistant to Caxton at Westminster, London, c. 1480. After Caxton's death in 1491, took over his house where he remained up to the end of 1500, when he moved to Fleet Street, his printing office being at the sign of the Sun. From c. 1509 had another shop in St. Paul's Church Yard at the sign of Our Lady of Pity. Died in 1535. (D.) Printed Higden's "Polycronicon" 1495, the first English printed book to contain printed musical notes (a short fragment of the stave containing eight notes), for which in Caxton's edition of 1482 a blank space was left to be filled in by hand, and in the edition of Peter Treveris 1527, the music was printed from a wood block. From the Sun in Fleet Street, Worde issued a York Manual,

1509. A book of twenty songs issued in 1530 has been incorrectly attributed to him, but the printer of this work is not known, as the only available portion of the imprint (in the Westminster Abbey Library) gives "Impryntyd in Londō at the signe of the black Morēs." (The British Museum Quarterly. Vol. XVI. No. 2. April, 1951. pp. 33-35.)
    D. S.

WORNUM (ROBERT). Musical instrument maker, music seller and publisher, London; Glasshouse Street, c. 1772-77; 42 Wigmore Street, c. 1777-1815. After his death, c. 1815, his son Robert continued the business as a pianoforte maker.
    K.
    Catalogue of Music. c. 1802. 1 p. fol. (B.M. 7896. h. 40. (19.))

WRAY (HUGH). Music seller and publisher, London; 37 Haymarket, c. 1832-34; 59 Frith Street, Soho, c. 1834-36. The Frith Street premises were afterwards occupied by Henry Lee.

WREN (J.). Bookseller, at the Bible and Crown, near Great Turnstile, Holborn, London. In 1750 reissued with new titles, volumes of "The Musical Miscellany" previously published by John Watts, 1729-31:—Vol. III as "The Harp," Vol. IV as "The Spinnet," Vol. V as "The Violin."

WRIGHT & CO. See Wright & Wilkinson.

WRIGHT & SONS. Music sellers, Royal Colonnade, Brighton. Published "Luleikha. A Set of favorite Waltzes . . . Composed . . . by Miss Mary Cunynghame," c. 1838; "The Sherwood-Forest Waltzes, composed by W. Gibbons," etc., c. 1838.

WRIGHT & WILKINSON. Music printers, music sellers and publishers, Catherine (or Catharine) Street, Strand, London, c. April 1783-c. May 1784 (some imprints: Wright & Co.): as Wright and Co. only, June 1784-February 1785. Advertised as "Successors to Mr. Walsh, Catherine Street, Strand," but they really succeeded Elizabeth Randall, whose address was 13 Catherine Street, Strand. Succeeded by H. Wright. Lowndes's London Directory 1784, gives Wright and Wilkinson at No. 12 Catherine Street, but there is no evidence whether this is a misprint or refers to Elizabeth Randall's premises at No. 13, which was the address of H. Wright.
    K. G.

WRIGHT (DANIEL) the Elder. Musical instrument maker, music printer, music seller and publisher, next door to the Sun Tavern, near (the corner of) Brook Street, near Holborn Bars, Holborn, London, c. 1709-35. From about 1729 the premises were known for a short time as The Golden Bass Violin, this sign being taken over by his son

Daniel in 1730. Wright the elder issued some works in conjunction with his son and Thomas Wright, probably a relative. John Johnson may have taken over some of his stock, as he issued some works from Wright's plates.

K. G.

A Catalogue of English and Italian Musick Vocal and Instrumental. c. 1734. 1 p. fol. (B.M. g. 679.)

See also Wright (Daniel) *the Younger*; Wright (Thomas).

WRIGHT (DANIEL) *the Younger*. Music printer and publisher, at the Golden Bass (Golden Bass Violin), near the Pump, the North Side of St. Paul's Church Yard (near Cheapside), London, 1730-c. 1734. Wright changed his sign to The Violin and Flute, c. 1734, and issued from there "The Compleat Tutor for ye Flute . . . by Daniel Wright M.M.", who may or may not have been the same person as the publisher. He was next door to Temple Bar c. 1735; probably gave up business c. 1740, or earlier. Published some works in conjunction with Daniel Wright the elder and Thomas Wright, probably a relative. John Johnson may have taken over some of his stock as he issued some works from Wright's plates.

K. G.

See also Wright (Daniel) *the Elder*; Wright (Thomas).

WRIGHT (E.). Musical instrument maker, seller of music paper, etc., teacher of the guitar and violin, probably published some music at her shop under St. Dunstan's Church, Fleet Street, London, c. 1740.

K.

WRIGHT (GRIFFITH). Printer and publisher, Leeds. Printed and sold "A Book of Psalmody, containing variety of Tunes . . . and fifteen Anthems . . . The ninth edition . . . By the Rev. Mr. John Chetham . . . MDCCLXVII."; the tenth edition was printed and sold by G. Wright and Son. 1779; and the eleventh edition by Thomas Wright.

P. III.

WRIGHT (HERMOND) or (HARMAN). Music printer, music seller and publisher, London; 13 Catherine (or Catharine) Street, Strand, February, 1785-1801; 386 Strand, 1801-03. Succeeded Wright and Co.; advertised as "Successor to Mr. Walsh"; some time after Wright ceased publishing his entire stock of plates was purchased by Thomas Preston, 97 Strand, London.

K. G.

WRIGHT (THOMAS). Music seller and publisher, at the Golden Harp and Violin (Harp and Violin), on London Bridge, 1732-34. Published in conjunction with Daniel Wright, senior and junior, to whom he may have been related.

[343]

WRIGHT (THOMAS). Printer, Leeds. Printed "A Book of Psalmody: containing variety of Tunes . . . The eleventh edition . . . By the Rev. John Chetham . . . MDCCLXXXVII." Son of Griffith Wright, and previously in the business of G. Wright and Son, who printed the tenth edition of the above work.
    K.

WRIGHT (WILLIAM). Musician and music seller, High Bridge, Newcastle-on-Tyne, c. 1800-05. Published a small amount of music.

WYAT or WYATT (JOHN). Bookseller, London; at the Golden Lion, St. Paul's Churchyard, 1690-91; at the Rose, or Rose and Crown, St. Paul's Churchyard, 1691-c. 1724. (P.) Published "The Christian Sacrifice of Praises, consisting of select Psalms and Hymns, with Doxologies and Proper Tunes. For the use of the Religious Society of Romney . . . London: Printed by William Pearson, for John Wyat, at the Rose in St. Paul's Church-Yard. 1724." His name appears in the imprint of "The Psalms of David in Metre: Fitted to the tunes used in Parish-Churches. By John Patrick . . . London, Printed for W. Churchill . . . J. Wyat . . . 1718"; also in the seventh edition, 1724.
    P. II.

WYBROW (W.) & (S.). Music sellers and publishers, at the Temple of Apollo, 24 Rathbone Place, London, c. 1825-27, or later.
    See also Wybrow (William).

WYBROW (WILLIAM). Music seller and publisher, London; at the Temple of Apollo, 24 Rathbone Place, c. 1821-43; 33 Rathbone Place, c. 1843-57. For a short period c. 1825-27, or later, became W. and S. Wybrow.
    K.

WYLIE (JOHN). Bookseller, Glasgow. Published "Minstrelsy: Ancient and modern, with an historical introduction and notes. By William Motherwell . . . MDCCCXXVII."; music engraved by A. Blaikie, Paisley.

WYNKYN DE WORDE. *See* Worde (Wynkyn de).

WYNNE (JOHN). Musician and music seller and printer, Cambridge. Printed and sold at his house in the Regent Walk, "Ten English Songs. Set to musick by Mr. John Wynne. 1754." Printed and sold by John Wynne at his music shop in Cambridge, "Six Sonate for the Violoncello e Basso, composed by Alexis Magito, Opera Prima", c. 1765. His name also appears as music seller in the imprints of a few other works. He was still in business in 1779.
    K.

An early example of a Thematic Catalogue. c. 1793

An early example of music printed by lithography. c. 1806-07

YANIEWICZ & GREEN. Music sellers and publishers, 29 Lord Street, Liverpool, c. 1810-12. Felix Yaniewicz was previously in business alone.
 K.
 See also Yaniewicz (Felix).

YANIEWICZ & WEISS. Music sellers and publishers, Liverpool; 60 Lord Street, c. 1817-27; 2 Church Street, c. 1827-29. The partners were Felix Yaniewicz and W. G. Weiss.
 K.
 See also Yaniewicz (Felix).

YANIEWICZ (FELIX). Violinist, composer, music seller and publisher, Liverpool; 25 Lord Street, c. 1801-05; 29 Lord Street, c. 1805-10; became Yaniewicz and Green, 29 Lord Street, c. 1810-12; partnership dissolved and Yaniewicz in business alone at 60 Lord Street, c. 1812-17; became Yaniewicz and Weiss, 60 Lord Street, c. 1817-27; 2 Church Street, c. 1827-29. Also had additional premises in London, 22 Devonshire Street, Bloomsbury, c. 1810; at his Pianoforte Rooms, 49 Leicester Square, c. 1811-12; W. G. Weiss continued the business as a music seller at 2 Church Street, Liverpool, c. 1829-?.
 K. G.

YARDLEY (RICHARD). Printer, London, 1589-c. 1593; in partnership with Peter Short, at the sign of the Star, on Bread Street Hill, who issued a number of musical works. Yardley and Peter Short succeeded Henry Denham.
 M.

YOUNG (H. R.). 157 Fenchurch Street, London. Printed and published c. 1815, "West-India Melodies; or Negro Tunes. Adapted for the Piano-Forte . . . now first collected and arranged by Philip Young . . . resident in Jamaica. Also: Three Waltzes and a Country Dance, by the same Author."

YOUNG (I.) & CO. Inverness. Printed for and sold by, c. 1813, "A Collection of Highland Music consisting of Strathspeys Reels Marches Waltzes & slow Airs with Variations original & selected for the Piano Forte Violin and Violoncello . . . by William Morrison."

YOUNG (JAMES). Printer, London, 1643-53. (P.) Printed "Choice Psalmes put into Musick for Three Voices . . . Compos'd by Henry and William Lawes . . . London, Printed by James Young for Humphrey Moseley . . . and for Richard Wodenothe . . . 1648." Son of Robert Young.
 K. P. I.

YOUNG (JOHN). Musical instrument maker and seller, music seller, music printer and publisher, at the Dolphin and Crown (Dolphin), at the West End of St. Paul's Church Yard, London, c. 1698-1730. Young may have been the same person as John Young appointed musician in ordinary to the King for the Viol da Gamba, May 23, 1673. (De Lafontaine.) He issued some works in conjunction with John Cullen.

YOUNG (ROBERT). Printer, at the sign of the Starre, on Bread Street Hill, London, 1629-43. Printed "A Briefe and short Instruction of the Art of Musicke . . . By Elway Bevin . . . 1631." May have printed an edition of the Sternhold and Hopkins versions of the Psalms, for the Company of Stationers, 1637. Young's premises were formerly occupied by Peter Short and later by Humfrey Lownes the elder; Young was apparently in partnership with Lownes for a little time before the latter's death in 1629. After Young's death his copyrights were transferred to his son James.
   P. I.

INDEX OF FIRMS IN PLACES OTHER
THAN LONDON

ENGLAND

ANDOVER
 Noyes

ARUNDEL
 Calkin (William)

ASHLEY, NEAR MARKET HARBOROUGH
 Scott (William)

BANBURY
 Calcut, *Mr.*

BARNSLEY
 Lord (Joseph)

BATH
 Ashley (John)
 Binns & Robinson
 Cruttwell (Richard)
 Farthing (A. C.)
 Frederick (William)
 George (James)
 Hazard (Samuel)
 Hume (John)
 Leake, *Mr.*
 Leake (James)
 Lintern (James) & (Walter)
 Loder (Andrew)
 Loder (John David)
 Mathews (James)
 Milson (Charles)
 Patton (Matthew)
 Robbens (Thomas S.)
 Simms (Henry)
 Steart (George)
 Wheatstone (Charles)
 White (John Charles)
 Whitehead (T.)
 Whitley (R. B.)

BEDFORD
 Smith (William)

BERWICK-ON-TWEED
 Taylor (Robert)

BIRMINGHAM
 Aris (Thomas)
 Askey (J.)
 Broome (Michael)
 Fletcher (William)
 Kempson (James)
 Smith (William Hawkes)
 Woodward (Michael)

BLANDFORD
 Glover (Hurst)
 Oakley (Thomas)

BRIGHTON
 Longman & Broderip
 Mott (Isaac Henry Robert)
 Wright & Sons

BRISTOL
 Hodges (Charles)
 Howell (Thomas)
 Keeler (Henry)
 Major (Richard)
 Morgan (I.)
 Naish (T.)
 Smith (Andrew P.)
 Sturge (Joseph)

BURY ST. EDMUNDS
 Gray (J.) & Crask (John)
 Green (W.)

CAMBRIDGE
 Archdeacon (John)
 Barford (Morris)
 Buck (John)
 Buck (Thomas)
 Daniel (Roger)
 Deighton (John)
 Dixon (William)
 Fletcher (Thomas) & Hodson (Francis)
 Hague (William)
 Hellendaal (Pieter)
 Hicks (Francis)
 Legatt (John)
 Legge (Cantrell)
 Macintosh (A.)
 Nicholls (George)
 Peppercorn (John)
 Pratt (Jonas)
 Simpson, *Mr.*
 Sippel (C.)
 Stevenson (Thomas)
 Wynne (John)

CANTERBURY
 Marsh (William)
 Saffery (James)

CARLISLE
 Jollie (Fra.)

CHELMSFORD
Buckland (James)
Green (W.)
Toft (Timothy) & Lobb (R.)

CHELTENHAM
Alder (Daniel)
Hale (Charles)
Harward (Samuel)

CHESTER
Taylor (Richard)
Thomas (Thomas)

CHESTERFIELD
Bradley (Job)

COLCHESTER
Keymer (William)

DERBY
Cantrell (William)
Fox (Samuel)

DEVIZES
Maynard, *Mrs.*

DORCHESTER
Gould (Samuel)

DURHAM
Andrews (Frances)

EAST DEREHAM
Barker (W.)
Philo (James)

EXETER
Lewis (George Herbert)
March (John)
Pilbrow (Tycho)
Roberts (William)
Score (W.)

FROME
Crocker (John) & (Edmund)

GAINSBOROUGH
Carlton (Oswald)
Lowe (John)

GLOUCESTER
Netherwood (R.)
Price (Thomas)
Raikes (Robert)
Wheatstone

GODALMING
Lemare (Frederick) & Son

GRANTHAM
Allen (William)
Scarmardine, *Mr.*
Wightman or Whiteman (Thomas)

GREAT BOWDEN
Harrot (John)

GREAT MILTON
Wilkins (Elizabeth)
Wilkins (Matthew)

GREENWICH
Martin (Charles)
Richardson (William)

GUILDFORD
Dixon (William)
Lemare (Frederick) & Son

HALIFAX
Dyson (William)
Fielding or Fielden (Martin)
Jacobs (E.)
Pohlman (Henry)
Whitley & Booth

HASTINGS
Hart (Joseph Binns)

HEREFORD
Child (Ebenezer)
Woakes (W. H.)

HERTFORD
Austin (R.)
Austin (Stephen)

HUDDERSFIELD
Dyson (William)
Lancashire (J.)

HULL
Ryles (Thomas)

IPSWICH
Shave (John)

KEW
Trotter (T.)

LANGTOFT, LINCOLNSHIRE
Cox (J.)

LEAMINGTON
Elliston
Hewett (John)

LEEDS
Booth (William)
Butterworth, Livesley & Co.
Clifford (W.)
Hopkinson (John) & (James)
Livesley (Christopher)
Muff (Joshua)
Ogle (Joseph)
Penrose (John)
Porter (Edward)
Swale (John)
Swallow (John)
Sykes (John)
Sykes (William)
Wright (Griffith)
Wright (Thomas)

LEICESTER
Ireland (John)
Valentine (Henry)

LICHFIELD
Bailey (Richard)

LINCOLN
  Knight, *Mrs.*
  Knight (John)
  Wood (William)

LIVERPOOL
  Banks (James) & (Henry)
  Fleetwood (Anthony)
  Gore (John)
  Hime (Humphrey)
  Hime (Morris) or (Maurice) &
    (Humphrey)
  Palmer (John B.)
  Pye (John Bridge)
  Sadler (John)
  Sibbald (William)
  Smith (James)
  Southwell (Nicholas)
  Ward (Cornelius)
  Yaniewicz & Green
  Yaniewicz & Weiss
  Yaniewicz (Felix)

LOUTH
  Boys (Dickinson)

LYNN (KING'S LYNN)
  Whittingham (W.)

MACCLESFIELD
  Rathbone (Josiah)

MANCHESTER
  Andrews (R.)
  Beale (Thomas)
  Clayton (William)
  Hime & Addison
  Hime & Hargreaves
  Hime, Beale & Co.
  Hime (Benjamin)
  Massey (Robert)
  Pickering (John)
  Pigot (James)
  Townsend (John)
  Ward & Andrews

MANSFIELD
  Heath (Joseph)

MARGATE
  Longman & Broderip

MARKET HARBOROUGH
  Clipsham (John)

MARLBOROUGH
  Smith

NEWARK
  Farnsworth (B.)

NEWBURY, BERKSHIRE
  Wimpey (Joseph)

NEWCASTLE-ON-TYNE
  Barber (Joseph)
  Charnley (William)

  Kinloch (Alexander Monro)
  Liddell (M.)
  Marshall (J.)
  Monro (Henry)
  Story (John)
  Wright (William)

NEWCASTLE-UNDER-LYME
  Chester (Charles)

NEWMARKET
  Stanly (R.)

NORTHAMPTON
  Dicey (William)
  Lacy (J.)
  Raikes (Robert)

NORWICH
  Solemne or Solempne (**Anthony de**)

NOTTINGHAM
  Ayscough (Anne)
  Ayscough (George)
  Ayscough (William)
  Farmer (Henry)
  Heath (Joseph)
  Willis (Richard)

NUNEATON
  Baraclough (John)

OXFORD
  Barnes (Joseph)
  Beesly (Michael)
  Bowman (Thomas)
  Cross (William)
  Davenport (James)
  Davis (Richard)
  Doe (Edward)
  Dollife (Francis)
  Firth (Richard)
  Graham (William)
  Hall (William)
  Hardy (Henry)
  Howell (Mary)
  Jung (Philip)
  Lichfield (Leonard)
  Marshall (William)
  Mathews (William)
  Munday (J.) *junior*
  Philips, *Mr.*
  Smith (Francis)
  Turner (William)
  Walpergen (Peter de)

PENZANCE
  Nibert (J. P.)

PETERBOROUGH
  Boucher (John)

PLYMOUTH
  Rowe (Peter Ellison)

PONTEFRACT
  Lord (Joseph)

PORTSEA
Woodward (William)

READING
Newbery (John)
Pocock (Charles)

RIPON
Austin (Richard)

ROCHESTER
French (Thomas)

ST. ALBANS
Boys (Anthony)

ST. IVES, HUNTINGDONSHIRE
Dicey (William)
Raikes (Robert)

SALISBURY
Banks (James) & (Henry)
Banks (W.)
Collins (Benjamin)
Easton (James)
Johnson

SEVENOAKS
Hodsoll (William)

SHEFFIELD
Chaloner (George)
Gales (Joseph)
Turner (Joseph)

SHERBORNE, DORSET
Cook (John)
Cook (Joshua)
Cruttwell (William)

SOUTHAMPTON
Baker (Thomas)

STAMFORD
Cook or Cooke (John)
Harrod (William)
Rogers (Andrew)

STOKESLEY
Pratt (William)

STOURPORT
Nicholson (George)

TAUNTON
Chauklin, *Mrs.*

TEWKESBURY
Harward (Samuel)

UPPINGHAM
Cook or Cooke (John)

WAKEFIELD
Barber (Abraham)
Lord (Joseph)

WALTHAM, LEICESTERSHIRE
East (William)

WARRINGTON
Booth (J.) & (W.)
Eyres (John)

WARWICK
Merridew (John)

WESTERHAM
Green (Henry)

WEYMOUTH
Benson & Barling
Rolls (Daniel)

WIMBORNE
Torbuck (George)

WINCHESTER
Colson (W.)
Edmund (John)
Robbins (James)

WINDSOR
Webb (William)

WISBECH
Leach (John)

WOODBRIDGE
Ridley (J.)
Smith (B.)

WORCESTER
Clements (J.)

YEOVIL
King, *Mr.*

YORK
Baxter (Thomas)
Bellerby (Henry)
Blanchard (William)
Gent (Thomas)
Hammond (Thomas)
Hardman (William)
Haxby (Thomas)
Hildyard (Francis)
Hildyard (John)
Jeeb (Robert)
Knapton, White & Knapton
Knapton (Samuel)
Knapton (Samuel) & (Philip)
Marsh (Thomas)
Robinson (John)
Sagg (William)
Todd (J.) & (G.)
Tomlinson & Sons
White (Grace)
White (John)

SCOTLAND

ABERDEEN
Angus (Alexander)
Brown (Alexander)
Chalmers (James) *the Elder*
Chalmers (James) *the Younger*
Daniel (James)
Davie & Morris

Davie (James)
Forbes (John)
Logan & Co.
Melvill (David)
Morris (Michael)
Paterson & Sons
Raban (Edward)

AYR
Paterson & Sons

BANFF
Banff Lithographic Press

DUMFRIES
Paterson & Sons

DUNDEE
Brown (W.)
Chalmers (James)
Milln (George)
Paterson & Sons

EDINBURGH
Allan (D.)
Anderson & Bryce
Anderson (J.)
Anderson (John)
Baillie (Alexander)
Balbirnie (William)
Ballantyne (James) & Co.
Bassandine (Thomas)
Beugo (John)
Bremner (Robert)
Brown (Thomas)
Bryson (James)
Brysson (John)
Calder (Thomas)
Cameron (Duncan)
Carmichael (Richard)
Charteris (Henry)
Cheyne (N. R.)
Churnside & Wilson
Clark (J.)
Constable (Archibald) & Co.
Cooper (Richard)
Corri & Co.
Corri & Sutherland
Corri (John)
Corri (Natale)
Croall (George)
Ding (Laurence)
Doig (Silvester)
Edward (William)
Elder (John)
Elliot (Charles)
Fleming (R.)
Fraser & Co.
Fryer & Thomson
Glass (John)
Glen (Alexander)

Glen (David)
Glen (John) & (Robert)
Glen (Thomas Macbean)
Gordon (William)
Gow & Galbraith
Gow & Shepherd
Gow (Nathaniel)
Gow (Nathaniel) & Son
Grant & Moir
Gray & Peter
Guthrie (Alexander)
Hamilton & Kincaid
Hamilton & Müller
Hamilton (John), c. 1795-1810
Hamilton (John), c. 1812-13
Hart (Andro)
Home (Robert)
Hutton & Balbirnie
Hutton (William)
Johnson & Anderson
Johnson (James)
Johnston (Alexander)
Lekprevik (Robert)
Liston (Edward)
Lizars (William Home)
Macintosh (A.)
MacLachlan & Stewart
Martin (Andrew)
Martin (R.)
Mather (J.)
Menzies (Robert)
Moir (John)
Muir, Wood & Co.
Muir (James)
Mundell & Son
Ogg (James)
Oliver & Boyd
Paterson & Roy
Paterson & Sons
Paterson, Mortimer & Co.
Penson, Robertson & Co.
Phinn (Thomas)
Pole (John Frederick)
Purdie (John)
Purdie (Robert)
Ramsay (Allan)
Read (James)
Robertson (Alexander)
Robertson (Daniel)
Rochead & Son
Ross (Robert)
Roy & Blake
Roy (Peter Walker)
Sands, Donaldson, Murray & Cochran
Shand (R.)
Sibbald (James)
Small, Bruce & Co.
Smith (James Taylor)
Smith (John)

Stevenson (Thomas George)
Stewart (Charles) & Co.
Stewart (Neil)
Sutherland (John)
Thomson (George)
Turnbull (Thomas)
Urbani & Liston
Vautrollier (Thomas)
Walker & Anderson
Walker & Hutton
Walker (George)
Watlen (John)
Whyte (William)
Wood & Co.
Wood, Small & Co.

GLASGOW
Adam (Alexander)
Aird (James)
Bain (W.)
Brown (James)
Carrick (A.)
Foulis (Andrew)
Gillies (James)
Greenshields, Brothers
Hamilton (William)
McFadyen (John)
McGoun (Archibald) *the Elder*
McGoun (Archibald) *the Younger*
Mitchison (William)
Niven, Napier & Khull
Paterson & Sons
Robertson (John) *junior*
Steven (James)
Taylor (Joseph)
Wood (John Muir) & Co
Wylie (John)

INVERNESS
Young (I.) & Co.

KILMARNOCK
Paterson & Sons

LEITH
Coke (William)

OBAN
Paterson & Sons

PAISLEY
Blaikie (Andrew)
Neilson (John)
Paterson & Sons

PERTH
Anderson (J.)
Bowie & Hill
Brown (J.)
Hill (Thomas)
Paterson & Sons

STIRLING
Anderson (William)

WALES
LLANDOVERY
Rees (William)

IRELAND
BELFAST
Hall (W.)
Malier (W. T.)
Simms & McIntyre

DUBLIN
Alday (Paul)
Aldridge (John)
Aldridge (Maria) & Co.
Allen (George)
Attwood (Elizabeth)
Bonham (George)
Bradley (Abraham)
Brent (John) & Powell (Stephen)
Brocas (John)
Browne (David)
Bunting, Walsh, Pigott & Sherwin
Bussell (Henry)
Button (Simon)
Christy (J.)
Cooke (Bartholomew) or (Bartlett)
Cooke (J.)
Cooke (T.) & Brenan
Cooke (T.) & Co.
Curry (William) *junior* & Co.
Curwen (Isaac) & Co.
Delany (John)
Dobson or Dopson (Eliphal)
Duffy (James)
Ellard (Andrew)
Gibson (William)
Goodwin (Jacob)
Gough (George)
Goulding, Knevett & Co.
Grierson (Boulter)
Guernsey & De Vine
Hardy & Walker
Hill (Joseph)
Hime (Morris) or (Maurice)
Hodges & Smith
Hodson (George Alexander)
Hoey (James)
Holden (Smollet)
Jones (William)
Kearns (Joseph)
Kelly (Ignatius)
Kirkwood (John)
Laurence or Lawrence (Peter)
Lee (Anne)
Lee (Edmund)
Lee (John)
Lee (Samuel)
Logier (Johann Bernard)

Lunch (C.)
Machen (J.)
McCalley (John)
McCalley (Mary)
McCullagh & McCullagh
McCullagh (Edward)
McDonnell
McGlashan & Gill
McGlashan (James)
McLean (John)
Mainwaring (William)
Moses (Marcus)
Mountain (Henry)
Neale or Neal (John)
Neale or Neal (William)
Pigott & Sherwin
Pigott (Samuel J.)
Powell (Samuel)
Power (William) & Co.
Rhames (Benjamin)
Rhames (Elizabeth)

Rhames (Francis)
Rice (John)
Robertson (John) & Co.
Robinson & Bussell
Robinson, Bussell & Robinson
Servant (Thomas)
Shade (Henry L.)
Shaw (John)
Sherwin (John Frederick)
Southwell (John)
Stewart (Graham)
Stokes (Joshua)
Thompson (Nathaniel)
Thornton (Robert)
Watson (A.) & (W.)
Watson (William)
Wheatley (Samuel)
White (Luke)
Willis (Isaac) & Co.
Woffington (Robert)
Wogan (Patrick)

M *

Agutter (Ralph)
Alexander (James)
Astor & Horwood
Astor (George)
Bainbridge & Wood
Bainbridge (William)
Ball (James)
Banks (James) & (Henry)
Barbe (Camille)
Barford (Morris)
Bates (Theodore Charles)
Betts (Arthur) *the Elder*
Betts (Arthur) *the Younger*
Blackman (Josiah)
Blackman (Josiah) & (S.)
Bland & Weller
Boosey (Thomas) & Co.
Booth (William)
Brasan or Bressan (Peter)
Briggs (John)
Brown or Browne (John)
Bryan (F.)
Buchinger, Buckenger or Buckinger & Sharp
Buchinger, Buckenger or Buckinger (Joseph)
Bull (Thomas)
Bury (Samuel) & Co.
Cahusac (Thomas) *the Elder*
Cahusac (Thomas) *the Younger*
Cahusac (Thomas) *the Younger* & (William Maurice)
Cahusac (William Maurice)
Card (William)
Carr (Elizabeth) & Buchinger, Buckenger or Buckinger (Joseph)
Carr (John)
Chappell & Co.
Clementi, Banger, Collard, Davis & Collard
Clementi, Banger, Hyde, Collard & Davis
Clementi, Collard & Collard
Clementi, Collard, Davis & Collard
Collard & Collard
Collett (Thomas)
Cooke (Bartholomew) or (Bartlett)
Cox (John)
Cramer, Beale & Chappell
Cramer (John)
Culliford & Barrow

Culliford, Rolfe & Barrow
Dale (Joseph)
D'Almaine & Co.
Davis (Joseph)
Davis (Richard) & (William)
Delany (John)
Distin (Henry)
Dodd (T.)
Drouet (Louis François Philippe)
Duke (Richard)
Eavestaff (William)
Ellard (Andrew)
Farn (Charles Joseph)
Flight & Robson
Forster (William) *the Elder*
Forster (William) *the Younger*
Ganer (Christopher)
Gange (George) & Co.
Gerock & Wolf
Gerock, Astor & Co.
Gerock (Christopher)
Gerock (Christopher) & Co.
Gibson (William)
Glen (Alexander)
Glen (David)
Glen (John) & (Robert)
Glen (Thomas Macbean)
Goulding, Phipps & D'Almaine
Goulding (George)
Hack (Robert)
Harbour (Jacob)
Hardman (William)
Hare (John)
Hare (Joseph)
Hawkes & Co.
Haxby (Thomas)
Hill (Henry)
Hill (Joseph)
Holland & Jones
Holland (Henry)
Holloway & Co.
Hopkinson (John) & (James)
Hunt (Richard)
Jenkinson (J.)
Johnson (John)
Jones (John)
Keith, Prowse & Co.
Keith (Robert William)
Key (Thomas)
Knapton, White & Knapton

Knapton (Samuel)
Knapton (Samuel) & (Philip)
Kohler (John)
Lawson (Henry)
Lawson (Joseph)
Lee (Edmund)
Lee (John)
Lindsay (Thomas)
Lintern (James) & (Walter)
Longhurst (James)
Longman & Bates
Longman & Broderip
Longman & Herron
Longman, Lukey & Broderip
Longman, Lukey & Co.
Longman (James) & Co.
Longman (John)
Longman (John), Clementi & Co.
Luff (George)
Lyon & Duncan
Lyon (Samuel Thomas)
Matthews & Co.
May (Charles)
Meares (Richard) *the Elder*
Meares (Richard) *the Younger*
Metzler & Co.
Metzler & Sons
Milhouse (William)
Monzani & Hill
Monzani (Tebaldo) or (Theobald)
Morris (Michael)
Mott (Isaac Henry Robert)
Motta & Ball
Muir, Wood & Co.
Neale or Neal (John)
Norman (Barak)
Paine (John)
Panormo (Louis)
Paterson & Roy
Paterson & Sons
Paterson, Mortimer & Co.
Peachey (George)
Phillips & Co.
Phillips (Thomas)
Pippard (Luke)
Potter (Samuel)
Power (James)
Power (William) & Co.
Preston (John)
Preston (Thomas)
Prowse (Joseph)
Prowse (Thomas)
Rauche (Michael)
Rawlins (Mickepher)
Rice (John)
Robinson (H.)
Rochead & Son
Rolfe (William)

Rudall, Carte & Co.
Rudall, Rose, Carte & Co.
Rudall (G.)
Satchell (J.)
Scates (Joseph)
Schuchart (Charles)
Scott & Co.
Simpson (James) & (John)
Simpson (John) 1734-c. 1749
Simpson (John) c. 1826-69
Small, Bruce & Co.
Smart (George)
Smith (Thomas)
Smith (William)
Southwell (Nicholas)
Stewart (Neil)
Thompson & Son
Thompson & Sons
Thompson (Ann) & (Henry)
Thompson (Charles) & (Samuel)
Thompson (Henry)
Thompson (Peter)
Thompson (Robert)
Thompson (Samuel)
Thompson (Samuel) & (Ann)
Thompson (Samuel, (Ann) & (Henry)
Thompson (Samuel), (Ann) & (Peter)
Thompson (Samuel), (Ann), (Peter) &
    (Henry)
Thorowgood & Horne
Thorowgood (Henry)
Tilley (Thomas)
Tolkien (Henry)
Townsend (John)
Turner (John Alvey)
Vernon (Charles)
Walmsley, Wamsley or Warmsley (Peter)
Walsh (John) *the Elder*
Walsh (John) *the Younger*
Warrell (William)
Waylett (Henry)
Weaver & Co.
Webley (Alexander)
Weller (E.)
Wheatstone (Charles)
Wheatstone (William)
Whitaker (Maurice)
Wigley (Charles)
Wolf (Robert) & Co.
Wood & Co.
Wood & Ivy
Wood, Small & Co.
Wood (George)
Woodward (Michael)
Wornum (Robert)
Wright (Daniel) *the Elder*
Wright (E.)
Young (John)

SUPPLEMENT

ADDENDA AND ERRATA

by CHARLES HUMPHRIES and WILLIAM C. SMITH

INTRODUCTION. p. 3, line 2; p. 3, line 21, Petrucci not Petrucchi. p. 19, last para delete:—Maurice Whitaker, who had been manager for Mrs. Simpson, succeeded Cox, while at the same time. p. 25, line 24, 1740 not 1749. p. 31, line 26, 1761-80 not 1762-80. p. 34, line 3, from bottom, 1836-92 not 1837-92. p. 35, line 10, Senefelder (1796).

ALLAN (DAVID). Lithographic printer and engraver, 187 Trongate, Glasgow. He lithographed "A Selection of Songs, Marches, etc. Composed by Hugh late Earl of Eglantin arranged for piano forte by John Turnbull," c. 1833.

ALLEN (G.). Music engraver, 5 Sadlers Wells, London. Engraved "Six Quartettos for two Violins a Tenor and Violoncello . . . by Iacob Herschel. Printed and sold by J. Dale, London." Advertised May 1788.

ALLEN (GEORGE). Add:—A Catalogue of Sacred Music. 1827. 1 p. fol. (B.M. h. 147.)

ARIS (THOMAS). Add:—"A Collection of twenty-eight Psalm Tunes in four parts by several authors . . . Collected printed and sold by Michael Broome & may be had of Thos. Aris Printer in Birming^m . . . 1753."

AUSTEN (STEPHEN). Add:—"A System of Divine Musick. Containing, Tunes to all the metres in the new version of psalms . . . By John Bellamy . . . London: Printed by Robert Brown . . . For the Author, and sold by him . . . and Mr. Stephen Austen . . . MDCCXLV."

BAKER (THOMAS). Add:—"XII Sonate A Violino e Basso di Felice Giardini . . . Baker Sculp. Londra, 1765";

BALDWIN (ANN) Mrs. Add:—Her name appears in the imprint of "A Book of Psalm-Tunes in Two, Three, and Four Parts . . . By John and James Greene of Wombwell in the Parish of Darfield. The Second Edition with large Additions . . . Printed by J. Heptinstall . . . and Sold by A. Baldwin . . . 1713."

BANISTER (HENRY JOHN). Stationer, music seller and publisher, London; 109 Goswell Street, c. 1824-30, with additional address 29 Thomaugh Street, Bedford Square, c. 1830. Edited and published "A new and complete edition revised and corrected of the Vocal Music of the late C. W. Banister," in monthly parts. Part I was issued July 1831 from 17 Hadlow Street, Burton Crescent; Part 2, etc. August 1831 to 1833, from 3 Huntley Street, Torrington Square. On some of the parts he is described as "Professor of the Violoncello at the Royal Academy of Music."

Catalogue:—New Music published by H. J. Banister. c. 1830. 1 p. fol. (B.M. h. 204. b. (2.))

BANKS (ALEXANDER). Bookseller and publisher of ballads, etc., Charing Cross, London, 1676-85. (P.II.) Published "The Loyal Scot. A excellent new Song. To an excellent new Scotch Tune. Printed for Alexander Banks . . . 1682."
P. II.

BARBER (ABRAHAM). Add:—*after* 1687:—Also the 3rd edition, 1698;

BARFORD (MORRIS). Cambridge. Add:—Printed and sold "Six Duets for a Violin & Violoncell. Composed by J. B. Breval. Op. XXI," c.1800.;

BEALE (THOMAS). Line 2. 6 St. Mary's Gate, c. 1813-28.

BEATNIFFE (RICHARD). Printer, bookseller and publisher, 1 Cockey Lane, Norwich, c. 1772-1818. Printed "Hymns and Spiritual Songs . . . by Edward Trivett. The second edition, corrected. With an addition of a great variety of new hymns . . . with tunes proper for the various meters, &c. Norwich: Printed by R. Beatniffe . . . and sold by the Author at Worstead, and by J. Gurney . . . London," c. 1772.
P. III.

BELL (GEORGE). Bookseller and publisher, 186 Fleet Street, London. Published "The Order of daily Service, with the musical notation as used in the Abbey Church of St. Peter, Westminster. Edited by Edward F. Rimbault . . . MDCCCXLIV."

BETTS (ARTHUR) *the Elder*. Line 3. c. 1823-38 not c. 1827-38. Line 4. c. 1844-September 1847. Died September 1847, aged 73. Succeeded his brother John Betts. Succeeded by his son Arthur Betts.

BETTS (ARTHUR) *the Younger*. Add:—27 Royal Exchange, September 1847-66, where he succeeded his father Arthur Betts.

BETTS (JOHN). Musical instrument maker and music seller, 2 North Piazza, Royal Exchange, London. May 1782-March 1823. His full name was John Edward Betts, generally known in his day as "Old John Betts" to distinguish him from his nephew Edward Betts, or "Ned Betts." He advertised May 1, 1782, "John Betts, real Musical-Instrument maker, begs leave to inform the Public . . . that he has taken Mr. Whitaker's late shop No. 2 North Piazza Royal Exchange . . .

that he served seven years apprenticeship with that great artist Mr. Duke, senr., and ten years after." His name appears in the imprints of a number of musical works; after his death in March 1823 the business was continued by his brother Arthur Betts, the Elder.

G.

BEUNGO (JOHN). Add:—Musician.

BICKHAM (GEORGE) *the Elder & the Younger*. Line 31. April 1738 to 1763.

BIGG (GEORGE). Line 6. MDCCLXXVII. (1777 not 1778.)

BINNS (JOHN). Printer, book and music seller, Briggate, Leeds. His name appears in the imprint of the single sheet song "The Vicar and Moses. Publish'd July 2nd. 1784 by J. Binns: Leeds, and J. Wallis . . . London."

BIRCHALL, LONSDALE & MILLS. Add:—Catalogue:—Index to Beethoven's Rondos and Airs with Variations. c. 1822. 1 p. fol. (B.M. Hirsch M. 762. (1.));

BLACKMAN (WILLIAM). Add:—Catalogue:—Sacred Music, lately published. c. 1843. 1 p. fol. (B.M. H. 1181. (22.))

BLANCHARD (WILLIAM). Line 6. MDCCLXXXIX. A second edition was issued in 1790.

BLAND (JOHN). Line 2. 45 Holborn, early in 1778-95. Add to Catalogues:—Catches, Glees, Canons, Canzonetts, etc. c. 1790. 1 p. fol. (B.M. G. 353. (8.)) Catalogues of Subjects or beginnings of the several works, for the harpsichord, piano forte or organ, which are printed and sold by J. Bland. London. c. 1790. (Check list of Thematic Catalogues, New York Public Library, 1954.)

BLUNDELL (JAMES). Add:—A number of his publications were reissued by S. A. and P. Thompson.

BOOKER (THOMAS). Stationer, 56 New Bond Street, London. His name appears in the imprint of "Six Sonatas for the Harpsichord or Piano Forte, with a Violin Accompanyment Obligate [*sic*] Composed . . . by Valentino Nicolai. Op: V. Printed and sold for the Author, at Mr. Booker's," etc. Advertised January 1780.

BOOSEY (THOMAS) & CO. Add:—Catalogues:—New Harp Music. c. 1845. 1 p. fol. (R.M. 16. b. (4.))
The real name of the founder of this firm was THOMAS BOOSÉE who emigrated from France at the time of the French Revolution and settled in London. In 1795 he opened a small bookshop and not until

1816 did he start the publication of music. In 1853 his sons, Charles and John succeeded to the business, the latter dying in February, 1893, at the age of sixty-one. In 1866 he founded the "Ballad Concerts," and in 1854 became the owner of the "Musical World" which lasted until 1890. (Le Ménestrel, April 30, 1893. C. Hopkinson. First Edition Book Shop.)

BOYCE. Music engraver, 63 Bunhill Row, London. Engraved "The Ladies Collection of Catches, Glees, Canons, Canzonets, Madrigals, &c. Selected from the Works of the Most Eminent Composers, By John Bland and Sold by him at his Music Warehouse, No. 45 Holborn. Boyce Sculp.," etc., c. 1787-90.

BOYS. (ANTHONY). Add at end:—Also third edition "Printed by J. Heptinstall for Anthony Boys to be sold at his shop in St. Albans . . . and by J. Hare . . . 1700."

BREWMAN (DRAPER). Printer, 13 Little New Street, Shoe Lane, London. Printed "An Account of the Origin and progressive Improvements of the Diatonic Scale, or System of Music . . . also the elements of tuning the harpsichord, organ, and piano-forte, with a new Scale. London: Printed by D. Brewman, for J. Carr," etc., c. 1790.

BREWSTER (EDWARD). Line 6. S. Keeble, not Kettle.

BRIDE (RICHARD). Exeter Change (Exchange).

BRISTOW (WILLIAM). Bookseller, Canterbury. His name appears in the imprint of "The Triumph of Britons, a new and constitutional song . . . written by James Alderson of Ashford. Set to music by George Philpot of Canterbury. Printed for the Authors & to be had of . . . Mr. Bristow . . . Canterbury," etc., c. 1800.

BRODERIP & WILKINSON. Add:—Catalogues:—No. 1. Music of the most esteemed Authors. c. 1801. 1 p. fol. (B.M. g. 453. (11.))

BROWN (W.) & CO. Stationers, 181 Fleet Street, London. Printed "(To be Continued) No. 1 Duo Concertante for Violins, Composed by W. Moorshead," etc., c. 1800.

BYE & LAW. Line 3. MDCC.XCVI. Also an edition dated 1804.

CARR (ELIZABETH) & BUCHINGER (JOSEPH). Add:—According to Dichter & Shapiro American Publishers &c., Benjamin Carr was the son of Joseph Carr who opened up in Baltimore in 1794.

CARR (J.) (JOSEPH). Add:—The same person as Joseph Carr who opened a music publishing business in Baltimore U.S.A. in 1794. His son Thomas took over the business before the death of Joseph on 27th October, 1819.

CARUSO, *Mr.* Line 5. 1765. (*The Public Advertiser*, Mar. 30.)

CHALK. *See* Meggy & Chalk.

CHALMERS & CO. *See* Chalmers (James) *the Younger*.

CHALMERS (JAMES) *the Younger*. Add:—"Translations and Paraphrases of several passages of Sacred Scriptures, collected and Prepared by a Committee appointed by the General Assembly of the Church of Scotland . . . MDCCLXVII."; "The Elements of Music to which is annexed a collection of the best Church Tunes . . . selected from the best Authors . . . by William Taas . . . J. Chalmers & Co. 1787."; The Psalms of David in Metre . . . with the Church tunes accurately set to music . . . J. Chalmers & Co.", c. 1790.

CHALONER (GEORGE). Line 2. 1847 not 1827.

CHAPMAN (LIVEWELL). Bookseller, London; at the Crown in Pope's Head Alley, 1651-61; Exchange Alley in Cornhill, 1665. (P.) Published "The Lutes Apology, for her Excellency: wherein is contained variety of Ayres, easie, pleasant, and delightfull. Newly set to the French Lute, by Richard Mathew, Lover of Musick, for the Benefit of the Industrious Practitioner, The first that hath been Published to the French Lute. London. Printed by Thomas Harper, for Livewell Chapman, at the Crowne in Popes-head Alley, 1652."
P. I.

CHAPPELL & CO. Add:—The premises at 50 New Bond Street were seriously damaged by fire May 6th, 1964, which destroyed a variety of musical instruments, a valuable library of music books, irreplaceable manuscripts, autographs, and paintings, but the business was re-established at the same address where it is carried on today with additional premises at 14 St. George Street, W. (*Musical Opinion*, June 1964, p. 523.)

CHAPPELL (SAMUEL). Add:—Catalogues:—New Vocal Music. c. 1830. 1 p. fol. (B.M. 1287. (5.)); New Pianoforte Music. c. 1833. 1 p. fol. B.M. g. 443. m. (15.)); New Italian and French Vocal Music. c. 1834. 1 p. fol. (B.M. 379. b. (20.))

CHARTERIS (HENRY). Add:—Printed "The CL. psalms of David in meter efter [*sic*] the forme that they ar used . . . in the Kirk of Scotland . . . with the Catechisme of M. John Caluine . . . 1594";

CHURCHILL (AWNSHAM) & (JOHN). Line 5. After 1698 Insert:— Published "The Psalms of David in Metre: Fitted to the tunes used in Parish-Churches. By John Patrick. London, Printed by J. H. for A. & J. Churchill . . . 1706." Also an edition in 1710.

CHURCHILL (JOHN). Bookseller, at the Black, Swan, Paternoster Row, London. Published "The Psalms of David in Metre: Fitted to the tunes used in Parish-Churches. By John Patrick. London, Printed for John Churchill . . . 1715." Also another issue in conjunction with Elizabeth Meredith in 1715. Brother of Awnsham Churchill with whom he was in partnership from 1690-1714.
P. II.

CLARE COURT. Line 1. c. 1818-20 not c. 1815-20. Add:—R. Major was in business at these premises during that time.
See Major (R.)

CLACHAR (WILLIAM). Bookseller, Chelmsford. His name appears in the imprint of "The Country Chorister containing seven Anthems, and thirty Psalm Tunes with Te Deum. Composed by George Ffitch of Great Dunmow Essex . . . Printed for the Author And sold by Messrs. Thompson's . . . London. Also by Mr. Clachar . . . Chelmsford," c. 1799.

CLARK (WILLIAM). Engraver, St. Ann's Lane, London. Engraved "Six Concertos, For the Violoncello, with Four Violins, one Alto Viola, and Basso Ripieno . . . by John Garth . . . Printed for the Author and Sold by John Johnson . . . J. Walsh . . . London, and R. Bremner in Edinburgh. MDCCLX."; "Twelve Songs Set to Music by William Jackson of Exeter. Opera Quarta . . . London. Printed for the Author and Sold at the Music Shops," c. 1765.

CLEMENTI, BANGER, COLLARD, DAVIS & COLLARD. Add:— Catalogue:—Clementi and Compyns. Collection of Rondos, Airs with Variations, Military Pieces, &c. [1-60.] c. 1810. 1 p. fol. (B.M. g. 232. b. (20.))

CLEMENTI, BANGER, HYDE, COLLARD & DAVIS. Add:—Catalogue: —Musical Publications. c. 1801. 1 p. fol. (B.M. g. 451. a. (3.))

CLEMENTI, COLLARD, DAVIS & COLLARD. Add:—Catalogue:— Clementi & Co. New Flute Music. 1821. 1 p. fol. (B.M. g. 525. (2.))

COCKS (ROBERT) & CO. Add:—Catalogues:—New Music, Elementary Works, &c. c. 1830. 1 p. fol. (B.M. g. 270. r. (23.)) Music for Violin, &c. c. 1835. 1 p. fol. (B.M. g. 270. r. (17.) No. 3.) New Violoncello Music. c. 1835. 1 p. fol. (BM. g. 270. r. (17.) No. 2.) Modern Classical Publications. 1837. pp. 12. (B.M. 7892. tt. 11.) Classical Oratorios, &c. c. 1845. 1 p. fol. (B.M. 271. d. (18.)) School Music for the Pianoforte. c. 1850 1 p. fol. (B.M. g. 545. j. (4.))

COLLIER & DAVIS. Musical instrument makers and music sellers, not Publishers.

COLLINS (FREEMAN). Printer, London and Red Well, Norwich, 1682-1713. (P.) Printed "The Book of Psalms In Metre Close and Proper to the Hebrew: Smooth and Pleasant for the Metre. To be sung in usual and known Tunes. Newly Translated with Amendments, and Addition of many fresh Metres . . . By William Barton Mr. of Arts, as he left it finished in his lifetime . . . London: Printed by F. Collins for the Company of Stationers, 1691."
P. II.

CONRAD (JOHN). Henrietta Street, London. His name appears in the imprint of "Choix nouveau d'airs à deux voix. Paroles francoises. Premier (Deuxieme) Cayer . . . À Londres Chez John Conrad Henriette Street. À Paris Chez . . . ceux qui le vendent," c. 1790.

COOPER (RICHARD). Edinburgh. Add:—"Six Solos for the Harpsicord Violin and German Flute also Song call'd Simplicetta Tortorella. Compos'd by Filippo Palma. Printed . . . for the Author," c. 1740.

CORRI (DOMENICO). Add:—Corri, in conjunction with Thomas Jones, issued a trade card advertising "The Musical Lounge and Apollo Circulating Libraries At D. Corri's Music Seller to the Royal Family; No. 28 Hay-Market, and at T. Jones's, No. 23 Bishopsgate Street." Some publications were issued bearing both names.

COVENTRY & HOLLIER. Line 3: dropped out 1849.

COX (JOHN). Line 10. *After* Bremner add:—Charles and Samuel Thompson, Henry Thorowgood (an apprentice of Cox) and John Walsh.

COXHEAD (JAMES). *See* Lee (Leoni) & Coxhead.

CRAMER, ADDISON & BEALE. Add:—Catalogue:—Pianoforte Instructions, Lessons &c., Exercises, Studies &c. c. 1835. 1 p. fol. (B.M. g. 443. g. (22.))

CROSLEY (JOHN). Bookseller, Oxford, 1664-1703. (P. II.) His name appears in the imprint of "The Psalter or Psalms of David Paraphras'd in Verse. And so design'd that by Two Tunes onely, the whole Number of Psalms (Four onely excepted) may be sung . . . The Second Edition, wherein the whole Number is Compleated. By Richard Goodridge. Oxford. Printed by L. Lichfield . . . for Jo. Crosley. 1684."
P. I.

CROSS (THOMAS). Add:—Issued "The Compleat Tutor to the Violin" in conjunction with John Young, 1699.

D., M. Engraver, Derby. "M.D. Derby Sculpt." appears on some leaves of "Divine Musick Scholars Guide . . . By F. Timbrell," c. 1725. Also in the c. 1730 and c. 1735 editions.

DALE (JOSEPH). Catalogues. Line 6. Hirsch M. 555.

D'ALMAINE & CO. Add:—Catalogues:—New Music. 1834. 1 p. fol. (B.M. H. 1287. (23.)); Vocal and instrumental arrangements of popular Operas. 1836. 1 p. fol. (BM. H. 450. (1.)); A Select Catalogue of new Pianoforte Music. 1837. 1 p. fol. (B.M. H.1251. (23.)); Jullien's Quadrilles, Waltzes, &c. 1844. 1 p. fol. (B.M. H. 1305. (3.))

D'ALMAINE (THOMAS). Line 2. Goulding, Phipps & D'Almaine.

DANIELL (WILLIAM). Bookseller, stationer, and printer, Bourn, Lincolnshire. Published c. 1833, the Song "England, Home of the Brave! Composed by Oscar Perry. Bourn: Published for the Author, by W. Daniell; and may be had of Preston . . . Soho. Printed with moveable music types, by J. Teuten . . . Soho, London."

DIETHER (JOHN). Line 2. New Lisle Street (or, Lisle Street).

DING (LAURENCE). Add:—"A Curious Collection of Scots Tunes with Variations for the Violin, and a Bass for the Violincello or Harpsichord . . . Edinburgh, Printed & Sold by L. Ding, No. 4 Parliament Square," c. 1793.

DOE (EDWARD). Add:—He was "privileged" by the University as a bookbinder 3 April 1717; from 1734 till his death (aged nearly 80) in 1769 he occupied a tenement belonging to the City "opposite Balliol."

DOWNING (JOSEPH). Printer and Bookseller, Bartholomew Close, near West Smithfield, London, 1670-1734. (P.) Printed and sold "Psalmodia Germanica: or, the German Psalmody. Part II. Translated from the High-Dutch . . . 1725."
     P. II, III.

DOWNING (M.). Add:—Probably widow of Joseph Downing.

DUFF & HODGSON. Add:—Catalogues:—Musical Index of favorite Songs. 1849. 1 p. fol. (B.M. H. 377. (12.)); Musical Index of Samuel Lover's popular Songs. 1849. 1 p. fol. (B.M. H. 377. (11.))

DUFF & HODGSON. Line 2. c. 1862-67. John Duff died March 7, 1867. Add:—Catalogues:—Musical Index of favorite Songs. 1849. 1 p. fol. B.M. H. 377. (12.)); Musical Index of Samuel Lover's popular Songs. 1849. 1 p. fol. (B.M. H. 377. (11.))

DUFF (CHARLES). Musician, music and musical instrument seller, Dundee; West side of Castle Street adjoining to the Theatre, 1815-c. 1817; 30 High Street, c. 1817-18; Opposite the English Chapel, Nethergate, c. 1818-21. In March 1821 announced sale of music and musical instruments. Previously in partnership with James Chalmers, 1808-15.

DUFF (CHARLES) & CHALMERS (JAMES). Music and musical instrument sellers, Dundee; 3 Castle Street, January 1808-March 1810; Near the bottom of Castle Street, March 1810-15. Partnership was dissolved by mutual consent, in 1815; Duff opened up on his own account at another address in Castle Street.

DUFF (JOHN) & CO. Line 1. Music sellers and publishers.

DUNCAN (JOHN). Bookseller, Dumfries. Engraved, printed and sold "A Collection of Psalm Tunes for the use of the Church of Scotland Compos'd in four parts (viz) Trible (sic) Contra Tenor Bassus. Engraven Printed and Sold By John Duncan . . . MDCCXXIII."

DUNCOMBE & MOON. Line 2. Holborn Hill (17 Holborn, opposite Furnival's Inn).

DUNLOP & WILSON. Booksellers, Glasgow. Their name appears in the imprint of "A Collection of Sacred Music Published for the use of The Episcopal Chapel in Glasgow by the Managers 1787. Sold at the Shop of Dunlop & Wilson," &c.

DYSON (WILLIAM). Add:—"A Book of Psalmody . . . The third edition . . . By John Chetham. London: Printed by William Pearson for William Dyson . . . MDCCXXIV."

EBERS (JOHN). See Hockham (Thomas) and Ebers (John).

EDDOWES (JOSHUA). Printer and bookseller, Shrewsbury, 1749-75. (P.) His name appears in the imprint of "The Psalm-Singer's Pocket Companion . . . With a plain and easy Introduction to Musick. By Thomas Moore . . . To which is added, A Collection of Hymns, Suited to all the different Metres of the Tunes . . . Printed for the Author, and sold by him at his House in Glasgow . . . By J. Eddowes in Salop . . . M.DCC.LVI."
P. III.

EDWARD (WILLIAM). Lines 1-3. "Six Solos for the Violin with, a Bass for the Violincello and Through Bass for the Harpsichord: Composed by Signior Guerini, Printed and Sold by Neil Steuart," c. 1765;

EDWARDS (GEORGE). Organist, teacher of the pianoforte and music seller, 31 Upper Arcade, Bristol. His name appears in the imprint of

"The Celebrated Fantasia, founded on Rossini's Overture to Semira-
mide . . . composed . . . by A. T. Huerta. Published for G. Edwards . . .
by S. Chappell," etc., c. 1830.

ERNEST, *Mr*. Music seller, Brighton. His name appears in the imprint
of "Twelve Favorite Canzonets, by the celebrated Aprile at Rome set
with accompanyments for the Piano Forte or Pedal Harp . . . by Philip
Seybold. Op. IV . . . Printed for the Author and sold by M^r. Ernest
at Brighthelmstone," c. 1785.

EUSTACE (JO.). Music seller? Oxford. W. N. H. Harding, Chicago, has
a Cluer music sheet (in a collection) with a pasted slip over the imprint; London, Printed for Jo. Eustace, near Paradise-Garden in
Oxford.

EVERINGHAM (ROBERT). Line 6. S. Keeble not Kettle.

EWER & JOHANNING. Line 6. Delete:—Jeremiah.

FALKENER (ROBERT). Add:—Harpsichord maker. Line 3. c. 1765-75
not 1770-75. Was the author and printer of "Instructions for playing
the Harpsichord . . . MDCCLXX." He issued a second edition in 1774.

FARN (CHARLES JOSEPH). Add:—Catalogue:—New Music. c. 1831.
1 p. fol. (B.M. G. 806. f. (70.))

FEATHERSTON (J.). Bookseller, Hexham. Sold "Several select portions
of the Psalms, from Tate and Brady's version. Collected For the use
of Churches, By a Clergyman. Together with their proper Tunes,
Revised and Corrected by W. Thompson . . . Newcastle: printed by
T. Slack, for W. Thompson; and sold by J. Featherston . . . M.DDC.
LXIII."
P. III.

FELTON (WILLIAM). Music seller, Ludlow. His name appears in the
imprint of "March, for a Military Band, in Score, likewise adapted for
the Piano Forte. With variations & an accompaniment for a flute
obligato . . . By Chas. Evans, Organist of St. Lawrence, Ludlow . . .
Op. 7. London Printed by Goulding Phipps & D'Almaine . . . Also
may be had of W. Felton Music Seller . . . Ludlow," c. 1803.

FENTUM (CATHERINE). Line 3. "C^e. F—m," or "Ka. F—m."

FINLAY (ROBERT) & (JOHN). Print sellers, booksellers and stationers,
Dilettanti Buildings, Glasgow. Published "Christian Vespers written
and composed by C. Hutcheson Esqre . . . 1832."

FITZPATRICK & COLES. Add:—Catalogue of Music. c. 1815. 1 p. fol.
(B.M. g. 443. x. (5.))

FLACKTON & CO. Stationers, Canterbury. Their name appears in the imprint of "The Triumph of Britons, a new and constitutional song . . . written by James Alderson of Ashford. Set to music by George Philpot of Canterbury. Printed for the Authors & to be had of . . . Messrs. Flacton (sic) & Co. Canterbury," etc., c. 1800.

FLETCHER (WILLIAM). Add:—"Printed for W. Fletcher. Three Duetts for two Violins. Composed by Sigr. Benda," c. 1775.

F—m, Cᵉ. (F—m, Ka.). *See* Fentum (Catherine).

FORSTER (WILLIAM) *the Elder*. Line 5. early in 1786—July 16, 1786. His son William took over the music portion of the business with the liberty to obtain work in his own behalf on 17th July 1786, being the day after his marriage. William Forster the elder continued in business as a musical instrument maker until his death in 1808. (Sandys and Forster. History of the Violin.)

FORSTER (WILLIAM) *the Younger*. Line 3. 17 July, 1786-1803, not c. 1800-03. He took over the music portion of the business established by his father.

FOUGT (HENRY). Add:—Catalogues:—New Music. 1769. [6 items.] 1 p. fol. (B.M. 221. (1.)); Åke Vretblad: "Henric Fougts engelska musiktryck." (*Biblis*, 1858, pp. 135-149.)

FRENCH (JOHN). Add:—"A Treatise of Music, containing the Principles of Composition . . . By Mr. Rameau . . . Translated into English," etc. c. 1775.

FULLER (JOHN). Bookseller and publisher, London, 1743-76; Dove in Creed Lane; Paternoster Row; Bible & Dove, Ave Mary Lane; Blowbladder Street, Cheapside. (P.) His name appears in the imprint of "A Collection of Psalm Tunes with a Thorough Bass for the Harpsicord or Organ with several Hymns, Anthems, & Divine Songs. Adapted to the Violin, & German Flute. London Printed by R. Williamson. and Sold by G. Keith . . . I. Fuller. Blowbladder Street," etc., c. 1765.
P. III.

GALBRAITH (J. MURRAY). Add:—Music seller, Edinburgh; 60 Princes Street, October 1826-27; 57 Princes Street, 1827-29. Published a small amount of music; formerly a tuner with Messrs. Broadwood, London; previously in partnership with Nathaniel Gow. *See* also Gow and Galbraith.

GALLOWAY (WILLIAM). Add:—Catalogue of new Music published. c. 1816. 2 pp. fol. (B.M. g. 272. t. (23.))

GAY'S (MR.) HEAD IN TAVISTOCK STREET, COVENT GARDEN, LONDON.
See Heney, *Mr*.

GEORGE (WILLIAM). Line 4. c. 1830-41. He resumed business for a short time at 6 Vere Street, Oxford Street, c. 1844-45.

GIRTIN (JOHN). Copperplate engraver, 11 Charles Street, Soho Square, London. Engraved, printed and published for the Author "The New grand O.P. Dance, with characteristic Figure, by that eminent Composer, O.P: M.D. now performing with universal applause at the Theatre-Royal Covent Garden . . . Nov. 23, 1809."

GOOD (RICHARD). Stationer, 63 Bishopsgate Without, London. His name appears in the imprint of "Twenty five Odes Hymn Tunes &c. in Four Parts. Composed by S. Porter. London Sold by R. Good . . . T. Conder . . . and J. Peck," etc., c. 1800.

GOUGH (GEORGE). Add:—Gough's Musical Circulating Library. Gough's Music and Instrument Warehouse, N⁰ 4 New Sackville Street.

GOULDING, PHIPPS & D'ALMAINE. Add:—Published as Goulding & Co. from 45 Pall Mall, before 1806.

GOULDING (GEORGE). Add:—Catalogue of new Music. 1792. 1 p. fol. (B.M. E. 81.)

GOW & GALBRAITH. Add:—J. Murray Galbraith continued the business on his own account.

GOW & SHEPHERD. Add:—Catalogue:—1800. 1 p. fol. (B.M. g. 229. c. (3.))

GREEN (JOHN). Add:—Published several editions of J. B. Logier's First and Second Companion to the Royal Patent Chiroplast or Hand-Director, and the Sequel to each book; and other works.
Catalogue:—Music published by J. Green. 1827. 8 pp. 4⁰. (B.M. 7895. g. (28.))

GURNEY (JOSEPH). Add:—"Hymns and Spiritual Songs . . . By Edward Trivett. The second edition, corrected. With an addition of a great variety of new hymns . . . with tunes proper for the various meters, &c. Norwich: Printed by R. Beatniffe . . . and sold by the Author . . . and by J. Gurney, Opposite Hatton-Garden, London," c. 1772.

GUTHRIE (CHARLES). Bookseller and stationer, Edinburgh; 8 Waterloo Place, c. 1821-32; 13 Waterloo Place, c. 1832-35. His name appears in the imprints of several works composed and published by Thomas Hamley Butler.

[368]

H., J. *See* Humphreys (John).

HAGUE (WILLIAM). Add:—Printed and sold "Duett for Two Performers on One Violin composed by Mr. Charles Hague," c. 1795; "The Gods of the Grape, written by a Gentleman. Compos'd by Is. Nicholls," c. 1800.

HALL (JOSEPH). Lithographer, Lothian Road, Edinburgh. Lithographed c. 1840, "The Pocket Companion for the German Flute. Containing a choice Collection of Scotch, Irish, English & foreign Duets, etc. from the works of the best composers."

HALL (W.). Music seller, 12 Macclesfield Street, Soho, London. Published c. 1780, "A Lesson for the Harpsichord or Piano-Forte. To which is added a favorite Air with Variations, after the manner of Felton Composed in the familiar Stile for the use of Scholars by John Webb . . . Printed & sold at W. Hall's Music Shop," etc.

HAMILTON (ALEXANDER). Line 4. Business continued by his son James.
    Catalogue:—Instrumental and Vocal Music. c. 1804. 2 pp. fol. (B.M. g. 431. a.)

HAMILTON (JAMES ALEXANDER). Line 5. Succeeded his father Alexander Hamilton.

HANNAM (JOHN). Add:—Musical Circulating and Instrument Warehouse.

HARDY (THOMAS). Add:—Published "An Ode on the King of Prussia and six songs. Set to Musick by Mr. Matts: Hawdon," &c., c. 1765. Samuel Knapton succeeded him in 1796.

HART (JOSEPH BINNS). Add:—Musical Repository, Royal Pelham Arcade, 1829-30; 1 (or 2) Castle Terrace, Wellington Square, 1831-40. Died 10 December, 1844 aged 50.

HAWES (WILLIAM). Line 5. c. 1825-28. Add:—Catalogue of new Music. c. 1830. 1 p. fol. (B.M. g. 443. d. (22.))

HAYES (JOHN). Printer to the University of Cambridge, 1669-1705. (P.) Printed "Some of the Psalms in Metre. Done by J. Patrick & by Mr. Brady & Mr. Tate . . . 1698."
    P. II.

HERON (CLAUDIUS). Add:—"Six Trios for two German Flutes, or two Violins with a Violoncello obligato figur'd for the Harpsichord & compos'd by Sigr: D'Hotel [Dothel?] Junr," etc., c. 1760.

HINTZ (FREDERICK). Musical instrument maker, London. His name appears in an advertisement October 1761, "Easy Lessons for the Harpsichord. Dedicated to the Honourable Mrs. Ingram. Composed by John Jones . . . To be had of the following musick-shops, viz Mr. Welcker . . . Mr. Hintzs, Newport-street," etc.; his name appears in the imprint of "Five Trios and One Quartetti for a German flute or Violin Violoncello obligato and a Bass Compose'd by Antonio Filtz. London To be had at Hummels Music Shop . . . And at Hintz Music Shop the Corner of Riders Court near Leicester fields," c. 1765. He was at "the Corner of Ryder's Court, Leicester Fields" in 1763. Hintz was the author of "A choice Collection of Psalm and Hymn Tunes set for the Cetra or Guitar by Frederick Hintz. London Printed by R: Bremner in the Strand, &c.," c. 1760.

HODGES (CHARLES). Line 2. c. 1800-32. Became Charles Hodges and Son, 1832-38. Succeeded by his sons Francis and Martin.

HODGES (FRANCIS). Music seller, 28 Clare Street, Bristol, c. 1846-58. May have published some music. Succeeded Francis and Martin Hodges.

HODGES (FRANCIS) & (MARTIN). Music sellers, 28 Clare Street, Bristol, c. 1838-46. Also known as Hodges Brothers. May have published some music. Took over the business from their father Charles Hodges, afterwards Charles and Son. Continued by Francis alone.

HODGSON, *Mr.* Bookseller? Skipton, Yorkshire. His name appears in the imprint of "A Book of Psalmody . . . The third edition . . . By John Chetham. London: Printed by William Pearson for William Dyson . . . and sold by him . . . and by Mr. Hodgson . . . MDCCXXIV."

HODSON (GEORGE ALEXANDER). Add:—Catalogue of Vocal and Instrumental Music. c. 1835. 1 p. fol. (B.M. 2835. a. (31.))

HOLDEN (SMOLLET). Add:—Dublin; 32 Arran Quay, 1805-06; 26 Parliament Street, 1806-18.

HOLE (WILLIAM). Add:—Thurston Dart (*Music and Letters*, Oct. 1956) ascribes Orlando Gibbons "Fantasies," c. 1720 to William Hole as engraver.

HOLLAND (HENRY). Add:—Also published as Holland & Co.

HOLLAND (WILLIAM). Print seller, 50 Oxford Street, London. Published "Marche des Marseillois. Chantée sur diferans theatres. Chez Frere Passage du Saumon. London. Pub. Novr. 10, 1792, by Willm. Holland," etc. With a head-piece engraved by Richard Newton, coloured by hand.

HOLLOWAY (THOMAS). Add:—Died July 7, 1867.

HOOKHAM (THOMAS) & EBERS (JOHN). Booksellers and stationers, 15 Old Bond Street, London, c. 1803-09. Their names appear in the imprints of some musical compositions by Augustus Meves. Ebers became manager of the King's Theatre, Haymarket, in 1821 and published his experiences in "Seven Years of the King's Theatre" in 1828.

HORNE. Add:—(ROBERT).

HOWELL. Silk Mercer, Marybon Street, Piccadilly, London. His name appears in the imprint of "A Collection of New Songs Sung at Rane-lagh by Mrs. Barthelemon and Master Blundell Mr. Barthelemon's Scholar. Composed by Mr. Barthelemon. London To be had of the Author at Mr. Howell's," etc.

HOWELL (THOMAS) *the Elder*. Music seller, Bristol; St. John Street (John Street), c. 1784-90; 12 Clare Street, c. 1790-1808. Published a small amount of music. Succeeded by his son Thomas.
    K.

HOWELL (THOMAS) *the Younger*. Music seller and teacher of music, Bristol; 12 Clare Street, c. 1808-18; 13 Clare Street, c. 1818-39; 55 Park Street, c. 1839-59. Published a small amount of music. Succeeded his father, Thomas Howell. (Substitute for previous entry under Howell (Thomas).)

HUMPHREYS (JOHN). Printer, Bartholomew Lane behind the Royal Exchange, London, 1697(?)-1724. Printed "The Psalms of David in Metre: Fitted to the tunes used in Parish-Churches. By John Patrick. London, Printed by J. H. for the Executor of Luke Meredith. 1706"; "The Psalms of David in Metre: Fitted to the tunes used in Parish-Churches. By John Patrick. London, Printed by J. H. for A. & J. Churchill . . . 1706." Also an edition in 1710.
    P. II.

ILIVE (JACOB). Printer and typefounder, London, 1730-63; Aldersgate against Aldersgate Coffee-House; London House, Aldersgate. (P.) Printed "A New Version of the Psalms of David Fitted to the Tunes used in Churches. By N. Brady . . . and N. Tate, Esq; Poet-Laureat to His Majesty. London: Printed by Jacob Ilive, for the Company of Stationers. 1741. And are to be sold at Stationers Hall near Lud-gate, and by most Booksellers."
    P. III.

IMLACH (JAMES). Bookseller, Banff. His name appears in the imprint of "Thirty New Strathspey Reels For the Violin or Harpsicord Com-

posed By Isaac Cooper . . . Sold by James Imlach Bookseller Banff," etc·
c. 1783.

ISAAC (MAYHEW) & CO. *See* Mayhew, Isaac & Co.

JAUNCEY (JOHN). Music engraver, printer and music seller. Add:—
"New Sacred Music, suited to the Grand Festival on the 7th Day of
July 1814, the Day of general Thanksgiving composed by John
Beaumont," c. 1814.

JOHNSON. *See* Newland and Johnson.

JONES & CO. *After* Finsbury Place add:— (Square). Published some
music and music books including "The Messiah . . . Arranged for the
Piano-Forte or Organ by D^r. John Clarke . . . 1835."

JONES (P.). Musical instrument maker? At the Golden Harp, New
Street, Covent Garden, near St. Martin's Lane, London. Printed for
and sold c. 1720, "A Favorite Solo for the Violin Composed by Dr.
Pepuch (*sic*) Never before Publish'd."

JONES (THOMAS). Music seller, 23 Bishopsgate Street. Add:—In
conjunction with Domenico Corri, issued a trade card advertising "The
Musical Lounge and Apollo Circulating Libraries at D. Corri's Music
Seller to the Royal Family, No. 28 Hay-Market, and at T. Jones's, No.
23 Bishopsgate Street." Some publications were issued bearing both
names.

JOPSON (JAMES). Printer, Coventry; Hay Lane; Over against the Black
Bull Inn, in High Street. Northampton; Gold Street; 1741-59. (P.)
Printed "Twelve Songs; three for Two Voices; with Symphonies for
the Violin, or German Flute. By John Barker, Organist of Holy-
Trinity Church. Coventry. Coventry: Printed by J. Jopson, in Hay-
Lane. MDCCXLI." ("Birmingham, Engraven and Printed by Michl.
Broome, at Purcell's Head in Litchfield Street," p. 16.)
    P. III.

JULLIEN (LOUIS ANTOINE). *After* New Bond Street, add:—(sometimes
as L. G. A. Jullien),

JUNG (PHILIP). Delete c. 1790-95. Add:—Born in Vienna and settled
in Oxford before 1789 in St. Mary's Hall until he removed to the New
Parade in the High Street on April 21 1793. Became bankrupt in
April 1796. Among his publications &c.

KEEBLE (S.). Wrongly entered under Kettle (S.).

KEITH (GEORGE). Add:—"A Collection of Psalm Tunes with a Thorough
Bass for the Harpsicord or Organ with several Hymns, Anthems, &
Divine Songs. Adapted to the Violin, & German Flute. London

Printed by R. Williamson. and Sold by G. Keith at the Bible in Grace-Church Street," etc., c. 1765.

KETTLE (S.). This entry should be under Keeble (S.). Line 5. Keeble not Kettle.

KNAPTON (SAMUEL). Line 2. c. 1796-1805 not c. 1797-1805.

KNIBB (THOMAS). Line 5. c. 1750 not c. 1745.

LATOUR (FRANCIS TATTON). Add:—Catalogues:—New Vocal Music. c. 1826. 1 p. fol. (B.M. H. 1221. (20.)); c. 1827. 1 p. fol. (B.M. H. 1278. (1.)); c. 1827. 1 p. fol. (B.M. H. 1280. (2.))

LAVENU & CO. *See* Lavenu (Elizabeth).

LAVENU & MITCHELL. Catalogues, line 4. c. 1808 not c. 1806.

LAVENU (ELIZABETH). Line 2. August 1818-c. 1821 . . . 24 Edward Street . . . Widow of Lewis Lavenu . . . c. 1828. Some publications have Lavenu & Co. in the imprint.

LAVENU (LEWIS). Line 4. c. 1811-August 1818, when Lavenu died, the business being continued by his widow Elizabeth Lavenu.
Catalogue:—A Collection of Periodical Duetts for two performers on one Piano Forte. c. 1808. 1 p. fol. (B.M. g. 443. e. (29.))

LAVENU (LOUIS HENRY). Line 2, delete Presumably. Line 3. Previously partner in and successor to the business of Moir and Lavenu.

LEA (H.). Music Publisher, 36 Strand, London, c. 1830-June 1840. The whole of his publications purchased by Thomas Prowse in June 1840.

LEE (JOHN). Line 2. Add *after* 70 Dame Street:—at the Corner of Eustace Street in Dame Street.

LEONE (GABRIEL). Printer, London? Printed and sold "Six Duets for two Violins. Dedicated to the Honourable Thomas Shirley Composed by Sigr. Emanuele Barbella," c. 1765.

LICHFIELD (LEONARD). Add:—*The Elder.*

LICHFIELD (LEONARD) *the Younger.* Printer, Oxford, Holywell, 1657-1686. Succeeded his father as Printer to the University in 1657. (P.) Printed "The Psalter or Psalms of David Paraphras'd in Verse. And so design'd that by Two Tunes onely, the whole Number of Psalms (Four onely excepted) may be sung . . . The Second Edition, wherein the whole Number is Compleated. By Richard Goodridge. Oxford Printed by L, Lichfield . . . for Jo. Crosley. 1684."

[373]

LINDSAY (THOMAS). Add:—Catalogue:—New Music for Flute and Piano-Forte. c. 1825. 1 p. fol. (B.M. g. 525. (7.))

LINLEY (FRANCIS). Add:—He added publications to the collections commenced by John Bland—"Linley's Continuation of Bland's Collection of Divine Music," "Bland's (continued by F. Linley) Harpsichord Collection without Accompts.," and "Bland's Collection (Continued by F. Linley) of Sonatas, Lessons, Overtures, Capricios, Divertimentos &c. &c."

LINTERN (JAMES) & (WALTER). Line 6. November 1817. Add:— Succeeded by George Packer.

LONGMAN (JOHN), CLEMENTI & CO. Add:—Catalogue:—Musical Publications. III. c. 1800. 1 p. fol. (B.M. h. 1747. (4.))

LONSDALE (CHRISTOPHER). Add:—He had a musical circulating library.

LOTHIAN (JOHN). Bookseller and stationer, 41 St. Andrews Square, Edinburgh. Published "The Edinburgh Musical Album. Edited by George Linley Esq . . . 1829."

LUMSDEN (JOHN). Stationer, 3 Argyll Street, Glasgow. Published "Apollonia Scottica: a Collection of favourite Scotch Songs, set to music for the voice, and arranged for the Piano-Forte, Violin, and German Flute. With a selection of the most approved Glees, Catches, &c. for three or four voices. By J. Robertson, Teacher of Music . . . 1823."

MC CALLEY (MARY). Add:—Her name appears as Mrs. Mc Cauley in the imprint of Thomas Kelly's "Hymns on various Passages of Scripture."

Mc CULLAGH (EDWARD). Line 2. Arcade (Royal Arcade).

MAJOR, (R.). Line 2. Add:—1. Clare Court, Drury Lane, c. 1818-20;

MAJOR (WILLIAM). Printer and stationer, St. John's Steps, Bristol. Printed "Glee inscribed to the M.W.G.M. His Royal Highness, Frederick Augustus, Duke of Sussex, &c. and the other royal, noble, and fraternal dignitaries of the Order of Free and Accepted Masons, assembled for the installation of the Provincial Grand Master for Somerset and the dedication of the new hall at Bath, September 23, A.L. 5819. A.D. 1819. The words by Brother M'Cleady. The music by Brother Nathan," etc.

MASON (JOHN). Wesleyan bookseller at the Wesleyan Book Room, 66 Paternoster Row, London. His name appears in the imprint of "A

Collection of Tunes . . . adapted to the Hymns in use by the Wesleyan
Methodist Societies; arranged . . . by Thomas Hawkes, of Williton,
Somerset . . . The whole revised and corrected by Mr. George Gay.
Printed and published for the compiler by Thomas Whitehorn,
Watchet; and sold by John Mason . . . London." The preface is
dated June 24, 1833.

MAUND (CHARLES). Add:—Catalogue of new Musical Publications.
c. 1844. 1 p. fol. (B.M. h. 931. (12, 13.)); c. 1845. 1 p. fol. (B.M. H.
1333. (10.))

MAURICE (D. S.). Printer and publisher, 4 Howford Buildings, Fenchurch Street, London, c. 1811-28. Printed by and for "The Vocal &
Musical Cabinet: containing the most approved Songs, Duets, Ballads
&c. &c. English, Scotch, & Irish . . . with the music . . . for the voice,
violin, German flute. Vol. 1. No. 1," etc., c. 1820.

MAY (J. A.). Music seller and teacher of music, Glasgow; 81 Hutcheson
Street, c. 1813-14; 17 Glassford Street, c. 1814-16; 9 Argyle Street
c. 1816-18; 3 Argyle Street, c. 1818-22. Published a small amount
of music.

MAYHEW, ISAAC & CO. Booksellers and publishers, At the Office of
the National Library of Standard Works, 14 Henrietta Street, London.
Printed and published "John Barnett's Library of Standard Music. In
weekly numbers," etc., c. 1835. Publications included "Artaxerxes,"
"The Beggar's Opera" and Mozart's "Il Don Giovanni."

MEGGY & CHALK. Chelmsford. Published "The Country Chorister:
By Mr. George Fitch, Great Dunmow, Essex: consisting of eight
Anthems, and thirty Psalm Tunes . . . 1801"; "Nine Psalm Tunes,
Six Anthems, and an Hymn. Comprising the supplement to the
Country Chorister. By Mr. George Fitch of Great Dunmow, Essex . . .
1803."

MELVILLE (GEORGE). Pianoforte maker and music seller, 14 Buchanan
Street, Glasgow, c. 1825-48. Published a small amount of music.

MEREDITH (ELIZABETH). *See* Churchill (John).

MEREDITH (LUKE). Line 8. *After* 1701 add:—Printed by J. H. for the
Executor of Luke Meredith, "The Psalms of David in Metre: Fitted
to the tunes used in Parish-Churches. By John Patrick . . . 1706."

MICHELLI (J.). Chichester. Published "The Lawyer's Glee, or Pauper's
Case. Set to Music by a Barrister of the Inner Temple . . . Printed
for J. Michelli, Chichester, by Goulding & Co . . . London," c. 1799.

MILTON. Engraver, London? Engraved "Musica di Camera or Some old Tunes new Sett, and some new ones compos'd for the Harpsichord . . . Fred: Nussen. London Printed for the Author. Opera 3^{tia}.," advertised March 1761. Also edition issued by J. Walsh c. 1765.

MOOR (A.). *See* Moore (A.).

MOOR (J.). Book and music seller, 1 Sloane Square, Chelsea, London. Published c. 1111 "Hymn to the Virgin in the Lady of the Lake by Walter Scott, Esq. Printed and sold by J. Moor," etc.

MOORE (A.). Pamphlet seller and publisher, near St. Paul's Church, London, c. 1720-47. Published "Duke upon Duke, An Excellent New Play-House Ballad. Set to Musick by Mr. Holdecombe . . . Printed for A. Moor . . . and sold by the Booksellers. 1720," etc.
P. III.

MOORE (RANDLE). Knutsford. His name appears in the imprint of "The Psalm-Singer's Pocket Companion . . . With a plain and easy Introduction to Musick. By Thomas Moore . . . To which is added, A Collection of Hymns, Suited to all the different Metres of the Tunes . . . Printed for the Author, and sold by him at his House in Glasgow . . . By Mr. Randle Moore in Knutsford . . . M.DCC.LVI."

MORI & LAVENU. Line 2. The partners were Nicholas Mori and his stepson Louis Henry Lavenu.

MORPHEW (JOHN). Bookseller, near Stationers' Hall, London, c. 1704-20. Printed and sold c. 1704, "Britain's Jubilee: A new congratulatory Ballad, on the Glorious Victories obtain'd by the Duke of Malborough [*sic*], over the French: Writ by the Famous Comedian, Mr. Escourt, and Sung by him to most of our Nobility, with great Applause."
P. II.

MUFF (JOSHUA). Line 1. Add:—and musical instrument maker. Add at end:—Succeeded by Agnes and Thomas F. Simms. Kirkstall Abbey House Museum has a set of water tuned musical glasses made by Muff.

MUIR (JAMES). Line 2. May 1796-98.

MURRAY & STUART. Engravers, Werburgh's Lane, Chester. Engraved "A Second Set of Hymns and Psalm Tunes in three and four parts; together with an Anthem," etc. By Edward Harwood. The Author. Chester. 1786. The engravers were probably Mrs. Murray and James Stuart.

MUSICAL LOUNGE AND APOLLO CIRCULATING LIBRARIES. *See* Corri (Domenico); Jones (Thomas).

NAISH (THOMAS). Line 1. Bridge Street, Bristol.

NAPIER (WILLIAM). Add:—Catalogues:—c. 1780. 2 pp. fol. (B.M. G. 137.)

NEALE OR NEAL (JOHN). Add:—Catalogues:—Books, printed and sold by Mr. Neale. c. 1729. 1 p. fol. (B.M. H. 178.)

NEELE (SAMUEL JAMES). Music engraver and copper plate printer, 352 Strand, London. Engraved "A Selection of the Favourite Scots Songs Chiefly Pastoral. Adapted for the Harpsichord with an Accompaniment for a Violin. By Eminent Masters . . . London. Printed for Willm. Napier. Neele Sc.," 1790, 91.; "Six Madrigals for Two, Three and Four Voices composed by William Jackson of Exeter. Opera XVIII. London. Printed for the Author. Neele Sculp.", 1798.; "Dr. Watts's Psalms and Hymns set to new music in three and four parts . . . Vol. I. (Dr. Watts's Psalsm & Hymns . . . in four parts . . . Vol. II.) Composed by Edward Miller . . . Neele Sc.", c. 1805.; "Two Glees," "The Sun had brightened Cheviot grey," and "Sweet Teviot on thy Silver Tide" . . . Composed . . . by Doctor John Clarke, of Cambridge. London. Printed by Wilkinson & Co . . . Neele Sculp," etc., c. 1808. "Two Glees "The feast was over in Branksome-Tower" . . . and "Is it the roar of Teviots Tide" . . . by Doctor John Clarke of Cambridge. London. Printed by Wilkinson & Co . . . Neele sculp," etc., c. 1808.

NEW MUSIC WAREHOUSE. 75 Long Acre, London. Printed and sold a Song c. 1804, "The Triad Alliance, or Rose Thistle & Shamrack [sic]. A Ballad written the Melody Composed & Sung by Brother George Nussey," etc.

NEWBERY (JOHN). Line 3. 1745-67 not 1746-67.

NEWLAND & JOHNSON. Music sellers and publishers, 26 Southampton Row, Russell Square, London, c. 1818-20.
    K. (To replace entry under Newland & Johnston.)

NICOLL (JAMES). Printer to the City and University, Aberdeen, 1710-1732. (P.) Printing house above the Meal Mercat, at the sign of the Towns Arms and shop in the End of the Broad-Gate. Printed "The Twelve Tunes for the Church of Scotland, Composed in four Parts, (Viz.) Treble, Contra, Tenor and Bassus. In a more Plain and Useful Method, than have been formerly Published. The Fifth Edition . . . with Bon-Accord Tune, Carefully Corrected according as they are Taught by the Master of the Musick School of Aberdeen . . . An. Dom. 1720."
    P. II.

NICHOLS (JOHN) & SONS. Printers, 25 Parliament Street, London. Printed "Some ancient Christmas Carols, with the Tunes to which they were formerly sung in the West of England. Collected by Davies Gilbert. 1822"; also the second edition, 1823.

NICHOLLS (SUTTON). Engraver, against the Angel in Aldersgate Street, London. Printed and sold illustrated single sheet song "Bacchus turn'd Doctor. written by Ben. Johnson," c. 1710.

NOVELLO & CO. Line 8. Add *after* 1906:—to February 1965, when the publishing, sales and distribution sides of the business were removed to Borough Green, Sevenoaks, Kent, where the printing works are which they acquired about 1961. After the removal from Wardour Street, editorial offices and showroom were opened up at 27 Soho Square, London.

NOVELLO (JOSEPH ALFRED). Last line but 2. In 1849 purchased plates of musical works (formerly owned by Thomas Preston) from the stock of Coventry and Hollier, when their partnership was dissolved.

OAKEY (HENRY). Music seller, at his Music Warehouse, 2 Charlotte Street, Rathbone Place, Oxford Street, London, c. 1838-40. He published at least one of his own compositions, "A Grand March," etc. (B.M. h. 721. d. (8.))

OLLIVIER (CHARLES). Line 2. 1836-53 not 1837-53. For many years assistant to Samuel Chappell.

PACKER (CHARLES). Music and musical instrument seller, Castle Street, Reading. His name appears on "Goulding, D'Almaine, Potter & Co's Select Collection of Country Dances, Waltzes &c, &c, for the Piano-forte. No. 42. To be had at Mr. C. Packers Harp, Piano Forte, and Music Saloon," etc., c. 1820.

PACKER (GEORGE). Music seller and musical instrument maker, 13 The Grove, afterwards Grange Grove, Bath, November 1817-c. 1841. May have published some music. Succeeded James Lintern.

PARSONS (RICHARD). Bookseller, Reading Room, Abingdon. His name appears in the imprint of "Congregational Psalmody, arranged & adapted to the public Services of the Church, by the Revd. T. H. Hawes . . . London, Published for the Editor, by W. Hawes . . . and sold by R. Parsons . . . Abingdon," etc. The preface is dated June 1844.

PEARCE & CO. Add:—Catalogue of new Music. c. 1808. 1 p. fol. (B.M. H. 2818. b. (45.))

PEARSON (WILLIAM). Add:—Dans Aldersgate-street, proche La Croix Blanche. (J. de Gouy's, "Le Compagnon Divin," c. 1699. (B.M. K. 3. b. (12.))

PEAT (ALEXANDER) & CO. Booksellers and stationers, 35 South Bridge Street, Edinburgh. Published c. 1825, "Complete Tutor for the German Flute with useful Directions, Lessons, Graces, etc. by the most eminent Masters."

PECK (J.) & (J.). Line 2. Falcon Square (Cheapside).

PINE (WILLIAM). Printer, Wine Street, Bristol, 1753-1803. (P.) Printed "Select Hymns with Tunes annexed: Designed chiefly for the use of the people called Methodists. The fourth edition, corrected. (Sacred Melodies or a choice collection of Psalms and Hymn Tunes with a short introduction.) Bristol: Printed by William Pine. M,DCC,LXXIII."
    P. III.

PLATTS (JAMES). Add:—On a trade card bearing the address 9 John Street, Gt. Portland Strt. London, he claims to be "The original Manufacturer of the Harmonica or Sticcado Pastorale and Spanish Castinets."

PORTER (EDWARD). Line 1. Briggate, August 1787-July 1796. Line 2. Lowerhead Row, July 1796-1837.

POWELL (SAMUEL). Line 2. Les Pseaumes.

PRESTON (JOHN). Last line. 1798-c. 1834, after the death of John Preston, January 1798.

PRESTON (THOMAS). Line 2. 1798-c. 1810.

PREVOST (NICOLAS). Bookseller and publisher, London, 1726-75; At the Ship in the Strand; Over against Southampton Street in the Strand. (P.) His name appears in the imprint of "Concerti Grossi Con due Violini, Viola e Violoncello di Concertini Obligati, e due altri Violini e Basso di Concerto Grosso Quali Contengono Preludii Allemande Correnti Gigue Sarabande Gavotte e Follia Composti della Seconda Parte del Opera Quinta D' Arcangelo Corelli per Francesco Geminiani To be Sold in London att Nicolas Prevost in ye Strand Price one Guinée," c. 1730. (Glasgow University Library.)
    P. III.

PRINCE. Musical Library, Brighton. This name appears in the imprints of "A Russian Polonese, for the Piano Forte. Composed by an Amateur. London. Printed by Goulding, Phipps & D'Almaine . . . Likewise may be had . . . at Prince's Musical Library, Brighton," etc., c. 1798; "A Russian March, for the Piano Forte. Composed on General Suvoroff's, Taking Ismael. London Printed by Goulding & C°. . . . Likewise may be had . . . at Prince's Musical Library, Brighton," etc., c. 1798.

PRITCHARD (WILLIAM). Bookseller, High Street, Carnarvon. Published "The Sacred Melodist; containing a prize Anthem &c. The whole composed and arranged by David Hughes . . . Y Perorydd Cysegredig . . . Carnarvon: Published for the Author, by W. Pritchard . . . 1843."

PROWSE (THOMAS). Line 3. c. 1860-67. Purchased the whole of the publications of H. Lea in June 1840. Died August 18, 1867.

RANSFORD (EDWIN). Add:—A Catalogue of Vocal and Instrumental Music. 1843. 1 p. fol. (B.M. H. 1310. (1.))

RASTELL (JOHN). Line 7. (B.M. K. 8. k. 8.)

READ (JAMES). Line 4. Neil not Niel Stewart.

REGENT'S HARMONIC INSTITUTION. Line 3. c. 1820-25. Line 6. c. 1825. Add:—Catalogue:—New and select Music. c. 1825. 1 p. fol. (B.M. g. 270. h. (25.))

RICHARDSON (JOHN). Bookseller, Leeds and Wakefield, 1700-05. (P.) His name appears in the imprint of "Tunes to the Psalms of David, in Four Parts: With an Introduction, fitted for the meanest Capacities. The like never before published. By S. S. and J. H. London: Printed by William Pearson, for Henry Playford . . . and Sold by John Richardson, Bookseller in Leeds, or at his shop in Wakefield. 1700."
P. II.

RICHARDSON (MOSES AARON). Bookseller, 101 Pilgrim Street, Newcastle-on-Tyne. Published c. 1840, "The Percy Quadrilles, for the Piano Forte, composed . . . by James Stimson, Organist of St. Andrew's Newcastle. Newcastle, Published by M. A. Richardson . . . London, R. Cocks & Co.," etc.

RICKMAN (THOMAS CLIO). Bookseller and stationer, 7 Upper Marylebone Street, London. Printed and sold "Naval Triumphs. An Heroic Song in Honor of the Gallant Officers & Brave Tars who command, and man, The Wooden Walls of Old England . . . The music by Mr. Yates," c. 1798.

RILEY (EDWARD). Add:—He emigrated to America and from 1806 carried on the same line of business in New York. Died August 1829.

ROBINSON (JOHN). 38 Stonegate, York. Add:—"La Tempesta, composed by Haydn, as performed at the York Musical Festivals, &c. for four Voices, with an accompaniment for the Piano Forte, arranged from the full score . . . by John Robinson, Organist of the Catholic Chapel, York. Printed by J. Robinson," etc., c. 1827;

ROOME (FRANCIS). Bookseller, Derby. Published "Parochial Harmony, or a Collection of Divine-Music in Score . . . Expressly composed for the use of Country Choirs, by J. Alcock, Junr. Batchelor in Music and Organist of Walsall . . . London. Printed for Francis Roome, Bookseller in Derby: Sold by Messrs. Thompson . . . M^r. Cahusac . . . 1777."

SANGUINETTE (ABRAHAM). Music seller, 31 Long Acre, London, c. 1784. May have published some music.

SAYER (ROBERT). Print seller, 53 Fleet Street, London. Published c. 1780, "Deux Concerto a violon principal premier second Alto et basse deux hautbois deux cors ad libitum. Composé par M^r. Crammer . . . London; Printed for Robt. Sayer . . . et a Versailles chez Blaizot au Cabinet litteraire."

SCHOLL (ANDRIES). London. Published "Sixteen maschradas performed at the weddings and feasts in Armenia collected by Mr. Dirk Vorstad of Delf in his travels through that country, and sett for a German-flute or violin with a thorough bass for the harpsichord. London. Printed for Andries Scholl, sold by Le Claire at Paris, Hummel's in Amsterdam, & Robt. Bremner in London, with "Js. Turpin Sculpt." at foot of p. 16. Advertised March 1763.

SHERWOOD (B.). Line 2. Conduit Street (near Hanover Square). Add: —Printed for and sold "IV Sonatas or Duets For two Violins Compos'd by an eminent Author," June 1758.

SIBBALD (WILLIAM). Line 1. 5 (or 6) Temple Bar, Liverpool, c. 1770- 1785 or later.

SILVESTER (RICHARD). Engraver and printer, 27 Strand, London. Printed and sold "The Singers Preceptor or Corris Treatise on Vocal Music . . . By Domenico Corri . . . Printed by & to be had of Mr. Silvester," etc. 2 vols. Preface dated Nov. 1, 1810.

SIMMONS & CO. Printers, booksellers and stationers, Canterbury. Their name appears in the imprint of "The Triumph of Britons, a new and constitutional song . . . written by James Alderson of Ashford. Set to music by George Philpot of Canterbury. Printed for the Authors & to be had of Messrs. Simmons & Co. . . . Canterbury," etc., c. 1800.

SIMMONS (MATTHEW). Bookseller and printer, London, 1636-54; Golden Lyon in Duck Lane; Goldsmith's Alley, [Cripplegate?] Next door to the Golden Lion, Aldersgate Street. (P.) Printed "The Book of Psalms in Metre. Close and proper to the Hebrew: smooth and pleasant for the Metre: Plain and easie for the Tunes. With

Musicall Notes, Arguments, Annotations, and Index . . . London, Printed by Matthew Simmons, for the Companie of Stationers. 1644."
P. I.

SIMMS (AGNES) & (THOMAS FITZWILLIAM). Pianoforte dealers and music sellers, 16 Commercial Street, Leeds, November 1846-c. 1850. Succeeded Joshua Muff.

SIMPKINS (WILLIAM). Engraver and printer, 251 Strand, London. Engraved "A First Collection of Catches, Glees, Canons &c. for three four & five Voices . . . by I. W. Callcott . . . Op. IV. Printed for Longman & Broderip . . . London . . . Simpkins Sculpt, etc., c. 1790. With no address. His name appears on a collection of Handel's Oratorio Songs (some 33 in number) "Sold at the Music Shops," probably issued by George Smart, Oxford Street, London, c. 1791. At 9 Clement's Inn, printed "Two Marches composed by I. Haydn, M.D. for Sir Henry Harpur, Bart, and presented by him, to the Volunteer Cavalry of Derbyshire, embodied in the Year, 1794, Printed for Sir Henry Harpur, Bart:," etc., c. 1794.

SIMPSON (JAMES). Musical instrument maker, music seller and publisher, at the Bass Viol and Flute, in Sweeting's Alley, near the East Door of the Royal Exchange, London, c. December 1764-c. 1767. Son of John and Ann Simpson who were at Sweeting's Alley 1734-c. 1749 and c. 1749-51 respectively. Took his son John into the business which became James and John Simpson c. 1767.

SIMPSON (JAMES) *Junior*. Line 6. c. 1767-95 not c. 1765-95.

SIMPSON (JAMES) & (JOHN). Musical instrument makers, music printers and publishers, at the Bass Viol and Flute, in Sweeting's Alley, near the East Door of the Royal Exchange, later 15 Sweeting's Alley, Cornhill, London, c. 1767-95. Some single sheet songs bear only the initials J. & J. S. James and John Simpson were presumably related to James Simpson junior. (To replace the original entry.)
K. G.

SKARRATT (ROBERT THOMAS). Add:—5 Eyre Street Hill, Clerkenwell, c. 1830;

SLACK (THOMAS). Printer and publisher, Union Street, Newcastle-on-Tyne, 1755-84. (P.) Printed "Several select portions of the Psalms, from Tate and Brady's version. Collected For the use of Churches, By a Clergyman. Together with their proper Tunes, Revised and Corrected by W. Thompson . . . Newcastle: Printed by T. Slack, for W. Thompson; and sold by J. Featherston, Bookseller, in Hexham. M.DCC.LXIII."
P. III.

SMART (GEORGE). Line 8. Walter Turnbull not William.

SMITH (ANDREW P.). Bristol; 18 Clare Street, c. 1816-20; 11 Clare Street, c. 1820-24.

SMITH (GEORGE). Music seller and musical instrument maker, Birmingham; 144 Snow Hill, c. 1834-50, 4 Colmore Row, c. 1851-54. May have published some music.

SMITH (JAMES). Glass cutter and manufacturer of Musical Glasses, 10 Nicolson Street, Edinburgh. Published "A Tutor for the Musical Glasses; containing, an introductory sketch of the original and progressive improvements of the instrument; scales and directions for playing; and a selection of the most approved melodies of Scotland, Ireland, and Wales, arranged as duets . . . By James Smith . . . Edinburgh: Printed for the Author, and to be had at his Shop . . . 1823."

SMITH (JAMES). Liverpool. Add:—He advertised on some of his publications that he had "A Musical Circulating Library on the London Principal at 47 Bold Street."

STANES (WILLIAM). Bookseller, Chelmsford. His name appears in the imprint of "The Country Chorister containing seven Anthems, and thirty Psalm Tunes with Te Deum. Composed by George Ffitch [sic] of Great Dunmow Essex . . . Printed for the Author And sold by Messrs. Thompson's . . . London. Also by . . . Mr. Stanes, Chelmsford," c. 1799.

STEUART (NEIL). See Stewart (Neil).

STEWART (NEIL). Add:—Steuart in some imprints.

Str: & Sk:; Str: & Skill. See Straight & Skillern.

STRAIGHT & SKILLERN. Line 5. "Str: & Sk:" and "Str: & Skill:" appear

STRAIGHT (S.). Line 3. c. 1800-19 not 1800-05.

STUART. See Murray & Stuart.

STUART (JAMES). Bookseller, Ormskirk. His name appears in the imprint of "The Psalm-Singer's Instructor: Being a Collection of most Single and Double Psalm-Tunes now in Use: With the Addition of several Tunes, and Hymns, Carefully Corrected, and Amended, and Full Directions how to Sing them with the Bassus, Counters, Trebles, and Medius's By Joshua Marsden. Liverpool: Printed by Samuel Terry, for James Stuart, Bookseller in Ormskirk. MDCCXIX."

TERRY (SAMUEL). Printer, Liverpool, 1712-20; Dale street, Cork, c. 1721-22; Limerick, 1722-25. (P.) Printed "The Psalm-Singer's Instructor: Being a Collection of most Single and Double Psalm-Tunes now in Use: With the Addition of several Tunes, and Hymns, Carefully Corrected, and Amended, and Full Directions how to Sing them with the Bassus, Counters, Trebles, and Medius's By Joshua Marsden. Liverpool: Printed by Samuel Terry, for James Stuart, Bookseller in Ormskirk, MDCCXIX."
P. II.

TEUTEN (JOHN). Printer, Dean Street, Soho, London. Printed with moveable music types, "England, Home of the Brave! Composed by Oscar Perry. Bourn: Published for the Author, by W. Daniell . . . Printed . . . by J. Teuten," etc., c. 1833.

THEAKSTON (SOLOMON WILKINSON). Book and music seller, Long Room Street, Scarborough. Published for the Author c. 1841, "A Set of Quadrilles, composed & arranged as Duets, for the Piano Forte . . . Alexander Peckett."

THOMAS (THOMAS). Line 4. MDCCCXLVIII. (1848 not 1858.)

THOMPSON (SAMUEL) (ANN) & (PETER). Add:—They reissued a number of publications previously published by James Blundell.

THORNE, *Mr.* Bookseller, Durham. His name appears in the imprint of "A Collection of Favourite Songs adapted for the Voice, Harpsichord, Violin, Guitar or German Flute, To which is added A Duett for two Violins Composed by W. Shield. Book 1st . . . London Printed for the Author, at Mr. Thorne's, Durham, and Sold by Longman, Lukey and Broderip," etc., c. 1775.

THOROWGOOD & HORNE. Musical instrument makers, music printers and publishers, London; at the Violin and Guitar, opposite Grocers Alley in the Poultry, January 1772-mid 1763; at the Violin and Guitar, near Mercer's Chapel, Cheapside, 1763-c. October 1764. Henry Thorowgood served an apprenticeship with John Cox and Robert Horne was previously employed by Messrs. Thompson, St. Paul's Churchyard. Henry Thorowgood continued the business alone. (To replace the original entry.)
K. G.

Henry Thorowgood, from Mr. Cox's, late Simpson's Music Shop in Sweeting's Alley, Royal Exchange, and Robert Horne, from Messrs. Thompson's in St. Paul's Church-yard; beg leave to inform their Friends, that they have opened a Shop, at the Sign of the Violin and Guitar, opposite Grocer's-Alley in the Poultry, where Merchants, Captains of Ships, Country Dealers, and others, may be supplied with all Sorts of Goods in the Musical Business, Wholesale and Retail.

Musical Instruments repaired in the neatest Manner. All orders executed with the utmost Punctuality. (Public Advertiser, Jan. 4, 1862.)

THOROWGOOD (HENRY). Musical instrument maker, music printer and publisher, London; at the Violin and Guitar, Mercer's Chapel, Cheapside, c. October 1764-December 1764; at the Violin and Guitar, under the North Piazza of the Royal Exchange (afterwards numbered 6 North Piazza, Royal Exchange in 1767), December 1764-c. 1780. The business under the North Piazza of the Royal Exchange was previously owned by William Curtis, but carried on in the name of his employeé Maurice Whitaker until August 1764. Purchased some of the stock-in-trade of John Cox and William Curtis, 1764. Published some music in conjunction with Richard Duke; some single sheet songs bear only the initials H. T. Previously in partnership as Thorowgood and Horne. (To replace the original entry.)
K. G.

TOLKIEN (HENRY). Add:—Published some music in conjunction with John B. Tolkien & Co. of Birmingham.

TOLKIEN (JOHN B.) & CO. Music sellers and publishers, 70 New Street, Birmingham, c. 1840-60. Published some music in conjunction with Henry Tolkien of London.

TONSON (JACOB) *third of the name* & (RICHARD) *the Younger*. Last line. c. 1736 not c. 1740. (Alexander's Feast.)

TONSON (RICHARD) *the Younger*. *See* Tonson (Jacob) *third of the name* & (Richard) *the Younger*.

TORRE & CO. Print sellers, 132 Pall Mall, London. Issued a number of musical works with an additional imprint reading "Imported from Vienna. Published & Sold by Torre & Co. 132 Pall Mall, London, July 15, 1785."

TRENKLEE (MICHAEL). Add:—"I think of thee ever. Ballad, Author Charles Jeffreys. Composer N. J. Sporle . . . Keith Prowse & Co . . . London." With lithographed titlepage dated 1836.

TURNBULL (WALTER). Catalogues:—Line 1. (B.M. g. 443. d. (16.)) Not g. 272. w. (21.) Add:—c. 1808. 1 p. fol. (B.M. g. 272. w. (21.)); c. 1808. 1 p. fol. (B.M. g. 272. w. (4.))

TURNER, *Mrs. See* Turner (M.).

TURNER (M.). Bookseller. At the old Post Office (Post-House), Russell (Russel) Street, Covent Garden, London. Her name appears in the imprints of "Musicus Apparatus Academicus, being a composition of two Odes with vocal & instrumental musick perform'd in the Theatre at Oxford Monday July the 13th. 1713. The words by the Reverend Mr. Joseph Trapp A.M. and set to musick by William Croft Dr. in Musick . . . London Printed for the Author, and . . . At Mrs. Turners," etc., c. 1720; "Sound Anatomiz'd, in a philosophical Essay on Musick . . . To which is added, A Discourse concerning the abuse of Musick. By William Turner. London, Printed by William Pearson . . . for the Author, and sold by M. Turner . . . and no where else in England. 1724."

TURNER (THOMAS). Music seller, Snow Hill, Birmingham. His name appears in the imprint of "Hail Source of Being. Harmonia sacra for four voices, the words taken from the Seasons, by James Thomson. Set to music & adapted for the piano forte, by George Beaumont. Sold by Mr. Woodward . . . and Mr. Turner . . . Birmingham," c. 1810.

TURPIN (JAMES). Add:—"A Cantata and Six Songs, Set to Music by Willm: Denby. Organist in Derby. (Turpin, Sculpt.) Printed for the Author, and sold by him at Derby; and Robt: Thompson. St: Paul's Church Yard," c. 1760.

TYLER (JOHN JAMES). Stationer, 204 Piccadilly, London, c. 1828-33. His name appears in the imprint of "A Collection of old and new Psalm Tunes as sung at St. James's Westminster. Arranged . . . by J. F. Burrowes. London. Published for the Author by Goulding & D'Almaine . . . and Sold by J. J. Tyler," etc., c. 1830.

VACHE (S.). Line 2. c. 1777-85 not c. 1780-85.

VALENTINE (HENRY). Add:—Music seller.

VINCENT (JOSEPH). Bookseller and printer, 90 High Street, Oxford. Published "Exercises intended to accompany the Art of reading Church Music . . . By William Marshall . . . M.DCCCXLIII."; "Cathedral Services, arranged for the Organ and Pianoforte, by William Marshall Mus.Doc. Oxon . . . 1847."

VOGLER (JOHN) & (GERARD). Line 2. Swallow Street (Burlington Gardens).

VOLLWEILER (GEORG JOHANN). Add:—His publications, which were few in number, included "The favourite Song in the celebrated Opera: Die Drei Freier (The three Suitors)," etc. (See illustration opposite p. 343.); "Woodland Hallò. Composed . . . by Miss Nina d'Aubigny von Engelbrunner."; "The favourite March from the Opera: La Clemenza di Tito by Mozart, arranged for the Piano Forte."

WALKER (THOMAS). Bookseller and music publisher, 79 Dame Street, Dublin, c. 1778-96. Published "The Hibernian Magazine"; with this were given musical supplements printed from moveable type—songs, country dances, etc. Published "Aileen Aroon made a Duett. As introduc'd by Miss Catley and Miss Wewitzer in the Beggar's Opera," c. 1780; "Woe's my Heart that we shou'd sunder." Song, c. 1780.
    K.

WALLIS (JOHN). Add *after* London:—c. 1780-1805. Published a Song "The Vicar and Moses. Publish'd July 2nd. 1784 by J. Binns: Leeds, and J. Wallis"; "Musical Domino, a new Game," containing instructions and engraved music, 1793; and a Song "Britons, to Arms . . . July 30, 1803."

WALTHOE (JOHN). Add:—He married the elder John Walsh's daughter Sophia, to whom Walsh left an annuity of £40, and £10 each to Sophia and John Walthoe for mourning.

WATSON (JAMES). Bookseller and publisher, London, 1728-c. 35; Over-against Hungerford Market in the Strand; Wardrobe Court, Great Carter Lane. (P.) Printed and sold "The Scotch Orpheus. Containing Fifty of the best Scotch Tunes, Engrav'd on Copper Plates, and transpos'd for the Flute, on the same Size and Paper as the last Edition of the Scotch Songs, Printed at London . . . London: Printed and Sold by J. Watson over-against Hungerford Market in the Strand. MDCCXXXI," etc.
    P. III.

WAUGH (JAMES). Add:—For a short time in partnership with William Fenner as Waugh and Fenner.

WAUGH (JAMES) & FENNER (WILLIAM). Booksellers, at the Turk's Head, Lombard Street, London. Their names appear in the imprint of "The Psalm-Singer's Pocket Companion . . . With a plain and easy Introduction to Musick. By Thomas Moore . . . To which is added, A Collection of Hymns, suited to all the different Metres of the Tunes . . . Printed for the Author, and sold by him at his House in Glasgow: By Mess. Waugh and Fenner . . . London . . . M.DCC.LVI."

WEAVER (SAMUEL). Musical instrument maker and music seller, &c.

WELCKER (PETER). Add after Catalogues:—Vocal and Instrumental Music. c. 1765, &c.

WELSH & HAWES. Line 3. c. 1825-28 not c. 1826-28.

WELSH (THOMAS). Line 7. c.1825-28 not c. 1826-28.

WESTLEY & DAVIS. Booksellers and stationers, 10 Stationers' Court (Stationers' Hall Court), London, c. 1826-37. Published a small amount of music. Partners were Francis Westley who was previously in business at the same address and A. H. Davis.

WESTLEY (FRANCIS). Add:—Succeeded Thomas Williams. Joined by A. H. Davis and continued as Westley & Davis.

WHAT (JOHN). Musical instrument maker and music printer, at the Golden Viol and Hautboy in St. Paul's Churchyard, London. His name appears in the imprint of "Pieces Pour le Clavecin Composées par G. F. Handel V^E. ouvrage . . . London, John What, Musical Instrument Maker and Musick Printer at the Golden Viol et hautboy in S^t. Pauls church yard. A Paris et Chez," etc. The copy of the work in the Conservatoire Royal de Musique, Brussels, contains a licence dated 20 March, 1739. What is assumed to be a fictitious name. Cecil Hopkinson: "Handel and France." Edinburgh, 1957. (*Edinburgh Bibliographical Society Transactions.* Vol. III. Part 4. 1957.)

WHEATSTONE (CHARLES). Catalogues:—Music, Vocal and Instrumental. c. 1805. 3 pp. fol. Add:—New Music. 1808. 1 p. fol. (B.M. g. 24. c. (4.)); Flute Music. c. 1808. 1 p. fol. (B.M. g. 280. k. (3.))

WHITAKER & CO. Add:—Stock in trade consisting of engraved music plates, copyrights, two printing presses and lease of the premises, were sold by auction by Mr. W. P. Musgrave September 20-23, 1824.

WHITAKER (MAURICE) (Maurice Philips Whitaker). Musical instrument maker, music seller and publisher, London; the sign of the Violin, under the Piazza next the North Gate of the Royal Exchange. c. 1760-August 1764; Under the Piazza, near (next) the North Gate of the Royal Exchange, opposite Bartholomew Lane, (Afterwards numbered 2 North Piazza, Royal Exchange, in 1767), September 1764-c. 1780. The music shop at the sign of the Violin, under the Piazza, which was carried on in Whitaker's name was owned by William Curtis, a musical instrument maker who had a house and warehouse in Threadneedle Street. On August 14, 1764, Curtis advertised "The Music Shop in the North Piazza, in which Maurice Philips Whitaker for some Time Past, officiated as my servant or Shopman, will, from this Time, be carried on by me alone." On August 27, 1764, Whitaker advertised "That being free from all Connection with William Curtis, begs leave to inform his friends . . . that he is now preparing a shop near his former one." At one time assistant to John Simpson in Sweetings Alley, and after Simpson's death was for several years, prior to 1760, chief manager for his widow and John Cox who married Mrs. Simpson. When Cox and his wife ceased business in June 1764, owing to the state of Mrs. Cox's health, Whitaker advertised "that he carries

on the same Business in every Branch therein, at his Music Shop."
Some songs bear only the initials M.W. (To replace the original
entry.)

K. G.

See also Betts (John).

WHITAKER (R. S.). Also published some music as Whitaker & Co.

WHITE (JOHN). Printer, York. Line 6. Add *after* 1687:—also the
3rd edition, 1698; delete also before the 4th edition.

WHITEHORN (THOMAS). Bookseller and publisher, Watchet. Printed
"An Introduction to Divine Service . . . Set to music and adapted to
general use by Thomas Hawkes, of Williton, Somerset." The work
bears an advertisement by the composer dated Sept. 21, 1831; Printed
and published "A Collection of Tunes . . . adapted to the Hymns in use
by the Wesleyan Methodist Societies; arranged . . . by Thomas Hawkes,
of Williton, Somerset . . . The whole revised and corrected by Mr.
George Gay. Printed and published for the compiler by Thomas
Whitehorn, Watchet: and sold by John Mason . . . London." The
preface is dated June 24, 1833.

WHITTEMORE (WILLIAM). Bookseller and publisher, London; 44
Paternoster Row, c. 1845-46; 28 Newgate Street, c. 1846-47; 24
Paternoster Row, c. 1847-48. Published a small amount of music.

WICKENS (MARTHA). Music seller, Oxford. Her name appears in the
imprint of "Congregational Psalmody, arranged to the public Services
of the Church, by the Rev^d. T. H. Hawkes . . . London, Published for
the Editor, by W. Hawes . . . and sold by . . . Mrs. Wickens . . . Oxford,"
etc. The preface is dated June 1844.

WIGLEY (CHARLES). Line 5. *After* c. 1811-16 add:—with additional
premises at 48 Ludgate Hill, c. 1814-16.

WILKINS (ELIZABETH). Line 2. c. 1775, not c. 1745.

WILLIAMS (T.) (THOMAS). Engraver, 43 Holborn, c. 1783-85, &c.

WILLIAMS (THOMAS). Bookseller and publisher, 10 Stationers' Court,
Ludgate Hill, London, c. 1800-18. Published and sold some musical
works. Succeeded by Francis Westley.

WILLIAMSON (R.). Add:—"A Collection of Psalm Tunes with a Thor-
ough Bass for the Harpsicord or Organ with several Hymns, Anthems,
& Divine Songs. Adapted to the Violin, & German Flute. London
Printed by R. Williamson. and Sold by G. Keith . . . I. Fuller . . . &
Lewer's Music-Shop," etc., c. 1765.

WILLIS (RICHARD) & (HENRY). Music sellers, Leeds. Removed on October 15, 1825 from Woodhouse Lane to 15 Albion Street, corner of Bond Street. (K.) Published c. 1825 "A Selection of antient and modern Psalm Tunes, Chants & Responses . . . Arranged for four voices with an accompaniment for the organ or piano forte by I. Greenwood, Organist of Parish Church, Leeds. Leeds, Published for the Editor by Messrs. Willis," etc.

WILSON. *See* Dunlop & Wilson.

WOODWARD (MICHAEL). Lines 2-4. Substitute *after* Birmingham:—
7 New Street, c. 1780-1811; Worcester Street, c. 1811-14; Union Street, c. 1814-20; 17 Bull Street, c. 1820-28; 7 Church Street, c. 1828-30.

WRIGHT (WILLIAM). Line 2, c. 1795-1805 not c. 1800-05.

WYBROW (WILLIAM). Add:—Catalogue of new Vocal Music &c. for selection, works of acknowledged merit. c. 1840. 1 p. fol. (B.M. H. 2815. f. (27.))

YOUNG (JOHN). Line 3. c. 1698-1732 not 1698-1730. Add at end *after* Cullen:—Thomas Cross, John Walsh and Joseph Hare.

INDEX OF FIRMS IN PLACES OTHER THAN LONDON

ENGLAND

ABINGDON
  Parsons (Richard)
BATH
  Packer (George)
BIRMINGHAM
  Smith (George)
  Tolkien (John B.) & Co.
  Turner (Thomas)
BOURN, LINCOLNSHIRE
  Daniell (William)
BRIGHTON
  Ernest, *Mr.*
  Prince
BRISTOL
  Edwards (George)
  Hodges (Francis)
  Hodges (Francis) & (Martin)
  Howell (Thomas) *the Younger*
  Major (William)
  Pine (William)
CAMBRIDGE
  Hayes (John)
CANTERBURY
  Bristow (William)
  Flacton & Co.
  Simmons & Co.
CHELMSFORD
  Clachar (William)
  Meggy & Chalk
  Stanes (William)
CHESTER
  Murray & Stuart
CHICHESTER
  Michelli (J.)
COVENTRY
  Jopson (James)
DERBY
  D., M.
  Roome (Francis)
DURHAM
  Thorne, *Mr.*
HEXHAM
  Featherston (J.)
KNUTSFORD
  Moore (Randle)

LEEDS
  Binns (John)
  Richardson (John)
  Simms (Agnes) & (Thomas Fitzwilliam)
  Willis (Richard) & (Henry)
LIVERPOOL
  Terry (Samuel)
LUDLOW
  Felton (William)
NEWCASTLE-ON-TYNE
  Richardson (Moses Aaron)
  Slack (Thomas)
NORTHAMPTON
  Jopson (James)
NORWICH
  Beatniffe (Richard)
  Collins (Freeman)
NOTTINGHAM
  Collier, or Collyer (John)
ORMSKIRK
  Stuart (James)
OXFORD
  Crosley (John)
  Eustace (Jo.)
  Lichfield (Leonard) *the Younger*
  Vincent (Joseph)
  Wickens (Martha)
READING
  Packer (Charles)
SCARBOROUGH
  Theakston (Solomon Wilkinson)
SHEFFIELD
  Simmons (Nevill)
SHREWSBURY
  Eddowes (Joshua)
SKIPTON
  Hodgson, *Mr.*
WAKEFIELD
  Richardson (John)
WATCHET
  Whitehorn (Thomas)

SCOTLAND

ABERDEEN
  Nicoll (James)

BANNF
  Imlach (James)

DUMFRIES
  Duncan (John)

DUNDEE
  Duff (Charles)
  Duff (Charles) & Chalmers (James)

EDINBURGH
  Galbraith (J. Murray)
  Guthrie (Charles)
  Hall (Joseph)
  Lothian (John)
  Peat (Alexander) & Co.
  Smith (James)

GLASGOW
  Allan (David)
  Dunlop & Wilson
  Finlay (Robert) & (John)

Lumsden (John)
May (J. A.)
Melville (George)

LEITH
  Hume (R. W.)

WALES

CARNARVON
  Pritchard (William)

IRELAND

CORK
  Terry (Samuel)

DUBLIN
  Walker (Thomas)

LIMERICK
  Terry (Samuel)

LIST OF MUSICAL INSTRUMENT MAKERS, AND REPAIRERS

Betts (John)
Collier & Davis
Curtis (John)
Falkener (Robert)
Hintz (Frederick)
Jones (P.)

Muff (Joshua)
Packer (George)
Simpson (James)
Smith (George)
Weaver (Samuel)
What (John)